TRILATERALISM

TRILATERALISM

The Trilateral Commission and Elite Planning for World Management

edited by Holly Sklar

SOUTH END PRESS   BOSTON

Grateful acknowledgement is made of the following for permission to reprint previously published and copyrighted material:

Takano Hajime: "A Guide to the Japanese Membership of the Trilateral Commission," excerpted from "Rockefeller's Men in Toyko: A Guide to the Japanese Membership of the Trilateral Commission," *AMPO: Japan-Asia Quarterly Review*, published by the Pacific-Asia Resources Center, Tokyo.

Michael Klare and the Bay Area Chapter of the Inter-University Committee: "Resurgent Militarism," earlier versions were published in 1976 by the Inter-University Committee to Stop Funding War and Militarism and in 1978 by the Institute for Policy Studies.

Marxist Perspectives and Fred Block: "Trilateralism and Inter-Capitalist Conflict," earlier version, "Cooperation and Conflict in the Capitalist World Economy," Spring, 1979.

Monthly Review and Jeff Frieden: "The Trilateral Commission: Economics and Politics in the 1970's," earlier version, December 1977.

The Nation, and Kai Bird: "Coopting the Third World Elites: Trilateralism and Saudi Arabia," earlier version, "Coopting the Third World Elites: Trilateralism Goes to Work," 9 April 1977.

The Nation and Alan Wolfe: "Capitalism Shows its Face: Giving up on Democracy," 29 November 1975.

Ramparts Press and Laurence H. Shoup: "Jimmy Carter and the Trilateralists: Presidential Roots," adapted from *The Carter Presidency and Beyond: Power and Politics in the 1980s*, Palo Alto, California, 1980.

Monthly Review Press, and Laurence H. Shoup and William Minter: "Shaping a New World Order: The Council on Foreign Relations' Blueprint for World Hegemony, 1939-1945," excerpted from Chapter 4, *Imperial Brain Trust: The Council on Foreign Relations and United States Foreign Policy*, New York, 1977.

The Scandinavian Institute of African Studies, Uppsala, Sweden, and Norman Girvan: "Economic Nationalists vs. Multinational Corporations: Revolutionary or Evolutionary Change?" from *Multinational Firms in Africa*, edited by Samir Amin, 1975.

William Tabb and the Union for Radical Political Economists: "The Trilateral Imprint on Domestic Economics," earlier version, *U.S. Capitalism in Crisis*, 1978.

All other articles were written for inclusion in this volume and appear with the authors' permission.

Library of Congress Catalog Card Number: 80-51040
ISBN: 0-89608-103-6 paper
ISBN: 0-89608-104-4 cloth
C-417

Cover design by Keith Sklar
Mechanical for cover by Jamie Kay and Keith Sklar
Keith Sklar is an artist living in San Francisco and working on community murals. Jamie Kay is a free-lance illustrator living in New York City.

South End Press   **Box 68, Astor Station**   **Boston, Ma 02123**

TABLE OF CONTENTS

ABOUT THE EDITOR

Holly Sklar is the co-author of the forthcoming study *U.S. Africa Policy for the 1980s: What the Think Tanks are Thinking*. She has co-designed popular workshops to demystify worldwide corporate strategies along with a slide show on global corporations focusing on the role of women as workers and consumers. Holly served on the steering committee of the October 1978 national conference, "Women and Global Corporations: Work, Roles, and Resistance," and lived and worked in an agricultural region of Bolivia from 1975 to 1976. She received her B.A. from Oberlin College and M.A. from Columbia University where she is presently in the doctoral program in Political Science.

Acknowledgements

This book has passed through many stages in the transition from a small packet of articles in 1977, through increasingly ambitious outlines, to this comprehensive reader. My special thanks to Leah Margulies, Dahlia Rudavsky, and especially Ros Everdell for ongoing support and assistance; to Lisa Wheaton, Terry Murphy, Mark Ritchie, and the National Coalition for Development Action with whom I launched the initial project; and to Earthwork/Center for Rural Studies and the New York CIRCUS for helping to meet the need for popular materials on trilateralism with their respective publications.

Most of the articles in this volume were specially solicited. Existing articles were generally revised and updated. I want to express my gratitude to all the contributors to this volume, without whom this project would not have been possible and with whom I am very privileged to have worked; to Peggy Newfield who typed and retyped the manuscript; and to Keith Sklar who designed the cover and promo poster. I also want to thank the following people who have encouraged and helped in many different ways: Karen Anderson, David Brooks, Carla Cassler, Susan Dorfman, Ruthann Evanoff, Nancy Goulder, Jamie Kay, Mark Kesselman, Aracelly Santana, Tracy Scott, Steve, Ellen Weiser, William Wipfler.

Generous contributions from the National Council of Churches Division of Overseas Ministries; the Board of Global Ministries and the Women's Division of the Methodist Church; and other organizations and individuals defrayed the many expenses incurred in researching and completing the manuscript. To all I am extremely grateful.

Finally, I want to thank South End Press, and especially Lydia Sargent, for taking an early interest in this work and giving it the space and assistance to develop. We came through the production stage with a combination of humor and commitment and I look forward to our future work in making this book available to as wide an audience as possible.

List of Tables

Foolish Attacks on False Issues
David Rockefeller Replies to Critics*

...To some extremists, the Trilateral Commission is pictured as a nefarious plot by an Eastern Establishment of businessmen in the service of multinational corporations, who will do almost anything including going into cahoots with the Kremlin for the sake of financial gain. The fact that many former members, including President Carter, are now members of the administration is hailed as proof of how devilishly well the conspiracy is working.

By contrast, the radicals at the other end of the spectrum view the Trilateral Commission as a scheme to subject the working people of the world to the machinations of rapacious capitalism. Both sides are inordinantly fond of the word "cabal" in describing our membership, and I, personally, am often singled out for special mention as the "cabalist-in-chief."...so let me put the record straight.

The Trilateral Commission now has 300 members from North America, Western Europe (almost entirely from the Common Market) and Japan. About one-fourth of the total are from the United States and include not ony businessmen, but labor union leaders, university professors and research institute directors, Congressmen and Senators, media representatives and others. There are about as many Republicans as Democrats. The members from other countries are drawn from a similarly broad base.

Among present and former U.S. members are the chairmen of the Republican National Committee, the president of the AFL-CIO, the chief editor of the *Chicago Sun Times* and others who would have difficulty hatching the same plot.

There are eight California members including Cap Weinberger, Arjay Miller and Philip Hawley. So if this is an Eastern Establishment, it's growing a pretty hefty West Coast branch.

It is gratifying and not surprising that many of our former members are now officials in the administration. The membership has always consisted of some of our most outstanding citizens. When a Commission member becomes a member of the administration, however, rules require that him or her resign. The same applies in Europe and Japan.

The Trilateral Commission does not take positions on issues or endorse individuals for office. It publishes a quarterly journal, holds plenary meetings that rotate from region to region, and gets task force reports that take well over a year each to prepare. To encourage lively and uninhibited debate and a full exchange of

*These remarks are from an excerpt of a speech Rockefeller gave to the Los Angeles World Affairs Council appearing in the *Wall Street Journal,* 30 April 1980.

views, we do not open Commission meetings to the public. But we do make available all reports.

My point is that far from being a coterie of international conspirators with designs on covertly ruling the world, the Trilateral Commission is, in reality, a group of concerned citizens interested in fostering greater understanding and cooperation among international allies.

Mean and small-minded attacks and the absurdities of the extremists don't bother me much. By this time, I've become relatively thick-skinned and quite able to fend for myself. But I regret that these misunderstandings have entered the political arena, and I do worry that misrepresenting the motives of good and dedicated people will only narrow instead of broaden participation.

In such an uncertain and turbulent world climate, our country—in shaping its role in the world—cannot afford to be sidetracked by foolish attacks on false issues. Rather, we must—all of us—work together to help frame a foreign policy that best reflects the courage and commitment that are cornerstones of this great nation.

David Rockefeller is the most conspicuous representative today of the ruling class, a multinational fraternity of men who shape the global economy and manage the flow of its capital. Rockefeller was born to it, and he has made the most of it. But what some critics see as a vast international conspiracy, he considers a circumstance of life and just another days work.

—Bill Moyers, "The World of David Rockefeller."*

[The purpose of the Trilateral Commission is to] seek a private consensus on the specific problems examined in the Trilateral analysis. Consensus-seeking must be a central element in the Trilateral process...the commission will seek to educate attentive audiences in the three regions, so that public opinion in Japan, North America, and Europe will come to reflect the private consensus.

—Gerard C. Smith, U.S. ambassador-at-large
for Non-Proliferation Matters.**

*Transcript of "The World of David Rockefeller," Bill Moyers' Journal, 7 February 1980 (WNET/Thirteen, 356 West 58th Street, New York, N.Y. 10019).
**From the Atlantic Community Quarterly, Fall 1974, p. 350, cited in Laurence H. Shoup, The Carter Presidency and Beyond, (Palo Alto, CA.: Ramparts Press, 1980).

PART I
AN OVERVIEW

TRILATERALISM: MANAGING DEPENDENCE AND DEMOCRACY— AN OVERVIEW *

Holly Sklar

Introduction

When Jimmy Carter became president of the United States in January 1977, he made an under-"Statement to the World" which began: "I have chosen the occasion of my inauguration as president to speak not only to my countrymen—which is traditional—but also to you, citizens of the world who did not participate in our election but who will nevertheless be affected by my decisions." With equal candor members of the Trilateral Commission—an organization in which Jimmy Carter was an active participant—might have added: "We have chosen the occasion of President Carter's inauguration to speak not only to our membership, the Business Roundtable, the Council on Foreign Relations, and other such elite planning organizations—which is traditional—but also to you, citizens of the world who are not familiar with our organizations and did not participate in our appointment but who will nevertheless be affected by our decisions."**

In 1973 the Trilateral Commission was founded by David Rockefeller, Chase Manhattan Bank chairman,*** Zbigniew Brze-

---

*I am especially grateful to Leah Margulies, Dahlia Rudavsky, Ros Everdell, Nancy Goulder, and Jane Fleishman for their comments on various drafts of this article. They helped me become clearer in my own mind and on paper.

Readers are encouraged to follow the authors' and editor's notes which appear at the bottom of the page for background information, extended discussion, and interesting sidelines. Reference notes are listed at the end of each article in this volume.

**Terms such as "businessman" and "chairman" (Carter uses "countrymen" above) appear throughout this paper. I want to make clear at the outset that these words are being used consciously. Very few women have been admitted into elite planning circles; there are virtually no women in the inner circles. Women were not admitted to the Council on Foreign Relations until 1970. The few women serving on the Trilateral Commission are highlighted in "Who's Who on the Trilateral Commission." No women serve as chief executive officers and only a handful have reached high positions in the corporations mentioned throughout this book. Understanding this, I think it is important not to mask the (white) male corporate elite in nonsexist terminology.

***See Appendix for background information on the Rockefeller family.

1

zinski, Carter's national security advisor, and other like-minded "eminent private citizens." Some 300 members (up from about 200 members in 1973) are drawn from international business and banking, government, academia, media, and conservative labor. (See "Who's Who on the Trilateral Commission" for a closer look at the participants.) The Commission's purpose is to engineer an enduring partnership among the ruling classes of North America, Western Europe, and Japan—hence the term "trilateral"—in order to safeguard the interests of Western capitalism in an explosive world. The private Trilateral Commission is attempting to mold public policy and construct a framework for international stability in the coming decades. Throughout this book, "trilateralism" refers to the doctrine of world order advanced by the Commission.

Shortly before Jimmy Carter's election in 1976, Richard Ullman wrote from inside the foreign policy establishment:* "In the U.S.— among elites, at any rate—trilateralism has become almost the consensus position on foreign policy."[1] But it was only at the time of Carter's election that the Trilateral Commission was given much media attention. "Sound the Alarm: the Trilateralists are Coming!" teased William Greider in a postinaugural article on the Carter Administration and the Trilateral Commission.[2] Jimmy Carter has picked no less than twenty-five trilateralists to serve in the highest posts of his administration.** Besides Brzezinski, founding director of the Trilateral Commission, we find: Vice-President Walter Mondale, (former) Secretary of State Cyrus Vance, (former) Ambassador to the United Nations Andrew Young, Secretary of Defense Harold Brown, and Chairman of the Federal Reserve Board Paul Volcker.*** (See Laurence Shoup, "Jimmy Carter and the Trilateralists: Presidential Roots.")

---

*Ullman was then director of the Council on Foreign Relations (CFR) 1980s Project. He is now the editor of *Foreign Policy,* published by the Carnegie Endowment for International Peace. (The CFR publishes the older establishment journal, *Foreign Affairs.*)

**"Trilateralist refers to active or inactive Trilateral Commission members as well as scholars who participate by heading up trilateral task force studies. Normally, when Commission members are appointed or elected to high public office they are listed in the organization's membership roster as "Former Members in Public Service." A complete list of trilateralists in government in the United States, Canada, Western Europe, and Japan appears in the "Who's Who" in this volume.

***In the wake of his so-called Thursday afternoon (cabinet) massacre, Carter accepted the resignation of one trilateralist, Secretary of the Treasury W. Michael Blumenthal, and appointed two others. Hedley Donovan, former editor-in-chief and a continuing director of Time Inc. (which encompasses *Time, Fortune, Life,* and the *Washington Star)* was named senior adviser on domestic and foreign policy and *media relations* (in his article on Carter and the trilateralists, Shoup discusses the

Trilateralists don't make a habit of speaking directly and openly to us, the mass of world citizens (whether they are in government or out of government). But from their publications and other statements as well as by their actions, we can glean a clear sense of their ideology, goals, and strategy. Key themes of trilateralism are captured in the following statements:

> The public and leaders of most countries continue to live in a *mental universe which no longer exists—a world of separate nations*—and have great difficulties thinking in terms of global perspectives and interdependence.
>
> The liberal premise of a separation between the political and economic realm is obsolete: *issues related to economics are at the heart of modern politics.*
> —Toward a Renovated International System
(Trilateral Task Force Report: 1977)
>
> *The vulnerability of democratic government* in the United States (thus) comes not primarily from external threats, though such threats are real, nor from internal subversion from the left or the right, although both possibilities could exist, but rather *from the internal dynamics of democracy itself in a highly educated, mobilized, and participant society.* [Italics ed.]
> The Crisis of Democracy: Report on the Governability
of Democracies to the Trilateral Commission
(New York University Press, 1975)*

---

instrumental role the media played—with Hedley Donovan's active leadership—in aiding Carter's election). Paul Volcker, former president of the Federal Reserve Bank of New York, mentioned above, became Federal Reserve chief (G. William Miller resigned that post to succeed Blumenthal at the Treasury Department). It is most interesting that the five leading candidates for Federal Reserve chief were all trilateralists. Bruce K. MacLaury, president of the Brookings Institution, remained in the running with Volcker. David Rockefeller; A.W. Clausen, chairman of the Bank of America; and Robert Roosa, partner in the investment banking firm of Brown Bros., Harriman, took themselves out of consideration (*New York Times,* 25 July 1979). Clyde M. Farnsworth reports that Volcker "was part of the Roosa 'brain trust' " and "also served in management positions at Chase Manhattan Bank." Rockefeller "and Mr. Roosa were strong influences in the [sic] Mr. Carter's decision to name Mr. Volcker for the Reserve Board Chairmanship." *(New York Times, 26 July 1979).*

Andrew Young resigned on 15 August 1979 under fire for meeting with the Palestinian Liberation Organization's representative to the United Nations. Cyrus Vance resigned on 28 April 1980 in a dispute over the hostage "rescue operation." Vance had earlier stated he would not stay on for a second term. The U.S.-Iran crisis is discussed in the conclusion to this volume.

Towards a Renovated International System "was conceived as a capstone [culmination] of the first three years of the Trilateral Commission's efforts." (*Fourth Annual Report.*) Since the report's completion, co-author Richard Cooper has become undersecretary of state for economic affairs and Robert Bowie, special consultant in the writing of the report, has become deputy director to the director of Central Intelligence for National Intelligence. Samuel Huntington, the co-author of

To put it simply, trilateralists are saying: (1) the people, governments, and economies of all nations must serve the needs of multinational banks and corporations; (2) control over economic resources spells power in modern politics (of course, good citizens are supposed to believe as they are taught; namely, that political equality exists in Western democracies whatever the degree of economic inequality); and (3) the leaders of capitalist democracies—systems where economic control and profit, and thus political power, rest with the few—must resist movement toward a truly popular democracy. In short, trilateralism is the current attempt by ruling elites to manage both dependence and democracy—at home and abroad.

What does trilateralism mean in practical terms for people in the United States and throughout the world? What are the links between trilateral design, government policy making, and actual events? Where are the gaps? What resistance does trilateralism face? These are some of the basic questions we must address. This article provides an overview of trilateralism and a foundation for the readings which follow. It is organized in six sections:

(1) Trilateral Origins: Western Business on the Defensive
(2) The New Corporate Empires: Spreading the Ideology of Profit, Stability, and the Trilateral Way
(3) Managing Third World Dependence: Revitalizing Imperialism
(4) East-West Relations: Rehabilitating the "Dropouts"
(5) Managing Western Democracy: Limited Democracy is "Governable" Democracy
(6) Challenges and Contradictions: The Struggle Continues

Trilateral Origins: Western Business on the Defensive

Trilateralism is rooted in a long tradition of elite ideology and corporate planning. For example, a private U.S. organization called the Council on Foreign Relations (CFR), founded in 1918, remains a powerful force in shaping public policy and perception. As the Council's 1919 handbook explains:

The Crisis of Democracy (a full-length book published by New York University Press) was appointed by Brzezinski to the National Security Council (see note on Huntington in "East-West Relations: Rehabilitating the "Dropouts" in this overview).

One rapporteur from each of the trilateral regions of North America, Western Europe, and Japan collaborate in writing the task force reports known as the *Triangle Papers;* see the list of publications in the bibliography to this volume.

It is a board of initiation—a Board of Invention. It plans to cooperate with the government and all existing international agencies and to bring them all into constructive accord.[3]

The CFR had its special chance to be a "Board of Invention" during and after World War II when it played a pivotal role in formulating U.S. war aims, constructing the post-World War II international economic and political order, and guiding U.S. policy over the last quarter century. (See Shoup and Minter.) In the postwar period, it was relatively easy to bring all parties into "constructive accord." Western Europe and Japan were in ruins; the U.S. emerged from the war as the unrivaled economic, military, and political power. Through massive economic and military assistance programs like the Marshall Plan and the North Atlantic Treaty Organization (NATO) Western Europe and Japan were reconstructed, following U.S. specifications, into stable trading partners and bulwarks against the "communist threat." The World Bank, the International Monetary Fund (see article by James Phillips), and other international organizations were founded during that early period. They became pillars of the postwar international trade and monetary system known as the Bretton Woods System (because it was established at Bretton Woods, New Hampshire in 1944); the Soviet Union and other "Socialist bloc" countries dropped out in the early stages when it became clear the system was to be designed mainly by and for the United States.

A lesser-known companion institution to the CFR is the Bilderberg Group. Bilderberg, founded in 1954, is a European-led organization which is well attended by heads of state and other "influentials" from Western Europe, the U.S., and Canada. The catch-word for the times was "Atlanticism" not "trilateralism"; Japan had not yet earned its place in the so-called "club of advanced nations" which formed the Atlantic Alliance. (See article by Peter Thompson for a look at postwar U.S.-European relations and Bilderberg's origins and activities through the present.)

Domestic stability and international stability were closely linked under the umbrella of the welfare/warfare state. (Alan Wolfe discusses this in Part VIII.) Policy makers and presidents like John F. Kennedy and Lyndon Johnson stepped up efforts to fight the world-wide "war on communism" (read "war for capitalism") alongside the domestic "war on poverty"—with the support of liberals, big labor, and big business. ("Cold War liberalism" is the name given to the dominant ideology of the postwar period.) Corporations reaped lush profits from domestic military production and rapidly expanded out into the empire which U.S. foreign aid remodelled and U.S. *guns* protected. Stability at home was maintained with varying doses of *butter* (expanding social welfare programs in the context of a prosperous economy) and political repression (McCarthy era of the 1950s; FBI and CIA counter-intelligence programs to disrupt and destroy progressive movements in the 1960s and 70s; systematic police brutality against Chicano/as, Blacks, Native Americans, and Puerto Ricans.)

With the sixties and early seventies came the collapse of the postwar international economic system and crisis in the welfare/warfare state. In advertising a 1979 feature story, "The Decline of U.S. Power: the New Debate Over Guns and Butter," *Business Week* exclaims:

> READ IT AND WEEP...Between the fall of Vietnam and the fall of the Shah of Iran the United States has suffered a series of shocks signaling a steady erosion of U.S. power throughout the world...The entire U.S.-created post-World War II global economic system is in danger of destruction.[4]

What are some of these shocks? Broad and militant protest and sustained political mobilization shook the stability of trilateral governments. The struggle for workers', students', and peasants' power brought France near revolution in May 1968—a climactic year throughout Western Europe, the U.S., and Japan. Watergate was a public display of government deceit and immorality. As trilateralists see it, a "crisis of democracy" plagued the West. (Carter sermonized about the continuing crisis in July 1979, calling it a "crisis of confidence"—in government, national purpose, the future—about which more will be said below.)

The rout of the U.S. military from Vietnam—formalized by the Paris treaty of 1973 and finalized with the fall of the Thieu regime in April 1975—undermined severely the U.S. role as global police for international capitalism. Domestic constraints were placed on direct and covert U.S. military action as the public said no to massive intervention abroad and Congress took steps to curb the imperial presidency and its zealous scouts, the CIA.*

The "oil shock" came with the October 1973 Arab oil embargo (against the U.S. and the Netherlands because of their support for Israel during the October War) and OPEC price hikes of 1973-74.**

---

*Kissinger and Ford, for example, wanted to escalate ongoing CIA operations in Angola where the U.S. supported factions backed by South Africa and Zaire(the FNLA and UNITA) fighting the MPLA, the rightful government of liberated Angola. (Angola became independent of Portugal in November 1975.) The Senate and House banned further covert aid in December 1975 and January 1976.

**Organization for Petroleum Exporting Countries: Algeria, Ecuador, Gabon, Indonesia, Iran, Iraq, Kuwait, Libya, Nigeria, Quatar, Saudi Arabia, United Arab Emirates, Venezuela (as of 1973).

OPEC's success awakened Third World and Western leaders alike to the potential of "commodity power" on the side of raw materials producers (and not just the "middlemen" corporations and consumer nations, as before). Oil gave OPEC the clout to force the rising Third World call for a *New International Economic Order* (NIEO) onto the Western agenda. (See first editor's note in Girvan article.)

> 1973 [observes Brzezinski] was the year in which for the first time the new nations—the Afro-Asian nations, so to speak, inflicted a political reversal on the advanced world...In some respects, if 1945 was the beginning of the existing international system, 1973 marked the beginning of its end and hopefully the beginning of its renovation and readjustment.[5]

But the post-World War II economic order began to disintegrate even before OPEC and Vietnam cracked the armor of Western imperialism. The new menace of "stagflation"—stagnant economic growth with associated widespread unemployment *plus* rampant inflation—proved immune to modern economic medicine, highlighting the deepening economic crisis of world capitalism. Trade rivalry was mounting among the U.S., Japan, and Western Europe. West Germany and Japan were fast becoming economic Frankensteins, challenging U.S. hegemony over the international capitalist system. By the mid-sixties the traditionally large U.S. trade surplus had begun to erode; by 1971 the U.S. was running trade deficits, importing more than it exported. A huge buildup of dollars outside the U.S.—a result of hegemonic military and foreign aid activities—became disruptive of international monetary relations. Through inflation and speculation the dollar weakened against the Japanese yen and West German mark. International economic reform was needed. But before mutually agreeable reforms could be initiated President Nixon and Treasury Secretary John Connally* unilaterally demolished the tottering Bretton Woods System on 15 August 1971 (an important date on the international business timeline), and attempted to reassert U.S. supremacy with a strongly protectionist "New Economic Policy."** (See article by Jeff Frieden for a perceptive review of these events leading up to the founding of the Trilateral Commission.)

---

*Connally was an unsuccessful candidate for the Republican presidential nomination in the 1980 elections.
**Protectionist measures are designed to defend (protect) the domestic economy and aid industries (e.g., steel and textiles) which are losing out in international trade competition. Examples include: quotas on imports, tariffs, direct subsidies for industry (increasingly important today).

The "Nixon shocks" violated the rules of "free trade"— the unobstructed flow of money, goods, and services between countries— enshrined in Bretton Woods. Indeed, such a harsh display of economic nationalism raised the specter of trade wars between the so-called free world powers, and horrified corporate captains such as David Rockefeller for whom international free enterprise is gospel.

On the political front, Nixon and Kissinger attended to the emerging U.S.-China-USSR triangle to the neglect of the Cold War alliance. Western Europe welcomed detente with the Soviet Union, but not at the expense of its special relationship with the U.S. The overtures to Peking marked by Kissinger's secret trip in July 1971 and Nixon's pageant in February 1972 came as a special shock to an uninformed Japan.

The Trilateral Commission was launched before all the tremors described above had yet registered on the economic/political seismograph. The Commission's aim is to "nuture habits and practices of working together" among the trilateral regions in order to: promote a healthy (i.e., mutually beneficial and not mutually suicidal) level of competition between the capitalist powers; forge a common front against the Third World and Soviet Union; "renovate" the international political economy in the interest of global business and finance; make trilateral democracy more "governable."

The trilateral regions, Commissioners point out, "have the largest shares of world trade and finance and produce two-thirds of the world's output." The Commission's overriding concern is that trilateral nations "remain the vital center" of management, finance, and technology (i.e. power and control) for the world economy—a world economy which (in Brzezinski's words) would "embrace" and "co-opt" the Third World and gradually reintegrate the Soviet Union, Eastern Europe, and China (known as the "dropouts" in trilateral lingo).

Trilateral Commissioners assert: *"history shows that every effective international system requires a custodian."* Today, the supereconomies—West Germany and Japan—must share the custodial role with the United States. Trilateralism, a form of "collective management" under U.S. tutelage, is the necessary response if corporate capitalism is to endure and prosper.[6]

The New Corporate Empires: Spreading the Ideology of Profit, Stability, and the Trilateral Way

Trilateralism is the creed of an international ruling class whose locus of power is the global corporation.* The owners and managers

*The term "global corporation" is being used in place of other common terms such as

of global corporations *view the entire world as their factory, farm, supermarket, and playground.* The Trilateral Commission is seeking to strengthen and rationalize the world economy in their interest.

Trilateral Commissioner George Ball (investment banker and former undersecretary of state) applauds the growing number of "cosmocorps" which are

> engaged in taking the raw materials produced in one group of countries, transforming these into manufacturing goods with the labor and plant facilities of another group, and selling the products in still a third group...[all] with the benefit of instant communications, quick transport, computors, and modern management techniques...[7]

These corporations control vast amounts of natural resources; monopolize the production of commodities vital to our daily lives, such as food and energy;* and dominate the research and development of new technology. (Michael Garitty discusses the devastating impact of corporate-controlled energy production on people and the environment focusing heavily on the pillage of resource-rich Indian lands and the mounting threat to Native American survival).

The economies of most countries are dwarfed by the economic power of the largest corporations and banks. Below, Table 1 ranks the top 130 industrial corporations and countries for 1976 (the last year for which complete data was available at this writing). A comparison with 1970 data is provided which especially highlights the gains of oil companies and oil-producing nations in the seventies. Table 2 examines the top fifty international banks. In 1976 some 40 percent of the total massive debt of non-oil producing Third World nations was owed to private banks like Chase Manhattan and Bank of America (about $75 billion; up from 28 percent of total debt, or $12 billion, in 1967).** Chairmen of the board, presidents, vice-

---

"multinational corporation" or "transnational corporation" which are used interchangeably in the popular vocabulary.

*For example, seven oil companies have long dominated the world's oil and natural gas supply. The so-called Seven Sisters include: Mobil, Gulf, Texaco, Exxon (Standard of New Jersey), Socal (Standard of California), BP (British Petroleum) and Royal/Dutch Shell. Oil companies have been steadily monopolizing other forms of energy: coal, nuclear, and solar. Describing concentration in the United States food industry, Susan George explains: "Economists generally agree that if 55% or more of a given market is controlled by four or fewer companies, then an oligopoly exists. This is the case for *every* major food category in the United States." For example, in the case of milk products the top four firms hold 70 percent of the market. Susan George, *Feeding the Few: Corporate Control of Food* (Washington D.C.: Institute for Policy Studies, 1979) pp. 27-28. In this volume, see Dahlia Rudavsky's analysis of trilateral food policies and the afterword by a U.S farmer.

**See, for example, Howard M. Wachtel, *The New Gnomes: Multinational Banks in*

Table 1
Top 130 Countries and Companies in 1976
Ranked by Gross National Product and Worldwide Company Sales[1]

Rank '76	'70[2]	Name Country/Company	Amount GNP/Sales (Billion $US)	Company Headquarters	Economic Sector/ or OPEC Member
1	1	• United States	1,694.9		
2	2	USSR	717.5		
3	3	• Japan	573.9		
4	4	• Federal Republic of Germany (West)	461.8		
5	5	• France	356.0		
6	6	• People's Republic of China	307.0		
7	7	• United Kingdom	233.5		
8	9	• Canada	182.5		
9	8	• Italy	180.6		
10	12	Brazil	143.0		
11	16	• Spain	107.2		
12	11	Poland	99.1		
13	15	Australia	97.3		
14	19	• Netherlands	91.6		
15	10	India	87.8		
16	13	German Democratic Republic (East)	75.8		
17	18	Sweden	74.2		
18	39	Iran	69.2		OPEC
19	20	• Belgium	68.9		
20	14	Mexico	65.5		
21	23	Switzerland	58.1		
22	17	Czechoslovakia	56.5		
23	29	• **Exxon**[3]	48.6	US	Petroleum
24	24	• **General Motors**	47.2	US	Motor Vehicle
25	33	Austria	42.2		
26	45	Turkey	41.3		
27	—	Saudi Arabia	40.9		OPEC
28	22	Argentina	40.7		
29	30	• Denmark	39.0		
30	25	Yugoslavia	37.7		
31	36	• **Royal Dutch/Shell Group**	36.1	Netherlands/ UK	Petroleum
32	32	Indonesia	36.1		OPEC
33	27	South Africa	33.7		
34	35	• Norway	31.4		
35	37	Venezuela	31.3		OPEC
36	—	Nigeria	30.9		OPEC

Rank '76 '70[2]	Name Country/Company	Amount GNP/Sales (Billion $US)	Company Headquarters	Economic Sector/ or OPEC Member
37 21	Romania	30.0		
38 31	● Ford Motor	28.8	US	Motor Vehicle
39 38	Finland	27.8		
40 54	● Texaco	26.4	US	Petroleum
41 48	● Mobil	26.1	US	Petroleum
42 43	South Korea	25.3		
43 —	Hungary	24.8		
44 42	Greece	23.6		
45 34	Bulgaria	21.6		
46 —	National Iranian Oil	19.7	Iran	Petroleum
47 66	● Standard Oil of California	19.4	US	Petroleum
48 69	● British Petroleum	19.1	UK	Petroleum
49 40	Philippines	18.0		
50 60	Taiwan	17.1		
51 —	Algeria	16.7		OPEC
52 61	Gulf Oil	16.4	US	Petroleum
53 47	● IBM	16.3	US	Office Equipment
54 52	Thailand	16.3		
55 —	● Portugal	16.1		
56 —	Iraq	16.0		OPEC
57 51	● Unilever	15.8	Netherlands/ UK	Food
58 44	● General Electric	15.7	US	Electrical
59 49	Colombia	15.7		
60 50	Chrysler	15.5	US	Motor Vehicle
61 —	Libya	15.1		OPEC
62 —	Kuwait	14.4		OPEC
63 58	Peru	13.4		
64 26	Pakistan	13.1		
65 —	New Zealand	13.1		
66 53	● ITT	11.8	US	Electrical
67 75	● Standard Oil (Indiana)	11.5	US	Petroleum
68 67	● Philips'	11.5	Netherlands	Electrical
69 46	Chile	10.9		
70 81	Democratic People's Republic of Korea (No)	10.8		
71 55	Egypt	10.7		
72 71	Malaysia	10.6		
73 —	● ENI	10.0	Italy	Petroleum
74 —	United Arab Emirates	10.0		OPEC
75 —	● Francaise des Petroles	9.9	France	Petroleum
76 —	Hong Kong	9.9		
77 59	Israel	9.7		

Rank '76 '70[2]	Name Country/Company	Amount GNP/Sales (Billion $US)	Company Headquarters	Economic Sector/ or OPEC Member
78 —	• Renault	9.4	France	Motor Vehicle
79 89	• Hoechst	9.3	W Germany	Chemicals
80 95	BASF	9.2	W Germany	Chemicals
81 —	Petroleos de Venezuela	9.1	Venezuela	Petroleum
82 91	Daimler-Benz	9.0	W Germany	Motor Vehicle
83 84	Morocco	8.9		
84 63	• US Steel	8.6	US	Metal Refining
85 64	• Volkswagenwerk	8.5	W Germany	Motor Vehicle
86 —	• Atlantic Richfield	8.5	US	Petroleum
87 77	• E.I. Du Pont	8.4	US	Chemicals
88 —	Bayer	8.3	W Germany	Chemicals
89 72	• Ireland	8.3		
90 70	• Nippon Steel	8.1	Japan	Metal Refining
91 86	Siemens	8.1	W Germany	Electrical
92 —	• Continental Oil	8.0	US	Petroleum
93 —	Cuba	8.0		
94 93	• August Thyssen-Hutte	7.9	W Germany	Metal Refining
95 —	• Toyota Motor	7.7	Japan	Motor Vehicle
96 —	Viet Nam	7.7		
97 —	Nestle	7.6	Switzerland	Food
98 —	ELF-Acquitaine	7.5	France	Petroleum
99 79	• Imperial Chemical Industries (ICI)	7.4	UK	Chemicals
100 —	Puerto Rico	7.4		
101 —	• Peugeot-Citroen	7.3	France	Motor Vehicle
102 —	Petrobras	7.2	Brazil	Petroleum
103 —	Bangladesh	7.0		
104 83	• Hitachi	6.7	Japan	Electrical
105 —	B.A.T. Industries	6.7	UK	Tobacco
106 —	• Nissan Motor	6.6	Japan	Motor Vehicle
107 92	• Proctor & Gamble	6.5	US	Soap & Cosmetics
108 —	Tenneco	6.4	US	Petroleum
109 90	• Union Carbide	6.3	US	Chemicals
110 —	Syria	6.3		
111 65	• Westinghouse Electric	6.1	US	Electrical
112 —	• Mitsubishi Heavy Industries	6.1	Japan	Industrial Equipment, Motor Vehicle
113 —	• Saint-Gobain-Pont- a-Mousson	6.0	France	Building Material
114 —	Singapore	5.9		
115 96	• Montedison	5.8	Italy	Chemicals

Rank '76 '70[2]	Name Country/Company	Amount GNP/Sales (Billion $US)	Company Headquarters	Economic Sector/ or OPEC Member
116 87	• Goodyear Tire and Rubber	5.8	US	Rubber
117 —	• Matsushita Electric Industrial	5.7	Japan	Electrical
118 —	Philips Petroleum	5.7	US	Petroleum
119 —	• Dow Chemical	5.6	US	Chemical
120 —	Occidental Petroleum	5.5	US	Petroleum
121 —	• International Harvester	5.5	US	Industrial and Farm Equipment
122 —	Eastman Kodak	5.4		Scientific Instruments
123 —	• Sun	5.4	US	Petroleum
124 —	AEG-Telefunken	5.4	W Germany	Electrical
125 —	Union Oil of California	5.4	US	Petroleum
126 85	• RCA	5.3	US	Electrical
127 —	Esmark	5.3	US	Food
128 94	• Bethlehem Steel	5.2	US	Metal Refining
129 —	Rockwell International	5.2	US	Aerospace
130 —	United Technologies	5.2	US	Aerospace

Summary:	Top 100	Last 30	Top 130
Companies	37	28	65
Countries	63	2	65

Other 1976 GNP Comparisons: Guatemala 4.4; Burma 3.8; Kenya 3.5; Bolivia 3.0; Panama 2.0; Jordan 1.8; Sierra Leone 0.6; Somalia 0.4.

[1] *Gross National Product* (GNP) = total value of a nation's annual output of goods and services. *Sales* include service and rental revenues but exclude dividends, interest, and non-operating revenues. All companies on list must have derived more than 50 percent of their sales from manufacturing and/or mining.

1976 is the last year for which *complete* data was available when this chart was compiled in 1979.

Sources: 1978 *World Bank Atlas;* 1977 *Fortune* Directory of the Largest Industrial Companies in the World.

[2] "Gross National Products of Countries and Net Sales of Companies Interspersed: Top 100, By Rank, 1970," in the Corporate Action Project's *Corporate Action Guide* (Washington D.C. 1974) p. 20.

[3] Formerly Standard Oil of New Jersey

Symbols:
• Country or Company Represented on Trilateral Commission through members and company officers or directors
— Not in top 100 of 1970 (or Not in existence)

Table 2   World's 50 Largest Banks

Rank 1976	Bank (Holding Company)	Home Country	Assets[a] (Billion $ US)		U.S. Banks Percentage of Foreign Earnings In Total Earnings	
			'76	'79	'70	'76
1	•BankAmerica Corp.	United States	72.2	108.4	15.0[c]	40.0
2	Citicorp	United States	63.1	106.4	40.0	72.0
3	•Caisse Nationale de Credit Agricole	France	52.7			
4	•Chase Manhattan Corp.	United States	45.0	64.7	22.0	78.0
5	Deutsche Bank	Fed. Rep. of Germany	44.4			
6	Credit Lyonnais	France	40.6			
7	Groupe BNP	France	40.6			
8	Banco do Brasil	Brazil	38.8			
9	•Dai-Ichi Kangyo Bank	Japan	36.9			
10	Societe Generale	France	36.5			
11	•Dresdner Bank	Fed. Rep. of Germany	35.9			
12	•Barclays Bank	United Kingdom	33.0			
13	Banca Nazionale del Lavoro	Italy	32.7			
14	•Fuji Bank	Japan	32.4			
15	•Sumitomo Bank	Japan	32.4			
16	Westdeutsche Landesbank Girozentrale	Fed. Rep. of Germany	30.9			
17	•Mitsubishi Bank	Japan	30.7			
18	•Manufacturers Hanover Corp.	United States	30.4	47.7	13.0	56.0

Rank 1976	Bank (Holding Company)	Home Country	Assets[a] (Billion $ US) '76	'79	U.S. Banks Percentage of Foreign Earnings In Total Earnings '70	'76
19	•Sanwa Bank	Japan	30.1			
20	National Westminister Bank	United Kingdom	29.1			
21	Royal Bank of Canada	Canada	28.6			
22	•J.P. Morgan and Co.	United States	27.9	43.5	25.0	53.0
23	Commerzbank	Fed. Rep. of Germany	26.8			
24	Chemical New York Corp.	United States	26.6	39.4	10.0	44.0
25	Canadian Imperial Bank of Commerce	Canada	26.0[b]			
26	•Bank of Tokyo	Japan	25.2[b]			
27	Bayerische Vereins Bank	Fed. Rep. of Germany	24.1[b]			
28	•Industrial Bank of Japan	Japan	23.7[b]			
29	Tokai Bank	Japan	23.2			
30	Algemene Bank Nederland	Netherlands	22.8			
31	•Mitsui Bank	Japan	22.7			
32	•Continental Illinois Corp.	United States	21.8	35.8	.2	23.0
33	Swiss Bank Corp.	Switzerland	21.6			
34	Union Bank of Switzerland	Switzerland	21.6			
35	Taiyo Kobe Bank	Japan	21.4			

Rank 1976	Bank (Holding Company)	Home Country	Assets[a] (Billion $ US)		U.S. *Banks* Percentage of Foreign Earnings In Total Earnings	
			'76	'79	'70	'76
36	Bankers Trust New York Corp.	United States	21.1	31.0	14.5[c]	64.0
37	Co-operative Central Raiffeissen-Boerenleenbank	Netherlands	20.8			
38	•Long-Term Credit Bank of Japan	Japan	20.6			
39	Amsterdam-Rotterdam Bank	Netherlands	20.5			
40	•Midland Bank Limited	United Kingdom	20.2			
41	•Bank of Montreal	Canada	20.1			
42	•Lloyds Bank	United Kingdom	20.1			
43	Banca Commerciale Italiana	Italy	19.9			
44	•First Chicago Corp.	United States	19.7	30.2	2.0	17.0
45	•Western Bancorp.	United States	19.7	29.7	na.	na.
46	Bayerische Hypotheken und Wechsel Bank	Fed. Rep. of Germany	19.6			
47	•Bayerische Landesbank und Girozentrale	Fed. Rep. of Germany	19.2			

Rank 1976	Bank (Holding Company)	Home Country	Assets[a] (Billion $ US)			U.S. Banks Percentage of Foreign Earnings In Total Earnings	
			'76	'79	'70	'70	'76
48	Daiwa Bank	Japan	18.9				
49	Bank of Nova Scotia	Canada	18.7				
50	•Bank fur Gemeinwirtschaft	Fed. Rep. of Germany	17.1				

•Bank represented on the Trilateral Commission through an officer and/or director

a Assets as of 31 December, 1976. Except: Japanese figures as of 30 September; Canadian figures as of 31 October.

Assets exclude contra accounts. Currencies have been converted at the rates of exchange which were current at the time the accounts were made.

b As of 31 March

c Estimate

Source: Compiled from Tables III-13 and III-14, *Transnational Corporations in World Development: A Re-examination*, produced for the United Nations Commission on Transnational Corporations, 20 March 1978 (order: E/C.10/38), by the United Nations Centre on Transnational Corporations, based on *The Banker*, June 1977 and *Who Owns What in World Banking, 1976-77* (London: Financial Times, 1976); and United States Senate Foreign Relations Subcommittee on Foreign Economic Policy, *International Debt, the Banks, and U.S. Foreign Policy* (Washington D.C., 1977); and 1976 annual reports of the banks in question.

presidents, and directors of most of those corporations and banks have served on the Trilateral Commission, as indicated in the previous tables. (Consult "Who's Who" for additional companies and more detailed information.)

Corporate allegiances are based on the dictates of worldwide economic growth and profitability. Mobility is the global corporation's chief asset. The Irving Trust Company advertises proudly: "The Multinational Corporation. The Sun Never Sets on it...The profit motive has propelled it on a fantastic journey in search of new opportunities." As a multinational bank, Irving Trust's job is "making sure the sun shines brightly" on corporate investment. The global corporation is most at home in a profit haven—a place where politicians are obliging, labor is cheap and "disciplined," tax breaks and tax "holidays" (which permit a corporation to go untaxed for up to 15 years and longer) are plentiful; and there are little or no governmental regulations (as in a "free zone" which is free of taxes and regulations), an absence of competition, ready supplies of local credit, and sustained political stability. (Norman Girvan explores the global corporation and the "transnationalized economy.")

Throughout the world we repeatedly see the relation between profit return and political repression. As one commentator wrote in *Fortune* about South Africa:

> South Africa has always been regarded by foreign investors as a gold mine, one of those rare and refreshing places where profits are great and problems are small. Capital is not threatened by political instability or nationalization. Labor is cheap, the market booming, the currency hard and convertible.[8] (See article by Carolyn Brown.)

It doesn't take nationalization and revolution to make a corporation pack up and leave. If the sun should start to set in the form of higher wage bills, taxes, and other profit ceilings, then the corporation will "run away" to another corner of the globe where the "sun shines brightly." We see this pattern within the United States when corporations move South where cheap nonunion labor remains a regional attraction.

Trilateralists want corporations to be free to pursue "the true logic of the global economy" (to use Ball's words). Global corporations, explains Ball, are "the best means yet devised for utilizing world-resources according to the criterion of *profit: an objective*

---

the Third World (Washington D.C.: Institute for Policy Studies, Transnational Institute. 1977).

standard of efficiency."[9] [Italics mine.] Capitalist economists continually refer to "the big tradeoff" between efficiency and equality:[10] more equality means less efficiency and vice versa. The simple Law of Private Profit holds that greed motivates effort; more effort means more output: more output enhances the "common good." To stoke the fires of greed, capitalist institutions, in the words of a prominent economist, "award prizes that allow the big winners to feed their pets better than the losers can feed their children." The logic of capitalist efficiency is one of the devices by which wealth and power are increasingly centralized. Two myths help sustain this inequality: the myth of "equality of opportunity" (which keeps people believing that at least their children will have a chance at the grand prize) and the idea that if someone is not successful it is probably their own fault (blame the victim, not the system).

The real tradeoff is between equality and *inequality* of resources and opportunity. Facts speak loudly and clearly in the United States, the most "affluent" society in the world. Today one-fifth of the population would be classified as poor if not for governmental assistance. There are now 24.7 million people—about 11.6 percent of the total population—with incomes below the federal poverty level according to the U.S. Department of Commerce (that figure would more than triple if the poor *above* the federal poverty level were counted).* In 1953, 1.6 percent of the adult population owned 32 percent of all privately owned wealth.[11] That figure has changed little in the twentieth century.** The U.S. standard of living is the fifth highest in the world—not first. The United States ranks fifteenth in infant mortality and literacy among the nations of the world and even lower on other measures of social welfare.[12] The U.S. imprisons people at a higher rate (per capita) than any other country in the West except South Africa! Private profit is the standard for a system which makes a mockery of democracy and a necessity of repression, condemning people to poverty and joblessness in the U.S. and throughout the free (for corporate profit) world.

---

*As with measures of unemployment, federal poverty indices mask the true extent of poverty in the U.S.
**Looking at income distribution alone does not give a clear picture of wealth inequities. In 1972, 15.9 percent of national income went to the top 5 percent.The top fifth received 41.4 percent while the bottom fifth received only 5.4 percent (the second quintile had 11.9 percent, third quintile 17.5 percent and the fourth quintile 23.9 percent). [See June Axinn and Herman Levin, *Social Welfare: A History of the American Response to Need* (New York; Dodd, Mead & Co., 1975) p. 277; see also A.B. Atkinson, *The Economics of Inequality* (Oxford: Clarendon Press, 1975).]

Spreading the Trilateral Way

Consumption is the locomotive of profit. In 1968 *Forbes* magazine (which proudly calls itself the "Capitalist Tool") featured the views of Nabisco's president, Lee Bickmore, on shaping "one world" of homogeneous consumption. Bickmore captured the corporate dream, looking forward to the day when

> Arabs and Americans, Latins and Scandinavians will be munching Ritz crackers as enthusiastically as they already drink Coke or brush their teeth with Colgate.[13]

Marketing—the art of repeatedly displacing and creating new "needs"—is the key to expanding consumption. But it is more. Marketing, like militarism, is a means of *managing social change.** Corporations not only advertise products, they promote lifestyles: lifestyles rooted in conspicuous consumption, patterned largely after the United States.** Corporate planners hope that enthusiastic consumption—of even the cheapest goods at the poorest income levels—will be a balm for exploitation endured in the workplace, serving the dual corporate aims of stability and profitability.

It would not be possible to build a one world market without a global mass communications system. Today advertisements, network news, entertainment, and educational programs are beamed via satellite to hundreds of millions of people around the world.*** Products, tastes, and norms develop in the trilateral regions and flow outward to the rest of the world. A "world information grid" is being built, helping, writes Brzezinski, to "broaden the scope of educa-

---

*This phrase comes from *Managing Social Change,* an unpublished reader or corporate strategy produced by the now disbanded New Haven IBI Collective: Leah Margulies, Judy Miller, Paul Seminen, Florika Remetier, and Joan Gabos, with the assistance of Stephen Hymer.

**Coca-Cola probably is the one product most symbolic and symptomatic of the American way of life, is going to China." So began a *New York Times* article (20 December 1978) on Coca-Cola's immediate plans for the Chinese market of "900 Million Potential Drinkers," closed since the revolution of 1949. Equally to the point, *Time* magazine began its feature story on normalization of U.S.—Chinese relations (15 January 1979, p. 34) with the comment: "Peking last week celebrated the advent of Sino-American relations with soda pop, champagne toasts, demands for free speech and free sex, and a binge of disco dancing—most of which, as the Chinese have been quick to learn, goes better with Coke."

***As early as 1968 the CBS *Annual Report* stated: "the CBS Newsfilm Service, using satellite delivery for major stores, expanded its penetration to 95% of the free world's [sic] television homes." The products and services of RCA [parent of NBC] are available in [at least] 143 countries—from Kenya to Saudi Arabia, Argentina to Yugoslavia, West Germany to the Philippines. See Herbert Schiller, *Communications and Cultural Domination* (New York: International Arts and Sciences Press, 1976) pp. 4 and 10.

tional-scientific and economic technological cooperation among the most advanced industrial nations that are becoming post-industrial and are in some regards moving into the *post-national* age."[14] [Italics mine.]

Trilateralists look forward to a pseudo postnational age in which social, economic, and political values originating in the trilateral regions are transformed into universal values. Expanding networks of like-minded government officials, businessmen, and technocrats*—elite products of Western education—are to carry out national and international policy formation. Functionally specific institutions with "more technical focus, and *lesser public awareness*"[15] [italics mine] are best suited for addressing international issues in the trilateral model. Trilateralists call this decision making process "piecemeal functionalism."[16] No comprehensive blueprints would be proposed and debated, but bit by bit the overall trilateral design would take shape. Its "functional" components are to be adopted in more or less piecemeal fashion, lessening the chance people will grasp the overall scheme and organize resistance.

Piecemeal functionalism is part of the Trilateral Commission's "broad global strategy for the management of interdependence." Trilateralists speak of "interdependence" in trade of vital commodities such as oil and food; in finance and technology; in communications and transport; in ecology; in social expectations; and in the threat of nuclear holocaust. The global strategy is set forth in the report seen by the Commission as the culmination of its first three years of work: *Toward a Renovated International System.* Commissioners argue that in today's "increasingly complex world, problems multiply at a rate for which man's outlook, habits, and decision making processes are not prepared."[17] Trilateralists have volunteered themselves to take the lead in "coping with pressing problems and shaping emerging conditions" with the aim of scientifically managing interdependence ostensibly in the common interest. In actuality, trilateralists are proposing a strategy for the management of *dependence.*

*A technocrat is a technician or specialist (scientist, economist, political scientist, engineer, computer analyst, etc.). Daniel Bell writes, "In the technocratic mode, the ends have become simply efficiency and output," (in Daniel Bell, *The Coming of Post-Industrial Society,* New York, Basic Books, 1973, p. 354) A *technocracy* may be defined as "the theory or doctrine of a proposed system of government in which all economic resources, and hence the entire social system, would be controlled by scientists and engineers." (Webster New World Dictionary, 1970.)

Trilateralism promises a pseudotechnocracy, where technocrats would serve the owner/managers of the global corporations. Profit would remain the force behind efficiency although it would be cloaked in the rhetoric of increasing productivity and enhancing the social welfare.

The managers of dependence would be the *Transnational Elite* which Brzezinski describes as being "composed of international businessmen, scholars, professional men, and public officials. The ties of these new elites cut across national traditions and their interests are more functional than national."[18]

At the international level, trilateral leaders would be responsible for *rule-making,* i.e., "establishing frameworks of rules, standards, and procedures." Elites from other countries would be increasingly incorporated into *management,* i.e., making "operating decisions— within the rules." "Such rule-making constrains operating decisions in such a way that national decisions aggregate into a consistent and beneficial whole rather than working at cross-purposes." [19] "By the period 1985-90," predicts one observer, "countries like Mexico, Brazil, India, Iran [sic], and Saudi Arabia will probably have joined the 'advanced nation club' for a number of functions of that club."[20] Other so-called "new influentials" include Nigeria, Venezuela, and Indonesia. Rhetorically Commissioners claim that trilateral states do "not set out to remake the world in their own image." Nonetheless, they pose this revealing "long run view of what is desirable" in the international order:

> ...building an international system that is pluralistic enough to *permit cultivation of the values of trilateral countries* in all those countries that choose to cultivate them. [Italics mine.][21]

In reality trilateral leaders hope to give countries little choice in the matter; "Cultivation" is a poor euphemism for imperialism. About Western imperialism Brzezinski observes:

> To be sure, the fact that in the aftermath of World War II a number of nations were directly dependent on the United States in matters of security, politics, and economics created a system that in many respects including that of scale, superficially resembled the British, Roman, and Chinese empires of the past...
> ...*The 'empire' was at most an informal system marked by the pretense of equality and non-interference...*By the late 1960s the earlier direct political/military dependence on the U.S. had declined (often in spite of political efforts by the U.S. to maintain it). *Its place has been filled by the pervasive but less tangible influence of American economic presence and innovation...It works* through the *interpenetration* of economic institutions, the sympathetic harmony of political leaders and parties, the shared concepts of sophisticated intellectuals, the mating of bureaucratic interests...[Italics mine.]*[22]

---

*Carrying his line of thinking further Brzezinski writes: "It is the novelty of America's relationship with the world—complex, intimate, and porous—that the

Brzezinski is right in stressing the economic/cultural side of imperialism, but wrong in implying that it displaces militarism. This is as much pretense as the admitted "pretense of equality and non-interference." The "American economic presence" is quite tangible and it occurs in the context of cultural, political, and military imperialism. By "interpenetration" Brzezinski means penetration of the weaker by the dominant system. (If "imperialism" didn't have such negative connotations, trilateralists would probably start using the term "interimperialism").

Countries are continually bombarded with images of the fantasy American Dream. In countless ways the message of the dominant system penetrates: the Western Way is the good way, national culture is inferior. This is the meaning of cultural penetration or cultural imperialism. Mass advertising, Voice of America radio, educational sponsorships are all designed to shape tastes, beliefs, practices, and aspirations in the image of the West.* Foreign economic and military aid are less subtle means of influencing other countries. Presidents like Harry Truman and John Kennedy have applauded the value of foreign aid in molding development to suit the needs of Western business (e.g. Truman's Point 4 Program and Kennedy's Alliance for Progress).** Military leaders have long been indoctrinated in Western

---

more orthodox, especially Marxist, analyses of imperialism fail to encompass." Like all imperialists, Brzezinski purports to know imperialism best. Karl Marx himself understood quite well "the complex, intimate, and porous nature of imperialism" but it was not in his class interest—as it is in Brzezinski's—to pretend that this "intimacy" is invited and not forced.

*The success of corporate promotion of infant formula is a cruel example of cultural imperialism. Companies use a variety of approaches to get Third World mothers to switch from breast-feeding to bottle-feeding of their newborn babies. "The smiling white babies pictured on the front of formula tins can lead her to think that rich white mothers feed their baby this product and therefore it must be better." The same message is broadcast over radio and painted on billboards. Companies court hospital personnel, give out free samples, send "milk nurses" to visit the mother in the hospital and at home; all to get the baby and mother hooked on infant formula from the start. "Poverty, inadequate medical care, and unsanitary conditions make bottle feeding, to quote a government nurse in Peru, 'poison' for babies..." See Leah Margulies, "A Critical Essay on the Role of Promotion in Bottle Feeding," *PAG* [Protein-Calorie Advisory Group of the United Nations] *Bulletin*, September-December 1978.

Fortune brings home the point about education in this comment about Saudi Arabia: "the ministers and second-level bureaucrats who run the country are mostly products of Western education—one wag has called them the "California Mafia" because so many of them attended universities in that state." (31 July 1978).

**As Loring Waggoner of the U.S. Agency for International Development put it, "We are first trying to create some Joneses and then get somebody to keep up with them. From "Goal in Laos: Creating Joneses to Keep Up With," *New York Times*, 22 February 1966; cited in *Managing Social Change, op.cit.*

capitalist values and trained in the methods of law and order and counterinsurgency at schools in the Panama Canal Zone and colleges like West Point (deposed Nicaraguan dictator Somoza attended West Point; as children he and his brother went to Lasalle Military Academy on Long Island).

If the sun never sets on the global corporation then neither must it be shadowed by national sovereignty and democratic popular control. "Peacefully working to conquer the world" is how Singer Sewing Machine Company has described its marketing strategy. But societies are not conquered and reconquered with products alone. Global corporations seem to be eclipsing the sovereignty of nations, big and small. Yet these new corporate empires depend on the political, economic, and repressive power commanded by the ruling class of the nation-state to maintain a "favorable investment climate."* Western governments, particularly the U.S., train and supply the military and police of other countries to keep the "sympathetic political leaders" Brzezinski described in power and suppress working class movements. When governments turn unfriendly the West attempts to discipline them if possible, depose them if necessary, preferably through economic and political maneuvers. Often in action, always standing by, are the military and covert action forces of the United States, France, and a host of junior forces: Morocco, Saudia Arabia, Israel, and so on. (See article on U.S. militarism by Klare et al.) In the following section we will look more closely at how the Trilateral Way is imposed on the Third World.

Managing Third World Dependence: Revitalizing Imperialism

Trilateralists have always known that "issues related to economics are at the heart of modern politics" and they are determined to consolidate a *world economy* in which all national economies beat to the rhythm of transnational corporate capitalism (all hearts leaping at the sight of corporate products and all minds thinking in the language of technocrats). Trilateral elites hope to guarantee a stable supply of raw materials, cheap labor, and an expanding market place for global corporations by strengthening the bonds which keep Third World "development" (read "underdevelopment") defined by and dependent upon the expansion of the leading capitalist economies.

The Third World calls for a New International Economic Order

---

*In the film *Controlling Interest* (a vivid portrayal of multinational corporations and their impact in the U.S. and abroad, produced by California Newsreel), George Ball explains in an interview that government helps business by keeping "economy free of obstructions."

(NIEO) to redress structural inequities and protect national economic (and political) sovereignty. The Commission is attempting to substitute a "Renovated International Economic System" renovated by and for Trilateral Inc. Christopher Makins (then deputy director of the Commission) calls this "gradualist or reformist approach" to international change the "middle way between the rock of conservatism and the whirlpool of revolution." He cautions those who advocate "profound economic, social, and political changes":

> too extreme measures could have a self-defeating effect by threatening to throttle the goose which can lay the golden eggs of growth.[23]

The trilateral goal is to reorient efforts to *redistribute* global resources into promotion of a so-called "new order for mutual gain" (a concept elaborated by Richard Cooper, undersecretary of state for economic affairs, among others).[24] This would be nothing more than the old order for trilateral gain thinly disguised by a few flourishes of affirmative action for Third World elites and whatever "trickle-down" effects an expanding world economy could afford. As always the rich in the rich and poor countries will get richer at the expense of the poor in all countries.

Largely in response to OPEC's early success, trilateral economist C. Fred Bergsten (Carter's assistant secretary of the treasury) illustrated the implications of Third World leverage over indigenous resources. He recommended that the United States respond to this "threat from the Third World" not with continued "confrontation and hostility" but "within a framework of generally cooperative relations."[25] (Norman Girvan analyzes the meaning of economic nationalism for the West and Third World peoples in "Economic Nationalists vs. Multinational Corporations: Revolutionary or Evolutionary Change?") The West had first attempted to split OPEC solidarity—without success. In 1975, Tom Farer (then serving as special assistant to the assistant secretary of state for InterAmerican Affairs) explained how a "strategy for accommodation" is analogous to the strategy used to diffuse class conflict in the industrialized West in the early twentieth century:

> In the years of bitter class conflict between capital and labor, before the ameliorations and compromises of the welfare state, many advocates of a hard line against the demands of labor invoked the alleged insatiability of those demands in support of a confrontational strategy...Nothing is better calculated to promote miscalculation than the pretense that the equilibrium of power has not shifted, that we can continue to dictate to the Third World on the terms which sufficed in the epoch of the Western imperium.[26]

Looking to the lessons of the past and faced with a volatile future, trilateralists seek new terms upon which to dictate to the Third World. (See article by Philip Wheaton for trilateralism's proposed terms for the Caribbean.) In discussing attitudes behind the rise of the modern welfare state—the terms upon which capital continues to dictate to labor—Commissioners observe that they are rooted "in ethical and philosophical values of the West as well as in *enlightened self-interest,* since *a minumum of social justice and reform will be necessary for stability in the long run."* [Italics mine.][27]

Accordingly, Commissioners describe the major tasks of their "strategy for the management of interdependence" as: "keeping the peace, managing the world economy, satisfying the basic human needs, and protecting human rights."[28] Regarding "basic human needs," Commissioners write:

> The alleviation of poverty is a demand of the basic principles of the West as well as simple *self-interest.* In the long run an *orderly world* is unlikely if great affluence in one part coexists with abject poverty in another while *"one world"* of communication, of mutual concern, and interdependence comes into being." [Italics mine.][29]

The regimes of countries which the Trilateral Commission calls "International Middle Class countries" or "new influentials" (mentioned above) are to be co-opted with an increased role and stake in international management and split from the ranks of Third World countries.[30] (See Kai Bird "Coopting the Third World Elites: Trilateralism and Saudi Arabia.")

In this trilateral scheme of divide and rule, the poorest countries (or "Fourth World"*) are to be pacified with a basic human needs approach. Symbolic minimal welfare programs would be administered through Western-dominated agencies such as the World Bank in accordance with a world development budget. Needless to say the terms of development would be dictated along lines which serve the global corporation in promoting an orderly world economy.

Corporate controlled economic growth operates according to the "Law of Uneven Development"—"the tendency of the system to

---

*The Trilateral Commission classifies as "Fourth World" those "resource-poor, low-income developing countries that lack large foreign exchange reserves, buoyant export prospects, or the ability to service credit on commercial or near-commercial terms." It "includes some 30 countries with nearly 1 billion people, among them India, Pakistan, Bangladesh, some tropical African countries, and a few countries in Latin America." In the "Third World" category "are countries like Mexico, Brazil, Turkey and Malaysia, which enjoy substantial foreign exchange reserves, high prices for their exports or ready access to capital markets." See *A Turning Point in North South Economic Relations* (Trilateral Commission, 1974), p. 13.

produce poverty as well as wealth, underdevelopment as well as development."[31] The gap between rich and poor countries widens. Workers and peasants grow increasingly impoverished as national income rises and a narrow strata at the top is enriched. Commissioners themselves admit (outside their classrooms and corporate PR activities): "meeting basic human needs is not necessarily the same as fostering economic development"; "a great deal of our past thinking on economic development has failed to put human beings in the center of transitional strategies"; and "rising per capita GNP figures may well obscure increasing misery within the state in question." Nonetheless, they promise more of the same, declaring: "countries that want economic development would be well-advised to welcome foreign firms on *appropriate* terms"[32] (i.e., terms appropriate and profitable for the corporations).

In discussing the goal of alleviating poverty, trilateralists conclude: "we do not have the human resources to eliminate poverty within the immediately foreseeable future; but we can contribute toward that end over a longer period of time." What they mean is that without steps to redistribute existing wealth and to reallocate the means of producing wealth, poverty and hunger are here to stay. (Dahlia Rudavsky analyzes the Commission's plans to cultivate more food for profit while perpetuating poverty.)

Trilateralists correctly note that "for the weaker developing countries, interdependence appears as a system of dependence...As they see it their entire economy and external trade have been shaped according to priorities defined by stronger industrialized states and not by their own needs."[33] They fear that "the idea of greater self-reliance, which is, in fact, an indispensable goal of development policy, could degenerate into a rejection of an integrated world economy if present trends continue."[34] In 1975, Brzezinski warned:

> ...today we find the international scene dominated on its overt plane more by conflict between the advanced world and the developing world than by conflict between trilateral democracies and the communist states...*the new aspirations of the Third and Fourth Worlds united together seems to me to pose a very major threat to the nature of the international system and ultimately to our own societies. That threat is the threat of denial of cooperation.*[35] [Italics mine.]

How do the trilateral powers keep Third World states "cooperative?" In the wake of World War II, old-style colonialism gave way to neocolonialism. The neocolonial state has formal political independence but "in reality its economic system and thus its political policy is directed from outside."[36] Instead of a single colonial master, the neocolonial state may have many new masters: Western governments (especially the U.S.), the International Monetary Fund, banking consortiums, global corporations. Western powers have intervened repeatedly to sabotage and smash governments which challenged the tightly woven fabric of dependency: Iran, 1953; Guatemala, 1954; the Congo (now Zaire), 1960; Brazil, 1964; Dominican Republic and Indonesia, 1965; Bolivia, 1970-71; Chile, 1973. (The 1961 Bay of Pigs invasion of Cuba, orchestrated by the CIA and top government and military officials with President Kennedy's approval, was defeated.)

Debt dependency is one of the neocolonial leashes around a Third World country's neck. The leash is let out to allow Western-directed development projects to gallop ahead—returning enormous profits to foreign corporations and banks. Or, the debt leash can be pulled in tight—as part of an economic and political *destabilization* campaign—to strangle a rebellious nation into submission.

Destabilization is the dominant system's "cure" for any government which threatens the economic freedom of international business as it becomes "more" responsive to the needs of its people. And the global doctors know just how painful their cure can be; it kills the body to save the cancer. The overthrow of Chile's democratically elected government is a case in point.*

*From a memo to Chilean President Frei, September 1970, in *Controlling Interest.* The case of Chile's destabilization following Salvador Allende's presidential victory is well documented. Nixon, Kissinger, and CIA director Richard Helms succeeded in their efforts to "make the economy scream" by orchestrating an economic blockade of the country—cutting off U.S. aid and all lines of international public and private bank finance and orchestrating economic and political sabotage within the country. Military assistance, however, was increased in order to encourage and enable the army to overthrow Allende's government and smash Chilean democracy to bring back "economic freedom."

More than 30,000 people were killed, including President Allende, resisting the military coup of September 11, 1973. Since then, over 2,000 people have "disappeared" and most are presumed dead. More than 100,000 people have been jailed for political reasons; torture is commonplace. Thousands of people have been forced to flee into exile.

Today hunger and starvation have replaced the community-based nutrition and food programs of the Allende government. Out of a sample of 19,000 children in a Church-sponsored study two-thirds were found to be malnourished in 1976. Infant mortality, reduced during the Allende years, jumped 18 percent during the first year of military rule. Before the coup unemployment had been reduced to 3.1 percent. By 1976 about one-fourth of the population had no income. A 1976 IMF study reveals the extent of income redistribution—from the poor to the rich—since the coup. In 1972, 63 percent of the total national income went to wage and salaried workers while property owners received 37 percent in the form of profits, dividends, and rent. By 1974, 62 percent went to the propertied sector and labor's share was cut to 38 percent. See for example: Orlando Letellier, "Chile: Economic 'Freedom' and Political Repression," a joint publication by *Race & Class*/ The Transnational Institute/Spokesman pamphlets, 1976 and Michael Moffitt, "Chicago Economics in Chile," *Challenge,* September-October 1977, reprinted by the Transnational Institute.

Three years before the coup U.S. Ambassador Korry communicated Washington's sinister promise:

> Not a nut or bolt shall reach Chile under Allende. Once Allende comes to power we shall do all within our power to condemn Chile and all Chileans to utmost deprivation and poverty...*

Events in Jamaica in the late 1970s reveal a newer brand of debt diplomacy—its more insidious style is preferred by trilateralists over the Chilean coup scenario. Even more than before, the International Monetary Fund acts as chief ambassador of Western capitalism in the art of debt diplomacy. The IMF is not the world's biggest loanshark, but it is the most important; the IMF "good housekeeping seal" is the green light for lending by banks, government agencies, and other international financial institutions like the World Bank. The U.S. and other trilateral countries control the IMF. (See article by James Phillips.)

The IMF program of economic stabilization spells austerity for the mass of the population. Measures are designed to entice foreign investment: so-called "luxury" social welfare programs like food and education subsidies are dismantled; wages are kept down. Harsh repression is often needed to carry out a forced cut in already meager living standards and redirect resources to the export business sector (the key sector for economic health in the IMF's view) which is largely foreign owned and controlled. Not surprisingly, the Commission has recommended a strengthening and expansion of the IMF's role in monitoring the international monetary system and managing "interdependence." As Franz Hinkelammert points out: "The Trilateral countries see 'interdependence' as a weapon in this conflict [between Western capitalism and the people of the Third World] and the use of this weapon is called destabilization."[37]

The "Human Rights" Strategy

When it comes to protecting human rights, Carter has launched the so-called Human Rights Campaign and committed the United States to "shaping a world order" that is "just," "peaceful," and "more responsive to human aspirations." The Commission uses this same rhetoric for the same purpose: it is a moral mask on the face of trilateralism with its goal of "shaping a world order" that remains responsive to corporate aspirations.* Trilateral states do not piously

---

*High sounding slogans like "making the world safe for democracy" have become familiar refrains in drowning out the true battle cry of U.S. interventionism. In 1961, for example, President Kennedy launched the "Alliance for Progress" in Latin America closely on the heels of the 1959 Cuban Revolution (which Kennedy

practice the human rights they preach—either inside or outside their borders.* Indeed, repression and counterinsurgency are the glue for the trilateral mask of reform.

Placing the Carter Human Rights Campaign in its proper historical context, James Petras observes:

> Morality is the recurring ideological expression of U.S. imperialism in a period of crisis: it is what is offered to the world in place of substantive changes in the world's economic and social order.[38]

When *substantive* change does occur it reflects a *failure* of the human rights policy, not a success. No case illustrates this more clearly than long-time Western support of the Shah's regime in Iran and its 1978-79 overthrow by the Iranian people. The Shah's regime received more U.S. military equipment than any other country in the world and was an economic bonanza for global corporations. With Saudi Arabia, the Shah's regime was to provide stability in the Middle East and moderation in OPEC policies, securing oil for the trilateral regions.**

Trilateralists caution that "in *many cases,* the support for human rights will have to be balanced against other important goals of world order."[39] [Italics mine.] They use detente with the Soviet Union as an example of where balance is needed. But the cases of countries like Iran, Nicaragua, South Korea, the Philippines, and South Africa are far more telling. Henry Kissinger bluntly explains the lesson to be

---

unsuccessfully tried to smash in 1961 with the CIA-led Bay of Pigs invasion). Stepped-up counterinsurgency assistance was coupled with mounting aid for economic development. The goal was to prevent "another Cuba" by defusing revolutionary potential where possible, crushing revolutionary movements where necessary.

*Remember the outcry when then U.N. Ambassador Andrew Young—one of the most candid and "enlightened" trilateralists—commented: "After all, in our prisons too, there are hundreds, perhaps even thousands of people who I would call political prisoners." He and we were reminded that "Human Rights" are a propaganda tool, being used then—at the time of the Soviet dissident trials (the U.S. press provided front page dramatizations)—as a Cold War weapon.

**When the Shah visited Washington D.C. in 1977, Carter toasted: "if ever there was a country which has blossomed forth under enlightened leadership, it would be the ancient empire of Persia which is now the great country of Iran" (with a little unmentioned help from the CIA which deposed the nationalist Prime Minister Mosadegh in 1953, brought the Shah back into power and then supported him until the final hour). The backdrop to the Shah's visit was a battle between anti-Shah and pro-Shah demonstrators; when tear gas drifted into the welcoming ceremonies, Carter apologized for the "temporary air pollution." *Washington Post* headlines begin to tell the story: "Human Rights on the Eclipse," "Iran Shifts Stand, Will Try to Keep Oil Prices Down," "Shah heads for U.S. with Arms List," "Helms as Consultant: Former Ambassador [and former CIA head] will be Go-between for Iranian Firms."

drawn from events leading to the overthrow of the Shah:

> The fundamental challenge of a revolution is this: *certainly wise governments forestall revolutions by making timely concessions;* indeed the very wisest governments do not consider adaptations as concessions, but rather as part of a natural process of increasing popular support. However, *once a revolution has occurred, the preeminent requirement is the restoration of authority.* These concessions, which had they been taken a year earlier might have avoided the situation, accelerated the process of disintegration...[Italics mine.][40]

Trilateral economics dictate unceasing exploitation. Still trilateralists rhetorically claim "a basic human solidarity with the oppressed." The lesson we must draw from events in Iran and around the globe is that human rights trilateral style is a move played in the game of world politics. It is never played "in solidarity with the oppressed" but only by and for the oppressor.

Keeping this point in mind, we see that two seemingly contradictory strategies are employed by trilateralists toward the same end: to keep conservative pro-Western Third World elites from being supplanted by progressive forces. First, there is maintenance of police states, or national security states as they are commonly known in Latin America, wherever they can remain stable and serve the needs of Western capitalism. Many of these regimes have served an increasingly important function as regional police and subimperialists under guidelines set forth in the Nixon Doctrine (explained in the article by Klare et al.).

Second, there is encouragement of "democratization" or "liberalization," as the Carter administration calls it. The goal is to transform client dictatorships into pro-Western subordinate forms of limited capitalist democracies (sometimes referred to as "new democracy" or "viable democracy").*

Liberalization is not a gift of the international ruling class. It comes of necessity when the revolutionary potential of the population is mounting under the unceasing repression and poverty of the police state; it entails the concessions Kissinger spoke of regarding Iran. Or it comes of necessity when local businessmen and landowners are closed out of wealth accumulation shared only with privileged foreign corporations. Often the ruling clique has a stranglehold on the economy (such as the Somoza family did in

---

*Arturo Sist and Gregorio Iriarte of the Bolivian Permanent Assembly for Human Rights wrote one of the earliest critical analyses of Carter's Human Rights Campaign and the transformation of National Security States to limited democracies (September 1977, La Paz, Bolivia). See the bibliography for references.

Nicaragua). If there is too much graft and patronage (and too much money leaving the country for Swiss bank accounts and foreign property) stymying the growth of the middle class and stunting economic development, then pressure mounts within the capitalist class and middle strata for a civilian government.

Democratization trilateral style requires the existence of a moderate alternative to military dictatorship, such as Antonio Guzman in the Dominican Republic (see article by Lisa Wheaton on events in the Dominican Republic). The moderate platform promises greater political freedom for the population while encouraging an expanding middle sector of entrepreneurs and consumers within a capitalist economy. By curbing the practices of arbitrary imprisonment, murder, exile, torture, and blanket censorship—focusing repression on the "extremists"—capitalists hope to defuse the popular struggle for universal economic and social rights (employment, food, housing, health, education) and true political participation. These rights go beyond what trilateralists see as the "minimum of social justice and reform" necessary for stability (and expanding markets) to directly threaten trilateral neoimperialism.

When liberation forces are strong, with widespread popular support, democratization has no chance of success. Witness the failure of the U.S. attempt to install the Bakhtiar regime in Iran or impose a conservative coalition government in Nicaragua (as the Sandinista-led victory drew near). In both cases, Washington was surprised when the people proved powerful enough to overthrow their respective dictatorships. Washington was again surprised when the people refused to hand their country back to U.S. caretakers. The trilateral strategy of democratization is a strategy of co-optation. It has a chance of success when power lies with the reformist elements in society, but not in the face of a broad-based revolutionary movement.

East-West Relations: Rehabilitating the "Dropouts"

The corporate one world economy must also include the Soviet Union, Eastern Europe, and China. Trilateralists want to see these regions they call dropouts return to the school of Western capitalism—at least for training in how to conduct international relations, if not domestic affairs as well.

U.S. recognition of the People's Republic of China in 1979, thirty years after its establishment, removed a roadblock to trilateral relations with China, as does normalization of relations between Japan and China, and Japan's friendship treaty with Russia. Recent business deals offer a glimpse of the enormous economic bonanza global corporations see in China's drive to modernize. China is not perceived as particularly threatening to the West so long as it remains on unfriendly terms with the USSR (it is assumed that China will be a regional power, not a world power, at least through the 1980s). The 1978 report, *An Overview of East-West Relations,* states: "The present degree of Sino-Soviet hostility...tends to benefit the West; and the West should help to ensure that the present situation continues to be worthwhile for China. In particular, it is clearly in the interest of the West to grant China favorable conditions in economic relations."[41]* The question for trilateralism is how best to play the so-called China Card in the continuing East-West conflict between the U.S. and the USSR. As trilateralists see it, the East-West conflict "combines the features of a power competition between the two superpowers of our time, and of an ideological conflict between rival political, economic and social systems based on fundamentally different values."[42] Trilateralists say to the Soviet Union: you can't beat the U.S.—especially in economic and ideological warfare—so why not join it. The hope is that the USSR will join the "Community of the Developed Nations" in defending the global interests of the industrialized rich countries against those of the Third World.

Trilateralists uphold the principles of both detente and deterrence. Within the Trilateral Commission there is disagreement over how warm should be the initiatives of detente, how powerful must be nuclear and conventional deterrence, and how much to link progress in one area to progress in the other.

The 1977 trilateral report, *Collaboration with Communist Countries in Managing Global Problems,* is optimistic about the prospect of widening cooperation with the USSR (and China) while winding down the arms race.[43] It explores opportunities for cooperative management on international problems: food, energy, the oceans, space, weather, earthquake warning, development aid, trade policy, and nonproliferation of nuclear weapons.

In contrast, the 1978 trilateral report (mentioned above) airs the views of the "hard line." It stresses the conflictual relationship between the Soviet Union and the West, arguing that detente is not the path to ending Soviet-U.S. rivalry but represents "necessary and useful efforts to limit the forms and range, the risks and burdens of a continuing conflict by negotiation and partial cooperation."[44] This report urges that the West make a concerted effort to shape Soviet (and Chinese) policies while containing Soviet economic and military power:

---

*China has been granted "most favored nation" trade status, which the USSR has long been denied. The most favored national principle stipulated that any trading concessions between any two countries must be granted (on an equal basis) to all countries which are part of the most favored nation trading agreement.

A stable world order is not a realistic objective for the West in a fundamentally unstable world. The only kind of peaceful world order that we can realistically envisage is one of *maximum flexibility for peaceful change*. As a *Basic Guideline* for its long-term relationship with Communist powers, *the West should seek to influence the natural processes of change worldwide in a direction that is favorable to its fundamental values.* This does not mean seeking a breakdown of the Communist regimes; but rather, given the difficult economic and political choices which keep facing them, particularly at a time of impending generation change in the Soviet Union, seeking to *influence the kind of choices that are possible and necessary within their given structure.* Through negotiations, in the framework of detente, on the limitation of armaments and of international violence, on terms for economic cooperation and communication across frontiers, *the West can shape the alternatives facing its negotiating partners in such a way as to make some choices more rewarding* to them than others. [Italics mine.][45]

An evenhanded policy toward the Soviet Union and China is in the trilateralists' best trading interest; but pressure for a hardhanded approach to the USSR has intensified in 1979 and 1980 (inside and outside the Commission). A centerpiece of the uneven approach to China and the USSR is growing U.S. military collaboration with the Chinese against a perceived Soviet threat: Pakistan (bordering Afghanistan), Thailand (bordering Cambodia), a U.S. green light for the Chinese invasion of Vietnam in early 1979. U.S. leaders continue to see the world divided into Soviet and U.S.-dominated "spheres of influence." While some trilateralists, like former UN Ambassador Andrew Young, oppose this view, most insist upon seeing all national liberation forces as Soviet pawns (or as pawns of Cuba which is painted as a Soviet proxy). The West continues to raise the specter of the Soviet bear whenever it feels that the U.S./Western sphere of influence is threatened: Zaire, Zimbabwe (Rhodesia), Nicaragua, Iran. (These issues will be discussed more extensively in the conclusion to this volume.)

Nonetheless, trilateralists are confident they can win the ideological and economic "competition" with the Soviet Union. They believe that the Soviet economy is declining and will reach a crisis state in the 1980s. More importantly, they believe that any country—whatever its economic system—will want Western products and technology (both Young and Brzezinski are vigorous proponents of this view). A recurring theme in business literature is that in trading with the West the elites of other countries will come to think like the West and act to shape their country in the West's image.*

Fortune described this "risk of infection" in an article about the Soviet Union

The meaning of detente for trilateralism is necessarily contradictory. The aim is to provide "maximum flexibility for peaceful change" favorable to Western capitalism. This means that moves will be made to relate more predictably and profitably with the Soviet Union and China. At the same time the U.S. will continue to press the arms race, maximizing the forms, range, and risk of nuclear annihilation. (Besides Klare et al., also see Wolfe's article in Part VIII for discussion of the domestic pressures on U.S. policy toward the Soviet Union.)

Managing Western Democracy:
Limited Democracy is "Governable Democracy"

Trilateralists are not only concerned with managing international events. They are determined to manage North American, West European, and Japanese democracy, fitting these societies ever more closely to the needs of global capitalism.

During the 1960s and 1970s ruling elites in the United States—and throughout the West—were challenged with militant protest from a wide cross-section of the public: workers, Native Americans, Blacks, women, poor people, students, Chicanos, Asian Americans, gays, environmentalists. The antiwar movement shook the bipartisan foreign policy consensus which was grounded in the Cold War and U.S. supremacy. Pressure mounted for a more equitable and democratic political, economic, and social system.

Protest was nonviolent and violent, organized and spontaneous, short-lived and enduring. Hundreds of thousands of people marched on Washington, a wave of riots hit major cities and universities were shut down. The ruling class response was often brutal. Protestors were beaten and jailed, leaders were murdered. Students, white and Black, were shot down at Kent State and Jackson State. Police brutality was widespread, especially in minority communities. The FBI escalated its counterintelligence program (COINTELPRO) against Black, Native American, and Puerto Rican liberation struggles; the New Left; the antiwar movement; and the Women's

---

entitled, "This Communist Internationale has a Capitalist Accent": "...an export sector would be linked to the economic and political world beyond the Soviet Union's closely guarded borders. The increased number of executives and managers assigned to it would of necessity spend long stretches of time living and working in the West, just as a carefully selected few do now. They would wheel and deal with Western businessmen, they would socialize with them, they would dress like them, talk like them, and inevitably some would start to think like them. The possibility of ideological infection from prolonged contact with the "Free World" has always terrorized Soviet leaders. It still does, and in the end, they may be unwilling to risk the political hazards of trade." See Herbert E. Meyer, "This Communist Internationale Has a Capitalist Accent," *Fortune* (February 1977), p. 148.

movement. The CIA carried out a covert action campaign within the U.S. and abroad against U.S. citizens assumed to be involved in antiwar activity known as Operation MHCHAOS (MH standing for matters related to internal U.S. security and CHAOS signifying its goal of infiltrating and destroying antiwar groups).

In 1975 the Trilateral Commission released its book-length study, *The Crisis of Democracy: Report on the Governability of Democracies to the Trilateral Commission*. Noam Chomsky best summarizes the theme: "Trilateral's RX for Crisis: Governability Yes. Democracy NO."[46]*

The 1960s are the point of departure for the trilateral analysis. Samuel Huntington, author of the chapter on the United States, describes this period as the "decade of democratic surge and of the reassertion of democratic egalitarianism."** What must follow, as the trilateralists see it, is the reassertion of elite rule and decades of public apathy. Thus, domestic items on the trilateral agenda include: reducing the expectations of the poor and middle class, increasing presidential authority, strengthening business-government cooperation in economic planning, stricter press self-regulation and government oversight, and pacification of rank and file labor.

The Crisis of Democracy contains sections on the United States, Western Europe and Japan with a joint introduction and conclusion followed by an important appendix. The appendix reviews the discussions of the Task Force Report at the plenary meeting in Kyoto, Japan in 1975 and outlines "Arenas for Action" which contain specific recommendations prepared as points of departure for the Kyoto discusion. The book was published in 1975 by New York University Press.

The Commission has attempted to put some distance between itself and the controversial *Crisis of Democracy* study; differing views were aired in *Trialogue* (Fall 1976). There are no disclaimers in its *Annual Reports* however. The 1975-76 report, for example, highlights the study, noting "Prime Minister Miki has given special attention to this report, and the Japanese office reports that 'governability' is becoming household jargon." In *Trialogue* (Spring 1976), co-author Huntington illustrates the report's importance, notably,"in lowering public expectations of what governments can achieve."

**Samuel Huntington is a Harvard professor who has had a role in confronting crises of democracy before. He was the architect of the program of "forced urbanization" (through bombing, burning, and strafing rural areas) designed to undercut the support base for the liberation forces during the Vietnam War. He resigned his post on the National Security Council (NSC) in August 1978 to become director of Harvard's Center for International Affairs. About Huntington's resignation, journalist Jim Hoagland writes: "Coming here on the campus-capital-campus shuttle that helped spawn Vietnam, Huntington was an acknowledged expert on military forces, structure and warfare. He leaves as an outspoken advocate of 'economic diplomacy' to force the Soviets to behave themselves." Following Huntington's recommendations, the NSC has been brought into the process of reviewing applications for sale of technology to the Soviet Union (*Washington Post*).

Below we will review key themes in the trilateral diagnosis and prescription for the crisis of democracy, when "the spirit of protest, the spirit of equality, the impulse to expose inequities were abroad in the land."

Diagnosis

"Truman had been able to govern the country with the cooperation of a relatively small number of Wall Street lawyers and bankers."[47]* Huntington concludes (regretfully) this was no longer possible by the late sixties. Why not? Presidential authority was eroded. There was a broad reappraisal of governmental action and "morality" in the post-Vietnam/post-Watergate era among political leaders who, like the general public, openly questioned "the legitimacy of hierarchy, coercion, discipline, secrecy, and deception—all of which are, in some measure," according to Huntington, "inescapable attributes of the process of government."[48] Congressional power became more decentralized and party allegiances to the administration weakened. Traditional forms of public and private authority were undermined as "people no longer felt the same compulsion to obey those whom they had previously considered superior to themselves in age, rank, status, expertise, character, or talents."[49]

Throughout the sixties and into the seventies, too many people participated too much:

> Previously passive or unorganized groups in the population, blacks, Indians, Chicanos, white ethnic groups, students, and women now embarked on concerted efforts to establish their claims to opportunities, positions, rewards, and privileges, *which they had not considered themselves entitled* [sic] *before.*[50] [Italics mine.]

Against their will, these "groups"—the *majority* of the population—have been denied "opportunities, positions, rewards and privileges." More democracy is not the answer: "applying that cure at the present time could well be adding fuel to the flames." Huntington concludes that "some of the problems of governance in the United States today stem from an *excess of democracy*...Needed, instead, is a greater degree of moderation in democracy."

---

*More explicitly, the report states: "(T)o the extent that the United States was governed by anyone during the decades after World War II, it was governed by the president acting with the support and cooperation of key individuals and groups in the Executive Office, the Federal bureaucracy, Congress and the more important businesses, banks, law firms, foundations, and media, which constitute the private establishment." (p. 92)

...The effective operation of a democratic political system usually requires some measure of apathy and non-involvement on the part of some individuals and groups. In the past, every democratic society has had a marginal population, of greater or lesser size, which has not actively participated in politics. In itself, this marginality on the part of some groups is inherently undemocratic but it is also one of the factors which has enabled democracy to function effectively. [Italics mine.][51]

With a candor which has shocked those trilateralists who are more accustomed to espousing the type of "symbolic populism" Carter employed so effectively in his campaign, the Governability Report expressed the open secret that effective capitalist democracy is *limited* democracy! (See Alan Wolfe, "Capitalism Shows Its Face.")

Huntington outlines the economic ramifications of the crisis of democracy. In the 1960s people put pressure on government—which was then, as it is now, being seen by more and more people as a captive of big business interests—to increase social welfare spending and regulate the economy in the interest of the greater population. Demands for improved education, social security, welfare, health care, and other social services snowballed into what the report calls an "overload" on the state. The state was already "loaded" down with responsibilities: expenditures for the Vietnam War and a global police force; welfare for business and the wealthy in the form of tax breaks, business subsidies, easy credit, etc., (a recent example of welfare for business is the deregulation of natural gas and oil). But with such a high level of popular mobilization, public interest lobbying efforts, and rising unionization among public employees, government was less inclined to say no to citizen and worker demands. Programs designed to defuse, channel and co-opt popular participation expanded rapidly. People in leadership roles were encouraged to work for change within the system as poverty program administrators, civil rights lawyers, and affirmative action officers.

At all levels government increasingly relied on deficit spending— spending more than the amount of revenue collected through taxes— to meet commitments. The Johnson Administration, for example, funded the Vietnam War by printing money and expanding the federal deficit—rather than attempting to raise taxes and revealing the extent of U.S. involvement. City and state officials went on debt-financed redevelopment sprees (like the New York City World Trade Center; urban renewal became known as urban removal to its many victims. Northeastern cities, especially, fell behind in efforts to keep mass transit and maintain other essential services in the face of rising expenses and a shrinking revenue and employment base (as higher income people escaped to the suburbs and big business ran away to southern and foreign low-wage-tax regions). Cities became increasingly dependent upon private banks which were glad to lend at higher and higher interest rates and strengthen their role in directing city development through institutions like New York City's Emergency Financial Control Board, established in September 1975. Their prescription for "fiscal crisis?" Impose austerity on workers and the poor and restore "investor confidence."

Inflation—already shooting up under the spending for the Vietnam War—continued spiralling. As Huntington sees it, the fiscal crisis of capitalism—a gap between state expenditures and revenues—is "a product of democratic politics."* The message behind this oversimplification is clear: in the trilateral analysis, the capitalist economy can only function well when it responds to the needs of the ruling class of bankers, businessmen and their support group of lawyers, technocrats, and policy-minded academics. A capitalist economy cannot withstand the pressure of democratic participation.

Prescription

How do the trilateralists propose to make democracy more governable? In the age where the media is considered the most effective means of reaching the "hearts and minds" of the population, steps must be taken to strengthen the symbiosis between media and government.

The Huntington report blames network coverage of the Vietnam War and exposure of the Pentagon Papers for undermining public confidence in government. Huntington uses a statement by Walter Cronkite to draw a lesson from the experiences of the sixties and seventies: the lesson is that "most newsmen" are "inclined to side with *humanity* rather than with authority and institutions."[52]

The media is almost wholly controlled by giant corporations like Time, CBS, RCA(NBC), ABC—which are in turn controlled largely by banks such as Chase Manhattan and Citibank**—which are very

---

*Huntington refers to James O'Connor's work, *The Fiscal Crisis of the State* (New York: St. Martin's Press, 1973). He wrongly purports to be improving on O'Connor's Marxian analysis. Alan Wolfe discusses both O'Connor's analysis and Huntington's reasoning in "Capitalism Shows Its Face" in this volume.

**In his article "Who Owns the Networks?" (*The Nation,* 25 November 1978) Peter Borsnan points out that "Chase and the other Rockefeller institutions are among the largest holders of network stock with substantial interests in all three networks [ABC, CBS, NBC]." For example, a 1973 Senate report on disclosure of corporate ownership (issued by Senators Muskie and Metcalf) found that Chase Manhattan controlled 14 percent of CBS. Brosnan points out that, with stock widely distributed among shareholders, institutions can wield great influence or outright control with 5 percent, sometimes 1 or 2 percent, equity.

much a part of the ruling class. (Media chiefs like Hedley Donovan of Time Inc.. are prominent Commission members.) Yet trilateralists point to an imbalance between government and media favoring the cause of "humanity" (i.e., the mass of the population not part of the ruling class). At times the press is too free to disclose information, such as in the case of the *Pentagon Papers* (it is less likely that Big Media will go too far in its role of tolerable criticism). Thus in an arena for action entitled "restoring a balance between government and media" Commissioners recommend more rigorous self-censorship. The right of the press to "print what it wants without prior restraint except in most unusual circumstances" is to be upheld.

> *But* there is also the need to assure government the right to withhold information at the source...Journalists should develop their own standards of professionalism and create mechanisms, such as press councils, *for enforcing these standards on themselves. The alternative could well be regulation by government.** [Italics mine.][53]

Trilateralists point to the media as one opposition power threatening the governability of democracy. An adversary culture among intellectuals (and student followers) is believed to be another. So-called "value-oriented intellectuals" traitorously "assert their disgust with the corruption, materialism and inefficiency of democracy and with the subservience of democratic government to 'monopoly capitalism.' " They do so in action as well as in words, taking part in causes like the antiwar movement, and, currently, the antinuclear movement. "This development," states the governability report, "constitutes a challenge to democratic government which is, potentially at least as serious as those posed in the past by the aristocratic cliques, fascist movements, and communist parties."[54] Upholding the values of the corporate system, in contrast, are the "technocratic policy-oriented intellectuals" who should be cloned on a global scale.

In reality, the adversary group of intellectuals is small. A much larger number are reproducing (aggressively or passively) corporate ideology in their roles as professors, sometime government officials, corporate directors and advisors, authors, and researchers. "Value-oriented intellectuals" threaten trilateralism by stepping outside the implicit bounds of liberal/moderate/conservative debate to question the very assumptions and legitimacy of the system itself.

---

*This statement should not be taken as implying that trilateralists desire *direct* press regulation. They much prefer that the corporations which dominate the media enforce their own codes of conduct.

Trilateralists write: "*By now higher education is the most important value-producing system in society.* That it works poorly or at cross-purposes with society should be a matter of great concern."[55] [Italics mine.] Higher education has always been a concern of the ruling class. Businessmen and bankers are the trustees of public and private educational institutions. Private colleges and universities are beholden to the gifts of corporations and rich alumni. Research is financially censored by private foundations. But with the sixties in mind, Commissioners urge a reexamination of higher education—hoping to make even less room for opposition and alienation to develop.

Like democracy, education must be limited—serving the needs of the ruling class. Education and work go hand in hand. Commissioners recommend that more teenagers be steered away from college toward vocational training and that an attempt be made to lower the career expectations of "surplus" people with college degrees. In both cases these measures are aimed first and foremost, not at the traditionally educated white male elite, but at minorities and women who fill the lower levels of the work force.

Labor's role is critical to the governability of capitalist domcracy. Regarding labor and social policies, Commissioners delineate two sets of problems in the "arenas for action": "First, the working structure of the enterprise, and, second, the content of the job itself." Not surprisingly, they suggest that reform efforts be focused on job content[56]—the more trivial aspects the better.

Presently, U.S. industrial relations are built upon the model of collective bargaining where "the relationship between Union and Management is adversarial." In the long run Commissioners see the need for more Western European-style "consensual" or cooperative industrial relations.*(William Tabb discusses the trilateral view of industrial relations in Part V.)

Trilateralists are fond of business unions, the type represented by the past and present Union leaders recruited onto the Commission: I.W. Abel (former president of United Steel workers), Lane Kirkland (president and former secretary-treasurer of the AFL-CIO), Sol Chaikin (president of the notoriously low-wage ILGWU), Leonard Woodcock (former president of the United Auto Workers and Carter's ambassador to China), and so on. Their job, like that of Third World strongmen, is to provide a docile labor force at the cheapest price possible.**

*This theme is expounded in the 1979 Task Force Report, *Collective Bargaining and Employee Participation in Western Europe, North America and Japan,* whose U.S. author was George C. Lodge of the Harvard Business School.
**"By the standards of today, the U.S. offers both cheap energy and cheap labor—

The governability of society at the national level depends upon the extent to which it is effectively governed at the sub-national, regional, local, functional, and industrial levels. In the modern state, for instance, powerful trade union "bosses" are often viewed as a threat to the power of the state. In actuality, however, *responsible union leaders with effective authority over their members are less of a challenge to the authority of the national political leaders than they are a prerequisite* to the exercise of authority by those leaders. If the unions are disorganized, if the membership is rebellious, if extreme demands and wild-cat strikes are the order of the day, the formulation and implementation of a national wage policy become impossible. [Italics mine][57]

A national wage policy would be one element of "effective planning for economic and social development" carried out by economists and planners representing business and government. In the draft report, *Industrial Policy and the International Economy,* (March 1979), the need for "voluntary concertation" between government and industry is stressed. Non-Japanese trilateralists are envious of the close and uncloseted business-government partnership known as Japan Inc. (giving Japan a competitive edge they resent).

A sound industrial policy must recognize that the enterprise sector is the prime mover in the economy...public policy can help to strengthen industry and facilitate the structural transformation of the economy. It can *contain or weed out the economic and social measures that reduce the dynamism of industry."* [Italics mine.][58]

Trilateralists would like to see a renewal of presidential executive branch authority, especially deference to its views on foreign policy and international economics. Congressional nation-mindedness in the era of "world order politics" has been duly lamented by the Trilateral Commission; they blame parochial interests in Congress for crippling Carter's first energy program and encouraging trade protectionism. The grueling controversy over the Panama Canal treaties, the pressure to recognize the Rhodesian "internal settlement" (see Prexy Nesbitt's article on Zimbabwe), and the heated debate over SALT 2 have all threatened the trilateral consensus. As

---

and the all-too-rare plus of political stability...In Germany, the Netherlands, Belgium, and Sweden, average wages for manufacturing workers now exceed comparable U.S. wages by as much as 20%." *Business Week,* 9 July 1979, pp. 50-52. This observation does not take into account the wider social benefits enjoyed in Western Europe such as socialized health care and education. The U.S. is the only major industrial country without national health care.

expressed in *Towards a Renovated International System:*

> since domestic politics is inevitably more shaped by national than external priorities, the political process produces varying degrees of parochialism which disregards the impact of national action on the outside world and shows little understanding of the requirements of interdependence...[59]

The democratic surge threatens the fabric of international relations by undermining the U.S. role as global police. A "government which lacks authority and which is committed to substantial domestic programs will have little ability, short of cataclysmic crisis, to impose on its people the sacrifices which may be necessary to deal with foreign policy problems and defense"[60] (such as the draft and social welfare cutbacks). Public awareness and opposition put a brake on U.S. interventionism in the post-Vietnam era. Only strong government (i.e., without strong opposition and oversight) can effectively rule in the interest of international capitalism.

> For a quarter-century the United States was the *hegemonic power* in a system of world order [writes Huntington]. The manifestations of the democratic distemper, however have already stimulated uncertainty among allies and could well stimulate adventurism among enemies...*A decline in the governability of democracy at home means a decline in the influence of democracy abroad.*[Italics mine.][61]

Once again the definition of democracy is clearly spelled out. The last sentence should read: a decline in the governability of democracy at home means a decline in the strength of imperialism abroad.

On the whole, trilateralists seem to be aware of limitations and contradictions within the capitalist form of democracy—even though their actions may often speak otherwise. In the "arenas for action" Commissioners recommend that governments give the "highest priority to establishing a minimum form of guaranteed subsistence for all citizens." In actuality, this is another form of welfare to business; income assistance allows business to pay low and subsistence wages to boost profits and cushions the high level of unemployment which is healthy for capitalism.* The governability report observes:

> the historical record indicates that democracy works best—indeed that it may only work—when there is a gradual but

---

*When unemployment is high workers are pacified with the threat of job loss. When there is little unemployment workers are in a much better position from which to bargain for improved wages, benefits, and working conditions and have greater chances of moving on to more attractive jobs (safer, higher pay, etc.). William Tabb discusses this point in his article, "The Trilateral Imprint on Domestic Economics."

relatively constant increase in the economic well-being of society.[62]

The dream of capitalism is to co-opt people with higher living standards without redistributing any wealth. Without co-optation, widescale repression is the only guarantor of gross inequality.

"If ever there was a democratic success story, it was written by the trilateral societies during the quarter-century following World War II" (when just such a period of relatively constant economic growth occurred) begins the conclusion of the *Crisis of Democracy*. Among the keys to that success were:

> sustained, and for some countries, spectacular economic growth; widespread social and economic amelioration, involving a *lessening of class conflict and assimilation of substantial portions of the population to middle-class values, attitudes and consumption patterns.* [Italics mine.][63]

The elimination of poverty and redistribution of wealth and power are not part of the "democratic success story." Consumption is. Class conflict did not give way to a classless society but was masked by the so-called *Consumption Community*. As prize-winning historian Daniel Boorstin describes in *Fortune* (1 September 1967):

> *A Consumption Community consists of people who have a feeling of shared well-being, shared risks, common interests, and common concerns that come from consuming the same kinds of objects...*As the advertisers of nationally branded and nationally advertised products are constantly telling us, by buying their products we are joining a special group—the Dodge Rebellion, the Pepsi Generation, those who throw in their lot with Avis because it is only No. 2...
>
> *...Consumption Community is non-ideological.* No profession of faith, no credo or orthodoxy, no ritual is required to join a Consumption Community...[64]

Capitalists hope to circumvent political revolution with the Dodge Rebellion and Pepsi Revolution. The binding ritual is consumption; the goal is to strive for a higher standard of living, the "publicly seen and known measure of how people do live and of how they *should* live." People not only pledge allegiance to brand names; they support the corporate system. Boorstin continues:

> *Consumption Community is democratic. This is the great American democracy of cash* which so exasperated the aristocrats of all older worlds. Consumption Communities, generally welcome people of all races, ancestry, occupations, and income levels, *provided they have the price of admission.* The boss and the worker both own Westinghouse washers...[all above italics mine.]

In reality of course there is no democracy of consumption. The boss and worker may both own a Westinghouse washer (though the boss might have a maid to do the wash in a more advanced model) but workers must sell their labor power to the boss. Class background, sex, and a host of other factors determine who is likely to have the "price of admission" to which Consumption Communities. Boorstin writes:

> The struggle for "civil rights" in the U.S. has been in large part a struggle for the right to consume—a struggle to enlarge and complete the democracy of consumption...

The continuing crisis of democracy reflects the failure of capitalism to deliver the goods to the mainstream as well as to Blacks and other people who have remained marginalized (the myth of the widening "Black Bourgeoisie" notwithstanding).* The sixties and seventies saw little affirmative action and much affirmative tokenism. Over the last decade we have seen a decline in real wage and living standards.**

When the masses of people demand a decent livelihood trilateralism would like it to suffice to say "let them eat symbolic democracy"; and when people demand true democracy, trilateralism responds with "let them vote for the consumer products of their choice," in the pseudodemocracy of consumption.

But the "crisis of democracy" reflects a struggle for much more than the right to consume either corporate products or liberal demo-

---

*On this point, see for example, Herbert Hill, "White Myths of Black Economics," *The Nation,* 6 December 1978. Hill points out that during the 1960s the gap in black and white income was somewhat narrowed but has widened again since the early 70s. He cites the important Bureau of the Census finding that "the income of the average Negro family with *three wage earners* is not significantly different from the family income of the average white family *with one wage earner.* [Italics mine.] *U.S. News and World Report* (21 August 1978) states that in 1976 Black family income was 59 percent of white family income. In 1977 it had dropped to 57 percent. As to the rising black middle class, Hill observes: "the proportion of black families earning $24,000 and up has steadily declined in recent years: from 12% in 1972 to 9% in 1976. Meanwhile the proportion of black families with incomes between $16,200 and $24,000 has remained constant at about 25%." *U.S. News and World Report* reveals that some 31.3 percent of all blacks are poor compared with 8.9 percent of all whites.

**Sidney Lens reports: "According to AFL-CIO statistics the average non-farm worker with three dependents took a cut of about $3.50 a week from 1972 to August 1978. His [sic] nominal wages soared from $121.09 to $184.09, but measured in 1967 dollars his real earnings (after federal taxes) shrank from $96.64 to $93.12. Construction workers fared worse, down by $15 a week, and those in finance and real estate lost $7 a week in real earnings. The only workers who did better were those in transportation and public utilities: over a six-year period their rates jumped by the grand sum of 40 cents a week." ("Disorganized Labor," *The Nation,* 24 February 1979).

cratic symbols. It reflects the desire of a growing sector of the population to translate freedom of speech into freedom to act. The ruling class tries to restrict the freedom of speech to freedom to burn off steam, to criticize and propose from a position of powerlessness— just as it means to confine the hard-won right to vote to the freedom to choose between candidates who are variations on the same theme.

The "crisis of democracy" reflects a struggle to assert democratic control over the political, economic, and social system. Capitalist democracy does not guarantee universal rights to decent food, housing, employment, childcare, education, or health care. There are no rights guaranteeing control over the fruits of one's labor and control over the work process itself. Why? Because these rights contradict the unequal distribution of wealth and power. Formal political democracy helps legitimize corporate capitalism.* True political democracy cannot exist without economic democracy and economic democracy cannot exist under capitalism.

Challenges and Contradictions: The Struggle Continues

The ruling class is not omnipotent. Ruling elites preserve their rule through a mixture of accommodation and force. Trilateralists hope to strengthen the weapons for military and economic policing of "subversive" citizens and upstart countries while improving the weapons of co-optation. There are two stereotypical views of how ruling elites generally react to progressive demands for change. Actually, both views, when taken together, approximate the truth. The first view holds that every reform is wrested by the oppressed from a kicking and screaming ruling class which attempts everything in its power to suppress progressive forces. The second holds that the ruling class is prescient and clever and acts quickly, even preemptively, to defuse revolutionary potential with timely minimal concessions, within a long-range strategy of co-optation. The fact is that ruling class elites do kick and scream in the face of change (particularly those capitalists who are most directly hurt; usually smaller labor-intensive businesses with local or national, rather than international, markets) even as more "enlightened" and politically conscious elites try to manipulate or manage social change in their own self-interest though a combination of reform and repression.

*This theme has been elaborated by contemporary writers such as Ralph Miliband (*The State in Capitalist Society, Marxism and Politics*) and Jurgen Habermas. In *Legitimation Crisis,* for example, Habermas distinguishes between "substantive democracy" (i.e. "the genuine participation of citizens in the process of political-will formation") and "formal democracy" which permits the state to gain "diffuse mass loyalty" while avoiding mass participation. (Boston: Beacon Press, 1973, pp. 36-37).

Like their chief economic instrument, the global corporation, the ruling class cherishes flexibility—indeed it depends on it. Brzezinski made this point in a *Washington Post* interview (14 March 1978):

> On the whole, my views are strategically consistent, tactically very fluid...I'm perfectly willing to change tactical positions because the world changes. Anybody who maintains that one has to be constant in one's views in every respect is a jerk.

What "history teaches us"—to use a phrase favored by trilateralists—is that ruling elites are deadly serious about seeing that any renovation of the international system is in their interest. They will use a variety of carrot and stick tactics to maintain political and economic control—domestically and internationally. Control techniques will be more vicious or less, depending on a combination of factors involving the state of the economy and, more importantly, the state of popular opposition. The more threatening and persistent the moves to counter their plans and build alternative models—the more violent will be their tactics of repression.

If this were a world of infinite resources and unlimited economic growth then the very best which the ruling class might concede to a substantial sector of the population is the world Aldous Huxley described in the preface to *Brave New World:*

> There is, of course, no reason why the new totalitarianisms should resemble the old. Government by clubs and firing squads, by artificial famine, mass imprisonment and mass deportation, is not merely inhuman (nobody cares much about that nowadays); it is demonstrably inefficient and in an age of advanced technology, inefficiency is the sin against the Holy Ghost. *A really efficient totalitarian state would be one in which the all-powerful executive of political bosses and their army of managers control a population of slaves who do not have to be coerced, because they love their servitude.* To make them love it is the task assigned, in present-day totalitarian states, to ministries of propaganda, newspaper editors and school teachers...[Italics mine.][65]

That these "new totalitarianisms" do not resemble the old is largely contingent upon the nurturing of a politically apathetic consumption community.

As more advanced weapons are being produced for the police state, more advanced means of psychological control are being developed. These behavioral controls operate in a variety of ways—from the CIA drug-testing program on unsuspecting human guinea pigs in the sixties to the proliferation of mind-altering drugs, behavior modification techniques, and brain operations on prisoners and mental patients. To so-called job-enrichment programs for "motivating employees." To a host of ventures in the realms of education, advertising, and military training.

In a 1973 memo on the Trilateral Policy Program then director Brzezinski recommended the study of "Control Over Man's Development and Behavior" as a theme for later consideration. More specifically such a task force would undertake to study "the social-educational implications of the availability, especially in advanced societies, of new means of social control."

The renovation trilateralism envisions is not smoothly underway. On the contrary, challenges and contradictions manifest themselves on all levels. Today the U.S. economy and the entire international capitalist system is fraught with deeply rooted problems like stagnation and rampant inflation. In 1979-1980 the Carter Administration attempted to engineer a controlled economic slowdown, hoping to avoid a damaging depression. The type of social Darwinism which a controlled recession would impose is just the sort big business wants to houseclean the economy—streamlining industry and labor for more efficient competition in the international arena.* (William Tabb discusses the rational behind recession and clearly analyzes Carter's trilateralist economic policies and their impact in Part IV.)

Carter's economic restructuring tools have included an enormous tax cut for "corporate America,"** tighter credit, natural gas and oil deregulation (on Carter's energy policy and its larger economic significance, see the article by Clawson and Kaufman), wage and price guidelines aimed squarely at labor, high unemployment, and a budget that is fat with military allocations (up after inflation is figured in, 3 percent on paper for 1979-80—and an average of nearly 5 percent through 1985—and more in practice), but "lean and austere" when it comes to human services (housing, welfare, food stamps, public jobs, and job training, community development, food and nutrition programs, etc. were cut by $2.5 billion in 1979; to put this in perspective—the cost of one new navy aircraft carrier or

---

*In part, streamlining means emphasizing high technology/high productivity/high profit industries like advanced electronics, aerospace, and energy over labor intensive/low technology/poorly competitive industries like textiles and steel.

**The tax cut included a cut in the corporate tax rate, a permanent investment tax credit, and a reduction in capital gains taxation. The *Nation* (7 October 1978) looked at this "Relief for the Greedy" and predicted that the 70 percent exemption on capital gains would result in an annual windfall of $4.2 billion—75 percent of it going to those making over $50,000, who represent the top 3 percent of the population. In capitalist logic it is this sector which will save and invest money most "productively."

trident submarine is $1.5 billion). About the poor, the *New York Times* (13 August 1979) editorializes:

> The shock of this winter's home heating costs will be felt with particular force by the poor. The poorest fifth of American families already spend 13 percent of their income on home energy (while the richest fifth spend 3 percent of theirs)...Necessity Stamps, for food, energy, or housing...would *allow recipients to decide for themselves how much hunger to trade for how much warmth.* [Italics mine.]*

Like women who were forced into chastity belts to protect the "property" of their husbands—the working class is forced to wear the austerity belt to protect the economic system they labor in: a system which is wrongfully the property of the ruling class.

The break-up of the welfare/warfare state duet has undermined the relative harmony of big labor and big capital. Cold War liberalism promised guns and butter. Now capitalists are trying to force workers to give back the gains of more prosperous periods. The debate over guns and butter is being waged increasingly with the language of class struggle. Rank and file militancy makes it clear that the working class will not be "content with forging for itself the golden chains by which the bourgeoisie drags it in its train."[66]

The simmering crisis of democracy was packaged for public consumption by President Carter as the "crisis of confidence." Carter—the man who was to renew faith in government and country—was shocked to find that in the summer of 1979 public trust had sunk below its Watergate low-point.** In his spiritual energy

---

*Poor families are already choosing between food, heat, shelter, health-care and other basic necessities. Hunger, cold, illness, and substandard housing are part of their everyday existence. Last winter, children and elderly persons died of exposure because their heat was shut off. The case of New York City is particularly illustrative of the impact of fiscal austerity on the poor. According to the Task Force Report on Welfare Issues (under Councilwoman Ruth Messinger's office) 1/11th of the nation's Public Assistance recipients live in New York City. One out of every seven people in New York City is on public assistance, 87 percent of whom are mothers and children. New York Community Council reports: "Currently it costs $441 per month (plus rent) for a four person public assistance family to maintain the same level of living that had been provided for them in the spring of 1969...The present basic cash grant of $258 per month (exclusive of rent) for a four person family has not changed in amount since it was fixed at that level in July 1974. Inflation since July 1974 has so eroded the purchasing power of the $258 non-rental grant that it is now worth only $198 in the market place." The report goes on to explain how food stamps are totally inadequate in closing the widening gap between income and need. (Community Council of Greater New York, "Some Facts about New York's Public Assistance Grant Levels," February 1979.)

**Patrick Cadell, President Carter's pollster, found "that the number of people who are long-term pessimists about the country which at the worst of Watergate was about 30 percent, was 48 percent now." The *New York Times* (3 August 1979) goes

address (15 July 1979) Carter sounded themes which Huntington had spelled out earlier:

> The erosion of our confidence in the future is threatening to destroy the social and political fabric of America...We've always had faith that the days of our children would be better than our own. Our people are losing that faith. Not only in government itself, but in their ability as citizens to serve as the ultimate rulers and shapers of our democracy...
>
> In a nation that was proud of hard work, strong families, close-knit communities and our faith in God, too many of us now tend to worship self-indulgence and consumption. Human identity is no longer defined by what one does but what one owns.
>
> But we've discovered that owning things and consuming things does not satisfy our longing for meaning...
>
> For the first time in the history of our country a majority of our people believe that the next five years will be worse than the past five years. Two-thirds of our people do not even vote...
>
> As you know there is growing disrespect for the government and for churches and for schools, the news media and other institutions...
>
> We were sure that ours was a nation of the ballot, not the bullet until the murders of John Kennedy and Robert Kennedy and Martin Luther King Jr. We were taught that our armies were always invincible and our causes were always just, only to suffer the agony of Vietnam. We respected the presidency as a place of honor until the shock of Watergate. We remember when the phrase "sound as a dollar" was an expression of absolute dependability until ten years of inflation began to shrink our dollar and our savings. We believed that our nation's resources were limitless until 1973, when we had to face a growing dependence on foreign oil. These wounds are still very deep. They have never been healed...[67]

Carter's failure to heal the wounds and rouse faith reflects the fact that distrust in government comes from knowledge that government does not serve people's needs (distrust is not just a personality disorder brought on by the shock of Watergate). Realizing people see government/oil company collusion behind the "energy crisis," Carter threw out OPEC as a scapegoat around which to rally the United States people "on the battlefield of energy" in the war for national

---

on to report more of the pollster's findings!:...57 percent of the people doubted they could have any impact on government decisions affecting their lives, and (that) 60 percent, as against 58 percent during Watergate, believed some major governmental figures were dishonest. Moreover only 10 percent believed the Government would do anything about inflation and taxes...Finally, an astonishingly low 6 percent expected to see significant progress in the next 5 years."

will.* But if people are rallying around anything, it is against nuclear power and corporate-controlled energy; not only in the U.S., but throughout Western Europe and Japan.

There was truth in Carter's speech—buried among the quotes from "ordinary people" he drew on for their populist effect. Carter said:

> And I like this one particularly from a black woman who happens to be the mayor of a small Mississippi town: "The big shots are not the only ones who are important. Remember, *you can't sell anything on Wall Street unless someone digs it up somewhere else first.*[Italics mine.]

The fact is that people are sick of "digging it up" to line the pockets of Wall Street investors. In an era of economic decline, the contradictions of capitalist democracy become that much clearer (and consumption worship, which Carter lamented, is no opiate).

Members of the higher echelons of the Trilateral Commission must be frustrated knowing that while they are not merely an advisory committee neither are they the executive committee of international capital (with the authority they are accustomed to in corporate hierarchies). (See Wolfe Part VIII and the concluding perspectives.) For trilateralism, relations between the big trilateral powers—the U.S., West Germany, and Japan—are not cozy enough. The threat of trade rivalries exploding into trade wars continues to loom over the Atlantic and Pacific horizons. (See Fred Block, "Trilateralism and International Capitalist Conflict.")

Aware that "protectionism" is on the rise, trilateralists take a harder look at underlying domestic and international economic conditions. They find that the trilateral countries are plagued by general "industrial malaise"; inflation and unemployment have remained high in the trilateral countries for over five years. Fundamental economic restructuring is placed squarely on the trilateral agenda for the 1980s:

> [It] may well be that the difficulties are not only cyclical, and hence amenable to demand management, but also *structural: They may require a reallocation of resources in the economy* which takes time and money to achieve. So long as structural changes are required, one could expect high unemployment or high inflation or both, as the forces for change press against established positions in the economy. [Italics mine.][68]

---

*Dependence on OPEC was blamed for gas lines and more: "It's a cause of the increased inflation and unemployment that we now face." Even *Business Week* scolded Carter for such meaningless rhetoric. For a more complete analysis of the "oil crisis" (and OPEC's role) from a corporate perspective see *Business Week,* "The Oil Crisis is Real This Time," 30 July 1979).

Observing the tasks of Carter's presidency, trilateralist Thomas Hughes (president of the Carnegie Endowment for International Peace) comments: "the essence of foreign policy is the management of contradictions."[69] Trilateralism is the current ruling class attempt to manage the contradictions which riddle the international capitalist system.

The Western capitalist prescription for development is a model which always leaves intact the dynamic of exploitation and the machinery of repression—regardless of what concessions or reforms may be instituted. It is a model which sees human labor as one more resource to be exploited (as cheaply as possible). It is a model which ties people to a treadmill of conspicuous consumption, warping the promise of human potential. It is a model which is built upon competition and advocates cooperation only in the self-interest of the most powerful. It is a model of development which buys stability for business at the price of shattered and stunted lives; offering people a t-shirt, a pair of sneakers, plastic dishes, maybe a radio or a watch, in place of freedom.

Where can we look for lessons? To our own histories which the ruling class has tried to bury under an invented history of myths and lies. To quote activist Emma Goldman (1869-1940):

> History teaches us that every oppressed class must gain liberation
> through its own efforts.

Oppression cannot be rationalized. In the end it must be overcome by the power of a people united in the struggle for their own liberation. This is the power trilateralism fears most. A crucial aspect of liberation is education and reeducation. With that in mind, this book examines the origins, goals, strategy, and impact of trilateralism. As a tool in understanding ruling class strategy and action, it can be a tool for organizing resistance.

Events in the U.S. and abroad—discussed more fully in the conclusion to this volume—should not discourage, but empower us. Trilateralism is not the triumph of corporate capitalism's "true world economy," where the weapons of war, torture and unceasing repression are traded as eagerly as toothpaste and soda; it is capitalism's defense. Together, we can build enduring democratic and socialist systems which are founded on the collective efforts of a "highly educated, mobilized, and participant society" and which put the needs and aspirations of ALL human beings—not the profits of the few—at the heart of economics and politics.

Appendix

The Rockefeller family is the most powerful family in the United States. Estimates of Rockefeller private assets have ranged from nearly $1.3 billion (calculated from disclosures at Nelson Rockefeller's vice-presidential confirmation hearings) to $5 billion and upwards. Rockefeller power lies in the many interlocking corporations, financial institutions, foundations, and leading individuals they control.* The fortune began with John D. Rockefeller Sr. (1839-1937; David Rockefeller's grandfather) and the Standard Oil Trust which monopolized the U.S. oil industry in the late 1800s. Today, the male heirs of John D. Rockefeller Sr. and the corporate offspring of Standard Trust continue to dominate politics, industry, finance, and philanthropy (the traditional role of women offspring in the Rockefeller patriarchy has been to marry into other influential families; "Rockefeller Wives" were influential inside and outside the family: Abby Aldrich Rockefeller, married to John D. Rockefeller 2nd, was co-founder of the Museum of Modern Art and Blachette Ferry Hooker Rockefeller, married to John D. Rockefeller 3rd, became president of the Museum of Modern Art).

As for corporations under the Rockefeller wing, in 1978 Exxon (Standard Oil of New Jersey) was the second largest corporation in the world, Mobil was the fifth largest; Socol (Standard Oil of California) was the eighth largest; and Standard Oil of Indiana was the seventeenth largest. That same year Chase Manhattan Bank was the third largest bank in the world; Metropolitan Life Insurance and Equitable Life Insurance, the second and third largest life insurance companies in the United States; and Eastern Airlines, the seventh largest transport company in the U.S. Powerful namesakes include the Rockefeller Foundation, Rockefeller Brothers Fund, Rockefeller University (formerly the Institute for Medical Research) and the huge real estate development project, Rockefeller Center Inc., located in New York City.

The late Nelson Rockefeller (died 1979; David's brother) was the chief exception to the Rockefeller rule to "operate primarily behind the scenes...laying out the long-range policies while leaving the details to loyal spokesmen of their interests in positions of public power." (See NACLA, *The Rockefeller Empire: Latin America,* reprinted from the NACLA newsletter April, May-June 1969, p.2.) Nelson Rockefeller was four-term governor of New York, 1958-1973. As governor, Rockefeller ordered state troopers to storm Attica Prison in 1971 after refusing to appear personally at the prison site, much less become involved in negotiations with rebelling prisoners. Ten hostages and thirty-three prisoners died in the assault and eight were wounded—all by trooper gunfire. Rockefeller's behavior was similar to his father's (John D. Rockefeller 2nd, 1874-1960) actions during

*As the authors of *The Rockefellers,* Collier and Horowitz, explain: "(T)he Mellons and a few other American families may have been richer but among the power elite whose rule stretched from Wall Street to Washington, the Rockefellers were without peer." (pp. 484-5.)

the Colorado Fuel and Iron Strike and Ludlow Massacre of April 1913. (There were 53 dead and many more wounded men, women, and children after a company of National Guard militia opened fire on the Ludlow workers' tent camp.) John D. Rockefeller 2nd defended his decision not to become involved in the long struggle, arguing that he was only a stockholder and not responsible for day-to-day operations; but he had been informed of and supported the management hard line throughout the strike. As for Rockefeller Sr. "(Y)ears earlier when he heard that Frick had ordered strikers at Carnegie's Homestead steelworks shot down, John Sr. had immediately fired off a telegram of support to the coke magnate" (Collier and Horowitz, p. 110). Rockefeller Sr. had turned to philanthropy and supported the Rockefeller Foundation to clean up the hated Rockefeller name. Rockefeller Jr. pushed philanthropy further and, after Ludlow, became a "statesman" in labor relations, promoting the pioneers in the insidious science of industrial relations and industrial management. (Collier and Horowitz, p. 141.)

Nelson Rockefeller had enormous impact on U.S. policy toward Latin America (where he and his family had vast investments) since the 1940s when he became the first Coordinator of Inter-American Affairs. After serving as undersecretary of the newly created Department of Health, Education and Welfare, Nelson became Eisenhower's special assistant for Cold War Strategy or "Presidential Coordinator of the CIA" (Collier and Horowitz p. 271). He was the long-time patron of Henry Kissinger and served as vice-president under Gerald Ford, but never made it in his bids for the Republican presidential nomination.

Laurence, a third brother, is the venture capitalist and conservationist-developer in the family. He was appointed to the Outdoor Recreation Resource and Review Commission in 1958 (bringing in aides from his two conservation organizations, Jackson Hole Preserve, Inc. and the American Conservation Association). The 1962 Commission report promoted the "policy of 'multiple use'; encouraging mining, lumbering, grazing and other industrial activities on recreation lands." (Collier and Horowitz, p. 382). Laurence was chairman of the New Citizens' [sic] Advisory Committee on Recreation and Natural Beauty under Johnson and the (renamed) Citizens' Advisory Committee on Environmental Quality under Nixon. Reaping profit from conservation and "multiple use" Laurence was a heavy investor in tourism development, especially luxury resorts, on beach and wilderness lands in Hawaii, Puerto Rico, the Virgin Islands, and elsewhere.

John D. Rockefeller 3rd (died 1978) was the philanthropist and "Mr. Asia." One of his special achievements was the Population Council, a foundation which supports projects to reduce the so-called population explosion, especially in the Third World. J.D. Rockefeller 3rd was a central figure behind private and public thinking of population reduction as the way to confront the problems of hunger, poverty, and scarcity of world resources while enhancing political stability in the Third World.

Among the four brothers' (excluding Winthrop, mentioned below) joint achievements was the three-year Rockefeller Panel Studies which produced *Prospect for America* a report whose "recommendations would be incorporated into both party platforms in the 1960 presidential elections and would exert a profound influence in the course of America's military politics and domestic affairs over the next troubled decade." (Collier and Horowitz p. 324). Winthrop Rockefeller (died 1973), the fifth brother went outside the family mainstream, moving to Arkansas and becoming a force in Arkansas' development as businessman, rancher, philanthropist, and governor (1967-1971) until his recurring problem of alcoholism added to his defeat for a third term. John D. (Jay) Rockefeller 4th (son of John D. Rockefeller 3rd) was elected Democratic governor of West Virginia in 1979 and serves on the Trilateral Commission with David.*

FOOTNOTES

1. Richard H. Ullman, "Trilateralism: 'Partnership' for What?" *Foreign Affairs*, 55:1 (October 1976), p. 11.
2. William Greider, "Trilateralists to Abound in Carter's White House," *Washington Post*, 16 January 1977.
3. Laurence H. Shoup and William Minter, *Imperial Brain Trust: The Council on Foreign Relations and United States Foreign Policy* (New York: Monthly Review Press, 1977), p. 15.
4. Ad appearing in the *New York Times*, 6 March 1979.
5. Zbigniew Brzezinski, "Trilateral Relations in a Global Context," *Trialogue* 7 (Summer 1975), p. 11.
6. C. Fred Bergsten, Georges Berthoin, Kinhide Mushakoji, *The Reform of International Institutions* (Trilateral Commission: Triangle Paper 11, 1976). The theme of "collective management" is developed earlier by Miriam Camps in a report for the Council on Foreign Relations, *The Management of Interdependence: A Preliminary View* (New York: CFR Council Papers on International Affairs 1974).
7. George Ball, "Cosmocorp: The Importance of Being Stateless," *Columbia Journal of World Business*, 2:6 (November-December 1967), p. 26.
8. John Blashill,"The Proper Role of U.S. Corporations in South Africa," *Fortune*, July 1972, p. 49.
9. Ball, *op.cit.*, p 28.
10. This phrase is used by Arthur M. Okun in the title of his book, *Equality and Efficiency: The Big Tradeoff*, Washington, D.C.: The Brookings Institution, 1975, p. 1.
11. Robert J. Lampman, *The Share of Top Wealth-Holders in National Wealth 1922-1956*, cited in Ferdinand Lundberg, *The Rich and the Super-Rich* (New York: Lyle Stuart, 1968), p. 7.

*For David Rockefeller's background see "Who's Who on the Trilateral Commission" in this volume. For an excellent, in-depth portrait of the Rockefellers, see the book cited frequently above: Peter Collier and David Horowitz, *The Rockefellers: An American Dynasty* (New York: Signet, 1976). Also, for a quick look at Nelson's impact on New York see Robert Fitch, "Nelson Rockefeller An Anti-Obituary" *Monthly Review*, June 1979. On the domestic and foreign activities of Chase Manhattan Bank see, for example, *NACLA Report*, "Chase's Rocky Road," April 1976.

12. From a report by SANE, A Citizen's Organization for a Sane World, cited in "The Nuclear Connection," a slide show by the Minneapolis Office of the American Friends Service Committee.

13. "One World," *Forbes*, 15 November 1968.

14. Zbigniew Brzezinski, *Between Two Ages: America's Role in the Technetronic Era*, (New York: Viking Press, 1970), p. 299.

15. *Reform of International Institutions*, p. 6.

16. Richard Cooper, Karl Kaiser, Masataka Kosaka, *Towards a Renovated International System*, The Trilateral Commission:Triangle Paper 14, 1977, p. 32.

17. *Ibid.*, p. 1.

18. Brzezinski, *Between Two Ages*, p. 59.

19. *Towards a Renovated International System*, p. 35.

20. Ullman, *op.cit.*, p. 13.

21. *Towards a Renovated International System*, p. 19.

22. Brzezinski, *Between Two Ages*, pp. 32-33.

23. Christopher J. Makins, "Is Reform an Illusion? A Trilateral Perspective on International Problems," *Trialogue 8* (Fall 1975), pp. 1-2.

24. Richard Cooper, "A New International Order for Mutual Gain," *Foreign Policy* 26 (Spring 1977).

25. C. Fred Bergsten, "The Threat from the Third World," *Foreign Policy* 11 (Summer 1973).

26. Tom Farer, "The United States and the Third World: A Basis for Accomodation," *Foreign Affairs*, October 1975, p. 97.

27. *Towards a Renovated International System*, p. 10.

28. *Ibid.*, p. 20.

29. *Ibid.*, p. 7.

30. *The Reform of International Institutions*, p. 9. See also Richard Gardner, Saburo Okita, B. J. Udink, *A Turning Point in North-South Economic Relations*, (Trilateral Commission:Triangle Paper 3,1974) and Richard Gardner, Saburo Okita, B. J. Udink, *OPEC, the Trilateral World, and the Developing Countries: New Arrangements for Cooperation, 1979-1980* (Trilateral Commission: Triangle Paper 7, 1975).

31. Stephen Hymer, "The Multinational Corporation and the Law of Uneven Development," in *International Firms and Modern Imperialism*, Hugo Radice, ed. (Baltimore: Penguin Books, 1975), p. 38.

32. For quotes see *Towards a Renovated International System*, pp. 26-28.

33. *Ibid.*, p. 9.

34. *Ibid.*, p. 17.

35. Brzezinski, "Trilateral Relations in a Global Context," *op.cit.*

36. Kwame Nkrumah, *Neo-Colonialism: The Last Stage of Imperialism*, (New York: International Publishers, 1966), p. ix.

37. Franz J. Hinkelammert, "El Credo Economico de la Comision Trilateral," in *Carter y la Logica del Imperialismo*, Hugo Assmann, ed. (Costa Rica: EDUCA, 1978), Volume I (of 2), p. 218.

38. James Petras, "President Carter and the 'New Morality,' " *Monthly Review*, June 1977, p. 38.

39. *Towards a Renovated International System*, p. 30.

40. *The Economist*, 10 February 1979, p. 32.

41. Jeremy Azrael, Richard Lowenthal, Tohru Nakagawa, *An Overview of East-West Relations* (Trilateral Commission Triangle Paper 15, 1978), p. vii.

42. *Ibid.*, p. 1.

43. Chihiro Hosoya, Henry Owen, Andrew Shonfield, *Collaboration with Communist Countries in Managing Global Problems: An Examination of the Options* (Trilateral Commission: Triangle Paper 13, 1977).

44. *An Overview of East-West Relations,* p. 3.

45. *Ibid.,* p. vi.

46. Noam Chomsky, "Trilateral's RX for Crisis: Governability Yes, Democracy No," *Seven Days,* 14 February 1977.

47. Michael J. Crozier, Samuel P. Huntington, Joji Watanuki, *The Crisis of Democracy: Report on the Governability of Democracies to the Trilateral Commission:* Triangle Paper 8 (New York: New York University Press, 1975), p. 98.

48. *Ibid.,* p. 93.

49. *Ibid.,* p. 75.

50. *Ibid.,* pp. 61-62.

51. *Ibid.,* pp. 113-114.

52. *Ibid.,* p. 99.

53. *Ibid.,* p. 182..

54. *Ibid.,* pp. 6-7.

55. *Ibid.,* p. 185.

56. *Ibid.,* pp. 185-6.

57. *Ibid.,* p. 163.

58. Draft report by John Pinder, William Diebold, Takashi Hosomi, *Industrial Policy and the International Economy* (Trilateral Commission, 1979), p. 88.

59. *Towards a Renovated International System,* p. 12.

60. *The Crisis of Democracy,* p. 105.

61. *Ibid.,* p. 106.

62. *Ibid.,* p. 174.

63. *Ibid.,* p. 157.

64. Daniel Boorstein, "Welcome to the Consumption Community," *Fortune,* 1 September 1967.

65. Aldous Huxley, *Brave New World,* (New York: Bantam Books, 1967), p.xii.

66. Richard Tucker ed., *Marx-Engels Reader,* "Wage Labor and Capital," p. 185.

67. "Transcript of President's Address to Country on Energy Problems," *New York Times,* 16 July 1979.

68. *Industrial Policy and the International Economy,* p. 1.

69. Thomas Hughes, "Carter and the Management of Contradictions," *Foreign Policy,* Summer 1978, p. 35.

PART II
THE TRILATERAL COMMISSION

This section brings the Trilateral Commission and its members to life. The stage is set by a review of the rise and decline of the postwar international economic system revealing the background conditions which led to the birth of the Trilateral Commission. A chronological account of the Commission's creation and early years is followed by a description of its goals, organization, funding, and programs. An extensive "Who's Who" provides a wealth of information about past and present trilateral participants, tracing their careers, corporate ties, and organization affiliations; government positions are highlighted. A preface to the Japanese "Who's Who" illuminates the Japanese Establishment.

The trilateral doctrine was born in a period of deep distress within the Establishment over the Nixon-Kissinger "shocks" to Western Europe and Japan. It was conceived as a counterstroke to the Nixonian foreign-policy concept of "pentagonalism" that viewed the world as dominated by five great powers—the United States, the Soviet Union, China, Japan and Western Europe. In that complex poker game, the United States was to be free to play a tough, independent and aggressive hand, shifting from coalition to coalition, depending strictly on the pursuit of American national self-interest.

—Leonard Silk
New York Times, 4 May 1979

Where trilateralism began as a formula and a forum for coordinating economic policy among the advanced market economies, it has come to mean something much more far-reaching—"a partnership between North America, Western Europe, and Japan," to quote Governor Carter. As such, trilateralism has two faces, one turned inward, the other turned outward.

The inward face has been concerned chiefly with preserving for the industrialized societies—indeed, expanding the advantages which, during the 1960s, flowed from openness and increased interdependence, while limiting their adverse consequences.

Trilateralism's outward face is turned toward the construction of a common approach to the needs and demands of the poorer nations, and the coordination of defense policies and of policies toward such highly politicized issues as nuclear proliferation, terrorism, and aerial hijacking, and such highly politicized geographical areas as the Middle East or Southern Africa...

The ultimate result—to quote Zbigniew Brzezinski, the former director of the Trilateral Commission—*would be "a community of the developed nations."**

—Richard Ullman
Foreign Affairs, October 1976

*[Italics added.]

chapter one

THE TRILATERAL COMMISSION: ECONOMICS AND POLITICS IN THE 1970s

*Jeff Frieden**

The Rise of International Finance Capital

Postwar U.S. foreign policy had as its keystone the reconstruction of Western Europe and Japan as future trade partners and front-line protection against the spread of socialism in Europe and Asia. In the interest of allowing these areas, especially Western Europe, to rebuild, the United States pumped billions of dollars in Marshall Plan aid into their economies. The U.S. also permitted and encouraged the formation of regional—and somewhat exclusive—organizations like the European Payments Union, the European Coal and Steel Community, the European Free Trade Association, and eventually the European Economic Community i.e. Common Market. (Thompson discusses these events in "Bilderberg and the West.")

What evolved was a system of international trade in which Japanese and Western European manufacturers found it relatively easy to sell their goods in the U.S. market—in competition with domestic U.S. industrialists—while U.S. manufacturers found it relatively difficult to export to the European and Japanese markets. The price, then, for a strong capitalist Western Europe was a Western Europe comparatively protectionist *vis-a-vis* U.S. imports; yet virtually the entire U.S. ruling class considered this price worthwhile to save the world from Creeping Communism. And the price was paid by U.S. exporters, whose share of "free world" trade fell from 23.3 percent in 1948 to 15.3 percent in 1970; Western European exports to the U.S. grew four times as fast as U.S. exports to Western Europe.[1]

*Jeff Frieden is a graduate student in political science at Columbia University and a director of the Independent Publishing Fund of the Americas. This is a revised and updated version of an article appearing in *Monthly Review,* December 1977.

But while domestically-based North American industries were finding it relatively hard to take full advantage of the growing Western European market due to tacit U.S. approval of a measure of European protectionism, the internationally-oriented corporations were thriving. For if there were restrictions on U.S. goods entering Western Europe, there were almost none on U.S. capital. U.S. private investment in Western Europe grew from $1.7 billion in 1950 to $16.2 billion in 1966 and $30.7 billion in 1972. Meanwhile long-term portfolio investments (i.e., stocks and bonds) of U.S. investors in Western Europe went from $1.3 billion to $4.5 billion to $5.9 billion, and short-term investment from $0.4 billion to $2.6 billion to $5.3 billion.

Little noticed by many was the increasing importance of U.S. banks in this massive internationalization of capital. The following table should suffice to show the skyrocketing importance of banking on the international scene:

International Activities of U.S. Commercial Banks
Selected Year-Ends
(Operating Data in Billions of Dollars)

	1960	1970	1974
Number of U.S. banks with foreign branches	8	79	129
Number of foreign branches	131	536	737
Assets (in billions of dollars) of overseas branches	3.5	52.6	155
Foreign assets as a percent of total assets	3.0	10.9	17.7

SOURCES: J. Backman and E. Bloch, eds., *Multinational Corporations, Trade, and the Dollar,* New York, 1974, p. 4; and Robert Z. Aliber, "International Banking: Growth and Regulation," *Columbia Journal of World Business,* Winter 1975.

Foreign investment in the United States also grew rapidly as European and Japanese corporations moved to tap the enormous North American market and enjoy labor costs which had become increasingly similar to European and Japanese scales. Direct investment by foreigners in the Unted States went from less than $8 billion in 1962 to $26.7 billion in 1975,[2] and foreign bank assets in the United States went from $5 billion in 1965 to $42 billion in 1974.[3]

It was clear by the mid-1960s that the most mobile, farseeing and important sectors of U.S., Western Europe, and Japanese imperialism were increasingly intertwined and ever more international. The dream of a world community seemed on the way to realization—if only a somewhat restricted community of billionaire banks and businesses.

The trend was noted early on by most influential U.S. and world businessmen and bankers, with David Rockefeller one of the central figures. With their worldwide investment base, loyal only to laws of maximum profit, subject to no national government, these forces raised their voices in the call for the elimination of any restrictions on free trade and investment. "Broad human interests," said "humanist" Rockefeller, "are being served best in economic terms where free market forces are able to transcend national boundaries."[4] "It is indeed time to lift the seige against multinational enterprises so that they might be permitted to get on with the unfinished business of developing the world economy."[5]

Indeed, international bankers, corporations, and investors have little need for tariffs and other trade barriers. Their interest lies in finding the most efficient, profitable, productive, and convenient spot for their investment to serve those "broad human interests," and then to put their capital to work untrammelled by such outmoded forces as trade barriers.

George Ball, undersecretary of state for Economic Affairs in the Kennedy Administration and a director of Lehman Brothers Kuhn Loeb, a large investment house, told the British National Committee of the International Chamber of Commerce in 1967:

> In these twenty postwar years, we have come to recognize in action, though not always in words, that *the political boundaries of nation-states are too narrow and constricted to define the scope and activities of modern business...*
>
> Except in extractive industries, most U.S. enterprises until recent times have concentrated their activities on producing for the national market, exporting only their surplus. Many still do. However, this is no longer adequate for the requirements of the world we live in. In order to survive, man must use the world's resources in the most efficient manner. This can be achieved only when *all the factors necessary for the production and use of goods—capital, labor, raw materials, plant facilities and distribution—are freely mobilized and deployed according to the most efficient pattern.* And this in turn will be possible only when national boundaries no longer play a critical role in defining economic horizons...
>
> By and large, those companies that have achieved a global vision of their operations tend to opt for a world in which not only goods but all the factors of production can shift with maximum

freedom. Other industries—some of great size and importance in the United States, such as steel and textiles—which have confined their production largely or entirely to domestic markets, anxiously demand protection whenever a substantial volume of imports begins to invade national markets.[6] [Italics ed.]

The internationalists, who, in the United States, concentrated their theoretical work in the Brookings Institution and the Council on Foreign Relations, their political work in the White House, and their economic work in the world's money markets, ran the show. Six rounds of General Agreement on Tariffs and Trade (GATT) negotiations, from 1947 to 1967, for example, brought tariffs on all dutiable U.S. imports down from their 1932 high of 59.0 percent to 9.9 percent in 1970.[7] But the war was not over, as future events were to show; support for free trade and an internationalization of capitalism was not universal.

For, as Ball acknowledged, some large industries were and still are mostly domestic; steel, textiles, and footwear are notable examples. For a variety of reasons these industries are unable or unwilling to compete internationally. And in times of economic difficulty, when the domestic market is contracting, domestic manufacturers of uncompetitive goods clamor for strict control on foreign imports.

Throughout the 1960s, however, business was relatively good; the U.S. market was expanding and foreign imports were not very menacing to U.S. domestic manufacturers. Yet storm clouds were on the horizon; as with weather, the gathering storm was something everyone talked about but was powerless to avert.

The Disintegration of the International Economic "System"

The postwar capitalist world, as we have seen, was based on the despotism—benevolent, perhaps, but despotism nevertheless—of the United States. The United States dominated the capitalist world, and the concessions and favors bestowed on its friends across the water were, after all, in its strategic interests. But little by little the king's favors enriched the courtiers, and the specter of an economic palace revolt became increasingly menacing.

We have reviewed this process in the trade and investment fields; let us now look at the cog in the machine that spelled its ultimate doom.

Even while World War II raged, U.S. leaders began to plan for the postwar reconstruction of the international economic system. The U.S. vision of the postwar capitalist world, of course, had the United States as leader and ruler. Weakened as they were by the war effort (which, paradoxically, actually strengthened U.S. capitalism) other capitalist powers—notably Britain—were unable to resist plans for a *Pax Americana.*

In this context, in July 1944, at a conference of forty-four nations in Bretton Woods, New Hampshire, the Anglo-American blueprint for an international monetary system was approved.

Although some of the actual terms of the agreement on the postwar monetary system approved at Bretton Woods were unworkable (notably the insufficient provisions for exchange-rate adjustments as needed and the lack of adequate provisions for an increase in gold reserves), by 1961 the international monetary system, managed by the International Monetary Fund (IMF) was in force along the general lines of the 1944 agreement. The full workings of the system are complex and beyond the scope of this essay, but we must look at its general outline.

At the center of the international monetary solar system shone the dollar; around it orbited the various national currencies. Their relationship to each other was fixed, defined by their relations to the American Sun; international transactions were carried out almost exclusively in dollars. This was fine so long as the Sun was the largest and most stable body in the system; but as the economies of Western Europe (especially of the Federal Republic of Germany) and Japan grew faster than that of the central body, the laws of gravity began to assert themselves. The German mark and the yen became ever stronger and challenged the hegemony of the dollar, and by the late 1960s the system could no longer be expected to perform its previous function as a medium for international exchange, and as a surrogate for gold. Similarly, the protective trade barriers were increasingly cumbersome for international finance. For a weakened U.S. economy especially, the EEC's relative protectionism, once a condition for European reconstruction, seemed unwarranted in view of Western Europe's considerable economic strength.

At the same time, the United States, in large part because of the enormous expense of maintaining and policing a global empire, had begun to accumulate a huge balance-of-payments deficit. The resulting overhang of dollars began to distort the entire structure of the international financial and monetary markets by the late 1960s.

International financiers agreed that reform was needed, that no national currency could completely dominate the system, and that national currencies should be pegged to correspond to their relative and interdependent strengths in a fluid manner. By 1970 serious discussion was underway to accomplish these and other changes, while continuing to move toward freer trade relations.

But these laborious discussions were destined to be destroyed by the increasingly serious economic crisis of the early 70s. In August

1971, the storm broke, in the form of President Richard Nixon's New Economic Policy. Its international components—referred to as the Nixon shocks—were aimed at dramatically altering the international monetary and trade systems.[8]

On the monetary front, Nixon suspended the convertibility of the dollar into gold and other reserves. This step—a clear violation of the Articles of Agreement of the IMF—was meant to achieve effective devaluation of the dollar relative to other currencies. With the dollar devalued, U.S.-made goods would cost less to foreigners and foreign-made goods would be less competitive on the U.S. market. With the dollar equivalent to four German marks, for instance, a U.S.-made ten dollar lamp would cost a German forty marks; if the dollar were devalued to three marks, the same lamp would sell for only thirty marks in Germany—with no particular effort on the part of the U.S. manufacturer necessary. Devaluation, then, was seen by Nixon as a way to improve the position of U.S. exporters and of domestic U.S. manufacturers competing with foreign imports.

On the trade front, too, Nixon struck out at the foreign firms competing with U.S. manufacturers for the U.S. market. Openly disregarding U.S. obligations under the General Agreement on Tariffs and Trade, he slapped a ten percent surcharge on most imports into the United States. Through the fall of 1971 Nixon stepped up the attack on imports by virtually ordering Japan, South Korea, Taiwan, and Hong Kong to reduce the pace of their imports of textiles into the United States. Japan and the Common Market were also asked in no uncertain terms to allow more U.S. goods to be sold at more competitive prices in their respective marketplaces.

The attack was successful. By the spring of 1972 Japan and other Asian nations had agreed to slow the growth of their U.S. sales of synthetic fibers, and both Japan and the EEC had agreed to relax their trade barriers to many U.S. products.

Nixon's methods were, however, extremely upsetting to the major representatives of transnational capitalist interests. Philip H. Trezise, assistant secretary of state for Economic Affairs since 1969, left the Administration and went to work for the Brookings Institution, that bastion of transnational theory. After twenty-seven years at the State Department, J. Robert Schaetzel, U.S. ambassador to the European Community since 1966, left his post in 1972 and began to write for the Council on Foreign Relations (CFR). And perhaps more significant, C. Fred Bergsten, a dynamic and brilliant darling of the financial capitalists, deserted his post as assistant for International Economic Affairs to Henry Kissinger, returned to the Brookings Institution and the CFR, and embarked on a campaign to point out the destructive nature of the Nixon shocks—in articles in the *Washington Post*, the *New York Times, Foreign Policy,* and *Foreign Affairs.* An article written for the latter in November 1971, three months after the Nixon bombshell, was quite blunt:

> In the summer of 1971, President Nixon and Secretary Connally revolutionized U.S. foreign economic policy. In so doing, they promoted a protectionist trend which raises questions about the future of the U.S. economy at least as fundamental as those raised by the abrupt adoption of wage-price controls. In so doing, they have also encouraged a disastrous isolationist trend which raises questions about the future of U.S. foreign policy...Both the U.S. economy and U.S. foreign policy for the relevant future hang in the balance...
>
> [Nixon] terminated the convertability of the dollar, shattering the linchpin of the international monetary system—on whose smooth functioning the world economy depends. He imposed an import surcharge, proposed both the most sweeping U.S. export subsidy in history and discriminated against foreign machinery by making it ineligible for the Job Development Credit, bludgeoned East Asia into "voluntary" restraint agreements on textiles and sought to extend and tighten the existing "voluntary" agreement on steel—completely revising the traditional position of U.S. administrations in resisting protectionism and leading the world toward ever freer trade...He violated the letter and the spirit of the reigning international law in both the monetary and trade fields...[9]

In September 1971 Bergsten, along with Richard Cooper and Richard Gardner,* two other leading transnational theorists, testified before the Subcommittee on Foreign Affairs, which issued a rather guarded report on the International Implications of the New Economic Policy in late February of 1972, noting:

> There was a consensus among the nongovernmental witnesses...that the tactics pursued in behalf of the "New Economic Policy" embodied a high-risk strategy *that could lead to the first international trade war since the 1930s...*
>
> There was a considerable body of opinion that the method of approach of the "New Economic Policy" unnecessarily harmed U.S. international relations. *Most significant was the apparent absence of any prior consultation with foreign nations, including our closest allies, on the measures announced.* Such a procedure undermines the basis for durable bilateral and multilateral relations of trust and cooperation between countries and in international organizations.[10] [Italics ed.]

---

*Bergsten became assistant secretary of the treasury for International Affairs; Cooper undersecretary of state for Economic Affairs, and Gardner ambassador to Italy under Carter.

Walter Scheel then West Germany's foreign minister, warned: "By its decisions on trade policy, the United States may bring about the disintegration of the Western world."[11]

The Nixon shocks, in fact, were a unilateral attempt to reassert U.S. economic dominance over Japan and Western Europe. Alliances, to be sure, were important, but the key was that Western Europe and Japan were on their own, open to U.S. attack or reconciliation as needed. In the vocabulary of the transnational "interdependence theorists," Nixon was following a policy of "economic nationalism" promoted by the more domestically-based and nationally-oriented industrial interests:

> By and large, the major political source of the recent resurgence of economic nationalism, particularly in the United States...[has been] relatively immobile domestic groups pressing the government for protection of their share of welfare in the competition with transnational competitors. It is not a situation in which foreign economic policy is used to enhance state power but in which short-term problems of the distribution of economic welfare, particularly for groups whose interests are hurt by increasing international transactions, exert strong pressure on foreign economic policy, *regardless* of the implications for interstate power or even the aggregate welfare of the national society.[12]

On the face of it, Nixon's view might seem an eminently realistic assessment of interimperialist rivalries in the midst of a severe economic and political crisis. In fact, the splintering of the industrial capitalist nations posed serious threats to those international players—the transnational financiers and corporations—with vested interest in free trade, free investment, and a fluidly interdependent capitalist economy worldwide, in which money was free to come, go, and make more money as it pleased.

It was not long before these transnational financial powers began to act. In a series of articles, conferences, and exchanges of opinion of the most important economic, political, and theoretical representatives of transnational capital—Zbigniew Brzezinski, David Rockefeller, George Ball, C.F. Bergsten, Richard Cooper, Richard Gardner, David Packard, Cyrus Vance, W. Michael Blumenthal, Sir Alec Cairncross, Don Guido Colonna di Paliano, Raymond Barre, Jean Ray, John Loudon, Chujiro Fujino, Saburo Okita (see "Who's Who on the Trilateral Commission")—it was generally agreed that the wounds caused by the Nixon shocks were not going to heal themselves and that transnational interests had to be more vigorously championed internationally. It was impossible, of course, for the international economic system to return to the *status quo ante,* or the scene of the crime, given the changed and changing scene. Nixon's economic policies; detente; an increasingly unsettled scene in Africa, Latin America, and Asia; and the emergence of OPEC and the oil crisis of 1973-74—all these factors had complicated and irreparably changed the capitalist world. But the international financial and corporate interests meant to see that these changes were dealt with so as not to threaten their transnational economic interests.

In early 1973, Rockefeller and Brzezinski launched the Trilateral Commission. (See "Creating the Trilateral Commission," following.)[13]

Is the Trilateral Commission a conspiracy? No more than the laws of capitalism conspire to assert themselves. The Trilateral Commission is the executive advisory committee to transnational finance capital. As Richard Falk has pointed out: "The vistas of the Trilateral Commission can be understood as the ideological perspective representing the transnational outlook of the multinational corporation," which "seeks to subordinate territorial politics to non-territorial economic goals."[14]

Before we move on to examine the Trilateral Commission's ideas, it might be in order to recall the political events of recent years.

The most striking event of the past decade was, of course, the Watergate affair and the scuttling of an entire administration. It is beyond the scope of this article to examine the direct relationship of transnational capital to Watergate; suffice it to say that, involved or not in Nixon's demise, the international financiers sighed with relief when Richard Nixon made his stumbling, feverish exit. The Ford Administration was much more reasonable, if somewhat noncommittal, and the 19 August 1974 appointment of Nelson Rockefeller as Ford's vice president spelled the final and definitive end to the turbulent Nixon shock years and the threat of a new protectionism—Vice-President Rockefeller being presumably closer to his brother David than to the excongressman from Grand Rapids. One can sense the cautious relief and guarded optimism in David Rockefeller's remarks to the Chamber of Commerce of the European Community in October 1975:

> I share your concern over the number of petitions which have already been filed under the anti-dumping and countervailing duty provisions of the 1974 Trade Act. I am equally distressed, both as a free trader and as an executive in an industry as vulnerable to reciprocity as banking, by the large number of bills in Congress that would inhibit the flow of foreign investments into this country...Most are outright protectionist and should be killed in committee...

Fortunately, there are no signs that these anti-trade measures are supported by the Administration. Furthermore, the White House decision, after some hesitation, to participate in the economic summit in Paris is a further substantiation of the Administration's attitude on trade.[15]

But it was widely felt that the Republican Party was dead, and especially with the possible convention victory of Ronald Reagan—who stood for everything the transnational imperialists had worked to eliminate—there were more than a few hints that the Commission had a hand in the strange rise to power of Jimmy Carter.[16] (See Shoup.)

Transnational Capital's Plan for a Better World

Interdependence is nothing new...but its present scale certainly is. Phenomena indicative of interactions across national frontiers have grown during the past generation even faster than output as a whole. Trade between the major economies, for instance, has increased about 8 percent annually, against an average annual growth of the global economy of about 5 percent. International production by integrated multinational companies has risen even faster, about 10 percent per year; over a fifth of the industrial output of market economy countries is now controlled by corporations which plan their investment, their fiscal transfers, their use of production capacity, their sales policy, etc., on a transnational basis.[17]

This excerpt from the first report of the Trilateral Political Task Force of October 1973 confirms the underlying reality of the Trilateral Commission's policy statements and programmatic declarations. In an increasingly complex international economic context, the choice for imperialist financiers is clear: either assert aggressively the subjugation of the entire capitalist world to the world and laws of finance, or risk the decay of interdependence and the rise of economic nationalism that would threaten the very basis of international financial capital's free-wheeling profit-making mechanism— open borders for capital flows:

The overriding goal is to make the world safe for interdependence, by protecting the benefits which it provides for each country against the external and internal threats which will constantly emerge from those willing to pay the price for more national autonomy. This may sometimes require slowing the pace at which interdependence proceeds, and checking some aspects of it. More frequently, however, it will call for checking the intrusion of national governments into the international exchange of both economic and noneconomic goods.[18]

First on the list of precious items to protect is foreign direct investment. The expansion of foreign investment has brought with it some unwanted side effects. "Host" countries, especially the neo-colonies, have an increasingly disturbing tendency to nationalize foreign businesses, or at least to tax them at something approaching reasonable rates. For obvious reasons, one of the Commission's imperatives is a safe atmosphere for foreign investment, i.e., docile neocolonial governments willing to enforce the superexploitation of their workforce. It has thus proposed "new international rules to check the efforts of national governments to seize for their own countries a disproportionate share of the benefits by foreign direct investment."[19] (See Girvan Part VII.)

Linked with this are the Trilateral Commission's ideas on trade policy, which can be summarized in a single familiar word: liberal-ization—"a progressive, across-the-board, and automatic reduction and elimination of tariffs on industrial products."[20] Similar if less drastic measures are recommended for non-tariff barriers to trade: import and export controls, confusing customs procedures, sub-sidies, "Buy American" campaigns and the like. The reasons are clear and consistent. Success has been slow to date, and the many protectionist pressures now being exerted on the government by U.S steel corporations, shoe manufacturers, and others highlight the political difficulties faced by transnational free traders.

International monetary reform was another priority on the transnational agenda, primarily because the system was in such disarray and this confusion was contributing to the strengthening of neonationalist forces. In mid-1973, coherent international monetary reform—or lack thereof—was the monkey wrench in the trans-national machine; indeed, the first task force report was on this topic. Although monetary policy continues to be important, it is no longer of paramount concern, as many of the Commission's recommen-dations (flexible exchange rates, the elimination of gold as a monetary vehicle within the IMF, increased use of the IMF's Special Drawing Rights, improvements in the use of short-term credit to offset balance-of-payments deficits) have since been adopted.

Perhaps the most interesting development in the Commission's plans has been its attempts to get a grip on turbulence in the Third World. An example was the tremendous problems posed by the accumulation of petrodollars by the OPEC countries. Such an accumulation of unused capital in OPEC coffers was serious, and much effort went into plans to recycle this capital toward the profit-making machinery of the transnational corporations. One early plan was the "Third Window," whereby the OPEC countries would—through the World Bank and with subsidies from the advanced capitalist countries—lend large sums of money to other Third World

countries to allow them to buy more goods produced by transnational corporations:

> A joint Trilateral-OPEC initiative that brings forth more
> capital for development would serve some very immediate
> Trilateral country interests. In a time of stagnant growth and
> rising unemployment, it is obviously advantageous to move funds
> from OPEC countries which cannot spend them on Trilateral
> country exports to developing countries who will.[21]

The history of this particular proposal indicates the powerful
influence of the Commission on international politics and economics. First raised in early 1974 by the Task Force on the Political
and International Implications of the Energy Crisis, it was fleshed
out later in the year and discussed with World Bank and IMF
officials in September of that year. In January 1975 the World Bank
called for further study of the Third Window plan; in February the
final task force report was published; in July 1975 the World Bank
accepted the proposal, which is now functioning, albeit only in part.
(See Phillips for a description of the Third Window.) International
commercial banks have also played a major role in "recycling" money
from OPEC treasure chests toward the fertile financial soil of
countries like Brazil and Mexico.

But it quickly became clear that no financial sleight-of-hand
would be sufficient to completely solve the energy problem, and
accordingly the task force called for a long-range program for the
trilateral countries to reduce dependence on OPEC petroleum. Their
proposals form the basis of President Carter's energy plan. (See
Garitty, and Kaufman and Clawson.)

More generally, since the energy crisis the Trilateral Commission's work has shifted and broadened its focus as the problems of
continuing imperialist domination of the neocolonies have become
more glaring. Thus more recent trilateral reports have emphasized the
need to integrate thoroughly the so-called developing world into
international capitalism. This integration takes many forms, from
allowing the neocolonies a symbolically greater voice in organizations like the IMF, to tying neocolonial economies even closer to
Western finance. Two well-known examples of trilateral theory in
action are the seemingly more relaxed African policy of the Carter
Administration on the one hand (see Nesbitt and Brown), and the
astronomical debt of many underdeveloped countries on the other
hand (see Phillips). Both—with different degrees of insidiousness—
serve to encourage and/or force Third World countries to act within
the economic and political limits prescribed by the major industrial
powers.

The Commission's proposals on these and other issues are complex and comprehensive; many are discussed elsewhere in this volume. Here it is enough to summarize once more their general game plan: a capitalist world dominated by the industrial capitalist nations (themselves dominated by transnational financial interests) cooperating in a concerted offensive against Third World revolutionism by pursuing the irredeemable integration of the neocolonies into international capitalist commodity, investment, and financial markets; and cooperating in presenting a common front to the socialist world on economic, political, and military matters.

The Trilateral Commission is not a cabal or conspiracy, as some would have it. It is the international forum for discussion and decision making of imperialist finance in an unstable age. With ties to every major imperialist government, every transnational bank and corporation, and every major imperialist think-tank, its power is significant—a concerted power based on a commonality of interests and concerns rather than a blood oath.

Achievements, Problems, and Prospects

We have emphasized that trilateralism is the political expression of one section of finance capital, a section made up of banks and corporations with investments, commitments, sales, and production on an *international* scale. Clearly there is another section of finance capital which does not support the policies for which trilateralism stands; this section is made up of primarily industrial corporations whose operations are confined to one nation, whose export sales and foreign production facilities are insignificant. And it is to this split in finance capital that many of trilateralism's most serious problems can be traced.

For a major component of trilateralism is the attempt to bribe, threaten, and cajole the people of the advanced capitalist countries into supporting the internationalization of capital. North Americans, West Germans, and Japanese all have to be convinced that their respective countries are friendly partners in a peace-loving alliance; that Japanese TV sets and German steel sold in the U.S. represent a boon to U.S consumers; that international economic interdependence is better than nationalism. It was not difficult to achieve this consensus in times of prosperity and economic expansion: incomes were rising, the lower prices of foreign-made goods were welcome, and the unemployment foreign competition might cause was only a distant threat.

But as the economy began to collapse in the early 1970s, for many people the problems of capitalist internationalism came to outweigh its advantages. Domestic manufacturers unable to sell their products looked to eliminate competitors, and when the crunch came and factories began to close, domestic industrialists were quick to blame unemployment on low-priced foreign competition.

Indeed, the recession of the 1970s has unleashed significant protectionist forces in every advanced capitalist country. And although Nixon's early protectionism may have been beaten down, today Jimmy Carter and like-minded national leaders around the world are finding it impossible to ignore the political strength of protectionism. (See Block.)

So far, the trilateralists have been able to keep protectionism and economic nationalism from destroying their carefully-woven fabric. But they have not been able to hold off recessionary economic forces, and recession has bred tensions between Western Europe, Japan, and the United States. As the recession deepens, these tensions may erupt into trade wars, restrictions on capital flows, and a general collapse of international money markets. Similar tensions—and similar actions harmful to transnational interests—may also be heightened and quickened by the effects of the crisis on Africa, Latin America, and Asia.

A house of cards, even if well planned and carefully constructed, is still just a house of cards. The Trilateral Commission's program for the international economy is careful and thoughtful; its plans have the backing of the world's most powerful bankers, industrialists, and politicians. Yet the triumph of trilateralism—truly transnational imperialist relations—is possible only in a period of general expansion. As the economy moves inexorably toward a general collapse, the plans for a transnational world economy will become less and less feasible. The trilateral house of cards will fall—not because it is poorly built, but because its architects assumed the impossible: that capitalism would forever expand.

FOOTNOTES

1. David P. Calleo and Benjamin Rowland, *America and the World Political Economy,* (Bloomington: Indiana University Press, 1973), pp. 147 and 150-1.
2. "Shifting Patterns of Foreign Direct Investment," *International Finance,* bi-weekly bulletin of the economics group of the Chase Manhattan Bank, 13 December 1976.
3. Robert Z. Aliber, "International Banking: Growth and Regulation," *Columbia Journal of World Business,* Winter 1975.
4. "Multinationals Under Seige," *International Finance,* 19 May 1975.
5. "The Importance of the Atlantic Connection," *International Finance,* 17 November 1975.

6. "Cosmocorp: The Importance of Being Stateless," *Columbia Journal of World Business,* 2: 6 (November-December 1967).

7. Robert E. Baldwin and David A. Kay, "International Trade and International Relations," in *World Politics and International Economics,* C. Fred Bergsten and Lawrence B. Krause, eds., (Washington, D.C.: The Brookings Institution, 1975), p. 100.

8. For a good summary of Nixon's 1971-1972 foreign economic policies, see Benjamin J. Cohen, "The Revolution in Atlantic Economic Relations: A Bargain Comes Unstuck," in *The United States and Western Europe,* Wolfram F. Hanrieder, ed., (Cambridge, Mass. 1974).

9. *Foreign Affairs,* January 1972.

10. *New Realities and New Directions in United States Foreign Economic Policy,* a report by the subcommittee on Foreign Economic Policy of the House Committee on Foreign Affairs, 28 February 1972.

11. The *New York Times,* 8 December 1971, p. 107.

12. C. Fred Bergsten, Robert O. Keohane, and Joseph S. Nye, "International Economics and International Politics: A Framework for Analysis," in *World Politics and International Economics,* p. 18.

13. Robert Manning, "A World Safe for Business," *Far Eastern Economic Review,* 25 March 1977, p. 39.

14. Richard Falk, "A New Paradigm for International Legal Studies," *The Yale Law Review,* 84:5 (April 1975).

15. "The Importance of the Atlantic Connections" *International Finance.* 17 November 1975.

16. Manning, *op. cit.*

17. *The Crisis of International Cooperation,* A report of the Trilateral Political Task Force to the Executive Committee of the Trilateral Commission, Tokyo, October 22-23, 1973. Rapporteurs: Francois Duchene, Kinhide Mushakoji, Henry D. Owen, (New York, 1974).

18. C. Fred Bergsten, Georges Berthoin, Kinhide Mushakoji, *The Reform of International Institutions,* (1976), p. 2.

19. *The Reform of International Institutions,* pp. 16-17.

20. *Directions for World Trade in the 1970s,* A report of the Trilateral Task Force to the Executive Committee of the Trilateral Commission, Brussels, 23-24 June 1974. Rapporteurs: Guido de Paliano, Philip H. Trezise, Nobuhiko Ushiba, (New York, 1974), p. 13.

21. *OPEC, the Trilateral World, and the Developing Countries: New Arrangements for Cooperation,* 1976-1980. A report of the Trilateral Task Force on Relations with Developing Countries to the Executive Committee of the Trilateral Commission. Rapporteurs: Richard Gardner, Saburo Okita, B.J. Udink, (New York, 1975), p. 6.

chapter two

FOUNDING THE TRILATERAL COMMISSION: CHRONOLOGY 1970-1977*

Holly Sklar

1970: Zbigniew Brzezinski wrote *Between Two Ages: America's Role in the Technetronic Era*** (New York: Viking Press), a forceful rationale for trilateralism. He called for the formation of "*A Community of the Developed Nations,*" composed of the United States, Western Europe, and Japan. These are the "most vital regions of the globe" because "they are in the forefront of scientific and technological innovation," and most advanced in "planetary consciousness" (p. 294).

From the start, Brzezinski stressed the important role of Japan: "Japan is a world power, and in the world of electronic and supersonic communications it is a psychological and political error to think of it as primarily an Asian nation. Japan needs an outlet commensurate with its own advanced development, not one that places it in the position of a giant among pygmies and that excludes it *de facto* from the councils of the real world powers" (pp. 297-8).

Brzezinski outlined "the broad and overlapping phases" in the formation of the Community of Nations: the first "would involve the forging of community links among the United States, Western Europe, and Japan, as well as with other more advanced countries (for example: Australia, Israel, Mexico). The second phase would include the extension of these links to more advanced communist countries," perhaps beginning with Yugoslavia and Rumania, (pp.

---

*This article is based largely on Trilateral Commission documents, particularly "Progress of Organization," Annex 2 (1) of "Trilateral Commission," 15 March 1973; *Annual Reports* 1-5; and *Trialogue.*
**A technetronic society, according to Brzezinski, is "a society that is shaped culturally, psychologically, socially, and economically by the impact of technology and electronics—particularly in the area of computors and communication." (p.9).

296-297)—the idea being that the Soviet Union would join up with the Western advanced nations or be beaten at the game of ideological, technological, and economic competition for the Third World and Eastern Europe.

The *"emerging community of developed nations would require some institutional expression."* The seeds of the Trilateral Commission as well as regular Western Economic Summit Meetings are found in Brzezinski's proposal for a "high-level consultative council for global cooperation, regularly bringing together the heads of governments of the developed world to discuss their common political-security, educational-scientific, and economic-technological problems, as well as to deal from that perspective with their moral obligations toward the developing nations. Some permanent supporting machinery could provide continuity to these consultations." Such a council "would be more effective in developing common programs than in the United Nations, whose efficacy is unavoidably limited by the Cold War and by north-south divisions"* (p. 297).

Brzezinski emphasizes that the traditional sovereignty of nation states is becoming increasingly unglued as transnational forces such as multinational corporations, banks, and international organizations play a larger and larger role in shaping global politics and the consciousness of the jet-age "transnational elite."

1971: Relations between North America, Western Europe, and Japan were not solidifying into a "community"; they were rapidly deteriorating. A dangerous low-point was reached in August at the time of the Nixon shocks to the international and economic political system. (See Frieden.)

In December, Brzezinski (then a Columbia University professor), organized the Tripartite Studies under the auspices of the Brookings Institution (Brookings, located in Washington D.C., is commonly known as the think-tank for Democratic administrations). Brookings scholars worked together with their counterparts from the Japanese Economic Research Center and the European Community Institute of University Studies on common problems. It was partly the impressive results of the Tripartite Studies which convinced David Rockefeller that trilateralism was a necessary and desirable

---

*Brzezinski further aired his views on trilateralism in the context of contemporary politics in two important articles. The first appeared in *Foreign Policy,* Summer 1971: "Half Past Nixon" (this was the article in which Brzezinski issued his famous Nixon Report Card). The second, "U.S. Foreign Policy: The Search for Focus," appeared in *Foreign Affairs,* July 1973.

process. Rockefeller "was getting worried about the deteriorating relations between the U.S., Europe, and Japan," and initiated the process which led to formation of the Trilateral Commission, recalls George Franklin who helped organize the Commission.*

Winter-Spring 1972: In the Winter Rockefeller proposed the creation of what he was then calling an "International Commission for Peace and Prosperity" in speeches before Chase Manhattan International Financial Forums in Western Europe and Canada. But the most enthusiastic and most crucial response came in the spring when Rockefeller and Brzezinski presented the idea of a trilateral grouping at the annual Bilderberg meeting. (See Thompson.) Michael Blumenthal, then head of the Bendix Corporation, strongly backed the idea.

May-June 1972: Rockefeller asked George Franklin to go to Western Europe and "explore there both degree of interest and possible participants." "As a result of interest found in Europe, David Rockefeller and George Franklin explore situation in Japan and find great interest there also."**

July 23-24, 1972: A seventeen-person planning group for the Trilateral Commission met at Rockefeller's estate, Pocantico Hills, in Tarrytown, New York. In addition to Rockefeller, Brzezinski, and Franklin, representatives from the U.S. included: C. Fred Bergsten, Senior Fellow at the Brookings Institution;*** Robert Bowie, Professor of International Affairs, Harvard; McGeorge Bundy, President of the Ford Foundation; Bayless Manning, President of Council on Foreign Relations; Henry Owen, Director, Foreign Policy Program at Brookings. Owen is cited as a key Commission conceptualizer and organizer by knowledgeable observers.

Representatives from Western Europe include: Karl Corstens, Christian Democratic Leader in the Bundestag, West Germany****; Guido Colonna di Paliano, President of La Rinascente and former member of the Commission of the European Community; Francois Duchene, Director of the Center for Contemporary European Studies, University of Sussex; Rene Foch, member of the Executive

---

*See Jeremiah Novak, "The Trilateral Commission," *Atlantic Monthly,* Summer 1977, for a review of these events.

**Up through 1975, all remaining quotes are from the Commission document "Progress of Organization" unless otherwise indicated.

***Positions at the time of the meeting. (See "Who's Who.")

****When Corstens was later elected president of West Germany his background as an ex-Nazi was raised by the media.

Committee, Partie des Republicans Independents; Max Kohnstamm, Director of the European Community Institute for University Studies.

From Japan, the members include: Kichi Miyazawa, member of the Diet and former Minister of Foreign Affairs; Kinhide Mushakoji, Professor of International Relations, Sophia University; Saburo Okita, President of Overseas Economic Cooperation Fund; and Tadashi Yamamoto, President of Japan Center for International Exchange.

Other early U.S. participants, not in attendance at the meeting, included: William Scranton, governor of Pennsylvania and former ambassador to the United Nations; William Roth, former chief trade negotiator under President Johnson; and Edwin Reischauer, ambassador to Japan under Kennedy and Johnson.

Fall 1972: Respective delegations designated Gerard Smith, former director of the Arms Control and Disarmament Agency, as United States chairman; Takeshi Watanabe, former president of the Asian Development Bank, as Japanese chairman; and Max Kohnstamm as European chairman. Brzezinski was selected as the director of the Commission to serve from July 1973. Partial funding was obtained from the Kettering Foundation to supplement the seed monies provided by David Rockefeller.

January-February 1973: Smith, Brzezinski, Franklin, and Kohnstamm held consultations with Watanabe and with Japanese planning groups in Tokyo: "Approval of the highest political and financial circles obtained." Formal funding proposal is submitted to the Ford Foundation "to support a major share of the intellectual and research aspect of the Commission's work and some of the administrative and 'selling' aspects." Other funding sources are explored. (See article following.)

July 1973: The Commission was officially inaugurated after a series of regional meetings and extensive consultations. (See chapter on Commission membership for list of founding members.)

October 20-23, 1973: The founding session of the Executive Committee was held in Tokyo. It was attended by Commission director Zbigniew Brzezinski; regional chairmen, Gerard Smith (North America), Takeshi Watanabe (Japan), and Max Kohnstamm (Western Europe); regional secretaries, George Franklin, Tadashi Yamamoto, and Wolfang Hager; task force rapporteurs Richard N. Cooper, Motoo Kaji, Francois Duchene, and Claudio Segre; and, for North America, Robert Bonner, Robert Bowie, Patrick Haggerty, Jean-Luc Pepin, Edwin Reischauer, David Rockefeller, Paul

Warnke, and Marina Whitman; for Japan Chujiro Fujino, Yukitaka Haraguchi, Kazuschije Hirasawa, Yusuke Kashiwagi, Kiichi Miyazawa, Kinhide Mushakoji, Saburo Okita, and Ryuji Takeuchi; and for Western Europe, P. Nyboe Andersen, Georges Berthoin, Marc Eyskens, Otto Lambsdorff, John Loudon, Cesare Merlini, Alwin Munchmeyer, Myles Staunton, Otto Grieg Tidemand, Sir Kenneth Younger, and Sir Philip de Zuleta. (See "Who's Who.")

A plenary session, with Japanese members, was also held. Japanese Prime Minister Tanaka gave the principal address. The "statement of purposes" formulated by the Executive Committee was adopted (reprinted in *Trialogue* no.2, November 1973).

May 30-1, 1975: First plenary meeting of the full Commission was held in Kyoto, Japan, attended by 113 members—following a consultation with Prime Minister Takeo Miki held on May 29 in Tokyo. Commission discussions were organized around the themes of "Global Redistribution of Power" and "the Trilateral Community: Key Problems and Prospects." The controversial draft Task Force Report on "The Governability of Democracies"—later published in book form as *The Crisis of Democracy* was a focal point of discussion.

Two and a half days of seminars on Japan, organized by the Japanese Office of the Commission, were held for North American and West European members before the plenary session. West European—Japanese relations are considered the weakest link in the Atlantic-Pacific Triangle. Meetings between Europeans and Japanese have continued on a regular basis.

By the time the Commission met in Kyoto the trilateral regions had faced new global shocks: the 1973 Arab oil embargo, 1973-74 OPEC price hikes, April 1975 liberation of Vietnam, rising Third World call for a New International Economic Order. For Brzezinski, Vietnam was the "Waterloo" of the "WASP-eastern seaboard-Ivy League-Wall Street foreign affairs elite" which had dominated foreign policy making before Nixon's administration. The trilateral problem was how to construct with little or no Third World participation an international system which would not be disrupted by Third World initiatives.*

---

*Earlier, Brzezinski had warned: "While it is difficult to fault the [Nixon] Administration's general priorities, one is struck by Washington's extremely limited interest in what is commonly described as the Third World. It may be true that the Kennedy Administration occasionally overdid its wooing of third-rate statesmen and fourth-rate countries [sic] but the Nixon Administration, far from establishing a balance, appears to be turning its back on most of mankind." (p. 10.)

mid-1975-mid-1976: The Commission's *Third Annual Report* states:

> In the United States, there was noticeably increased emphasis on trilateral ties as the cornerstone of American foreign policy—as evidenced in the pronouncements of both Secretary of State Henry Kissinger and presidential candidate Jimmy Carter, an active Commission member*—and "trilateralism" seems to have become a recognized word in the foreign policy lexicon. The Rambouillet (November 1975) and Puerto Rico (June 1976) 'summits' indicated a clearer recognition of the importance of economic cooperation among the economies of the trilateral regions." (p.1) [See Novak for a look at the summits.]

Serving under President Ford, Kissinger (now a member of the Executive Committee of the Commission) moved further away from the unilateralism which Nixon attempted to fashion and closer to the trilateral approach. Concerning the Third World, his earlier confrontationist approach took on more of the trilateral rhetoric of cooperation.

Carter regularly expounded trilateralism in his foreign policy addresses during the campaign. An oft-quoted remark he made in his autobiography *Why Not the Best* (New York: Bantam Books, 1975) reads "Membership on this Commission has provided me with a spendid learning opportunity, and many of the other members have helped me in my study of foreign affairs." Early on Brzezinski became Carter's principal tutor. (See Shoup.)

mid-1976-mid-1977: The Commissions *Fourth Annual Report* exclaims: "*An increase in the Trilateral Commission's impact, resulting in large part from the number of Commissioners entering various governments, was perhaps the principal feature of the year 1976-1977.* This entry into government was most spectacular in the case of the United States...The interest in these appointments resulted in greatly increased exposure for the Commission's work— as reflected in particular by the wide press coverage received by the Commission, and in a substantial boost in the circulation of its reports and other published material." [Italics ed.] In this period the North American mailing list grew from 1700 to 2300 individuals.

Widened press exposure presented some problems: "Although the net result was a substantial boost in the public's interest in the Commission and in the dissemination of its work, some of this

---

*One Carter activity which pleased the Commission was "his distributing some 400 Task Force Reports to Democratic candidates for office in the 1974 United States elections," as cited in the *First Annual Progress Report,"* p. 6.

coverage tended to give a largely distorted image of the Commission's role—sometimes raising the old conspiracy theories." Because of this greater public relations efforts were directed at the press and the public—promoting the image that the Commission was an unofficial grouping of concerned citizens trying to suggest ways to address pressing world problems for the good of all humanity.

At the 9-11 January plenary session in Tokyo, trilateralists discussed the task force report *Towards a Renovated International System*. The *Fourth Annual Report* calls it "a broad overview which was conceived as a capstone of the first three years of the Trilateral Commission's efforts" (p. 2). By 1977 the trilateral prescription for revitalizing the world economic and political order had been spelled out.

chapter three

THE COMMISSION'S PURPOSE, STRUCTURE, AND PROGRAMS— IN ITS OWN WORDS *

Holly Sklar

I. Purpose

A. To Foster Cooperation Among the Trilateral Regions

The introduction to the Commission prospectus cautions that "domestic concerns—in Japan, Europe, and the U.S.—make it difficult to resolve [these] problems in ways which will not drive these regions apart...But...because of their *technological and economic interdependence,* these areas have sufficient common interests to make up a *community in fact, if not in form...*

"The choice between these two directions—between drifting apart and closer cooperation among the three advanced regions— will shape the world of the future. *A private group can play a role in making that choice.* To this end, David Rockefeller had proposed the formation of a Trilateral Commission of leading private citizens from Japan, Europe, and North America *"whose primary objective, as I see it, would be to bring the best brains in the world to bear on the problems of the future."*[2]

B. To Shape Governmental and Non-Governmental Action

"Inaugurated in July 1973, the Trilateral Commission is a policy making organization."[3] The Commission seeks "to formulate and propose policies which the regions and nations within the Regions could follow in their relations with one another, in their foreign relations in general, and in the solution of common domestic problems including particularly relations and problems involving

---

*The material compiled by the editor in this section is drawn from the following Commission documents: *Constitution of the Trilateral Commission,* 1973; *The Trilateral Commission,* a prospectus issued 15 March 1973; *Statement of Purposes,"* issued by the Executive Committee of the Trilateral Commission, October 1973; Trilateral Commission *Annual Reports* 1-6; Financial Statements; *Trialogue;* and regular Information Brochures.

(1) economic matters, (2) political and defense matters, (3) developing countries, and (4) Communist countries,"[4] and "to foster understanding and support of Commission recommendations both in governmental and private sectors in the three regions."[5]

C. To Renovate the International System

"The renovation of the international system will be a very prolonged process. The system shaped after World War II was created through an act of will and human initiative in a relatively restricted period of time. One power had overwhelming might and influence, and others were closely associated with it. In contrast, a renovated international system will now require a process of creation—much longer and more complex—in which prolonged negotiations will have to be initiated and developed. *In nurturing habits and practices of working together among the trilateral regions, the Commission should help set the context for these necessary efforts.*"[6]

D. Critics Answered

The Trilateral Commission dismisses criticism of its basic aims with these remarks:

> "This cooperation does not involve setting up a supergovernment to run the 'advanced world'; it means the developed regions coming closer together in joint programs and institutions to meet common needs. It does not envisage a new anti-Communist alliance; indeed, at some point in the future the more advanced Communist states might choose to become partners. It does not foreshadow a rich man's club. Working more closely together the industrial areas may not only sustain their own security and prosperity but also provide more effective assistance to poor nations."[7]

II. Structure

A. Membership

Initially, about 180 and now some 300 "eminent private citizens (Commissioners)"—from the three regions "sharing common concerns about the future of the Regions and the world."[8]

"The need for diversity, professionally and geographically will be met as well as the need for *men and women of sufficient standing to influence opinion leaders both public and private in favor of the Commission's recommendations.*"[9]

B. Leadership*

    1. Director / Coordinator

        During the first three years of the Commission's operation there was a central director—Zbigniew Brze-

*See list of officers in "Who's Who."

zinski—with heavy responsibilities in the area of policy studies based in the North American office (New York). It was agreed that the Commission administration would "proceed in a more decentralized manner in the new phase." Now there is a "Coordinator" chosen by the Executive Committee—George Franklin—who oversees the overall operation of the Commission but the "responsibilities of the European (Paris) and Japanese (Tokyo) offices have been considerably strengthened, notably in managing task forces."[10]

2. Regional Chairman

The three regional chairmen are the "chief executive officers in charge of the Commission's activities." Succeeding chairmen are chosen by Executive Committee members from the respective Regions.

3. Executive Committee

The Executive Committee is the "principal policy organ of the Commission." It initiates policy studies in consultation with the director; reviews task force recommendations; makes policy decisions and implements Commission proposals.

The Executive Committee is composed of the regional chairmen, any deputy chairmen, and thirty other Commissioners divided amongst the three regions as follows: eleven from North America (nine from the U.S. and two from Canada); twelve from Western Europe; and seven from Japan.

4. Program Advisory Board

The advisory board is a small informal group of Commissioners which advises the director and regional chairmen on policy studies.

C. Meetings

The founding session of the Executive Committee was held in October 1973 in Tokyo (symbolic of Japan's initiation in the "advanced nation club"). The full Commission first met May 30-31, 1975 in Kyoto, attended by 113 members. Subsequent plenary meetings took place in May 1976 in Ottawa, Canada; January 1977 in Tokyo; October 1977 in Bonn, West Germany; July 1978 in Washington D.C.; and April 1979 in Tokyo. The Washington meeting was attended by 200 Commissioners and invited experts. Plenary meetings are now held about once every nine months and generally last two to three days. Keynote speakers address selected themes and members discuss any final or interim reports presented by the trilateral task forces.

Consultations with heads of state, high government officials, and prominent politicians of the host nation are a regular feature of plenary meetings, Executive Committee meetings, and regional meetings. Meetings are regularly reviewed in *Trialogue* and in the *Annual Reports.*

D. Duration

The Commission was originally expected to operate for a limited period of three years—sufficient time, it was hoped by Rockefeller and others, to forge a new framework for the foreign and domestic policies of the trilateral regions. But in December 1975 and again in July 1978, the Commission renewed its three-year mandate (through July 1982). In fact, if not in form, the Commission has longer-range plans.

E. Funding

Seed monies were provided by David Rockefeller and then supplemented with grants from the Kettering Foundation, the Ford Foundation, the Lilly Endowment, the Rockefeller Brothers Fund, and the Thyssen Foundation. Other individuals and corporations provided smaller contributions. According to Commission Financial Statements, between 30 June 1974 and 30 June 1976 David Rockefeller gave $109,328; David Packard (chairman of Hewlett-Packard) gave $88,438; and George Franklin gave $41,920. In the same period, the Ford Foundation provided $500,000, the Lilly Endowment, $300,000; the Rockefeller Brothers Fund, $150,000; the Kettering Foundation, $40,000; the Thyssen Foundation, $94,978. General Motors, Sears Roebuck, Caterpillar Tractor, Deere, and Exxon gave $30,000 each. Texas Instruments gave $20,000 and Coca Cola, Time, CBS, and the Wells Fargo Bank gave contributions ranging from $3500 to $7500. *Total receipts* for the 1974-76 period were $1,577,133.

For the second three-year period—1 July 1976 through 30 June 1979—the Commission received $631,295 from foundations; $93,500 from corporations, $125,500 from individuals; $25,703 from investment income. The Commission also received Canadian contributions of $28, 440 and European and Japanese contributions of $78,375. New corporate donors listed in this second period include: Honeywell, Cargill, Cummings Engine, Kaiser Resources, Bechtel, and Weyerhauser.

F. Regional Headquarters

North American Office	European Office	Japanese Office
345 East 46th Street	151 Boulevard Haussman	Japan Center for
New York, New York 10017	75008 Paris, France	International Exchange
Telephone: (212) 661-1180	Telephone: 764-6609	4-9-17 Minami-Azabu
		Minato-ku, Tokyo, Japan
		Telephone: 446-7781

III. Programs
A. Policy Studies

One of the purposes of the Commission is "to involve leaders in the private sector of each region in cooperative study of important issues affecting the Regions." Trilateral Policy Studies are carried out by the task forces. Task forces are appointed by the director in consultation with the regional chairmen and consist of representatives from all Regions. "*The operation of this 'trilateral process' in the preparation of reports is a vital aspect of the Commission's efforts to nurture habits and practices of working together among the three regions.*"[11]

Task force members and special consultants include Commissioners and non-Commissioners who are "leading experts in the subject chosen for study." Generally, three Rapporteurs (one from each region) are jointly responsible for coordinating the project and drafting the final reports. Before publication in the form of *Triangle Papers,* the task force report is reviewed by the Executive Committee and, if possible, a plenary meeting of the Commission. At the front of each report is a list of persons consulted and a schedule of activities.

Task force report "format—an average of 40 pages—and their *clear emphasis on policy recommendations are designed to make them useful to the busy and influential reader.*"[12] Summaries are provided at the start of each report. (See bibliography for list of reports.)

B. Impact Meetings

Impact meetings are hosted by the Commission in order to: *"sharpen the impact of its work among decision-makers"* and to generate favorable press coverage of the task force findings. Meetings take place with the press; congresspersons, senators, and parliamentarians; Executive and congressional staffers; embassy officials; leaders of international organizations and political bodies, e.g., the Commission of the European Communities; experts in related fields; and top government officials. Politicians serving on the Commission play a key role in organizing formal and informal gatherings with legislators and legislative aids. In this fashion the circle of "influential persons" directly in contact with the Commission is widened considerably.[13]

C. Trialogue

Trialogue is the Commission's quarterly bulletin of trilateral and world affairs. It contains valuable information and articles on Commission activities including discussion of task force reports; the progress of Commission policy recommendations; plenary sessions and Executive Committee meetings; major speeches; governmental events such as the London summit (Winter 1977-78, #16); and special topics such as "The Politics of Human Rights" (Fall 1978, #19).

The Winter 1980 issue marks the " 'coming of age' of *Trialogue* as an important quarterly journal of North American/European Japanese affairs." *Trialogue* is now being distributed on a paid subscription basis, "with three issues devoted each year to topical international problems high on our nations' agendas, and a fourth issue covering in detail that year's plenary conference of the Trilateral Commission."

Trialogue is one indication that the Commission is just entering its maturity.

FOOTNOTES

1. Trilateral Commission, "The Industrialized Democratic Regions in a Changing International System," a statement found in the Commission brochure and appearing on the rear cover of the two volumes of collected Commission Task Force Reports, (New York: New York University Press, 1977 and 1978).
2. Trilateral Commission, "The Trilateral Commission," 15 March 1973, pp. 1-3.
3. "The Industrialized Democratic Regions," *op. cit.*
4. "Constitution of the Trilateral Commission," Attachment B, April 1973, pp. 1-2.
5. "The Trilateral Commission," p. 4.
6. "The Industrialized Democratic Regions, *op.cit.*
7. "The Trilateral Commission," pp. 1-2.
8. Constitution, p. 1.
9. "Fourth Annual Report," October 1977, p. 11.
11. *Ibid.,* p. 6.
12. *Ibid.,* pp. 10-11.
13. Impact Activities are reviewed in the Annual Reports. Citation given is from the "Fifth Annual Report," p. 8.
14. Memorandum to *Trialogue* readers from George S. Franklin, 19 November, 1979.

"The men organizing the Commission want it to take new looks at things. But not for abstract purposes: like the old Monnet Committee,* they want to bring about action, and hence they want the new body to be a marriage of the intellectual and the influential."

—"The New Atlantis," *The Economist,* also cited in Trilateral Commission brochure.

If after the inauguration you find Cy Vance as Secretary of State and Zbigniew Brzezinski as head of national security, then I would say that we failed. And I'd quit.

—Hamilton Jordan, Carter's White House Chief of Staff during the 1976 campaign.

---

*For information about Jean Monnet's Action Committee for a United Europe, see Peter Thompson, "Bilderberg and the West" in this volume. Max Kohnstamm, European Chairman of the Trilateral Commission from 1973-75 was the long-time vice-president of the Action Committee and a close associate of Monnet.

chapter four

WHO'S WHO ON THE TRILATERAL COMMISSION
*Holly Sklar & Ros Everdell**

Table of Contents

*Ros Everdell is co-director of the Food and Hunger Hotline in New York City. She works with the Committee to End Sterilization Abuse (CESA) and the People's Initiative on Food, Land and Justice.

Trilateral Commission Officers

Director/Coordinator	Deputy Director
Zbigniew Brzezinski, Director 1973-76	Christopher Makins 1975-76
George Franklin, Coordinator 1977-	

North American Officers

Chairman	Deputy Chairman	Secretary
Gerard Smith 1973-76	Mitchell Sharp 1977-	George Franklin 1973-76
David Rockefeller 1977-		Charles Heck 1977-

European Officers

Chairman	Deputy Chairman	Secretary
Max Kohnstamm 1973-75	Francoise Duchene 1974-76	Wolfgang Hager 1973
George Berthoin 1976-	Egidio Ortona 1976-	Hanns Maull 1977-78
		Martine Trink 1979-

Japanese Officers

Chairman	Deputy Chairman	Secretary
Takeshi Watanabe 1973-	Nobuhiko Ushiba 1977-	Tadashi Yamamoto 1973-

Trilateralists in the Carter Administration
(As of January 1977 unless otherwise indicated)*

1. Lucy Wilson Benson, Undersecretary of State for Security Assistance (resigned 1980)
2. C. Fred Bergsten, Assistant Secretary of the Treasury for International Affairs
3. W. Michael Blumenthal, Secretary of the Treasury (resigned July 1979)
4. Robert R. Bowie, Deputy to the Director of Central Intelligence for National Intelligence (resigned 1979)
5. Harold Brown, Secretary of Defense
6. Zbigniew Brzezinski, Assistant to the President for National Security Affairs
7. Jimmy Carter, President
8. Warren Christopher, Deputy Secretary of State
9. Richard N. Cooper, Undersecretary of State for Economic Affairs
10. Lloyd N. Cutler, White House Counsel (September 1979-)
11. Hedley Donovan, Senior Advisor Domestic and Foreign Policy and Media Relations (July 1979-)
12. Richard N. Gardner, Ambassador to Italy

---

*Many of these names appear on the Commission's list of "Former Members Now in Public Service". Some members did not resign from the Commission upon assuming office; two (Bergsten and Huntington) have participated in the Commission as Task Force leaders but are not regular members.

13. Richard Holbrooke, Assistant Secretary of State for East Asian and Pacific Affairs
14. Samuel P. Huntington, Coordinator of National Security, National Security Council (resigned August 1978)
15. Sol Linowitz, Special Mid East Negotiator; Director, President's Commission on World Hunger; Co-Negotiator of Panama Canal Treaties
16. Walter Mondale, Vice President
17. Henry Owen, U.S. Ambassador at Large, Special Representative of President for Economic Summits
18. Elliot L. Richardson, U.S. Ambassador at Large with Responsibility for U.N. Law of the Sea Conference
19. John Sawhill, Deputy Secretary of Energy (August 1979-)
20. Gerard C. Smith, U.S. Ambassador at Large for Non-Proliferation Matters
21. Anthony M. Solomon, Undersecretary of the Treasury for Monetary Affairs (resigned 1980)
22. Cyrus R. Vance, Secretary of State (resigned April 1980)
23. Paul C. Warnke, Director, U.S. Arms Control and Disarmament Agency; Chief Disarmament Negotiator (resigned 1979)
24. Leonard Woodcock, Ambassador to Peking
25. Andrew Young, Ambassador to the United Nations (resigned August 1979)
26. Paul A. Volcker, Chairman of the Federal Reserve Board (July 1979-)

Trilateralists in the Ford Administration

1. William T. Coleman, Jr., Secretary of Transportation
2. Elliot L. Richardson, Secretary of Commerce

Canadian Trilateralists in Government Since 1973

John Allen Fraser, Postmaster General; Minister of Environment
Claude Masson, Head, Division of Planning & Research, Department of Trade and Commerce
Jean-Luc Pepin, P.C., Chairman of the Anti-Inflation Board of Canada; Co-Chairman, Task Force on Canadian Unity

West European Trilateralists in Government Since 1973

Svend Auken (Denmark), Minister of Labor
Raymond Barre (France), Prime Minister and Finance Minister
Lord Carrington (U.K.), Secretary of State for Foreign and Commonwealth Affairs
Michel Debatisse (France), Food and Agricultural Minister
Herbert Ehrenberg (W. Germany), Minister of Labor and Social Affairs
Marc Eyskens (Belgium), State Secretary for Budget and Flemish Regional Economy; Minister of Cooperative Development
Bernard Hayhoe (U.K.), Parliamentary Undersecretary of State in the Defense Ministry
Count Otto Graf Lambsdorff (W. Germany), Minister of Economics
Jean-Philippe Lecat (France), Presidential Spokesman; Minister of Culture and Communications
Evan Luard (U.K.), Parliamentary Undersecretary of State for the Foreign Office

Ivar Norgaard (Denmark), Minister of Foreign Economic Affairs and Nordic Affairs; Minister of Commerce; Minister of Environment

Michael O'Kennedy (Ireland), Minister of Foreign Affairs

Henri F. Simonet (Belgium), Foreign Minister

Thorvald Stoltenberg (Norway), Secretary of State, Ministry of Foreign Affairs

Olaf Sund (W. Germany), Senator for Labor and Social Affairs

Michael Woods (Ireland), Minister for State in the Office of Prime Minister

Japanese Trilateralists in Government Since 1973

Koichi Kato, Deputy Chief Cabinet Secretary

Kiichi Miyazawa, Chief Cabinet Secretary; Minister of Foreign Affairs; Director of Economic Planning Agency

Nobuhiko Ushiba, Minister of External Economic Affairs; Representative for Multilateral Trade Negotiations; Advisor to Ministry of Foreign Affairs

Saburo Okita, Minister of Foreign Affairs

Women With the Trilateral Commission

Doris Anderson	Canada	1973-
Anne Armstrong	US	1977-78
Lucy Wilson Benson	US	1973-76, 1980-
Antoinette Danis-Spaak	Belgium	1978-
Carla Anderson Hills	US	1978-
Ann L. Hollick	US	Author
Mary T.W. Robinson	Ireland	1973-80
Martine Trink	France	European Secretary
Martha Wallace	US	1978-
Marina v. N. Whitman	US	1973-

Executive Committee Members
(Comparing 1973 and November 1979 Committees)

U.S. '73	U.S. '79	W. Europe '73	W. Europe '79	Japan '73	Japan '79
I. W. Abel	William T. Coleman	Giovanni Agnelli (Italy)	Giovanni Agnelli (Italy)	Chujiro Fujino	Chujiro Fujino
Harold Brown	George S. Franklin	P. Nyboe Andersen (Denmark)	P. Nyboe Andersen (Denmark)	Yukitaka Haraguchi	Takashi Hosomi
Patrick E. Haggerty	Robert Ingersoll	Klaus Dieter Arndt (W. Germany)	Georges Berthoin (France)	Kazushige Hirasawa	Yusuke Kashiwagi
Edwin O. Reischauer	Henry A. Kissinger	Kurt Birrenbach (W. Germany)	Henrik N. Boon (Netherlands)	Yusuke Kashiwagi	Kiichi Miyazawa
David Rockefeller	Bruce K. MacLaury	Francesco Campagna (Italy)	Paul Delouvrier (France)	Kiichi Miyazawa	Keichi Oshima
William M. Roth	Charles W. Robinson	Marc Eysken (Belgium)	Horst Ehmke (W. Germany)	Kinhide Mushakoji	Kiichi Saeki
William M. Scranton	David Rockefeller	Max Kohnstamm (Netherlands)	Michel Gaudet (France)	Saburo Okita	Ryuji Takeuchi
Gerard C. Smith	William M. Roth	John Loudon (Netherlands)	Max Kohnstamm (Netherlands)	Ryuji Takeuchi	Nobuhiko Ushiba
Paul C. Warnke	William M. Scranton	Mary T. W. Robinson (Ireland)	Baron Leon Lambert (Belgium)	Takeshi Watanabe	Takeshi Watanabe
		Otto Grieg Tidemand (Norway)	Roderick MacFarquar (U.K.)		
Canada '73	**Canada '79**	Sir Kenneth Younger (U.K.)	Egidio Ortona (Italy)		
Robert W. Bonner	Robert W. Bonner	Sir Philip de Zulueta (U.K.)	Mary T. W. Robinson (Ireland)		
Jean-Luc Pepin	Mitchell Sharp		Otto Grieg Tidemand (Norway)		
			Sir Philip de Zulueta (U.K.)		

Description of Format

With each person's name is a biographical sketch including: dates of Commission membership and any trilateral positions; current and former job positions; organizational, political, business, and academic affiliations; and trilateral publications.

Dates of Commission membership appear just after the person's name. They are preceeded by an entry in parentheses showing years on the Executive Committee, where applicable. An abbreviation signifying the person's major occupational category follows. Where applicable, Trilateral Commission positions are given on the line underneath the person's name.

Then job positions are listed in chronological order, from most current to earliest in the past. The first entry(ies) is (are) the most current position(s) found in the references checked (see bibliography) and/or listed on the Commission membership roster on which the person last appears. Where dates were not available, the word "past" appears in parentheses to indicate the *first* past position listed.

Then information appears (without dates) following the italicized entries: *mbr, dir, Tr, gov.* This means the person *is* or *has been* a member, director, trustee, and/or governor of the organizations, universities, and/or corporations listed. *Directorships of companies are listed separately* for quick reference.

Trilateral Commission publications of all trilateral authors are listed at the end of the biographical sketch.

Symbols, abbreviations, and unfamiliar terms used in the sketch are explained below.

List of Symbols
(appearing at left of name)

* Current or former member of Executive Committee 1973-1980
o Member or officer as of March 1980
+ Member or officer as of September and/or November 1973

Abbreviations of Major Occupational Categories*
(appearing at far right after name)

acd	educational or research institution
bank	banking (private or public)
bus	business (including agriculture)
lab	labor union
law	law
med	media
org	private organization (foundation, think tank, civic group, etc.)
pol	politics (elected or appointed position in government, officer of political party)

---

*It should be understood that persons often wear more than one professional 'hat', moving easily between business, government, and academia, in a given period, or pursuing different careers at different times. The biographical sketches of George Ball and Sol Linowitz, to name two, illustrate this point.

General List of Abbreviations and Names

Adm.	Administrator/Administration	Dir.	Director
Adv.	Advisor/Advisory	dir.	on board of directors
AEC	Atomic Energy Commission	EC	European Communities
AEI	American Enterprise Institute for Public Policy Research	Econ.	Economic(s)
Af.	Affairs	ECOSOC	United Nations Economic and Social Council
AI	Atlantic Institute for International Affairs	ECSC	European Coal and Steel Community
AID	Agency for International Development	Ed.	Editor
Am.	American	EEC	European Economic Community
Amb.	Ambassador	EM	European Movement
Appt.	Appointed/Appointment	EPA	Environmental Protection Agency
Assoc.	Associate/Association	Euratom	European Atomic Energy Commission
Asst.	Assistant	Exec.	Executive
Atl. Cl.	Atlantic Council	ExIm Bank	Export-Import Bank
Bd.	Board	FEA	Federal Energy Administration
BIS	Bank of International Settlements	Fed.	Federation
Brookings	Brookings Institute	FTC	Federal Trade Commission
Bundestag	West German Parliament	Fund.	Foundation
Bus.	Business	Gen.	General
Carnegie Peace	Carnegie Endowment for International Peace	Georgetown CSIS	Georgetown University Center for Strategic and International Studies
CCES	Center for Contemporary European Studies	Gov.	Governor
CFDT	French trade union	gov.	on Board of Governors
CFR	Council on Foreign Relations	Govt.	Government
Ch.	Chairman/Chairwoman	Hon.	Honorary
Chase Bank	Chase Manhattan Bank	IBRD	World Bank (International Bank for Reconstruction and Development)
Cl.	Council	ICFTU	International Confederation of Free Trade Unions
Co.	Company	IESC	International Executive Service Corps.
Col.	College	IISS	International Institute for Strategic Studies
Com.	Committee	ILO	International Labor Organization
Comn. EC	Commission of the European Communities	IMF	International Monetary Fund
Conf.	Conference	Ind.	Industry
Cons.	Consultant	Inst.	Institute
Coord.	Coordinator	Intl.	International
Corp.	Corporation	Invest.	Investment
Coun.	Counsellor	J.	Journal
COWPS	Council on Wage and Price Stability	JFEA	Japan Federation of Employer's Association
Ctr.	Center	Johns Hopkins UCES	Johns Hopkins University Center for European Studies
Dail	Irish Parliament		
Del.	Delegate		
Dem.	Democrat		
Dep.	Deputy		
Dept.	Department		
Dev.	Development		
Diet	Japanese Parliament		

Keidanren	Japan Federation of Economic Organizations
Kennedy Ctr.	Kennedy Center for School of Government, Harvard University
Lat. Am.	Latin America
Man.	Managing/Manager
Mbr.	Member
Mfg.	Manufacturing
Min.	Minister
Mvt.	Movement
MP	Member of Parliament
NASA	National Aeronautics and Space Administration
NATO	North Atlantic Treaty Organization
Natl.	National
NSC	National Security Council
OAS	Organization of American States
OECD	Organization for Economic Cooperation and Development
OEEC	Organization of European Economic Cooperation
OPIC	Overseas Private Investment Corporation
Org.	Organization
Perm.	Permanent
Plan.	Planning
Pol.	Political
Pres.	President
Prof.	Professor
Prog.	Program
Prvt.	Private
Ptnr.	Partner
Reg.	Regular
Rel.	Relations
Rep(s).	Representative(s)
Repub.	Republican
Res.	Research
RIIA	Royal Institute for International Affairs (or Chatham House)
Sci.	Science
SDP	Social Democratic Party
Sec.	Secretary
Sen.	Senator
Soc.	Society
Sr.	Senior
Tech.	Technology
Tr.	Trustee
tr.	on board of trustees
U.	University
UN	United Nations
UNA	United Nations Association
UNESCO	United Nations Educational, Scientific and Cultural Organization
V.	Vice
VP	Vice President
W.	West
Wilson Ctr.	Woodrow Wilson International Center for Scholars

Regional Membership 1973-79

Country*	Total No. of Members Between 1973-79	Total Membership 1973	Total Membership 1979	No. of 1973 Commissioners who are on in 1979**
U.S.	116	59	80	35
Canada	23	8	14	4
Western Europe	170	60	129	36
Belgium	10	5	7	3
Denmark	5	1	3	1
France	28	8	20	5
Ireland	12	6	9	3
Italy	17	10	15	8
Luxembourg	1	1	-	-
Netherlands	10	3	8	1
Norway	4	3	3	2
Spain***	13	-	13	-
U.K.	39	9	30	5
W. Germany	31	14	21	8
Japan	94	63	76	50
Totals	403	190	299	125

*Portuguese members were first admitted in 1980 and are not recorded here.

**While most members have served without interruption, some left temporarily to assume government position and then rejoined.

***Spanish members were first admitted in 1979.

Breakdown by Major Occupational Category 1973-1979

Category	U.S.	Canada	W. Europe	Japan	Total
bus	24	8	48	43	123
pol	24	5	63	9	101
bank	12	3	22	18	55
acd	22	3	14	16	55
lab	6	1	9	3	19
med	6	1	10	3	20
law	10	2	2	-	14
org	11	-	2	2	15

UNITED STATES

*+ I. W. Abel (Exec. Com. 73-79)   73-79 lab
  Pres. United Steelworkers of America (65-77); VP AFL-CIO

o+ David M. Abshire   73- acd
  Ch. Georgetown CSIS (62-70, 73-); Ch. U.S. Bd. for Intl. Broadcasting (74-77); Pres.
  Appt. Conglomerate Comn. on Org. of Govt. for Conduct of Foreign Policy (73-76);
  Asst. Sec. of State, Congressional Rel. (70-73); Dir. Res. Repub. Policy Comn (58-60)
  dir.: AEI, Atl. Cl.   *mbr.:* CFR, IISS
  dir.: Am. International Underwriters Overseas

o Gardner Ackley   77- acd
  Prof. Pol. Econ. Michigan U. (69-); Amb. to Italy (68-69); Pres. Cl. Econ. Adv.
  (62-68)
  mbr.: Bd. Natl. Bureau Econ. Research, Joint Cl. on Econ. Education
  dir.: Banco di Roma

o+ Graham Allison   73- acd
  Dean, Kennedy Ctr. Harvard; Cons. Rand Corp.
  mbr.: CFR

o+ John B. Anderson   73- pol
  House of Reps. (60-80); Joint Com. Atomic Energy; House Repub. Conf; lawyer
  mbr.: CFR   *Tr.:* Trinity Col.

+ Ernest C. Arbuckle   73-77 bank
  Ch. Wells Fargo Bank; Ind. Adv. Cl. Dept. of Defense (69-72); Pres. Comn. on Intl.
  Trade and Invest. Policy (70-71); Ch. Stanford Res. Inst. (66-70); Adv. Com. ExIm
  Bank; Dean, Grad School Bus. Stanford U. (58-68)
  dir.: Owens-Illinois, Safeway Stores, Hewlett Packard, Utah Intl.

Anne Armstrong   77-78 org
  Co-Ch. Reagan Campaign; VCh. Adv. Board and Mbr. Exec. Com. Georgetown
  CSIS; Amb. to UK and N. Ireland (76-77); Adv. Cl. Bicentennial Adm. (75-76);
  Coun. to Nixon and Ford (72-74); Repub. Natl. Com. (68-73)
  mbr.: Alliance to Save Energy, CFR   *dir.:* Atl. Cl.   *gov.:* AI
  dir.: General Motors, Braniff Intl., American Express, General Foods

o+ **John Paul Austin**   73-   bus
Ch. Coca-Cola Co. (70-); Ch. Bd. Trustees Rand Corp; Pres. C.C. Export (59-62);
lawyer
mbr.: Bus. Roundtable, Bus. Cl., Twentieth Century Fund, Smithsonian Institution,
United Negro Col. Fund, Atlanta U. Ctr., Comn. on Fund. & Prvt. Philanthropy
dir.: Morgan Guaranty Trust, General Electric, Continental Oil, Dow Jones, NYC
General Electric, South Mills, Trust Co. Georgia, Adela Invest., Federated Dept.
Stores

o+ **George W. Ball**   73-   bank
Sr. Man. Dir. Lehman Brothers Kuhn Loeb (68-); Special Adv. on Iran (78); Perm.
Rep to UN (68); Under Sec. of State (61-66); Assoc-Gen. Cl. Lend-Lease Adm.;
Under Sec. Econ. Af. (61); Pol. Adv. to Adlai Stevenson; lawyer; Dir. U.S. Strategic
Bombing Survey, London (44-45)
mbr.: Bilderberg Steering Com., CFR   *gov.*: AI
dir.: Burlington Industries, AMAX

o+ **Lucy Wilson Benson**   73-76, 80-   org
The Continental Group (80-); Under Sec. of State for Security Assistance (77-79);
Pres. League of Women Voters (68-74); Co-Ch. Urban Coalition (73-75)
Tr.: Natl. Urban League, Brookings, Alfred P. Sloan Fund, Mitre Corp., Smith Col.
gov.: Common Cause, Am. Natl. Red Cross
dir.: Catalyst, Women's Action Alliance

o+ **W. Michael Blumenthal**   73-75, 80-   bus
V. Ch. Burroughs Corp. (March 1980-end 1980 when he becomes Ch. of Burroughs);
Sec. of Treasury (77-79); Ch. Bendix Corp. (72-77); Pres. Bendix Intl. (67-70); State
Dept. Special Trade Negotiator (63-67); Dep. Asst. Sec. of State for Econ. Af. (61)
Tr.: Rockefeller Fund   *dir.*: Atl. Cl., CFR
mbr.: Bilderberg, US-China Trade Adv. Com., Japan-US Econ. Rel., Com. to Fight
Inflation   *dir.*: Equitable Life Assurance

o+ **Robert R. Bowie**   73-76, 79-   acd
Dir. Harvard Ctr. for Intl. Affairs (57-77, 79-); Dep. to the Dir. of Central Intelli-
gence for Natl. Intelligence (77-79); Coun. Dept. of State (66-68); Asst. Sec. of State,
Policy Plan. (55-57); Gen. Counsel to the U.S. High Comn. W. Germany (50-51);
Prof. Law Harvard U. (45-55)   *mbr.*: CFR
Special Consultant, *Towards a Renovated International System* (77)

o **John Brademas**   75-   pol
House of Reps. (58-); Mbr. Com. on House Adm. and Com. on Education and
Labor; Minority Whip (76-78); Chief Dep. Majority Floor Whip (73-77); Exec. Asst.
Adlai Stevenson (55-56); Harvard U.   *mbr.*: CFR, Central Com. World Cl. of
Churches; Adv. Cl. U. of Notre Dame; Bd. of Visitors JFK School of Gov't, Bd. of
Overseers Harvard U.   *Tr.*: St. Mary's Col., Amherst U.

o **Andrew Brimmer**   77-   bank
Pres. Brimmer and Co. (76-); Visiting Prof. Grad. School Bus. Adm. Harvard U.
(74-76); Pres. Assoc. for Study of Afro-American Life and History (70-73); gov.
Federal Reserve Bd. (66-74); Asst. Sec. Econ. Af. (65-66); Dep. Asst. Sec. Dept of
Commerce (63-65)   *Tr.*: Ford Fund, Natl. Urban League, Tuskegee Inst., Atlantic
U. Ctr.   *mbr.*: CFR   *dir.*: Bank of America, Intl. Harvester, DuPont, United Air
Lines, American Security and Trust Co.

William E. Brock III   76-79 pol
Ch. Republican Natl. Com. (77-); Senate (70-77); Rep.-Tennessee (62-70)

*+ **Harold Brown** (Exec. Com. 73-76)   73-76 acd
Sec. of Defense (77-); Pres. California Inst. of Tech. (69-77); mbr. SALT talks
(69-77); Sec. of Air Force (65-69); Dir. Defense Res. and Engineering, Dept. of
Defense (61-65); Pres. Sci. Adv. Com. (61); Group Leader to Dir., Radiation Lab. at
Livermore (52-61)   *mbr.*: CFR   *dir.*: IBM, Times-Mirror Corp., Schroder Banking
Corp.

+ Zbigniew Brzezinski (Dir. Trilateral Comn, 73-76)   acd
  Asst. to Pres. for Natl. Security Affairs (77-); COWPS (77-); Energy Resources Cl.
  (77-); Intl. Inst. for Peace and Conflict Res. (62-77); Dir. Columbia U. Res. Inst. for
  Intl. Change (61-77); Cons. State Dept. and Rand Corp. (62-76); Policy Plan. Cl.
  State Dept. (66-68); Ford Fellow (70); Dir. Foreign Policy Task Force, VP Humphrey
  (68); Prof. Gov't, Ctr. for Intl. Af. Harvard U. (53-60)
  mbr.: Bilderberg, IISS, NAACP   *dir.*: CFR, Amnesty Intl., *Foreign Affairs,
  Foreign Policy*

o John F. Burlingame   80-   bus
  VCh. General Electric Co.

o Arthur F. Burns   78-   bank
  Sr. Adv. Lazard Freres and Co., Distinguished Scholar in Residence AEI; Ch. Com. to
  Fight Inflation; Ch. Bd. gov., Federal Reserve Bd. (70-78); Pres. Adv. Com. on
  Labor-Management Policy (61-66); Pres. Cl. Econ. Adv. (53-56)   *mbr.*: CFR

  George Bush   77-78 pol
  Adjunct Prof. Rice U.; Dir. of Central Intelligence (76-77); Chief, U.S. Liaison
  Office in Peking (74-75); Ch. Repub. Natl. Com. (73-74); Amb. to UN (71-72);
  Repub. House of Rep. (67-71)   *dir.*: Atl. Cl., CFR   *Tr.*: Trinity U.
  dir.: First Intl. Bank, London and Houston; Eli Lily Corp.; Texas Gulf; Purolator

o Philip Caldwell   79-   bus
  Ch. Ford Motor Company   *mbr.*: Intl. Adv. Com. Chase Manhattan

o Hugh Calkins   78-   law
  Ptnr. Jones, Day, Reavis and Pogue   *mbr.*: CFR, American Law Inst.
  dir.: Brown and Sharpe Manufacturing Co., Premier Industrial Corp., Jeffrey Co.

+ Jimmy (James E.) Carter   73-76 bus
  U.S. President (77-); Gov. Georgia (71-74); State Senator (62-66); W. Central Georgia
  Area Plan and Dev. Comn. (64); Pres. Plains Dev. Corp. (63); peanut farmer and
  warehouser; Deacon and Sunday School teacher Plains Baptist Church

o Sol Chaikin   77-   lab
  Pres. Intl. Ladies Garment Workers Union (75-); VP AFL-CIO (75-); Del. to ILO (76)
  dir.: Atl. Cl., Com. on Present Danger
  mbr.: Bus. Roundtable, Brookings, Natl. Urban Coalition

+ Lawton Chiles   73-76 pol
  U.S. Senate (71-); Florida State Senate (66-70); Florida State Rep. (58-66)
  mbr.: Dem. Natl. Com.

+ Warren Christopher   73-76 law
  Dep. Sec. of State (77-); Ptnr. O'Melveny and Myers (58-67, 69-77); Dep. Attorney
  Gen. (67-69); Gov's. Comn. on Los Angeles Riots (65-66); Cons. State Dept., econ.
  problems; Del. Geneva Conf. on Cotton Textiles (61)   *mbr.*: CFR
  Tr.: Harvard U., Stanford U.   *dir.*: Pacific Mutual Life, Southern California Edison

+ Alden W. Clausen   73-76 bank
  Pres. Bank of America (70-); Treasury Adv. Com. on Reform of Intl. Monetary
  System   *mbr.*: Bus. Roundtable, Bus. Cl., Adv. Cl. Japan-U.S. Econ. Rel., Natl. Cl.
  U.S.-China Trade, Stanford Res. Inst.   *Tr.*: Harvard Bus. School

o William S. Cohen   77-   pol
  U.S. Senate (73-); lawyer (66-72)

*o+ William T. Coleman, Jr. (Exec. Com. 77-)   73-74, 77- law
  Sr. Ptnr. O'Melveny and Meyers (77-); Ch. NAACP, Ch. Legal Defense and Educa-
  tional Fund; Sec. Transportation (75-77); Sr. Ptnr. Dilworth, Paxsin, Kalish, Levy
  and Coleman; Cons. Arms Control Agency (63-75); numerous gov't consultantships
  Tr.: Rand Corp, Brookings   *mbr.*: CFR, Stock Exchange, Bd. of Overseers Harvard
  U.   *dir.*: IBM, Chase Manhattan Bank, Pepsi Co., AMAX, American Can Co., Pan-
  Am, Pennsylvania Mutual Life, Phila. Electric Co., INA Corp.

o+ Barber B. Conable Jr.   73-   pol
  House of Reps. (65-); Ways and Means, Budget Com; Ch. House Repub. Policy Com;
  NY State Senate (63-65); lawyer

+ **Richard N. Cooper**   73-76   acd
  Under Sec. of State for Econ. Af. (77-); Provost and Prof. of Intl. Econ. Yale U.
  (63-77); Dep. Asst. Sec. State for Intl. Monetary Af. (65-66); Cl. of Econ. Adv.
  (61-63)   *dir.*: Atl. Cl.   *mbr.*: CFR, Bilderberg   *Towards a Renovated International
  System* (77), *Towards a Renovated World Monetary System* (73)

○ **John Cowles Jr.**   78-   med
  Ch. Minneapolis Star and Tribune Co. (73-); Assoc. Press (66-75); Ch. *Harper's*
  Magazine (68-72); Urban Coalition, Minneapolis (68-70); Pres. *Harper's* (65-68);
  Minneapolis Civil Liberties Union (56-61)
  mbr.: CFR, AI, Adv. Bd. Pulitzer Prizes Columbia U., Bus. Cl.
  dir.: German Marshall Fund, Harper and Row Publishers Inc., Des Moines Register
  and Tribune Co.

  Alan Cranston   77-78   pol
  U.S. Senate (69-); VP Carlsberg Financial Corp. (68); Pres. Homes for Better Am.
  Inc. (67-68); Controller California (59-67)

○+ **John C. Culver**   73-   pol
  U.S. Senate (75-); House of Reps. (64-74); Legislative Asst. to Sen. Edward Kennedy
  (62-63)   *mbr.*: CFR

○ **Gerald L. Curtis**   74-   acd
  Dir. East Asian Inst. Columbia U.

+ **Lloyd N. Cutler**   73-79   law
  White House Counsel (Sept. 79-); President's Special Counsel on SALT hearings
  (June 79-); Ptnr. Wilmer, Cutler and Pickering (62-79); Ptnr. Cox, Langford,
  Stoddard and Cutler (46-62); Co-Ch. Com. Civil Rights Under Law (71-73); Exec.
  Dir. Natl. Comn. on the Causes and Prevention of Violence (68-69); Ch. D.C. Com.
  on Adm. Justice Under Emergency Conditions (68); Lend-Lease mbr. N. Africa
  Econ. Bd. (43)   *dir.*: CFR   *Tr.*: Brookings   *mbr.*: Bd. Visitors School for
  Advanced Intl. Studies, Stanford Res. Inst.   *dir.*: Kaiser Industries, Alza Corp.,
  Southeast Bank Corp.

  John C. Danforth   77-78   pol
  U.S. Senate (77-); Attorney Gen. Missouri (68-76); Bryon, Care, McPheeters, and
  McRoberts (66-68); ordained deacon Episcopal Church (63)

+ **Archibald K. Davis**   73-76   bank
  Ch. Wachovia Bank and Trust Co. (56-74); dir, Federal Reserve Bank of Richmond
  (50-56)   *mbr.*: Intl. Adv. Bd., R.J. Reynolds Industries Inc.   *dir.*: AT&T,
  Wachovia Bank and Trust Co., Royal Cotton Mills, Seller Mfg., Wachovia Corp.,
  Southern Railway Co., Sellers Dying Co., Jordan Spinning Co., Chatham Mfg. Co.,
  Media General Inc.

+ **Emmett Dedmon**   73-77   med
  VP and Ed. Dir., Field Enterprises Inc; VP and Ed Dir. *Chicago Sun-Times* and
  Chicago Daily News (68-); Ed. *Chicago Sun-Times* (65-68)

+ **Hedley W. Donovan**   73-79   med
  Sr. Adv. Domestic and Econ. Af. and Media Relations (79-); Liaison to Pres. Comn.
  for a Natl. Agenda for the 80's; Ed.-in-Chief Time Inc. (64-79); Lecturer on Press
  Harvard U.; Man. Ed. *Fortune* (45-59)   *Tr.*: Ford Fund, Carnegie Peace, NYU, Mt.
  Holyoke Col.   *dir.*: CFR. *Time Time, Life, Washington Star*

○+ **Daniel J. Evans**   73-   acd
  Pres. Evergreen State College (77-); Gov. of Washington (65-77); Adv. Cl. on Inter-
  gov't Rel. (72-); Bus. exec. (53-65)   *mbr.*: Carnegie Cl. on Policy Studies in Higher
  Education   *Tr.*: Carnegie Fund for Advancement of Teaching

○ **Thomas S. Foley**   77-   pol
  House of Reps. (64-); Special Counsel Interior and Insular Af. Com. U.S. Senate
  (61-64); Attorney Gen. Washington (60-61); Dep. Prosecuting Attorney Spokane
  County (58-60); Ptnr. Higgins and Foley (57-58)

∗○+ **George S. Franklin (Exec. Com. 79-)**   74-   org
  Trilateral Commission Coordinator (77-), North American Sec. (73-76); Exec. Dir.
  CFR (53-71); division World Trade Intelligence, Dept. of State (41-44); Asst. to
  Nelson Rockefeller (40)   *dir.*: CFR, Atl. Cl.

o Donald M. Fraser   75- pol
Mayor of Minneapolis (79-); House of Reps. (62-78); Counsel, Mbrs. of Congress for
Peace Through Law; Ch. Democratic Study Group (69-71); Minnesota State Senate
(54-62); Ptnr. Lindquist, Fraser and Magnuson (50-62); Mbr. Del. to UN (75)
mbr.: CFR, Comn. on Role of Future Pres. Primaries (76-), Intl. Rel. Com., Dem.
Nominees Bd.

Richard N. Gardner   75-76 acd
Amb. to Italy (77-); Prof. Columbia Law (57-61, 65-77); Adv. Law of Sea Conf. (71);
Pres. Comn. on Intl. Trade and Invest. Policy (70-71); Asst. Rep. UN; Dep. Asst. Sec.
State Intl. Org. Af. (61-65); Law Practice, Coudert Brothers (54-57) *mbr.*: CFR
*OPEC, The Trilateral World and the Developing Countries: New Arrangements for
Cooperation 1976-80* (75), *A Turning Point in North-South Economic Relations* (74)

o John H. Glenn Jr.   78- pol
U.S. Senate (75-l); VP Corporate Development and dir. Royal Crown Cola Co.
(62-74); Project Officer, fighter and design branch, Navy Bureau Aero (56-69);
Astronaut Project Mercury NASA (59-64) *mbr.*: Society of Experimental Test
Pilots, Intl. Academy of Astronauts *Tr.*: Muskingum Col.

*+ Patrick E. Haggerty (Exec. Com. 73-75)   73-75 bus
Hon. Ch.,Texas Instruments (76-); Ch. Natl. Cl. on Educational Res. (73-74)
mbr.: Intl. Adv. Com. Chase Bank; Exec. Com. Rockefeller U.; *Tr.,* mbr. Exec. com.
U. Dallas; Bus. Cl. *dir.*: A.H. Belo Corp.

o Philip M. Hawley   78- bus
Pres. Carter Hawley Hale Stores Inc.; Ch. Los Angeles Energy Conservation Com.
(73-74) *Tr.*: California Inst. of Tech. *dir.*: Atlantic Richfield, Bank of America,
Bank America Corp., Pacific Telephone and Telegraph Co., NT and SA

Charles B. Heck   77-78 org
North American Sec. (77-); Editor *Trialogue* (74-76); Asst. to Zbigniew Brzezinski;
Brookings; Carnegie Peace

o Walter W. Heller   78- acd
Prof. of Econ. U. Minnesota (50-); Cons. Congress Budget Office (75-); Ch. and mbr.
OECD Group of Fiscal Experts (64-68); Treasury Com. Intl. Monetary Arrangements
(65-69) *dir.*: Northwestern Natl. Life Insurance, Intl. Multifoods, Commercial
Credit Corp., Natl. City Bank of Minneapolis

o+ William A. Hewitt   73- bus
Ch. Deere and Co. (64-) *mbr.*: Chase Manhattan Intl. Adv. Com., CFR, AI, Bus.
Cl., Wilson Ctr., Stanford Cl. *dir.*: IESC, US-USSR Trade and Econ. Cl.
Tr.: Carnegie Peace *dir.*: AT&T, Continental Oil, Continental Illinois, Natl. Bank
and Trust

o Carla A. Hills   78- law
Sr. Resident Ptnr. Latham, Watkins and Hills; VCh. Adv. Comn. Intergov't Rel.
(75-); Sec. of Housing and Urban Dev. (75-77); CoCh. Alliance to Save Energy; Ptnr.
Munger, Tolles, Hills and Rickerhauser (62-74)
mbr.: Carnegie Com. Public Broadcasting *Tr.*: Brookings, Wilson School of Public
and Intl. Affairs *dir.*: IBM, American Airlines, Standard Oil, Signal Co.

o James F. Hoge Jr.   78- med
Chief Ed., *Chicago Sun-Times* (76-); Ch. Exec. Cl. Adlai Stevenson Ctr; Adv. Cl.
Aspen Prog. Communications and Soc. *mbr.*: CFR

Richard C.A. Holbrooke   74-76 org
Asst. Sec. of State for East Asian and Pacific Af. (77-); Man. Ed. *Foreign Policy*
(72-77); dir. publications, Carnegie Peace (72-77); Coord. foreign policy and defense
issues, Carter-Mondale Pres. Campaign (76); Cons. Comn. Org. Gov't for Conduct
of Foreign Policy (74-75); Peace Corps (70-72); State Dept. (62-69)
mbr.: CFR, IISS

o Hendrik S. Houthakker   77- acd
Prof. of Econ. Harvard U. (60-); Cl. of Econ. Adv. (67-68)

o+ **Thomas L. Hughes**   73- org
Pres. Carnegie Endowment for Intl. Peace (71-); Ed. Bd. *Foreign Policy*; State Dept.
(61-71); Coun. Humphrey (55-58); U. lecturer (53-58)   *dir.*: Atl. Cl.   *mbr.*: CFR,
IISS, Harvard Ctr. for Intl. Studies

*o **Robert Ingersoll** (Exec. Com. 77-)   77- bus
U.S. Ch, U.S.-Japan Econ. Relations Group; Dep. Ch. Bd. of Trustees, U. Chicago;
Dep. Sec. State (74-77); Amb. Japan (72-74); Ch. Borg-Warner Corp. (58-72); Asst.
Sec. State East Asia (74); VP Chamber of Commerce   *mbr.*: CFR, Bus. Cl.
dir.: Atlantic Richfield, Honeywell, Kraft, Caterpillar Tractor, Weyerhauser, Borg-
Warner, First Natl. Bank Chicago, Burlington Northern, Marcor

J.K. Jamieson   74-76 bus
Ch. Exxon Corp. (-75)   *mbr.*: CFR, Bus. Cl.   *dir.*: Chase Manhattan Bank,
Equitable Life

o **D. Gale Johnson**   78- acd
Provost and Prof. of Econ. U. Chicago (76-); Natl. Comn. on Population Growth
and Am. Future (70-72); Adv. Bd. State Dept. Policy Plan. Cl. (67-69); Cons. AID
(62-68); Pres. Natl. Adv. Com. on Food and Fiber (65-67); Agricultural Adv. Office
Pres. Special Rep. for Trade Negotiations (63-64)   *mbr.*: Cl. of Acd. Adv. AEI
*Reducing Malnutrition in Developing Countries and Increasing Rice Production in
South and Southeast Asia* (78)

+ **Edgar F. Kaiser**   73 bus
Ch. Kaiser Industries Corp. (67-); Ch. Stanford Res. Inst.; Pres. Kaiser Industries
Corp. (56-67)   *dir.*: US-USSR Trade and Econ. Cl.;   *mbr.*: Bus. Cl.
dir.: Kaiser Steel Co., Kaiser Aluminum and Chemical Corp., Kaiser Cement and
Gypson Corp., Kaiser Resources Ltd., Natl. Steel and Shipbuilding Co., Bank
America Corp., Hindustan Aluminum Co., Volta Aluminum Corp., Mysore Cements
Ltd.

o **Edgar F. Kaiser Jr.**   76- bus
Ch. Kaiser Steel Co. (79-); Pres. Kaiser Resources Ltd. (73-); Special Asst. to Sec. of
Interior (69); AID-Vietnam (67-68)   *mbr.*: CFR   *dir.*: Tornoto-Dominion Bank,
Kaiser Resources Ltd., Daon Dev. Corp.

o+ **Lane E. Kirkland**   73- lab
Pres. AFL-CIO (79-); Sec.-Treasurer AFL-CIO (69-79); Co-Ch. Com. on Present
Danger; Comn. on Natl. Agenda for 80's (Carter); Comn. CIA Activities Within U.S.
(Ford); Comn. on Financial Structure (Nixon); Blue Ribbon Defense Comn. (Nixon);
Gen. Adv. Com. Arms Control and Disarmament Agency; Comn. on Fund. and
Prvt. Philanthropies; Natl. Comn. on Critical Choices for Am (Rockefeller)
Tr.: Rockefeller Fund, Brookings, Am. Inst. for Free Trade Dev.
dir.: African-Am. Labor Ctr., Carnegie Peace, CFR   *mbr.*: Bilderberg

*o **Henry A. Kissinger** Exec. Com. 77-)   77- acd
Ch. Intl. Adv. Com. Chase Bank (77-); Prof. Georgetown U. (77-); Coun. Georgetown CSIS; Sr. Fellow Aspen Inst. (77-); Cons. NBC (77-); Cons. Goldman Sachs and
Co. (78-); Sec. of State (73-77); Pres. Asst. for Natl. Security Af. (69-74); NSC
(69-75); Arms Control and Disarmament Agency (61-68); Prof. Gov't Harvard U.
(59-69)   *dir.*: CFR, Atl. Cl.   *mbr.*: Bilderberg Steering Com.

o **Joseph Kraft**   79- med
Syndicated Columnist *Washington Post, Chicago Sun-Times*, etc. (63-); Staff writer
Harper's (62-65), *New York Times* (53-57)   *mbr.*: CFR

o **Sol M. Linowitz**   75- law
Mideast Negotiator (79-); Sr. Ptnr. Coudert Brothers (69-); Dir. Pres. Comn. on
World Hunger (78-); Head of Comn. for U.S.-Lat. Am. Rel.; Ch. Natl. Cl. Foreign
Policy Assoc.; Co-Negotiator of Panama Canal Treaties (77); Amb. to OAS and
Inter-Am. Com. for the Alliance for Progress (66-69); Ch. Xerox Corp. (58-66)
mbr.: CFR   *dir.*: Pan-Am World Airways, Marine Midland Bank, Time Inc.,
Midland Corp., Dreyfus Marine; *Tr.*: Mutual Life Insurance Co.

○ **Winston Lord** 78- org
Pres. CFR; Dir. Policy Plan. Staff State Dept. (73-77); Mbr. Staff NSC (69-73); Mbr. Staff Intl. Security Af. Dept. of Defense (67-69)   *gov.*: AI   *dir.*: Atl. Cl., CFR
mbr.: Bilderberg Steering Com.

*○+ **Bruce K. MacLaury** Exec. Com. 77-) 73- org
Pres. Brookings (77-); Pres. Federal Reserve Bank of Minneapolis (71-77); Dep. Under Sec. for Monetary Af., Treasury Dept. (69-71)
mbr.: CFR, Bilderberg Steering Com.   *Tr.*: Joint Cl. Econ. Education, Brookings
dir.: Dayton Hudson Corp.   *Major Payments Imbalances and International Financial Stability* (79)

○+ **Paul W. McCracken** 73- acd
Prof. of Bus. Admin. U. Michigan (48-); Ch. Cl. of Econ. Adv. (69-71); Dir. Res., Federal Reserve Bank of Minneapolis (43-48)   *mbr.*: CFR, Cl. of Acd. Adv. AEI, Com. to Fight Inflation   *dir.*: Dow Chemical

○ **Arjay Miller** 77- acd
Pres. Natl. Comn. on Productivity; Dean Grad School of Bus. Stanford U. (69-); Adv. Comn. on U.S. Trade Policy; Pres. Ford Motor Co. (63-68)
mbr.: IESC, UNA, Conference Board, Urban Inst., Eisenhower Exchange Fellowship   *Tr.*: Brookings   *dir.*: Ford Motor Co., Wells Fargo Bank, *Washington Post,* Levi Strauss and Co., Utah Intl., Trans World Airlines, SRI Intl.

+ **Wilbur D. Mills** 73-74 pol
Shea, Gould, Climenko and Casey Tax Counsel Firm (77-); House of Reps. Arkansas (39-77); Ch. Ways and Means Com.   *mbr.*: Com. to Fight Inflation

+ **Walter F. Mondale** 73-76 pol
Vice President (77-); NSC (77-); Regent, Smithsonian Inst. (77-); U.S. Senate (64-77); Attorney Gen.-Minn. (60-64); lawyer (56-60)   *mbr.*: CFR, Bilderberg

+ **Lee L. Morgan** 73-79 bus
Ch. Caterpillar Tractor Co. (77-)   *mbr.*: CFR, EC-U.S. Bus. Cl.; Adv. Cl. on Japan-U.S. Econ. Rel., Bus. Roundtable, Chase Intl. Adv. Com.
dir.: 3M Co., First Natl. Bank of Chicago, Commercial Natl. Bank, Central Illinois Light Co., First Chicago Corp.

○+ **Kenneth D. Naden** 73- bus
Pres. Natl. Cl. of Farmer Cooperatives (75-)

○ **Joseph S. Nye Jr.** 79- acd
Kennedy School of Gov't, Harvard U.

*+ **Henry D. Owen** (Exec. Com. 77-78) 73-78 acd
Special Rep of Pres. for Econ. Summits, U.S. Amb. at Large; Mbr. NSC.; Dir. Foreign Policy Studies Prog., Brookings (69-77)   *mbr.*: CFR
Collaboration With Communist Countries in Managing Global Problems: An Examination of the Options (77)

○+ **David Packard** 73- bus
Ch. Hewlett-Packard Co. (72-); Co-Ch. Com. on Present Danger (73); Dep. Sec. of Defense (69-71)   *dir.*: Atl. Cl.;   *Tr.*: AEI   *mbr.*: Intl. Adv. Com. Chase Bank, Bus. Cl., Bus. Roundtable   *dir.*: U.S. Steel, Standard Oil, Caterpillar Tractor, TWA

○ **Gerald L. Parsky** 77- law
Ptnr. Gibson, Dunn and Crutcher; (past) Asst. Sec. of Treasury for Intl. Affairs

○ **William R. Pearce** 77- bus
V.P. Cargill Inc.   *mbr.*: CFR

+ **John H. Perkins** 73-77 bank
Pres. Continental Illinois Natl. Bank and Trust Co. (73-); Ch. Continental Illinois Venture Corp.; Ch. Continental Illinois Overseas Corp.
dir.: Pillsbury Co., Continental Bank Intl., Continental Intl. Finance Corp.

o+ Peter G. Peterson   73- bank
    Ch. Lehman Brothers Kuhn Loeb (73-); Ch. Comn. on Fund. and Prvt. Philan-
    thropy; Sec. of Commerce (72-73); Asst. to Pres. for Intl. Econ. Policy (71-72); Pres.
    Bell and Howell (58-71); Marketing Exec. (47-58)   *dir.*: CFR   *mbr.*: Brookings, Atl.
    Cl., Com. on Econ. Dev.   *dir.*: American Express, General Foods, 3M Co., RCA,
    Illinois Bell, Black and Decker Mfg. Co., First Natl. Bank of Chicago, Lehman
    Corp., U. Bell Telephone

*o+ Edwin O. Reischauer (Exec. Com. 73-75)   73- acd
    Prof. and Dir. of Japan Inst. Harvard U. (50-61, 66-); Ch. Harvard-Yenching Inst.
    (70-); Amb. to Japan (61-66); Dir. Harvard-Yenching Inst. (56-61)

    Elliot L. Richardson   74   pol
    Amb. at Large with Responsibility for UN Law of the Sea Conf. (77-); Sec. of
    Commerce (76-77); Amb. to U.K. (75); Fellow, Wilson Ctr., Smithsonian Inst. (74);
    Attorney Gen. U.S. (73); Sec. of Defense (73); Sec. HEW (70-73); Under Sec. of State
    (69-70); Attorney Gen.-Mass. (67-69)   *dir.*: CFR

 o John E. Rielly   79- org
    Pres. Chicago Council on Foreign Relations

*o+ Charles W. Robinson (Exec. Com. 77-)   73-74, 77- bank
    VCh. Blyth, Eastman, Dillon and Co.; Ch. Energy Transition Corp.; (Past) Dep. Sec.
    of State; Sr. Man. Dir. Kuhn, Loeb and Co; Pres. Marcona Corp.
    dir.: Atl. Cl.   *mbr.*: CFR

*o+ David Rockefeller (Exec. Com. 73-)   73- bank
    Trilateral Comn. North American Ch. (77-); Ch. Chase Manhattan Bank N.A. (69-
    retiring April 1981); Ch. Rockefeller Brothers Fund (80-); Head of Coalition of N.Y.
    Businessmen (79-); Ch. Exec. Com. Rockefeller U. (75-); Ch. Cl. of the Americas
    (65-70); Ch. of Bd., CFR; VP, CFR (50-70); Ch. N.Y. Chamber of Commerce; N.Y.
    Econ. Dev. Cl.   *dir.*: CFR; Rockefeller Center   *Tr.*: U. Chicago   *mbr.*: Bilder-
    berg, Bus. Cl., Bus. Roundtable

 o John D. Rockefeller IV   77- pol
    Gov. West Virginia (77-); Ch. Comn. on Coal (Carter); Ch. White House Conf.
    Balanced Natl. Growth and Econ. Dev. (78-); Pres. W. Va. Wesleyan Col. (73-75);
    Asst. to Asst. Sec. State for Far Eastern Af. (63)
    Tr.: Rockefeller Fund   *mbr.*: CFR

o+ Robert V. Roosa   73- bank
    Ptnr. Brown Bros. Harriman and Co. (65-); VCh. Rockefeller Fund; Ch. Brookings;
    Ch. Brookings Trust (75-77); Under Sec. for Monetary Af., Treasury (61-64); Federal
    Reserve Bank of N.Y. (46-60)   *dir.*: CFR, Atl. Cl.   *mbr.*: Adv. Com. Intl. Finance
    Corp.   *Tr.*: Sloan Kettering Inst., Brookings   *dir.*: Anaconda, Texaco, American
    Express, Owens-Corning Fiberglass Corp., Brown and Harriman Intl. Bank

*o+ William M. Roth (Exec. Com. 73-)   73- bus
    Roth Properties; Fellow, Kennedy Ctr. Harvard (69-); Special Rep. on Trade
    Negotiation (67-69); Ch. Pacific Natl. Life Assurance (60-63); Matson Navigation
    (52-61)

o+ William V. Roth Jr.   73- pol
    U.S. Senate (71-); Rep.-Delaware (61-71); Repub. Natl. Com. (61-64)
    mbr.: CFR, Adv. Bd. Georgetown CSIS

 + Carl T. Rowan   73-76   med
    Columnist *Chicago Daily News*, Publishers-Hall Syndicate (65-); Dir. U.S. Informa-
    tion Agency (64-65); Amb. to Finland (63-64); Dep. Asst. Sec. State for Public Af.
    (61-63); Staff Writer *Minneapolis Tribune* (50-61)

    John C. Sawhill   77-79 acd
    Dep. Sec. of Energy (79-); CoCh. Aspen Inst. Com. on Energy; Pres. NYU (75-79);
    Adm. FEA (73-75); Assoc. Dir. Natl. Resources, Office of Man. and Budget
    mbr.: CFR   *Energy: Managing the Transition* (78)

○ Henry B. Schacht   76- bus
Ch. Cummins Engine Inc. (77-); Pres. Comn. for a Natl. Agenda for the 80's (79-)
Tr.: Rockefeller Fund   *mbr.*: CFR; Bd. of Overseers, Harvard U.; Harvard Bus.
School Assoc.; Com. on Econ. Dev.; Urban Inst.; Western Highway Inst.
dir.: CBS, Potomac Assoc. Inc., Kirloskar Cummins (India)

○ J. Robert Schaetzel   79- pol
V.Ch. Atlantic Inst.; Amb. to European Communities (66-72); Dep. Asst. Sec. of
State for Atlantic Af. (62-66); State Dept. (45-62)   *mbr.*: CFR   *dir.*: Atl. Cl.
The Problem of International Consultations (76)

*○+ William W. Scranton (Exec. Com. 73-75, 77-)   73-75, 77- pol
Pres. Comn. for a Natl. Agenda for the 80's (79-); Pres. Intelligence Adv. Com.; Adv.
Comn. Dept. of State; Adv. Comn., Civil Service Comn.; Amb. to UN (76-77); Cons.
to Pres. (74-76); Pres., Gen. Adv. Comn. Arms Control and Disarmament (69-76);
Ch. Northeast Natl. Bank of Pa. (73-76); Ch. Natl. Liberty Corp. (69-71); Ch. Pres.
Comn. on Campus Unrest (70); Amb. and Ch. Del. INTELSAT (69); Special Envoy
Middle East (68); Gov. of Pennsylvania (63-67); House of Rep. (60-62); Asst. to Sec.
State (59-60); Ch. Northeast Pa. Broadcasting Co. (52-69); Pres. Scranton-Lacka-
wanna Trust (53-56)   *mbr.*: CFR, Urban Inst.   *Tr.*: Yale U.
dir.: IBM, American Express, Sun Oil, Scott Paper, Mutual of New York, Bethlehem
Steel, Cummins Engines, *New York Times*, Northeast Natl. Bank of Penn., Southeast
Banking, Miami, Ryan Homes

○ Mark Shepherd Jr.   77- bus
Ch. Texas Instruments Inc. (76-); Ch. Adv. Cl. Japan-U.S. Econ. Rel.
mbr.: CFR, Iran-U.S. Bus. Cl., Pres. Export Cl., Georgetown Ctr. Conf. Bd., AEI,
Intl. Cl. of Morgan Guaranty Trust Co.   *Tr.*: Southern Methodist U., Com. for
Econ. Dev., AEI   *dir.*: U.S. Steel, Republic Natl. Bank of Dallas

*+ Gerard C. Smith (Exec. Com. 73-76)   73-76 pol
Trilateral Comn. North American Ch. 73-76; Amb. at Large for Non-Proliferation
Matters (77-); Rep. Intl. Atomic Energy Agency (77-); Counsel, Wilmer, Cutler and
Pickering (73-77); Dir. Arms Control and Disarmament Agency (69-72); Foreign
Policy Cons. Washington Ctr. Foreign Policy Res. (61-69); Asst. State Dept. (61-68);
Asst. Sec. State (57-61); Asst. to Sec. State for Atomic Af. (54-57); AEC (50-54)
mbr.: CFR   *Tr.*: Brookings   *dir.*: Atl. Cl.

+ Anthony M. Solomon   73-76 pol
Pres. Federal Reserve Bank New York (April 80-); Under Sec. of Treasury for
Monetary Af. (77-); Pres. Intl. Invest. Corp. for Yugoslavia (68-73); Asst. Sec. State
Econ. Af. (65-69);Dep. Asst. Sec. State for Lat. Am. and Dep. Asst. AID Adm. for
Lat. Am. (63-65); Ch. AID Mission to Bolivia (63); Pres., Rosa Blanca Food Products
Corp.   *mbr.*: CFR

○ Edson W. Spencer   77- bus
Pres. Honeywell Inc.   *mbr.*: CFR   *dir.*: Ford Fund, Carleton Col.
dir.: Northwest Bancorp., Intl. Harvester

○+ Robert Taft Jr.   73- law
Ptnr. Taft, Stettinius and Hollister; U.S. Senate (71-76); Mbr. Senate Com. on
Foreign Af. and Subcom. on Europe; House of Rep. (55-62)

○+ Arthur R. Taylor   73- bus
General Ptnr. Arthur Taylor & Co.; Ch. American Assembly; Pres. CBS (72-76);
Exec. VP Intl. Paper (71-72); Exec. VP First Boston Corp. (66-70)
mbr.: CFR, Bilderberg Steering Com.   *dir.*: Rockefeller Ctr., Ctr. for Inter-
American Relations   *Tr.*: Brown U. Asia Society   *dir.*: Investors Diversified
Services Inc.

○ James R. Thompson   77- pol
Gov. of Illinois (77-); Counsel, Winston and Strong (75-77); Office of Attorney Gen.
(69-75); VP Americans for Effective Law Enforcement (67-69); President's Task
Force on Crime (67); dir. Chicago Crime Comn.

○ **Russell E. Train**   77- bus
Exec. VP Union Carbide (79-); Sr. Assoc. Conservation Fund (77-); Adm. EPA
(73-77); Ch. Cl. on Environmental Quality (70-73); Chief Negotiator UN Conf.
Human Environment (72); Under Sec. Interior (69-70)   *mbr.*: CFR, Cl. on Solar
Biofuels   *Tr.*: German Marshall Fund, Intl. World Wildlife Fund, Princeton U.

○ **Philip H. Trezise**   76- acd
Sr. Fellow Brookings (71-); Pres. Japan-U.S. Society (73-76); Asst. Sec. of State for
Econ. Af. (69-71); Amb. OECD (66-69); Dep. Asst. Sec. State for Econ. Af. (61-65);
U.S. Embassy Tokyo (57-61)   *dir.*: Atl. Cl.   *mbr.*: CFR, Washington Policy Cl.
Intl. Management and Dev. Inst.   *dir.*: Bank of Tokyo Trust Co.
Directions for World Trade in the Nineteen-Seventies (74)

+ **Cyrus R. Vance**   73-76 law
Sec. of State (77-80); V.Ch. Bd. of CFR (73-76); Ptnr. Simpson, Thacher, and Bartlett
(70-77); State Dept. (67-69); Paris Peace Talks on Vietnam (68-69); Korea (68);
Cyprus Envoy (67); Dep. Sec. of Defense (64-67); Sec. of Army (62-63); General Cl.
Dept. Defense (61-62); Ptnr. Simpson, Thacher and Bartlett (46-61)
dir.: CFR, Am. Assembly   *mbr.*: Bilderberg   *Tr.*: Rockefeller Fund, Yale U.,
Urban Inst., One William St. Fund   *dir.*: IBM, Pan Am, World Airways, New York
Times Co.

Paul A. Volcker   77-79 bank
Ch. Federal Reserve Bd. (79-); Pres. Federal Reserve Bank of N.Y. (75-79); Under
Sec. Monetary Af. (69-74); Dep. UnderSec. Monetary Af. (63-65); Chase Manhattan
Bank (57-68); Treasury Dept. (61-63)   *mbr.*: Federal Natl. Mortgage Assoc.
Tr.: Rockefeller Fund   *dir.*: CFR, Am. Cl. on Germany, Am. Friends London
School of Economics

○ **Martha R. Wallace**   78- org
Exec. Dir. Henry Luce Fund Inc.   *dir.*: CFR

○ **Martin J. Ward**   77- lab
Pres. United Assoc. of Journeymen and Apprentices of the Plumbing and Pipe
Fitting Ind. of U.S. and Canada   *dir.*: Com. on Present Danger

*○+ **Paul C. Warnke** (Exec. Com. 73-76)   73-76, 79- law
Ptnr. Clifford and Warnke (69-77, 79-); Dir. Arms Control and Disarmament Agency
(77-79); Chief Disarmament Negotiator (SALT); Dir. Exec. Com. Intl. Voluntary
Services (72); Dept. of Defense (66-69); Covington and Burling (48-66)
dir.: CFR   *mbr.*: Adv. Com. Yale Econ. Growth Ctr.

○ **Glenn E. Watts**   77- lab
Pres. Communications Workers of America (74-); VP Exec. Cl. AFL-CIO (74-);
Dept. of Labor (75-); Sec. United Way of Am. (71-)
mbr.: Pres. Comn. for a National Agenda for the 80's; gov. bd. Common Cause;
Natl. Com. on Coping with Interdependence, Aspen Program; Natl. Labor Com. for
U.S. Savings Bonds (75-); Natl. Adv. Bd. Labor Cl. for Lat. Am. Advancement (75-)
Tr.: Ford Fund, George Meany Ctr. for Labor Studies   *dir.*: American Arbitration
Assoc.

○ **Caspar W. Weinberger**   77- bus
VP and Gen. Counsel Bechtel Corp. (75-); Sec. of HEW (73-75); Coun. to Pres. (73);
Dir. Office Management and Budget (70-73); Ch. FTC (70); Heller, Ehrman, White
and McAnliffe (47-69); California Repub. Com. (60-64); Ca. State Legislature (52-58)
dir.: Pepsi Co., Quaker Oats Co.

○ **George Weyerhaeuser**   77- bus
Pres. Weyerhaeuser Co. (66-)   *mbr.*: Japan-California Assoc., Bus. Cl.
dir.: Boeing Co., Puget Sound Natl. Bank, Equitable Life Assurance Society

○+ **Marina von Neumann Whitman**   73- bus
Chief Econ. and VP General Motors Corp. (79-); Prof. of Econ. U. Pittsburgh (71-);
Sec. Commerce Econ. Adv. Comn.; Cl. on Econ. Adv. (70-73); Bd. of Overseers
Harvard U.   *dir.*: Atl. Cl., Brookings, CFR   *mbr.*: Cl. of Acd. Adv. AEI,
Bilderberg Steering Com.   *dir.*: Procter and Gamble Co., Westinghouse Electric,
Manufacturer's Hanover Trust

o+ Carroll L. Wilson   73- acd
    Mitsui Prof. Problems of Contemporary Tech. Alfred Sloan School of Management;
    Dir. Workshop on Alternative Energy Strategies MIT (74-); Dir. World Coal Study:
    ECOSOC (64-70); Ch. OECD Com. on Sci. Res. (61-70)l; Pres. Metals and Controls
    Corp. (57-58); Pres. Climax Uranium Co. (51-54); AEC (47-51)
    dir.: CFR   *Tr.*: Ch. World Peace Fund of Boston   *dir.*: Millipore Corp., Hitchener
    Mfg. Corp.

*o Thornton A. Wilson (Exec. Com. 78)   78- bus
    Ch. Boeing Co. (72-)   *mbr.*: Bus. Cl.   *gov.*: Iowa State U. Fund

+ Arthur M. Wood   73-77 bus
    Past Ch. Sears, Roebuck and Co.   *mbr.*: Bus. Cl.   *dir.*: Sears, Quaker Oats,
    Continental Illinois Corp., Allstate Insurance, Simpson, Moemart Dev. Co.

+ Leonard Woodcock   73-76 lab
    Amb. to Peking (79-); Chief Liaison Mission in Peking (76-79); Pres. emeritus UAW
    (77-); Pres. UAW (70-77)   *mbr.*: NAACP

Andrew Young   76 pol
    Pres. Young Ideas Inc.; Amb. to UN (77-79); Dem. Rep.-Georgia (72-77); Ch.
    Atlantic Community Rel. Comn. (70-72); clergyman (55-)
    dir.: Martin Luther King Jr. Ctr. for Social Change, Field Fund, Southern Christian
    Leadership Conf. (61-70); *mbr.*: CFR

CANADA

o+ Doris H. Anderson   73- med
    Pres. Canadian Adv. Cl. on Status of Women; Ed. *Chatelaine* Magazine (58-77)
    dir.: MacMillan Publishing Co.

o Michel Belanger   76- bank
    Pres. Provincial Bank of Canada; Pres. Montreal Stock Exchange (73-)
    dir.: C.D. Howe Research Inst.

+ Russell Bell   73-76 lab
    Research Dir. Canadian Labour Congress

+ Bernard Bonin   73 acd
    Dir. Institut d'Economie Appliquee, Ecole des Hautes Etudes Commerciales

*o+ Robert W. Bonner (Q.C.) (Exec. Com. 73-)   73- bus
    Bonner & Fouks Vancouver; Ch. British Columbia Hydro Comn.; Ch. MacMillan
    Bloedel Ltd.   *dir.*: IBM Canada, Intl. Nickel Co., Montreal Trust, Canadian Cable-
    Systems Ltd., J. Henry Schroeder Canada Ltd.

o Claude Castonguay   78- bus
    Pres. Fonds Laurentien; Ch. Bd., Imperial Life Assurance Co.; (Past) Minister in
    Quebec Govt.

George Creber   74 bus
    Pres. The Consumer Gas Co. (75-); Pres. George Weston Ltd. (69-74)
    dir.: Home Oil Co., Scurry-Rainbow Oil Ltd., Rothmans of Pall Mall Canada Ltd.,
    Huron Eire Mortgage Corp., Canada Trust Co., Canada Trustco Mortgage Co.,
    Cygnus Corp., Chubb Industries

o Louis A. Desrochers   75- law
    Ptnr., McCuaig and Desrochers, Edmonton   *dir.*: Bank of Montreal, L'Assurance-
    Vie Desjardins

o Peter Dobell   74- acd
    Dir. Parliamentary Ctr. for Foreign Af. and Foreign Trade, Ottawa

o Claude A. Edwards   77- pol
    Mbr. Public Service Staff Rel. Bd. (76-); Pres. Public Service Alliance of Canada
    (66-76); Econ. Cl. Canada (75-76)

o+ Gordon Fairweather   73- pol
   Chief Commissioner of Canadian Human Rights Comn. (77-); (past) MP-
   Conservative Party

   Brian Fleming   76 law
   Policy Adv. to the Prime Minister (76-); Stuart, Macken and Covert, Halifax (71-76);
   Rep. to Helsinki (66)

   John Allen Fraser   78-79 pol
   Postmaster General (79-); Min. of Environment (79-); MP

 o Donald Southam Harvie   78- bus
   Dep. Ch. Petro Canada   dir.: Standard Life Assurance Co., Molson Industries
   Ltd., Bank of Montreal, Northern Telecom Ltd., Penartic Oils Ltd.

o+ Alan Hockin   73- bank
   Exec. VP, Toronto-Dominion Bank (72-); (past) Alternative Exec. dir. IMB/IBRD;
   Permanent Del. to NATA and OEEC (52-53) mbr.: Canadian Inst. of Intl.
   Affairs   dir.: Morgan Stanley & Co., Acadia Life Insurance

 o Michael Kirby   77- acd
   Pres. Inst. for Research on Public Policy, Montreal; (past) Bd. of Comn. of Public
   Utilities, Nova Scotia

 o Donald S. Macdonald   78- bus
   McCarthy and McCarthy (77-); Min. of Finance (75-77); Canadian Inst. of Intl.
   Affairs   mbr.: Bilderberg Steering Com.   dir.: Shell Can Ltd., Dupont of Canada
   Ltd., Boise Cascade Corp., McDonald Douglas Corp.

 o Darcy McKeough   80- bus
   Pres. Union Gas Ltd., Chatham, Ontario

   Claude Masson   74-77 bus
   Head, Division of Planning and Research, Dept. of Trade and Commerce (77-79); V.
   Ch. Hudson's Bay Oil & Gas. Co. (59-73)

 + J. R. Murray   73 bank
   Pres. Federal Bus. Development Bank.; V. Ch. Foreign Invest. Review Agency
   (74-75); V. Ch. Hudson's Bay Oil & Gas. Co. (59-73)

   Arne R. Nielsen   74 bus
   Pres. & Gen. Man. Canadian Superior Oil Ltd. (68-); (past) V.P. & Dir.Saskatchewan
   Pipe Line Co.   mbr.: Natl. Adv. Com. on Petroleum   dir.: Toronto-Dominion
   Bank, Mobil Oil Canada Ltd., Rainbow Pipe Line Co., Ltd., Petrogras Processing
   Ltd.

*+ Jean-Luc Pepin, P.C. (Exec. Com. 73-75)   73-75 pol
   CoCh. Task Force on Canadian Unity (77-79); Pres. Interimco Ltd. (73-75); Min. of
   Ind., Trade & Commerce (68-72); Ch. Anti-Inflation Bd. of Canada; Min. of Mines
   and Technology Surveys (65-66)   mbr.: Canadian Inst. of Intl. Affairs
   dir.: Westinghouse Canada Ltd., Bombardier Ltd., Power Corp. of Canada, Collins
   Radio Co. of Canada

*o Mitchell Sharp (Exec. Com. 77-)   77- pol
   North American Dep Ch. (77-); Comn. Northern Pipeline Agency (78-); Min. of
   External Affairs (68-74); Min. Finance (65-68); Min. of Trade and Commerce (63-65);
   V.P. Brazilian Traction, Light & Power Co., Ltd. (58-62)   dir.: BRASCAN

   Maurice F. Strong   76-77 bus
   Ch. Petro-Canada (76-); Pres. CIDA (66-); Exec. Dir. UN Environment Prog.
   (73-77);   Tr.: Rockefeller Fund, Rockefeller U.   Alt. gov.: Asian Dev. Bank

North American Officers and Authors Who Are Not Regular Commission Members

   Jeremy R. Azrael   U.S. acd
   Prof. Political Science, Ch. Com. Slavic Area Studies U. Chicago
   An Overview of East-West Relations (78)

Carl E. Beigie   Canada   acd
Exec. Dir. C. D. Howe Research Inst.
Seeking a New Accommodation in World Commodity Markets (76)

C. Fred Bergsten   U.S.   acd
Asst. Sec. of Treasury for Intl. Econ. Af. (77-); Sr. Fellow Brookings (72-77); Visiting
Fellow CFR (67-68, 71-72); Asst. Intl. Econ. Af. to NSC (69-71); State Dept. Bureau
Econ. Af. (63-67)   *mbr.*: CFR, IISS, Bilderberg   *dir.*: OPIC (77-); Consumers
Union (76-77); AI (73-77); Overseas Dev. Cl. (74-77); Ctr. for Law and Social Policy
(73-77); World Watch Inst. (75-77)   *The Reform of International Institutions* (76)

John C. Campbell   U.S.   acd
Sr. Research Fellow Dir. of Studies CFR (77-78); Adv. State Dept. (63-)
Energy: The Imperative for a Trilateral Approach (74)
Energy: A Strategy for International Action (75)

William Diebold   U.S.   acd
Sr. Research Fellow, CFR   *Industrial Policy and the International Economy* (79)

Albert Fishlow   U.S.   acd
Prof. Econ. and Dir. Concilium on Intl. and Area Studies, Yale U.
*Trade in Manufacturers With Developing Countries: Reinforcing North-South
Partnership* (80)

Ann L. Hollick   U.S.   acd
Exec. Dir. Ocean Policy Project, Johns Hopkins U.   *mbr.*: CFR
A New Regime for the Oceans (76)

Samuel P. Huntington   U.S.   acd
Dir. Harvard Ctr. Intl. Affairs; Coord. of Natl. Security, NSC (77-78); Founder and
Ed. *Foreign Policy*; Assoc. Dir. Inst. War and Peace Studies, Columbia U. (59-62);
Cons. Policy Plan. Cl. State Dept.; Cons. AID; Cons. Office Sec. of Defense
mbr.: CFR   *The Crisis of Democracy: Report on the Governability of Democracies
to the Trilateral Commission* (75)

Douglas M. Johnson   Canada   acd
Prof. Law Dalhousie U.   *A New Regime for the Oceans* (76)

George C. Lodge   U.S.   acd
Prof. Bus. Admin. Harvard Bus. School (63-); Asst. Sec. of Labor for Intl. Af.
(58-61); U.S. Dept. of Labor (54-61); journalist   *mbr.*: CFR   *Collective Bargaining and Employee Participation in Western Europe, North America and Japan* (79)

Richard Nelson   U.S.   acd
Prof. Econ. Yale U.   *Labor Market Problems and Policies in Modern Trilateral
Societies: Reducing Unemployment and Smoothing Adaptation* (80)

Joseph J. Sisco   U.S.   acd
Pres. American U.; Asst. Sec. of State for Near East-South Asia; Under Sec. of State
for Political Af.   *dir.*: Tenneco   *The Trilateral Countries and the Middle East* (81)

Western Europe—Belgium

○ Guido de Clercq   80-   acd
Gen. Dir. Catholic U. of Louvain

○ Willy de Clercq   78-   pol
Ch. Party for Freedom and Progress; Mbr. European Parliament

○ Antoinette Danis-Spaak   78-   pol
Mbr. Chamber Reps. Brussels; Ch. Dem. Front of French Speaking Bruxellois; Mbr.
European Parliament

+ R. Ewalenko   73   bank
Dir. Belgium Natl. Bank

*+ Marc Eyskens (Exec. Com. 73-76)   73-76   pol
Min. of Cooperative Dev.; Former State Sec. Budget and Flemish Regional Econ.;
Commissary Gen. Catholic U., Louvain (76)

o+ Jozef P. Houthuys   73- lab
        Ch. Belgian Confederation of Christian Trade Unions

o+ Daniel E. Janssen   73- bus
        Dep. Dir. Gen. Belgian Chemical Union Ltd.   dir.: Societe Generale de Banque
        mbr.: Bilderberg Steering Com.

*o+ Baron Léon J. G. Lambert (Exec. Com. 77-)   73- bank
        Ch. Groupe Bruxelles Lambert S.A.   gov.: AI   mbr.: Bilderberg Steering Com.

 o Jean Rey   74- bus
        Minister of State; Ch. Sofina (71-); Pres. Comn. EC (67-70); Pres. EM (74-); Pres.
        External Rel. EEC (58-67); Min. Econ. Af. (54-58); lawyer gov.: AI dir.: Philips

    Henri F. Simonet   77   pol
        Foreign Minister (77-); VP EEC (73-77); Min. Econ. Af. (72-73); MP (68-73)

 o Luc Wauters   74- bank
        Ch. Kredietbank, Brussels (66-); Prof. Finance Antwerp U. (52-); Pres. monetary
        panel European League for Econ. Cooperation;   dir.: Intl. Monetary Conf.
        mbr.: AI   dir.: Antwerpse Diamant Bank, Cie Belge d'Assurance Credit, Inst. de
        Reescompte et de Garantie, Gevaert Photo-Products, Williams and Glyn's Bank Ltd.

Western Europe—Denmark

*o+ P. Nyboe Andersen (Exec. Com. 73, 76-)   73, 76- bank
        Chief Gen. Man. Andelsbanken A/S; (past) Min. for Econ. Af. and Trade; MP

    Svend Auken   77   pol
        Minister of Labor; (past) MP; spokesman on labor market

 * Ivor Norgaard (Exec. Com. 74)   74   pol
        Minister of Environment (79-); Exec. Com. SDP (61-); Min. of Commerce (77-79);
        Min. of Foreign Econ. Af. and Nordic Af. (71-77); VP European Parliament (74-75);
        Danish Natl. Bank (68-76); Min. of Econ. Af. (65-68); Ed. Aktuelt (61-64); AEC
        (56-65)

 o Erik Ib Schmidt   78- pol
        Perm. Undersec. of State; Ch. Riso Natl. Laboratory

 o Erik Seidenfaden   77- med
        Dir. Danish Fund, U. Inst. Intl. of Paris (66-); diplomatic columnist Berling ske
        Tidende (68-); Ed. Information (46-65); Correspondent The Times
        mbr.: Cl. IISS (65-76)

 o Niels Thygesen   79- acd
        Prof. of Econ., Econ. Inst., Copenhagen U.

Western Europe—France

 + Raymond Barre   73-76 pol
        Prime Minister and Finance Min.; Min. of Trade (76); Prof. U. Paris; Gen. Cl. Bank
        of France (73); VP Comn. EC (67-72)

*o+ Georges Berthoin (Exec. Com. 74-)   73- org
        Trilateral Comn. European Ch. (76-); Pres. European Movement (78-); Lec. NATO
        Defense Col., Rome; Chief Rep. Comn. EC to U.K. (71-73); Dep. Chief Rep. EEC
        and Euratom to U.K. (68-70); Hon. Dir.-Gen. Comn. EC; Principal Prvt. Sec. to
        Jean Monnet (52-55); Pres. ECSC   dir.: Aspen Inst., Berlin; Adv. Bd. Johns
        Hopkins UCES, Italy   mbr.: Bilderberg
        The Reform of International Institutions (76)

 + Jean Boissonat   73   med
        Ed.-in-Chief, L'Expansion

 o Marcel Boiteux   79- bus
        Ch. French Electricity Bd.

Rene Bonety   74-77   lab
Adv. Econ. Research Dept., French Electricity Bd.; Econ. and Social Com., EEC
(73); Exec. Com. CFDT [trade union] (62-73)

o Hérve de Carmoy   79-   bank
Chief Exec. Officer, BCT, Midland Bank, Paris; Gen. Man. Midland Bank, London

o+ Jean Claude Casanova   73-   acd
Counsellor to the Prime Min.; (past) Prof. Pol. Sci., Inst. of Political Studies; Dir.
Studies Natl. Fund of Pol. Sci.   *mbr.*: Res. Adv. Cl. AI

Roger Chinaud   74   pol
Pres. Republican Independent Group (73-); VP Intl. Paneurop Union (76)

Michel Crépeau   76-78   pol
Mbr. French Natl. Assembly; Mayor of La Rochelle; (past) VP, Natl. Movement de
Radicaux de Gauche

Michel Debatisse   74-79   lab
Food and Agriculture Minister (79-); Former Ch. French Natl. Farmers Union

*o+ Paul Delouvrier (Exec. Com. 75-)   73-   pol
Pres. de l'Establissement Public Charge de l'Amenagement du Parc de la Villete (80-);
Ch. French Electricity Bd. (69-79); Prof. Inst. Pol. Studies (48-); Prefect of Paris
(66-69); Dir. Gen. of Algeria (58-60); Financial Dir. of European Iron and Steel
Comn. (55-58); EEC (53); Pres. West Atlantic Assoc.

o Jean P. Dromer   77-   bank
Pres. and Dir. Gen. Intl. Bank of Western Africa; Dir. Gen. Natl. Bank of Paris (68)

o Francois Duchene   76-   acd
Trilateral Comn. European Dep. Ch. 74-76; Dir. Sussex European Research Ctr.
U. Sussex (74-); Dir. IISS (69-74); economist   *gov.*: AI   *mbr.*: Res. Adv. Cl. AI

o Pierre Esteva   74-   bus
Pres. Union des Assurances de Paris; Dir. of Cabinet (68-71); Tech. Coun. to Pres.
Pompidou (67-68); Financial attache U.S. (54)   *dir.*: Peugeot-Citroen

o René Foch   76-   pol
Principal Coun. French Delegation to OECD; Natl. Del. on Intl. Questions of the
Independent Repub. Party

+ Jacques de Fouchier   73-78   bank
Pres. Co. Financiere de Paris et des Pays-Bas (Dutch)   *dir.*: Xerox, Paribas, Credit
Natl., BSN-Gervais Darone, Thomson Brandt, Pechinery-Uquine-Kuhlman, Rand
Selectior

*o Michel M. Gaudet (Exec. Com. 77-)   74-   bus
Pres. Federation Francaise des Societes d'Assurances; Pres. Comite Europeen des
Assurances; VP EC (76-); Councillor of State (73); Dir. Gen. EEC Legal Services
(52-69);   *dir.*: Finextel

Pierre Jouven   74-75   bus
Pres. Pechiney-Ugine-Kuhlmann Co.; (past) VP Rhone-Porlenc; Dir. Credit Comn.
of France

o Jacques Lallement   79-   bank
Dir. Gen. Credit Agricole, Paris

Jean-Phillipe Lecat   74, 76   pol
Min. Culture and Communications; (past) Pres. Spokesman; Mbr. Cl. of State
(63-66, 74-); Sec. State of Econ. (73-74); Min. of Information (74)

o+ Robert Marjolin   73-   pol
V. Ch. Bd. of Gov. Atlantic Inst.; Prof. Political and Economic Sci. (67-69); VP
Comn. EC (58-67); Sec. Gen. OEEC (48-55)   *mbr.*: Intl. Adv. Com. Chase Bank;
European Adv. Cl. General Motors; Adv. IBM; Adv. American Express
dir.: Royal/Dutch Shell Francaise, Rebeco

○ Roger Martin   74- bus
     Pres. Saint-Gobain-Pont-a-Mousson Co. (70-79) *dir.*: Co. Finance Suez Credit
     Industry and Commerce, French Electricity Bd., Rhone-Poulenc, Agence Hondas,
     Certain Teed

○ Thierry de Montbrial   78- acd
     Dir. French Inst. of Intl. Relations; Prof. Econ. Ecole Polytechnique, Paris
     mbr.: Bilderberg Steering Com.

○ Bernard Pagezy   74- bus
     Pres. and Dir. Gen. Societes d'Assurances du Groupe de Paris; (past) Pres. Gen. de la
     Paternelle-Vie; Dir. Gen. Africa Co.; Bank Casablanca (63-65); Dir. Schneider
     S.N.C.F.

○ Francois de Rose   77- pol
     Amb. of France; Pres. and Dir. Gen. Societe Nouvelle Pathe Cinema; Amb. to North
     Atlantic Cl. (70-75); Amb. to Portugal (64-69); AEC (50-64) *gov.*: AI, IISS

○ Baron Edmond de Rothschild   74- bank
     Pres. Compagnie Financiere Holding; (past) Pres. Israel-Euro Co.; Dir. Rothschild
     Bank *mbr.*: Bilderberg

○+ Roger Seydoux   73- pol
     Amb. of France; (past) Pres. Adm. Cl., Fondation de France; Pres. Commercial
     Bank of Madagascar; Amb. to USSR (68-73); Amb. NATO (67-68); Amb. to UN
     (62-67); Amb. to Morocco (60-62); Amb. to Tunisia (56-57); VP UNESCO (48)

Western Europe—Ireland

+ Frederick Boland   73-76 bus
     Chancellor Dublin U.; (past) Ch. IBM; Pres. UN General Assembly (60-61); Perm.
     Rep. to UN (56-64); Amb. to UK (50-56); Ch. Irish Comn. Justice of Peace
     dir.: Guiness, Inv. Bank of Ireland, Irish Distillers

○ Richard Conroy   79- pol
     Mbr. Senate

+ Barry Desmond   73-78 pol
     MP and Labor Party Whip (69-); (past) Official, ICFTU; Sponsor, Irish Anti-
     Apartheid; Ch. Labor Party

*○ Garret Fitzgerald (Exec. Com. 80-)   77- pol
     MP and Leader of Fine Gael Party (77-); Foreign Min. (73-77); Man. Intelligence Unit
     (61-72) *mbr.*: Bilderberg   *The Trilateral Countries and the Middle East* (81)

○+ Michael Killeen   73- bus
     Man. Dir. Industrial Dev. Authority; Irish Export Bd. (57-69) *dir.*: Shannon Free
     Airport Dev. Co.

○ Liam Lawlor   79- pol
     Member Parliament

○ Dan Murphy   77- pol
     Sec. Gen. Civil Service Exec. Union, Dublin (68-); Dept. Transportation and Power
     (65-68)

+ Michael O'Kennedy   73-76 pol
     Min. of Foreign Affairs (77-); Min. of Transport. and Power (73); MP in Dail (69-);
     Mbr. Senate (65-); lawyer; VP Irish Cl. of European Party in Senate

*+ Mary T. W. Robinson (Exec. Com. 73-80)   73-80 pol
     Mbr. Senate (69-); Exec. Com. Irish Cl. of EM (69-); lawyer (69-)

○+ Myles Staunton   73- pol
     Mbr. Senate

○ T. Kenneth Whitaker   77- pol
     Mbr. Senate; Gov. Central Bank of Ireland (69-76); Sec. Dept. of Finance (56-69);
     Pres. Econ. and Social Res. Inst.; Ch. Natl. Ind. Econ. Cl. (64-71)

Michael Woods   78-79   pol
    Min. for State in Office of Prime Min. (79-); MP

Western Europe—Italy

*o+ Giovanni Agnelli (Exec. Com. 73-)   73-   bus
    Pres. FIAT Ltd. (66-); Ch. Inst. of Finance and Ind.; Ch. Agnelli Fund   *gov.*: AI
    mbr.: Bilderberg Steering Com., Intl. Adv. Com. Chase Bank, Intl. Mfg. Assoc.
    dir.: Medisbanca, Torino Ind. Assoc., *La Stampa*

  o Giovanni Auletta Armenise   79-   bank
    Ch. Banca Nazionale dell'Agricultura

 o+ Piero Bassetti   73-   pol
    Chamber of Deputies; (past) Pres. Regional Govt., Lombardy

  + Franco Bobba   73-75   bank
    Dir. Co. Turin; Ch. Capital Finance S.A.; Dir. Gen. Econ. and Financial Af. EEC;
    Past Del. to Rome Treaties; Min. Foreign Af. responsible for European Integrity (50)
    dir.: European Invest. Bank

  o Guido Carli   77-   bank
    Pres. Confindustria; OECD (75); EEC Monetary Com. (60-75); Dir. BIS (60-75);
    Gov. Bank of Italy (59-75); Min. Foreign Trade (57-58); IMF (47)   *mbr.*: Bilderberg
    gov.: Asian Dev. Bank, IBRD, AI

 o+ Umberto Colombo   73-   acd
    Pres. Natl. Com. for Nuclear Energy; Dir. Gen. Res. and Dev. Division, Montedison
    (71-79); Pres. European Ind. Res. Man. Assoc.   *dir.*: Com. for Scientific Policy-
    OECD (72-75), Montecatini G. Donegani Res. Inst. (67-71)
    *Reducing Malnutrition in Developing Countries; Increasing Rice Production in South
    and Southeast Asia* (78)

 o+ Guido Colonna di Paliano   73-   bus
    Past Pres. La Rinascente (dept. stores); Mbr. Comn. EC (64-70); EEC (64-67); Dep.
    Sec. Gen. NATO (62-64); Amb. Norway (58-62); Dep. Dir. Political Af., Ministry of
    Foreign Af. (56-58)   *gov.*: AI   *dir.*: FIAT Spa, Solvay et Cie S.A. Compagnia
    Generale di Elettricita, Exxon. *Directions for World Trade in the Nineteen-Seventies* (74)

*o+ Francesco Compagna (Exec. Com. 73-75)   73-   pol
    Chamber of Deputies; (past) Under Sec. State, Ministry of Mezzogiorno

  + Francesco Forte   73-78   bus
    Pres. Tescon SpA.; (past) Prof. Financial Services, U. of Turin

 o+ Giuseppe Glisenti   73-   bus
    Pres. La Rinascente; (past) Pres., Dir. Gen. Radio Audizione Italian

  o Giorgio La Malfa   78-   pol
    Pres. Comn. on Ind. and Commerce, Chamber of Deputies

 o+ Arrigo Levi   73-   med
    Columnist, *La Stampa*, Turin; *The Times*, London
    The Trilateral Countries and the Middle East (81)

  o Pietro Merli-Brandini   79-   lab
    Sec. Gen., Italian Confederation of Free Trade Unions

 o+ Cesare Merlini   73-   acd
    Dir. Inst. for International Affairs, Rome

 *o Egidio Ortona (Exec. Com. 76-)   76-   bus
    Trilateral Comn. European Dep. Ch. (76-); Pres. Honeywell Information Systems
    Italia (75-); Amb. to U.S. (67-75); Sec. Gen. Ministry of Foreign Af. (66-67); Dir.
    Gen. Econ. Af. Ministry Foreign Af. (61-66); Perm. Rep. UN (58-61); Pres. UN
    Security Cl. (59-60); U.S. Embassy (44-58); Del. to IBRD, IMF (47-55)   *gov.*: AI
    dir.: Aeritalia (75-)   *The Problem of International Consultations* (76)

  o Federico Sensi   77-   pol
    Amb. of Italy; (past) Amb. to USSR; Pres. INGENS, SpA.

o Paolo Vittorelli   77- pol
  MP; Dir. Avanti

Western Europe—Luxembourg

+ Pierre Pescatore   73-76 law
  Mbr. European Court of Justice (67-); Prof. Law U. of Liege; Min. Foreign Af.
  (50-67); Del. to UN (46-52) *mbr.*: Inst. de Droit Intl.

Western Europe—Netherlands

o E. K. den Bakker   79- bus
  Ch. Nationale Nederlanden

*o Henrik N. Boon (Exec. Com. 77-)   77- pol
  Ch. Netherlands Inst. for Intl. Af.; Amb. Italy (52-58, 71-79); Amb. to NATO
  (61-70); Amb. to Venezuela (58-61)

o Karel Fibbe   ●   78- bus
  Ch. Overseas Gas and Electricity Co., Rotterdam *dir.*: Royal/Dutch Shell,₁
  Ahold, Centrale Sviker Maatschappij

+ Andre Kloos   73-76 med
  Ch. Socialist Radio and Television Network VARA (71-); Ch. Dutch Trade Union
  Fed. (62-71)

*o+ Max Kohnstamm (Exec. Com. 73-)   73- pol
  Trilateral Comn. European Ch. (73-75); Principal, European U. Inst., Florence (73-);
  VP Action Com. for a United Europe (56-); Ministry Foreign Af. (48-62); ECSC
  (52-56); Principal Sec. Queen Wilhelmina (45-48) *mbr.*: Bilderberg Steering Com.,
  Res. Adv. Cl. AI *gov.*: AI

*+ John Loudon (Exec. Com. 73-75)   73-75 bus
  Ch. Royal/Dutch Petroleum Co. (65-); Ch. Intl. Adv. Com. Chase Bank (65-); Ch.
  Bd. of Gov. AI; VCh. Royal Netherlands Blastfurnaces and Steelworks (71-); Ch.
  Shell Oil Co. (57-65) *mbr.*: European Adv. Com., Ford Fund. *dir.*: Chase Bank,
  Shell Petroleum Co. Ltd., Orion Bank, Itek Corp., Estel NU Hoesch-Hoogovens

o Ivo Samkalden   77- pol
  Former Mayor of Amsterdam

o W. E. Scherpenhuijsen Rom   77- bank
  Ch. Nederlandsche Middenstandsbank N.V.

o Th. M. Scholten   78- bus
  Ch. Robeco Inv. Group, Rotterdam

o Edmund Wellenstein   77- pol
  Co-Pres. EEC Development Comn. Intl. Conf. Econ. Cooperation (76-); Dir. Gen.
  External Af. Comn. EC (73-76); Dir. Gen. Foreign Trade EEC (68-70); ECSC
  (53-67); Ministry Foreign Af. (50-62); Queen's Cabinet (46-50)

Western Europe—Norway

o Preben Munthe   77- acd
  Prof. of Econ., Oslo U.; Official Chief Negotiator in Negotiations between Labor
  Unions and Ind.

o+ John Christian Sanness   73- acd
  Prof. Norwegian Inst. of Foreign Af.; Prof. Philosophy of History; Labor Mbr.

+ Thorvald Stoltenberg   73-75 pol
  Sec. of State, Ministry of Foreign Af.; (past) Intl. Af. Sec., Norwegian Trade Union
  Cl.; UnderSec. Min. of Defense and Min. of Trade and Shipping

*o+ Otto Grieg Tidemand (Exec. Com. 73-)   73- bus
  Ship owner; Mbr. Conservative Party; Min. of Trade and Shipping (70-71); Min. of
  Defense and Min. of Econ. Af. (65-70) *mbr.*: Bilderberg Steering Com.

Western Europe—Portugal

○ Antonio Vasco de Mello (Exec. Com. 80-)   80-   bus
   Ch. Companhia Portuguesa de Trefilaria, SARL; Pres. Confederation of Portuguese
   Ind.

○ Francisco Lucas Pires   80-   pol
   VP Central Social Democratic Party (CDS)

○ Paulo de Pitta e Cunha   80-   acd
   Prof. Econ. Faculty of Law U. Lisbon; Ch. Portuguese Assoc. for the Study of
   European Integration

Western Europe—Spain

○ Luis Maria Anson   79-   med
   Pres. Agencia EFE, Madrid; Pres. Natl. Federation of Press Assoc.

○ Claudio Boada Villalonga   79-   bus
   Ch. Bank of Madrid; Ch. Altos Hornos de Vizcaya; (past) Ch. Natl. Inst. of Ind.,
   Madrid

○ Jaimé Carvajal   79-   bank
   Ch. Banco Urquijo, Madrid

○ José Luis Ceron   79-   bus
   Ch. ASETA; Former Pres. Spanish Bd. of Trade

○ Carlos Ferrer (Exec. Com. 80-)   79-   bus
   Ch. Spanish Confederation of Employer's Org.; Ch. Ferrar Intl.

○ Antonio Garrigues   79-   bus
   Dir. Assoc. para el Progreso de la Direcion [management] Madrid   gov.: AI

○ Carlos March Delgado (Exec. Com. 80-)   79-   bank
   Ch. Banca March, Madrid; VCh. Juan March Fund.

○ Alfonso Osorio   79-   pol
   Mbr. House of Reps.; (past) VP Spanish Gov't.

○ Antonio Pedrol   79-   pol
   Mbr. Spanish Senate; Ch. Consejo General de la Abogacia [Law] Espanola

○ Pedro Schwartz   79-   acd
   Dir. Inst. de Economia de Mercado, Madrid

○ Jose Antonio Segurado   79-   bus
   Ch. Intl. Relations Comn., Spanish Confederation of Employers' Orgs.; Ch. SEFISA

○ Ramon Trias Fargas   79-   pol
   Mbr. House of Reps.; Ch. Convergencia Democratica de Cataluna

○ José Vila Marsans   79-   bank
   Dir. Banco Central, Barcelona; Ch. Sociedad Anonima de Fibras Artificiales

Western Europe—U.K.

+ Alastair Burnet   73   med
   Political Ed. Independent TV News (63-64, 76-); Ed. *Daily Express* (74-76); Lead
   Writer *The Economist* (65-74)

Lord Carrington   78-79 pol
   Sec. of State for Foreign and Commonwealth Af. (79-); House of Lords (74-); Sec. of
   State for Energy (74); Sec. of State for Defense (70-74); Min. of Aviation Supply
   (71-74); Ch. Australia and New Zealand Bank (67-70); Opposition Leader, House of
   Lords (64-70); Min. Without Portfolio of Foreign Office; Leader, House of Lords
   (63-64); First Lord of Admiralty (59-63) *dir.:* Rio Tinto Zinc, Barclays Bank,
   Hambros Bank, Cadbury Schweppes, Amalgamated Metal Corp.

○ **The Earl of Cromer**   74- bank
  Advisor, Baring Bros. and Co. (74-); Amb. to U.S. (71-74); Ch. London MultiBank;
  Ch. Intl. Adv. Cl. Morgan Guaranty Trust; U.K. Exec. Dir. IMF (59-60)
  dir.: IBRD, Intl. Dev. Assoc. (54-61) *gov.*: AI, Bank of England (61-66)
  dir.: Shell, IBM, Imperial Group, Intl. Finance Corp., Peninsular and Oriental Steam
  Navigation Co.

○ **Geoffrey Drain**   80- pol
  Gen. Sec. Natl. Assoc. for Local Gov't. Offices (NALGO)

G. Eastwood   77-78 lab
  Gen. Sec. Assoc. Patternmakers and Allied Craftsmen, London

Max H. Fisher   74-80 med
  Ed. *Financial Times* (73-) *mbr.*: RIIA (77-)

○+ **Sir Reay Geddes**   73- bus
  Ch. Dunlop Holdings Ltd. (68-); Gov't. Adv. Cl. on Intl. Dev.; Natl. Econ. Dev. Cl.
  (62-65) *gov.*: AI *mbr.*: Intl. Adv. Com. Chase Manhattan *dir.*: Shell Transport
  and Trading, Bank of England, Midland Bank, Pirelli, Rank (transport and trading)
  Org.

○ **Ronald Grierson**   77- bus
  Dir. General Electric Co. Ltd.; Dir-Gen. Ind. and Tech. Af. EEC (73-74); Ch. Orion
  Bank (71-73); Dir. Warburgs (58-68) *mbr.*: RIIA

○ **Lord Harlech**   74- bus
  Ch. Harlech Television; Comn. Bank of Wales; Ch. EM; Amb. to U.S. (61-65); Min.
  State for Foreign Af. (57-61)

Bernard Hayhoe   77-79 pol
  Parliamentary Under Sec. of State in Defense Ministry (79-); MP (70-); VCh.
  Conservative Intl. Office (73-); VCh. Conservative Group for Europe (73-76);
  Conservative Res. Dept. (65-70)

○ **Denis Healey**   79- pol
  Mbr. Parliament; Former Chancellor of Exchequer; Ch. IMF Steering Group under
  Prime Min. Callaghan

○ **Edward Heath**   79- pol
  Mbr. Parliament; Former Prime Min.

○ **Terence Higgins**   79- pol
  Mbr. Parliament; Former Min. of State and Financial Sec. to Treasury

+ **Roy Jenkins**   73 pol
  Pres. Comn. European Communities (77-); MP (48-77); Sec. State for Home Dept.
  (65-67, 74-76); Dep. Leader of Labor Party (70-72); Chancellor of Exchequer (67-70);
  Min. Aviation (64-65)

○ **Lord Kenneth Keith of Castleacre**   77- bus
  Mbr. House of Lords (80-); Ch. Rolls Royce Ltd. (72-80); VCh. Beechams; Chief
  Exec. Hill Samuel; Group Ch. (70-); Natl. Econ. Dev. Cl. (64-71); M.D. Phillip Hill
  (59-62) *dir.*: The Times

○ **Henry N. L. Keswick**   77- bus
  Ch. Matheson and Co. Ltd. (75-); Proprietor *The Spectator* (75-); Ch. China Assoc.
  mbr.: Great Britain China Comm. *dir.*: British Bank of Middle East, Sun Alliance
  and London Assurance Ltd., Robert Fleming Holdings Ltd.

○ **Sir Arthur Knight**   77- bus
  Ch. Natl. Enterprise Bd.; Ch. Courtaulds, Ltd. (75-); Economic Com. CBI (65-72)
  mbr.: RIIA, Bilderberg *dir.*: Pye, Rolls Royce

○ **Mark Littman**   77- bus
  Queen's Counsel, Rio Tinto Zinc Corp.; Dep. Ch. British Steel Corp. (71-80); Mbr.
  Royal Comn. Legal Services; lawyer (47-67); Queen's Counsel (61) *dir.*: Rio Tinto
  Zinc Corp., Commercial Union Assurance Co., British Natl. Oil Corp., British
  Enkalon Ltd., Granada Group Ltd., Amerada Hess Corp.

○ Evan Luard   74-75, 79- pol
   Parliamentary Under Sec. of State for Foreign Af. (76-79); MP (66-); Fellow, Oxford

*○ Roderick MacFarquhar (Exec. Com. 77-)   77- med
   MP (74-79); Ed. *China Q*; Ed. Bd. *New Statesman*; BBC Reporter/Producer (63-74)

   Christopher Makins   75-76 pol
   Trilateral Comn. Deputy Director (75-76); Fellow of All Souls College, Oxford
   (63-); First Secretary of British Emb. in Washington (71-75); East European and
   Soviet Dept. and Near Eastern Dept., Foreign and Commonwealth Office, London
   (68-70); British Emb. in Paris (65-68)

+ Reginald Maudling   73-78 pol
   MP (50-); Home Sec. (70-72); Chancellor of Exchequer (62-64); EEC negotiator
   (58-59)   *mbr.*: Bilderberg

   Sir Frank McFadzean   74-76 bus
   Ch. British Airways (76-); Ch. Trade Policy Res. Ctr. (71-); Ch. Shell Transport and
   Trading Co. (72-76); Ch. Shell Canada (71-76)   *dir.*: Beecham Group, Royal
   Dutch/Shell and Co.

○ David Owen   80- pol
   MP; (past) Foreign Sec.; Labor Party Speaker for Energy in House of Commons

○ Sir John Pilcher   74- org
   Ch. Brazil Fund (76-); Ch. Japan Society; Foreign and Colonial Inv. Trust; Amb. to
   Japan (67-72); Amb. to Austria (65-67); Asst. Under Sec. State Foreign Office
   (63-65); Amb. to Philippines (59-63)

○+ Julian Ridsdale   73- pol
   MP (54-); Ch. Anglo-Japanese Parliamentary Group (64-); VCh. UN Parliamentary
   Group (64-); Parliament Under Sec. Air (62-64)

○+ Sir Frank K. Roberts   73-78, 79- bus
   Adv. Dir. Unilever Ltd. (68-); Pres. British Atlantic Comn. (68-); VP Atlantic Treaty
   Org.; Adv. Intl. Af. Lloyd's of London (68-77); Amb. W. Germany (63-68); Amb.
   USSR (60-62); Permanent Rep. North Atlantic Cl. (57-60); Amb. Yugoslavia (54-57)
   mbr.: Bilderberg, CCES *gov.*: AI *dir.*: Dunlop, Mercedes-Benz, Hoechst

○+ Lord Eric Roll of Ipsden   73- bus
   Ch. S. G. Warburg and Co. Ltd. (67-); Natl. Econ. Dev. Cl.; Perm. Sec. Econ. Af.
   (64-66); Exec. Dir. IMF, IBRD (63-64)   *gov.*: AI   *mbr.*: Bilderberg Steering Com.
   dir.: Bank of England, Times News Ltd., Common Market Trust, Comn. Dev.
   Finance

○ John Roper   77- pol
   MP (70-); Ch. Labor Comn. for Europe; Econ. Lecturer, Cl. Inst. of Fiscal Studies
   (75)

○ Lord Shackleton   77- bus
   Dep. Ch. Rio Tinto Zinc Corp. Ltd. (75-); Leader House of Lords and Lord Privy
   Seal (68-70); Min. Defense Royal Air Force (64-67); MP (46-55)

○ Sir Andrew Shonfield   75- acd
   Prof. of Econ., European U. Inst., Florence (78-); Dir. RIIA (72-77); Ch. British
   Social Sci. Res. Cl. (69-71); Dir. Studies RIIA (61-68); Econ. Ed. *Observer* (58-61);
   Foreign Ed. *Financial Times* (49-57)   *mbr.*: Res. Adv. Cl. AI, Intl. Res. Cl.
   Georgetown CSIS   *Collaboration with Communist Countries in Managing Global
   Problems: An Examination of the Options* (77)

○ J. H. Smith   78- bus
   Dep. Ch. British Gas Corp.

○ G. R. Storry   74- acd
   Prof. Far East Ctr., St. Anthony's College, Oxford

○ John A. Swire   74- bus
   Ch. John Swire and Sons Group; Ch. Hong Kong Assoc. (75)   *dir.*: British Bank of
   Mid East, Royal Insurance Co.

○ Peter Tapsell   79- pol
    Mbr. Parliament; former Junior Conservative Spokesman on Foreign and Commonwealth Af.; Conservative Spokesman on Treasury and Econ. Af.

○ Sir Anthony F. Tuke   74- bank
    Ch. Barclays Bank Ltd. (72-); Ch. Com. of London Clearing Bankers (74-79); VP Inst. of Bankers (73-)

○ Sir Mark Turner   79- bus
    Ch. Rio Tinto Zinc Corp. Ltd. (75-); Brinco (76-); Ch. Bank of America Intl. Ltd. (71-76); Ch. British Home Stores (68-76)

○ Sir Frederick Warner   77- bus
    Dir. Guinness Peat Overseas Ltd.; Mbr. European Parliament; Amb. to Japan (72-75); Amb. to UN (69-71); Min. NATO (67-68); Amb. to Laos (65-67) *dir.*: Chloride Group Ltd., Mercantile General Insurance Co., Yard Farms

○ Alan Lee Williams   77- pol
    Dir. Gen. English Speaking Union; MP (66-70, 74-79); Dir. British Atlantic Com. (71-74); Dep. Dir. EM (70-71); VCh. Labor Party Foreign Af. Group (68-70) *gov.*: AI

*+ Sir Kenneth Younger (Exec. Com. 73-75)   73-76 law
    Lawyer; Dir. RIIA (59-71); Min. State for Foreign Af.; Labor MP (45-59)

*○+ Sir Philip de Zulueta (Exec. Com. 73-)   73- bus
    Ch. Antony Gibbs Holdings Ltd. (76-); Private Sec. to Avon and Macmillan; (past) Chief Asst. to Prime Min.; Private Sec. Home (55-64); Asst. Sec. Treasury (62) *dir.*: Hills Samuels

Western Europe—West Germany

*+ Klaus Dieter Arndt (Exec. Com. 73)   73 pol
    Mbr. Bundestag

○ Kurt H. Biedenkopf   78- pol
    Dep. Ch. Christian Democratic Union; Mbr. Bundestag

*○+ Kurt Birrenbach (Exec. Com. 73-79)   73- bus
    Pres. German Foreign Policy Assoc.; VCh. August Thyssen-Hutte AG (73-); Ch. Thyseen Stiftung; VCh. AI; VP Europa Union; Thyseen Vermogensverwaltung Gmblt

Fritz Dietz   75-76 bus
    Pres. German Assoc. Wholesale and Foreign Trade; (past) owner sugar importers and wholesalers *mbr.*: Econ. Adv. Com. Konzertierte Aktion

+ Werner Dollinger   73-76 pol
    Mbr. Bundestag (53-); Mbr. Christian Socialist Union/Christian Democratic Union (53-); Min. Posts and Telecommunications (66-69); Min. Federal Property (62-66)

*○ Horst Ehmke (Exec. Com. 78-)   77- pol
    Dep. Ch. Parliamentary Fraction of Social Democratic Party; Mbr. Bundestag; (past) Min. of Justice

* Herbert Ehrenberg (Exec. Com. 74-76)   74-76 pol
    Min. Labor and Social Af. (76-); Mbr. Bundestag (76); Lecturer social science; Ch. Econ. and Financial Policy Com. of SDP

+ Wolfgang Hager   73 acd
    Dir. of Studies European Community Inst. for U. Studies; Trilateral Comn. European Sec. (73); staff aide, EC Commissioner Dahrendorf; Sr. Fellow, Res. Inst. of German Society for Foreign Policy
    Seeking a New Accommodation in World Commodity Markets (76)

○ Hans Hartwig   77- bus
    Ch. German Assoc. for Wholesale and Foreign Trade

+ **Karl Hauenschild** 73-76 lab
Pres. German Chemical-Paper-Ceramics Workers Union (70-); Natl. Exec. Bd.
German Trade Union Confederation *mbr.*: Labor Cl. SDP

o **Diether Hoffman** 79- bank
Speaker of Bd., Bank fur Gemeinwirtschaft A.G., Frankfurt/Main

o **Ludwig Huber** 78- bank
Pres. Bayerische Landesbank, Girozentrale Munich

o **Horst K. Jannott** 77- bus
Ch. Munich Reinsurance Society *dir.*: Dresdner Bank A.G.

Hans-Jurgen Junghans 77-78 pol
Mbr. Bundestag

o+ **Karl Kaiser** 73- acd
Dir. Research Inst. of the German Society for Foreign Policy; Prof. Pol. Sci.,
Cologne U.; Res. Assoc. Harvard U. Ctr. for Intl. Af. (63-68) *mbr.*: Comn. of
Experts for European Questions; Res. Adv. Cl. AI
Towards a Renovated International System (77)

o **Norbert Kloten** 79- bank
Pres. Central Bank of State of Baden-Wurttemberg

o **Erwin Kristoffersen** 77- lab
Dir. Intl. Division, German Fed. of Trade Unions

*+ **Count Otto Graf Lambsdorff** (Exec. Com. 77) 73-77 pol
Min. of Economics (77-); Mbr. Bundestag (72-); lawyer (55-71) *dir.*: insurance co.

+ **Eugen Loderer** 73-75 lab
Pres. German Metal Workers' Union; Mbr. SDP *dir.*: Volkswagenwerk AG,
Rohren AG, Mannesmann

o **Richard Lowenthal** 77- acd
Prof. Intl. Relations, Free U. Berlin; Visiting Prof. Berkeley (77-78), Columbia U.
(64-65, 75-76), Oxford (72-73), Tel Aviv (71-72), Harvard U. (59-60); journalist in
U.K.; foreign affairs commentator *The Observer*
An Overview of East-West Relations (78)

o **Hanns W. Maull** 77- med
Trilateral Comn. European Sec. (77-78); journalist; writer, *Bayerischer Rundfunk*;
Research Fellow at IISS and CCES (73-76) *Energy: Managing the Transition* (78)

o+ **Alwin Münchmeyer** 73- bank
Ch. Bank Schroder, Munchmeyer, Hengst and Co.; (past) Pres. German Banking
Fed.; Federal Min. of Econ.; Ch. Alternate Credit AG, Foreign Trade Adv. Bd.

*o **Karl-Heinz Narjes** (Exec. Com. 80-) 77- pol
Mbr. Bundestag; (past) Ch. Econ. Com. State Ministry

o **Friedrich A. Neuman** 77- bus
Ch. State Assoc. Ind. Employers Societies, North-Rhine Westphalia; Owner,
Neuman Eschweiler metal manufacturer

o **Konrad Porzner** 79- pol
Mbr. Bundestag; Parlamentarischer Geschaeftsfuehrer der Sozialdemokratischen
Bundestagsfraktion [Parliamentary Leader of Social Democratics in Bundestag]

o+ **Gerhard Schröder** 73- pol
Mbr. Bundestag (49-); Ch. Foreign Af. Com. of Parliament (69-); Min. of Defense
(66-69); Foreign Min. (61-66); Min. of Interior (53-61); Reorganizer of Iron and Steel
Ind. (47-53)

o+ **Hans-Günther Sohl** 73- bus
Ch. August Thyssen Hutte AG (73-); VCh. Wirtschaftswereinigung Eisen und
Stahlindustrie; VPres. Bundesverband der Deutschen Industrie; (past) Pres. Federal
Union of German Ind. *dir.*: Dresdener Bank AG

o+ Theo Sommer   73- med
   Ed.-in-Chief *Die Zeit* (73-); Lecturer Econ. Rel. U. Hamburg (67-70); Head of Plan.
   Staff Ministry of Defense   *mbr.*: Bilderberg Steering Com., IISS

   Olaf Sund   76 pol
   Sen. for Labor and Social Af., Land Gov't. of Berlin

o+ Heinz-Oskar Vetter   73- lab
   Ch. German Fed. of Trade Unions (69-); Mbr. European Parliament; European Fed.
   of Trade Unions (74-); VP ICFTU

o+ Otto Wolff von Amerongen   73- bus
   Pres. Otto Wolff AG; Pres. German Fed. of Trade and Ind.; (past) Pres. German
   Chamber of Commerce; VP Foreign Trade Adv. Bd.; Federal Ministry of Econ.
   mbr.: Bilderberg Steering Com. *dir.*: Exxon

European Officers and Authors Who Are Not Regular Commission Members

Guy de Carmoy   France acd
Prof. European Inst. Bus. Adm., Fontainebleau   *Energy: The Imperative for a
Trilateral Approach* (74)   *Energy: A Strategy for International Action* (75)

Jean Carriere   France bus
Dir-Gen. SEITA; Former Alternative Exec. Dir. World Bank
*Trade Manufacturers with Developing Countries: Reinforcing North-South
Partnership* (80)

Michel Crozier   France acd
Founder and Dir. Ctr. de Sociologie des Organisations; Sr. Res. Dir., Ctr. Natl. de la
Recherche Scientifique; Former Reg. Cons. to French Gov't. on econ. plan., educ.
and public admin.   *The Crisis of Democracy* (75)

Michel Hardy   U.K.   law
Legal Adv., Comn. EC   *A New Regime for the Oceans* (76)

Johan Jorgen Holst   Norway acd
Dir. of Res., Norwegian Inst. of Intl. Affairs   *A New Regime for the Oceans* (76)

Alexandre Lamfalvssy   Belgium bank
Econ. Adv. and Head of Monetary and Econ. Dept., BIS; Exec. Dir. Banque
Bruxelles Lambert (65-75)   *Major Payments Imbalances and International Financial
Stability* (79)

Heinz Markmann   W. Germany acd
Dir. Econ. and Social Sci. Inst. of German Fed. of Trade Unions
*Labor Market Problems and Policies in Modern Trilateral Societies: Reducing
Unemployment and Smoothing Adaptation* (80)

John Pinder   U.K.   acd
Dir. Policy Studies Inst.   *Industrial Policy and the International Economy* (79)

Benjamin C. Roberts   U.K.   acd
Prof. Industrial Relations, London School of Econ. and Pol. Sci.; Ed. *British J. of
Industrial Relations* (63-); Pres. Intl. Ind. Rel. Assoc. (67-73)   *Collective Bargaining
and Employee Participation in Western Europe, North America and Japan* (79)

Claudio Segre   France bus
Co. Europeenne de Placements; Comn. EC; Assoc. Dir. Lazard Freres and Cie; Pres.
Dir. Gen. of Lazard S.A.; Lazard Bank
Towards a Renovated World Monetary System (73)

Martine Trink   France med
Trilateral Comn. European Sec. (79-); Economic Reporter, *Le Figaro*

B. J. Udink   Netherlands bus
Man. Dir. of OGEM Holding N. V.; Min. of Transport (72-73); Min. Housing and
Physical Plan. (71-72); Min. for Aid to Developing Countries (67-71)   *A Turning
Point in North-South Economic Relations* (74)   *OPEC, the Trilateral World and
the Developing Countries: New Arrangements for Cooperation 1976-80* (75)

A Guide to the Japanese Membership
Takano Hajime

Three Japanese attended the planning session of the Trilateral
Commission held at the Rockefeller Estate in 1972:** Saburo Okita, an
economist who has been working with successive Japanese governments in
economic planning since the end of World War II; Kinhide Mushakoji, an
academic who studied at the University of Paris and Princeton; and Kiichi
Miyazawa, a Liberal-Democratic Party (LDP; the governing party) politician who has been involved extensively in international trade and industry
affairs and was a top contender for prime minister after Ohira's death.

Miyazawa became acquainted with David Rockefeller when he went to
the U.S. to study just before the start of the Pacific War. While the other two
Japanese participants were selected by Tadashi Yamamoto, director of the
Japan International Exchange Center, on the request of George Franklin,
Miyazawa was invited by Rockefeller himself.

The involvement of Japan in the Trilateral Commission highlighted its
growing economic importance. Nonetheless, the three Japanese elites had
reservations about participating. While they were personally flattered by the
Rockefeller invitation and proud that Japanese leaders would finally be
allowed to enter the exclusive salons of Western elites, they were also
anxious that Japan might be forced to assume increasing responsibility for
safeguarding the Western-dominated world order. Miyazawa, realist that he
is, was fully aware that while the Japanese economy had expanded rapidly,
it was not as solid as it should be, but had grown somewhat like an
overweight child: its bones are too thin and the weight is more water than
muscle.

Japan's role in what has been called the "shadow world government"
was formalized in 1973 when the Trilateral Commission held its first general
meeting in Tokyo. The Japanese committee of the Trilateral Commission
was organized by Okita, Miyazawa, Mushakoji, and Yamamoto, who
became Japanese secretary of the Commission. Takeshi Watanabe—
politically colorless, but well-connected and experienced—became Japanese
chairman. Nobuhiko Ushiba became vice-chairman of the Commission,
retiring (temporarily) when he was appointed Minister for External
Economic Affairs in the Fukuda Cabinet.

---

*Takano Hajime has worked with the Pacific-Asia Resources Center, PARC. These
are (edited) excerpts from an article which appeared in the English-language
quarterly, *AMPO,* published by PARC, Tokyo, Japan, 1978. Japanese names are
given as they appear in the Trilateral Commission Membership List. In the original
article, Saburo Okita, for example, is printed Ohkita Saburo, with surname first.
**See "Creating the Trilateral Commission" for full listing.

The Ushiba family typifies the Japanese Establishment. Nobuhiko Ushiba's elder brother, Tomohiko, started his career as a politician after he graduated from Oxford University and became Cabinet secretary for Konoe Fumimaro (known as "the most tragic Prime Minister" of the prewar days). He served as a board member of Japan Exim Bank after World War II and is presently an adviser to the Long-Term Credit Bank of Japan (formerly the Hypothec Bank of Japan). The second eldest brother, Michio, is an adviser to Mitsubishi Corporation and Mitsubishi Motors Corporation. Nobuhiko's younger brother, Daizo, is a Harvard-educated medical doctor who used to be the director of the medical college of Keio University. Nobuhiko himself pursued a career in diplomacy and became ambassador to the U.S. in 1970. Since retirement, he has been director of both the Sony Corporation and the Nippon Credit Bank. The matrimonial connections of these four brothers and their sons and daughters range from a chamberlain of the Emperor; to the Tokugawa family; to Yoshisaburo Ikeda, president of the Industrial Bank of Japan; to Yoshihiro Inayama, chairman of the Nippon Steel Corporation; to Susumu Kajita, the Japanese agent of Soriano & Company.

Among the first 74 Japanese members (there have been slight changes from the original membership but the basic character has not been altered), there are several people who, like Watanabe, Okita, Miyazawa, and Ushiba, held positions involving negotiation with the United States during the occupation days and thus established their own channels to the U.S. Establishment: Yusuke Kashiwagi, president of the Bank of Tokyo and an influential member of Japan's monetary mafia and Ryuchi Takeuchi, former ambassador to the United States and adviser to the Minister for Foreign Affairs. Dr. Mukaibo Takashi, a member of the government's Atomic Energy Commission and president of Tokyo University, has played a decisive role in bringing Japan's future nuclear development in line with U.S. strategy.

Another group is composed of academicians, most of whom are so-called pro-U.S. academicians, educated in the U.S. at universities such as Harvard, Columbia, MIT, and Princeton.

Most members of the Japanese Committee of the Trilateral Commission are executives of large banks and corporations, particularly of the emerging Japanese MNCs (mostly trading companies and giant manufacturers): Sony; Mitsubishi Corporation (the leader of the Mitsubushi group, the largest conglomerate in Japan); Mitsui & Company; Nippon Steel; Toyota Motor Company; Nissan Motor Company; Hitachi Ltd.; Sumitomo Chemical Company; Toray Industries Inc.; Sumitomo Shoji and C. Itoh.* Banks with representatives include: Mitsui Bank, Mitsubishi Bank, Fuji Bank, Sumitomo Bank, Sanwa Bank, and Daiichi Kangyo Bank.

---

*ed. note: The pillars of Japan Inc., a tight business-government partnership, are the "Zaibatsu," giant financial-industrial combines like the Mitsubishi Group, Mitsui Group, and Sumitomo Group, and business federations like "Keidanren," the Federation of Economic Organizations (all represented on the Commission). The top ten Japanese transnational corporations include: Mitsui, Mitsubishi, Marubeni, C. Itoh, Sumitomo Shoji Kaisha, Nissho-Iwai, Matsushita Electric Industrial, Toray Industries, Honda Motor, and Sony.

The younger generation, the future leaders of the country's financial world, like Noboru Gotoh, Seiji Tsutsumi, and Akio Morita are quite active in Commission activities.

Japan

o+ **Isao Amagi**   73- org
   Dir. Gen., Japan Society Promotion of Sci.; Adv. to Min. Education; (past) V. Min. of Education; Dir. Japan Scholarship Fund.

o+ **Yoshiya Ariyoshi**   73- bus
   Bd. Counsellor, Nippon Yusen, K.K.; (past) Ch. Nippon Yusen Kaisha; VCh. AI

o **Shizuo Asada**   77- bus
   Pres. Japan Air Lines Co. (71-); Exec. Dir. Keidanren; Adm. VMin. of Transport (61-63) *dir.*: Keidanren *mbr.*: Exec. Com. Intl. Air Transportation Assoc., Japan Econ. Res. Ctr.

o+ **Yoshishige Ashihara**   73- bus
   Ch. Kansai Electric Power Co.

o+ **Toshiwo Doko**   73- bus
   Ch. Keidanren (74-); Pres. Tokyo Shibaura Electric Co. (65-); Ch. Ishikawajima-Harima Heavy Ind. (64-74) *gov.*: AI *dir.*: Ishikawajima do Brasil Estaleiros SA

o+ **Jun Eto**   73- acd
   Prof. Tokyo Inst. of Tech. (71-); Visiting Lecturer Princeton (63-64) *dir.*: Rockefeller Fund

o+ **Shinkichi Eto**   73- acd
   Prof. Intl. Relations, Tokyo U.

*o+ **Chujiro Fujino** (Exec. Com. 73-)   73- bus
   Ch. Mitsubishi Corp. (74-) *mbr.*: Japan Foreign Trade Cl., Intl. Adv. Com. Chase Bank; Intl. Adv. Bd. R. J. Reynolds Industries

o+ **Shintaro Fukushima**   73- med
   Ch. Kyodo News Service

o+ **Noboru Gotoh**   73- bus
   Ch. TOKYO Corp.

+ **Toru Hagiwara**   73-79 pol
   Adv. to Min. of Foreign Af.; (past) Amb. to France

o **Nihachiro Hanamura**   78- bus
   V. Ch. Keidanren

o+ **Sumio Hara**   73- bank
   Exec. Adv. Bank of Tokyo (77-); VP and Dir. Japan Econ. Cl. for Asian Foreign Af. (73-); VP Japan Tariff Assoc. (68-); Ch. Bank of Tokyo (73-77); Japan Chamber of Commerce and Ind. (75-); Adv. Natl. Personnel Authority (75-) *mbr.*: External Dev. Cooperation Cl. (69-); Japan-U.S. Econ. Cl.; Adv. Bd. Sperry Rand Corp. (74-); Rockefeller U. (73-)

*+ **Yukitaka Haraguchi** (Exec. Com. 73-78)   73-78 lab
   Ch. Central Exec. Com. All Japan Fed. and Metal Mine Labor Unions

o+ **Norishige Hasegawa**   73- bus
   Ch. Sumitomo Chemical Co. (77-); VP Keidanren; Pres. Nippon Aluminum Co. *dir.*: Japan Com. for Econ. Dev., JFEA *gov.*: AI *mbr.*: Econ. Cl., Exec. Com. Japan-U.S. Econ. Cl., Visiting Com. Ctr. for Intl. Studies MIT

* **Yoshio Hayashi** (Exec. Com. 75-76)   75-76 pol
   Mbr.: Diet

o+ **Teru Hidaka**   73- bus
   Ch. Yamaichi Securities Co.

○ Kosuke Hiraoka   79- bus
   VP Komatsu Ltd.

*+ Kazushige Hirasawa (Exec. Com. 73-76)   73-76 med
   TV News Commentator, Japan Broadcasting Inc.

○ Gen Hirose   77- bus
   Pres. Nihon Life Insurance Co. Ltd.

○+ Hideo Hori   73- org
   Pres. Assoc. for Employment Promotion of Handicapped; (past) Pres. Employment
   Promotion Projects Corp.

+ Teizo Horikoshi   73 bus
   Exec. Dir. Keidanren (54-); Ch. Nippon Usiminas Co. (76-); Pres. Securities and
   Exchange Cl.; Min. of Finance (61-); Auditor Toho Mutual Life Insurance Co. (59-)
   dir.: Bank of Japan

*○ Takashi Hosomi (Exec. Com. 78-)   78- bank
   Adv. Industrial Bank of Japan Ltd.

+ Shozo Hotta   73-78 bank
   Hon. Ch. Sumitomo Bank Ltd. (71-); Adv. to Min. of Foreign Af.; (past) Exec. Dir.
   Keidanren; Roving Amb. in Europe (57) *Adv.*: Kansai Electric Power Co.,
   Sumitomo Electric Ind. Ltd., Sumitomo Atomic Energy Ind. Ltd. *dir.*: Nippon
   Electric Co., Sumitomo Real Estate, Mitsui-OSK Lines

○ Hosai Hyuga   77- bus
   Pres. Kansai Econ. Fed. (77-); Coun. Bank of Japan (77-); Ch. Sumitomo Metal Ind.
   Ltd. (74-); Exec. Dir. Keidanren (64-); Sumitomo Group (31-41, 41-); Sec. to Min. of
   State and Min. of Finance (41)

○+ Shinichi Ichimura   73- acd
   Prof. Econ., Kyoto U.

○ Yoshizo Ikeda   77- bus
   Ch. Mitsui and Co. Ltd.

+ Hiroki Imazato   73-77 bus
   Ch. Nippon Seiko K.K.

○+ Yoshihiro Inayama   73- bus
   Ch. Nippon Steel Corp. (73-); Ch. Keidanren; VCh. Intl. Iron and Steel Inst. (73-);
   Ch. Japan Steel Exporters Assoc.; Pres. Japan Iron and Steel Fed.; (past) Pres.
   Yawata Works and Yawata Iron and Steel Co. Ltd. (61-70)

○+ Kaoru Inouye   73- bank
   Ch. of Sr. Exec. Com., Dai-Ichi Kangyo Bank Ltd. (76-); Exec. Dir. Keidanren;
   Auditor Furukawa Electric Co. Ltd.; Exec. Coun. Tokyo Chamber Commerce and
   Ind. *dir.*: Asahi Mutual Life Insurance Co., Taisei Fire and Marine Insurance Co.,
   K. Hattori and Co.

○+ Rokuro Ishikawa   73- bus
   Pres. Kajima Corp.

○+ Tadao Ishikawa   73- acd
   Pres. Keio U.; Prof. Dept. Pol. Sci. Keio U. (76)

○ Joji Itakura   77- bank
   Counsellor, Mitsui Bank Ltd. (74-); Ch. Tokyo Bankers Assoc. Ltd.

○+ Yoshizane Iwasa   73- bank
   Ch. Japan-U.S. Econ. Cl.; Coun. Fuji Bank Ltd. (75-); VP Keidanren (63-); VCh.
   Japan Natl. Com. Pacific Basin Econ. Corp.

○+ Motoo Kaji   73- acd
   Prof. Econ. Tokyo U.; (past) Prof. Am. Studies Tokyo U.
   Toward a Renovated World Monetary System (73)

○+ Fuji Kamiya   73- acd
   Prof. Intl. Relations Keio U.; (past) Dir. Inst. of Modern Intl. Rel. Keio U.

*o+ Yusuke Kashiwagi (Exec. Com. 73-)   73- bank
Pres. Bank of Tokyo Ltd. (77-); Ch. Bank of Tokyo and Detroit Ltd.; VMin. Finance
Intl. Af. (68-71); Special Adv. to Min. of Finance *mbr.*: Intl. Monetary Conf.
dir.: Sony Corp., Saudi Intl. Bank

Koichi Kato   77-78 pol
Dep. Chief Cabinet Sec.; (past) Mbr. Diet

 + Ryoichi Kawai   73-78 bus
Pres. Komatsu Ltd.

o+ Katsuji Kawamata   73- bus
Ch. Nissan Motor Co. Ltd. (73-); Ch. Nissan Diesel; Ch. Nissan Shatai; VP
Keidanren; Ch. Japan Automobile Manufacturers Assoc. (62-72) *gov.*: JFEA

 + Kazutaka Kikawada   73-76 bus
Ch. Tokyo Electric Power Co. Inc.

o+ Kiichiro Kitaura   73- bank
Ch. Nomura Securities Co. Ltd.

o+ Koji Kobayashi   73- bus
Ch. Nippon Electric Co. Ltd. (76-); Exec. Dir. Keidanren (66-); VP Japan Telecommunications Independent Fed. (74-); Ch. Nippon Electric Yamagata Ltd.; Ch.
Nippon Electric Tohoku Ltd. (73-); Ch. Nippon Aviotronics Co. Ltd. (69-)
gov.: JFEA

 o Yotaro Kobayashi   80- bus
Pres. Fuji-Xerox

 + Kenichiro Komai   73-78 bus
Ch. Hitachi Ltd. (71-); Ch. Japan Consulting Inst. (65-); (past) Ch. Tokyo Atomic
Industrial Consortium; Exec. Dir. Keidanren (62)
gov.: JFEA (62-) *dir.*: Japan Atomic Power Co.

 o Shinichi Kondo   76- bus
Adv. Mitsubishi Corp.; Amb. to Canada (69-72); Dep. VMin. of Foreign Af. (67-69);
Amb. to New Zealand (64-67); Del. to UN (65); Amb. to Denmark (61-63)
Energy: The Imperative for a Trilateral Approach (74)
Energy: A Strategy for International Action (75)

o+ Fumihiko Kono   73- bus
Counsellor Mitsubishi Heavy Industries Ltd.; VP Keidanren
dir.: Mitsubishi Shoji Kaisha Ltd., Mitsubishi Steel Co. Ltd., Mitsubishi Atomic
Power Industrial Inc.

o+ Masataka Kosaka   73- acd
Prof. Law, Kyoto U.; Res. Assoc. IISS (73); Visiting Scholar Harvard U. (60-62)
mbr.: Res. Adv. Cl. AI *Towards a Renovated International System* (77)

o+ Fumihiko Maki   73- bus
Principal Ptnr. Maki and Assoc., Design, Planning and Dev. (64-); Lecturer Dept.
Urban Engineering U. Tokyo (64-); Assoc. Prof. Harvard U. (62-66)

o+ Shigeharu Matsumoto   73- bus
Ch. Intl. House of Japan Inc. (65-); Man. Dir. Japan Assoc. for Am. Studies (68-);
Dir. Nippon Light Metal Co. (57-75); Coun. Inst. of Asian Econ. Af. (60-); Gen.
Ptnr. Matsumoto, Kojima and Matsukato; VP Natl. Com. of Japan for UNESCO
(57-63); Ed. Domei News Service (40-45) *gov.*: Japan Broadcasting Corp. (61-65)

 + Masaharu Matsushita   73-76 bus
Ch. Matsushita Electric Co. Ltd. (77-); Ch. Matsushita Electronics Corp. (72-); Ch.
Matsushita Communication Industrial Co. (70-); Ch. Matsushita Electric Corp. of
America (74-); Pres. Electronics Industries of Japan (68-70)
dir.: Kansai Com. for Econ. Development (75-) *dir.*: Matsushita Real Estate Co.,
Matsushita Seiko Co., Matsushita Reiki Co.

 o Daigo Miyado   77- bank
Ch. Sanwa Bank Ltd. (76-)

*o+ Kiichi Miyazawa (Exec. Com. 73-74, 77, 79-)   73-74, 77, 79- pol
Chief Cabinet Secretary (80-); Mbr. Diet; Min. State and Dir. Gen. Econ. Planning
Agency (77-79); Min. Foreign Af. (74-76); Min. Intl. Trade and Ind. (70-71); Min.
Econ. Planning (62-64, 66-68)

o+ Akio Morita   73- bus
Ch. SONY Corp. (76-)
gov.: AI *mbr.*: Intl. Cl. Morgan Guaranty Trust Co., Rockefeller U. Cl., Finance
Com. SONY Corp. Am.   *dir.*: IBM World Trade Americas/Far East Corp.

o+ Takashi Mukaibo   73- acd
Pres. Tokyo U.; (past) Prof. Engineering Tokyo U.

*+ Kinhide Mushakohji (Exec. Com. 73-78)   73-78 acd
VRector, UN U.; Prof. Pol. Sci. Sophia U.; Dir. Inst. of Intl. Relations Sophia U.
(69-75); Sr. Pol. Sci. Res. East-West Ctr.; Visiting Prof. Northwestern U.
The Crisis of International Cooperation (74)
The Reform of International Institutions (76)

o   Norihiko Nagai   77- bus
Pres. Mitsui O.S.K. Lines

o+ Yonosuke Nagai   73- acd
Prof. Political Science, Tokyo Inst. of Tech.

o+ Shigeo Nagano   73- bus
Hon. Ch. Nippon Steel Corp. (73-); Ch. Nippon Steel Corp. (70-73); VP Pacific Basin
Econ. Cl. (70-); Coun. Japan Dev. Bank (70-); Pres. Fuji Iron and Steel Corp. (50-70);
Pres. Japan Chamber of Commerce and Ind. (69-); Coun. Min. of Foreign Af.; Hon.
Pres. Japan Iron and Steel Fed.; Ch. Prime Min. Cl. for Foreign Econ. Cooperation
Adv.: JFEA (70-) *mbr.*: Keidanren

o+ Eiichi Nagasue   73- pol
Mbr. Diet

o   Nobuyuki Nakahara   78- bus
Man. Dir. Toa Nenryo Kogyo, K.K.

o+ Toshio Nakamura   73- bank
Ch. Mitsubishi Bank (70-); Ch. Fed. of Bankers Assoc.; Auditor Mitsubishi Heavy
Industries Ltd.; Auditor Mitsubishi Petrochemicals Co. Ltd.
Tr.: Keizai Koyukai *dir.*: London Honda Motor Co., Orion Bank, Mitsubishi
Warehouse and Transport Co.

+   Ichiro Nakayama   73-80 acd
Pres. Japan Inst. of Labor

o+ Sohei Nakayama   73- bank
Counsellor, Industrial Bank of Japan (70-); Ch. Com. for Energy Policy Promotion;
Pres. Overseas Technical Cooperation Agency; Exec. Dir. Keidanren
mbr.: Exec. Com. Japan Com. for Econ. Dev. *dir.*: Keidanren, Mitsushita Electric
Industrial Co.

o   Akira Ogata   77- med
Former Chief News Commentator, Japan Broadcasting Corp. (NHK)

o+ Yoshihisa Ohjima   73- bus
Pres. Arabian Oil Co. Ltd.; (past) VMin. of Intl. Trade and Ind.

o   Kazuo Oikawa   79- lab
Gen. Pres. Japan Telecommunications Workers Union (Zendentsu); VCh. Gen. Cl.
of Trade Unions of Japan (SOHYO)

*+ Saburo Okita (Exec. Com. 73-79)   73-79 pol
Min. of Foreign Af. (79-); Ch. Japan Econ. Res. Ctr. (73-79); Special Adv. Intl. Dev.
Ctr. of Japan (73-); Pres. Overseas Econ. Cooperation Fund (73-77); Pres. Intl. Dev.
Ctr. of Japan (71-73); mbr. UN Comn. on Dev. Plan.; Dir. Gen. Dev. Bureau
(62-63); Dir. Gen. Plan. Bureau
A Turning Point in North-South Economic Relations (74)
*OPEC, The Trilateral World and the Developing Countries: New Arrangements for
Cooperation, 1976-80* (75)

*o Keichi Oshima (Exec. Com. 79-)   79- acd
    Prof. Nuclear Engineering, Tokyo U.; Science, Tech. and Ind. OECD (74-76)
    mbr.: Adv. Com. Japan AEC; Ministry Intl. Trade; Ind., Sci., and Tech. Agency;
    Econ. Plan. Agency; Ministry of Transportation
    Energy: Managing the Transition (78)

*o+ Kiichi Saeki (Exec. Com. 78-)   73- acd
    Ch. Nomura Research Inst. of Tech. and Econ.

o+ Kunihiko Sasaki   73- bank
    Dir. and Hon. Ch. Fuji Bank Ltd. (75-)

+ Kiichiro Sato   73   bank
    Counsellor, Mitsui Bank Ltd.

o Yukio Shibayama   77- bus
    Ch. Sumitomo Corp.

o Masahide Shibusawa   78- acd
    Dir. East-West Seminar

o Yoshihito Shimada   77- bus
    Pres. Takahashi Fund.; (past) Pres. Japan Petroleum Dev. Corp.

o Ichiro Shioji   79- lab
    Pres. Confederation of Japan Automobile Worker's Union (Jidosha-Soren)

o Tatsuo Shoda   77- bank
    Ch. Nippon Credit Bank Ltd.

o Binsuke Sugiura   78- bank
    Ch. Long Term Credit Bank of Japan Ltd. (71-)

  Toshisuke Sugiura   77-78 bank
    Pres. Long Term Credit Bank of Japan Ltd.

o Chusuke Takahashi   79- bank
    Exec. VP Sumitomo Bank

*o+ Ryuji Takeuchi (Exec. Com. 73-)   73- pol
    Adv. Min. of Foreign Affairs; (past) Amb. to U.S.

o+ Eiji Toyoda   73- bus
    Pres. Toyota Motor Co. (67-); Exec. Dir. JFEA (67-); Exec. Dir. Keidanren (67)
    mbr.: Japan Motor Industrial Fed. (72-) *dir.*: Aishin Seiki Co., Chujoda Fire and
    Marine Inst. Co., Hichi Steel Works Ltd., Toyota Machine Works Co., Toyota
    Motor Sales Co., Toyota Motor Sales U.S. Inc., Towa Real Estate Co., Toyota
    Automatic Loom Works, Toyota Central Res. and Dev. Lab. Inc.

o Seiki Tozaki   77- bus
    Pres. C. Itoh and Co.

o+ Seiji Tsutsumi   73- bus
    Ch. Seibu Dept. Store Inc.

+ Kogoro Uemura   73-78 bus
    Hon. Pres. Keidanren

o+ Tadao Umesao   73- acd
    Dir. Natl. Museum of Ethnology; Prof. Ethnology Kyoto U. (75)

*o Nobuhiko Ushiba (Exec. Com. 74-77, 79-)   74-77, 79- pol
    Trilateral Comn. Japanese Dep. Ch.; Rep. of Japanese Gov't. for Multilateral Trade
    Negotiations (79-); Adv. to Min. Foreign Af. (64-70, 79-); Min. External Econ. Af.
    (77-79); Amb. to U.S. (70-73); Co-Ch. Japan-U.S. Econ. Rel.; Amb. to Canada
    (61-64); Dir. Gen. of Econ. Af., Bureau of Min. Foreign Af. (57-61)
    Directions for World Trade in the Nineteen-Seventies (74)
    The Problem of International Consultations (76)

+ Jiro Ushio   73-76 bus
    Pres. Ushio Electric Inc.

o+ Shogo Watanabe   73- bus
    Ch. Nikko Securities Co. Ltd.

*o+ **Takeshi Watanabe** (Exec. Com. 73-)   73-   bank
Trilateral Comn. Japanese Ch.; Adv. Bank of Tokyo (73-); Ch. Trident Intl. Finance
Ltd. (72-77); Pres. Asian Dev. Bank (66-72); Exec. Dir. IBRD and IMF (56-60); Min.
Japan Embassy U.S. (52-56)

+ **Tadashi Yamamoto**   75-78   acd
Trilateral Comn. Japanese Secretary (73-)   *dir.*: Japan Intl. Exchange Ctr.

Eme Yamashita   77-78   pol
Former VMin. Intl. Trade and Industry

o **Toshihiko Yamashita**   79-   bus
Pres. Matsushita Electric Industrial Co. Ltd.

o+ **Kizo Yasui**   73-   bus
Sr. Adv. Toray Industries Inc. (71-); VP Keidanren (74-); Pres. Mitsui Petrochemicals
Co. (61); Dep. Pres. Mitsui Bank (59)

o **Hirokichi Yoshiyama**   79-   bus
Pres. Hitachi Ltd. (71-); Ch. Tokyo Atomic Industrial Consortium

Japanese Officers and Authors Who Are Not Regular Members

Masao Fujioka   bank
Exec. Dir. Ex-Im Bank of Japan; Asian Dev. Bank (66-69); IMF (60-64)

Tadashi Hanami   acd
Dean, Faculty of Law, Sophia U.
*Labor Market Problems and Policies in Modern Trilateral Societies: Reducing
Unemployment and Smoothing Adaptation* (80)

Takashi Hosomi   bank
Adv. Ind. Bank of Japan; Ch. IBJ Intl. Ltd.; Spec. Adv. to Min. Finance (71-74)
Industrial Policy and the International Economy (79)

Chihiro Hosoya   acd
Prof. Intl. Relations, Hitosubashi U.
*Collaboration with Communist Countries in Managing Global Problems: An
Examination of the Options* (77)

Hideo Kitahara   pol
Former Amb. to France   *The Trilateral Countries and the Middle East* (81)

Tohru Nakagawa   pol
Former Amb. to USSR (65-71)   *An Overview of East-West Relations* (78)

Shigeru Oda   acd
Prof. Intl. Law. Tohoku U.   *A New Regime for the Oceans* (76)

Hideaki Okamoto   acd
Prof. Ind. Rel., Hosei U.   *Collective Bargaining and Employee Participation in
Western Europe, North America and Japan* (79)

Sueo Sekiguchi   acd
Sr. Staff Econ. Japan Econ. Res. Ctr.   *Seeking a New Accommodation in World
Commodity Markets* (76)   *Trade in Manufacturers with Developing Countries:
Reinforcing North-South Partnership* (80)

Toshio Shishido   acd
Pres. Nikko Res. Ctr.   *Reducing Malnutrition in Developing Countries: Increasing
Rice Production in South and Southeast Asia* (78)

Joji Watanuki   acd
Prof. Sociology, Sophia U.; assoc. with Inst. of Intl. Rel. for Advanced Studies on
Peace and Dev. in Asia   *The Crisis of Democracy* (75)

Bibliography

Atlantic Institute for International Affairs—Information Brochure, January 1979

Canadian Who's Who, 1979 (Vol. XIV, Kieran Simpson, ed., U. of Toronto Press)

Council on Foreign Relations, *Annual Report, 1977-78*, Membership List, List of Officers and Directors, 1978-79

Peter Dreier and Steve Weinberg, "Journalism Has a Problem: Newspapers Share Directors With the Institutions They Cover" and "Who They Are: the Names and Ties of the Directors of the 25 Largest Newspaper Companies", *Columbia Journalism Review*, November/December 1979, pp. 51-68

Takano Hajime, "Rockefeller's Men in Tokyo: A Guide to the Japanese Membership of the Trilateral Commission", *Ampo*, Tokyo

Jane's Major Companies of Europe, Jonathan Love, ed. (London: Jane's Yearbooks, 1976)

Roy Laishley, "An Introduction to Trilateral Commission Members", *The Global Theater*, The International Coalition for Development Action, November 1977

New York Times, Business Week, and other newspapers and periodicals, primarily from the United States

Laurence Shoup, *The Carter Presidency and Beyond* (Palo Alto, CA: Ramparts Press, 1980), Appendix lists of officers, directors, trustees, and/or members of the Business Council, 1977; Business Roundtable, 1978; Brookings Institution, 1976; and Atlantic Council, 1978

Standard & Poor's Register

The Bankers' Almanac and Year Book 1977-78 (New York: International Publications Service, 1978)

The Japan Biographical Encyclopedia and Who's Who 1964-65 (3rd ed., Rango, Tokyo Press)

The International Who's Who 1978-79 (42nd ed., London, Europa Publications)

Peter Thompson, "Bilderberg and the West", in this volume

Trialogue, 1-22 (1973-80)

Trilateral Commission Membership Lists 1973-79

Various Company Annual Reports

Who's Who in America 1978-79

Who's Who in the World 1978-79 (4th ed., Chicago, Marquis)

PART III
ELITE PLANNING: WORLD WAR II THROUGH THE 1980s

Elite planning organizations have been around for a long time. It should come as no surprise that those who dominate wealth and power plan and act together to defend and strengthen the economic/political system which serves them. But for most of us this section holds many surprises—about the U.S. role in World War II, the international system and government policy making. In the capitalist democracies of the trilateral regions elite interest masquerades as the "national interest." The articles below strip away the mask and expose how the U.S-based Council on Foreign Relations, the West European-North American Bilderberg Group, and the Trilateral Commission shape the policy making process and influence the course of national and international events.

In speaking of public enlightment, it is well to bear in mind that the Council has chosen as its function the enlightment of the leaders of opinion. These, in turn, each in his own sphere, spread the knowledge gained here in ever-widening circles.

—Council on Foreign Relations
1951 Annual Report*

Here above national and international bureaucracies and beyond the brief tenures of most elected governments, a useful level of meetings and exchanges of views has come into being—a sort of *European-Japanese-American Establishment*. Problems can be attacked there that are beyond the narrow scope of nation-state interests and transcend the time horizons of a legislative session...[Italics ed.]

—Theo Sommer, *Die Zeit*
excerpted in the 1979-80
Trilateral Commission Brochure

*Cited in Shoup and Minter, *Imperial Brain Trust, p. 13.*

chapter one

SHAPING A NEW WORLD ORDER:
THE COUNCIL ON FOREIGN RELATIONS'
BLUEPRINT FOR WORLD HEGEMONY

Laurence H. Shoup & William Minter*

Near the end of the Second World War, two of its senior directors wrote that the Council on Foreign Relations (CFR or Council) had "served an increasingly useful function in the period of the twenties and thirties; but it was only on the outbreak of World War II that it has proved to come of age."[1] They were referring to the Council's successful efforts, through its special War and Peace Studies Project, to plan out a new global order for the postwar world, an order in which the United States would be the dominant power. The War and Peace Studies groups, in collaboration with the U.S. government, worked out an imperialistic conception of the national interest and war aims of the United States. The imperialism involved a conscious attempt to organize and control a global empire. The ultimate success of this attempt made the United States for a time the number one world power, exercising domination over a large section of the world—the American empire.

The process of planning a new international system was decision making of the most important kind. Such blue-printing was by its very nature *determining the national interest of the United States.* [Italics editor.] Those having this crucial function were the most powerful of the society. The Council and government planners began with certain assumptions, excluding other alternatives. These assumptions became intentions and were ultimately implemented by government actions....

---

*This article is excerpted by the editor from the chapter of similar name in *Imperial Brain Trust: The Council on Foreign Relations and United States Foreign Policy* (New York: Monthly Review Press, 1977). Laurence Shoup is the author of *The Carter Presidency and Beyond,* (Ramparts Press, 1980). William Minter is on the staff of *Africa News* and author of *Portuguese Africa and the West,* (Monthly Review Press, 1972).

The main issue for consideration was whether the U.S. could be self-sufficient and do without the markets and raw materials of the British Empire, Western Hemisphere, and Asia. The Council thought that the answer was no and that, therefore, the United States had to enter the war and organize a new world order satisfactory to the United States....

The War and Peace Studies Project

The fast-paced events of the first two years of the Second World War set the context for the early period of postwar planning. With the outbreak of war in September 1939, Council leaders immediately began considering the need for advanced planning to deal with the difficulties which the United States would face during the war and the eventual peace. Council Director Isaiah Bowman, who had been a key figure in the "Inquiry"—the postwar planning done during World War I*—was particularly adamant about the need for adequate preparation this time, so that previous mistakes would not be repeated.[2]...

Less than two weeks after the outbreak of the war, Hamilton Fish Armstrong, editor of *Foreign Affairs*, and Walter H. Mallory, the executive director of the Council, traveled to Washington D.C., meeting with Assistant Secretary of State and Council member, George S. Messersmith on 12 September 1939. They outlined a long-range planning project which would assure close Council-Department of State collaboration in the critical period which had just begun. The Council would form several study groups of experts to focus on the long-term problems of the war and to plan for the peace. Research and discussion would result in recommendations to the department and to President Franklin D. Roosevelt and would not be made public.[3]...

By mid-December 1939, details of the organization, purpose, scope and procedure of the Council projects had been worked out....A central steering committee was established to unify and guide the work of the groups. Norman H. Davis, President Roosevelt's ambassador-at-large, was chairman of this committee, with Armstrong as vice chairman, Mallory as secretary, and Alvin H. Hansen, Jacob Viner, Whitney H. Shepardson, Allen W. Dulles, Hanson W. Baldwin, and Bowman the other members. These last six men, together with the vice-chairman Armstrong, headed the five study groups which were established—Economic and Financial,

---

*ed. note: The Inquiry was established by President Wilson and led by his Chief adviser, Colonel Edward House. See footnote 3 in Thompson's article, "Bilderberg and the West," for further discussion of the Inquiry.

Political, Armaments, Territorial, and Peace Aims. Hansen, Professor of Political Economy at Harvard University, and Viner, Professor of Economics at the University of Chicago, led the Economic and Financial Group. Shepardson, a corporate executive who had been secretary to Edward M. House in 1919 at the Versailles Peace Conference, did the same for the Political Group. Dulles, an international corporate lawyer (and later CIA director) who had worked closely with Davis in disarmament negotiations during the 1930s, was co-rapporteur of the Armaments Group along with Baldwin, military correspondent for the *New York Times*. The Territorial Group's leader was Bowman, America's leading geographer and president of Johns Hopkins University. Armstrong later headed the Peace Aims Group, established in 1941.[4]...

The study groups averaged about ten to fifteen men each between 1940 and 1945. Almost 100 individuals were involved in this work during these six years.[5] Through these individuals, at least five cabinet level departments and fourteen separate government agencies, bureaus, and offices were interlocked with the War and Peace Studies Project at one time or another.[6]... The aim of the vast undertaking, to which the Rockefeller Foundation alone gave over $300,000 in a six-year period, was to directly influence the government...*[7]

The Council leaders also met regularly with the State Department's postwar planners once the department had established its own structures for such long-term thinking. In so doing, they formalized long-standing personal relationships with many of the top policy-makers. For example, the economist Leo Pasvolsky, special assistant to the secretary of state in charge of postwar planning during the war years, was familiar with most Council leaders. He had joined the

---

*During mid-1940, key members of the Council exerted their influence in yet another way by creating an ad hoc pressure organization. This body was called the Century Group because it met at the Century Association, an upper class club in New York.... At a 25 July 1940 meeting, the Century Group decided that something had to be done to aid Britain, specifically the transfer of fifty destroyers to Great Britain in exchange for bases on British possessions in the Western hemisphere and a pledge never to surrender its fleet to Germany.[8] Miller took the lead in approaching the government with this suggestion. He and four others traveled to Washington on 1 August 1940. Some met with President Roosevelt, others with various cabinet members. The next day the president discussed the Century Group's idea with the cabinet. At this meeting it was decided to explore the suggestions with the British. In this way the negotiations began which culminated in the Destroyers for Bases agreement in early September 1940.[9] The Century Group, in the words of historian Robert A. Divine, "had broken the logjam on the destroyer issue."[10] The Destroyers for Bases agreement marked the end of any pretense of American neutrality during World War II: the United States government had definitely taken sides...[11]

Council on Foreign Relations by 1940 and was quite close to it during the war years...[12]

Beginnings of Grand Scale Planning: Summer and Fall 1940

The German army's sweep across the French countryside to victory in May and June 1940 shocked the Council and government planners. They were suddenly faced with an entirely new situation. Germany might expand farther and defeat Britain, capturing its fleet and empire. Led by the Council, U.S. policy makers began grand-scale contingency planning to deal with this and other eventualities.

The key question which had concerned U.S. leaders for almost ten years centered on the problems of self-sufficiency and economic warfare. Was the Western hemisphere self-sufficient, or did it require trade with other world areas to maintain its prosperity? How self-contained was the Western hemisphere compared to German-controlled Europe? How much of the world's resources and territory did the United States require to maintain power and prosperity? The importance of this Council's concern should be emphasized because these are questions that have been debated for some years by Marxists and liberals. Marxists have argued that these things were and are essential to United States capitalism as presently organized, and that U.S. foreign policy is largely based on these needs. The CFR's conclusions, as we shall see, effectively support the Marxist position and shaped U.S. policy accordingly.

In the summer of 1940, the Council, led by the Economic and Financial Group, began a large scale study to answer these questions. The world was divided into blocs and the location, production, and trade of all important commodities and manufactured goods were compiled for each area. About 95 percent of all world trade in every commodity and product was included.[13] The self-sufficiency of each major region—the Western hemisphere, the British Empire, Continental Europe, and the Pacific area—was then measured, using net export and import trade figures...[14]

Using this type of analysis, the self-sufficiency of the German-dominated Continental European bloc was found to be much higher than that of the Western hemisphere as a whole.[15] To match this economic strength the Western hemisphere had to be united with another bloc...

The degree of self-sufficiency of the new region, initially called the Western hemisphere, British Empire and Far East bloc, was substantially greater than that of any other feasible union... The Council planners thus concluded that, as a minimum, the U.S. "national interest" involved free access to markets and raw materials in the British Empire, the Far East, and the entire Western hemisphere. They now turned their attention to making sure that the government of the nation at large defined the "national interest" in the same way.

Policy Recommendations: Mid-October 1940

Out of the conceptualization of the national interest developed during the summer and early fall of 1940 ensued the type of military, territorial, and political policy necessary to ensure a satisfactory functioning of the American economic system. In mid-October 1940, the Economic and Financial Group drafted a comprehensive concluding memorandum (number E-B19) summarizing its work and drawing out all possible implications for the United States policy. The purpose of this recommendation to President Roosevelt and the Department of State was "to set forth the political, military, territorial and economic requirements of the United States in its potential leadership of the non-German world area including the United Kingdom itself as well as the Western hemisphere and Far East."[16]...

The Problem of Japan

The major impediment to integrating the non-German world was Japan's refusal to play the subordinate role which the United States had assigned to it. All War and Peace Studies Groups recognized that Japan was an expanding power and a threat to Council plans. On 23 November 1940, the Economic and Financial Group discussed possible actions against Japan to prevent that country's takeover of Southeast Asia and destruction of American access to that part of the non-German world. Aid to China to entangle Japan's military machine there and economic sanctions were considered.[17] This raised two questions: how much would Japan be hurt by such sanctions, and what would Japan do politically, economically, and militarily if it were hurt?

Having pressed their discussion to the limits of economic analysis, a special meeting of all War and Peace Studies groups and government representatives was called on 14 December 1940...[18]

Despite some disagreement, there were enough areas of consensus to issue a summarizing memorandum to President Roosevelt and the Department of State suggesting what policy the nation should pursue in the Far East. This memorandum is very important for an understanding of the role of the Council in the process of postwar planning. It was the initial recommendation to the government aimed at the implementation of the Council's proposals for a worldwide non-German bloc dominated by the United States. In addition, as a policy suggestion concerned with the means rather than the ends of policy, it can be used as a test case to determine whether there was a correspondence—and likely a cause and effect relationship—between the Council recommendations and governmental actions.

The aide-memoire, numbered E-B26, which came out of the December 14 meeting, was issued on 15 January 1941, under the title of "American Far Eastern Policy." It began by stating that it was in the national interest of the United States to check a Japanese advance into Southeast Asia, and that this could best be done by taking the initiative rather than waiting for Japanese action. The main interests of the United States in Southeast Asia were twofold. The first was economic: "The Philippine Islands, the Dutch East Indies, and British Malaya are prime sources of raw materials very important to the United States in peace and war; control of these lands by a potentially hostile power would greatly limit our freedom of action."[19] Secondly, strategic considerations demanded prevention of Japanese occupation of Southeast Asia, since Japanese control would impair the British war effort against Hitler, threatening sources of supply and weakening the whole British position in Asia. Many would view it as the beginning of the disintegration of the British Empire, and Australia and New Zealand might decide to concentrate on home defense.[20]

The program which the Council proposed to stop the Japanese move southward had three aspects. First was to give all possible aid to China, especially war materials, in order to pin down Japanese troops in that country. Second, the defenses of Southeast Asia should be strengthened by sending naval and air forces and by making an agreement with the British and Dutch for defense of the area. Finally, Japan should be weakened by cutting off some of its supplies of war materiel.[21]...

On 28 January 1941, Pasvolsky gave Secretary of State Cordell Hull a copy of this Council recommendation.[22] The two most important aspects of these suggestions—aid to China and embargo of Japan—were implemented by government action within seven months.[23] These policies, which the Council proposed and the government adopted, had extremely important ramifications, leading to American entry into World War II.

The Grand Area

The Grand Area, as the United States-led non-German bloc was called during 1941, was only an interim measure to deal with the emergency situation of 1940 and early 1941. The preferred ideal was even more grandiose—one world economy dominated by the United States.[24]...

A 24 July 1941 memorandum to the president and Department of State outlined the Council's view of the national interest, describing the role of the Grand Area in U.S. economic, political, and military policy. The memorandum, number E-B34, summarized the Grand Area concept, its "meaning for American policy, its function in the present war, and its possible role in the postwar period."[25]...The Economic and Financial Group had found a self-contained United States-Western hemisphere economy impossible without great changes in the U.S. economic system.

To prevent alterations in the United States economy, the Council had, in the words of group member Winfield W. Riefler, "gone on to discover what 'elbow room' the American economy needed in order to survive without major readjustments."[26] This living space had to have the basic raw materials needed for the nation's industry as well as the "fewest possible stresses making for its own disintegration, such as unwieldy export surpluses or severe shortages of consumer goods."[27] The extensive studies and discussions of the Council groups determined that, as a minimum, most of the non-German world, the Grand Area, was needed for elbow room. In its final form, it consisted of the Western hemisphere, the United Kingdom, the remainder of the British Commonwealth and Empire, the Dutch East Indies, China, and Japan itself...[28]

In E-B34 the Economic and Financial Group stressed the significance of the economic integration of the Grand Area. All member countries had to be able to prosper within the region, or instability would inevitably result.... Memorandum E-B34 stated:

> In the event of an American-British victory, much would have to be done toward reshaping the world, particularly Europe. In this the Grand Area organization should prove useful. During an interim period of readjustment and reconstruction, the Grand Area might be an important stabilizing factor in the world's economy. Very likely the institutions developed for the integration of the Grand Area would yield useful experience in meeting European problems, and perhaps it would be possible simply to interweave the economies of European countries into that of the Grand Area.[29]

The Grand Area was thus considered a core region, which could always be extended to include more countries...

At the end of recommendation E-B34, the Economic and Financial Group outlined the key topics for future study on integrating the Grand Area. Leading the list were financial measures—the creation of international financial institutions to stabilize currencies, and of international banking institutions to aid in investment and development of backward areas.[30] They had thus identified at a very early date the need for the International Monetary Fund and the World Bank, which they were to specifically suggest in February 1942...

Evidence for the Council's key role in setting and implementing American war aims from mid-1941 to mid-1944 is even greater than for the earlier period.

The International Setting, 1941-1944

Internationally the period from mid-1941 to 1944 was marked by intensified warfare and stepped-up planning for the postwar world. Germany attacked the Soviet Union in June 1941. Three months later, the United States began an undeclared naval war against Germany in the Atlantic. During the second half of 1941, the danger of conflict in the Pacific heightened as Japan prepared to push south and west from its bases in Indochina. In the year following the 7 December 1941 attack on Pearl Harbor and U.S. entry into full belligerency, the nadir of Allied fortunes was reached. During 1943 and 1944, however, the Axis powers suffered sharp and increasingly disastrous reverses as their complete defeat and the end of the war approached.

After mid-1941, both the Council and the government assumed that the defeat of the Axis was both necessary and inevitable... A new world order with international political and economic institutions was projected, which would join and integrate all of the earth's nations under the leadership of the United States....

The Council and American Entry into the Second World War

...President Roosevelt agreed with the State Department-Council on Foreign Relations view [on Japan], stressing the danger to British and U.S. raw material supplies which Japanese expansion posed. The president stated during the second half of 1941 that a Japanese attack on British and Dutch possessions in the Far East would immediately threaten the vital interests of the nation and "should result in war with Japan."[31] Prime Minister Churchill also emphasized the need to prevent Japanese movement south, which would cut the lifelines between the Dominions and England. Such a blow to the British government, he argued, "might be almost decisive."[32] Thus the top governmental policy makers on both sides of the Atlantic agreed that their joint interests demanded that Japan be prevented from capturing Southeast Asia.

Japan also saw its essential national interests joined with the fate of Southeast Asia. Japan had its own equivalent of the Grand Area, called the Greater East Asia Co-Prosperity Sphere. Japan's new order involved control over the Dutch East Indies (which it coveted as the finest pearl in the prospective colonial booty), China, Indochina, Thailand, Burma, Malaya, the Philippines, and certain Pacific Islands.[33] The Japanese felt that control of these areas was necessary to attain economic self-sufficiency, especially in raw materials. They planned to eventually create a self-contained empire from Manchuria on the north to the Dutch East Indies in the south, for the same economic reasons the United States and Britain wanted to dominate the region.[34]

The three great European colonial powers—Britain, France, and the Netherlands—controlled Southeast Asia in 1941. Since only Britain, much weakened by its struggle with Germany, was still an independent power, Japan recognized a prime opportunity to secure present and future economic needs. In late July 1941 Japanese leaders decided to move into southern Indochina as a first step toward control of all of Southeast Asia. The U.S. reaction was forceful: Japanese assets in the United States were frozen and a total economic embargo, including oil, was imposed. Britain and the Netherlands government-in-exile followed suit.[35] The Council had recommended this policy in January 1941. The seriousness of this action was well known at the time. Many people had previously warned that it would provoke Japan into war, since it cut off many raw and finished materials, including oil, which that country had to have to survive as a great power.[36]... The Japanese were informed that there would be no relaxation of the embargo until Japan gave up the territory it had fought for years to gain in China.[37]

The American stand [on China] weakened the moderates in Tokyo and, joined with the previously mentioned factors, made war inevitable. There were several reasons for the U.S. position. First, U.S. minimum living space, the Grand Area, included China. The Council felt that China's economic development could lay the basis for a peaceful Far East during the postwar period, since its industrialization would create a large demand for Japanese and U.S. production, giving great aid to both countries in solving surplus and unemployment problems. This meant that Japan had to restore the territorial integrity of China.[38] In addition, as we shall see in more detail shortly, the long-range war aims of the United States, which became fixed during this time, involved a single world economy, an open door world, the maximum possible U.S. living space...

Final negotiations took place during November, culminating in the ten-point plan from the United States to Japan on 26 November 1941. This memorandum took a hard line, visualizing a return to the status quo of 1931 by demanding a Japanese withdrawal from China and Indochina in return for resumption of trade relations.[39] With its oil supplies getting low because of the trade embargo, Japan had to choose between submission and war.

Roosevelt and his advisors, expecting Japan to advance south, had concluded that this movement would endanger the U.S. national interest and had to be stopped, by a United States declaration of war and armed intervention if necessary. Roosevelt told Harry Hopkins that a Japanese attack on the Netherland East Indies should result in war between the United States and Japan.[40] On November 28, the War Council made up of Hull, Secretary of War (and longtime) Council member) Henry L. Stimson, and Secretary of the Navy Frank Knox, decided that Roosevelt should inform Congress and the American people that if Japan attacked Singapore or the East Indies, the security of the United States would be endangered and war might result.[41] It was agreed that Hull, Stimson, and Knox should draft this projected message to Congress. The idea behind the message was to persuade Congress and the public that Japanese expansion constituted such a threat to the national interest of the United States that military counteraction was necessary.[42]...

[Roosevelt] faced the difficult task of persuading Congress and the American people that war for these ends was justified. How to convince the American people that an attack on British and Dutch colonies in the South Pacific "was tantamount to an attack upon our own frontiers," was a tremendous difficulty for the President.[43] Nevertheless, during the last week of peace, Roosevelt gave Britain assurances of armed support in case of Japanese aggression.[44] The assault on Pearl Harbor on 7 December 1941, which came because the Japanese had correctly calculated that the United States was likely to declare war when they moved further into Southeast Asia, made the whole problem moot.

Merger of Council and
State Department Planning in 1941-1942

In late 1941 the Department of State created a special committee to carry out postwar planning. The Advisory Committee on Postwar Foreign Policy was, Undersecretary Wells wrote, a "new approach to a problem that the Department had previously handled in a wholly desultory fashion."[45] The Council had a central role in establishing the Advisory Committee, in which its leading planners filled key positions...

The Advisory Committee set the value framework for all key decisions on the postwar world made during 1942, 1943, and 1944. It dealt with fundamental issues of national policy, such as the needs of U.S. economy and society, the relationship of these requirements to the rest of the world, and the role of international organizations...

The original Advisory Committee was (thus) an amalgam of people with close ties to New York (10), the Council on Foreign Relations (8), and to the Department of State (9). The East Coast was in control, with other sections of the country unrepresented. White, Anglo-Saxon upper class businessmen, lawyers, and technocrats dominated the committee. The working class generally—labor, consumers, small business, minorities, and ethnic groups—had virtually no representation. Table I summarizes information about the original Advisory Committee.[46] (See Appendix to this article.)

Those at the top of the department and those from the Council made up the core of the Advisory Committee decision-makers who decided the fate of the postwar world. The core group consisted of Hull, Welles, Davis, Taylor, Bowman, and Pasvolsky. They were the people, who, beginning in early 1943, became known as the Informal Political Agenda Group, which President Roosevelt called "my postwar advisors."[47] They were the senior men, who selected, planned, and guided the agenda for the entire Advisory Committee and also drafted the United Nations Charter...[48]

The Grand Area and United States War Aims

Military conflicts are fought to determine who will shape the peace following victory, and on what basis. Therefore the complex of assumptions and goals, labeled for the sake of convenience as war aims, are most crucial for understanding long-range foreign policy. Analysis and description of these aims throw light on both the origin and consequences of the conflict.

The Grand Area concept and the means which the Council proposed to integrate this territory became the initial basis for United States war aims. Two problems faced the Council and government planners in regard to these goals. First, the American people had to be inspired and mobilized to enter the war and win it. This involved issuing plausible propaganda. Secondly, the detailed and specific means for integration of an expanded Grand Area into a United States-dominated world order had to be devised. This involved working out the mechanics for new international institutions.

The CFR's War and Peace Studies groups recognized at an early date the difference between these two types of problems. The Economic and Financial Group pointed out in July 1941 that "formulation of a statement of war aims for propaganda purposes is very different from formulation of one defining the true national interest."[49] While this group's main concern was with the latter function, it did give the government ideas on how to deal with the former. In April 1941 the group suggested to the government that a statement of U.S. war aims should now be prepared, coldly warning:

> If war aims are stated *which seem to be concerned solely with Anglo-American imperialism, they will offer little to people in the rest of the world, and will be vulnerable to Nazi counter-promises.* Such aims would also strengthen the most reactionary elements in the United States and the British Empire. The interests of other peoples should be stressed, not only those of Europe, but also of Asia, Africa, and Latin America. This would have a better propaganda effect.[50] [Italics ed.]

Since such propaganda statements had to be at least close to actual U.S. interests, the war aims declaration had to be vague and abstract, not specific. The statement which resulted was the Atlantic Charter of August 1941. It was the public war aims statement of the United States, and its reason for being was propaganda.[51] The generalized aims it advocated were those which people everywhere would agree were laudable: freedom, equality, prosperity, and peace. The Council had made suggestions about what should be in such a public statement, and a member of the Council—Undersecretary of State Sumner Welles—was President Roosevelt's chief adviser on the Atlantic Charter.

With the entry of the United States into World War II, U.S. planners were virtually unanimous in the belief that the nation should claim a dominant position in the postwar world. As usual, however, the leaders of the Council on Foreign Relations were stating this view most clearly. Council director and Territorial Group leader Isaiah Bowman wrote Hamilton Fish Armstrong, a week after the entry of the United States into the war, that the Council and the U.S. government now had to "think of world-organization in a fresh way. To the degree that the United States is the arsenal of the democracies it will be the final arsenal at the moment of victory. It cannot throw the contents of that arsenal away. It must accept world responsibility... The measure of our victory will be the measure of our domination after victory."[52] The next month, in January 1942, Bowman further asserted that at a minimum, an enlarged conception of American security interests would be necessary after the war in order to deal with areas "strategically necessary for world control."[53]

Council president Norman Davis, now chairman of the Department of State's security subcommittee of the Advisory Committee on Postwar Foreign Policy, asserted in early May 1942 that it was probable "the British Empire as it existed in the past will never reappear and that the United States may have to take its place."[54] Gen. George V. Strong, a member of Davis' subcommittee who had worked on the War and Peace Studies Project during 1940, used even stronger language during the same discussion. He expressed the opinion that the United States "must cultivate a mental view toward world settlement after this war *which will enable us to impose our own terms, amounting perhaps to a pax-Americana."*[55] [emphasis added.] He went on to say that the nation must adopt a tough attitude toward its allies at the expected peace conference. Davis agreed with Strong, adding that the United States could "no longer be indifferent as to what happens in any part of the world."[56]

The reason for this emphasis on global hegemony for the United States was the same one that the Council had stressed in 1940 and 1941: the economic life of U.S. society as presently organized was very closely connected with the outside world. The economy of the nation, as it had been for some time, was geared to the need for large export markets, the loss of which—barring a transition to a form of socialism—would cause a lowering of the national income and greatly reduced employment.[57] The haunting specter of depression and its political consequences made the planners pay careful attention to the relationship between international and domestic economic policies...[58]

The first document produced by the economic subcommittee of the Advisory Committee on Postwar Foreign Policy stressed the danger of another world depression and the need to provide confidence in world economic stability.[59] This necessarily meant that U.S. planners had to concern themselves with the politics and economics of other nations. At a minimum the United States had to be involved in the internal affairs of the key industrial and raw materials-producing countries. If one or a few of these nations did not cooperate in a new worldwide economic system, they might not develop rapidly enough to enlarge their purchases from the United States, thereby increasing the likelihood of a depression. The various countries' economies had also to be efficient; otherwise they could not pay for more imports. The political and security side was also connected with this basic economic dilemma. Davis's subcommittee laid great stress on "the impossibility of providing security to the world unless developments in other fields would be such as to provide a sound basis for international cooperation."[60]

The IMF and World Bank

Clarification of the objectives of U.S. policy gave rise to ideas for specific methods of solving the concrete problems of American and world capitalism. Ideas for international economic institutions—the International Monetary Fund (IMF) and the International Bank for Reconstruction and Development (World Bank) were worked out first. (See Phillips.)

The Council had proposed that economic means would play a key role in integrating the Grand Area.[61] In several recommendations during 1941, the CFR's War and Peace Studies groups proposed that international economic and financial institutions were needed to assure the proper functioning of the proposed world economy.[62] Recommendation P-B23 (July 1941) stated that worldwide financial institutions were necessary for the purpose of "stabilizing currencies and facilitating programs of capital investment for constructive undertakings in backward and underdeveloped regions."[63] During the last half of 1941 and in the first months of 1942, the Council developed this idea for the integration of the world.

In October 1941 Winfield W. Riefler of the Economic and Financial Group presented a design for an International Development Authority to stimulate private investment in underdeveloped areas. The Authority would be run by nine directors—three American, three British, and three representing international bodies. A new world judicial organization would settle disputes. The greater investment gained by international guarantees would develop resources and raise living standards in poorer regions and at the same time increase overseas purchasing power and, thus, the demand for United States exports.[64] Following Riefler's scheme was one which Alvin H. Hansen suggested on 1 November 1941: an international Reconstruction Finance Corporation should be jointly established by many governments during the war. This body would also promote investment, both in backward areas and in the more developed countries. The corporation would float bonds guaranteed by the government to tap private money now withheld from foreign investment because of the risk. To guide the investment, an international resources survey would be undertaken to discover where development might most usefully be initiated.[65]

The Council advanced these proposals by drafting a recommendation, dispatching it directly to President Roosevelt and the Department of State...

While it was the Council which initially proposed during 1941 and 1942 the idea of international economic institutions to integrate the new world order, it was Harry Dexter White of the Treasury Department who worked out the actual technical details which led to the International Monetary Fund and the World Bank. Although not a Council member, White probably had contact with its ideas, perhaps through Viner, who was a Treasury adviser, or through Hansen, who was active in many federal agencies. In any event, White produced a memorandum on the subject of both a monetary fund and bank by March 1942.[66] This was the plan which Secretary of the Treasury Morgenthau gave to Roosevelt in mid-May.[67] Following discussions with Secretary Hull, a special interdepartmental committee was established to refine the plan. This was the Cabinet

Committee, which began meeting on 25 May 1942. The Cabinet Committee organized a group of experts, called the American Technical Committee, which did the actual planning work.[68] These two committees, largely responsible for the final form of the Monetary Fund and the World Bank, were centered in the Treasury Department and had only informal ties with the State Department's Advisory Committee on Postwar Foreign Policy. There was a considerable overlapping of personnel, however, between the two groups. White served as the Treasury Department's man on the economic subcommittee of the Advisory Committee. Acheson, Berle, Feis, Pasvolsky of the State Department, and Cohen of the White House staff were on either the Cabinet Committee or the American Technical Committee, which White chaired. The Council was well represented on these latter two committees by the last three men and by Hansen, who attended many of the Technical Committee's meetings.[69] A full-blown international conference to establish a monetary fund and world bank convened at Bretton Woods, New Hampshire in 1944 creating institutions whose aim was integration of the expanded Grand Area states. (See Frieden.)

The Council and the Origins of the United Nations

Council leaders recognized that in an age of rising nationalism around the world, the United States had to avoid the onus of big-power imperialism in its implementation of the Grand Area and creation of one open door world. Isaiah Bowman first suggested a way to solve the problem of maintaining effective control over weaker territories while avoiding overt imperial conquest. At a Council meeting in May 1942, he stated that the United States had to exercise the strength needed to assure "security," and at the same time "avoid conventional forms of imperialism."[70] The way to do this, he argued, was to make the exercise of that power international in character through a United Nations body.[71] As we shall see below, the Council planners had a central role in the creation of this United Nations organization.

The planning of the United Nations can be traced to the secret steering committee established by Secretary Hull in January 1943. This informal Agenda Group, as it was later called, was composed of Hull, Davis, Taylor, Bowman, Pasvolsky, and, until he left the government in August 1943, Welles.[72] All of them, with the exception of Hull, were members of the Council on Foreign Relations. They saw Hull regularly to plan, select, and guide the labors of the Department's Advisory Committee. It was, in effect, the coordinating agency for all the State Department postwar planning...[73]

In late 1943, the Agenda Group began to draft the U.S. proposal for a United Nations organization to maintain international peace and security. The position eventually taken at the Dumbarton Oaks Conference was prepared during the seven-month period from December 1943 to July 1944. Once the group had produced a draft for the United Nations and Hull had approved it, the Secretary requested three distinguished lawyers to rule on its constitutionality. Myron C. Taylor, now on the Council's board of directors, was Hull's intermediary to Charles Evans Hughes, retired chief justice of the Supreme Court, John W. Davis, Democratic presidential candidate in 1924, and Nathan L. Miller, former Republican governor of New York. Hughes and Davis were both Council members and John W. Davis had served as president of the Council from 1921 to 1933 and a director since 1921. The three approved the plan, and on 15 June 1944, Hull, Stettinius, Davis, Bowman, and Pasvolsky discussed the draft with President Roosevelt. The chief executive gave his consent and issued a statement to the American people that very afternoon.[74]

Although the Charter of the United Nations underwent some modification in negotiations with other nations at the Dumbarton Oaks and San Francisco conferences during 1944 and 1945, one historian concluded that "the substance of the provisions finally written into the Charter in many cases reflected conclusions reached at much earlier stages by the United States government."[75] The Department of State was clearly in charge of these propositions within the U.S. government, and the role of the Council on Foreign Relations within the Department of State was, in turn, very great indeed.[76] The Council's power was unrivaled. It had more information, representation, and decision making power on postwar questions than the Congress, any executive bureaucracy except the Department of State, or other private group.[77] It had a very large input into decisions on the International Monetary Fund, the World Bank, and the United Nations. The formulators of the Grand Area had indeed been able to gain positions of strength and put their plans for United States hegemony into effect.

The CFR-Ruling Class Conception of the "National Interest"

Leaders of the United States have always declared that the foremost objective of their policies has been the promotion of the country's collective interest—the "national interest." As Secretary of State Charles Evans Hughes put it in the 1920s, "foreign policies are not built upon abstractions. They are the result of practical conceptions of national interest.[78] The national interest is rarely an objective fact, however, as is indicated by the truism that in every country it is always redefined after a revolution.... Since those in power define the national interest as the preservation of the existing set of economic, social, and political relationships and of their own rule, the national interest in a capitalist society is little more than the interest of the upper class. The Council, as a key organization of this class, was in the lead in defining its class interest. One has to transcend its values, assumptions, and goals in order to question its formulation of the national interest.

The U.S. capitalist class, through the Council, had proposed to preserve and extend U.S. capitalism by a policy of empire-building—overseas expansion of United States power....It was clear, however, that there was an alternative...The fact was that the need for such export markets could be largely obviated by public ownership of the chief means of production, and democratic planning to assure all in the country both employment and adequate consumption.

The United States was the most self-sufficient nation in the world during the 1930s and 1940s. Council theorists recognized this fact during the depression. In 1937 Eugene Staley wrote a book called *Raw Materials in Peace and War* under the auspices of the Council-dominated American Coordinating Committee for International Studies.... Staley concluded that in regard to raw materials the "United States is more nearly capable than any other great power (unless it be the Soviet Union) of meeting its normal demands from resources within its boundaries."[79]...

The ruling class, through the Council, had successfully put forward a particular conception of the United States national interest. This perspective did not in reality uphold the general interest of the people of the nation, but rather the special interests of a capitalist economic system controlled by and benefiting the upper class. Simply stated, the Council theoreticians argued that the United States needed living space to maintain the existing system without fundamental changes in the direction of socialism and planning. Council member Henry R. Luce put the issue more bluntly when he stated in his famous February 1941 *Life* article that "tyrannies may require a large amount of living space. But Freedom requires and will require far greater living space than Tyranny."[80]

Appendix
Members of the Advisory Committee on Postwar Foreign Policy

Member	Primary Occupation (Position at time)	Importance in official postwar planning	Council member during war	Known level of CFR involvement	Involved in War and Peace Studies?
Cordell Hull	Politician (Secretary of State)	Great	No	--	No
Sumner Welles	Career government official (Undersecretary of State)	Great	Yes	Slight	No
Norman H. Davis	Banker (Ambassador-at-Large)	Great	Yes	Great	Yes
Myron C. Taylor	Corporation Executive	Great	Yes	Great	No
Isaiah Bowman	University President (Johns Hopkins)	Great	Yes	Great	Yes
Leo Pasvolsky	Economist (Special Assistant to the Secretary of State in Charge of Postwar Planning)	Great	Yes	Moderate	Yes
Dean Acheson	Lawyer (Asst. Sec. of State specializing in economic matters)	Great	No, but had joined by 1948	--	No
Hamilton Fish Armstrong	Editor	Great	Yes	Great	Yes
Adolf A. Berle	Lawyer (Asst. Sec. of State)	Great	No, but had joined by 1946	Slight	No
Benjamin V. Cohen	Lawyer (State Dept. Officer)	Moderate	Yes	Moderate	Yes
Herbert Feis	Economist (State Department Advisor on Intl. Econ. Affairs)	Moderate	Yes	Moderate	No
Green H. Hackworth	Lawyer (State Dept. legal advisor)	Moderate	No	--	No
Harry C. Hawkins	Economist (Chief of Division of Commercial Policy, State Dept.)	Moderate	No	--	No
Ann O'Hare McCormick*	Journalist	Moderate	No	--	No

* McCormick had no direct relationship to the Council since women were then barred from that body. She was on the Editorial Board of the *New York Times*.

FOOTNOTES

Abbreviations found in Notes

FDRI	Franklin D. Roosevelt Library, Hyde Park, New York.
HLWRP	Hoover Library on War, Revolution, and Peace, Stanford Ca.
HSTI	Harry S. Truman Library, Independence, Missouri.
JHUL	Johns Hopkins University Library, Baltimore, Maryland.
MDLC	Manuscript Division, Library of Congress, Wash. D.C.
NUL	Northwestern University Library, Evanston, Illinois.
PUL	Princeton University Library, Princeton New Jersey.
R.G. 59	Record Group 59, Records of the Department of State, National Archives, Wash.
SUL	Stanford University Library, Stanford, California.
YUL	Yale University Library, New Haven, Connecticut.

1. John W. Davis and George O. May to Philip C. Jessup, 22 June 1944, Philip C. Jessup Papers, Box 114, MDLC.

2. William Diebold, Jr. interview, 1 November 1972; Isaiah Bowman to Lionel Curtis, 2 November 1939, Franklin D. Roosevelt Papers, President's Personal File 5575, FDRL.

3. George S. Messersmith, "Memorandum of Conversation, September 12, 1939," Decimal File 811.43 Council of Foreign Relations/220 Exhibit A, R.G. 59; Walter H. Mallory to Laurence H. Shoup, 5 June 1973.

4. CRF, *The War and Peace Studies of the Council on Foreign Relations, 1939-1945* (New York: CFR, 1946), pp. 19-24.

5. *Ibid.,* pp. 9-24.

6. *Ibid.,* pp.12-13. The State, War, and Navy Departments were directly represented. Viner was a Treasury Department adviser during these years, Hansen headed postwar planning at the Federal Reserve Board, and Upgren joined the Commerce Department in 1941 to head postwar planning there.

7. Harley Notter, *Postwar Foreign Policy Preparation, 1939-1945,* (Washington D.C., 1949), p. 56, footnote 24.

8. *St. Louis Post-Dispatch,* 22 September 1940: 3C; Robert A. Divine, *Reluctant Belligerent: America's Entry into World War II* (New York, 1965), p. 90; Mark L. Chadwin, *The Hawks of World War II* (Chapel Hill, 1968), pp. 74, 78, 86, and 94; Francis P. Miller, *Man From the Valley* (Chapel Hill, 1971), pp. 95, 102.

9. Divine, 1965: p. 90; Chadwin, 1968: pp. 74, 78, 86, and 94; Miller, 1971: pp. 95, 98, and 102; William L. Langer and S. Everett Gleason, *The Challenge to Isolation, 1937-1940* (New York, 1952), pp. 749-751.

10. Divine, *op.cit.,* p. 90; Chadwin, *op.cit.,* p. 74; T.R. Fehrenback, *FDR's Undeclared War 1939-1941* (New York, 1967), p. 160.

11. Divine, *op.cit.,* p. 91.

12. CFR, *By-Laws with List of Officers and Members,* 1938; Francis P. Miller Interview, 13 October 1972; Diebold Interview, *op.cit.*

13. Memorandum E-B18, 6 September 1940, CFR, *War-Peace Studies,* NUL; memorandum E-B18, supplement I, 6 September 1940, CFR, *War-Peace Studies,*

NUL. E-B18, supplement I is fifty pages long and illustrates well the very detailed work being done by the Group.

14. *Ibid.*

15. Memorandum E-B18, supplement I, *op.cit.*

16. Memorandum E-A10, 19 October 1940, CFR, *War-Peace Studies,* Baldwin Papers, Box 117, YUL.

17. Memorandum E-A11, 23 November 1940, CFR, *War-Peace Studies,* HLWRP; a memorandum of the Territorial Group (T-B20, 11 October 1940) had previously raised this possiblity, the aim being to stop Japanese expansion into the Western Pacific. It argued that such a move by Japan might cut off United States sources of raw materials in Southeast Asia.

18. Memorandum E-A11, *op.cit.;* memorandum E-A12, 14 December 1940, CFR, *War-Peace Studies,* HLWRP.

19. Memorandum E-B26, 15 January 1941, CFR, *War-Peace Studies,* NUL.

20. *Ibid.*

21. *Ibid.*

22. A copy of E-B26 with a note attached addressed to Secretary Hull.

23. Langer and Gleason, *The Undeclared War, 1940-1941* (New York, 1953), p. 490, footnote 62, p. 493. A total embargo on Japan was instituted by the United States, Britain, and the Netherlands in late July 1941.

24. Memorandum E-A17, 14 June 1941, CFR, *War-Peace Studies,* HLWRP.

25. Memorandum E-B24, *24 July 1941, CFR, War-Peace Studies,* NUL.

26. Memorandum T-A14, 17 June 1941, CFR, *War-Peace Studies,* Baldwin Papers, YUL.

27. Memorandum E-B34, 24 July 1941, CFR, *War-Peace Studies,* NUL.

28. *Ibid.*

29. Memorandum E-B34, 24 July 1941, CFR, *War-Peace Studies,* NUL.

30. Memorandum E-B34, 24 July 1941, CFR, *War-Peace Studies,* NUL.

31. Sumner Welles, *Seven Decisions that Shaped History* (New York, 1951), pp. 89, 91. Also see Franklin D. Roosevelt, "Defense and the Far West," *Vital Speeches of the Day,* 7 (15 August 1941), pp. 649-650; Langer and Gleason, 1953, p. 646; F.C. Jones, *Japan's New Order in East Asia: Its Rise and Fall, 1937-1945* (London, 1954), p. 247; Joseph C. Grew, *Turbulent Era: A Diplomatic Record of Forty Years, 1904-1945,* vol. II (Boston, 1952), p. 1259.

32. United States Department of State, *Foreign Relations,* 1941, vol. I., pp. 355-356.

33. Langer and Gleason, 1953, pp. 29. 52; Nobutaka Ike, *Japan's Decision for War, Records of the 1941 Policy Conferences* (Stanford, 1967), pp. 78, 162.

34. Jones, *op.cit.,* p. 224; Akira Iriye, *Across the Pacific: An Inner History of American-East Asian Relations* (New York, 1967), pp. 201, 207-209; Divine, *Causes and Consequences of World War II* (Chicago, 1969), pp. 115; Ike, *op.cit.,* XIX and pp. 78-81.

35. Paul W. Schroeder, *The Axis Alliance and Japanese-American Relations, 1941* (Ithaca, 1958), pp. 52-53.

36. *Ibid.;* Welles, *op.cit.* p. 81; Roosevelt, *op.cit.,* p. 650

37. Also see Langer and Gleason, 1953, p. 862; Arnold A. Offner (comp.), *America and the Origins of World War Two, 1933-1941* (Boston, 1971), pp. 149-153; Arthur S. Lonk, *American Epoch: A History of the United States Since the 1890's* (New York, 1963), vol. II: pp. 506-507.

38. Memorandum E-B33, 20 June 1941, CFR, *War-Peace Studies,* NUL.

39. Iriye, *op.cit.,* p. 219; Cordell Hull, *Memoirs* (London, 1948), Vol. II: p. 1083.

40. Langer and Gleason, 1953, pp. 915, 935; Robert E. Sherwood, *Roosevelt and Hopkins: An Intimate History* (New York, 1948) p. 428.

41. Richard W. Leopold, *the Growth of American Foreign Policy* (New York, 1962), p. 591.

42. Langer and Gleason, 1953, pp. 913, 932.

43. Langer and Gleason, 1953, pp. 860-887; Leopold, 1962, p. 592.

44. Raymond Esthus, "President Roosevelt's Commitment to Britain to Intervene in a Pacific War," in *America and the Origins of World War II, 1933-1941,* Offner (comp.) op. cit. pp. 217, 220.

45. Welles, op. cit. p. 182.

46. Table compiled from Laurence H. Shoup, "Shaping the National Interest: The Council on Foreign Relations, the Department of State, and the Origins of the Postwar World, 1939-1943," Evanston, Illinois, Northwestern University, Ph.D. Dissertation (history), 1974, pp. 201-205.

47. Notter, 1949, p. 172.

48. *Ibid.* , p. 247.

49. Memorandum E-A18 (19 July 1941, CFR, *War-Peace Studies*, Baldwin Papers, YUL.

50. Memorandum E-B32, 17 April 1941, CFR, *War-Peace Studies,* NUL.

51. Langer and Gleason, 1953, p. 681; Theodore A. Wilson, *The First Summit: Roosevelt and Churchill at Placentia Bay 1941* (Boston, 9169), p. 173.

52. Bowman to Armstrong, 15 December 1941, Bowman Papers, Armstrong File, JHUL.

53. Memorandum T-A21, 16 January 1942, CFR, *War-Peace Studies* Baldwin Papers, YUL.

54. Minutes S-3 of the Security Subcommittee, Advisory Committee on Postwar Foreign Policy, 6 May 1942, Notter File, Box 77, R.G. 59. As early as October 1940, Davis had argued that the British Empire was collapsing and that the United States would be the "heirs of the Empire." See Nancy H. Hooker (ed.) *The Moffat Papers: Selections from the Diplomatic Journals of Jay Pierrepont Moffat (Cambridge, Mass., 1956), p. 333.*

55. *Minutes S-3 of the Security Subcommittee, Advisory Committee on Postwar Foreign Policy, 6 May 1942, Notter File, Box 77, R.G. 59.*

56. *Ibid.*

57. See James Weinstein, *The Corporate Ideal in the Liberal State,* (Boston, 1968), for a detailed study of corporate upper class concern with this question during the early years of this century. See William Appleman Williams, *The Tragedy of American Diplomacy* (New York, 1972) for the development of this dependency during the nineteenth and twentieth centuries.

58. This was true of top-level men like Cordull Hull, Sumner Welles, and Henry Morgenthau, Jr., as well as of the members of the State Department planning committees. Welles said, for instance, that economic barriers caused "the present world collapse." See United States, Department of State, *Foreign Relations 1941,* 1:353; for an example of Hull's view, see United States, Department of State, *Foreign Relations 1942,* 1:201-202; Morganthau stated in May 1942 that a lack of economic cooperation would cause another world war. United States, Department of State, *Foreign Relations 1942,* 1:177.

59. E-Document 1, "Postwar Economic Problems," 19 February 1942, Notter File, Box 88, R.G. 59.

60. "S Minutes 16" of the Security Subcommittee, Advisory Committee on Postwar Foreign Policy, 23 October 1942, Notter File, Box 76, R.G. 59.

61. Memorandum E-B34, 24 July 1941, CFR, *War-Peace Studies,* NUL.

62. Memorandum P-B23, 10 July 1941, CFR, *War-Peace Studies*, NUL.

63. Memorandum P-B23, 10 July 1941, CFR, *War-Peace Studies*, NUL.

64. Memorandum E-A21, 11 October 1941, CFR, *War-Peace Studies*, Baldwin Papers, YUL.

65. Memorandum E-A22, 1 November 1941, CFR, *War-Peace Studies*, Baldwin Papers, YUL.

66. John P. Young, "Developing Plans for an International Monetary Fund and a World Bank," *Department of State Bulletin 23* (November 1950), p. 779.

67. United States, Department of State, *Foreign Relations 1942*, 1:174-177.

68. Notter, 1949, pp. 141-143; Young, 1950, p. 779 ft. nt. 3.

69. *Ibid.*

70. Memorandum T-A25, May 20, 1942, CFR, *War-Peace Studies*, HLWRP.

71. *Ibid.*

72. Notter, 1949, pp. 169-170; entry for 4 January 1943 in Harley A. Notter, "Recollections: Notes January 1942-December 1943," Notter File, Box 1, R.G. 59.

73. Notter, 1949, p. 171.

74. *Ibid.* p. 247; Divine, *Second Chance:* The Triumph of Internationalism in America (New York, 1967), p. 192.

75. Ruth B. Russell, *A History of the United Nations Charter: The Role of the United States, 1940-1945* (Wash. D.C. 1958), p. 2.

76. *Ibid.* pp 21-22, 205.

77. The Council continued to have access to all top secret information during the 1942-1944 years, despite continued warnings by Pasvolsky to his staff about the need to maintain the "strictest confidence" about the postwar planning work of the department. Even the existence and organization of the committees, as well as their thinking, were "not under any circumstances to be the subjects of comment to anyone outside the members of the Division itself." Memorandum, Pasvolsky to staff members of the Division of Special Research, 22 December 1942, Notter File, Box 4, R.G. 59.

78. Quoted in Charles A. Beard, *The Idea of National Interest* (New York, 1934), p. 1.

79. Eugene Staley, *Raw Materials in Peace and War* (New York, 1937), p. 37.

80. Henry R. Luce, "The American Century," *Life* 10 (17 February 1941) p. 64. Luce's article is reprinted in John A. Garraty and Robert A. Divine, *Twentieth Century America: Contemporary Documents and Opinions* (Boston, 1968), pp. 470-476.

chapter two

BILDERBERG AND THE WEST
Peter Thompson*

Introduction

Western Europe, the United States and Canada have experienced a considerable degree of coherence in policy and outlook since World War II. Foreign policies, particularly, have been coordinated *vis-a-vis* both socialist countries and the colonies and the neocolonies of the Third World. Such cooperation, whatever its limitations, had never before been achieved although these same countries had long been the dominant world powers.

The U.S.-led Western empire of the last four decades has worked through a number of international economic, political, and strategic institutions, some of which claim to be universal: the United Nations, the International Monetary Fund (IMF), the World Bank, the Organization for Economic Cooperation and Development (OCED), the North Atlantic Treaty Organization (NATO). But it is the secret gatherings of powerful West Europeans and North Americans known as the Bilderberg meetings which have filled, to some degree, the need to *coordinate* the transnational system of the West.

Bilderberg's name comes from the group's first meeting place, the Hotel de Bilderberg of Oosterbeek, Holland, in May 1954. Participants in the meetings over the last twenty-five years have included most of the top ruling class actors in the postwar history of Western Europe and North America (unlike the Trilateral Commission, Japanese participants are excluded). Prince Bernhard of the Netherlands remained Bilderberg chairman until he was implicated in the Lockheed bribery scandal.[1] The handling of the embarassing

*This article is edited from the preliminary draft of a longer work by Peter Thompson of the London Collective, State Research (9 Poland St. London, W1, UK). The author would like to thank Holly Sklar for turning a mass of research into an article. Extensive footnotes with additional supplemental material as well as references appear at the end of the article.

Bernhard revelations was a private affair, like all of Bilderberg's operations. The 1976 meeting scheduled for April 22-25 in Hot Springs, Virginia was cancelled to avoid undo publicity and Bernhard resigned his position in August 1976. In April 1977 the annual gatherings resumed, continuing through the present.

There is certainly room for disagreement about the role of the Bilderberg meetings in the flow of events since its founding in 1954. In my view, Bilderberg is neither a world super-government; nor is it merely a club where incidental shoptalk takes place, as some portray it. Top executives from the world's leading multinational corporations meet with top national political figures at Bilderberg meetings to consider jointly the immediate and long-term problems facing the West. Bilderberg itself is not an executive agency. However, when Bilderberg participants reach a form of consensus about what is to be done, they have at their disposal powerful transnational and national instruments for bringing about what it is they want to come to pass. That their consensus design is not always achieved is a reflection of the strength of competing resisting forces—outside the ruling capitalist class and within it.

Bilderberg is not the only means of Western collective management of the world order; it is part of an increasingly dense system of transnational coordination. The foreign policies of nation-states, particularly economic and monetary policies, have always been a highly elitist matter. Policy options are proposed, reviewed, and executed within the context of a broad bipartisan consensus that is painstakingly managed by very small circles of public and private elites.

Democratic interference in foreign policy is avoided, in so far as possible, throughout the Western capitalist democracies. Where necessary, a consensus is engineered on issues which must get congressional/parliamentary approval, but wherever possible executive agreeements between governments are used to avoid the democratic process altogether.[2] Nonetheless, in the long run, orchestration of affirmative public opinion on foreign policy matters is often necessary for the effective pursuit of foreign policy objectives. Failure to cultivate public support can lead to trouble for the policy makers when—as in the case of the Vietnam War—broad sectors of the public democratically challenge ruling class policy. More commonly, though, policies are pursued with impunity.

Bodies like the U.S. Council on Foreign Relations (CFR); the British Royal Institute for International Affairs, commonly known as "Chatham House"; and transnational counterparts like Bilderberg and the Trilateral Commission play a crucial role in formulating policy directions, molding establishment consensus, and even testing for likely opposition. These institutions propogate the resulting policy positions throughout their network of authoritative channels (university publications, public officials, forums, etc.) setting the limits of respectable foreign policy debate.[3] How well or poorly this elite apparatus works can be evaluated by considering postwar U.S. policy toward Europe and by assessing the role of Bilderberg in pushing Western Europe toward closer regional unification and toward deeper alliance with the United States and Canada.

Reconstructing Europe

Europe—a region whose shape has been greatly altered with each World War—has long been a concern of the U.S. ruling class. In the 1920s U.S. leaders pushed for a "United States of Europe," a stable entity which would be far more appropriate for a managed world economy.[4] But, a unified Europe never materialized and neither did a smoothly functioning international economic system. Intracapitalist rivalries and beggar-thy-neighbor economic policies marked the 1920s and led into the global depression of the 1930s. The withdrawal of U.S. loans to Germany in 1928 for the purpose of speculating with these funds on the booming New York Stock exchange was a factor in the German economic slump and the rise of Hitler. Even after Munich, future Bilderberg members were appeasers of Hitler and of his fascist supporters in their own countries.* Moreover, U.S. firms such as Standard Oil of New Jersey (Exxon) continued to cooperate with Nazi Germany through German firms such as I.G. Farben even after the Council on Foreign Relations and the Roosevelt Administration had decided upon war with Hitler.[5]

The 1930s demonstrated the need for multinational management of world capitalism. This vision was brought to fruition in the 1940s.[6] As the "arsenal of democracy," the U.S. had supplied war materiel to the Allies (including the Soviet Union) under a scheme called lend-lease. This allowed the transfer of materiel without immediate payment, but fostered enormous indebtedness. In 1945,

---

*ed. note: The Munich Pact, an agreement signed in 1938 in Munich, Germany by Great Britain, France, Italy, and Germany ceded the Czech Sudentenland to Nazi Germany. The pact is regarded as the epitome of mistaken political appeasement for shortly thereafter Hitler invaded Prague, the capital of Czechoslovakia. The lesson enshrined in Western strategic thought was that if aggression was not blocked at the outset it would escalate. President Johnson, for example, called up the memory of Munich in justifying the "domino theory" for Southeast Asia; President Carter to rationalize the harsh (hysterical) U.S. response to Soviet intervention in Afganistan in early 1980.

the U.S. abruptly cut off lend-lease to both the Soviet Union and Britain leaving them in precarious straits and affording the U.S. additional leverage in architecting the postwar world.

The central feature of U.S. policy toward Europe was its perception of Europe as a unified economy and polity; Germany was recognized to be of primary importance. The decision to divide Germany into East and West was taken by future Bilderbergers. Denazification was forgotten in the push to expand the western zone of Germany as the core of the European economy.[7] (The German Federal Republic came into being in 1949, with Bonn as the capital.)

Once European reconstruction was seen as urgent for the solidifying of the West, steps followed quickly. In June 1947, U.S. Secretary of State, General George C. Marshall, announced that if the European countries *jointly* produced one plan for European recovery the U.S. would finance it. By providing Europe with the wherewithal to buy goods and services from the U.S., the foundation for the United States of Europe would be established and the risk of postwar depression in the U.S. would be forestalled.[8] The so-called Marshall Plan was approved by Congress in 1948, with $17 billion in aid for European recovery.

The Marshall Plan pushed for rapid removal of economic controls and promoted political, economic, and military integration of Europe. The Organization of European Economic Cooperation (OEEC) prepared the joint plan submitted to General Marshall and coordinated intergovernmental assessment of national economic policies. The OEEC was transformed into the Organization for Economic Cooperation and Development (OECD) in 1961, with the U.S. and Canada included as fully participating members. The European Coal and Steel Community (ECSC)—a common market in coal, iron, and steel—was formed in 1950, removing a major historic reason (disputes over industrial resources) for French-German warfare. The ECSC was supplemented by the broader European Economic Community (EEC) known as the "Common Market." The EEC, established with the Rome Treaty in 1957, was designed to eliminate market barriers and unify trade and farm policies, creating one large free-trade zone. The Common Market's six original member nations—France, West Germany, Italy, Belgium, the Netherlands, and Luxembourg, were joined by Britain, Denmark and Ireland in 1972. (In May 1979, Greece was elected as the tenth member, effective as of January 1981. Spain and Portugal may follow—ed.)

Postwar strategic alliances were also being strengthened. The Truman Doctrine had been enunciated by President Truman in March 1947: the U.S. would provide assistance for combatting internal or external Communist threats anywhere in the world. Quickly, the U.S. replaced Britain in aiding Greece and Turkey. This was the start of a chain of military alliances, the most important of which is the North Atlantic Treaty Organization (NATO). NATO requires its thirteen European members to jointly assess their military requirements with Canada and the United States. It is the core of Western military planning; together with the Marshall Plan NATO served as the basis for the making of *Atlantic Europe*—the Europe closely integrated in the Atlantic Alliance with the United States. The *European Movement* led by Joseph Retinger and other Bilderberg founders became the unofficial political arm of Atlantic Europe, as we will see in the following section.

Bilderberg is Founded

> Bilderberg has its inception in the brilliant brain of Dr. Joseph Retinger...an extraordinary character who flitted through Europe talking on intimate terms with Prime Ministers, labour leaders, industrial magnates, revolutionaries and intellectuals—in short all the non-Communist rulers and would-be rulers of the free nations of Europe.[9]

During World War II, Retinger was top aide to General Sikorski, head of the Polish government in exile in London. After discussions with several men who were to become postwar leaders in the European Movement (including Bilderbergers van Zeeland and Pipinelis mentioned below), Retinger "suggested regular meetings of the foreign ministers of the Continental countries."[10] In these meetings, from October 1942 to 1944, the postwar customs union Benelux (Belgium, Netherlands, and Luxembourg) was born; Benelux represented an early move toward postwar European unity.

After the war, Retinger explained his concern for European unification in a meeting at Chatham House: "The end of the period during which the white man spread his activities over the whole globe saw the Continent itself undergoing a process of internal disruption," he explained. At the end of two World Wars "there are no big powers left in continental Europe, [whose] inhabitants after all, represent the most valuable human element in the world." Europeans, Retinger suggested, had rejected both Hitler's New Order and Communism; but the permanent solution to European weakness was to move towards a federal union of neighboring European countries, in which the states would "relinquish part of their sovereignty."[11] At this time Retinger was secretary general of Belgian Prime Minister Paul van Zeeland's Independent League for Economic Cooperation (ILEC; also called the Economic League for European Cooperation ELEC, and other varients). ILEC later became one of the constituent organizations of the European Movement and Retinger became its secretary general. Soon after his Chatham House speech, Retinger talked to W. Averell Harriman, U.S. ambassador to England, who arranged for him to go to the United States to secure U.S. support for ILEC:

> I found in America a unanimous approval for our ideas among financiers, businessmen and politicians. Mr. Leffingwell, senior partner in J.P. Morgan's [bank—Leffingwell preceeded John J. McCloy* and David Rockefeller as the CFR's chairman of the board 1946-53 and had been a CFR director since 1927]. Nelson and David Rockefeller, Alfred Sloan, Chairman of the Dodge Motor Company, Charles Hook, President of the American Rolling Mills Company, Sir William Wiseman, partner in Kuhn Loeb, George Franklin [Rockefeller in-law, executive director of the CFR 1953-71 and Trilateral Commission coordinator] and especially my old friend Adolf Berle Jr. were all in favor, and Berle agreed to lead the American section [of ILEC]. John Foster Dulles [Secretary of State under Eisenhower] also agreed to help us."

Dulles and Berle had both assisted the wartime exile governments. "Later on," says Retinger, "whenever we needed any assistance for the European Movement, Dulles was among those in America who helped us most."[12]

Returning to Europe, Retinger took up his job as secretary general of the European Movement while the Marshall Plan was getting under way. The European Movement (EM) consisted of a series of existing pro-European organizations with a central apparatus and national council super-imposed upon it. Thanks to the importance of European unity in U.S. policy, the EM received considerable support from U.S. government secret funds and private sources via the American Committee for a United Europe (ACUE)—and other institutions.[13]

---

*John J. McCloy, who initiated the European Youth Campaign, was the top wartime planner of civil affairs in Europe. He revamped the World Bank to suit Wall Street wishes as its president 1947-49. (See Bruce Nissen's article in, Steve Weissman, *The Trojan Horse*, Ramparts Press, 1973, pp. 48-51). He then became U.S. High Commissioner for West Germany, 1949-52. Apparently he was also Eisenhower's first preference for secretary of state, but Senator Robert Taft vetoed this, claiming that every Republican candidate for president since 1936 had been nominated by the Chase Bank. (Peter Collier and David Horowitz, *The Rockefeller's*, Signet, 1976, p. 270). McCloy was chairman of the board of Ford Foundation 1953-65 and with Shepard Stone made it into a powerful force in international affairs. McCloy became chairman of the Chase Manhattan Bank 1953-60 and of the CFR until David Rockefeller took over in 1970. (McCloy was also a Warren Commission member).

As Retinger explains it the Cold War produced in "the 'Western World'...the necessity of an ever closer collaboration to protect their moral and ethical values, their democratic institutions and even their independence against the growing Communist threat." The U.S., Retinger went on, had taken the lead with the Marshall Plan and NATO had followed on the heels of the Truman Doctrine in 1949.[14] "...The Korean crisis [the Korean War started in June 1950 and was used to scare Europeans into accepting a rearmament program which included German rearmament] demonstrated how far-seeing the statesmen both in the United States and in Europe had been when they decided on close collaboration between both sides of the Northern Atlantic."[15]

But the road to European unity was difficult. By 1952 the EM was experiencing difficulties as opposing tendencies grew in the U.S. and in Continental Europe. Retinger registers the traditional elitist complaint: "Political decisions of such magnitude are rarely understood by the public at large. The new policy was attacked from the outset by elements in the various countries which saw advantages in sowing discord in the Western ranks...objections based on nationalist and isolationist sentiments were voiced and a certain distrust of the U.S. grew in Western Europe, paralleled by a similar feeling in the U.S. towards the European countries."[16] Retinger observed:

> The rising tide of anti-Americanism in practically every country of Western Europe...was not confined to Communist-influenced or left-wing circles, but was equally prevalent among conservatives and liberals. The United States was disliked, feared, and sneered at with a unanimity that was remarkable...This feeling threatened the solidarity of the Western World's defenses against Communism."[17]

Retinger was one of those who "realized that unless this tendency [of anti-Americanism] were checked forthwith, it could...lead to a disastrous weakening of the Western position."[18] He decided to do something about it; he resigned as secretary general of the European Movement, retaining however an honorary role.

"Retinger always believed that public opinion follows the lead of influential individuals. He much preferred working through a few carefully selected people to publicity on a massive scale."[19] Retinger had plenty of influential friends. He consulted ex-Belgian Prime Minister Paul van Zeeland who had moved on from Benelux and ILEC to become president of the OEEC as well as Paul Rykens, chairman of Unilever, the huge food and soap transnational and wartime adviser to the exiled Dutch government in London. Rykens suggested that Prince Bernhard would be interested also. This proved to be the case.

Retinger's plan for Atlantic-European reconciliation was "to get the leaders of opinion in the most important European countries to make an appraisal of where the Americans were wrong..." Then, "at a completely private meeting of top-level people from both continents ...to present this frank critique to leaders of American opinion and give them an opportunity to answer the indictment."[20] (Retinger's idea was not a particularly new one. A similar process had been undertaken by the CFR and Chatham House.)[21]*

To get the most important figures in the push towards European, U.S., and Canadian unity together with similarly important Americans was a sensible way to set about reaching Atlantic European consensus or at least narrowing the points at issue at a time of growing rift: over German rearmament, U.S. policy in South East Asia, the Cold War, McCarthyism, and the process of European integration. To lay the groundwork for such a gathering a European critique was prepared of U.S. policy and behavior.[24] Prince Bernhard sent it to some American friends, including, most importantly, William Averell Harriman.[25]**

*Retinger, Prince Bernhard and Rykens drew up a list of top people in NATO European countries seeking "two people from each country who would give the conservative and liberal slant."[22] The resulting group consisted of Paul van Zeeland and Alcide de Gasperi (the architect of postwar Italian Christian Democracy), both prime ministers of their countries and presidents of honor in the European movement; Antoine Pinay, right wing French prime minister; three important leaders of anticommunist social democracy: British Labor Party leader Hugh Gaitskell, Max Brauer, the Mayor of Hamburg (heavily involved in German anticommunist Labor politics), and Guy Mollet, leader of the French socialists; Sir Colin Gubbins, who as head of Britain's wartime S.O.E. (Special Operations Executive—the model for the U.S. Office of Strategic Services (OSS) which in turn provided people and practices for the Central Intelligence Agency (CIA) which was set up in 1947) worked closely with Retinger and many of the others in governments in exile in London in his role of assisting antiNazi resistence movements; diplomats Pietro Quaroni of Italy and Panayotis Pipinelis of Greece; top German corporate lawyer Rudolf Miller, who had been chief German economic administrator in the British American "Bizonia" of occupied postwar Germany; and Otto Wolff von Amerongen, the Cologne head of the family firm Otto Wolff A.G. (whose father had been an early and substantial contributor to Hitler); and conservative Danish politician and publisher of Denmark's top daily newspaper, Ole Bjon Kraft, then Denmark's Foreign Minister.[23]

**Harriman's father had left him the Union Pacific Railroad and he went into banking, first establishing W.A. Harriman Bank in the twenties, and than Brown Brothers, Harriman. A friend of Franklin D. Roosevelt's top aide, Harry Hopkins, Harriman worked in the New Deal National Recovery Administration (N.R.A.) and then headed the Business Advisory Council to the U.S. Department of Commerce. Even before the United States declared war on Japan, Harriman was a key figure in building up the war industry. President Roosevelt made him his representative and defense expediter in London before the Lend-Lease Act passed in March 1941.

Connections made (or continued from as far back as World War
I) in the lend lease supply programs between U.S. officials and
businessmen and their European counterparts continued into
postwar European history and do much to illuminate Bilderberg.
Harriman was among the most important Americans in Europe
throughout the war, arranging the lend lease supply of the Soviet
Union as well as Britain. Jean Monnet, "the father of Europe,"
headed the combined British-French supply committee until the
French collapse in summer 1940. Then he went as Churchill's
appointee to the British supply council in Washington and drafted
the "Victory Program" of war production for Roosevelt (in 1943 he
went to Algeria for the joint Munitions Assignments Board,
becoming commissioner on armaments, supply and reconstruction in
the French Committee on National Liberation). Harriman, Monnet,
and the British civil servant Edwin Plowden were NATO's "Three
Wise Men" who, in 1951, worked out the procedures by which
NATO's fifteen nations jointly negotiate their defense budgets to this
day. Early in 1948, Harriman—after serving briefly as Truman's
commerce secretary—became the top Marshall Plan administrator
in Europe, heading the Economic Cooperation Administration
which shaped the domestic and European policies of all the
recipient nations. Jean Monnet was at that time heading the French
Plan for industrial modernization. After completing the NATO job,
Monnet directed the first stage of French, German, Italian and
Benelux economic integration, as head of the European Coal and
Steel community (ECSC). Harriman followed the NATO job by
heading up the Mutual Security Administration (successor to the
Economic Cooperation Administration), the means of rearming
Europe at the peak of the Cold War, until Truman lost the 1952
elections. Retinger had met Harriman "when he came to London in
connection with the Lend Lease Act of 1941."[26]

When consulted about the European critique of the Americans,
Harriman made clear that he thought further activity should wait
until after the 1952 presidential elections (Harriman knew Eisenhower wanted to use the critique against Truman and the Democrats)
Soon after Eisenhower's victory, Prince Bernhard set off to the
United States to organize the American end of Bilderberg. When he
finally got around to seeing his old friend, Walter Bedell (Beetle)
Smith, Eisenhower's wartime chief of staff, Smith, who was then
director of the Central Intelligence Agency (CIA) apparently asked:
"Why the hell didn't you come to me in the first place."[27] Nonetheless
there was some delay due to "Beetle" Smith's role in organizing the
new Eisenhower Administration. Smith "turned the matter over to
C.D. Jackson, special assistant to the president for psychological

warfare" (i.e. presidential coordinator for the CIA)[28] "and things really got going."[29]* Jackson went to John S. Coleman, president of the Burroughs Corporation (which had mass produced the Norden bomb sight during the war.) Coleman was a member of the important Committee for a National Trade Policy and an advocate of total abolition of U.S. tariffs as a means of increasing the economic integration of the West. The Committee for a National Trade Policy undertook to draft an American reply to the European critique. Several of its members presented this reply to the first meeting at the Bilderberg Hotel and Coleman briefly became the U.S. chairman of Bilderberg.

The First Meeting

The first Bilderberg meeting filled the last three days of May 1954. That month in Geneva, the international conference to settle the war in Korea had taken up the question of the future of Vietnam following the Vietnamese defeat of the French at Dien Bien Phu in February.** At their first meeting, Bilderbergers covered the following broad areas, which remained focal points of discussion for successive meetings: Communism and the Soviet Union; Dependent areas and peoples overseas; Economic policies and problems; and European integration and the European Defense Community.***[31]

Among the people at the first meeting were David Rockefeller; J.H. Heinz II (his son, J. Heinz III is one of the two richest members of the U.S. Senate); Dean Rusk, then head of the Rockefeller Foundation and later secretary of state under Kennedy and Johnson; Joseph E. Johnson, head of the Carnegie Endowment for International Peace and U.S. secretary of Bilderberg; Denis

---

*C.D. Jackson had been president of the Committee for a Free Europe which runs the anticommunist Radio Free Europe transmitters in Germany. Previously he was publisher of *Fortune* magazine, managing director of *Time-Life*, and deputy head of psychological warfare at Eisenhower's wartime headquarters. Jackson chaired the U.S. committee of the International Chamber of Commerce on European Economic liberalization. He also worked with a committee of businessmen of the Marshall Plan nations which gave the business seal of approval to the OEEC plans for a European Payments Union. Jackson was well placed, therefore, to get U.S. Bilderbergers together.

**The conference decided on temporary partition of Vietnam pending elections two years later and probable reunification. The United States refused to sign this settlement, engaged as it was in the clandestine construction of the Dien regime in Saigon.

***The European Defense Community (EDC) was rejected by the French National Assembly three months later, so West Germany was brought into NATO instead of France.

Healey, Britains Labor Party minister of defense 1964-70 and Chancellor of the Exchequer (Treasury) 1974-1979;* Winston Churchill's close European collaborator Lord Boothby; and the Bilderberg organizers mentioned above.[32] Prince Bernhard told his biographer that "it was a beautiful meeting because sparks were flying like crazy between Americans like C.D. Jackson and Britishers like Sir Oliver Franks and Denis Healey and Hugh Gaitskell."[33]

McCarthyism was a prime topic of discussion as anticommunism was a Bilderberg hallmark but, nonetheless, McCarthy's demagoguery was seen as dangerous. Many Europeans "seemed genuinely fearful that the United States was heading for a Fascist dictatorship." Jackson calmed their fears.** George McGhee, senior State Department official and Bilderberg executive member, claimed that "the really bad misunderstandings between Europeans and Americans were dissipated at the first Bilderberg."

Bilderberg Participants

From the start, Bilderberg has been run by a very small core group. When, in 1956, a steering committee was set up to help Prince Bernhard arrange further Bilderberg meetings it was not in any way an elected committee. It could not be—because there was no acknowledged membership. Joseph Retinger explained, "the Prince centralizes all Bilderberg activities, appoints all the members of the steering committee and, after consultation with these members, decides on those to be invited to the yearly conferences."[35]

The permanent core group of officials consisted of Prince Bernhard (who remained permanent chairman of meetings until his resignation in August 1976), the U.S. chairman, European and North American secretaries, and a treasurer. Retinger was permanent secretary until his death in 1960, when Bernhard's close associate, E.H. van der Beugel took over. Van der Beugel was director of the

---

*ed. note: Healey was the number two person in the Callaghan government and a key Labor Party link to international organizations. He was, for example, chairperson of the IMF steering group, when, in 1977, the U.K. received a dose of IMF medicine in return for loans. The IMF agreement was pushed through over heated opposition within the Labor Party. Healey has been a member of the Trilateral Commission since 1979.

**Jackson pointed out that in the American system of government and politics, "we are bound to get this kind of supercharged emotional freak from time to time," like Father Coughlin and Huey Long. When a U.S. senator went on the rampage, party discipline was non-existent and there was no way to stop him. "Whether McCarthy dies by an assassin's bullet or is eliminated in the normal American way of getting rid of boils on the body politics...by our next meeting he will be gone from the American scene."[34]

Dutch bureau for the Marshall Plan 1947-52 and became president of KLM Royal Dutch Airlines in 1961. He now heads the International Institute of Strategic Studies in London. Paul Rykens, of Unilever, was treasurer until his death in 1964, when Johannes Meynen, another Bernhard associate took over. C. Fritz Karsten, managing director of the Dutch AMRO (Amsterdam/Rotterdam Bank) is now Bilderberg treasurer. Former British Conservative Prime Minister Lord Hume, has been chairman since Bernhard's demise. The U.S. secretary from the beginning has been Joseph E. Johnson, a member of the State Department's policy planning committee for the Marshall Plan and a CFR director (1950-74) as well as a long time president and trustee of the Carnegie Endowment for International Peace. In 1955, Dean Rusk and W. Bedell Smith[36] of the CIA oversight committee became U.S. co-chairmen, replacing John Coleman of Burroughs. They, in turn, were replaced by Arthur Dean* and H.J. Heinz II in 1957.

Retinger paints this portrait of Bilderberg participants: "Any citizen of a country that believes in defending Western ethical and cultural values, and who himself shares these ideals, is eligible to be invited to Bilderberg meetings." But, "the success of the meetings depends primarily on the level of the participants." So invitations are "only sent to important and generally respected people who through their special knowledge or experience, their personal contacts and their influence in national and international circles can help to further the aims set by Bilderberg." Party political balance is sought, but labor and socialist representation is small, coming from the right-wing of the social democratic sector.** According to Retinger, the composition for any meetings "should reflect the general opinion prevailing in the various countries with regard to the subjects discussed...[so] roughly one third...are politicians and statesmen, one fourth or one fifth businessmen, the remainder consisting of intellectuals, trade unionists, diplomats, officials and other leaders of

---

*Arthur Dean became the senior partner of the top corporate law firm Sullivan and Cromwell when John Foster Dulles became a U.S. Senator in 1944, and Eisenhower's secretary of state in 1953; (another senior partner, Allen Dulles, replaced W. Bedell Smith as director of the CIA). Dean negotiated the Korean War truce at Panmunjon in 1953. He is trustee of the Asia Foundation, well known conduit for CIA money into Asia studies; was a director of the CFR, 1955-72; and chairman of the Institute of Pacific Relations, 1950-52.[37]

**ed note: In reference to the 1977 Bilderberg meeting, it is reported that: "When asked why none of the new Eurocommunists had come one of the organizers answered simply enough: 'we didn't invite them.'" See Steve Weissman and Robert Eringer, "The World's Most Exclusive Club Gets Down to Business," *Seven Days*, 6 June 1977, pp. 22-23.

public opinion such as representatives of the press."[38] Retinger curiously omits specific mention of bankers, who are among Bilderberg's most influential participants. Needless to say, when Retinger speaks of the "general opinion" he means only elite opinion. Retinger's longtime secretary, John Pomian, observes:

> ...during the first 3 or 4 years the all important selection of participants was a delicate and difficult task. This was particularly so as regards politicians. It was not easy to persuade the top office holders to come...Retinger displayed great skill and an uncanny ability to pick out people who in a few years time were to accede to the highest offices in their respective countries...today there are very few figures among governments on both sides of the Atlantic who have not attended at least one of these meetings.[39]

Bilderbergers have played key roles in the development of the European Movement, the unsuccessful European Defense Community, and various organizations—ECSC, EEC, and Euratom, the European Atomic Energy Commission*—subsumed under the European Community. These supranational quasi-technical bodies have real powers of executive action which extend well beyond national political processes. When the European Coal and Steel Community came into being in 1952, Jean Monnet became its "High Authority." Max Kohnstamm, private secretary to Prince Bernhard's mother-in-law, Queen Wilhemina, until 1948, and then head of the German Bureau of the Dutch Foreign Office and Dutch representative in the Schuman Plan (ECSC)** negotiations, became "Secretary to High Authority" under Monnet.[40] Monnet resigned from the ECSC in 1955 to push for further unification through his Action Committee for a United States of Europe (ACUSE). Kohnstamm became the vice-president of ACUSE which had extensive overlaps with Bilderberg.[41] In 1973 Kohnstamm became the first European chairman of the Trilateral Commission, until his resignation at the end of 1975. George Berthoin is another important Bilderberger. He went from the prefecture of Alsace-Lorraine, France to become Monnet's private secretary at the ECSC, 1951-55. Then he left to represent the

---

*The European Atomic Energy Commission was set up at the Messina Conference of 1955 (where the EEC was first agreed to).

**ed. note: "The first new proposal, made explicitly in 1950, 'as the first step in the federation of Europe,' was the Schuman plan to combine the coal and steel production of France and Germany under a common High Authority, open to other European countries." After Britain declined to join the negotiations agreement was reached by France, Germany, Italy, Belgium, the Netherlands, and Luxembourg to set up the ECSC. Cited in William Ashworth, *A Short History of the International Economy*, London: Longman, 1975, p. 284.

ECSC and later the European Community in London. Berthoin has replaced Kohnstamm as European chairman of the Trilateral Commission. Officials of the European Community—normally the president goes—have attended all Bilderberg meetings. A few of these officials include: Walter Hallstein, first EEC president and former German Foreign Affairs Minister; Jean Ray, first president of the unified European Communities; and Rolf Dahrendorf, former Commissioner for External Affairs. Similarly, officials from the OECD, NATO, the IMF, World Bank, and GATT regularly attend. It should come as no surprise, then, that when asked by Prince Bernhard's biographer for an example of a Bilderberg accomplishment, steering committee member, George McGhee (past chairman of policy planning council in the State Department and then undersecretary of state for political affairs in the Kennedy Administration) replied: "I believe you could say the [1957] Treaty of Rome which brought the Common Market into being, was nurtured at these meetings."[42]

From the early 1960s the OECD—Japan joined in 1964—developed into an official forum in which the West worked out global economic issues before taking their common positions to negotiations and forums where Third World and socialist-bloc countries would be represented. Thorkil Kristensen, first OECD secretary general participated in Bilderberg meetings. With Bilderberg guidance, the OECD has solidified its role as the rich nations club; the Trilateral Commission has put forth recommendations for futher enhancing the OECD's role. (The European and U.S. authors of *The Reform of International Institutions,* the 1976 trilateral report in which the OECD is discussed, are Bilderbergers: George Berthoin and Fred Bergsten, current U.S. assistant secretary of the treasury for international affairs).

Let's look more closely at how Bilderberg meetings function. At the meetings "subjects...are introduced by rapporteurs who have prepared papers that are circulated before the meetings...A confidential report is drafted after each conference" for all living participants and past participants. "No names are mentioned," just the speaker's nationality and a short summary of his contributions.[43] Speakers at the meetings are supposed to limit themselves to five minutes.

While some of the participants have known each other for decades, efforts are made to deepen and broaden contacts among Bilderbergers. There is "the unwritten rule that anybody who has ever been to a Bilderberg Conference should be able to feel that he can, in a private capacity, call on any former member he has met." Moreover one sees "at least twenty percent new faces at each meeting" which "makes possible an expanding continuation of association," undoubtedly easing the difficulties of collective management of Western institutions in times of crisis.[44] Informal discussions may well be more significant than formal discussions. "To establish closer contact between participants, it is considered of the utmost importance to have a hotel in a secluded location...at the exclusive disposal of the participants." The only time participants left the Bilderberg Hotel at the first meeting was to go to Prince Bernhard's palace for cocktails. The need for a secluded hotel is usually easily met by each national group that organizes a conference, there being plenty of hotel-owning Bilderbergers (e.g., the 1974 meeting was held at Edmond de Rothschild's Mont d' Arbois Hotel, Megeve, France).

Bilderberg works through a consensus process rather than through formal resolutions and voting.[45] Bilderbergers are in positions of such considerable executive power that if a consensus is reached and acted upon, the advanced capitalist West is likely to act more or less as a unit. Where there is no such consensus, the real interests at stake, and the constantly repeated injunction not to act divisively can produce a similarly cohesive effect. At the 1974 Bilderberg conference in France—six months after the October War and the oil price rise—a British keynote speaker gave "credit for the constructive handling of such a wide range of economic and monetary problems...to the emergence of transnational forces, i.e., effective relationships among individuals and organizations in the private and public sectors." A German participant remarked:

> Half a dozen knowledgeable people had managed, in effect, to set the world's monetary system working again, [after the oil price rise quadrupled OPEC revenues] and it was important to try to knit together our networks of personal contacts. We had to resist institutionalism, bureaucratic red-tape, and the creation of new procedures and committees. *Official bodies should be put in the position of ratifying what had been jointly prepared in advance.*[46] [Behind closed doors, that is. Italics ed.]

The 1950s

Four Bilderberg meetings were held in the first two years. Each began with a review of important events for the West. At the second Bilderberg in March 1955 at Barbizon in France—during the post-Stalin thaw in the Cold War and before the abortive summit meeting between the U.S., USSR, Britain, and France—Bilderbergers discussed "Communist infiltration in various Western countries." Moves to ban Communist parties were in full swing in a number of countries, notably West Germany (successful) and Australia (unsuccessful, but very intimidating). On the same theme, the second agenda item was political, ideological, and economic relations with the uncommitted (for or against the USSR) nations. This was three weeks before the first meeting of the Non-Aligned Nations in Bandung, Indonesia.*

In September 1955 in Germany, Bilderbergers discussed whether further moves towards European and Atlantic cooperation or integration were possible through the structure of the NATO military alliance. NATO already provided joint military planning among thirteen European nations and the U.S. and Canada, and West Germany had just joined. (Eight months later, NATO's top political meeting of foreign ministers of the North Atlantic Council appointed three of their number to report on how to extend NATO nonmilitary cooperation and develop greater Atlantic unity.) It was a busy three days. Participants also dealt with European unity as a separate item; political, strategic, and industrial aspects of atomic energy;[47] reunification of Germany; East-West trade; the expansion of international trade and last but not least, "the political aspects of convertability" of currencies.

Following up their concern with the Bandung Conference of the Non-Aligned Nations a year earlier, the May 1956 Bilderberg meeting devoted itself to the causes of the growth of anti-Western (i.e. antiimperialist) blocs, in particular within the United Nations;** the role of anticolonialism in relations between Asians and the West; a common approach by the Western world toward China and the emergent nations of South and East Asia; the Communist campaign for political subversion or control of the newly emancipated countries of Asia. (No room there for deviant speculations that the Asian liberation movements might in fact be nationally based, much less legitimate).

The time set by the Geneva Accords for elections and reunification of Vietnam was approaching and the West was involved in counterrevolutionary warfare (overtly or covertly) in Vietnam,

---

*ed. note: At the Asian-African Conference held in Bandung, countries first pressed for international recognition as a group of non-aligned nations—that is, neither aligned with (nor dominated by) the West *nor* the Soviet Union. The Conference established principles of "Economic Cooperation" to foster Third World development.

**ed. note: Western elites have grown increasingly upset with the idea that the United Nations is no longer ruled by the Western powers (led by the United States). This frustration is registered within Bilderberg as well as the Trilateral Commission. About Bilderberg's process, Caroline Moorhead observes: "No invitations go out to representatives of the developing countries. 'Otherwise you would simply turn us into a mini-United Nations,' said one person [a Bilderberger] with scorn. And more revealingly, 'we are looking for like-thinking and compatible people. It would be worse to have a club of dopes.' " (Moorehead, "An Exclusive Club, Perhaps Without Power, but Certainly With Influence: The Bilderberg Group," *The Times*, London, 18 April 1977.)

Malaya, Indonesia and the Philippines. Any criticism heard by Bilderbergers at this meeting (and it is hard to see who might have offered it) did not affect the later escalation of the war in Vietnam by the U.S. government whose foreign policy posts were dominated by Bilderbergers and CFR members.* Indeed the Kennedy and Johnson Administrations with Bilderberg/CFR guidance, shifted U.S. military priorities from super-power confrontation to Third World counterinsurgency, making Vietnam their test of "manhood." Although unsuccessful in Vietnam, counterinsurgency led to the installment of numerous pro-West military regimes in Latin America and Southeast Asia.

Shortly after these discussions of the West's problems with the Third World, President Nasser of Egypt nationalized the Suez Canal and the Suez Crisis erupted. Egypt had been effectively a British colony since the canal was built, but the British puppet regime was overthrown by moderately nationalist officers in 1952. In September 1956, the British, French and the Israelis invaded Egypt—without U.S. participation—with the aim of toppling Nasser and installing another puppet regime. The United States refused to support the invasion, forcing the aggressors to retreat, and adhere to U.N. resolution of the conflict. Not surprisingly, when the Bilderbergers met five months later, "at St. Simons, 1957, the French, British, and Americans almost came to blows over Suez," when they discussed what the agenda simply called "the Middle East."[48] Concern over the state of the West (i.e. concern over European unity and unity between Europe and the U.S.) is a constant Bilderberg theme. The Suez Crisis was a perfect example of the disastrous consequences of disunity in the Atlantic Alliance.

Meeting in Italy in October 1957, Bilderbergers explored "unity and division in Western policy" and looked into developments in tropical Africa. In the late fifties there were serious disagreements between the United States and European speakers about the importance to the West of holding the Chinese Islands, Quemoy and Matsu, for Chaing Kai Shek, President of Taiwan. A bit later, the issue of trade with Cuba also produced heated debate. (This issue went far beyond the realm of debate in the early sixties when agents of the CIA sabotaged shipments from England to Cuba.) After Francis Gary Power's CIA U-2 spy plane was shot down, provoking cancellation of the 1960 Kennedy-Krushchev summit meeting, Bil-

*ed. note: Kennedy/Johnson Secretary of Defense Robert MacNamara; Secretary of State Dean Rusk; National Security Adviser McGeorge Bundy; and CIA Directors Allen Dulles, John McCone, and Richard Helms, were all CFR and/or Bilderberg participants and leaders.

derbergers discussed "the world situation after the failure of the Summit."

NATO Strategy

In addition to political disagreements about Cold War strategy, technical matters of military structure, capabilities, and tactics were discussed frequently at Bilderberg meetings. In 1957, the subject of "modern weapons and disarmament in relation to Western security" topped the agenda. (This was soon after Henry Kissinger's book for the Council on Foreign Relations, *Nuclear Weapons and Foreign Policy,* was published.) At this conference Bilderberg stalwart, Denis Healey, later Britain's defense secretary, arranged funding for the London-based Institute of Strategic Studies which began operating in 1958.[49] The renamed International Institute of Strategy Studies was headed by Francois Duchene between 1969 and 1974.

In 1958 the whole meeting was given over to "the future of NATO defense," and in 1961 the question of leadership of the West was split into discussions of "NATO in the world [sic] policy of the member countries" and "the role and control of nuclear weapons within NATO." Problems arose over the creation of common nuclear policy for the alliance without a "European finger on the trigger." The British and French were determined to sustain independent nuclear deterrents; the U.S. opposed this, pushing Europe-based conventional forces instead. At the 1964 meeting "NATO strategy" and "sharing of responsibility for nuclear deterrent" again came up for debate.

In March 1966 Bilderbergers again discussed the question, "should NATO be reorganized and if so, how?" The following year NATO governments finally came around to the American position and adopted officially as NATO strategy "flexible response": meet force with like force. This meant more conventional troops and non-nuclear weaponry. Official doctrine until then was massive retaliation to *any* incursion. But by the latter sixties this automatic Armageddon had lost much of its credibility. NATO was deeply involved in the process of West Germany's *Ostpolitik* which entailed the formal settlement of German boundaries and final ending of World War II. Detente became the theme of the 1970s. Nixon and Brezhnev signed the first SALT Treaty in 1972. In May 1973, in Sweden, the Conference on European Security and Cooperation was then getting underway so the Bilderbergers spent a session discussing their conflicting expectations about it. Eventually, in 1975, it produced the Helsinki Agreement.

The 1960s: Atlantic Economic and Political Problems on the Rise

Each year, but particularly in the early sixties, Bilderbergers argued about the implications of the growing economic strength of the EEC. The EEC's Common Agricultural Policy (CAP), which prevented the U.S. from selling its farm surpluses within the Common Market in order to foster internal agricultural development, was a continuing source of conflict. The U.S. hoped the Common Market would be seen as part of a process toward global tariff reductions and increased economic integration (a process to continue in the Kennedy Round and most recent Tokyo Round of GATT negotiations).[50] French obstructionism was a major Bilderberg preoccupation ever since President de Gaulle had vetoed British entry into the EEC and had withdrawn from NATO military planning. American worries about Europe becoming an independent "Gaullist" superpower were aired. The balance of economic power in the West was shifting.

Throughout the late sixties and seventies, Bilderbergers discussed internal as well as external security and stability. In 1968, Bilderberg was scheduled to take up the issue of "internationalization of business," but other issues were bearing more heavily on the participants. President Johnson had announced his retirement to coincide with the initiation of Peace Talks on Vietnam (with Harriman as chief U.S. negotiator). The student revolt in France was to bring that country to a halt within a fortnight with worker support.

Having missed the boat in its programming for 1968, Bilderberg attempted to catch up in 1969 by addressing "elements of instability in Western society." At that meeting participants also worked through disagreements in the West over the handling of the 1968 Russian invasion of Czechoslovakia. In 1970, just before the Nixon/Kissinger invasion of Cambodia which toppled neutralist Prince Sihanouk and produced a storm of antiwar protest on and off university campuses, Bilderbergers set themselves to strategically considering the "future function of the university in our society." Numerous Bilderbergers were (and are) involved in education. From the U.S., participants included Paul Samuelson, MIT professor, noted author and government consultant in economics and resource planning; Graham T. Allison, now dean of the Kennedy School at Harvard University; and Andrew Cordier, dean of the School of International Affairs at Columbia University 1962-68, and acting president during the student occupation of 1968 among others.[51]

In April 1971 Bilderbergers extended their preoccupation with "current problems of social instability" into the more creative realm of "the contribution of business in dealing with" these problems. "The possibility of a change of the American role in the world and its consequences" was another issue of importance. In August 1971 Nixon formally broke with central agreements of the postwar economic system so carefully architected by the Bilderbergers and other elite planners. (See Frieden.)

Bilderberg and the Trilateral Commission

By the 1970s, Bilderbergers were regularly discussing trilateralism. But, while the Trilateral Commission emphasized economic matters, military/strategic discussions were commonplace at Bilderberg.

Such differences reflect changed historical conditions. Bilderberg originated as part of the thrust toward Western coordination in the midst of the Cold War. Anticommunism provided the ideological justification of joint military planning through Nato. Successive secretary generals of NATO have all been regular Bilderberg attendees. The Trilateral Commission emerged at a time when intracapitalist economic and north-south (industrialized West-Third World) problems were threatening to tear the system apart.

Bilderberg and the Trilateral Commision have somewhat different modes of operation. While both organizations have closed meetings, Bilderberg is far more secretive in all its activities.* Bilderberg does not publicly lobby for its views as an organization in the way the Commission does. Whereas the Commission is explicitly organized as a pressure group, made up of influential individuals who are not (for the time being) in government, Bilderberg participants encompass many heads of state, other top government officials and royalty. They feel confident attending on a regular basis *because of* the strict secrecy and confidentiality of the Bilderberg. Retinger portrayed the significance of Bilderberg for government officials and international relations this way:

> The improvement of international relations is primarily the task of statesmen and diplomats through bilateral contacts and international conferences. But the scope and possibilities of these official contacts are limited and certainly do not specifically cover

---

*Bilderberg marks the material it send to members "personal and strictly confidential" and "not for publication" as part of an attempt to restrict circulation. These reports do not contain hard facts, however, and are written in rather bland language. After the meetings long reports (60-70 pages) are circulated to all living participants. These contain short summaries of the papers distributed in advance of the meetings as well as summaries of discussion.

the entire field that the originators of Bilderberg had in mind. Moreover, statesmen, diplomats and politicians are bound by their instructions: they must defend specific interests and standpoints, even if they do not personally agree with them...None of these disadvantages arises in...Bilderberg...Even if a participant is a member of a government, a leader of a political party, an official of an international organization or of a commercial concern, he does not commit his goverment, his party or his organization by anything he may say...he can express his views on all the matters under discussion...Thus, Bilderberg offers a framework of a unique kind in so far as it provides a platform for men from both sides of the Atlantic to exchange opinions and views.[52]

President Eisenhower told Prince Bernhard's biographer that "I always had one of my people go to the Bilderberg Conferences. [ie., Gabriel Hauge*] I'm in favor of...any study of that kind which helps international understanding. The Bilderberg meetings enlightened me; I'd get viewpoints from other than official channels...There were so many points of view that somebody had to be wrong; but it was still important to know them."[53] President Kennedy "virtually staffed the State Department with...Bilderberg alumni"—Secretary of State Dean Rusk, Undersecretary of State George W. Ball, George McGhee, Walter Rostow, McGeorge Bundy, Arthur Dean—and Paul Nitze at the Pentagon.[54] Furthermore, many of the Trilateral Commissioners in the Carter Administration are also Bilderbergers, including Vice President Mondale, Secretary of State Vance, National Security Advisor Brzezinski, and Treasury Secretary Blumenthal. David Aaron, Deputy National Security Advisor, attended the 1977 Bilderberg. He and British Foreign Secretary, David Owen, were then engaged in efforts to find an Anglo-American solution for Zimbabwe (Rhodesia).

Bilderberg avoids attention in order to maintain the highest effectiveness at the top-levels of policy making. Efforts to influence public opinion are indirect, in contrast to the Trilateral Commission which takes both indirect and direct action, such as publishing its findings in concise form and arranging meetings with influential non-members. Retinger comments:

> Bilderberg does not make policy. Its aim is to reduce differences of opinion and resolve conflicting trends and to further understanding, if not agreement, by hearing and considering various points of view and trying to find a common approach to major

*Hauge was director of the CFR from 1964—and its treasurer. He was Eisenhower's White House domestic policy chief and is chairman of Manufacturers Hanover Trust.

problems. Direct action has therefore never been contemplated, *the object being to draw the attention of people in responsible positions to Bilderberg's findings.*[55] [Italics ed.]

The object is not to "draw the attention" of the greater population to Bilderberg activity. Bilderberg's existence is often denied, even by foreign ministry officials. Apart from planted newspaper articles, no Bilderberg publications are available to the public. The extent of media blackout is remarkable; insight into how this is achieved comes from a confidential memo of the steering group meeting in preparation of the 1964 conference at Williamsberg. George Nebolsine, of Coudert Bros. law firm (to which Sol Linowitz, a career negotiator and trilateralist, belongs) explains that

"this meeting was to be attended by three Prime Ministers, besides Washington high brass, Congressmen, etc., and that a searching curiosity by newspapers must be anticipated. To protect H.R.H. [Prince Bernhard] I suggested that we prepare a rather full account, including some names, and put it in the hands of two or three friendly newspapers as a safeguard against stories being published in other papers of an irresponsible character. We should also have a short release in advance of the meeting so that we are officially on record with our story."

Another, more direct, means of dealing with the problem of unauthorized coverage was employed in England in 1967. Press Baron Cecil King, chairman of the International Publishing Corporation (which was the largest daily circulation press in Britain) and chairman of the Newspaper Proprietors Association requested his fellow proprietors to see that "on no account should any report or even speculation about the content of the conference be printed."[56]

Bilderberg secrecy has produced tendencies in the literature towards conspiratorial fantasy on the one hand—especially on the right, which sees Bilderberg as a Jewish/Communist conspiracy to subvert free enterprise and Anglo-American civilization[57]—and offhand dismissal of its importance on the other. For instance, press coverage of the Bilderberg meeting in England just before the London Economic Summit of 1977 summed it up as a giggle plus a yawn and added a list of names of people who attended. The conspiratorial views encouraged by the on-going secrecy are, however, apparently not sufficient to make Bilberberg close up shop now that the Trilateral Commission has been established. Top government officials continue to attend: Chancellor Helmut Schmidt, NATO chief Joseph Luns, and Undersecretary of State for Economic Affairs Richard Cooper attended the 1977 meeting in Torquay, England.

Bilderberg remains a West European-North American endeavor; its central figures have acted as a permanent leadership. We noted above that Prince Bernhard was chairman from 1954-76 until his disgrace; Retinger, secretary-general until his death in 1960; Rykens, treasurer until just before his death in 1964; and Joseph E. Johnson has been U.S. secretary since 1954. The same continuity is seen in the steering committee.

The Steering Committee of 25-30 leading Bilderbergers continues to handpick participants, plan meetings, and solicit discussion papers. After a decade or so, the original group had been reduced by death and nonattendence, but many new recruits became permanent members. When Retinger died, van der Beugel (who has recently moved to the International Institute of Strategic Studies, London) took over as European secretary and has kept that position since. Giovanni Agnelli, head of FIAT; Otto Wolff von Amerongen, top German industrialist; and the Turkish diplomat Nuri Birgi have all been on the steering committee for two decades. Well into their second decade are David Rockefeller; the Belgian Baron Snoy et d'Oppuers, long-term secretary general of the Belgian Ministry of Economic Affairs and first chairman of the Marshall Plan's OEEC council; Emilio Collado, the U.S. representative on OECD's business and industry advisory committee, a longtime executive of Exxon and director of J.P. Morgan and Morgan Guaranty Trust Banks; Gabriel Hauge; Canadian Anthony G.S. Griffin, step-son of long-term prime minister Sir William Mackenzie, chairman of Home Oil and host of the 1977 Bilderberg meeting in England; and Sir Frederick Bennett, British secretary of the Steering Committee. Of these, Agnelli, Otto Wolff and Rockefeller are Trilateral Commission executive committee members. Moreover, Rockefeller is chairman of the board and Hauge is treasurer of the Council on Foreign Relations.

More recent additions to the steering committee complete its current shape: Hans Igler, president of the Austrian industrialists federation; Victor Umbrecht, director of the Swiss drug company Ciba-Geigy; George Ball, managing director of the top investment bank Lehman Brothers Kuhn Loeb and senior Kennedy foreign policy advisor; William Bundy, longtime editor of the CFR's *Foreign Affairs* and top Vietnam War planner. Then there is Lord Eric Roll, a British Civil servant who was involved in the wartime Combined (US-UK) Food Board and UK delegations to the OEEC, NATO, EEC (during Britain's entry negotiations), U.S. Treasury, IMF, and World Bank. (He is also Director of the Bank of England and chairman of S.G. Warburg, the merchant bank, and of the Common Market Trust.) Other members include: Edmond de Rothschild, the French banker; top German columnist Theo Sommer; former chairman of C.B.S. Arthur Taylor; Denmark's *Berlingske Tidende* chief editor Niel Norlund; Norwegian ship-owner Otto G. Tidemand; Belgium's chief executive of Belgian Chemical Union Ltd. Daniel Janssen; and Max Kohnstamm.

A closer look at just one steering committee figure is worthwhile for it reveals means by which Bilderbergers help shape policy. Sir Frederick Bennett is not exactly well known, but he has long been on Bilderberg's steering group and was the host of the 1974 Bilderberg meeting. Besides being a Conservative M.P. in England, Bennet has been a member of the Rhodesian bar since the forties. The Muldergate trial has drawn attention to his strong South African connections.* Sir Frederick told the London *Guardian* (24 March 1979) that Dr. Dennis Rhoodie, brother of fugitive ex-secretary of the South African Department of Information Eschel Rhoodie, had "many times in the past" asked him to suggest names of MP's who might want to go to South Africa. Bennett is the chairman of the London-based Foreign Affairs Research Institute (FARI) whose purpose is "the propagation of warnings about the Soviet danger."[58] People's News Service (London, 17 April 1979) quotes reliable sources saying that FARI was set up by the South Africans in 1976 and subsidised to the tune of 85,000 pounds per year. (The London *Guardian* quoted the same figure.)

Dr. Eschel Rhoodie, in explaining his Department of Information secret projects has said that Western trade unionists were bribed to help make ineffective the International Confederation of Free Trade Unions (ICFTU) week of action against apartheid in 1976. The main form this was going to take in Britain was a Union of Post Office Workers' boycott of telecommunications with South Africa for a week in favor of recognition of Black trade unions there. The postal workers' action was prevented by a court injunction brought by the National Association for Freedom (NAFF) whose director, Robert Moss, is a FARI board member who has also

---

*ed. Note: "Muldergate" refers to the influence buying scandal which has shaken South Africa since late 1978. Cornelius (Connie) Mulder directed the Information Department's covert world-wide campaign to influence policy and bolster South Africa's public relations image, in his post as Information Minister. Mulder appointed Eschel Rhoodie to the Information Department's top administrative post from where, since late 1972, he has led the information campaign. State President John Vorster was implicated in the secret information projects by a government-appointed inquiry and was forced to resign in June 1979 (Vorster had been South African Prime Minister for 12 years until September 1978). Before the revelations, Mulder was almost certain to be future prime minister but the scandal forced him to resign his Cabinet post and give up the chairmanship of the powerful Transvaal Province National Party. (See Brown.)

allowed his articles on Angola, for instance, to be used in huge press advertisements for South Africa paid for by the Department of Information (acting as The Group of Ten). Bennet, too, is a council member of NAFF, as are fellow Bilderbergers Sir John Foster, a barrister, and Sir Paul Chambers, ex-chairman of Britain's huge Imperial Chemical Industries. Both NAFF and FARI have closely interlocking boards with the London Institute for the Study of Conflict (ISC) which produces monthly extreme right wing analyses of conflict situations around the world and sells the hard-line politics as security information.[59] Bilderberg connections with this apparatus are many, for these kinds of activities were fairly central to the building of the anticommunist Atlantic European consciousness which was the West's ideological armor until the late 1970s.

Conclusion

The 1966 revision of Retinger's Bilderberg prospectus ends by emphasizing the changes in the world since the first full meeting in 1954:

> In the early fifties enthusiasm for, and confidence in, European unification justified the expectation that an economically and possibly a politically and militarily integrated Europe would be in a position to speak with one voice with the United States. There was every reason to expect that Bilderberg's activities would considerably facilitate and help to consolidate this process. When, shortly after the first Bilderberg Meeting, it became evident that military and political unity of Europe would not be achieved in the near future and when, in the early sixties [with President de Gaulle's 1963 veto of British entry to the Common Market] even the propects of achieving the desired economic integration became increasingly gloomy with the subsequent danger of a division of Europe into two blocs [the six nations of the Common Market or EEC and the Seven of the EFTA, the European Free Trade Association*], a new situation confronted Bilderberg. The problem was no longer limited to straightening out misunderstandings between the United States and Europe, it also became increasingly necessary to deal with the task of preventing divergences between the European countries themselves. How has Bilderberg reacted?...the organization has continually adapted to changing circumstances, [thanks to its permanent steering committee, secretariat and flexible selection of participants].[60]

*ed Note: EFTA was established in July 1960 by the U.K., Scandinavian countries, Switzerland, Austria and Portugal. They then disagreed with the defined goals of the Common Market.

The 1977-79 meetings reflected changing world circumstances. The 1977 Bilderberg meeting in Torquay, Devon—just before the economic summit in London—discussed (unsurprisingly): North American and Western European attitudes toward the future of the mixed economies in the Western democracies, and the Third World's demand for restructuring the world order and the political implications of those attitudes. In Princeton, in April 1978, topics were: Western defense and its political implications, and the changing structure of production and trade and consequences for the Western industrial countries. In Vienna in April 1979, there was another meeting and in April 1980 Bilderbergers met again. Bilderberg has work ahead of it. Like the Trilateral Commission, the CFR, and other elite institutions, Bilderberg is attempting to study and resolve the problems of the 1980s, strengthening the foundation for Western capitalist prosperity in the decades beyond.[61] As Retinger put it earlier:

> It may be assumed that in taking decisions on problems affecting the interest of the United States, Canada, and Western Europe, those responsible will certainly bear in mind the discussions they attended in the confidential and friendly atmosphere of Bilderberg.[62]

FOOTNOTES

1. Prince Bernhard was born in 1911, the German Prince of Lippe-Biesterfeld. He studied law and international trade and joined the German chemicals trust, I.G. Farben, in the mid-1930s (I.G. Farben was broken into constituent chemical companies after the war: Bayer, Hoechst, and BASF are among the biggest chemical transnational corporations.) Bernhard worked in the I.G. Farben, intelligence system, department "NW7", under a man called Frank Fahle (who was to become postwar Lockheed agent in West Germany). I.G. Farben had been at the core of Nazi Germany's preparation for war. For example, I.G. built a synthetic fuel and rubber plant at Auschwitz. I.G.'s patent deals with Standard Oil of New Jersey (Exxon) prevented U.S. preparation for synthetic rubber production, among other things. The wartime Truman Committee hearings made clear that this had held back war preparedness in the U.S., particularly since the Japanese cut off the most important supplier of natural rubber, Malaya, at the time of Pearl Harbor. On I.G. Farben's wartime role, see Joseph Borkin, *The Crime and Punishment of I.G. Farben,* (Free Press, 1978.)

Herman J. Abs, whom David Rockefeller called "the leading banker of the world" (no doubt in a fit of modesty), worked closely with I.G.'s NW7 in arranging takeovers of industrial property in occupied countries through the Deutsche Bank as Hitler took over Europe. Bernhard probably knew him before, as well as after the war.

Bernhard married Princess Juliana of Holland in 1937. During the war Holland was occupied and the royal family stayed in London (except for future Queen Juliana who was sent to Canada). Bernhard was busy in exile as top military liaison with other allied forces, and in raising funds and buying planes for Dutch forces. On his several trips to the U.S. he met President Roosevelt, many future Bilderbergers, executives of the purchasing boards (probably including Jean Monnet) and heads of aircraft companies; he flew a Lockheed-20 that he piloted himself.

In London he met Joseph Retinger and was involved in the discussions which produced the customs union between Belgium, the Netherlands, and Luxembourg, (Benelux) after the war. Among his advisers was Paul Rykens. Thus, the initiators of Bilderberg were already in contact. As victory approached, Bernhard was made head of the Dutch forces under Eisenhower. He was deeply involved in the European Movement, helping Retinger with its first big Conference at the Hague in 1948, and, when the associated European Youth Campaign got under way, welcoming the delegates to its first conference in 1952. After the war, the royal family's substantial holdings in certain Dutch companies (and in Exxon) assured Bernhard of a prosperous life in business and as Prince of the Netherlands, he had a considerable stipend from the Dutch government. But it seemingly wasn't enough.

The Lockheed story broke by accident. Lockheed's auditors Arthur Young and Co. started checking the accuracy of Lockheed's accounting in the late sixties. They wanted receipts for bribes, commissions, etc., and made up work-sheets summarizing these payments. Among the receipts were those for payments to Bernhard's Paris friend Poupette who received no less than $100,000 early in 1970. When both the Securities Exchange Commission and the Church Committee were investigating Lockheed's payments, they both wanted the worksheets, and the SEC subpoenaed them. The Church Committee was supposed to get only a set with the names excised, but by mistake Arthur Young's lawyer supplied a set with the names. Ensuing investigations showed that Bernhard received $1 million by 1962 thanks to Lockheed's European sales director Fred Meuser (who had been in Bernhard's wartime airforce squadron) for his supposed assistance in selling the "widow-maker" Lockheed Starfighter. Bilderberger Franz Joseph Strauss was West German Defense Minister at the time of the Starfighter deal. [In July, 1979 he was chosen to run against Helmut Schmidt as the Christian Democratic Union candidate for Chancellorship; he did not win, however, likely because he is such an ultra-rightest—ed.] The evidence is unclear about whether, as one Ernst Jauser claims, he also received Lockheed cash for sundry other services totalling another million by this time. Later, when Lockheed was trying to sell its Orions in 1967, Lockheed's Carl Kotchian offered Bernhard half a million dollars if he could alter the Dutch decision to buy the French Atlantique instead. Apparently, for his "honesty" in saying that he could not reverse that decision, Kotchian decided to give him $100,000 anyway! In 1973 Meuser again suggested to Lockheed brass that Bernhard could sell Orions to the Dutch and in December 1974 a fixed commission of $1 million was agreed to provided at least four aircraft were bought. Unfortunately for Bernhard, the Dutch government went for defense cuts instead. It's no wonder Bernhard's Bilderberg was such a strong pro-NATO force. Incidentally, Bernhard was not a one-company man. Bilderberger Tom Jones, the chief executive of Northrop, also paid Bernhard $750,000 for alleged services rendered. Perhaps the easiest sources for all this material are David Holton's *The Lockheed Papers* (London: Jonathan Cape, 1978) and Anthony Sampson's *The Arms Bazaar* (London: Hodder and Staughton, 1977).

2. The Trilateral book on *The Crisis of Democracy* is one of the latest in a long line of executive branch complaints about "popular" or congressional interference with foreign policy: e.g. Congressional rejection of the League of Nations in 1920, and of the International Trade Organization in 1948.

3. At the Peace Conference at Versailles, 1920, a pioneering United States think-tank called "The Inquiry" and similar groups in other countries did such useful

strategic work that they decided to form continuing foreign affairs bodies to carry on the efforts. See Gelfand, *The Inquiry*; Council on Foreign Relations, *Annual Reports*; and Stephan King-Hall, *Chatham House: A Brief Account of the Origins, Purposes, and Methods of the Royal Institute of International Affairs* (London: Oxford University, 1937). Among the Trilateral Commissioners long involved in these planning networks are Henry Owen, foreign policy studies director of the Brookings Institution, serving in the Carter Administration as special ambassador-at-large, responsible for Summit preparation and follow-up; Peter Dobell, director of the Canadian Parliamentary Centre for Foreign Affairs; Karl Kaiser, director of the Research Institute of the German Society for Foreign Policy; Cesare Merlini, director of the Italian Institute for International Affairs; J.C. Sannes, director of the Norwegian Institute for International Affairs; Andrew Shonfield, director, and Sir Kenneth Younger, former director of Chatham House; Saburo Okita, chairman of the Japan Economic Research Center, and others in Japan.

4. See F.A. Southard, *American Investment in Europe*, (New York: Houghton Mifflin, 1931); Southard is a Bilderberger. Also Paul Hutchinson, *The United States of Europe* (Christian Century Publishing Co., 1929).

5. See footnote 1; also see Gabriel Kolko, "American Business and Germany 1930-1941," *Western Political Quarterly*, December 1962.

6. William Diebold Jr., *The United States and the Industrial World, American Foreign Economic Policy in the 1970s* (New York: Praeger, 1972), p. 5.

7. See John H. Herz, "The Fiasco of Denazification in Germany" *Political Science Quarterly* (December 1948) pp. 569-594, and Joseph F. Napoli, "Denazification from an American's Viewpoint," *The Annals* (July 1949), pp. 115-123.

8. After its defeat, Japan was occupied by the U.S. alone. Geopolitically Japan is a defined area under a single government. There was no need for such an informal supranational network as Bilderberg. In Europe, on the other hand, Germany was under Four-power occupation. Britain and France, the other Western powers in Germany, were both dependent on U.S. financial aid for their own reconstruction. "Europe" consisted of a score of nations and there were substantial boundary problems along with problems of unstable political structures and alignments.

9. The authorized biography by Alden Hatch, *H.R.H. Prince Bernhard of the Netherlands* (London: George Harrap, 1962) pp. 212-213. This book contains a chapter on Bilderberg.

10. John Pomian (Retinger's longtime secretary), *Joseph Retinger: Memoirs of an Eminence Grise* (University of Sussex Press, 1972), p. 106. This book sets the formation of Bilderberg in the context of Retinger's central role in the European Movement.

11. J.H. Retinger, *The European Continent?* (London: Hodge, 1946). The idea of federating Europe and its empire into one grand English-speaking civilization has early roots; some of which are traced in C. Carrol Quigley's *Tragedy and Hope* (1967).

12. Pomian, *op.cit.,* p. 212. David Astor, long-term postwar editor of the London *Observer* and Bilderberger, when approached in 1947 for a contribution to the European Movement, instead gave Retinger a 500 pound per annum income for seven years—a substantial stipend in those days. (Pomian, pp. 208-209).

13. The American Committee for a United Europe (ACUE) provided nearly half of the funds for the European Movement (EM) between 1947 and 1952, according to the doctoral thesis of F.X. Rebattet, who, as son of the man who followed Retinger as secretary general of the EM had access to EM archives. Source: EM archives, Fin/8/6 "European Movement" EMC Treasurer's Report, 1949-1953.)

This funding continued beyond the period covered by the Rebattet thesis. Most of it went to the European Youth Campaign, which was initiated by John J. McCloy, U.S. High Commissioner in Germany (later a Bilderberger), who delegated Shepard

Stone (also a Bilderberger) to counter a major youth rally in East Berlin in 1951. "Wild Bill" Donovan, who had headed the wartime OSS, the predecessor of the CIA, was chairman of ACUE at this time and Allen Dulles, who was to replace "Beetle" Smith as CIA chief in the Eisenhower Administration, was its vice-chairman. Thomas W. Braden became executive director with Dulles. Braden was in Allan Hovey Jr. (Bilderberger), ACUE's representative in Europe, told Rebattet that he was well aware of the CIA funding. Rebattet found that five-sixths of the money raised by ACUE was from the U.S. government. Braden explained that the top European statesmen in the European Movement "knew and approved of CIA funding" (*Sunday Times*, London, 25 May 1975).

In a 1967 article in the *Saturday Evening Post*, "I'm glad the CIA is immoral," Tom Braden described how he gave "$15,000 to Irving Brown [another Bilderberger of the AFL-CIO] to pay off his strong-arm squads in Mediterranean ports, so that American supplies could be unloaded against the opposition of Communist dock workers...I...gave Walter [Reuther, also a Bilderberger] $50,000 in $50 bills. Victor spent the money, mostly in Germany, to bolster labor unions there...We had placed an agent in a Europe-based organization of intellectuals called the Congress for Cultural Freedom. Another agent became an editor of *Encounter*. The agents could not only propose anti-Communist programs to the official leaders of the organizations but they could also suggest ways and means to solve the inevitable budgetary problems. Why not see if the needed money could be obtained from American foundations. As the agents knew, the CIA-financed foundations were quite generous when it came to the national interest."

14. Joseph Retinger, *Bilderberg Meetings* (November 1966) as revised by Arnold T. Lamping, a Dutch diplomat who became Bilderberg's Deputy Secretary. p. 3.

15. Retinger, p. 4.

16. *Ibid.*

17. *Ibid.* p. 214.

18. *Ibid.* p. 4.

19. Pomian, p. 250.

20. Hatch, p. 215.

21. The Council on Foreign Relations and Chatham House published the results of their own evaluation processes concluding with a five-day meeting in September 1952 in *Britain and the United States* (rapporteurs H.L. Roberts and P.A. Wilson, 1953). Each of the groups—the CFR Americans and Chatham House British—"set down its interpretation of the other."

22. Hatch, p. 215.

23. Versions of this list are found in Retinger, p. 5.; Hatch, p. 215; and Pomian, p. 251.

24. Hatch, pp. 215-216 lists the people who prepared papers for the critique.

25. Retinger, p. 5; Hatch, p. 216.

26. Pomian, p. 135.

27. Hatch, p. 216.

28. In September 1953, President Eisenhower made C.D. Jackson his assistant for psychological warfare. He also made his wartime chief of staff (later Truman's director of the CIA), W. Bedell Smith, chairman of the Operations Coordinating Board. "Beetle" Smith was John Foster Dulles' number two in the State Department. Jackson was the Eisenhower White House's representative on the Operations Coordinating Board, OCB, (*Current Biography*, 1953, p. 581). That Board replaced the Psychological Strategy Board and later became infamous as the Forty Committee. Whatever the title, the task is clear. The OCB was the CIA control committee, supposedly under the National Security Council and the President. In bureaucrat bland it was said to be "binding closely together the critical functions of conceiving, developing and implementing high national strategy." (*New York*

Times, 4 September 1953). Jackson, the presidential coordinator for the CIA, had the job of giving "assistance in the development of increasing understanding and cooperation of all peoples." When Jackson gave up this job, Nelson Rockefeller picked up the load. He in turn was replaced by Dillon Anderson, who explained the position thus: "Eisenhower...preferred not to know about clandestine operations such as the...overthrow of the democratically elected Arbenz regime in Guatemala because of the difficulty he experienced in presenting the cover story at press conferences." So he appointed Jackson to authorize the dirty work (see *The Rockefellers,* by Peter Collier and David Horowitz, Signet paperback, 1976, p. 271).

29. Hatch, p. 216.

30. *Ibid.*

31. Retinger, p. 13. All subsequent citations of subject titles come from this document or, since 1966, from succeeding documents.

32. Pomian, pp. 252-253; Retinger passim; Hatch, pp. 215-216.

33. Hatch, p. 217.

34. Hatch, p. 218. Major-General Sir Kenneth Strong, longtime British intelligence chief, in his book *Intelligence at the Top* (London: Cassel, 1968, p. 229) gives a virtually identical view of the McCarthy problem—but in his account it is Eisenhower telling him: "McCarthys had appeared from time to time...one had the choice of killing them by some act or other, or letting them exhaust themselves... Eisenhower was sure that sooner or later McCarthy would destroy himself."

35. Retinger, p. 8.

36. See note 28 on C.D. Jackson.

37. "On January 14, 1954, Arthur H. Dean called a press conference after he had heard charges of 'appeasement' against him by Senator Herman Welker (R) of Idaho. Dean defended his membership in the Institute of Pacific Relations (which had been called a Communist front) and said that he had remained a trustee of the institute in order to get evidence on Frederick Vanderbilt Field's (alleged) Communist activities, "and then a number of trustees and myself forced his resignation." Dean added (truthfully enough, to judge by his record) "I am and always have been consistently anticommunist. Communism...should be fought tooth and nail" (*New York Times,* 15 January 1954).

38. Retinger, pp. 9-10.

39. Pomian, pp. 254-255.

40. Francois Duchene, former deputy European chairman of the Trilateral Commission and Paul Delouvrier of the Trilateral Commission both worked for the ECSC in the fifties, as press attache and finance director respectively.

41. ACUSE met once a year and issued statements, but all the year Monnet moved about working on deals that would further European unity and confront problems. Apart from Kohnstamm, its vice-president, and Duchene who ran its documentation center in Paris, some of the ACUSE people in Bilderberg are Rayner Barzel, top German CDU politician; Mollet and Pinay of the original Bilderberg group; Italians Malagodi, La Malfa and Rumor; Belgian trade union bureaucrat August Cool; top German business politician (CDU, Thyssen chief since 1954), eleven of the European Defense Community Plan; Marjolin; Pierre Uri; and Guido Carli (former Bank of Italy head, now head of industrials organization ·Confindustria), Kurt Kiesinger, and Helmut Schmidt.

42. Retinger, p. 9.

43. Retinger, pp. 13-14.

44. *Ibid.* p. 12.

45. Hatch, p. 223.

46. Citations are taken from the Report of the 1974 Megeve, France Bilderberg meeting, pp. 18, 30.

47. 1955 was the year Eisenhower's "Atoms for Peace" initiative made headway in the international scientific conference in Geneva August 8-20. The International Atomic Energy Agency was part of the package; the Messina Conference had agreed to proceed to set up Euratom in May; and in June, the OEEC established a working group on peaceful uses of the atom.

Konrad Adenauer had committed W. Germany on joining NATO "not to manufacture in its territory...atomic, biological and chemical weapons" but it was to provide South Africa with a key to the manufacture of nuclear weapons by allowing it access and assistance to uranium enrichment technology through the Karlsruhe Nuclear Centre. "It was at the Geneva conference that nuclear co-operation between West Germany and South Africa was initiated." Today, Frank Barnaby, director of the Stockholm International Peace Research Institute (SIPRI), points out that "if South Africa acquires a national nuclear force then other African countries are likely to wish to counter the threat by acquiring nuclear weapons." Zdenek Cervenka and Barbara Rodgers, *The Nuclear Axis: Secret Collaboration Between West Germany and South Africa* (London: Julien Friedmann Books, 1978), pp. 37, 39, and xv.

48. Hatch, p. 222.

49. In summer 1956, the retired chief of British naval intelligence, Sir Anthony Buzzard; top scientist, Lord (Professor P.M.S.) Blacket; Denis Healey and others started discussing the problems with the existing NATO strategy of "massive retaliation" with nuclear weapons if deterrence failed. After a conference in Brighton in January 1957 they decided to set up a center in London "which would make possible a better trans-Atlantic dialogue with the new generation of American strategic experts." According to a biography of Denis Healey: "To set up a British centre for strategic studies, however, needed money. Healey's international contacts were decisive in getting it." "I met Shep Stone, head of the social and political studies part of the Ford Foundation at a meeting of the Bilderberg Group in Fiuggi, Italy, the day the Russians launched their first Sputnik," remembered Healey. "I took him out for a walk in a heavy mist under the wet plane trees, and said we were starting this thing and we would like about $10,000 to keep it afloat. He told me they never looked at anything under $100,000, but he was interested in the idea, so if we revamped it and put in a formal request it would stand a good chance." "When Healey returned to London...he played an active part in setting up the Institute for Strategic Studies...By the end of 1958 the I.S.S. had begun its work, with the Ford Foundation giving $150,000 over three years, as a strategic think-tank." Healey had become really concerned about nuclear weapons around 1954, and wrote on them for *Encounter* in 1955...With the formation of the I.S.S. he began making Britain a forerunner in Europe in understanding nuclear strategy, and with Alastair Buchan [the first director of I.S.S.] he began making defence thinking respectable in Europe." (See Bruce Reed and Geoffrey Williams, *Denis Healey and the Politics of Power* (London: Sidgwick & Jackson, 1971, p. 139ff.) Also see a brochure from the ISS called "The International Institute of Strategic Studies," section on development of the institute.

The importance of the influence that could be wielded through the informal coordinating role of bodies like Bilderberg and the Trilateral Commission in bringing the foreign affairs and strategic studies apparatus together with top political, banking, industrial, scientific, and media figures can hardly be overstated. The Center for Strategic and International Studies at Georgetown University, Washington D.C. (among other institutes) is also closely linked to Bilderberg/ Trilateralists. Henry Kissinger is a counselor; David Abshire of the Trilateral Commission is its chairman; Ray Cline, former deputy director of the CIA, is an executive director; at least five Trilateral Commissioners are listed on its note-paper.

50. For a discussion of U.S. investment in Europe see Servan-Schreiber, *The American Challenge.*

51. Many Bilderbergers were able to contribute knowledgeably to that discussion. For

example: James A. Perkins worked in the Foreign Economic Administration during the war, went to Swarthmore as vice-president, then to the Carnegie Corporation 1950-1963, and became President of Cornell University 1963-1969. He has since been head of the Center for Educational Inquiry and of the International Council for Educational Development, and a member of both the Carnegie Commission on Higher Education, 1967-1973, and of the Carnegie Council Policy Studies in Higher Education since 1974. Frank Darknell's short study of "The Carnegie Council for Policy Studies in Higher Education" (*Insurgent Sociologist*, Spring 1975), pp. 106-114, throws some light on the significance of Perkin's activities. Perkins is close to the Chase Manhatten Bank and a former trustee of the Rand Corporation. Don K. Price has been with the Social Sciences Research Council, the Pentagon's Research and Development Board, and the Ford Foundation. He has been a Harvard professor and dean of the Kennedy graduate school since 1958 (before Allison); trustee and then chairman of the Twentieth Century Fund; trustee of Vanderbilt University, Rand, and the Rhodes Trust since 1968. Paul Samuelson, MIT professor, has been a government consultant to the National Resources Planning Board and War Planning Board during the war (also at the MIT Radiation Laboratory); consultant to the Treasury Department, RAND, the Federal Reserve Bank, and President Kennedy's Council of Economic Advisers. Samuelson's economic text is standard fare in college and university economic courses. Graham T. Allison has recently replaced Don K. Price as Harvard Dean of the Kennedy School and is a RAND consultant. Allison is with the Center of International Affairs which was also Kissinger's, Bowie's and other academics' home base. Andrew Cordier was dean of the Graduate School of International Affairs at Columbia University 1962-1968 and acting president during the student occupation in 1968. He was (he tells us) in the State Department as an expert on international security 1944-1946 (with Joseph E. Johnson and Dean Rusk, and adviser to all the presidents of the U.S. General Assembly, 1946-1962. At the U.N. he was also special representative of the U.S. secretary general in Korea in 1952 and in the Congo in 1960. He was also a trustee of Johnson's Carnegie Endowment for International Peace. So it was no mere academic discussion at Bilderberg on the topic at hand.

52. Retinger, pp. 6-7.
53. Hatch, p. 223.
54. Hatch, pp. 223-224.
55. Retinger, p. 9.
56. See the articles on Bilderberg by Robert Eringer, "The West's Secret Power Group," *Verdict* (a former British Monthly) November, 1976.
57. The U.S. extreme Right and fascist groups in Europe (e.g. Britain's "Nazis," the National Front) have attacked the Bilderberg/Trilateral Commission/Council on Foreign Relations connection in true Hitler style, seeing it as Jewish finance league with the "commies" to subvert good U.S. (British or whatever) free enterprise and nativist values. Gary Allen's *None Dare Call It Conspiracy* has sold four million copies in various languages. Other contributors along these lines include Anthony C. Sutton's books, *National Suicide: Military Aid to the Soviet Union, Wall Street and the Bolshevik Revolution* ("powerful and wealthy Americans bankrolled the establishment of the first Communist state") and *Wall Street and F. D. R.* (the super-rich designed the New Deal as a "fascist-socialist government that would eliminate competition"). Sutton's latest book, with Patrick M. Wood, is *Trilaterals Over Washington*. Gary Allen contributed his "shocking account of a security risk who became Secretary of State" in *The Kissinger File* and *The Rockefeller File*; and a heavy, if not weighty, tome by Phyllis Schafly and Admiral Chester Ward called *Kissinger on the Couch* purports to show "how he became the principal force in the SALT disarmament agreements that have relegated the United States to second

place in nuclear weapons" (which, of course, they have not). *The Naked Capitalist* by W. Cleon Skousen is fairly typical of the distortion and fantasy of the extreme Right documents a plot to create a collectivist dictatorship in America." To them Quigley is effectively a Commie in the State Department—"a highly placed socialist" who "had admitted the existence of a conspiracy among the super-rich." Skousen's book turns Quigley's liberal imperialist views and view of the radical right on their heads.
58. Geoffrey Steward-Smith, director of FARI, and deputy director Ian Grieg are well known professional anticommunists. Ian Gilmour, Prime Minister Thatcher's Foreign Office spokesman in the House of Commons, is on the FARI board.
59. ISC published a "reds under the beds" study of communists in the British labor movement just before the February 1974 election for example. ISC was formed when Brian Crozier, its director, came aboard with a library from the CIA-funded Forum World Features news service (which in turn had started life as the newsletter of the CIA-funded Congress for Cultural Freedom, the Cold War intellectuals' front.
60. Retinger, p. 16.
61. See for example, the 1974 Bilderberg record, p. 57.
62. Retinger, p. 17.

Two Additional Sources

1. The activities of individual Bilderbergers are widely covered in the press, reflecting their importance. Some members list their participation in Bilderberg in their *Who's Who* entries, but for the most part this is left unsaid in their continuing publicity.
2. An article by Eugene Pasyonowski and Carl Gilbert, "Bilderberg the Cold War International," (originally published by Temple University Free Press) was entered into the U.S. *Congressional Record* (Vol. 117, 15 September 1971; H.R. pp. E9615-24) by Representative John R. Rarick of Louisiana. The article adheres to a more conspiratorial interpretation than the present writer.

chapter three

TRILATERALISM AND THE SUMMITS
Jeremiah Novak*

> We do not like to call ourselves neo-federalists—that irritates too
> many sensitive souls. We call ourselves neo-functionalists who
> attain control over domestic policies by coordinating functional
> areas. But yet, there is an aspect of neo-federal supranationalism
> to our program.
>
> —Karl Kaiser
> Trilateral Commisioner

Far faster than people realize, the domestic and foreign policy
of the United States is being influenced by a supranational directory,** operating on a governmental and private basis under the
aegis of the Trilateral Commission.[2] Inherent in the idea of trilateralism is a neo-federalist supranational unit to which individual
nation-states are subordinated. The Commission's second report,
The Crisis of International Cooperation, called for the formation of
an advisory commission of three heads of state to set policy for the
trilateral nations: "The international system which depended for its
leadership in the past on the United States alone now requires a truly
common management."

---

*This article is based on extensive interviews with Trilateral Commission partici-
pants and knowledgeable observers in late 1976, 1977, and early 1978.[1] Jeremiah
Novak is economic columnist for *The Asia Mail*; he spent fifteen years as an
executive for multinational corporations (including five years in Asia) before turning
to journalism. This is a condensed version of the original article.
**The executive body in charge of the French government from 1795 to 1799, during
the French Revolution (1789-1799), was called the "directory." Generally, the term
refers to a body of directors or a directorate.

The 1974 Winter edition of the Commission's magazine *Trialogue* shows a picture of Commissioners with President Ford as he listens to trilateral recommendations. One outcome of this meeting was the Rambouillet Conference of December 1975 where, after similar meetings with trilateralists, the President of France, the Chancellor of West Germany, the Prime Ministers of Britain, Japan, and Canada, and the Chairman of the European Economic Community (EEC), held their first summit meeting. The Rambouillet summit was the first precedent-setting institutional meeting of the trilateral supranational directory.[3] Subsequent meetings have been held in San Juan (Puerto Rico), London, Bonn, and Tokyo. Indeed, the summits have become an annual affair and, as we shall see below, have developed a permanent organizational machinery.

Analysis of the economic summit as an institution has lagged behind analysis of the Commission itself. The summits are the outcome of the Commission which most expresses its supranational character. Most importantly, they are a structure for implementing policy at the highest levels. In addition to the actual summits, two other distinct institutions put trilateralism into practice: the International Summit Preparatory Group and the Organization for Economic Cooperation and Development (OECD), which acts as a secretariat.

In an interview in *Trialogue* in the Winter of 1977-78, Henry Owen, Carter's special ambassador-at-large responsible for summit preparation and follow-up (also director of Foreign Policy Studies at the Brookings Institution and former chief of policy planning in the State Department during the Vietnam War), said that the summit agenda always includes domestic economic policy, monetary relations, trade, energy, and North-South relations. These issues, according to Owen, "are at the heart of the matter. They don't change from year to year."

At the first summit meeting attended by the Carter Administration, held in London in 1977, the primary item on the trilateral agenda was coordination of internal economic policies. The basic goal was to have all three major economies—the U.S., West Germany, and Japan—stimulate their economies simultaneously. U.S. exports would be augmented through greater demand in Japan and Western Europe. Following this agreement, President Carter directed an increase in the government deficit and spurred the Federal Reserve to increase the money supply. This policy fostered an economic upturn in the United States.

At the Bonn summit in July 1978, U.S. policy was challenged by other participants who felt that stimulatory policies had gone too far and were exacerbating a decline of the dollar. For Japan and Western

Europe a deflated dollar represented a "tariff" on their exports because it meant that U.S. consumers paid higher prices for imported goods. In keeping with summit deliberations Carter announced on 24 September 1978 a reduction in spending by the Federal government and a new "voluntary wage and price policy." On October 1, four months after Bonn, the president asked the Federal Reserve to raise interest rates and announced that the United States would borrow $30 billion in foreign currency denominated bonds to stabilize the dollar. In January 1979 the president went to Congress with an "austerity" budget, pledging to keep the budget deficit below $30 billion. And in April 1979 Treasury Secretary Michael Blumenthal called for higher interest rates and a slowdown in economic growth.

The leaders of Western Europe and Japan had also urged the president to raise oil prices through decontrol and reduce consumption of imported oil. In April 1979 Carter asked Congress to decontrol oil prices, receiving praise from the trilateral allies. (See Kaufman and Clawson, and Garitty.)

These examples from the London and Bonn summits help demonstrate how the directory effects policy at home. The directory determines growth and monetary guidelines; each nation is expected to adhere to these guidelines by pressing their legislatures and taking administrative actions to insure they are accomplished. For example, for over three years French Prime Minister Raymond Barre has been executing an austerity program for hitherto government subsidized industry in line with summit guidelines for the French economy. One immediate result: thousands of French steelworkers have been laid off.

Summitry can influence the poverty or progress of nations. It is not part of the constitutional process but a transcendence of the constitutional process. This point is brought home in a 1978 interview conducted by this author with trilateralists Karl Kaiser, Director of the Foreign Affairs Council of West Germany, and Richard Cooper, undersecretary of state for International Economic Affairs. In the trilateral report, *Toward a Renovated International System*, Cooper and Kaiser called for a special committee of experts to coordinate summit agenda and follow-up. This semi-secret committee, known as the preparatory group is discussed below:

Reporter: Is it true that a committee led by Henry Owen of the U.S. and made up of representatives of the U.K., U.S., West Germany, Japan, France, and the EEC is coordinating the economic and political policies of the trilateral countries?

Cooper: Yes. They have met three times.

Reporter:	Yet, in your recent paper you state that this committee should remain informal because to formalize "this function might well prove offensive to some of the Trilateral and other countries which do not take part." Who are you afraid of?
Kaiser:	Many countries in Europe would resent the dominant role that West Germany plays at these meetings.
Cooper:	Many people still live in a world of separate nations, and they would resent such coordination.
Reporter:	But this committee is essential to your whole policy. How can you keep it a secret or fail to try to get popular support?
Cooper:	Well, I guess it's the press' job to publicize it.
Reporter:	Yes, but why doesn't President Carter come out with it and tell the American people that economic and political policy is being coordinated by a committee made up of Henry Owen and six others? After all, if policy is being made on a multinational level, the people should know.
Cooper:	President Carter and Secretary of State Vance have constantly alluded to this in their speeches.
Kaiser:	It just hasn't become an issue.

A few weeks after this interview the names of the preparatory committee appeared in the press. Clyde Farnsworth of *The New York Times*, who was present at the above interview, met with Owen and elicited the names of the other members of this International Summit Preparatory Group: Bernard Clapper, governor of the Bank of France; Sir John Hunt, parliamentary secretary to then British Prime Minister Callaghan; Dr. Deiter Hiss, president of the Landeszentralbank of Berlin; Hiromichi Miyazaki, Japanese deputy minister for Foreign Affairs; Umberto Larocca, Foreign Affairs Advisor to the Prime Minister of Italy; and Robert Johnstone, deputy undersecretary, Canadian Department of External Affairs.[4]

The preparatory group, I ascertained in interviews with Owen, Cooper, and Kaiser, is the "pivotal organization" because its members set the agendas for the summits. They select what is to be discussed; present the assembled directory with options, note the decisions taken, and follow up to monitor and report on each nation's progress.

An older institution, the Organization for Economic Cooperation and Development (OECD) serves as a type of secretariat for the preparatory committee and the summit directory, providing economic data and analysis. According to C. Fred Bergsten, co-author of the trilateral report, *The Reform of International Institutions,* the OECD should be responsible for "the coordination of domestic economic policies among the industrialized countries. To this end the

OECD should initiate an annual consolidating on the outlook for economic development and economic policy plans in each of the member countries...An interchange on such subjects, at strategic times in the decision making process *by responsible officials* could have an important effect on improving policy *within* each country and in avoiding conflicts between the efforts of different countries." [Italics mine.]

Most North-South issues revolve around the international economy which itself is expressed in the operations of the IMF, the World Bank, and GATT. It is not surprising to find that many of the trilateral pamphlets deal with strategies to reform these institutions; implementing reform is not so difficult as the trilateral nations control the voting of the IMF and World Bank. (See Phillips.)

For example, at the Rambouillet summit in December 1976, a decision was made to amend the articles of the International Monetary Fund to permit the IMF to regulate floating exchange rates and to gradually introduce a new international money to replace the dollar: the SDR, (Special Drawing Right). Six weeks after the summit, the trilateral nations pushed through their Rambouillet decisions at an IMF meeting in Kingston, Jamaica.*

After the London summit, where it was decided that the IMF needed a new fund for emergency financing, the trilateral countries developed the Witteveen Facility which could be used to help Third World countries that could not pay off their loans to private banks. The summit established the facility in order to prevent failure of the private banking system; knowingly *The Wall Street Journal* called the fund the Bankers' Relief Act of 1977.

At the Bonn summit it was decided to press for rapid completion of the new multilateral trade agreements. As the trilateral nations account for the majority of world trade, the developing nations would have to conform or suffer the consequences. In April 1979, a new trade accord (the Tokyo Round) was signed by the trilateral nations over the protest of Third World nations who saw that they favored the rich countries.

Proposals found in trilateral pamphlets became embodied in summit decisions which are in turn subscribed to by the United States and other participants. The U.S. is a part of the trilateral process, not outside it. The effect of this technique is to present to the Congress,

---

*In 1978, at the Bonn Summit, it was decided to distribute $12 billion worth of SDRs on the basis of contributions. This gave the United States nearly $2 billion of foreign exchange just before Carter announced his austerity program to protect the dollar. This "new money" was then used to purchase excess dollars in international private currency markets.

IMF amendments, World Bank commitments, trade agreements and commodity agreements as previously elaborated at the summits. Congress can either pass or refuse to act on these agreements, but it cannot substantially reformulate them.[4]

Increasingly, economic decisions flow from the Trilateral Commission to the preparatory committee to the OECD to the summit. Policy implementation is sought—rather successfully—through congressional/parliamentary approval or administrative fiat. Policy does not reflect the needs of people in the U.S. or other trilateral countries. It is time that people become aware of what goes on around the summits, or the directory will take even greater power.

FOOTNOTES

1. The basic thrust of this article is based on extensive interviews with various Trilateral Commission participants in August 1976, 1977, and early 1978. These include Richard Cooper, Karl Kaiser, Jean Francois-Poncet, Nobuhiko Ushiba, C. Fred Bergsten, George Franklin, Francois Sauzey, Scott Powers, Charles Heck. Others with knowledge of the role of the summits who were interviewed are Ed Fried, American director of the World Bank; J.J. Pollak, research director of the IMF; Congressman Henry Reuss of the House Banking Committee; Congressmen Henry Gonzales and Michael Harrington of the House Committee on International Financial Institutions.

2. For an extended discussion of the Trilateral Commission and its origins see Jeremiah Novak, "New World Economic System Dawns," *Christian Science Monitor,* 14 February 1977, and "Outline for Remaking World Trade and Finance," *Christian Science Monitor,* February 15, 1978. Also see, by same author, "The Trilateral Connection," *Atlantic Monthly,* July 1977, and "Trilateralism," *America,* 5 February 1977. The essence of these articles is to stress the economic restructuring of the world order as being the central thrust of trilateralism. Simon Serfaty, "Brzezinski: Play it Again, Zbig," *Foreign Policy,* Fall 1978, notes: "Even as a conceptual abstraction, trilateralism had evolved rather erratically, starting first in the mid-1960s (in *Alternative to Partition*) as a 'cooperative community' that would include 'America and Russia as the peripheral participants, and West Europe and East Europe as the two halves of the inner core.' In the late 1960s (in *Encounter*) it grew into a 'larger community' that would embrace 'the Atlantic states, the more advanced European communist states (including the Soviet Union), and Japan,' before being reduced to the more developed, industrialized, and non-communist states in the early 1970s. But as an action policy, while there was wide agreement on the very principle of consultation and cooperation, divergencies among the allies were inevitably to emerge at the level of practice. These were the same economic, strategic, and political divergences that have characterized the postwar history of trilateral relations and that no amount of consultation can truely bridge."

3. *Trialogue,* Winter 1974, p. 1. Also a discussion with Henry Owen of the preparatory group in which he said, "The Rambouillet summit set a precedent which

laid the groundwork for all future summits." See Clyde Farnsworth's article on Henry Owens, *New York Times,* (2 July 1978).

4. See hearings before the subcommittee on International Policy and Trade of the Committee on International Relations, 20, 21 September 1977, testimony of Jeremiah Novak, p. 96. For further discussion of the internal and external effects of trilateral summits see: "The London Economic Conference, " *America,* 11 June 1977; "Trilateral Reform and Social Justice," *America,* 3 September 1977; "Beyond North and South," *Worldview,* May 1979; "Trilateralism," *The Asia Mail,* April 1977; "A New Perspective on World Hunger," *America,* 13 May 1978; "Other Perspectives on World Hunger," *America,* 24 June 1978, all by Jeremiah Novak.

PART IV
INSIDE THE UNITED STATES: CARTER IS NO HYPOCRITE TO THE TRILATERALISTS

Jimmy Carter sprinted to the presidency preaching morality and compassionate government in the big bad world of Watergate, the Vietnam War, poverty, and police states. His campaign image was a populist peanut farmer set against closed Establishment politics. This section opens with an account of how the trilateralists helped Carter capture the presidency. Straightforward analysis of economic, energy, and military policy illustrates the trilateral impact on people living and working in the United States. Recession and the "politics of less," resurgent militarism, and Native American colonization are three sides of the exploitative system trilateralism serves.

"If you think this economic system is working—then ask someone who isn't."

—bumper sticker

Don't ask:

...a political and economic elite who have shaped decisions and never had to account for mistakes nor to suffer from injustice. When unemployment prevails, they never stand in line looking for a job. When deprivation results from a confused welfare system, they never do without food, or clothing, or a place to sleep. When the public schools are inferior or torn by strife their children go to exclusive private schools. And when the bureaucracy is bloated and confused, the powerful always manage to discover and occupy niches of special influence and privilege.

—Jimmy Carter, 1976
Acceptance Speech for Democratic Nomination

chapter one

JIMMY CARTER AND THE TRILATERALISTS: PRESIDENTIAL ROOTS

*Laurence H. Shoup**

Introduction

There are two levels of political process which need to be considered in any analysis of U.S. election campaigns. The first, which gets greater attention in the news media and academic writings is best labeled the party politics level. This is the familiar world of political bosses and their machines, party elites, advertising agencies merchandising a candidate to the voters, and the often carnival-like atmosphere of grass roots campaigning. The second level, much less reported—at least partly because it takes place behind the scenes—is actually more important than the first. It is best called the ruling class level of U.S. politics. This term refers to the ways in which an upper class can control the political process. This level includes the world of large-scale fund raising from wealthy upper class individuals, the networks of influential people developed by exclusive private clubs and policy-planning groups, and the media's merchandising of favored candidates through manipulation of the definition of news.

These two levels of politics are, of course, interconnected, and always interact in some fashion—a successful politician has contacts with both realms and attempts to reconcile them—but they do represent different traditions, constituencies, and purposes and thus are conceptually distinct. This ruling class level of U.S. politics is the central focus of this article. This analysis will show how a small group of wealthy and powerful people—members of the corporate upper

*This article is adapted from the first part of *The Carter Presidency and Beyond: Power and Politics in the 1980s* (Palo Alto, Ca.: Ramparts Press, 1979) by Laurence H. Shoup.

199

class—shaped the 1976 presidential selection process, and helped Jimmy Carter gain power. Carter did have to struggle at the party politics level: in primaries, in the delegate selection process, and so on, in order to be nominated and elected; but his ties to the Eastern Establishment, the dominant sector of the ruling class, were the key to his success and therefore will be the main focus of this article.*

Major party presidential *nominations* are the critical stage of the process of the presidential choice, because it is at this stage that alternatives are excluded and the voters' choices narrowed to only two individuals. The several years before the primaries begin and, in some cases, the primaries themselves, are crucial to this nominating process. During this early period, the mass communications media, political financiers, polls, pollsters, and party leaders produce an unofficial nominee or, at most, several *viable, serious* candidates.[1] This study will therefore focus on the several years prior to March 1976. By late March 1976, Jimmy Carter ranked so high in the public opinion polls and was gathering support so rapidly that he had virtually clinched the nomination.

During this early period two things were essential to the success of candidate Carter. First, adequate financing was needed to hire a staff, to travel, to disseminate campaign literature, to buy advertisements—in short, to supply all the necessities of a modern political campaign. Second, favorable coverage from the mass communications media—both print and broadcast—was absolutely vital. As two authorities in this field put it: "if the mass communications media do not pay attention to a person, he has no chance of becoming president."[2] Media coverage, or the lack of it, also plays a major role in raising money, since journalists and media commentators label a candidate a winner or loser, serious or not, viable or not, and political financiers, like voters, take note of these appraisals. Favorable media coverage was especially crucial to Carter since he was one of the least known candidates in the field.

In 1973, leaders of the Establishment were looking for a southern representative and invited Carter to join the Trilateral Commission.** This gave Carter access to individuals who could aid his

---

*The term Eastern Establishment refers to the complex of institutions controlled by upper-class families—leading banks, law firms, industrial and media corporations, influential private policy planning organizations like the Council of Foreign Relations and the Trilateral Commission, private clubs, top foundations and universities—centered on the northeast coast of the United States, especially in New York City, but also Boston, Philadelphia, Washington, D.C., and a few smaller cities.
**ed. note: Writing in *The Black Scholar* ("James Carter and the Trilateral Commission: A Southern Strategy," May 1977, pp. 2-7), Mark Allen reports:

campaign with financial support, advice on strategy and policy positions, and favorable coverage in the mass communications media.

Carter, the Atlanta Establishment, and the National Power Structure

Jimmy Carter was a wealthy landowner and agribusinessman when he launched his political career in the early 1960s. By the time of his 1970 campaign for governor, Carter was personally close to, and supported by, central figures of the Atlanta Establishment—the upper class leadership group which runs that city and which has great influence throughout Georgia and the entire southeastern United States. These leaders of the Atlanta Establishment included individuals like Charles Kirbo of the King and Spaulding law firm; J. Paul Austin, chairman of Coca Cola; Philip H. Alston, Jr., of the Alston, Miller and Gaines law firm; David and E. Smyth Gambrell, wealthy and socially prominent lawyers; lawyer Robert Lipshutz, a leader of the reform wing of the city's Jewish community; Robert and Anne Cox Chambers, key executives of the main media (newspapers, radio and television) group in the state; as well as others. This group of people provided the core of Carter's support during his race for governor, helped him run the state government, and provided, both directly and through their wide contacts, the bulk of the money which allowed Carter to enter the presidential race.[3] They also supplied another key element in Carter's campaign: introductions to leading figures of the Eastern Establishment, and at the same time, assurances that those leaders would find Carter trustworthy. Several members of Carter's early support group in Atlanta—Gambrell, Kirbo, Austin, and others—have close links with the Rockefeller family or with the broader Eastern Establishment. The Gambrell

---

Rockefeller and Brzezinski "were considering Carter, Florida's [governor] Reuben Askew, and former North Carolina Governor Terry Sanford as their representative of the New South to sit in the White House...Brzezinski was later to tell Peter Pringle of the *London Sunday Times*, 'It was a close call between Carter and Reuben Askew of Florida, but we were impressed that Carter had opened trade offices for the state of Georgia in Brussels and Tokyo. That seemed to fit perfectly into the concept of the Trilateral'."

Since then Askew has received a trilateral education in international business affairs. He was appointed U.S. Trade Representative on 2 October 1979. As a result of a controversial reorganization plan adopted by the Carter Administration, the U.S. Trade Representative unequivocally becomes responsible for overall trade policy and takes over from the State Department in representing the U.S. in international bodies like the Organization for Economic Cooperation and Development (OCED). See "Can Askew Deliver on Trade?" *Business Week,* 15 October 1979.

family, for example, is a major stockholder in Eastern Airlines, where Laurence Rockefeller is the single biggest individual stockholder. The elder Gambrell is on Eastern's board of directors, and his law firm is general counsel for Eastern. Laurence Rockefeller or his representative, Harper Woodward, has long been on the Eastern board with Gambrell. Thus, the Gambrell and Rockefeller families, as two main elements of the group controlling Eastern Airlines, are in close touch with each other; and they provided an early link between Carter and the Rockefellers.

These and similar connections led, by 1971, to meetings between Carter and both David Rockefeller and Hedley Donovan, then editor-in-chief of *Time* magazine and now Carter's senior adviser on domestic affairs and media relations. Carter was consequently no stranger to these national leaders when they decided to form the Trilateral Commission in the Spring of 1973. At that time, David Rockefeller, with George S. Franklin Jr., a Rockefeller in-law, Zbigniew Brzezinski, Henry Owen, Robert Bowie, and Gerard C. Smith—the last four, now members of the Carter Administration— selected members for the Commission. To advise them on the best Southerners to include they consulted contacts in that part of the United States. Franklin, Brzezinski, Owen, Bowie, and Smith were all leading members of a premier organization of the Eastern Establishment: the Council on Foreign Relations (see the article by Shoup and Minter). The Council has a number of affiliated organizations, called the Committees on Foreign Relations, made up of local leaders in thirty-seven cities around the nation.[4] Franklin called upon one of the leaders of the Council's Atlanta Committee—a group reflecting that city's power structure—to set up an advisory group to recommend possible members for the Commission. This was done and, on 13 April 1973, this body of prominent Atlantans recommended Carter for membership.[5]

Jimmy Carter was a very active member of the Trilateral Commission, attending all the regional sessions and the first plenary meeting in Japan in May 1976.[6] For this last session, Carter paid his air fare and other expenses from campaign funds and then was reimbursed by the Commission. In other words, Carter saw his journey to Japan as a campaign trip and the Commission's reimbursement represented a campaign contribution of $1,323.44.[7] For a period of several years Carter personally phoned the Commission's headquarters to keep up with the latest reports, and even passed out trilateral pamphlets when he worked with the Democratic National Committee in 1974.[8]

Carter and his leading advisers recognized the Commission's importance to his candidacy. Carter said in his autobiography that

"service on the Trilateral Commission gave me an excellent opportunity to know national and international leaders in many fields of
study concerning foreign affairs."[9] He added that "membership on
this Commission has provided me with a splendid learning opportunity..."[10] Gerald Rafshoon, Carter's media and advertising specialist, told one reporter that Carter's early trilateral tie was "most
fortunate" for Carter and "critical to his building support where it
counted."[11] In addition, Carter's entire foreign policy, much of his
election strategy, and some of his domestic policy has come directly
from the Commission and its leading members. The architect of
Carter's foreign policy from 1975 to the present has been Zbigniew
Brzezinski, first Commission director. Brzezinski wrote Carter's
major speeches during the campaign, and, as the president's national
security adviser, heads foreign policy—with assists from fellow
CFR leaders and Trilateral Commissioners like Vance, Brown,
Blumenthal, and a few others. The watchword for Carter's foreign
policy from 1975 on was "clear it with Brzezinski." Carter would
always ask when given a memorandum on foreign policy, "has
Brzezinski seen this...?"[12]

Less well known than his reliance on the Commission for his
foreign policy is the fact that Carter used Commission sources for
much of his campaign strategy. Brzezinski stressed as early as 1973
that the 1976 Democratic candidate "will have to emphasize work,
the family, religion, and, increasingly, patriotism, if he has any desire
to be elected."[13] Samuel P. Huntington's 1975 Commission report on
U.S. democracy (see Wolfe Part IV) seems to have been even more
important in setting Carter's campaign strategy. Huntington, a long-
time friend of Brzezinski and a Carter adviser during the campaign
became coordinator of security planning for the National Security
Council in the Carter Administration until resigning in August
1978.[14] To become president, Huntington argued, a candidate should
cultivate "the appearance of certain general characteristics—honesty, energy, practicality, decisiveness, sincerity, and experience."[15] His
next piece of analysis was even more striking. After reviewing the
political history of the 1960s and 1970s, Huntington summed up the
experience by saying:

> the "outsider" in politics, or the candidate who could make
> himself or herself appear to be an outsider, had the inside road to
> political office. In New York in 1974, for instance, four out of five
> candidates for statewide office endorsed by the state Democratic
> convention were defeated by the voters in the Democratic
> primary; the party leaders, it has been aptly said, did not endorse
> Hugh Carey for governor because he could not win, and he won
> because they did not endorse him. The lesson of the 1960s was
> that American political parties were extraordinarily open and

extraordinarily vulnerable organizations, in the sense that they could be easily penetrated, and even captured, by highly motivated and well-organized groups with a cause and a candidate.[16]

Needless to say, Carter was an "insider" who campaigned as an "outsider." As Carter himself expressed it, his campaign did best "whenever we'd project ourselves as the underdog fighting the establishment...fighting a valiant battle..."[17] And as president, Carter has followed several of Huntington's suggestions on domestic policy, such as tightening control over the Democratic Party and lowering expectations about what government can and should do.

One of the Commission's main initial objectives, as stated in its own publications, was to gain governmental influence in each of the three industrial capitalist sectors of the world: the U.S., Western Europe, and Japan. Only then could plans and policies be put into effect. As a 15 March 1973 memorandum put it, one of the objectives of the Commission's work would be "to foster understanding and support of Commission recommendations both in governmental and private sectors in the three regions."[18] In choosing members, Rockefeller and other leaders of the Commission stressed the need to find and recruit "men and women of sufficient standing to influence opinion leaders both public and private in favor of the Commission's recommendations."[19] Carter was thus only one of many who Commission leaders felt could be influential in the future. Commission founders also chose other politicians for membership such as Senators Walter Mondale and Robert Taft Jr.; Governor Daniel J. Evans; former Governor William W. Scranton; and Elliot Richardson. They were clearly trying to cover as many future possibilities as they could by involving a spectrum of politicians—both Democrats and Republicans—in their work.

Carter's Trilateral/Eastern Establishment connection helped him win both campaign funding and media attention. New York campaign contributions became an important supplement to Georgia funds during the second half of 1975 and throughout 1976. The main group of Carter backers, individuals who hosted gatherings or served on the Wall Street Committee for Carter, collectively made up an impressive list of socially and financially prominent people.[20] They were connected to each other and interacted socially through common membership in various institutions of the Eastern Establishment—elite social clubs, the Council on Foreign Relations (which had thirty-six members and ten directors on the Trilateral Commission in 1976), corporate boards of directors, etc. These members and their positions as of 1976 included: *Roger C. Altman,* a partner in Lehman Brothers investment banking firm (the firm's chairman,

Peter G. Peterson, is a member of the Commission and a director of the CFR); *John Bowles*, a banker and member of the Metropolitan Club, which has Trilateral Commissioners and numerous CFR leaders as members (Bowles first met Carter through Mike Troter, a close friend who was a lawyer with the Alston, Miller and Gaines law firm in Atlanta)[21]; *C. Douglas Dillon*, of Dillon Read investment banking firm, a director of the CFR, trustee of the Committee for Economic Development, the Brookings Institute and the Business Council, and a member of Chase Manhattan Bank's international advisory board, and the Links and Century Clubs; *Henry Luce III*, a director of *Time* magazine (along with Hedley Donovan) and a member of the Yale and University Clubs (which have other Commissioners as members); *Howard Samuels*, "Baggies" tycoon and Democratic party official; *Theodore C. Sorenson*, a corporate lawyer and active member of the CFR; and *Cyrus Vance*, a director of several leading corporations, early Trilateral Commissioner, and vice-chairman and a director of the CFR.

However, in all likelihood, an even more important result of Carter's trilateral tie was the inside track for favorable media coverage it gave him. As one journalist put it, this connection gave Carter "an opportunity to convince the corporate and media leaders that he was not a rustic yahoo, but a man to be taken seriously."[22] The media establishment did indeed take the Carter candidacy seriously, as will be seen below.

Carter's Media Coverage

During the 1976 campaign it was widely recognized by the candidates and their key staff members, by political reporters, and by academic observers that coverage by the mass communications media was the critically important factor determining the outcome of the race for the presidency. In a nation where the average voter has little contact with parties or politicans, newspapers, magazines, radio, television, and other media are the major intermediaries between the candidate and the electorate. Most voters learn nearly all of what they know about a candidate from these sources. This is particularly true of primary campaigns, where the party label is not a factor in the people's choice. No matter how long or hard national candidates may campaign, they cannot make contact with more than a tiny fraction of voters. The news media is their only hope for wide exposure. The owners and managers of the mass communications media are thus an important part of the U.S. political structure, wielding great power, especially during the pre-primary and primary periods of the campaign. The establishment media have the power to define the bounds of respectable presidential candidates. As Theo-

dore White put it, the "hereditary press barons...can make politicians—and on many occasions, break them."[23]

Hamilton Jordan, Carter's campaign manager, clearly recognized these facts. He wrote in a memorandum to Carter in November
1972 that "an eastern liberal news establishment," consisting specifically of the *New York Times* and the *Washington Post*,

> has tremendous influence. The views of this small group of
> opinion-makers in the papers they represent are noted and
> imitated by other columnists and newspapers throughout the
> country and the world. Their recognition and acceptance of your
> candidacy as a viable force with some chance of success could
> establish you as a serious contender worthy of financial support
> of major party contributors.[24]

He added in another memorandum two years later that the press
plays a "very special and powerful role." Its interpretation of results
during the first few primaries will "begin to make 'winners' of some
and 'losers' of others."[25] Jordan concluded that "hopefully, good
press in the early primaries will have solved some of our name-
recognition problem and given Jimmy Carter some depth to his new
national image."[26]

Jordan had put his finger on Carter's key problem: that he was
an unknown, even obscure, figure. In various public opinion polls
taken in the fall of 1975, Carter placed so low among Democratic
voters that his name was not even listed when the poll results
appeared in magazines and newspapers.[27] In the December 1975
Gallup Poll, for example, Carter was reported together with all
others with 7 percent or less (with Edward M. Kennedy listed) or 4 per-
percent or less (without Kennedy).[28] This put Carter behind Kennedy, Humphrey, Wallace, McGovern, Jackson, Muskie, and Bayh,
who were the most popular Democratic presidential possibilities.[29]

As late as the Gallup Poll taken during 23-26 January 1976,
Carter was still the first choice of only 4 percent of Democratic
voters.[30] It was at this point that his poll ratings took off. He jumped
to 12 percent by the end of February (after the New Hampshire
primary), behind only Wallace and Humphrey; and to 26 percent by
the second week in March (after the Florida and Massachusetts
primaries), only one percentage point behind front-runner Humphrey.[31]

Starting from an incredibly low-level of recognition and voter
support in January 1976, Carter had far surpassed Jackson, Wallace,
and the other Democratic contenders in the polls and nearly equalled
Senator Humphrey's popularity by early March.

By mid-March 1976, Carter was not only far ahead of the active
contenders for the Democratic presidential nomination, he also led

President Ford by a few percentage points.[32] In the space of only a few months, Jimmy Carter went from a virtual unknown to one of the most popular politicians in the entire nation, on par with men who had been prominent in national life for decades. This is certainly the most astonishing rise ever in twentieth century U.S. politics. Carter's sudden prominence in early 1976 was all the more significant when it is remembered that, typically, about 80 percent of voters make up their minds about whom they will vote for *before* the general election campaign begins. It is therefore during the pre-primary and primary period that presidents are really made.[33]

Only favorable media coverage of the Carter campaign— attention which led to a positive impression of Jimmy Carter—could have accounted for his rise to almost instant popularity. Such media favoritism was commented on by many people during 1975 and early 1976. Carter himself recognized that he had, on the whole, received good press. In early May 1976 he said, "I think the press has treated me well. And I would not be where I am now had the press not accommodated some of my errors."[34] As early as January 1975 Rex Gramun, a Georgia political commentator who later joined Carter's White House staff, noted Carter's favorable press coverage, pointing out that the *New York Times*, the *Washington Post*, and the *Wall Stree Journal* had all had front page stories on Carter's announcement for the presidency and that all together over one hundred newspapers and magazines around the world ran stories on Carter.[35] The tone of these stories was generally upbeat, treating Carter seriously, and some, like syndicated columnist Gary Wills, "lauded Carter."[36] A few months later the *Atlantic Constitution* reported that Carter "has gotten a good press from the national news media...a score of newspapers across the nation have kind things to say about Carter's presidential effort."[37] National news columnists like Joseph Kraft and Tom Wicker both pointed out in mid-January 1976 that Carter was, in Kraft's words, "the media candidate for the Democratic presidential nomination."[38] Wicker added that Carter had received a "good press" and was being "promoted" by the media as the "surprise" of the campaign.[39] Reporter Elizabeth Drew added in a March 1976 report that "the press, on the whole, has been kind to Carter and has played an important part in his buildup."[40] Some of Carter's competitors for the nomination also noticed what Morris Udall called an "incredible flow of press" beginning in the fall of 1975.[41] Thus, *before* Carter had won a single state caucus or primary, many media observers commented on his favorable press coverage. Not one of these leading mass media organizations ever mentioned Carter's trilateral connection, despite its importance.

What these observers and participants in the campaign were

noticing was the fact that leading media outlets—especially those
most closely connected to the Eastern Establishment such as the *New
York Times* and *Time* magazine, as well as CBS and NBC news—
were very favorable to the Carter candidacy in their news reporting.
A detailed content analysis of their campaign news coverage, too
lengthy to reproduce here, shows this to be the case.[42] The reason for
such favorable treatment of Carter's candidacy was that he was
known to be a centrist and internationalist, a thoroughly reliable
man from the point of view of the ruling class. All the leading media
corporations have numerous directors and owners who are members
of Eastern Establishment organizations, including the Commission
itself; leading corporations and banks; exclusive gentlemen's clubs
like the Links, and private policy planning organizations like the
Council on Foreign Relations. The word was quickly passed that
Carter was the best Democratic presidential candidate from the point
of view of establishment leaders; their media outlets projected a
favorable image to the public to help Carter win the election.

Conclusion

The central point of this article is that Jimmy Carter, using a
combination of charm, hard work, middle-of-the-road policy positions, and a keen sense of where power lies in the U.S., built his
political career by gaining support, first from the Establishment of
his local area, and then from the dominant sector of the national
ruling class. Traditional democratic constituencies like labor, intellectuals, minorities, ethnics, and big city machines provided support
as time went on but the key to Carter's victory was the early support
given by upper class groups centered in Atlanta and New York,
especially the latter's large financial and media corporations.

The makeup and locus of power in Carter's administration supplies strong additional evidence of the validity of this perspective. The
individuals Carter chose to fill the central policy making positions in
his administration were overwhelmingly from Eastern Establishment
organizations: the Trilateral Commission, the Council on Foreign
Relations, and the Committee for Economic Development.[43] In
addition, at least six assistant secretaries of State and Treasury are
also either Commissioners or CFR members, as are numerous
ambassadors, advisers, and government negotiators. These men
make the most important foreign, economic, and domestic policy
decisions of the U.S. government today; they set the goals and
direction for the administration.* (See "Who's Who.")

---

*It is an interesting comment on the close class connections at the uppermost levels

The Eastern Establishment—through the Trilateral Commission, the Council on Foreign Relations, and key media corporations—helped elect Jimmy Carter president. What does this mean for the future? It means increased ruling class control over U.S. politics, leaving minorities, the women's movement, the Left and even traditional Democratic Party constituencies like unions and liberals with less and less influence. This increased control is deemed necessary by Eastern Establishment leaders in order to give them freer reign to address the domestic and international crises facing the capitalist system during the late 1970s and throughout the 1980s.

The shape of their plans to deal with these problems add up to an increased appetite for authority, discipline, and control. The U.S. ideological climate has shifted to the right over the past few years, providing the basis for a forced decline in the living standards of the working class. This trend bears close watching and appropriate action by all those who desire a more, rather than less, democratic world.

FOOTNOTES

1. See James D. Barber, ed., *Choosing the President* (New York, 1974), p. 36; William R. Keech and Donald R. Matthews, *The Party's Choice* (Washington, D.C., 1976), pp. vii and p. 1; and Arthur T. Hadley, *The Invisible Primary: The Inside Story of the Other Presidential Race: The Making of the Candidate* (Englewood Cliffs, N.J., 1976).
2. Keech and Matthews, *The Party's Choice*, pp. 9-10.
3. See Laurence H. Shoup, *The Carter Presidency and Beyond: Power and Politics in the 1980s* (Palo Alto, Ca.: Ramparts Press, 1979), Chapter one.
4. Council on Foreign Relations, *Annual Report 1976-1977* (New York, 1977), p. 93. For a detailed analysis of the Council, see Laurence H. Shoup and William Minter, *Imperial Brain Trust: The Council on Foreign Relations and United States Foreign Policy* (New York, 1977).
5. George S. Franklin to S. Dan Schwartz, 10 January 1978. A copy of this letter is in the possession of the author.
6. *Washington Post*, 16 January 1974, p. A4.
7. Report of Committee for Jimmy Carter to the Federal Election Commission, 14 October 1975, Schedule A, Part 4, page 1; letter to Madeleine Jablonski, Office of the Trilateral Commission, to Laurence H. Shoup, 8 November 1977.

---

of the American power structure that, when Henry Kissinger left the government in 1977, he immediately became a director of the Council of Foreign Relations and a member of the executive committee of the Trilateral Commission, as well as chairman of the International Advisory Board of the Chase Manhattan Bank.

8. *Washington Post*, 16 January 1977, p. A4. *Los Angeles Times*, 24 January 1977, p. 13.

9. Jimmy Carter, *Why Not the Best?* (Nashville, Tenn., 1975), p. 140.

10. *Ibid.*, p. 127.

11. Robert Scheer, "Jimmy, We Hardly Know Y'All," *Playboy*, November 1976, p. 192.

12. *Los Angeles Times*, 23 January 1977, p. 1.

13. *Los Angeles Times*, 24 January 1977, p. 13.

14. *Newsweek*, 21 June 1976, p. 22.

15. Michel J. Crozier, Samuel P. Huntington, and Joji Watanuki, *The Crisis of Democracy: Report on the Governability of Democracies to the Trilateral Commission* (New York: New York University Press, 1975), p. 96.

16. *Ibid.*, p. 89.

17. Martin Schram, *Running for President: A Journal of the Carter Campaign* (New York, 1977), p. 6.

18. The Trilateral Commission, *The Trilateral Commission* (New York, 15 March 1973), p. 4.

19. *Ibid.*, p. 7.

20. John Bowles to Laurence H. Shoup, 12 January 1978.

21. References to Carter's New York supporters were drawn from: *Atlanta Constitution*, 5 November 1975, p. 1A; the *New York Times*, 15 March 1976, p. 36; 29 March 1976, p. 23; and 28 May 1976, p. A12; *Business Week*, 12 April 1976, pp. 87-88; *San Francisco Sunday Examiner and Chronicle*, 31 October 1976, Sunday Punch Section: 8; and from reports of the Committee for Jimmy Carter to the Federal Election Commission.

22. *Washington Post*, 16 January 1977, p. 13.

23. Theodore White, *The Making of the President 1972* (New York, 1973), p. 255.

24. Martin Schram, *Running for President 1976: The Carter Campaign* (New York, 1977), p. 64.

25. Jules Witcover, *The Pursuit of the Presidency 1972-1976* (New York: Marathon, 1977), pp. 135-136.

26. *Ibid.*, p. 137.

27. See *U.S. News and World Report*, 22 September 1975, pp. 53-54; Leslie Wheller, *Jimmy Who: An Examination of Presidential Candidate Jimmy Carter: The Man, His Career, His Stands on the Issues,* 1976; *Los Angeles Times,* 26 October 1975, p. 15.

28. *Los Angeles Times*, 14 December 1975, p. 16.

29. *Ibid.*

30. Princeton Survey Research Center, Inc., *Gallup Opinion Index #129,* April 1976, p. 4.

31. *Ibid.*

32. *New York Times,* 29 March 1976, p. 1; *Gallup Opinion Index #129,* April 1976, pp. 3-4

33. Elihu Katz, "Platforms and Windows: Broadcasting's Role in Election Campaigns," *Journalism Quarterly* (Summer 1971), p. 306.

34. Robert W. Turner, *I'll Never Lie to You: Jimmy Carter in His Own Words* (New York, 1976), p. 10.

35. *Atlanta Constitution*, 6 January 1975, p. 2A.

36. *Ibid.*

37. *Atlanta Constitution*, 13 April 1975, pp. 1A and 22A.

38. *Atlanta Constitution*, 15 January, 1976, p. 4A.

39. *New York Times*, 20 January 1976, p. 36.
40. Elizabeth B. Drew, "Reporter in Washington D.C.," *New Yorker*, 31 May 1976, p. 64.
41. Schram, *Running for President*, p. 19.
42. See *The Carter Presidency and Beyond*, Chapter three.
43. Drawn from official lists in Trilateral Commission reports, Annual Reports of the Council on Foreign Relations, and news reports.

chapter two

THE TRILATERAL IMPRINT ON DOMESTIC ECONOMICS
William Tabb*

A guiding purpose of the Trilateral Commission is to assist in finessing the structural crisis of U.S. and world capitalism. But in this attempt to finesse the crisis the Trilateral Commission faces a struggle—not only from workers but from within the ruling class. On the one side are the global corporations. On the other side are national and regional producers who stand to be squeezed out with the further centralization and concentration of capital.

Capitalist interests look very different to the few dozen truly global corporations whose profitability requires open access to all nations. Such firms have little in common with small business with its fear of unions, of government interference, and of tax burdens. The multinational giants have learned to pursue more sophisticated low-cost policies (including multiple sourcing and subcontracting to competitive sector firms, programmed de-skilling, and bureaucratized work rules and procedures), and they are quick to relocate plants in cheap labor regions. They have learned to let the unions do much of their work for them in disciplining labor and inculcating proper attitudes toward work.

The giant firms learned long ago how to use government intervention to their advantage—to assure themselves access to foreign markets on favorable terms, to arrange intricate export subsidies and insurance against nationalization, to manipulate other governments through foreign aid and military intervention, to finance research and development, to pay the costs of reproducing

*An earlier version of this paper appeared in *U.S. Capitalism in Crisis* (New York: Union for Radical Political Economics, 1978). It has been substantially revised and updated for inclusion in this volume. William Tabb is Associate Professor of Economics at Queens College (CUNY).

labor power (such as education and social insurance) and to stabilize the national economy and polity to promote economic and ideological hegemony. Global corporations have seen special tax treatment initiated so that the more business they do the lower their taxes.

Public debate over protectionism, the tax rebellion, and labor legislation all pit multinational capitalists against most of the rest of the business community. This sharpening of intracapitalist conflict (see Block) must be seen within the broader context of the economic crisis of world capitalism: overcapacity, intensification of competition, heightening interimperialist rivalry, economic stagnation, rampant inflation and high unemployment.

I shall argue that the Carter Administration's economic policy fits into the global aspirations of trilateralism and that Carter is neither conservative nor liberal in the traditional sense of these categories. He is embarked on an economic policy very different from the welfare liberalism of a Kennedy or a Johnson, and which goes well beyond the conventional budget cutting and special-interest favoring of Nixon and Ford.

First, I describe the conservative-liberal impasse and argue that these traditional polarities are dialectically united; then I discuss the novel combination of old economic instruments and the emergence of new tools which are being developed by the newer new economics. The former refers to the undercutting of labor's power and real wages and the establishment of a new buffer fraction in the U.S. population. The latter discusses the continued drift into corporatist planning and the adoption of wage-price-investment controls. Finally, I shall discuss the prospects for an alternative future.

The Conservative-Liberal Impasse

Carter has accepted the conservative, Nixon-Ford Administration's contention that increased government spending on nonproductive activities is inflationary. This position suggests that Keynesianism is a one-sided policy of constant overstimulation.* In this view, good intentions must give way to realism, for if we expand government spending and provide more and more for our citizens, two sorts of problems follow. First, to the extent that more flows

---

*ed. note: In the post-World War II period the dominant Keynesian theory (named after British economist John Maynard Keynes, whose later work was much more radical in its promotion of a planned full-employment economy than the brand of Keynesianism practiced in the United States) promised enduring prosperity through governmental economic intervention. Government would safeguard against depression and "prime" the national economy with high government spending, credit expansion, and lower taxes to stimulate consumption.

through the public sector, less is available to private enterprise. To the degree that larger and larger deficits are funded through the money markets, private corporations are either forced to pay more (and this, of course, both discourages investment and is passed on to consumers in higher prices), or they are crowded out of financial markets altogether because the government can outbid them. Thus the private sector is weakened with the growth of the public sector.

A second argument is equally important to the conservatives: to the degree to which the federal government raises welfare benefits, extends unemployment compensation to cover longer periods of joblessness, provides food stamps and so on, it undercuts the incentive to work. The incentive to work was, in earlier days, also called the whip of hunger. By either name, it forced U.S. workers into unsafe and unpleasant work and work under oppressive conditions at low pay. To the extent that workers may have less inclination to work in the fields from sunup to sundown or to operate a sewing machine in a sweatshop or to wash dishes in the dirty kitchen of some elegant hotel, the effect of the welfare state on work incentives is a major concern. So is its impact on wage rates; under existing conditions where jobs are stratified and pay scales hierarchical, an increase in legal minimum wage for entry-level jobs has profound effects. In order to restore the original differentials in pay, other wages are forced up. Thus, for example, if well-paying public sector jobs were made available in significant numbers, they would wreak havoc in the labor market for low-wage employment. This explains the outcry against the Humphrey-Hawkins Bill as originally written and the emasculated form in which it was finally passed.*

Conservatives point out—and again I think they are correct on this point—that in periods of sustained full employment labor discipline breaks down, worker productivity drops, and there is strong upward pressure on wages. Put otherwise: when a range of job

---

*ed. note: Humphrey-Hawkins has gone through major revisions since it was first introduced in 1975 as the Equal Opportunity and Full Employment Act. The bill originally stated that "all adult Americans able and willing to work have the right to equal opportunities for useful paid employment at fair rates of compensation" and required the federal government to pursue "such policies and programs as may be needed to attain and maintain full employment." The bill has been watered down to the point where it is unrecognizable under intensive pressure from business. The right to employment for all became a hazy goal of "full employment" at 3 percent unemployment (measured in artificial terms, which systematically underestimates real conditions). Even the rhetoric of the bill Carter endorsed and Congree passed promised continued hard times for workers. See for example, Richard Child Hill, "Left with the Democrats? The Rise and Demise of a Full Employment Bill," *U.S. Capitalism in Crisis, op.cit.,* pp. 275-283.

choices exists, worker-quit-rates go up in the most oppressive and low-paying jobs and all workers feel more confident in demanding paygrade promotion and improved safety conditions. They collude more widely and more openly in slowing down the work pace, knowing there is less management can do about it. With a booming economy and full order book, strikes are far more costly to management, less necessary for labor. The presence of what Marx called the reserve army of the unemployed restricts worker maneuverability: the threat of involuntary conscription into the unemployed ranks improves worker attitudes in ways management finds congenial to higher profits. While long recessions are costly to capital, intermittent employment is less harmful and may perhaps be useful. Finally, from a profit point of view, the lower the cost of production the better. Therefore, so long as markets exist, it is better for capital as a whole to keep wages low. The Keynesian logic was to cut taxes in order to build purchasing power; the conservatives prefer to hold down wages, increase profit margins, and foster investment.

This line of thinking leads to the notion of the political business cycle wherein a downturn is induced to discipline labor. The public of course is presented with another story, which insists that deflationary policies are needed to fight the rampant wage-price spiral. The blame is laid on workers who find the strength to fight for wage increases during high employment periods which will match and ideally get ahead of price increases. But before wage increases impinge on profits to the extent that such costs can no longer be passed on to consumers, the business press will call for, and the government will initiate, deflationary policies producing higher levels of unemployment.

The liberal Keynesian view challenges the conservative position on a number of essentials. At the theoretical level Keynesians argue that budget deficits during a recession are helpful because they increase aggregate demand and keep output and profits up. More pragmatically, they put forth a stagnationist analysis: where would the U.S. be now if there had not been strong federal intervention and spending on the interstate highway program, FHA (Federal Housing Authority) and VA (Veteran's Administration) mortgages, and aerospace-military spending? Would the postwar suburban-auto-military-led economic expansion have taken place so successfully, leading the U.S. to world supremacy and the much vaunted American way of life?

But the treatment itself has nurtured disorder. The present economic malady results from the cure to post-Great Depression stagnationist fears. Military spending in the long run proves parasitic on a formerly healthy civilian economy, eating up investment funds and employing many of the best scientific minds to produce items which add little to the U.S. standard of living. Mobility has also meant a sick form of suburban sprawl, urban decay, environmental degradation, pollution, and wasteful patterns of energy use.

Domestically, the postwar pattern of growth through suburbanization and highways has increased sales for the major U.S. firms, from GM to GE. These markets, if not totally saturated, are certainly limited, since their goods are no longer in the income range of many Americans. New home ownership, for example, is proving to be, for most young families, an unobtainable goal.

To some extent, these trends have been offset by a series of temporizing measures such as credit expansion and deficit spending. These solutions now constrain policy options. Consider the following: in 1950 consumer installment credit (excluding mortgages) was less than $15 billion. By 1965 such debt was over $70 billion and by 1975 more than $160 billion, an incredibly rapid rise in debt for U.S. families. By 1979 consumers were spending about a quarter of their disposable income to meet debt payments. Consumer debt is one piece of a fragile world credit structure.

Only in one year since 1960 has the federal budget been balanced. While deficits were $3-4 billion not so many years ago, it was $40-odd billion in 1975 and $60-plus billion a year later. It was a big deal when in 1979 President Carter submitted a budget which attempted to hold the line on government spending and proposed to keep the deficit below $30 billion. In doing so he was, as even his advisors noted, courting a recession. The system was and remains on the horns of a dilemma, for to slow the rate of debt creation is to risk depression. Other nations are in very desperate shape, and are staving off bankruptcy only because the U.S. and other Western powers are rolling over their debt. (These include industrialized countries like Italy as well as Third World countries.) Soaring energy and food prices aggravate the situation. The former is the joint domain of the stormy marriage between OPEC and the Seven Sisters,* while the latter is increasingly a U.S. monopoly. It should also, however, be noted that the OPEC price rise of ten percent for 1979—prices paid in dollars—would just about keep the oil producers up with the U.S. rate of inflation. After 18 months of steady oil prices this was a very good deal for the U.S. and its trilateral partners. Oil prices fell for most of these countries since OPEC prices are quoted in dollars and almost all capitalist currencies have done very well against the dollar.

*ed note: These are the seven major oil companies—Mobil, Gulf, Texaco, Exxon, Socal, British Petroleum (BP), and Royal/Dutch Shell.

At the same time the long postwar period of European recovery, rebuilding, and export boom is coming to an end. World capacity has, at least temporarily, outrun demand—despite a vast pumping-up credit-creation operation by national governments, international funding agencies, and private banks—with the latter operating in an increasingly shaky Euro-currency market.*

Under such conditions, fiscal conservatism has a superficial plausibility in a world of capital mobility and global corporations. Just as within the U.S. the Northeast must hold taxes and wages down to discourage runaway shops (the alternative being to move to social control of investment and production decisions), so, too, many nations must remain competitive or lose out internationally to more attractive sites for capitalist investment. The attack on social welfare spending is part of this phenomenon.

The social wage is the income in transfers and in kind as provided by the government—the wide panoply of health, housing, education, old age benefits and others. If the economic surplus of the society can be transferred from working class consumption to the business sector, then both present profit rates and the prospects for future profits will tend to increase as capitalists plow a portion of their profits into investment. Reducing bureaucracy and controlling Big Government inefficiency are admirable goals, but they are more an ideological cover than the real reason for fiscal conservatism. An overtaxed U.S.A. has become increasingly receptive to the economics of less and wary of big spenders in government. This does not reflect a lessened desire for the services of a sensibly organized welfare state but rather an awareness that government is inefficient, and the benefit/cost ratio of the tax dollar is far lower than it should be. But if Big Government has its drawbacks, it also has important advantages to capital. And if higher profits are desirable in the present system, they are not necessarily guaranteed in the long run by the lowering of real wages and imposing greater work force discipline. For this reason Carter is hardly ready to abandon Keynesian stimulation as a mindless conservatism might suggest. Rather, in a more directly class-biased way than his predecessors, he chooses to direct government economic policies not merely to fostering the accumulation process in general, a policy of all presidents since F.D.R., but to financing the structural transformation of the world economy by fostering the ability of U.S.-based multi-

*ed. note: Eurocurrencies are currencies such as the U.S.-dollar, German deutsche mark, or Swiss franc held and traded outside their country of origin, mainly in Western Europe. These markets are not regulated by any national or international agencies.

nationals to invest on a world scale with minimal restrictions, and to do so in a way coordinated for maximum stability with the junior partner nations of Japan and Western Europe. The task is not to expand the economy; this would trigger rampant inflation and increase the danger of system collapse. Rather, the task is to ensure the hegemony of U.S.-based multinational capital while transforming the domestic economy. In this context Carter's economics is critical of traditional Keynesians. It is not that Keynesians have been wrong in the past so much as that their prescriptions (from the trilateral perspective) are wrong for the present.

At the risk of appearing somewhat mechanistic, I would suggest that liberals and conservatives are each half-right. In a period of no growth or slow growth, the Democrats are right to spend lots of money, stimulate the economy, run deficits, and intervene actively. In periods of inflation, the Republicans are correct to warn of the dangers of pyramiding debt, wasteful government spending, and the need for discipline. But unfortunately for policy makers in the newer new economics—necessitated by the current crisis—a half-truth and another half-truth do not add up to the whole truth. Without rapid debt creation and inflation, the U.S. would have endured even higher rates of unemployment and unused productive capacity. Keynesianism may have its deep and perhaps insurmountable problems, but the conservative alternative promises permanent austerity and eventually a deep depression.

Zapping Labor

What I shall call the Trilateral Approach to the domestic economy is a new policy thrust which attempts to move beyond the impasse I have described, to adopt a new combination of old instruments and to develop new ones. It basically seeks to create space to transform the U.S. economy. Space for change is created, in the felicitous phrase of a high ranking wage-price administrator of the Nixon years, by zapping labor—forcing down the real wages of U.S. workers and cutting the services they have come to expect from their government. Lowered expectations, the politics of less, benign neglect: these are the continuing policies which it is hoped will allow for a restructuring of economic relations. The goals of restructuring are to generate capital to modernize the U.S.'s aging plant capacity, to relocate production away from the highly unionized and politically more demanding Northeast, to develop new energy sources through the biggest government giveaway in U.S. history (to the oil companies), to reorient our transportation system, and to develop space for some Schumpeterian technological breakthroughs. Key elements of the Establishment have essentially accepted the long wave thinking of some radical economists—which predicts a severe economic downturn following a long period of relative prosperity— and are looking for ways to lower costs of production and to lay the conditions for generating a new wave of economic expansion. We understand Carter's policies in this light.

During his campaign for the presidential nomination, Mr. Carter worked hard to make himself more acceptable to the liberal elements of his party. He talked tax reform and full employment. He spoke out against the political and economic elite. In his acceptance speech to the Democratic Convention, he delivered what was in his own words a populist message. Throughout the campaign Carter sought to convey lineal descent from the New Deal of Franklin Delano Roosevelt. Once elected, however, his cabinet appointments drew heavily on Establishment insiders. He held numerous and well-publicized meetings with the major power brokers. Corporate executives, suspicious of irresponsible Democrats, were invited to meet with Carter's economic advisers and with congressional Democrats chairing key tax and banking committees to be reassured.

In spite of instances of symbolic populism, Carter moved very slowly in areas of tax and welfare reform, national health, and other priorities of the liberal agenda. With the continuation, indeed the worsening, of stagflation (and the deepening Dollar Crisis), Carter was widely criticized for the dismal performance of his Administration in the area of economic policy, and he moved to provoke a domestic slowdown. Cutting social spending, jobs for the poor, and aid to the cities, Carter moved to punish the victims of economic crisis by a voluntary wage-price control program—an effective means of zapping labor. In its details the program was even more anti-labor than the Nixon program had been. Carter, in short, had turned out to be a fiscal conservative.

Actually, none of this should be confusing. The best way to view Carter, I am suggesting, is to see that he has pursued, albeit in a somewhat muddled fashion, the policies outlines above—trying to create the conditions for restructuring and, above all, disciplining American labor. As has been suggested, this policy precedes Carter. (The forcing of a lower standard of living also antedates the OPEC price increases.)

There is an important dialectic at work here regarding the imperative of multinational business and the role of the nation-state. Even though formal and informal transnational decision making bodies are becoming increasingly important, the national state is a critical intervening agency, mediating the desires of globally oriented capital and its conflicts with smaller locally, regionally, and nationally oriented capital on the one hand, and the working class on the other. Struggles over tariff protection and state subsidies, restrictions on capital mobility must be seen in these terms. For example, some U.S. television producers are against being protected from foreign T.V.—indeed, they *are* the foreign producers using cheaper labor to service the U.S. market from abroad. For workers, too, the state is the level at which important struggles are waged. It is the state that says there must be wage control and that there are to be cuts in social services. The rationale is that the U.S. must stay competitive. Thus the globalization in the arena of decision making by increasingly mobile multinationals impacts on workers and smaller producers in ways which are addressed by national governments. The working class movement is forced to unite with workers in all nations, not because of stirring polemics, but because of concrete material needs in an era of monopoly capital. The nation-state is the jurisdiction through which capital disciplines labor and plays off groups of workers against each other. By fighting cutbacks in social expenditures, efforts to limit the right to strike and so on, workers make demands which make clearer the class position of the state apparatus Thus, the political struggles and the class struggle become one. This is the goal and the hope of the Left movement.

This is especially true in light of a second phenomenon with deep political implications: a cycle of regional impoverishment affecting increasingly large parts of the U.S. in much the same way as it does poorer countries. The process of industrializing agricultural nations and parts of nations, such as Puerto Rico and the Mexican side of the Rio Grande, entails capital penetration of a low wage area, the establishment of infrastructure at government expense, the building of plants and installing of machinery to exploit local labor. Over time, as the surplus labor of the area is absorbed, as workers organize and demand more of the surplus they produce, as multinational penetration drives up the cost of living and likewise wages if living standards are not to drop, as more and more things must be purchased in the money economy (e.g. food is no longer grown individually, homes must be rented or bought from construction companies and real estate people), the firms move on to more profitable areas, leaving behind a depressed region no longer able to meet its needs. The disinvestment of much of the industrial Northeast is a process akin to the one we have been describing.

In the early days of industrialization, unions were a grave threat to Big Business. Oftentimes the police and judicial apparatus of the state came down hard on the side of capital against workers, sharpening the relationship between political struggle and class struggle. Since the great union organizing drives in basic industries succeeded in the 1930s, large capital has come to accept the inevitability of unions and has worked to turn them into institutions to control and discipline labor. In the post-World War II period one of the central functions of the Cold War was to force American socialists, communists, and other militants who had built the CIO out of positions of leadership in the trade union movement and to support class-accommodationist business unionism and even gangsterism.

Management and unions struck a bargain. The productivity deal which supplanted class politics called for multi-year contracts to promote labor peace and security of seniority and retirement benefits to buy loyalty and give workers a stake in the company. Most importantly the company was given control of the production process and was more or less free to introduce new technologies which would hold down the need for labor, but the workers who continued to have jobs with the company would share some of the gains through higher wages. (See Tabb Part V.) The outcome has been that a smaller and smaller proportion of the work force is organized. The multi-divisional corporations moved first to subcontracting parts to nonunion shops and finally to moving plants to nonunion areas and actively fighting unionization efforts. The trade union movement today is paying the price of its earlier accommodations. Viewed as authoritarian structures, dominated by white males more interested in the steady inflow of dues and labor peace than they are with the well-being of their members, and viewed by the general public as arrogant and selfish, the AFL-CIO Executive Council pronouncements seem hardly a threat to a president bound on a policy of forcing down the real wages of U.S. workers.

At the present time these collaborationist policies are being deeply questioned. Labor isn't doing very well in the deal. With increased international competition and a general situation of excess capacity (in steel, for example) workers in each country are being told by the transnational corporation that they must work harder to meet foreign competition. The workers compete to produce more for lower wages and the transnational corporation profits. It is no wonder that union officials are having a difficult time selling the productivity deal to members. Output rises, accompanied by layoffs, but the gains just set new norms which must be surpassed. While union leaders, fearing plant closings, are afraid to push demands, rank-and-file militance increases as seen in the number of wildcat strikes and the prevalence of insurgent campaigns like the challenge by steel worker Ed Sadlowski for the union presidency on the platform: "The workers and the boss have nothing in common. It's a class question...The boss is there for one damn purpose alone, and that is to make money, not to make steel, and it's going to come out of the worker's back." The alternative to growing worker opposition to their victimization in the restructuring of the world economy is to stay with the old leadership rather than risk a real confrontation with capital.

The increased interdependence of the world economy is the single most important factor in the present historical period. After a period of rapid expansion of the world economy based on exports and growing world markets, we have reached a situation where not everyone can keep growing through export surpluses. Japan and West Germany do well, but Britain and Italy are in real trouble. Just as the Northeast competes with the Sunbelt of the Southwest United States, so too do all of the nations which are part of the international division of labor compete with each other.

Trilateral economics takes note of these depressing trends and seeks to "optimize," given the severe "constraints" of a declining capitalism. The point is to grab as much of the pie as possible and the crisis of world capitalism offers both the need and the possibility. The trilateralists want to do this while pursuing international stability through a sophisticated trilateral bargaining process.

Holding Down Wages

Three observations about this newer economics help clarify its effect on the relation between capital and workers. First, that within its possibilities, it is working. Given the nature of the crisis (a severe and very deep one), U.S. capital is doing well. Second, U.S. labor is doing very badly. No longer the junior partner in imperialist adventures, U.S. unions—and even more so the vast majority of unorganized workers—are the victims of a crisis they have had little to do with, and they are being made to appear as the scapegoat. Third, the standard of living of most U.S. workers will continue to be outpaced by the growth of corporate profits and priorities. Let us examine each of these points.

We are being told that wages in the U.S. must be kept down and social spending cut back because of international competition. The seesawing of comparative advantage between the U.S. and other capitalist nations is an aspect of the international economy which merits attention. Just as U.S. monetary policy cannot avoid giving close consideration to the effect of interest rates and monetary policies on U.S. financial accounts, so too do relative rates of wage inflation affect the balance of trade accounts. The degree to which U.S. labor costs rise at a faster or slower rate than our major trading partners is of the greatest significance. A large part of the Ford Administration rationale in the economic area was to hold down both wage earnings and the aforementioned social wage in order to favor U.S. business.

As I shall argue, real wages continue to go down. The timing of new wage controls reflects the intensity of trade union efforts to catch up. When business feels pressure from labor they turn to the state. New controls were not instituted until 1978 largely because the corporate sector did not feel the need for them until then. A review of the financial press through 1976-78 will help set the background for a discussion of the present period.

In a fascinating cover story titled "1976: Labor's Year of Compromise," *Business Week* (1 December 1975) noted that five basic industries (auto, trucking, rubber, electrical equipment, and construction) would be negotiating contracts in what, given the power of the unions involved, "should be an industrial relations nightmare." The story starts out noting: "One thing is sure. The unions are talking of huge wage increases to make up for the income erosion since 1973. Between January 1973 and July 1975, the Consumer Price Index increased 27.1 percent, while average hourly earnings of workers in industry rose only 20.2 percent. Union leaders are under enormous pressure from the rank-and-file to deliver both on the inflation catch-up issue and on job security." But don't worry, says *Business Week*, corporate leaders are optimistic about relatively low cost contracts. It is union leaders who are worried about how to sell bad contracts to the workers. "Labor's moderation since controls expired in early 1974 is one hint. Instead of exploding, wage gains have surprisingly run behind inflation in the past 2-2½ years." That is, with high levels of unemployment, workers are grateful they have jobs, don't risk losing them, and lack the confidence to press for higher wages.

A year later the business press had the same story. As the *Citibank Newsletter* (December 1976) says of 1976: "Many prognosticators feared that rapidly climbing labor costs would fuel a rise in the overall inflation rate, as labor leaders sought to make up the ground that wages had ceded to inflation over the past three years...[but] Against the backdrop of a near 9% unemployment rate, the rate of increase in compensation was far more moderate than generally predicted."

It is important to note that not only did the data *not* support a blame-the-unions theory of inflation but also that the business press fully recognized this to be the case. A similar analysis is presented in the December 1976 *Morgan Guaranty Survey* to explain record high corporate profits. "Contributing importantly to that better showing was a degree of moderation in wage inflation that surprised most analysts." When writing for its corporate readership alone, business reviews dismiss the influence of labor costs and of costly disruptive strikes, pointing out that idle days due to work stoppages amount, after all, to only a small fraction (less than a half of one percent) of total work time for the U.S. economy. While it may be important for the general public to believe that workers' greed causes economic crises—and applaud punishing measures—such an explanation is rejected by the financial community's serious analysts.

Perhaps such wage moderation had come after an extended period of labor gains? No, that was not the case. The expectation that workers would have sought higher gains in 1976 was based, as W. J. Usery, Jr., Director of the Federal Mediation and Conciliation Service put it, on "need not greed." The average worker had the lowest purchasing power in ten years, and workers badly needed to catch up.

We see also that U.S. workers have been losing out relative to workers elsewhere. Of the industrialized capitalist nations unit labor costs over the 1970-77 period rose by 44 percent in the U.S.—half the rate as in Britain and less than a third as fast as in Germany, Japan, and the other major competitors. These statistics (computed by Citibank economists) suggest that the relative docility of the AFL-CIO has not helped its members. It is also clear that U.S. workers have not caused the inflation. In comparing worker-management earnings Census Bureau surveys show the following: While in 1962 managers earned 27 percent more than workers, by 1974 they earned 49 percent more; and employer-provided fringe benefits for non-production personnel make the growing difference even greater. This manager-administrator group is increasing in size and in purchasing power, setting up what *Business Week* has called "the new two-tier market for consumer goods."

The upper-tier has been composed of college graduates who act as forepersons in white collar and service jobs. While part of management, they represent a growing stratum of higher paid workers who function to keep production running smoothly or do technical, sales, or other sorts of nonproduction work. It is clearly cheaper to expand the ranks of management and social control employees while holding down wages of other workers. A new middle class is created with relative privilege and a greater stake in existing stratification and hierarchical forms of organization.

At the same time, conspicuous consumption leads others to demand similar affluence; these new consumer products are also desired by the general workforce. One effect of the proliferation of new products and rapid style changes is to increase the cost of living and the amount needed to insure an adequate standard. Coupled with the rising cost of fringe benefits, especially of health care which was once exclusively the perk of executive positions, wage pressures are severe. The basic wage required for a working class standard of living appears to be rising. Perhaps that is responsible for much of what the corporate sector sees as wage drift resulting in a permanent inflation, or a basic inflation of 5-6 percent, which persists despite high levels of unemployment.

The two-tier phenomena follows the Brazilian model in which rapid growth is facilitated by keeping the lid on wages and making better use of nontraditional labor resources (urbanizing peasants in one case; women, teenagers, and regional relocation of industry away from high wage areas in the other). A second element is establishing a larger middle class buffer of better paid professionals, expanding the number of salaried employees who watch over lower-tier workers. The intermediate role of this group is mirrored in their pro-corporatist political and social attitudes.

Sorting through statistical trends to isolate the movement toward a Brazilian model is made difficult by interregional patterns. Industry is moving out of the higher wage Northeast to the South, West, and Southwest. Superficially, this points to an increasing equality of national income distribution, taken by itself. In class terms, it represents the effort of capital to lower the wage bill. On the race front, factories are not locating in the heavily Black areas of the South, but rather where antiunion attitudes prevail, largely outside of the large cities and away from Black communities which have come to grasp the importance of collective action in race issues and easily apply the lesson to struggles at the workplace. Interregional competition like ethnic, racial, and sexual divisions continue to play a key role in holding down working class organization. While the general attack on labor income intensifies the need for class unity, it can, in the absence of a clear Left analysis and movement, lead to scape-goating and to increased intraclass tensions (the "antis"—busing, abortion, affirmative action, etc.—of the New Right are cases in point).

Regulation and Class Struggle

The business press tells us how the auto industry is positively throttled with regulations that divert money and manpower from production. General Motors, we are told by *Fortune* magazine (4 December 1978) employs 24,000 people who report to various regulators, and the poor company "is having to spend billions each year on downsizing alone." Most Americans reject such an analysis. Downsizing means saving gas and the raw materials which go into producing cars. It was Detroit's refusal to build high quality, durable small cars which led to the import boom and to federal regulation. They ignored consumer preference and resource considerations because profits were higher on bigger cars. Regulation is not throttling industry so much as it is an uphill battle to bring selfish corporations into some semblance of responsibility to social goals.

There are similar protests by the financial press against new rules concerning noise levels, coke-oven emissions, possible carcinogens in the steel industry, and to chemophobia, the fear of being poisoned by the chemical industry's poisons which has led to passage of the Toxic Substances Control Act. There are similar complaints about the comprehensive mine-safety regulations passed in 1969 which have lowered productivity in the coal industry (and reduced deaths in the mines by over a third, although mining in the U.S. is still far more dangerous than in Europe). There is also complaint about land reclamation laws which require reforestation to protect the homes of miners in the valleys from landslides caused by stripping the hills. In all of these regulations and thousands more, people are being protected to some degree from the effects of the profit system. Business is counterattacking and blaming such regulation for the drop in productivity in U.S. industry.

There are two things to say about this charge. First, it is untrue. Second, even if it were true, it would be no reason to remove such regulations. It is not true because very very little of the drop in productivity is explained by increased regulations (or by more women and teenagers in the labor force, another prevalent scape-goating idea). The drop in U.S. productivity came very suddenly, in 1974, and seems more linked to the general onset of world economic crisis.

The corporations clearly do not like restrictions on their ability to maximize profits. Yet their insistence that dangerous chemicals in our food and unsafe conditions on the job are necessary to bring economic growth helps us to question the validity of their measure of growth. Each year that the Gross National Product goes up the quality of life goes down. The form of growth favored by the corporations is capital intensive and resource wasteful. They accuse opponents of wanting to undercut our standard of living. Yet it is they in their selfish singlemindedness who are destroying the planet and undercutting the ability of local governments and even nations to democratically decide their own future. The market annuls demo-cracy by defining the decisions which are central to life as private while the ones we are allowed to vote on become increasingly meaningless.

Business understands and does not like the idea that society through democratic process could channel investment into those areas the electorate would prefer—say a livable environment which by creating full employment and providing a basic adequate living standard would undercut the decay of our cities and reverse the crime statistical trends, and perhaps save the air, water, and other natural resources from pillage by the profit motive. Mobil Oil, which uses its non-taxed dollars to buy a column on the Op Ed page of the *New York Times,* sees the matter clearly, although obviously the political stress is quite different: "When governments tax away private savings, they also keep those savings from being invested in new factories or farms. So the power to tax is also the power to channel investment...As government grows larger and bureaucracy proliferates, the natural allocation of resources by a free-market economy is increasingly distorted. In the United States, government growth has meant massive expenditures for the increased regulation of business and other non-productive pursuits. The money spent on regulation and compliance with regulation is channeled away from the kinds of investment that spur productivity and economic growth."

Later in this column (titled "The Leaky Bucket," Part 2 of their series on "The Standstill Economy"), they describe how bureaucrats writing position papers on energy don't produce any energy, and neither do energy industry executives assigned to complying with regulations. Such public service messages are a small, though significant, part of their continuing efforts to be sure governmental policies subsidize them at the public expense and that the general public accepts their propaganda that regulation hurts rather than helps. We can expect more efforts of this sort to misrepresent the purpose of social regulation. In point of fact most regulation still favors corporations by restricting competition and protecting profits. While the federal budget for social services is cut, tax expenditures (special treatment through exclusions and exemptions) have led to the corporate income tax share of federal taxes falling from 25 percent of total revenues to less than half that today. Adjusting for the effect of state and local income and social security deductions, weekly spendable earnings—while more than doubling in money terms between 1965 and 1978—actually *fell* for the average worker. With rising energy costs (because of deregulation of domestic prices allowing domestic producers windfall gains to match OPEC price increases), rising interest costs on consumer credit and home mortgages, and rising food prices—all heavily influenced by government policies—we can expect a continued attack on our living standard. It is the combination of allowing the powerful to use their market power to raise prices and lower the quality of products, on the one hand, and the increasingly regressive tax structure, on the other, which is forcing down the living standard of working people.

On both of these issues—productivity and taxes—the corporate position has gained acceptance, thanks to media support and generous public relations and electoral campaigns. Yet opposition to corporate ideology and policy prescription is also growing as citizens see that the tax rebellion has brought them a higher share of taxes (since the legislation of tax reduction has mostly favored business and the rich) and the lower budgets means a deterioration of public services. In most parts of the capitalist world Left movements— Socialist, Communist, and Labor parties and factions—resist such cuts. In the U.S. many ordinary citizens have voted to cut taxes because here individualist solutions are more frequently relied upon as a way to solve problems. One can anticipate that as such shortsighted policies are shown to hurt, most Americans too may come to understand that some forms of collective resistance to economic hardship is imperative and will come to identify the problem not as being "the poor" or other workers, but the dominance of privately controlled transnational corporations. In the absence of such a Left alternative the corporate sector has been successful in forcing the burdens of the current crisis onto working people. In 1979 there seems to be some consensus in the business press and among leading figures such as Arthur Burns that a recession was the best way to protect profit margins. This is *not* to say that corporations prefer a stagnant economy to a dynamically growing one. Rather, given the slowdown, overcapacity, and need for restructuring (to remove the inefficient smaller firms so that after further centralization the basis will be laid for a new period of expansion) corporate spokespeople see a recession as a good thing—a period of adjustment to both shake out weaker competitors and prevent labor from successfully making wage demands to catch up with rising prices.

Support for the notion of the political business cycle is found in the December 1978 *Morgan Guaranty Survey,* which points to the dramatic slowing of productivity, the continued strength of the economy as measured by capacity utilization and the rising unit labor costs (9 percent in the last year, which combined with only a 1 percent increase in productivity would cause a profit squeeze if corporations were not raising their prices). For Morgan it is labor costs which have exerted heavy pressures on prices, with no let-up in sight. The policy lesson to be learned from the past year? "Perhaps the most important one is the danger of government pursuit of anti-inflationary policies in a timid way for fear of inducing a business slump. Such a "recession obsession" has dominated government policy for many years, but it was especially apparent in 1978." More simply put, the need is to cut the growth in wages by increasing unemployment. This was the business community consensus President Carter acted upon in the early months of 1979 to slow growth and create unemployment.

The ways Carter is doing this are by cutting social spending and enforcing wage controls. Since debate over wage and price controls will be with us for some time, and because their adoption is an important marker on the road to more comprehensive forms of planning it is important to understand their nature. The way such controls are applied in a capitalist economy can never be neutral. The extent to which they favor capital versus labor is an indicator of the strength, the degree of class consciousness and power of the contending forces. By blaming workers for inflation, or even in saying "workers may not have created inflation but holding down wages is crucial to slowing inflation," the state favors capital and undermines labor's standard of living, autonomy, and ability to defend itself.

The AFL-CIO is quite right that Carter's voluntary guidelines if followed would hurt labor even more than Nixon's 1971-74 controls. Nixon's controls did not count any improvement in benefits won by unions in measuring wage increases; catch-up pay increases were allowed; and cost-of-living increases were estimated as they occurred over the course of the year (rather than at the beginning of the year before they occurred, as under Carter). Most of all, under Nixon, some steps were taken to hold down the rate of price increases.

Editorial writers, led by the *New York Times* (11 December 1978) criticized Mr. Meany for his efforts to "undermine the President's embryonic wage-price guideline program." The *Times* calls his criticism that the program is too hard on wages and too soft on prices, "premature and unfortunate." In response to Meany's call for mandatory controls, the *Times* says that the President's threat of denying government contracts to recalcitrant firms "could turn out to be mandatory in all but name." But of course this is far from true.

Union settlements are highly visible and so in 1979 as contracts for teamsters, petroleum workers, electrical, and auto workers come to be negotiated, public and private pressure is strong to limit demands. Meanwhile, the Council on Wage and Price Stability says it will monitor the largest 400 firms. Its staff couldn't possibly do that. It is too small and does not have the power to compel firms to submit the data it needs to determine whether cost increases are justified. Nor has it asked for that power. It doesn't want it. Most huge firms don't have to worry about price increases even if they are scrutinized; they merely lower the cost of poorly selling products a bit so that the average increase doesn't look so bad. By changing the size of candy bars or new designs, companies can argue they are producing a different product and are within the guidelines. The inevitable result is increasing prices but lower real wages.

The media generally pictured AFL-CIO head, George Meany,* as unreasonable for not giving Mr. Carter's voluntary wage-price guidelines a chance. Mr. Meany's position itself was rarely stated. It was that if there must be any controls let them be compulsory—on wages yes, if necessary, but also on prices and profits. As the AFL-CIO Executive Council October 1978 policy statement said, Mr. Carter's price guideline "is so flexible as to be non-existent and is without effective enforcement" and noted that "dividends, capital gains, unearned income from tax shelter—all are completely free to climb without limit. Commodity speculators remain free to drive up the prices of food and other raw materials. Banks and other financial institutions remain free to speculate at will against the American dollar. Professional fees are not effectively controlled, and there is no mechanism for halting rapid increases in rents." Is there anyone who doubts this? The one sided coverage by the media exhorting "let us pull behind the president," and denunciations of greedy unions prevents any reasoned discussion of the issues.

Despite Mr. Meany's hopes, however, mandatory controls too would not be in labor's interest. Experience under the Nixon controls show the difficulty of establishing guidelines and controlling prices. Not only can companies "change" models, product mix, specifications, terms of sales, and so on, but profit rates can also be juggled on paper by allowable costs and pass-through provisions making exceptions wide enough to drive a truck through. Further, since imports (including oil and industrial raw materials), agricultural products, and interest rates are all exempt from controls, food, housing, and energy costs will continue to soar, as will health care and other essential services.

In the Nixon wage-price controls experience labor was burned badly. They were not meaningful participants in a tripartite labor-business-public decision making structure because the public and business were both represented by the same sort of antilabor individuals. By 1974 George Meany was opposed to wage price controls but if they were to be enacted again he also wanted profit controls, interest rate controls, and controls of dividends and executive compensation as well as real enforcement of price controls. Full controls would mean investment decisions would also have to be negotiated. A key reason Carter has favored voluntary controls is so that he can avoid the concessions labor would demand in exchange for accepting compulsory wage ceilings. [Trilateralist Lane Kirkland succeeded Meany who died in January 1980-ed.]

If output does slow down we can expect firms to spread their continuing overhead costs over fewer units sold so that we will have higher not lower prices. Under Carter's guidelines passing on production costs is accepted and so firms will protect their profit rates by increasing their profit margins.

In sum, capitalism has only one way to solve crisis: take from the poor and give to the rich, cut capital gains and taxes, and increase depreciation allowances, and hope the corporations will use the money to create jobs and economic growth. Simple minded marxism? Hardly. This is the consensus opinion of leading economists and the unquestionable policy of the government. Will it work? No and yes. Will it avoid a recession? No, nothing economists or government officials have tried for the last hundred years has prevented the fairly regular appearance of recessions and depressions. Yes, it will work to get the economy going again, after a recession-depression. Given these realities is some form of state economic planning a good thing?

Reality and Appearance in Economic Planning

The economic policy of trilateralism is everywhere more or less the same—investment credits and other forms of subsidy for corporations to modernize their plant capacity and to do it pretty much on the private sector's terms: some stimulus, some wage-price controls, some planning. The exact combination is a matter of the concrete situation in a given nation-state at a given time. The pressure, as I've argued, is for a secular increase in all of these policy interventions by the state. I have argued also that the nation-state role is two-fold: to subsidize capital accumulation and to discipline labor. The apparent paradox is that as corporations outgrow the state and come to treat each nation as only one profit center in a global operation, they also rely more heavily on the state to discipline workers in each country. National austerity is the outcome as government officials act to lower the real wage of workers in each nation. Just as South Carolina competes with Mississippi and Massachusetts for plant location, so do Spain, Britain, and Italy. As international capital mobility increases, the importance of the nation-state for capital does not diminish. The police power of the state supplements economic policy. Realism is the ideological cover for wage cuts. Dividing the working class of the world to play one group against the others is the class content of national austerity.

A significant group of liberal economists, labor leaders, and corporate executives came together during the 1974-75 crisis period to discuss and formulate a rationale, and then formally presented from the "Initiative Committee on Economic Planning," in broad outlines a proposal which, if adopted, would move the U.S. toward a European style approach to government planning. The proposal had impressive support: Wassily Leontief and Robert Roosa, Henry

Ford II and Leonard Woodcock, men prominent on Wall Street and in the corporate boardrooms, as well as leading academic economists. As the economy seemed to recover, their initiative faded. Because of the liberal caste of the support and the seeming cogency of their major argument (that gathering information about possible needs, discussing sensibly and democratically ordering priorities, will mean a more healthy economy than the alternative of not thinking out and gathering information on needs and resources), opponents were hard-pressed intellectually to object—although they sensed that the seemingly innocuous proposal, lacking, as it did, any coercive elements, was indeed the camel's nose under the tent flap and that more formal procedures were sure to follow.

I myself must break with these would-be public interest planners, not because I doubt their sincere intentions but because I think that planning is the camel's nose of corporatism. (See Kaufman and Clawson). While the global firms are right to fear some restrictions from such a formalization of big business/big government/big labor coordination as compared to the present less structured working arrangement, they will also pretty much be the dominant element in any national planning—just as they were in the NRA boards and as their counterparts now dominate planning in Europe. After all, the system is capitalism, even if narrow private profit is sometimes limited in the interests of the larger system. Union members would do better than unorganized labor; they would be represented by "responsible" officials who would be presumed to speak for all workers. But those not in unions, almost 80 percent of the labor force, would not be a central concern to the AFL-CIO hierarchy, which would continue to press for higher wages for the organized. Even union members would become more powerless; the demand that they give up their most powerful instrument, the strike, in the national interest (lest it interfere with production to the detriment of the public welfare) would be difficult to resist.

Instead of both labor and business being organized on a broad oppositional basis, labor would appear as an interest group selfishly concerned with its private gain at the expense of the common good. On the other hand, corporations would call for more investment to create jobs and increase output, for the betterment of all.

Liberal advocates of planning hope that they would gain influence over the goals of the planning apparatus and turn it in truly responsive directions: rebuilding cities, rural redevelopment of depressed areas, day care centers, and so on. In a limited sense they are right; the planning mechanism would be more responsible to the system and it would perform better than unreformed capitalism, with the anarchy of the marketplace in its modern form dominated by huge corporations which benefit from growth in periods of expansion and which have the wherewithal to outlast smaller competitors in the downturns. But is this the best we can do? It seems to me that Jimmy Carter will be able to convince the American people that it is. The struggle will be, in the main, between the farsighted liberals at the Trilateral Commission with technical backup from the Brookings Institution, on the one side, and the Association of Commerce and Industry smaller capitalists, with support by the American Enterprise Institute, on the other.

An Alternative Alternative

What this sort of incomes policy or corporatist planning does not deal with at all is what economic goals should be pursued. It can be confidently predicted that these mechanisms would be used to play out the current patterns of investment and consumption priorities. Yet, because of the wasteful expense of holding up a bloated capital structure and an energy-intensive growth pattern, the prospect is for continued stagflation. It seems clear that progressive forces have the opportunity to articulate an alternative vision of growth—one which speaks to our needs to conserve resources, to stimulate productive and more satisfying utilization of our labor power, and to develop more fulfilling forms of collective consumption and community.

Such an alternative is logically synonymous with the traditional bill of reordering priorities which most of us can recite by heart. If the argument that I have been making is correct—that full employment is prevented by capital's preference for a reserve army of laborers to hold down wages and by the development of a two-tier economy, and that the stimulus capable of doing much for the lower tier heightens inflation due to monopoly power and increased absorption of surplus by the top tier—then direct job creation is a sensible approach to break this structural pattern. If workers in different countries are being played off against each other in order to extract new concessions for capital—and they are giving up more and more and getting less and less—then an alternative model of growth is overdue. Further, revenue sharing—decentralized to the community level for neighborhood-controlled health, child care and educational facilities, for example—promotes energy-saving and labor-intensive activities, and so is desirable in and of itself.

There is a sickness which distorts basic economics and fundamental questions of common sense to suggest that environmental protection is bad but military spending good for the economy. Traditional liberal arguments in this area seem very much to the point. The Council on Environmental Quality reports that without the environmental programs in effect in 1976, the unemployment rate would be 0.4 percent higher, or about 400,000 workers more. Other estimates put the effects of private and public environment protection spending at a million additional jobs for the U.S. work force. This of course does not prevent private firms, who fear their profits would be hurt by ecologically grounded restrictions, from arguing (as we have seen above) that workers and consumers would be hurt by conservationist measures.

The bottle, can, beverage, glass, and metal industries spent millions of dollars to fight bans on throwaway bottles. In Massachusetts, while a Federal Reserve Bank study predicted such a ban would not affect prices and would lead to a net gain in jobs, bottle manufacturers sent their employees to the polls with "Save My Job" placards. Bottle bills were defeated in Massachusetts and Colorado. Nuclear power and utility issues took the same turn as corporations and utility companies told voters that, without cheap energy, companies would leave. Unions often joined with management in such efforts to promote a better business climate.

Disregard for environmental amenities lowers the quality of life and leads to an exodus of those who can afford to leave for healthier areas. These costs are measurable. A firm which produces noxious chemicals which pollute the air requires people living nearby to paint their homes more and more often, wash their clothes and their cars, and to dust and mop more frequently. It uses people's lungs as filters— at no cost to the firm but without the consent of the rest of us. The use of outmoded, dangerous, and under-maintained equipment may cost the firm less, but its workers pay dearly for the added profits. The true "output" of the firm is not just the item it sells but also the deteriorated environment and the impaired health of the worker and area resident. Some of these costs can be measured in dollar terms, others occur in the form of eye damage, cancer, white lung disease, black lung disease, and so on. While the incident of such externalities is measurable, the firm prefers to think it to be its "right" to make others pay for them.

At the social level, consider the decision to pay bondholders, lay off massive numbers of employees, and cut public services in New York City. The rising rate in crime and drug use (as well as in family breakup, mental illness and suicide) can be correlated with this decision. The fast-growing industries are locksmiths, installers of burglar alarms, trainers of police dogs, rent-a-cop business. All add to GNP, but the quality of life deteriorates. We must surely feel uncomfortable with GNP measures which say that such expenditures increase our well-being.

Just as pollution devices are called wasteful, but annual model changes and planned obsolescence and product proliferation good, so too the business community would have us believe that money spent on employing people and maintaining a decent livelihood is wasteful, but funds for guards and fences to keep out desperate people are good. There are alternatives to the self-defeating policy of subsidizing these huge corporations and the pattern of energy wasting, environmentally harmful, and socially irresponsible behavior they demand. But the liberal critique, where correct does not go far enough; it faces the necessity of reform, but not of radical restructuring.

It is possible that there will be a meaningful third force in the struggle; but this is far from certain. This third presence would be an anticorporatist Left rooted in four major constituencies which, to this point have not coalesced: Nader populists (consumer advocacy and ecological action groups); social movements and community action organizations (civil rights, feminism, housing, neighborhood community development corporations); the left groupings (the remnants of the New Left and refugees from sectarian party formations); and the progressive trade unions and labor officials plus individual mavericks in more conservative unions, militant rank-and-file groups, Black caucuses, and so on. The potential constituency for such an anticorporatist movement is vast. The degree to which it will be mobilized into a more united, ideologically coherent, and politically effective instrument of social change is difficult to predict. It is not merely a matter of developing an alternative analysis, a socialism rooted in the U.S. experience which speaks in the language and to the felt needs of the nation's working people. Nor is it only a matter of hard-headed, realistic, effective leadership emerging. Just as the corporatism it will face is produced by the conditions of deep and sustained crisis in which the nation finds itself, so too will an opposition movement be forged.

If events continue to move as they have in Europe and the Third World, and U.S. policy makers continue to side systematically with the forces of reaction , as they have in Chile, Vietnam, Greece, and Southern Africa, then the loss of legitimacy of the U.S. system, of its political parties and its economic institutions will continue. As the welfare state is chipped away and workers find they are being asked to make sacrifice after sacrifice in the name of realism, the politics of less may start to be questioned on a broad scale. This is an unsettling period precisely because it appears that just such a major leap is required. The forces represented by the Trilateral Commission have put forth one alternative: the question is whether a democratic alternative can be presented to challenge such a corporatist future— an alternative to symbolic populism and corporate dominance.

If one accepts the argument that much of the inflationary pressure comes from the present heavy consumer durables patterns of consumption, then it makes no sense that the form of stimulus should go primarily to the top tier of our dual economy as is now the case. Such a pattern is not to the advantage of the majority of people; it leads only to continued stagflation. Up until now, people-oriented use of resources was viewed by liberals as a matter of preference. I think there is a strong argument that such a pattern of use is also the better course in strictly macroeconomic terms. The giant corporations, of course, stand unalterably opposed. What is at stake is not just a test of profits, but it is, in a profound sense, a test of democracy. If the Carter corporatist policies are pursued, it will be a defeat for the majority of people in the U.S. Socialism, far from being a dream, emerges in the present conjuncture as the best realistic alternative.

In summary: the pattern of economic growth which mainstream economists, including many liberals, are advocating does not challenge the wasteful patterns of resource use, the continued gross under-employment of our labor force, or the lack of popular participation. The conservative logic—a crackpot realism of belt-tightening, lowering expectations, triage, and planned shrinkage—seems to be gaining a strong following at the expense of liberal Keynesianism. An alternative model of economic growth which would meet human needs and put social goals first is feasible and, from an economic standpoint, far more sound. Rather than subsidizing the capital intensive growth of the giant corporations, where fewer and fewer workers produce more and more goods which cannot be sold, job creation must be labor intensive and democratically determined. Such a pattern of growth is also resource-conserving as against the corporatist pattern of growth which is energy-wasting and ecologically a disaster. Social justice is efficient in terms of real long-term needs. A general thrust of this kind will help almost all people, not only the most oppressed groups, and so it unites rather than divides. The one problem, and needless to say it is hardly a small one, is that such a proposed pattern for future economic development must confront corporate capitalism, must wrest from it the surplus that the global corporations would prefer to move to their enclaves in Brazil, South Korea, and elsewhere. The connection is also, unfortunately, all too clear; that U.S. foreign policy has maintained governments in power which provide the stability of police-state-enforced low wages. Workers of the world are going to have to unite. Those of us in the U.S. are in some ways further behind Third World workers and European workers. But, if what has been presented here is accurate, then it may increasingly become the case that rather than take a hands-off attitude toward the production process, asking only for greater redistribution after the fact, social movements will develop in the U.S. which are increasingly forced to adress control of the production process as well. Poverty will be overcome then not through various forms of income transfers but by including people productively in the society in the first instance.

The left alternative seeks social control over the investment decision, the recapture of the social surplus currently appropriated by the global corporations, and the end to restructuring premised on the desires of capital. The negative goals include ending disinvestment in older regions; halting the generation of problems associated with too rapid growth in other regions; and reducing environmental pollution, mindless destruction of natural amenities, and depletion of nonreplenishable resources. More positively the democratic socialist vision is one of rebuilding the social and economic infrastructure of community—neighborhood government; schools run by parents, students and teachers; factories run by workers, socially responsible experts, and consumers. The social surplus allows for such a development, and as I have argued above, the corporate solution is technically far more problematic. In Europe, a Left alliance is struggling to strengthen itself and spell out a common program. In the U.S. the immediate task is more primitive: it is to put the possibility of democratic socialism on the agenda. Everywhere the problem is the same: control of the global corporations and extension of democratic control to the economy.

chapter three

THE U.S. COLONIAL EMPIRE IS AS CLOSE AS THE NEAREST RESERVATION: THE PENDING ENERGY WARS

*Michael Garitty**

Early in 1973 three events took place that at the time did not seem closely related: President Richard Nixon released the details of Project Independence; David Rockefeller and Zbigniew Brzezinski formed the Trilateral Commission; and the FBI and Federal troops occupied Wounded Knee. Today the interrelated nature of these events is clear.

Under the aegis of the Trilateral Commission the Carter Energy Program has succeeded Project Independence.** The goal is to make the trilateral world as free from dependence on the vast mineral resources of the Third World as is possible (and profitable). For this imperialism must come home to roost. Appropriately, the chicken has made its nest right in the middle of the Northern Great Plains (Montana, Wyoming, and the Dakotas) and the Rocky Mountain states (Colorado, Utah, Arizona, and New Mexico), home (and second home) to many Indian Peoples. Wounded Knee was no

*Michael Garitty works with the Black Hills Alliance in Minneapolis, Minnesota. This article is an edited version of a much longer paper written for this book; the author's earlier draft appeared in *Akwesasne Notes*, Winter 1980.

**ed. note: In August 1979, John Sawhill, then president of New York University and a member of the Trilateral Commission, was appointed deputy secretary of Energy under Charles Duncan Jr. (former President of Coca-Cola and Deputy Secretary of Defense). Sawhill is the co-author of the latest Trilateral Commission report on energy: *Energy: Managing the Transition.* "From late 1973 to early 1975, Dr. Sawhill was Administrator of the U.S. Federal Energy Administration, an agency created in the wake of the oil embargo and a forerunner of the current Department of Energy," according to the Trilateral Commission. Sawhill advised Carter on energy matters before assuming his current post. He is head of the Interagency Task Force on Energy Supplies. While president of N.Y.U. Sawhill served on the New York City Emergency Financial Control Board. (*New York Times*, 17 August 1979.)

isolated incident, but part of the continuing struggle by Indian peoples to survive centuries of genocide and plunder and regain self-determination.

Project Independence

The forerunner of the Carter energy plan and the first vehicle for restructuring the industrial might of the U.S.—with OPEC very much in mind—was "Project Independence." David Rockefeller and other Trilateral Commission founders were at odds with Richard Nixon over his New Economic Policy (in Part II, Frieden reviews how Nixon's economic program conflicted with the transnational corporate interests Rockefeller represents); but the plan for energy independence fits right in with the trilateral recipe for a healthy and ever-expanding capitalism. With Project Independence the old industrial North would be left behind in the pollution and acid rain while the corporate might of the nation would head for the sunny, mineral rich, and non-unionized West and Northern Great Plains. A major restructuring of the social, economic, and cultural base of the Mid-West was planned.

Under Project Independence nuclear power output was to increase ten-fold between 1973 and 1985; coal production was to jump from 600 to 960 million tons per year; oil production from 10.9 to 14 million barrels per day; and natural gas production from 23 to 27 trillion cubic feet per year. Project Independence elaborated the policy that a national energy crisis necessitated the stripping of western coal on a crash basis and contained "a major leasing program for mineral rights to Federal lands involving 10 million acres per year by 1978."[1] The plan provided government and corporate decision makers with a rationale for immediate "development" of the vast fossil fuels in the largely rural and sparsely populated West; but the actual pace of exploitation disappointed the planners. Today, eagerly awaiting the Energy Mobilization Board (EMB)—a pillar of Carter's Energy Program—the energy conglomerates are dusting off their long-dormant, massive oil-shale, and synthetic fuel projects.*

*For instance, in Wyoming, Atlantic Richfield (ARCO), Gulf Oil, Panhandle Eastern Pipeline Co. and Texaco are pushing schemes for coal gasification. In Montana, Burlington Northern (largest holder of coal reserves in the nation),[2] Tenneco, Utah International Inc., Gulf, and Mobil Oil are doing the same. In Colorado, Occidental Petroleum, Gulf Oil, Superior Oil of Indiana, Union Oil of California, Colony Oil, and Mobil Corporation are looking for shale that could produce as much as 1.5 billion barrels of oil.

Already the result of the Project Independence mandate has been vast underground and surface coal and uranium mines; coal-fired electrical generating plants; experimental coal gasification plants; oil, natural gas, water and coal-slurry pipelines; and numerous other acitivities now planned, under construction, or in operation in and around small communities throughout the West. A significant number of these projects are found on Indian lands guaranteed sovereign by almost 400 treaties—treaties which are legally binding under the U.S. Constitution.[3] Energy "development" is taking place on Indian lands, as well as on federal holdings, because the mineral rights and labor come cheap; profits are high. The Council of Energy Resources Tribes (CERT)—a concoction of the Bureau of Indian Affairs (BIA) and puppet Tribal Councils about which more will be said later—estimates that its twenty-three member western Indian Nations control 33 percent of the low sulphur strippable coal reserves, 80 percent of the uranium, and 3 to 10 percent of the oil and gas reserves in the United States. As of 1974, only 23.5 percent of oil and gas leases, 36 percent of the coal leases, and fewer than 1 percent of uranium leases on Indian lands were producing. That leaves a lot of resources just waiting to be torn from the ground of reservations like Fort Berthold, Wind River, Fort Peck, and Fort Belnap.[4] (I will use the word reservation as little as possible as it symbolizes the colonial treatment of the Indian people by the U.S. government. A reservation is not the same as an Indian Nation: the Great Lakota (Sioux) Nation, for example, is now composed of only seven reservations, mostly in South Dakota.)

The position of the Indian Nations in relation to transnational corporations and the U.S. government parallels that of many Third World nations—the U.S colony of Puerto Rico, among them. (See Philip Wheaton.) Pressing economic needs, high unemployment and underemployment are all part of the dependency syndrome so common to the Third World. The FBI, the BIA, and other arms of the U.S. government work together to beat a smooth path for the pillage of Indian resources. But before discussing this let's look more closely at the structure of the energy industry and the overall impact of energy production.

Big Oil Corners the Energy Market

Following the OPEC oil embargo and the energy crisis of 1973, coal and uranium reserves in the U.S. became dominated by a small number of firms. (See Bird Part VI.) The energy giants—many of which are represented on the Trilateral Commission*—began swal-

*Energy companies with officers or directors on the Trilateral Commission between

lowing up the smaller firms in take-overs and driving those who wouldn't cooperate out of business. In testimony before the Senate Subcommittee on Antitrust, Monopoly and Business Rights on 22 May 1979, S. David Freeman, chairman of the board of the Tennessee Valley Authority (TVA) portrayed the situation as follows:

> TVA operates the Nation's largest electric generating system. In fiscal year 1978, 60% of our power came from coal-fired generating plants and 12% from nuclear...As we finish the nuclear units we have under construction, we expect to be using 6 to 7 million pounds of uranium per year by the late 1980s...*Increasing oil company dominance of uranium and coal is not just an academic matter to TVA*...We actually see the changes in bargaining strength when our independent fuel suppliers are acquired by the energy companies; and we have felt the tremendous injury caused by skyrocketing coal and uranium prices.

In coal, prior to the early 1960s, oil companies did not generally own coal or coal companies. Today, however, energy companies own about 100 billion tons of coal reserves. Continental Oil has 13.7 billion tons of reserves; Exxon has 10 billion tons; Phillips Petroleum has 8 billion tons; El Paso Natural Gas has 5.2 billion tons; and 12 of the top 13 oil companies control a total of 57.5 billion tons of coal reserves. *6 of the top 15 national coal*

1973 and 1979 are listed below. Note: all persons named are currently serving, or have served in the past, on the boards of directors of the respective company, unless another position is indicated. Consult "Who's Who" for further biographical information.
Anaconda (Robert V. Roosa); Atlantic Richfield (Philip M. Hawley, Robert Ingersoll); Bethlehem Steel (William R. Scranton); Burlington Northern (Robert Ingersoll); Cargill Inc. (William R. Pearce, vice-president); Caterpillar Tractor (David Packard, Robert Ingersoll); Climax Uranium Co. (Carroll L. Wilson, former president); Continental Oil (John P. Austen, William Hewitt); Cummins Engine Co. (Henry B. Schacht, chairman; William Scranton); Exxon Corp. (J. K. Jamieson, chairman); Kaiser Resources Ltd. (Edgar F. Kaiser, Jr. president); Kaiser Steel Co. (Edgar F. Kaiser, Jr., chief executive); Standard Oil (Carla A Hills, David Packard); Sun Oil (William Scranton); Texaco (Robert Roosa); 3M Company (Lee L. Morgan, Peter G. Peterson); Union Carbide (Russell Train, former head of the EPA, now vice-president of Union Carbide); U.S. Steel (Mark Shepard, Jr., David Packard); Utah International (Ernest C. Arbuckle, Arjay Miller); Westinghouse (Marina v. N. Whitman); Weyerhauser (George Weyerhauser, president; Robert Ingersoll). In addition, Carroll L. Wilson (mentioned above) is director of MIT's Workshop on Alternative Energy Strategies and director of the World Coal Study; former president of Metals and Controls Corps; and served on the Atomic Energy Commission (1947-51). John D. Rockefeller IV is the chairman of President Carter's commission on coal. Joseph J. Sisco, a director of Tenneco, is the U.S. member of the trilateral task force on the Middle East.

producers are now owned by major oil companies and only 2 of the first 15 are independent companies. Continental Oil owns the second largest national producer, Consolidation Coal, with production of 47.9 million tons in 1977; Standard Oil of California owns a 20% interest in AMAX, the third largest producer; Occidental Petroleum owns Island Creek, the fourth largest producer; Ashland Oil and Hunt Petroleum own Arch Mineral, the seventh largest producer; Standard Oil of Ohio owns the 13th largest producer, Old Ben Coal; Pittsburg and Midway Coal Mining, the 15th largest producer is owned by Gulf.

The top four firms (in the Northern Great Plains) control over ½ of (the) market's production. *Oil companies account for 38% of the (coal) production from the Northern Great Plains...*[5] [Italics ed.]

"Worse," Freeman said, "the same group of energy companies which dominate the coal markets also dominate the uranium market." (See chart below.)

Estimated Uranium Reserve Holdings, 1977

	Percent of Reserves	
	Oil Firms	Non-Oil Firms
Kerr McGee	33.5	
Gulf Oil	18.5	
United Nuclear		9.6
Conoco - Pioneer Natural Gas	5.8	
Phelps Dodge (Western Nuclear)		5.5
Getty Oil	4.6	
Exxon	4.0	
Lucky Uranium		4.3
Atlantic Richfield (Anaconda)	3.6	
Phillips Petroleum	2.8	
Rio Algom Mines		2.1
Standard Oil - Ohio	1.0	
Union Pacific		1.0
Union Carbide		1.0
Standard Oil - Calif. (Amax)	.7	
TOTAL	74.5%	23.5%
Others*		2%

* would include Texaco, Standard Oil of Indiana, Union Oil and Tenneco, all of which are known to have uranium reserves.

The fact that the coal industry is monopolized by a few oil companies means that technology is being revolutionized under their capital and control. Production is shifting from underground to stripmining and relocating from Appalachia to the Great Plains and Rocky Mountains.* In stripmining, output per day is 100 percent greater than in underground mining, average recovery 60 percent higher, and operating costs 30 percent lower. The total strippable reserves of the 8-state region is estimated at 86,281,000,000 tons, or 63 percent of all the strippable reserves in the U.S.[6] The Great Plains and Rocky Mountain States are already on their way to joining Appalachia** as *national sacrifice areas* to the greed of the corporate elite. (*Before* Carter's energy speech, coal production in the region was expected to increase sevenfold in a 25 year period.) The Bureau of Mines and the Office of Coal Research have been allocating grants to U.S. energy giants to improve techniques first developed in Germany in the 1940s for gasification and liquefacation of coal (since this means lower transportation costs for the industry, the railroads, particularly Burlington Northern, frown on this form of government welfare for the energy companies). The western U.S. is the perfect place to develop this new technology: more than 90 percent of U.S. low-sulphur coal reserves are found there (over half in the massive Fort Union Coal Formation of Wyoming lying very close

*ed. note: *Business Week* highlights these trends in a feature story "The Oil Majors Bet on Coal" (24 September 1979): "Thanks to a careful acquisition strategy that began 15 years ago, all oil companies now own 25% of all the coal in the country, and *the oil industry has the future of coal in its grip.* And big oil has big plans for coal. From a modest 22% production share in 1978, oil companies have embarked on an ambitious expansion program that will put their share of national production at almost 50% by 1985...And the main coal-producing regions will shift from East to West—underground mines in Appalachia will give way to the huge Western strip mines that oil companies will be developing...In effect, the oil companies are turning their backs on the problems of Eastern underground coal mining—tangled labor relations..., backward management, declining productivity, and black lung disease..." *Business Week* quotes S. David Freeman whom they see as the chief opponent to Big Oil's move into coal. "Big oil has the strength to keep fuel supplies short and prices high. *They can even keep the sun from rising as an energy competitor.*"[Italics mine.] At the same time as the energy giants are helping keep federal research and development of solar technology abysmally low, they are buying up solar companies and necessary raw materials such as copper.

**ed. note: Poverty is central to any basic description of Appalachia, an area endowed with rich natural resources. To cite *Webster's New World Dictionary*, Appalachia is "the highland region of the eastern U.S. including the central and southern Appalachian Mountains and the Piedmont Plateau from northern Pennsylvania through northern Alabama; it is characterized generally by economic depression and poverty."

to the surface). Of the low-sulphur reserves accessible to stripmining, 87 percent are in Wyoming, Montana, New Mexico, and North Dakota, much of it on land owned by the federal government and Indian Nations, as revealed in the chart below.

Estimated Ownership of Coal Lands in Five Southwestern States[a]

	Ownership (in Percentages)					
State	U.S. Gov't	State Gov't	Indian Tribes	Western Railroads	Private	Total
Wyoming	48	12	0	20	20	100
Utah	67	15	1	0	18	100
Colorado	36	14	6	20	24	100
Arizona	0	0	100	0	0	100
New Mexico	34	18	40	5	3	100
Total	45	13	13	12	17	100

[a]Provisional estimates based on incomplete data.

Source: Thomas D. Duchesneau. *Competition in the U.S. Energy Industry.* A report to the Energy Policy Project of the Ford Foundation (Cambridge, Mass.: Ballinger, 1975). p. 81. Found in *Native Americans and Energy Development.*

Principal Nuclear Engineering and Construction Firms and their Market Share

company (owner)*	ranking 1978**	net profits ($000,000)	market share ('77)
1. Bechtel Corporation, San Francisco, Ca. (*Bechtel Group of Companies*, S.F., Ca.)	(privately-held		
2. Stone & Webster Engineering, Boston, Ma. (*Stone & Webster, Inc.*, N.Y., N.Y.)	information not available)		24.0%
3. United Engineers & Constructors, Philadelphia (*Raytheon Co.*, Lexington, Ma.)	175	113.2	10.5%
4. Ebasco Services, Inc., New York, N.Y. (*Enserch Corp.*, Dallas, Tx.)	283	74.1	8.9%
5. Daniel International, Greenville, S.C. (*Fluor Corp.*, L.A., Ca.)	278	75.5	6.2%
6. Brown & Root, Inc., Houston, Tx. (*Halliburton Co.*, Dallas, Tx.)	35	355.1	6.2%
7. Offshore Power Systems, Inc. (*Westinghouse Electric Corp.*, Pittsburgh, Pa.)	47	271.3	3.8%
Top 3			74.8%
Top 7			99.9%

(source: *Electrical World*, "1978 Nuclear Plant Survey," 15 January 1978 and Energy Research Group, U/Mass, Amherst, Ma.)

*when different from company
**Forbes Profits 500

Found in Anna Gyorgy and friends, *No Nukes: everyone's guide to nuclear power,* (Boston: South End Press, 1979), p. 159.

The Mineral Leasing Act of 1920 and the Omnibus Tribal Leasing Act of 1938 authorized the federal government, through the secretary of the interior and the BIA, to

> lease public and Indian lands and mineral rights to private corporations. By 1973, the Federal Government had leased 680,854 acres of public and 258,754 acres of Indian land, containing over 20 billion tons of coal, to the corporations. Leasing halted in 1973 and did not begin again until late spring of 1979, because there was criticism of the fact that 70% of the land leased was going to only 15 multinational oil companies—Shell, Sun, ARCO, Gulf, Exxon, Mobil, etc.[7]

The ban was lifted by Secretary of the Interior Cecil Andrus.[8]

Corporations with headquarters in New York, Chicago, Houston, and Minneapolis in large part determine the underdevelopment of rural areas, both Indian and non-Indian. White farmers and ranchers also see their livelihoods disappearing as giant feed-lots, grain companies, and energy producers dominate more and more of the rural economy. (See "The U.S. Connection: Conversation with a California Farmer.") The vast quantities of energy resources in the West hold only a false promise of economic and social recovery for the rural residents.

The energy produced is delivered to cities many hundreds of miles away while land blight, increased water scarcity, and water and air pollution have become standard features of the landscape of the energy-rich resource areas. During the development stage, jobs are most often awarded to skilled employees who leave at the end of the construction phase. The transient workers who swell towns like Gillette, Wyoming, and Colstrip, Montana, five, ten, or twenty times pre-boom size, live in mobile homes or house trailers and generally buy their food, clothing, and entertainment in larger cities. Housing, sewers, roads, lighting systems, schools, teachers, police, fire services, and the like are grossly inadequate. The corporations responsible for the energy development assume none of the social and physical infrastructure costs; rather they are borne by residents through bond liquidation and local property taxes. Local residents are never involved in the planning phases of pending energy development, and they are misinformed of the human, social, fiscal, and environmental costs inherent in the development. The North Central Power Study, reviewed below, provides a good illustration of how corporations weigh "costs" and "benefits" to the detriment of people and environment.

The North Central Power Study and Water Use

Two years before the launching of Project Independence a document was released with little ceremony which has since been called "the essence of Project Independence": The *North Central Power Study* (NCPS).[9] The study investigated the "feasibility of constructing large mine-mouth [plants located right next to the underground source of their fuel] thermal plants located in the substantial coalfields just east of the Rocky Mountains and, by the use of extra-high-voltage transmission lines deliver economical power to major load centers."[10] The conclusion of the report was that, yes, it could and should be done on a massive scale, glossing over any detrimental environmental effects.*

To run the mammoth plants would take more water than is available in the semi-arid environment of the Northern Great Plains. A series of water studies was undertaken. In 1976 the draft study entitled *Water for Energy* reaffirmed the goals of the NCPS (which by then was being called "inoperative" by bureaucrats and utility executives).[13] It studied the impact "caused by depletion of 1 million acre-feet of water on the main-stem Missouri River system" for energy-related industrial purposes. The report concluded that "maximum potential industrial development by the year 2000 would disturb 188,000 acres of land; about 131,000 acres for mining, and the rest for facilities sites, pipelines, and transportation routes."[14] It went on to outline disruptions to agricultural production, plant and wildlife, and pollution of the surface and ground water supply. 2035 is the last year (water) service contracts for industry would terminate. By then there won't be a drop of water anywhere near the Northern Great Plains fit to drink. Already the water flowing in the underground aquifer systems is being allocated at rates far exceeding the natural rate of regeneration by rainfall.[15] The fact that most of the water under study is Indian water guaranteed by treaty was not mentioned.

Energy companies are planning to use as much as 10 to 35 million acre-feet of water a year in the Northern Great Plains alone.

---

*In all the report proposed 42 new coal-fired generating plants, 13 of which would be 10,000 megawatts—5 times larger than any plant now in existence. Of the 42 plants, 21 were sited in eastern Montana, 15 in Wyoming (all of those were to be 10,000 megawatts), 5 in North Dakota, and one each in South Dakota and Colorado.[11] In addition, the NCPS suggested a massive network of transmission lines radiating outward from the plants to Seattle, Portland, Minneapolis-St. Paul and a dozen other cities in as many states. These transmission lines were to be 765 kilovolt lines (765,000 volts) "for best economy" for the eastern, and 500 kv for the smaller western system.[12]

How much is that? The Missouri River has only 18½ million acre-feet flowing through it each year. Companies also plan to ring the area with powerlines carrying electricity to and from the immense generating plants. What harm will a 765 kilovolt line do to the people and other living things in the vicinity? The farmers of northwestern Minnesota think they have a pretty good idea. That's why they have toppled 10 powerline towers and have shot out over 40,000 glass insulators along the line so far.* In all, the energy-exploiting corporations plan to tear up more than 250,000 acres of fragile Plains soil in the next 30 years with enormous machines called draglines (space age steam shovels).**

This is just the beginning, as *The Rape of the Great Plains* argues:

> For if the nearly 100 coal and energy companies—and the Department of the Interior—now deeply involved in the exploitation of plains coal have their way, the huge area known as the Northern Great Plains will have to be renamed *"A National Sacrifice Area..."*[19]

The energy exploiting companies claim they will see to the reclamation of the land after they have stripmined it. But this too is an empty promise; they cannot reclaim the fragile soils of the West and Mid-West where rainfall is often at or below 10 inches a year, and the ecosystem is delicately balanced.

The *Water for Energy* study is more than a plan for ecological catastrophe. It also reveals the next installment of the white man's five hundred year campaign of genocide and plunder against the indigenous peoples of this continent. The report sees an end to the Indian Peoples' "special relationship with land," and a "shift from an agricultural to mining/light industry/trade service economy." The

---

*The farmers contend that the high-voltage lines will shrivel crops; prevent seeds from germinating; cause spontaneous abortions in livestock; stop cows from giving milk; cause headaches, exhaustion, skin irritation, nosebleeds in humans; and scare off wildlife. Anything metal become electrified and shocks are common. The farmers say they know when the line is in operation just by looking to see if their horses and cows are roaming free in the pastures or huddled as far away from the lines as they can get.[16] The right-of-way for one of these giants is wider than a football field is long, and they will ultimately criss-cross the nation unless stopped.[17]

**These machines are as tall as 16 story buildings, weigh 27 million pounds, and can move 220 cubic yards (325 tons) of "overburden" (i.e., wildlife habitat, cropland, or home) in a single pass; they can scoop up a full load every minute. Draglines are electric and use enough electricity to fully power a city the size of Rapid City, South Dakota. On the average, these machines will have to rip down through 100 or 150 feet of "overburden" just to uncover the coal seams of the Great Plains.[18]

effects of the report on the Native Americans would "contribute to bringing Indians into the mainstream of American life." Although it is euphemistically referred to as "disappearance or loss of tribal cultural heritage/values (cutural degradation)," the report is talking about destruction of the Indian Nations.[20]

An Energy Mobilization Board is one means of insuring that the sacrifices of the Indian People and Northern Great Plains are carried out.

The Energy Mobilization Board

In his 15 July 1979 speech to the nation, Carter proposed the creation of an Energy Mobilization Board (EMB) to "cut through the red tape, the delays and the endless roadblocks to completing key energy projects." Public hearings and environmental impact statements (EIS) would surely be seen as red tape and delays. Following the speech, Fish and Wildlife Service Director, Lynn Greenwalt, said that it is no longer up to environmental agencies to decide whether a project will be built—only to suggest how the project's impact on people and the environment can be swiftly minimized.[21]

The EMB would facilitate disastrous programs such as the crash synfuel project. To reach the synthetic fuel goals set by the Carter program would require the construction of dozens of coal gasification and liquefacation plants in the west and exploitation of all Colorado's extensive oil shale. An oil shale industry producing one million barrels of oil a day would consume 10 percent of the Colorado River water now being used by the western states for irrigation. A million barrels per day production would require moving about a billion tons of earth a year—about the same amount dug up to build the Panama Canal.[22] Carter wants the U.S. to be producing 2.5 *billion* barrels of synthetic oil a day from coal by 1990.

A representative of the National Association of Manufacturers was caught in a most candid moment after hearing a briefing in Washington on the contents of Carter's speech just before it was delivered. He commented "we sure as hell better convince those people in Colorado that cross-country skiing is more fun than downhill skiing, because we're going to have to level the state."[23] Moreover, vastly increased mining and burning of coal could only make the current acid rain situation worse for a larger part of the U.S. and Canada.[24]

The Energy Mobilization Board has cleared both houses of Congress. The version approved by the House of Representatives is the stronger of the two "fast track" bills, empowering the board to override Federal environmental, conservation, and other substantive laws with the approval of the president and Congress. Whatever the final compromise bill, the Board will most likely be composed of four members. It isn't too hard to imagine who would sit on such an important board; former Secretary of Energy Schlesinger's name has come up often. Other Board members would probably include a friendly banker and labor leader and a mild-mannered environmentalist.

Carter's synfuels project may be cut back but the EMB is alive and well.* The intent remains clear. "We will protect our environment," Carter said, "but when this nation critically needs a refinery, or a pipeline, we will build it." And much more. What Carter didn't say was that much of this development is going to take place on Indian lands.

Indian Nations and Energy Resources

For hundreds of years the Northern Great Plains/Rocky Mountain area was considered a worthless part of the Great American desert. That is precisely why most of the remaining indigenous peoples of this country were relocated there. Today, the new Mexico Indian Environmental Education Project estimates that the Navajos, Hopi, Pueblos, and other western Nations own 100 percent of all the coal in Arizona, 40 percent in New Mexico, 6 percent in Utah, and 1 percent in Colorado (as seen in the chart above). The Department of Energy (DOE) estimates are a little more conservative, figuring that Indians hold title to as much as 25 percent to 50 percent of all uranium in the country, one-third of all low-sulfur strippable coal, and 2 percent of all domestic oil and natural gas.[25]

The developing of the west and its natural resources is a sordid story of conquest, broken treaties, corruption, and murder on such a vast scale that it can only be characterized as genocide. In the last century the Indian's land was given to the railroads, and exploited for coal and gold.** Today, what remains of the Indian land base is

---

*ed. note: In November 1980 Congress voted final approval for a massive $19 billion synthetic fuel program. The same energy measure authorized a token $1 billion for solar energy and conservation programs. According to the *New York Times* (10 November 1979), "The legislation provides funding for a major portion of President Carter's energy program and was a resounding victory for the Administration."

**From the mid-1850s to the 1870s the early robber barons (Jay Gould, Jim Hill, et. al.) were given vast tracts of land grants (6,400 to 12,800 acres per mile of track laid) totalling an incredible 155 million acres. In addition to the land, the railroad tsars received millions in government subsidies and bonds (an undetermined amount of which found its way back into the pockets of the ever-obliging Congressmen from whence it came).[26] The railroads brought white people to "settle" the land and on the return trip east brought coal, oil, and timber to burgeoning industry.

wanted for uranium and water (as well as coal and gold). To better understand the present, we must look also to the past.

Broken Treaties and Genocide

In 1830 the Removal Act was passed by Congress giving legal sanction to the wars of genocide being fought at that time. The Act gave President Jackson the "right" to remove every Indian east of the Mississippi to west of the Mississippi; thousands died or were murdered during this forced march. By the turn-of-the-century the Indian population had plumetted to 235,000. The best estimates of the total population at the time of Columbus' arrival put the number at between 8 to 12 million; the total North American Indian population today is just over a million. Along the way hundreds of Indian Nations have vanished from the face of the earth or been "terminated" by the U.S. government.* The Winnebago, Huron, Ottawa, Potawatomie, Wyandot, Shawnee, Kickapoo, Delaware, Peoria, Miami, and countless others are now remembered by whites only as the name of some town, lake, county, or recreation vehicle.**

In 1887 the Dawes Allotment Act was passed. What land remained for the Indians was soon to be taken away. The Act decreed that Indian land heretofore owned in common by members of the Nation would be parcelled out among individual owners with the condition that they accept government control over their lives and give up the traditional ways.***Each male head of family was to receive 160 acres; each child or other dpendent family member was allot-

---

*Termination is the 145-year-old government policy whereby sovereign Indian Nations are decreed to no longer exist, whether or not they exist in reality. The actual purpose is to terminate the Nations' Treaty Rights. The policy abolishes the Tribal Government and forces the members of the heretofore sovereign Nation to seek a place in the mainstream of white society as individuals rather than as co-existing, separate national cultural groups. The Choctaw, terminated in 1830, was the first Indian nation to be dissolved by the unilateral act of another sovereign state. A new, more sophisticated effort to implement this policy began in the 1940s and culminated in the Act of 1954, which ordered the termination of the Menominee Nation of Wisconsin. With termination, government assistance for education, health, welfare, and taxes ceases. See Rozanne Dunbar Ortiz, *The Great Sioux Nation* (1977), p. 4.

**A similar situation is now in progress in Latin America where the transnationals' greed for raw materials is leading to the eradication of tribes of the Amazon River Basin by the Brazilian junta. In Bolivia, Argentina, Chile, Paraguay, Uruguay, etc. Indian lands are being opened up for "development" and Indian people are being driven into the capitalist economy as cheap labor. The Ache Indians of Paraguay provide one of the more blatant examples of the genocide being practiced against indigenous peoples around the world. See Richard Arens, *Genocide in Paraguay*, Temple University Press, Philadelphia, 1976.

***Traditional is a term much misunderstood by whites. The word does not imply an individual who wishes only to return to the life-style of a hundred years ago.

ted 80 acres. Under this scheme millions of acres were left over to be grabbed up by the Government and white settlers. In all, 118 reservations were divided up. Thirty-eight million acres were taken outright by the Government while 22 million acres were declared surplus and opened for settlement. Worse yet, Indian owners were forced to sell an additional 23 million acres between 1887 and 1934 because of inability to pay taxes and mortgage payments and the need to pay off debts and support their families. By 1934 when the Act ended, Indian people had lost almost two-thirds of their land: 90 million acres.[27] But that's not all. When the BIA examined the remaining Indian lands, 14 million acres were found to be critically eroded, 17 million acres severely eroded, and 25 million acres slightly eroded. Not a single acre of the remaining 56 million acres was judged to be uneroded![28]

Genocide is not a thing of the past. Hundreds of Indian activists have been murdered in recent years (as we shall discuss later). Hundreds of Indian women are being sterilized against their wishes or entirely unbeknownst to them in public health service clinics each year; full-blooded Indian women are the special target of the doctors.* And from colonial times through the present, Indian children have been forcibly separated from their families and shipped off to boarding schools and foster homes to be raised as whites.

The gift of the smallpox-laden blanket has been replaced by free sterilization and cancer-causing uranium mine tailings for use in building the *hogan* (sod house). Leasing acts—like the Mineral

---

Traditional means the strengthening and retention of the cultural and political integrity of the Nation and development of the values that made Indian Nations great in the past. Traditional implies unity among all areas of human endeavor, i.e., religion, science, medicine, politics, etc. The earth is sacred and is to be protected for the unborn. All living species have as much right to live and enjoy the riches of life on earth as any other species of living thing, including human beings. The earth cannot be bought and sold; land can only "belong" to those people who are part of the land. Agreements over land rights and usage are considered sacred by traditional peoples who represent a majority of Native Peoples. Also, one does not have to be an elder to be traditional. It does not come with age, but is an attitude or state of mind. See Ortiz, *Great Sioux Nation*, pp. 201-202.

*ed. note: "Overall, at least 25 percent of the Native women of childbearing age have been steralized, although the toal population numbers less than one million. Recent reports estimate that the percentage sterilized in one tribe alone, the Northern Cheyenne, is close to 80 percent." In the U.S. colony of Puerto Rico the picture is the same. According to a 1968 study "over 1/3 of all women in Puerto Rico of child bearing age had been sterilized." Ruthann Evanoff, "Reproductive Rights and Occupational Health," *WIN*, 16 August 1979. See also *Akwesasne Notes*, late winter 1979, p. 29.

Leasing Act and the Omnibus Tribal Leasing Act mentioned earlier—sanction pillage of the mineral resources the Dawes Act had neglected.

Leases and the Imposed Tribal Structure

The plight of the Navajo Nation illustrates the devastating impact of leases for energy development.[29] The Navajo Tribal Council (headed by Peter MacDonald) entered into a long series of oil, natural gas, and helium leases which provided the energy companies with enormous profits and filled the pockets of a few official tribal leaders at the expense of the well-being of the tribe.[30] Until 1976 the secretary of the Interior and the BIA had overseen all leasing of Indian land and resources to the energy-exploiting corporations under a system called trusteeship. All the leases followed a consistent pattern. They were let at fixed prices and were valid as long as the mineral being extracted was found in the ground in sufficient quantity. There were no escalator clauses for royalty rates to take account of the rising price of minerals. Indian nations were not allowed to tax the corporations. Commonly, state governments glean more revenues from corporate activity on Indian land than the Indian Nations receive in royalties and leases.*

The fact that the Navaho Tribal Councils could sign over vast tracts of Indian land to the companies is testament to the Tribal Reorganization Act of 1934. That act brought "democracy" to the reservation through the tribal structure.** The tribal structure is essentially that of a business corporation but with "democratically elected" officials. Elections are consistently boycotted by traditional

---

*In 1976 the Navajo received $12.8 million in coal royalties, while taxes paid by the corporations to Arizona totalled $18.5 million.[31] The state also receives $10.5 million a year in taxes from the Navajo coal-fired power plant, while the Navajos get $2.5 million for the coal used, rent, and right-of-way. They get nothing for the water used in cooling the plant; those rights were signed away in an earlier agreement with the Salt River Project. The Navajos get less than ¼ the revenue the state gets even though the plant and the coal are on Indian land. The plant uses water guaranteed by the Treaty and the smokestacks hopelessly pollute the formerly pristine environment of the reservation.[32] For their coal lease with Utah International Inc., the Navajos get the same royalty of 15 cents per ton as when the lease was signed 22 years ago.[33]

**The 1934 Indian Reorganization Act was set up under FDR and administered by Commissioner of Indian Affairs John Collier. Up until that time, the Indian Nations, beginning in 1884, were not allowed to own land communally, or to govern their affairs in any way. The BIA proclaimed itself trustee of Indian affairs. Roosevelt and Collier offered the separate reservations some control of their own affairs and the right to own land communally, if each reservation would set up a "tribal council" and a "tribal structure." (continued)

people; voter turnouts are low. The BIA completely ignored the already existing governmental structure inherent within each separate nation and maintained complete supervisory and financial control and veto power over the tribal council. Regional and national organizations of these "tribal councils" entrench the colonial network.[34]

The 1934 Act came on the heels of the 1924 Citizenship Act which sought to make Native peoples U.S. citizens. Native peoples were not then, and are not now, U.S. citizens. By treaty, they are members of sovereign nations which exist within the borders of the U.S. But in reality the situation is quite different. The reservations are domestic colonies, as are the Bantustans of South Africa and the aboriginal homelands in Australia. The elected tribal governments are colonial governments under the thumb of the BIA.* The BIA evolved from an arm of the War Department in the late 1700s to an arm of the Interior Department today. The switch was made in 1849. The BIA's original purpose was to oversee the extinction of the race. Now it pays more attention to the immediate goal of ripping off Indian water, land, and resources for the corporations.

Indian Water Rights

Indian water rights are guaranteed by treaty and aboriginal rights. The U.S. Supreme Court affirmed this in the *Winters Doctrine* of 1908, ruling that Indian nations have a right to as much water as is necessary to irrigate their lands, and that even where this right may have gone unexercised it takes precedence over all other claims. It doesn't work that way in the real world.

For decades the federal government worked hand-in-hand with the railroads to bring settlers into the west and take Indian lands and water. Now the railroads have been replaced by the energy giants and agribusinesses who are pushing the states to quantify the amounts of water available to the Indian people so limits can be established that will negate the intent of the treaties and the Winters Doctrine. There are some twenty-two bills now awaiting congressional attention that

---

The BIA is overseen by the Secretary of the Interior who can make decisions on just about any aspect of Indian life. The House Committee on Interior and Insular Affairs participate in Indian Affairs by approving the BIA's budget and expenditures of individual tribal funds from the Treasury. Indian nations are also subject to various constraints of state and local governments.

*The Indian people have never lacked sophistication about their rights, resources, or the true motives of the government and corporations. The "tribal councils" are simply puppets of the U.S. government, whether or not individual Indians who sit

in one way or another will take more land, water, and treaty rights away from Native Peoples.*

For all too real examples of domestic colonialism at work we need only turn to the nearest reservation.

Indian People Pay the Price of Energy Development

What is left today after years of energy development on the Navajo reservation is an environmental and health disaster. The Four Corners coal-fired plant has been in operation since 1963. In 1973 this plant alone was spewing out 383 tons of fly ash, 1,032 tons of sulphur dioxide, and an undetermined amount of nitrogen oxide each day.[35] Pollution control equipment notwithstanding, the five generating plants in the area emit 40 tons of particulates a year—100 times the emissions allowable in Los Angeles County—creating a lethal haze that was the only human-made thing visible on earth to the returning Apollo 15 astronauts. In testimony about energy development in the Four Corners area, Arizona Public Service President William P. Reilly admitted that there was a pollution problem in the area; but that "development" provided an "opportunity" for a "minority" to "play a role in our free enterprise system."[36]

In addition to the coal strip mines and the coal-fired power plants are five abandoned uranium processing mills with radioactive tailing piles totalling 240 acres of over 10 million tons (tailings are the sandy remains after uranium ore has been milled out). The federal government estimates that 85 percent of the radioactivity of the uranium extracted remains in the tailings.[37] The government is just beginning to acknowledge the dangers of this low-level ionizing radiation, although many scientists and lay people alike have warned for years of the severe health effects the tailings can have.[38]

Abandoned mines now belong to the Navajo Nation.** The corporations who are responsible for the radioactive mills and

---

on the councils wish it that way. Indian affairs, especially around natural resources, cannot be understood without a clear understanding of this basic fact and the U.S. Government's exploitation of that fact.

*The stakes are high. At a recent meeting of the National Conference of State Legislatures in Carson City, Nevada, Indian legal suits to regain their treaty water rights were an urgent topic for discussion. The assistant attorney general of Washington, Charles Roe, estimated that if all Indian suits in the western U.S. were upheld, the economic impact on the states and corporations would be "in the billions."

**As if the above was not enough to assure that Four Corners will soon be unfit for human habitation, Pacific Lighting Corporation and Texas Eastern Transmission (together they form WESCO), El Paso Natural Gas and Continental Oil Company plan to build six coal-gasification projects in the same area as the Navajo Indian Irrigation Project.[39]

tailing piles assume no responsibility under the law. To add injury to injury, while the mines were producing in the 1950s and 60s, the corporations encouraged the Navajo miners to use the radioactive tailings to build houses, schools, and other public buildings. Let's look more closely at uranium production on Indian lands.

Uranium

Uranium is the essential ingredient of the nuclear fuel cycle. Without uranium ore, there would be no nuclear weapons or nuclear reactors. Therefore, the easiest way to stop the proliferation of nuclear weapons and nuclear power plants is to keep the uranium in the ground where it belongs. Unfortunately, that is becoming harder and harder to do given the escalating drive by the transnationals to acquire and mine every bit of uranium ore they can find.

North American Indian tribes own reserves of uranium so vast that if taken as a whole, they would be the fifth largest uranium-owning nation in the world. If ranked by production, Indian tribes would rank fourth in the world. Since 1948, 53,835 tons of uranium— 10 percent of the world's total—has come from Indian lands. In 1976, 25 percent of all U.S. uranium-308 (yellowcake) was produced from Indian lands. As of 1978, 1,185,000 acres of Indian land were under lease for uranium exploration and development. Breakdown of Indian land leases (according to the DOE) is as follows: Colorado, 162,000 acres; New Mexico, 786,000 acres; Washington, 57,000 acres; and Wyoming, 180,000.[40] Most of the uranium in the U.S. is located in the Wyoming Basin and the Colorado Plateau, which contains New Mexico's Grants Mineral Belt, the largest uranium-producing area in the world.* The Nuclear Regulatory Commission (NRC) estimates that New Mexico has 30 percent of the probable uranium reserves in the country, followed by Wyoming (15 percent), Colorado (11 percent), Utah (14 percent), and Texas (10 percent). South Dakota, California, Arizona, Nevada, and Washington have another 11 percent scattered among them. (The fastest growing area for uranium exploration and mining is the state of Washington, specifically around the Spokane reservation.) Over half of Grant's Mineral Belt is on Indian land, including part of the Navajo Nation, Laguna Pueblo, Ramah Navajo, Cononcito Navajo, Jemez Pueblo,

---

*Since 1959, when mining began in the Grants region, production of uranium ore has totalled more than 55 million tons. In 1977, U.S. production of Uranium-308 totalled 14,900 tons—of which 6,800 came from the Grants Mineral Belt.[41] Half that is from Kerr-McGee's two mines at Church Rock and Ambrosia Lake.[42]

Zia Pueblo, and Zuni Pueblo.*

To take one example, the Jackpile mine operated by Anaconda (ARCO) is on the land of the Laguna Pueblo in New Mexico. Since the early 1950s when Anaconda opened the mine, it has become the largest open-pit mine in the U.S., stretching a full five miles in length.**[46] The Rio Paguate used to pass through a beautiful agricultural valley next to the Pueblo village of Paguate. Now it runs through the Anaconda Jackpile mine and its waters are turned green by the discharged effluent. It is this water that the people must drink and give to their livestock; stomach cancer is on the rise. Although the mine has been in operation for 25 years, not one foot of the Pueblo's land has been "reclaimed." The reason is simple: reclamation of radioactive soil is impossible.[48] The mine has produced 80 million tons of uranium-308, devastating 2,800 acres of the Pueblo. Anaconda's "Bluewater" processing mill has left 75 acres (13 million tons) of tailing to the mercy of the desert wind and rain.[49]

The total labor force of the Pueblo is only 970, 447 of whom work in the mines and a smaller number in the mill complex. The fact that five of every seven workers are employed in uranium production may help explain why more than 100 Laguna babies born in recent years suffer from some form of birth defect (reported by a staff member on the Senate Committee on Indian Affairs).[50]

The Sacrifice of Indian Miners

Red Rock was home to traditional Navajos who were totally unaccustomed to the logic and practices of the representatives of the energy giants who wanted their land. The energy-exploiting corporations and the Atomic Energy Commission (AEC) took full advantage of this. In 1945, the Trinity Test Site in New Mexico confirmed the viability of the atomic bomb. In 1948 the AEC authorized purchase of uranium to stockpile for nuclear weapons and provided cash incentives for corporations to find as much uranium as they could.

---

*Close to 750,000 acres of Navajo and Pueblo land has been leased for exploration. Exxon alone has 400,000 acres leased near Red Rock on Navajo land. Thirteen other energy companies have leases in the area: Continental Oil (CONOCO), Anaconda Copper (ARCO), Grace Oil, the Hearst's Homestake Mining, Humble Oil, Hydro Nuclear, Kerr-McGee, Mobil Oil, Pioneer Nuclear, Phillips Petroleum, Marathon Oil, and Gulf Oil.[43] Thirty-six mines and 6 processing mills are now in operation in the region. Twenty-six more mines are slated by 1985[44] along with at least 4 more mills.[45]

**Anaconda holds a total of 7,500 acres of leases on the Pueblo lands. In addition to the pit operation, two underground mines on the property together produce 1,300 tons per day of ore.[47]

On reservations like Red Rock there were no taxes, regulations or laws regarding mining activities. Nicer still, for the corporations, there was a population of very cheap labor, ignorant of radioactivity and its dangers. In the sixties the AEC discontinued its price supports and incentive program. At once the price of uranium dropped to around six dollars a pound (it has since risen dramatically).[51] With no more government assured profits to reap, the corporations closed their mines, left millions of tons of radioactive tailings, threw hundreds of miners out of work and left for higher profits in other countries. Any cleanup attempt was left to the Navajo Nation. According to the Government Accounting Office (GAO), this will cost the Navajos over $21 million—which takes on more meaning when we note that Navajos received less than $1 million in total royalty payments. What happened to the miners?

Some 100 Navajos were hired by Kerr-McGee, in 1954, given minimal training, and sent in to dig uranium ore. A few more were employed at a nearby processing mill in Shiprock.

"The company came around and said there were jobs opening up, but they didn't tell us a thing about dangers of uranium mining," recalls former miner Terry Light, "The labor came cheap back then. [Miners were paid $1.60 an hour.[52] The white men really took advantage of the Navajos who needed jobs."[53] "They chased us in there like we were slaves," recalls another miner. "I remember that it used to be so dusty that we were always spitting up black stuff and how when we went home we all had headaches from breathing all that contamination."

"Those mines had 100 times the level of radioactivity allowed today," says LaVerne Husen, director of the Public Health Service in Shiprock. "They weren't really mines, just holes dug outside into the cliffs. Inside the mines were like radiation chambers, giving off unmeasured and unregulated amount of radon."[54] [Italics mine.]

In 1965, the Indian Health Service hospital at Shiprock reported that two Navajo uranium miners had died of lung cancer (carcinoma). By 1970, eight had died. By 1974, eighteen had died. At this writing, twenty-five miners have died, and forty-five more have radiation-induced lung cancer, a disease that until Kerr-McGee came along was unknown among the Navajos.[55] In a seven-year study completed in 1972, no cases of lung cancer were found in a review of 50,000 chest x-rays of Navajos. But rates of lung cancer have now soared because of exposure to radiation.*

*In a paper entitled "Uranium Mining and Lung Cancer Among Navajo Indians," Dr. Gerald Buker states that the risk of lung cancer has increased by a factor of eighty-five among Navajo miners.[56]

Oscar Sloan, a former miner living in an isolated community near Monument Valley, Arizona, says that "all the people here have used the uranium wastes to build our homes. The company never told us they were dangerous. Some white men came here a couple of years ago and said we shouldn't live in our houses. They said the Government would get us new houses because our houses were radioactive, but they never did. I don't want to live in this house anymore, but I have no place else to go."[57]

Kerr-McGee denies responsibility for any of the deaths and refuses to pay medical expenses. Kerr-McGee representative, Bill Phillips, told a Washington reporter, "*I couldn't tell you what happened at some small mines on an Indian Reservation, we have uranium interests all over the world.*"[58] Amanda Spake of *Mother Jones* asked government officials about the situation. They all denied any responsiblity for the deaths, except one who denied that the mines *ever existed.* Although the ore was mined for the AEC, the NRC denies any responsibility because the old AEC regulated the uranium only after it was taken out of the ground.*[59]

Still the Indian people are sent into the mines of the energy giants. In 1975, 3,400 underground miners and 900 stripminers were employed by the uranium industry. Hundreds are employed on Navajo lands. On the Spokane lands one out of four in the work force has worked or is working in the mines. And now the government is paying the companies to train an Indian workforce. An article in *Business Week* (1 November 1977) entitled "Manpower Gap in the Uranium Mines" explains how the Labor Department pays Kerr-McGee to train Navajo miners:

> By 1990, the [uranium] industry will need 18,400 underground miners and 4,000 above-ground...Once on the job, Kerr-McGee estimated that it costs approximately $80,000 per miner in training, salary and benefits, as well as the costs for trainees who quit. To try and trim these costs and create an ample labor force, Kerr-McGee is now operating a training program at its Church Rock mine on the Navajo Reservation. The $42 million program is financed by the Labor Department and is expected to turn out

---

*The U.S. Government has shown callous disregard for the health and safety of its citizens on many occasions. Misinformed soldiers were used as guinea pigs in the atomic bomb tests in New Mexico and the Pacific. Surrounding communities were exposed to high levels of radioactive fallout. The genocidal bombings of Hiroshima and Nagasaki were followed by a clean-up operation which exposed hundreds or more civilians and soldiers to dangerous levels of radioactivity. See Howard L. Rosenberg, "The Guineapigs of Camp Desert Rock," *The Progressive,* June 1979; "Compass," *East-West Journal;* and the film *Paul Jacobs and the Nuclear Gang,* distributed by New Times Films, New York City.

100 Navajo miners annually. Labor Department sponsors hope the program will help alleviate the tribe's chronic unemployment which is estimated at about 40%.

Uranium miners—Indian and non-Indian—are part of the great national sacrifice to corporate wealth. In a 1973 study of 3,400 uranium miners (780 of whom were Indians) over a twenty year period, it was found that the group could expect 600 to 1,100 lung cancer deaths above what would normally be expected for other occupations.[60] Other reports indicate irradiation through uranium mining has resulted in the premature death of one out of every six uranium miners from lung cancer or radiation related illnesses.[61] The primary goal of the energy-exploiting corporations is profit maximization. Through government subsidies, paid for by the taxpayers, even the financial costs of uranium exploration and development are socialized (we have seen how the human and environmental costs are socialized), while the profits are monopolized.*

The Nuclear Fuel Cycle and Recent Catastrophes

The Navajo miners and other uranium miners are victims of the front end of the nuclear fuel cycle. The dangers associated with the fuel cycle are slowly becoming more and more well known. The near meltdown at Three Mile Island brought us, again, to the brink of nuclear disaster.** The public has been lied to about the real levels of radioactivity released (and still being emitted) and their long-term health dangers.*** Other recent catastrophes have been covered up

---

*For example, the DOE's Grand Junction office administers the National Uranium Resource Evaluation Program (NURE). On-site contractor for the program is the Bendix Field Engineering Corp with occasional help from the USGS, various universities and the DOE laboratories. The purpose of the multifaceted project conducted by NURE is to evaluate all uranium potentials in the country. Funding was $33 million in 1977, $55 million in 1978, and $78 million in 1979.[62]

In addition to NURE there is the information and aid provided by the U.S. Geological Survey; NASA's Landsat and other mineral exploration satellites; the Departments of Interior, Agriculture, and Energy research sections; and guaranteed free liability insurance, subsidies for research and development work, low-cost fuel enrichment for reactors, price guarantees and other direct subsidies.[63]

**See, *We Almost Lost Detroit*, by John G. Fuller (Reader's Digest Press, 1975), for a look at what happened at Windscale, England in 1957 and at the Fermi I reactor near Detroit, Michigan in 1966. Other accidents which rival Three Mile Island occurred at TVA's Browns Ferry, Alabama reactor in 1975 and the Duane Arnold reactor near Cedar Rapids, Iowa in June of 1978.

***For in-depth examination of the true aftermath of Three Mile Island see: Bill Keisling and Ed Perrons, "Corporate Meltdown," *The Progressive*, June 1979, p. 12; Ernest Sternglass, "The Whole Truth About Three Mile Island," *The Progressive*, June 1979; and Harvey Wasserman, "The Antinuclear Movement Approaches Critical Mass," *New Age*, June 1979, p. 22.

with virtual media blackouts.

The United Nuclear mine at Churchrock has recently been shut down by the worst spill of radioactive material in the history of uranium mining in this country. In one of the few stories on the catastrophe, the *Washington Star* of 31 August 1979 reported that over 100 million gallons of highly radioactive liquid waste and 1100 tons of equally radioactive solid waste spilled into the dry river bed of the Rio Puerco River (a tributary of the Little Colorado which flows to the Colorado) when a tailings pond dam broke open on 16 July 1979.* "Substantial amounts of uranium, thorium and radium" were released into the dry river bed, eventually coursing 80 miles into Arizona before being absorbed by the soil. Hundreds of Navajo families live and graze their livestock near the river. There were indications that United Nuclear officials knew of cracks in the dam months before the 6,000 foot dam suffered a twenty foot breach that is now endangering the lives of so many Navajo people. The local papers reported that the normally dry river was overflowing its banks on the day before the spill.

Unfortunately, this spill will have little effect on the mining and milling activities in the area. The governor of New Mexico decided not to declare the site a disaster area or even admit that an emergency situation existed for fear of hurting the uranium mining industry in his state. The area may see seventy-five new mines and twenty new mills by the end of the next decade.[64]

The same day the dam burst, preliminary hearings were scheduled to begin in Washington, D.C. on a suit filed in December 1978 by ninety-nine Navajo traditionals, an Acoma Indian, and the organization, Friends of the Earth, to stop all uranium mining on Indian land until the federal government prepares an environmental impact statement for the area of the San Juan Uranium Basin. The suit claims that the defendants have evolved a national uranium exploration and development policy that has never been subject to public review and is therefore in violation of the National Environmental Policy Act (NEPA). NEPA requires an EIS for all federal actions that significantly affect the environment. The suit also demands the federal government study appropriate alternatives to uranium production.[65]

---

*A tailings pond is a euphemism for a radioactive waste dump. Great amounts of water are used in the process of mining and milling uranium. After becoming polluted with radioactive effluent, the water and other solid wastes are discharged into an earthern coffer dam adjacent to the mine or mill site. It was this type of waste dump which broke open and flooded the Rio Puerco in Church Rock.

Resistance

In the forefront of resistance and the struggle for Indian liberation are the men and women of the American Indian Movement (AIM) and Women of All Red Nations (WARN). AIM was born, in the words of Bill Means of the International Indian Treaty Council, "out of the dark violence of police brutality and the voiceless despair of injustice in the courts of Minneapolis." The movement quickly spread to the reservations and other urban centers with large uprooted Indian populations. The men and women of AIM and WARN are working together to see Indian people in the U.S. and throughout the world have a sense of pride in their culture and themselves, to stop the BIA and welfare agencies from taking Indian children from their homes and cultures, to stop forced sterilizations, and to regain self-determination over their lives and land.

The history of AIM is a chronicle of abuse and injustice by the FBI and state and local police.* These government forces have attempted to crush the organization by murdering its leaders and members (including Richard Oakes, Larry Casuse, Buddy Lamont, Pedro Bissonette, Frank Clearwater, Wesley Bad Heart Bull, Anna Mae Aquash, Joe Stuntz, the unborn child of Joanne Yellow Bird, Dallas Thundershield, and *hundreds* more as well as several unsuccessful attempts on the life of Russell Means, Clyde Bellecourt, and Leonard Peltier); sapping individual and organizational energy with never-ending successions of indictments and costly trials—often lasting years—on entirely fabricated charges (Russell Means has endured thirteen trials and over thirty indictments, been shot twice and stabbed twice, and served time for a conviction on a phony riot charge; Clyde Bellecourt has been indicted 42 times); and imprisoning as many members as possible (Leonard Peltier, Dick Marshall, Ted Means, and hundreds of other political prisoners are serving long prison terms on trumped-up charges). Yet, this chronicle of systematic repression has not received public attention. The Select Committee to Study Governmental Operations with Respect to Intelligence Activities headed by Senator Frank Church did not included one word about the FBI's policy of terror against AIM, although the infamous Counter-Intelligence Program (COINTEL—

*Following the government's seige of Wounded Knee there were 562 arrests by federal authorities and 185 grand jury indictments. Nonetheless, only eleven felony convictions were successfully engineered by federal prosecutors. The usual conviction rate for the Eighth Circuit where most of the trials took place is 78.2 percent. The Wounded Knee conviction rate was a comparatively minor 7.7 percent.

PRO) was rightly discussed in relation to the Black Panthers and New Left groups.

Governmental violence has always followed AIM activity. In late 1972 there was a takeover of the Bureau of Indian Affairs in Washington; records documenting the BIA's misconduct over the years were made public.[66]

In the winter of 1973, several hundred Oglala Lakota and AIM supporters from around the country came to Wounded Knee, South Dakota, at the request of the traditional Lakota leaders. All other means of changing conditions on the Pine Ridge Reservation had failed. The U.S. Government responded to their act of self-determination with armored personnel carriers, helicopters, automatic rifles, and other Viet Nam-era weapons. But for seventy-one days no federal police or BIA officials had any authority at Wounded Knee. Despite countless gun battles, negotiating sessions, and the government's blockade of all food, fuel, and medical supplies, a self-governing community was built and maintained.[67] As Russell Means says about his days at Wounded Knee, for once "I walked in Freedom."

Over one hundred years earlier the warriors of several Indian Nations had defeated the army under General Custer in the Big Horn Mountains. The battle has gone down in the history books of white North America, but the true account of its causes and consequences is little known by non-Indians. It is a story of the discovery of gold in the Black Hills of South Dakota, broken treaties, the decimation of the Great Sioux Reservation, and genocide against the Lakota, Cheyenne, and Arapaho Peoples.*

*In the early 19th century, gold seekers, homesteaders, and the U.S. Cavalry opened the Bozeman Trail through the heart of the Great Plains Indian lands. The Lakota, Cheyenne, and Arapaho resisted, and the U.S. government bargained for peace in an attempt to gain through treaty what could not be won on the battlefield. In 1868 the Ft. Laramie Treaty was signed (under General Sherman), and the U.S. agreed to abandon its forts along the Bozeman Trail and close the trail permanently. The Indians agreed, for the first time, to boundaries on their land. The Indians saw the Treaty as a permanent guarantee of their sovereignty. It provided the unceded Indian Territory from which whites were excluded, stretching from the Missouri River west to the Powder River hunting grounds into the Wyoming Big Horn Mountains and from the Canadian border south into Nebraska. Part of this land, the western half of South Dakota and part of North Dakota formed the Great Sioux Nation. The 1868 Treaty was to last forever: "for as long as the grass shall grow." Forever lasted for six years, when a military expedition led by General George Custer confirmed that large amounts of gold were to be found in the Black Hills. Time for a new treaty. In 1876 the U.S. broke the Treaty and took most of the Lakota lands in Nebraska, Wyoming, Montana, and North Dakota, leaving only a small portion of South Dakota. The sacred Black Hills were annexed for gold mining. In 1886 the "Great Sioux Nation" was reduced to seven small reservations. In the winter of 1875-1876

Today uranium is the treasure sought in the sacred Black Hills of the Lakota. First discovered in 1951, it has been mined for many years leaving 3½ million tons of radioactive tailings in Fall River County only a few miles away from the Pine Ridge Reservation. Twenty-seven corporations including Union Carbide, Exxon, Kerr-McGee, Westinghouse, Mobil, Rio Algom and the public TVA operate in the seven western counties of South Dakota stolen from the Lakotas. Today corporate interests are being opposed by Lakota traditionals, white ranchers, and farmers (who fear that the area's water will either be used up in the mining and milling operations or left so contaminated by radioactivity that it will be unfit for humans, crops or livestock), AIM and WARN members, non-Indian activists, and environmentalists, who have come together in the Black Hills Alliance. The Alliance was formed early in 1979 to challenge the activities of the energy companies and to see that the original 1868 treaty is respected.

What could be the first in a new wave of violent confrontations between the U.S. government and Indian people is shaping up at Big Mountain on Black Mesa. 6,500 traditional Navajos and 60 Hopi have been ordered by a federal judge in Tucson to leave the lands they have lived on for centuries. At issue is the 2 million acres of the Hopi-Navajo Joint Use Area (JUA). (President Chester Arthur decreed the JUA in 1882.) In 1977 Federal Judge James Walsh ruled the land should be split between the two peoples. He required all members of either group to relocate if they were not living on designated lands. If

---

the Secretary of the Interior declared that any Sioux found off the reservation area would be considered hostile; the army was sent to enforce this. That summer the Lakota, Cheyenne and Arapaho gathered for the sun dance in the Big Horn Mts. It was this camp—said to be the largest gathering of native peoples ever to have taken place in the hemisphere—that Custer stumbled upon. Sitting Bull, a Hunkpapa Lakota, and Crazy Horse, an Oglala, led the attack on Custer. After the victory the Nations separated seeking to avoid more fighting and hoping the white man would honor the treaty and go away. But the Lakota were ultimately forced by hunger to return to the Government Indian agencies. The white man had virtually exterminated the buffalo upon which the Lakota had depended for subsistence.

Then came the Ghost Dance which prophesied the return of the slaughtered warriors and buffalo and told of a coming purification in which the whites would disappear and the earth would be new again. The government agents and the military saw the Ghost Dance as the beginning of an uprising. Sitting Bull was killed by BIA police and troops were sent into the reservations in another violation of the treaty of 1868. In December 1890 some of Sitting Bull's people who had fled their camp after his murder joined with Big Foot's Minneconjou Lakota. Together they sought Red Cloud's Oglala at Pine Ridge. They were intercepted by the restored Seventh Cavalry at Wounded Knee, about 18 miles from the Pine Ridge Agency. On 29 December 1890, after disarming the Indians, the Seventh Cavalry murdered all 300 Lakota

the 6,500 Navajos and 60 Hopi do not move, an attempt will be made to forceably evict them. Traditional peoples from other nations and members of the American Indian Movement (AIM) have pledged their support of the Navajo and Hopi traditionals that do not intend to move.

What is behind the judge's ruling? Every square foot of the JUA sits atop a massive coal deposit. The disputed area is only a few miles from the Peabody mines. A statement regarding the JUA was drafted at the June 18-24 International Treaty Council Conference at Big Mountain, declaring: "We the people of Big Mountain do hereby recognize that the real purpose of the laws and disputes created is to remove...the traditionals from their lands to make it possible to mine coal that lies beneath the entire Joint Use Area." The International Indian Treaty Council which has NGO (Non-Governmental Organization) status at the United Nations will make the JUA relocation a top priority of the current session (October 1979).

Other likely sites for resistance include: the Colville and Spokane Reservations (over uranium); the Western Shoshone lands in Nevada (over water); the Santee Sioux lands at Prairie Island in Minnesota (where Northern States Power has built two nuclear reactors); the Upper Skagit, Sauk-Suiattle, and the Swinomish Tribal Communities (where a nuclear power plant could be located in the middle of thier ancestoral homeland in the Skagit Valley on the shores of the Skagit River); the Pine Ridge Reservation (where the Lakotas are faced with uranium mining and possible oil and gas exploration); the Pima and Papago lands of Arizona (over the stealing of their water for industrial purposes); the Wind River Reservation of Wyoming and Fort Belnap, Fort Peck, Blackfoot,

---

men, women, and children. The white press called it the last "battle" of the "Indian Wars."

In 1902 the 1886 Dawes Allotment Act was applied to the Pine Ridge Reservation. By 1970, the Pine Ridge Reservation was a patchwork of white and Indian-owned land. Of its 3 million acres the tribal government owned a half million, whites owned 1 million and the Oglalas owned only 1½ million. Of those who still own their ancestral lands, 83% have been forced by poverty to lease part or all of their holdings. Over the years the Oglalas on Pine Ridge have been coerced by BIA policies into an assimilation process. Welfare and other benefits were withheld if parents refused to send their children to BIA or mission schools where Indian dress, customs, and language are forbidden. Early on, Indian religion was *outlawed* and Christian missionaries were encouraged, often with grants of free land, to work among the Indians to destroy the roots of the old ways. (Today there are 137 churches on Pine Ridge, one for every 100 people.) The policy of genocide has been so successful that at the time of World War II Adolph Hitler is said to have modelled his "final solution" around the colonial Indian policies of the U.S. government as well as those of the British in India.[68]

Crow and Northern Cheyenne Reservations of Montana (over coal and uranium exploration and mining); the Flathead lands of Montana (over the building of a high-voltage transmission line from the Colstrip, Montana coal-fired plants through the reservation); the Duck Valley Reservation of Northern Nevada (over water rights) where Tina Trudell, wife of AIM leader John Trudell, their three children and Tina's mother were all murdered in a fire earlier this year; and the Mohawk lands of New York (which at this writing are surrounded by state police attempting to arrest traditional members for resisting the takeover of their homelands by the state (*Akwasasne Notes* is produced here); and the Shoshone lands of Nevada (because the MX missile system is to run through disputed lands). The list could go on and on until every reservation in the country was named.

At the Big Mountain meeting discussed earlier, AIM co-founder Clyde Bellecourt summed up the present situation of the American Indian by saying:

"When you look at it you see that our relationship to the U.S. Government is the same as the Iranian or Vietnames Peoples' before their revolutions. It's the same everywhere. The push to take Indian lands has never stopped."[69]

Conclusion

The U.S.-based energy corporations are preparing for what may prove to be a final assault on the remaining land-base of North America's indigenous people.* The battlelines are drawn; the Northern Great Plains, Rocky Mountain States, and the Four Corners areas are the battlegrounds. It is in these sparsely-populated areas that the energy wars of the 1980s are going to be fought. They will be fought for the same reasons as the Indian Wars of the last century: water, land, and minerals. Successive U.S. governments have chosen to violate, rather than enforce, the treaties which *forever* guarantee sovereignty over these resources. As before, resistance will take place every step of the way. The difference this time around is that a significant number of non-Indian men and women will offer their help in the coming struggle.

Native people have never ceased their struggle for self-determination. The survival of us all—Indian, white, Black, Hispanic,

*Exploitation and genocide against the Indian people of what is now Canada has not been the subject of this paper. The fact that multinational energy corporations are exploiting vast deposits of high grade uranium ore in the Saskatchewan territory of the Dineh People is just one example of continuing injustice there.

Asian American—is being threatened by the men who control the transnational corporations and have organized the Trilateral Commission.* It is time to decide which side we will be on.

FOOTNOTES

1. *Project Independence: A Summary*, Federal Energy Administration—Office of Strategic Analysis, 1 November 1974.
2. Burlington Northern Railroad, Form 10-K, 1978, p. 43.
3. Larry B. Leventhal, "Indian Sovereignty—It's Alive," in *The Great Sioux Nation*, Rozanne Dunbar Ortiz, ed., (American Indian Treaty Council Information Center, NY, 1977), p. 206.
4. Joseph G. Jorgensen, "Energy, Agriculture, and Social Science in the American West," *Native Americans and Energy Development*, (Cambridge, MA: Anthropology Resources Center, 1978).
5. "Statement of S. David Freeman, Chairman of the Board of Directors of the Tennessee Valley Authority Before the Senate Subcommittee on Antitrust, Monopoly, and Business Rights on May 22, 1979," available from TVA, Knoxville, TN.
6. Wallace McMartin, "Western Coal: Energy vs. Agriculture," Reprint #938, North Dakota Agricultural Experiment Station, from *Farm Research*, January-February 1979, pp. 12-17.
7. Jorgensen, *op. cit.*
8. *New York Times*, 24 June 1979, p. 16.
9. Kenneth Ross Toole, *The Rape of the Great Plains: Northwest America, Cattle and Coal*, (Boston: Atlantic Monthly Press, 1976), p. 22.
10. *Ibid.*, p. 2.
11. *North Central Power Study*, Volumes I and II, Bureau of Reclamation, October 1971.
12. Toole, *op.cit.*, p. 19.
13. *Toole's findings refute this.*

*ed. note: The bond of exploitation and resistance stretches form the uranium mines of Namibia and South Africa to the mines of western United States. Rio Algom, mentioned above, is a subsidiary of Rio Tinto Zinc which is heavily represented on the Trilateral Commission. (See Brown Part VI.)

14. *Water for Energy, Final Environmental Impact Statement*, Bureau of Reclamation, Department of Interior, 1 December 1977, p. i.

15. See Bob Alvarez, *Water for Industry in the Missouri River Basin*, Environmental Policy Center, Washington, D.C., Lou Cannon and Joel Kotkin, "The Embattled West," *The Manchester Guardian Weekly*, July 15 and July 22, 1979, for a discussion of the Oglala Aquifer.

16. See Harvey Wasserman, "Revolt of the Boll Weevils," *Rolling Stone*, 9 August 1979, p. 38.

17. Toole, *op. cit.*, p. 6.

18. *Ibid.*, p. 1.

19. *Ibid.*, p. 4. For an elaboration of the term "national sacrifice area" see "Rehabilitation Potential of Western Coal Lands," National Academy of Sciences Report, 1974.

20. *Water for Energy*, p. 3-119.

21. Joan Nice, "Carter Energy Steamroller Threatens Environment," *High Country News*, 27 July 1979, p. 11.

22. *Ibid.*, p. 2.

23. Bruce Hamilton, "Carter Energy Mobilization Demobilized by Congress," *High Country News*, 10 August 1979, p. 6.

24. Robert Ostmann, "Threat From Acid Rain Worsens," *The Minneapolis Star-Midweek*, 17 July 1979, p. 1. Also see Gene Likens, Richard Uright, James Galloway, Thomas Butler, "Acid Rain," *Scientific American*, October 1979.

25. Ann Crittenden, "Tribes study options for development of resources," *Minneapolis Tribune*, 12 August 1979, p. 3D.

26. Dee Brown, *Hear That Lonesome Whistle Blow*, (New York: Bantam Books, 1977), pp. 39-41, 44-46, 56-57, 64, 75, 175-176, 205.

27. Bruce Johansen and Roberto Maestas, *Wasi'chu: The Continuing Indian Wars*, (New York: Monthly Review Press, 1979), p. 30.

28. Peter Farb, *Man's Rise to Civilization*, 2nd edition, (New York, E. P. Dutton, 1st edition, 1968, 1978), pp. 231, 232.

29. Nancy J. Owens, "Can Tribes Control Energy Development?" *Native Americans and Energy Development*, p. 57.

30. Harris Arthur, Preface to *Native Americans and Energy Development*, p.2.

31. Owens, *op. cit.*, p. 53.

32. *Ibid.*

33. Gerald F. Seib, "Indians Awaken to their Lands' Energy Riches and Seek to Wrest Development from Companies," *Wall Street Journal*, 20 September 1979, p. 40.

34. Jimmie Durham, "Native Americans and Colonialism," *Guardian*, 28 March 1979, p. 19.

35. Richard O. Clemmer, "Black Mesa and the Hopi," *Native Americans and Energy Development*, p. 20.

36. *Ibid.*, p. 30.

37. Bob Rankin, "Congress Debates Cleanup of Uranium Mill Wastes," *Congressional Quarterly*, 19 August 1978, p. 2180.

38. See Karl Z. Morgan, "Cancer and Low Level Ionizing Radiation," *Bulletin of the Atomic Scientists*, September, 1978, pp. 30-41 and Helen Caldicott, *Nuclear Madness* (Autumn Press, 1978).

39. The Los Alamos Scientific Labs in New Mexico have proposed that parts of the Southwest be cut into energy districts and that human habitation be forbidden in those areas.

40. Winona La Duke, "How Much Development?," *Akwesasne Notes*, Late Winter 1979, p. 5.

41. Richard Hoppe, "A stretch of desert along Route 66—the Grants Belt—is chief

locale for U.S. uranium," *Engineering and Mining Journal*, November 1978, pp. 73-93.

42. *Ibid.*, p. 76.

43. Tom Barry, "Bury My Lungs at Red Rock," *The Progessive*, February 1979, pp. 25-27.

44. *Energetic New Mexico—The Power State*, Albuquerque Chamber of Commerce, 1977.

45. *Draft Generic Environmental Statement on Uranium Milling*, Volumes I and II, Nuclear Regulatory Commission, April 1979, p. 3-14.

46. Barry, *op. cit.*, p. 27.

47. Hoppe, *op. cit.*

48. *Akwesasne Notes*, Late Winter 1979, p. 6, and Summer 1979, p. 31.

49. Hoppe, *op. cit.*, pp. 86-88.

50. Newsletter of the Native American Solidarity Committee (NASC), Spring 1979, pp. 12, 13.

51. Uranium is now selling for $43.25 a pound on the open market.

52. *Akwesasne Notes*, Late Winter, p. 4.

53. This is so even though the information was available in the U.S. from the beginning of the 20th century and available to Europeans since the 1600s from the experiences of pitchblende miners.

54. Barry, *op. cit.*, p. 28.

55. Winona La Duke, "The History of Uranium Mining," *Black Hills—Paha Sapa Report*, 1:1, p. 2.

56. Barry, *op. cit.*, p. 28.

57. *Ibid.*, p. 26.

58. La Duke, *op. cit.*

59. *Ibid.*

60. Anthony S. Schwagin and Thomas Hollacher, "Lung Cancer Among Uranium Miners," *Nuclear Fuel Cycle*, (Union of Concerned Scientists, Cambridge, MA, 1973).

61. Michael Best and William Connally, "An Environmental Paradox," *The Progressive*, October 1976, p. 20.

62. *Engineering and Mining Journal*, November 1978, p. 128.

63. See *The Nation*, April 1977.

64. Christopher McLeod, "New Mexico's Nuclear Fiasco," *Minnesota Daily*, 8 August 1979, p. 5.

65. *Akwesasne Notes*, Late Winter, p. 19.

66. See "Trail by Broken Treaties: BIA I'm Not Your Indian Any More," *Akwesasne Notes*, 1973.

67. See "Voices From Wounded Knee," *Akwesasne Notes*, 1974.

68. *Wasi-chu*, pp. 24-25.

69. Ron Ridenhour, "Defending a Sacred Mountain," *Minneapolis Star Saturday Magazine*, 21 July 1979, p. 6.

chapter four

RESURGENT MILITARISM
Michael Klare*
and the Bay Area Chapter of the
Inter-University Committee

The U.S. is being plunged into another era of confrontation, intervention, and resurgent militarism. The Pentagon's unremitting crusade for increased military appropriations gains momentum with each new budget year, and the Carter Administration has pledged to reduce social spending in order to augment the nation's war coffers. Although U.S. policy makers appear committed to eventual adoption of a new strategic arms limitation pact with the Soviet Union (SALT-II), they have launched new nuclear weapons programs which will surely spur comparable Soviet moves and thus further inflame an already volatile arms race. And despite denials that the United States seeks a first-strike nuclear capability against the USSR, the introduction of new counterforce weapons like the M-X missile will make such an attack appear increasingly plausible, and thus push us all closer to the brink of a nuclear catastrophe.

Along with the increased danger of atomic war, we also face a growing risk of U.S. involvement in future *non-nuclear* conflicts. As the government of Shah Mohammed Reza Pahlavi collapsed in

*Michael Klare is director of the Militarism and Disarmament Program of the Institute for Policy Studies, Washington, D.C., and author of *War Without End: American Planning for the Next Vietnams* (Alfred Knopf, 1972). This is an edited version of an essay originally written and published by the Inter-University Committee to Stop Funding War and Militarism in 1976. Work on the current version began in July 1978 and was completed in December (published as an IPS Issue Paper), with an update in January 1979. The members of the Inter-University Committee who participated in drafting the two versions are: Jonathan Cobb, Howard Dratch, Madeline Duckles, Daniel Ellsberg, Todd Gitlin, David Gold, Vivian Gold, William Kornhauser, Jon Livingston, Will Rigaan, Jerry Sanders, Charles Schwartz, Alan Wolfe, and Carol Wolman. Substantial editorial assistance was also provided by Robert Borosage, Stephen Daggett and Delia Miller of the Institute for Policy Studies, and Eric Prokosch and Diana Roose of NARMIC.

Iran—and along with it the U.S. policy of converting selected Third World regimes into regional gendarmes—U.S. strategists began planning an expanded U.S. police presence abroad. President Carter has already called for the formation of a rapid-reaction strike force for possible use in the Middle East and Africa, and the Pentagon budget will be raised in order to finance the procurement of additional conventional (i.e., non-nuclear) munitions. And given the growing tendency of conservative leaders to exploit the Soviet threat issue for political gain, it is increasingly likely that the Carter Administration will engage in military show of force operations to demonstrate that it has the will to stand up to the Russians in contested areas abroad.

As always the public's awareness of these issues is blurred by the government's omnipresent cloak of secrecy and by the media's persistent failure to challenge the myths of national security. In the Congress, meanwhile, Republicans and Democrats argue only over the *velocity* of the unquestioned arms buildup, leaving the real questions of war or peace in the thermonuclear age largely unexplored. And, over the past few years, promilitary forces have often dominated public discussion of war-peace issues through a lavishly-funded grassroots campaign designed to persuade us that the United States is about to fall behind in the superpower arms race.

But while the promoters of militarism represent powerful political forces, we should not assume that their future success is guaranteed. The great majority of Americans stand to suffer enormously from this new militarism—not only from the very real prospect of thermonuclear war, but from the progressive deterioration of our quality of life and through curbs on our civil liberties. We believe that the great majority can be rallied to defeat resurgent militarism. In order to overcome this scourge, however, we must first isolate the forces behind it and point out the majority's stake in an alternative direction. These are the tasks to which the authors set themselves in writing this article.

What follows is a preliminary analysis of the origins and consequences of the present resurgence of militarism in our society. It was written *before* the Soviet intervention in Afghanistan became the golden opportunity to justify this resurgent militarism. The article is organized into four sections: in the first, we analyze the U.S.'s changing strategic position in the post-Vietnam world; in the second, we identify the components of the militarist response to that position; in the third, we look at the political-economic forces which underlie the new militarism; and finally, we examine the consequences of resurgent militarism in the United States. While we recognize that any comprehensive analysis of the world political situation would require an assessment of the possible role played by other international actors—particularly the Soviet Union and the Peoples Republic of China—our concern here is with the emerging political situation in *this* country and with the options we will face in our own lives.

U.S. Response to the Changing World Strategic Environment

The U.S. defeat in Vietnam, and concurrent changes in the world political-economic environment, have significantly altered the U.S. global power position. The Pentagon's failure to overcome the guerilla forces of the National Liberation Front severely undermined the presumption of U.S. invincibility which, by itself, was once considered sufficient to ward off any challenges to U.S. interests abroad. Domestic resistance to overseas military entanglements has further reduced the perceived credibility of future U.S. police-type operations abroad. The simultaneous emergence of strains in U.S. economic performance—the declining value of the dollar, rampant inflation, the waning competitiveness of U.S. products on the world market—has also eroded Washington's political clout. And while the United States remains the world's preeminent military power, there is widespread agreement that *relative* U.S. military advantage has diminished, and with it, Washington's capacity to manage world events.

In a sense, the decline in U.S. influence is not so much the result of specific events—such as the Vietnam catastrophe or the drop in value of the dollar—as it is an inevitable consequence of the growing diffusion of power throughout the world at large. With the collapse of the old colonial systems, many new nations have entered the world community—which has become that much harder to manage or dominate. These new actors have adapted the prevailing socio-economic systems to local conditions, thus producing a variety of compromises between socialism and capitalism and thereby adding to the complexity and unpredictability of international relations. The simultaneous appearance of divisions between the major capitalist powers on the one hand, and between the Soviet Union and China on the other, has further eroded the authority of the great world powers. Clearly, in this new environment of shifting alliances and power-relationships, there are obvious limits to the influence enjoyed by any single power—no matter how militarily advanced.

These developments have profound implications which can only be fully appreciated in the context of a more detailed review of changes in U.S. global power position over the past fifteen years. Three key developments, in particular, must be examined.

U.S. Lead in the Superpower Arms Race Has Diminished

In contrast to the situation which prevailed during the Cuban missile crisis of 1961, when the United States enjoyed overwhelming superiority in every category of strategic (i.e., nuclear) weaponry, the U.S. and the USSR today enjoy parity in most *quantitative* measures of nuclear strength. While the United States still enjoys a significant lead in the *qualitative* measures of strategic power (e.g., in the accuracy, reliability, and survivability of its nuclear delivery systems), the growth in the size of the USSR's nuclear arsenal has diminshed the U.S.' *perceived advantage* in strategic weaponry. That is not to say that America's nuclear war-making potential has in any way been reduced: both superpowers have long possessed sufficient firepower to destroy the world many times over, and both continue to expand their arsenals at rapid rates. What *has* changed is that the gap between U.S. and Soviet capabilities has narrowed over the last fifteen years.

At the same time as it was closing the gap in strategic weaponry, the Soviet Union was also expanding its conventional (i.e., non-nuclear) arsenals. The Soviet Navy has been transformed from a coastal defense force into a true ocean-going fleet, and Soviet ground forces have been re-equipped with advanced tanks, missiles, and artillery. Some military analysts have asserted that this buildup represents a Soviet intent to engage Western forces in a classical military confrontation, but a more realistic assessment suggests a political, rather than military orientation. The modernization of Soviet ground forces in Europe, for instance, is intended to demonstrate Moscow's determination to safeguard the prevailing (Soviet-dominated) political order in Eastern Europe rather than to signal an aggressive design on Western Europe. And Soviet naval forces are being used to show the flag and demonstrate Moscow's resolve to protect its new-found allies in Africa and Asia. While these forces would, of course, be available for combat in any future East-West conflict, it is their political (or, in the words of former Navy chief Admiral Elmo Zumwalt, their para diplomatic*) potential that most troubles U.S. strategists. By restricting America's capacity to use the threat of force to intimidate Third World governments, Russia has deprived Washington of a favored instrument of coercion and thus further diminished U.S. perceived global power.

---

*In a 1974 statement before the Senate Armed Services Committee, Admiral Zumwalt, then Chief of Naval Operations, asserted that "It is now evident, even to the most casual observer, that the historically land-oriented Soviet Union has embraced naval power as a major element of their foreign policy. They have acquired the ability to compete most effectively with us in the peacetime, paradiplomatic use of naval power."

Domestic Support for U.S. Intervention Abroad Has Declined

Before Vietnam, the U.S. public generally supported Washington's aggressive Cold War policies. Today, as a result of the Indochina debacle, there is significant domestic opposition to the extended use of U.S. combat forces abroad. Although many Americans would probably support "surgical" operations of the *Mayaguez* type,* resulting in relatively few U.S. casualties, there is little enthusiasm for any commitments that might lead to more costly and prolonged military involvements. This popular aversion, in turn, has led Congress to place new restraints on presidential war-making powers and on potential U.S. involvement in proxy wars of the Angola type. And while some politicians have proposed a relaxation of these restraints, to permit a U.S. military response to growing Soviet and Cuban involvement in Africa, Congress has so far resisted such efforts.**

The Vietnam War also provoked widespread dissent within the military, and ultimately led to the abolition of conscription. While formation of an all-volunteer army has alleviated some of the military's personnel problems, however, it has failed to produce a dependable disciplined force. Desertion, insubordination, and drug abuse continue at Vietnam-era levels, while recruitment quotas are going unfulfilled. Given the high cost of an all-volunteer service and the failure to recruit sufficient qualified personnel, it is almost inevitable that the Pentagon will attempt to reinstate the draft—a move that is certain to precipitate widespread political opposition among students and the middle class. [Draft registration began in July 1980; resistance is high—ed.]

---

*In May 1975 a U.S. ship, *the Mayaguez,* and a crew of 40 were seized by Cambodia. According to a *New York Times* editorial (23 February 1979), "The United States sent in the Marines and bombers, against nearby territory. Commentators applauded. Pollsters found President Ford's reputation for strength improved. Muscles had been duly flexed.

What might restraint have accomplished? And what was protected?...During the attacks, 41 American servicemen were killed and 50 wounded [and many more Cambodians]. And two minutes before the surprise attacks were launched, Cambodia had started broadcasting an announcement that it was releasing ship and crew."

**ed. note: For example, in the face of efforts to escalate CIA involvement in Angola during the Ford Administration, the Senate banned further covert aid in December 1975, and the House followed suit on January 16. According to correspondent Elizabeth Drew, Brzezinski "has brought up the idea from time to time that perhaps the United States should cause trouble for [now deceased] Agostinho Neto, the leader of Angola." He "has raised the question of whether the congressional restrictions are still applicable; the CIA has told him that they are." From "A Reporter at Large: Brzezinski," *The New Yorker,* 1 May 1978.

The Third World Has Emerged as a Significant Political-Economic Force

The Arab oil embargo of 1973 demonstrated to the First and Second Worlds that some countries of the Third World have acquired the will and occasionally the wherewithal to challenge them on critical international issues. This new muscle-flexing by once powerless nations reflects a major shift in political, economic, and military power from the industrialized nations of Europe, North America, and Japan to the underdeveloped countries of Asia, Africa, and Latin America. Although most Third World nations remain critically dependent on the industrialized countries for capital, technology, and markets for their products, some have gained new leverage by forming producers' organizations like OPEC, and by voting as a bloc in the United Nations and similar groups. The growing scarcity of raw materials has also intensified the competition between the advanced industrial powers for access to these materials, thus further enhancing the Third World's bargaining position.

The Third World's new leverage is due also to changes in the world power balance. The U.S. defeat in Southeast Asia, along with the American public's aversion to further Vietnam-type adventures, has diminished the likelihood of future U.S. interventions and thus encouraged many Third World governments to adopt more assertive and independent foreign policies. At the same time, the growth of Soviet and Chinese power has increased the options available to Third World countries in seeking economic and political allies. Dramatic increases in Third World military spending has, moreover, endowed some of the wealthier countries with impressive military capabilities. Israel's military forces, for instance, are now better equipped than those of some NATO powers, and it is likely that several Third World countries will follow India's lead in developing a nuclear weapons capability. In short, the relatively simple bipolar world predicated by Cold War analysts has given way to a more complex and demanding environment in which many actors (and combinations thereof) play significant and often unpredictable roles in world affairs.

These developments have profoundly altered the way in which U.S. leaders view the world around them. Whereas once they viewed the "Free World" as a hospitable environment in which there were no insurmountable barriers to the attainment of U.S. objectives, today they see it as hostile or at least contested territory where there are severe constraints on U.S. maneuverability. This altered consciousness is manifest in a 1972 statement by Admiral Thomas H. Moorer, then chairman of the Joint Chiefs of Staff, in an appearance before the Senate Appropriations Committee:

Our relative military power throughout the world has peaked and is declining. We no longer possess that *substantial strategic superiority* which in the past provided us with a significant margin of overall military power that we could, *with confidence,* protect our interests worldwide. Henceforth, we will have to chart our course with much greater precision and calculate our risks much more cautiously. (Emphasis the authors.)

This shift in America's relative power position has led its leaders to impose much tighter cost-effectiveness controls over the employment of U.S. forces abroad, and, as in the case of Angola, to accede to the loss of marginal interests wherever the political-economic costs of continued involvement outweigh any potential gains.

Caution at the margins has been accompanied, however, by a renewed sense of commitment to the *core interests* upon which America's world paramountcy and economic prosperity rest. First and foremost of these interests is the continued solidarity of the three leading centers of capitalist production—Western Europe, the United States, and Japan—in the face of rising demands from poorer nations. (Such, indeed, was the fundamental premise upon which the Trilateral Commission was founded and upon which President Carter's foreign policy is largely based.) At the same time, U.S. leaders are committed to the principle of U.S. supremacy *within* the trilateral alliance, and thus America's core interests also include continued U.S. control over the Middle Eastern oil supplies, without which European and Japanese economies would collapse.

Although top United States policy makers differ over the precise boundaries of U.S. core interests (there is some disagreement, for instance, as to whether they include the preservation of white minority rule in South Africa), all are committed to taking whatever steps are necessary to protect these basic interests and to ensure continued U.S. dominance within the trilateral alliance. And while these leaders perceive a wide variety of threats to U.S. interests abroad, including those arising from competition between the advanced capitalist countries and from growing economic nationalism in the Third World, they emphasize the Soviet threat above all others for a number of reasons:

1. The Soviet Union is perceived by U.S. policy makers as the principal long-range threat to U.S. domination of its "core" interests abroad.
2. The Soviet military buildup is the only credible basis for increased military spending at home.
3. Soviet aid is benefitting Third World governments and liberation movements which have resisted U.S. domination, including those in Angola, Ethiopia, Cuba, and Afghanistan.
4. The preservation of the U.S. military lead over the USSR is seen

as the *sine qua non* of continued U.S. leadership within the capitalist world as well as of its capacity to coerce antagonistic powers in the Third World, since the *credibility* of U.S. power is seen as resting, in the main, on its ability to outface the Soviets in a showdown.

5. The durability of the U.S. quasi-alliance with China likewise hinges on continued U.S. military superiority *vis-a-vis* the USSR.

Given these perceptions, top U.S. leaders from both major parties agree on the urgent need to widen the U.S.' nuclear lead over the Soviet Union and to strengthen its conventional war-fighting capability. As we shall see later, this effort has led U.S. policy makers to adopt dangerous new strategies and tactics which have quickened the tempo of militarism in this country and which greatly increase the risk of U.S. involvement in future conflagrations abroad.

The Drift Towards War

While U.S. leaders are committed to enhancing America's global military advantage, they face unprecedented political, military, and economic hurdles in achieving this goal. Given the sustained buildup in Soviet military capabilities and the growing diffusion of power throughout the world at large, true military superiority—of the sort the U.S. enjoyed at the end of World War II—appears unattainable. Even a doubling of the U.S. defense budget (in the unlikely event that American taxpayers could be persuaded to pay for such a move) would not restore that margin of overall military power whose loss Admiral Moorer so laments. Indeed, the very concept of superiority becomes meaningless when both superpowers already have sufficient nuclear weapons to destroy each other several times over. In their efforts to strengthen U.S. military capabilities, therefore, U.S. leaders have sought new technologies and strategies which enhance U.S. clout while respecting the objective limits to military growth.

As soon as the Vietnam War ended, Pentagon officials embarked on a multi-billion dollar effort to re-equip U.S. forces with the latest military hardware.* The objective of this drive was to increase the

---

*Indeed, some analysts believe that U.S. military leaders were, in the end, happy about the disengagement from Vietnam because they felt that ten years of war spending had diminished U.S. overall military preparedness (by pre-empting funds needed for arms modernization), and thus viewed the termination of hostilities as an opportunity to replace their obsolete hardware with modern equipment. With the war over, these officials persuaded Congress to approve development of a whole new generation of combat systems—including the XM-1 Main Battle Tank, the YAH-64 Advanced Attack Helicopter, and the F-16 Air Combat Plane, thus ending hopes for a "peace dividend" in the form of reduced military spending.

overall war-making capabilities of U.S. forces while simultaneously reducing military manpower levels in accordance with the switch to an all-volunteer service. Emphasis was placed on the development of "smart bombs," man-portable rockets, and other hardware that would enable small but heavily-armed U.S. forces to overcome much larger enemy forces. At the same time, U.S. scientists were ordered to develop new tactical nuclear weapons like the neutron bomb which could be used against discrete enemy forces without causing wide-spread damage to non-military facilities, and also to enhance the hard-target capabilities of strategic nuclear weapons (i.e., their capacity to destroy hardened military installations like missile silos and under-ground command bunkers.)

All these developments, and others described below, have added new muscle to the U.S. military apparatus. They have not, however, altered the basic ratio of forces between the United States and poten-tial adversaries—as measured in *numbers* of tanks, *numbers* of aircraft, *tonnage* of war fleets, etc. Accordingly, U.S. policy makers have also sought new strategies and tactics which enhance U.S. leverage while retaining the present balance of forces. In particular, they have emphasized the employment of surrogate troops to augment U.S. forces, and the use of threats and bluff to intimidate potential adversaries, and, thus, presumably to eliminate the need for direct military action. Under the Nixon Doctrine, many U.S. soldiers were withdrawn from potential combat zones in the Third World while massive shipments of U.S. arms were used to convert selected clients like Iran and Indonesia into regional police powers.* U.S. naval

---

*When first promulgated in July 1969, the Nixon Doctrine called for the gradual withdrawal of U.S. combat forces from Asia and the assumption of a "forward defense role by the ground forces of our clients (liberally supported, of course, by U.S. air and naval forces)." As noted by President Nixon in his 1970 "State of the World" address, the Doctrine's operative phrase held that in cases of non-nuclear conflict, "we shall furnish military and economic assistance when requested and as appropriate, but we shall look to the nation directly threatened to assume the primary responsibility of providing the manpower for its defense." By 1973, however, the Doctrine had been given a much wider interpretation: instead of applying merely to Asia, it has been extended to the entire globe; and instead of referring exclusively to military resources and options, it encompasses the whole spectrum of foreign-policy operations...Stated in more pragmatic terms, the revised Doctrine envisions the United States at the center of a whole new galaxy of power relationships and alliances in which armed combat will be delegated—insofar as possible—to the weaker and poorer nations while *detente* and collaboration will govern relations between the richer and stronger nations (including those in the Communist bloc)...In most Third World areas, the primary defense responsibility will be delegated to indigenous military and paramilitary forces (assisted by U.S. military advisors, police, and intelligence specialists, and U.S. civilian technicians

doctrine was revamped to stress the "presence" mission of the Navy—
i.e., the use of gunboats to threaten insubordinate Third World
governments with possible U.S. military action should they fail to heed
Washington's instructions. In the nuclear area, U.S. strategists
introduced the "Counterforce" doctrine, which envisions limited
nuclear strikes against Soviet missile forces—thereby calling into
question the survivability of the USSRs second-strike deterrent capability (thus increasing Moscow's perceived vulnerability, and enhancing the United States' presumed bargaining position).

These doctrinal innovations are intended to strengthen U.S.
relative power position while avoiding a major buildup of forces.
By using surrogate forces instead of its own, by threatening the use
of military force rather than employing it directly, and by suggesting
a U.S. readiness to wipe out Russia's nuclear deterrent, Washington
hopes to promote U.S. interests with a minimum commitment of
U.S. resources. But there are inherent limitations to such stopgap
measures: client regimes can collapse in the face of domestic unrest
(witness the revolution in Iran), gunboat diplomacy can inspire
resistance rather than compliance, and nuclear brinkmanship can
trigger unpredictable and dangerous countermoves. These strategies
can only work, moreover, when Washington demonstrates its
resolve to back up its clients and to carry out its threats when things
fail to work according to plan—and thus we could be forced to
engage in combat merely to protect the credibility of the entire
scheme.

By introducing new weapons systems and military strategies,
U.S. leaders have attempted to enhance U.S. global power position
while staying within the current budgetary restraints. In their
search for shortcuts, however, they have increased the risk of U.S.
involvement in future military conflicts abroad. In this section, we
will show how U.S. policies and related international developments
are pushing the world ever closer to global conflagration. Five key
trends, in particular, strike us as ominous:

---

and other white collar mercenaries working for the CIA and Defense Contractors
and to the interventionary troops of selected regional powers. U.S. military
involvement, when authorized, will normally consist of air or sea operations in
support of allied ground forces, or quick surgical assaults by U.S. shock troops
lofted abroad by huge jumbo jets and backed by abundant U.S. airpower."
Excerpted from Michael T. Klare, "U.S. Military Strategy after Vietnam," *Monthly
Review*, March 1974 and "From Containment to Cost-effectiveness: American
Interventionism After Vietnam," 1975, by the editor.

The U.S.-Soviet Rivalry

Top U.S. policy makers, as noted earlier, have come to reaffirm the primacy of the U.S.-Soviet rivalry, and consider U.S. supremacy in this contest to be a prerequisite for future efforts to discipline U.S. allies and dependents. Thus, the purely local consequences of any given conflict, as in Angola and Zaire, will often be discounted in favor of its possible strategic implications. In Western Europe, for instance, any electoral victories by Communist parties—no matter how independent of Moscow—will be perceived by Washington as weakening NATO and thereby contributing to Soviet strength.

Given this perception, U.S. policy makers have accelerated the development of new strategic weapons (the M-X missile, the cruise missile, the Trident-II missile, etc.), while increasing the American military commitment to NATO. And, while U.S. leaders are unlikely to risk a direct clash with Soviet forces, there is a growing inclination to confront forces which they consider to be Soviet proxy forces—e.g., the Cubans in Africa—in order to demonstrate the U.S. will to resist Soviet probes in the Third World. Such a move is becoming increasingly plausible because U.S.-Soviet relations have become a major domestic political issue—in that groups like the Committee on the Present Danger have attacked incumbent officials for being excessively soft in the face of what they describe as Soviet aggressiveness—and thus U.S. leaders will feel increasingly disposed to demonstrate American resolve in the event of a future crisis like the May 1978 upheaval in Zaire.

The Nuclear Arms Race

In contrast to the situation that prevailed in the 1950s and 1960s, when U.S. nuclear forces were ostensibly principally geared for massive retaliation in the unlikely event of an all-out Soviet attack on the United States, recent developments in U.S. strategic doctrine and weapons technology make thermonuclear war more thinkable, and thus more likely, than at any time since the U.S. lost its nuclear monopoly. Under the Counterforce doctrine introduced by then Secretary of Defense James R. Schlesinger in 1974, the Pentagon has accelerated deployment of counterforce weapons (so-named because they are designed to strike against Soviet *strategic forces*—ICBM complexes, nuclear submarine bases, etc.—in contradistinction to countervalue weapons, which are aimed at Soviet cities and factories). Ostensibly, these new weapons will be used to deter a Soviet pre-emptive strike against U.S. missile silos by offering U.S. leaders the option of responding with a limited counterstrike against Soviet forces—a response which is theoretically more credible than an all-out retaliatory attack against Soviet cities (which would surely trigger a comparable Soviet attack against U.S. cities). Since, however, even a limited nuclear exchange would produce many millions of casualties on both sides and thus almost inevitably trigger all-out retaliation, the introduction of counterforce weapons would not appear to enhance the U.S. deterrent to Soviet attack (which rests, as before, on the maintenance of an invulnerable, second-strike arsenal aimed at Soviet population centers).

But beyond that, some U.S. military leaders believe that the development of counterforce weapons would provide the United States with additional military options in responding to *other sorts of* Soviet moves and thus enhance Washington's bargaining position in a crisis. Because the use of counterforce weapons would theoretically be a more credible response to hypothetical Soviet probes against U.S. allies than the use of city-busters, these leaders believe that the possession of such weapons would increase Moscow's uncertainties as to possible U.S. reactions to such moves and would help discourage any Soviet risk-taking. Indeed, as suggested earlier, the introduction of Counterforce was intended to offset Soviet gains in nuclear weaponry by purposely increasing Moscow's uncertainties about U.S. moves and thus enhancing Washington's maneuverability and leverage in crisis situations. For such tactics to work, however, Moscow must be convinced that Washington is prepared to actually order a nuclear strike, and thus U.S. strategists are busy inventing scenarios in which the use of atomic munitions is kept limited—and thus would somehow be more acceptable than in a full-scale war. But however rational such strategems may appear to Pentagon officials, it is obvious that they increase the risk of nuclear Armaggedon. For when a crisis arises, the levels of tensions and uncertainty on both sides will quickly escalate, making negotiations more difficult while increasing the risk of miscalculation, thus bringing us all closer to the brink of annihilation.

In addition, the deployment of counterforce weapons raises the possibility that Washington could order a surprise first-strike attack against the Soviet Union designed to incapacitate Moscow's retaliatory capability. But even if a fully-effective first-strike capability appears unattainable at this time (because U.S. antisubmarine forces cannot yet locate and destroy all Soviet missile submarines simultaneously) the development of counterforce weapons such as the proposed M-X missile suggests a U.S. drive for such a capacity. Once deployed, the existence of such weapons would be perceived by Moscow as a direct threat to their deterrent forces, and thus could conceivably prompt the Soviets to launch their own missiles in a crisis (to prevent their destruction by a U.S. pre-emptive strike), or, conversely, could tempt Washington to order an attack of its own in expectation of just such a Soviet strike. Thus, even with leaders of both superpowers committed to a policy of nuclear restraint, the deployment of counterforce weapons by *either* side increases the perceived vulnerabilities of the other and thus increases the risk of war.

This drive to improve U.S. offensive capabilities and to expose Soviet vulnerabilities is proceeding despite President Carter's cancellation of the B-1 bomber and his efforts to negotiate a new SALT agreement with the USSR. In place of the B-1, Carter has spurred development of the nuclear-armed cruise missile—a weapon which can be fired from a wide variety of launching platforms (conventional aircraft, surface ships, submarines, and mobile ground systems) and thus is relatively immune to detection by existing surveillance systems—making its control under future SALT agreements extremely problematical. Furthermore, existing Minuteman ICBM warheads are being replaced by the much more accurate and powerful Mark-12A, investing the current U.S. ICBM force with significantly improved counterforce capabilities. And discussion of a new version of the Trident submarine-launched missile (Trident-II) and of a new manned strategic bomber reveals a commitment to the development of even more potent weapons. These programs will proceed whether or not a new SALT treaty is signed (indeed, many analysts believe that they are the price Carter has agreed to pay to insure Pentagon support for the arms pact), thus pushing us into a deadly new round in the arms race while nullifying the restraining impact of a new SALT agreement when and if it is adopted.*

Increased Military Spending

Despite President Carter's pre-election pledge to reduce U.S. military spending, the defense budget will reach new heights in the years to come. Projected Pentagon spending for Fiscal 1980 was set at

---

*According to Michael Klare: "Carter's choice for the new director of the Arms Control and Disarmament Agency, Gen. George M. Seignious, has called for the acquisition of new nuclear weapons. Even if a SALT treaty is adopted, Seignious told reporters in December 1978, the Pentagon will 'require additional money to modernize the strategic systems we have.' (The *New York Times*, 14 December 1978.) The appointment of Seignious to replace Paul Warnke as head of the A.C.D.A. has drawn heavy criticism from disarmament activists, who point to his membership on the Coalition for Peace Through Strength, a pro-military lobby that has campaigned against adoption of the SALT Treaty." From "Potomac War Fever: Letter from Washington," *The Nation,* 3 February 1979; see also A. Lin Neumann, "Peace Groups Attack Hawk in Doves Coop," in *In These Times,* 7-14 February 1979.

$124 billion, "real" increase (after accounting for inflation) of 3 percent, and the total will keep rising each successive year in line with President Carter's pledge to strengthen our NATO-oriented forces. Furthermore, as the Pentagon proceeds into production of costly new weapons systems now in the development stage—the M-X missile, and M-1 tank, Trident-II, and the nuclear-powered Strike Cruiser—the defense budget will have to expand at an even faster pace, reaching $200 billion well before the end of the decade.

Defense expenditures at these projected levels will ensure the continued prominence of the military-industrial complex within the U.S. economy, and will discourage any effort to convert arms facilities to civilian use. And since federal revenues are not expected to grow as rapidly as projected military spending, due to taxpayers' resistance and the sluggish state of the economy, the Pentagon and its corporate partners will find themselves in increasing competition with other sectors for scarce government funds. In order, then, to defeat anticipated efforts by trade unionists, urban politicians, minority groups and others to protect existing social benefits (many of which are threatened by the current budget crunch), the pro-military forces feel compelled to step up their anti-Soviet propaganda and to take other steps to create a climate favorable to their escalating fiscal demands. Notwithstanding the domestic origins of these militaristic pressures, their consequences for U.S. foreign policy and the evolution of U.S. relations with the Soviet Union will be profound; adoption of a new SALT agreement, for instance, could be blocked entirely by right wing forces opposed to any checks on the growth of the U.S. strategic arsenal.

Conventional Forces and Tactical Nuclear Weapons

Even while Washington is pushing ahead with development of new nuclear weapons, the Pentagon is continuing to strengthen its conventional forces. Given the perceived primacy of defending U.S. core areas, this buildup is concentrated in Europe, the Mediterranean, the Persian Gulf, and along the key maritime routes connecting these areas to U.S. ports. And while U.S. leaders insist that they will always search for a negotiated solution to conflicts arising abroad, Defense Department officials acknowledge that they are prepared for a wide range of contingencies, including a ground war in Europe and an over-the-beach assault on uncooperative oil kingdoms in the Middle East. Such planning received renewed urgency folowing the collapse of the Pahlavi dynasty in Iran, and with it, the U.S. strategy of using Iranian forces as regional gendarmes in the Persian Gulf area. In a commentary on the implications of the Iranian debacle, Secretary of Defense Harold

Brown told the *Washington Post* on 2 January 1979 that the United States may be forced to use its own troops to protect its oil supplies in the event of a future Mideast crisis. "I think that's a worse problem than it was in the 1950s and 1960s. You say how could it be worse than Vietnam? What I'm saying is that our vital interests are more likely to be involved than in retrospect they probably were (in Vietnam). We're more interdependent; we're more resource-dependent on the outside world." Given this fact, "We might have a very difficult time avoiding the choice between active participation in conflict...or a severe damage to our national interests and resources." To demonstrate that he was not talking in abstract terms, Brown revealed that "planning is going ahead" for a highly mobile, hard-hitting specialized force for use in conflicts outside of the NATO theater.

In the intervention scenarios now being developed by the Pentagon, heavily-armed U.S. shock troops will be flown to an incipient battlefield as quickly as possible, and will employ PGMs (precision-guided munitions, or smart weapons) and other sophisticated arms to secure U.S. objectives quickly before significant political opposition has a chance to develop. Such blitzkrieg tactics could be used in selected Third World areas to protect U.S. interests threatened by nationalistic forces, or to rescue pro-U.S. regimes from internal revolt. And while the duration of such conflicts may be short, the use of PGMs and other modern arms could result in high levels of violence and destruction—as demonstrated by the October War of 1973, when an estimated 100,000 soldiers were killed or wounded and 2,000 tanks destroyed in only 17 days of fighting.

At the same time that conventional weapons are approaching the destructiveness of atomic weapons, a new generation of mini-nuclear munitions are being developed to further erode the firebreak between conventional and nuclear weapons. By combining small nuclear warheads with precision-guided targeting systems, the Pentagon hopes to introduce a new breed of "surgical" nuclear munitions whose effects would be confined to a limited area—and whose use would, presumably, therefore, be considered more acceptable in future conflicts. Of the many horrors in this deadly new arsenal, none is more pernicious than the neutron bomb—a so-called enhanced radiation device which kills human beings through radiation poisoning while sparing buildings from harm. Although President Carter has precluded immediate deployment of the neutron device, he has authorized the stockpiling of neutron bomb components so as to permit near-instantaneous production of the actual weapon at some future date.

Worldwide Militarism and Trilateral Arms Exports

The spread of advanced military hardware and nuclear technology from the advanced countries to the Third World has, over the past few years, attained flood proportions. According to the U.S. Arms Control and Disarmament Agency, Third World military spending quadrupled between 1965 and 1976, and now tops $100 billion per year. The value of Third World arms imports, meanwhile, has risen from $2.5 billion in 1965 to $9.8 billion in 1976, and is expected to reach much higher in the years ahead. Not only are Third World countries buying more weapons than ever, they are also ordering the most sophisticated types available. Thus, countries which only a few years ago were armed with obsolete hand-me-downs acquired through various aid programs are now receiving the world's most advanced missiles, PGMs, fighter planes, and warships. And, as demonstrated by the October War, these deliveries insure that future conflicts will be fought at ever-increasing levels of violence and destructiveness.

The booming trade in conventional arms is being fueled by a variety of political and economic factors, including the arms suppliers' desires to acquire political leverage over recipient governments, and the efforts of the industrial nations to reduce their balance-of-payments deficits *vis-a-vis* the OPEC nations. At present, four nations—the U.S. (with 49 percent of the market), the USSR (28 percent), France (5 percent) and Great Britain (4 percent)—dominate the world arms trade. Increasingly, however, other producers—including some Third World nations—are joining the weapons trade on their own. As competition between the arms producers for foreign markets has intensified, moreover, so have their efforts—legal and otherwise—to induce Third World governments to acquire increasingly costly and sophisticated military hardware. Thus, despite President Carter's promise to reduce arms sales, U.S. military exports reached record levels in 1979 and are expected to continue rising in the years ahead.

Similar dynamics can be found in the nuclear field, causing an ever-increasing flow of atomic technology to the non-nuclear powers. At least fourteen "developing" nations now possess or are building nuclear reactors and a number of them—including India, Israel, and South Africa—have acquired the technology to convert spent reactor fuel into weapons-grade material. And despite the highly-publicized efforts of the existing nuclear powers to halt the proliferation of atomic munitions, it is unlikely that they can prevent still more countries from joining the nuclear club in the 1980s and 1990s. As in the case of the conventional arms trade, efforts to halt the transfer of nuclear technology are being hampered by giant corporations intent on increasing exports.

Unless a serious effort is made to control the trade in conventional and nuclear military technology, the prognosis is for an ever-increasing rate of militarization in the Third World and an attendant increase in the risk of war. Moreover, since the major arms producers are increasingly involved in the supply of military technical services (training, maintenance, logistical support) to Third World armies, there is growing danger that the great powers will be drawn into otherwise local conflicts. (The severity of this risk was clearly demonstrated by the October War of 1973, when both Russian and American military personnel were dispatched to the battlefronts to supervise the unloading of emergency arms shipments.) And while U.S. officials argue that timely arms deliveries can actually be used to *prevent* war, by offsetting local arms imbalances, the rate of arms trafficking has become so great that such balancing acts appear increasingly ephemeral—and dangerous.

These developments present a frightening picture of the world to be. Yet many U.S. leaders advocate policies which will accelerate rather than reverse these trends. In the following section, we will examine the various political and economic forces which promote militarism in our society.

The Political-Economic Forces Behind Resurgent Militarism

The accelerating drift towards militarism and confrontation is taking place at a critical juncture in U.S. political history. During and after World War II, a governing consensus was established which has dominated U.S. politics until very recently.This consensus,forged by the various interest groups which formed the core of the Democratic Party (which had become the majority party during the New Deal), was based on support for the Welfare State and a foreign policy of rigid anticommunism. Together, these two principles can be described as Cold War liberalism. Under this banner, leaders of both major parties joined in promoting limited social reforms at home and expanded U.S. military commitments abroad. This alliance was based, however, on one essential precondition: an expanding U.S. economy.

Two events undermined this consensus. First, U.S. foreign policy suffered an unprecedented defeat in Vietnam. Not only was the war costly both in political and economic terms, but it also shattered a central element of the expansionist ideology—the presumption of U.S. invincibility. Second, the economic downturn of the 1970s marked the end of the long postwar boom. Because it is now impossible to have both more butter and more guns, U.S. rulers are being forced to favor one or the other. Events of the past few years suggest that most major political interests have chosen to favor guns. Cold War liberalism is rapidly becoming a Cold War without the liberalism. In announcing a projected Fiscal 1980 Defense Department budget of $124 billion, the *New York Times* noted on 16 November 1978, that "Administration sources said that the Defense Department was especially gratified because Carter has decided to cut about $15 billion out of the normal growth of a range of social and domestic programs" while raising military spending by some $12 billion. "Officials indicate that the 'guns and butter' argument waged within the administration has now, in fact, been settled by Carter in favor of the Defense Department."

From the breakup of the original Cold War consensus, two forces have emerged: one pushing for a sharp and immediate move to the right, the other advocating a more tempered but nevertheless militaristic policy. The first represents a continuation of the prevailing right wing momentum. It is pushing for an aggressive, confrontational foreign policy that implies a dramatic increase in the militarization of U.S. life, an increase that has already begun. The locus of these interests is the right wing of the Democratic and Republican Parties, and groups further to the right. Their economic backbone is the high-technology, military-oriented industries which have become such an important segment of U.S. capitalism since World War II. These industries require heavy public expenditures to keep afloat, and military/space contracts—because they do not involve competition with the "private" sector—have traditionally provided the means to this end. Located primarily in the South and the West, these industries supply much of the money and personnel for right wing political forces in the U.S. Their allies in the CIA, the Pentagon, and key committees of Congress peddle their interests with persistence and enthusiasm. They have also managed to convince some labor and community leaders that the best solution to unemployment is more government contracts for their companies, thereby creating the appearance that a broad coalition supports continued military spending.

On foreign policy issues, the Right can call on other allies. Groups like the Committee on the Present Danger and the Coalition for Peace Through Strength have mobilized many politicians— including some with impressive liberal credentials—for an acrimonious assault on the policies of detente. Many pro-Israeli groups have also joined this effort in the belief that continued U.S. aid to Israel can best be assured in an atmosphere of heightened East-West tension. And many of the Cold War intellectuals who were discredited by their support for the Vietnam War have discovered that it is once again fashionable to publish studies depicting the emerging Soviet threat.

Recently, the Right has experienced its greatest gains on the domestic front, by exploiting grassroots opposition to big government and high taxation, and by promoting profamily causes (antiabortion, anti-ERA, antigay rights) which have attracted a dedicated band of crusaders. Although these issues are apparently devoid of foreign policy implications, it is not too difficult to detect reverberations of militarism in the Right's domestic platform, and reactionary social attitudes in its military policies. Prominent militarists like James Schlesinger [who served as Carter's Energy Secretary until August 1979—ed.] have charged, for instance, that the public's preoccupation with U.S internal problems—inequality, urban decay, poverty, pollution, etc.—has undermined its will to resist future Soviet incursions elsewhere.*

The influence of the Right on U.S. policy is clear. During Gerald Ford's last year as president, a substantial growth in military spending, the *Mayaguez* incident, and renewed talk of limited nuclear war—all bore witness to this influence. But militarists in the Republican Party were not satisfied; the further to the right that Ford moved, the more rightward Reagan had to go in order to outflank him. The result was a 1976 Republican foreign policy plank that criticized Ford's own reactionary administration for not being hawkish enough. Even before the election, the Right had succeeded in forcing a return to the language of nuclear brinkmanship that prevailed in the 1950s. In 1975, for example, Secretary Schlesinger was able to threaten the use of tactical nuclear weapons against North Korea, and have Ford back him up.

None of this is particularly surprising. What is remarkable is the surge that the Right has experienced since Jimmy Carter assumed office in 1977.

At first, Carter's election and trilateralist policy suggested a relaxation of Cold War militarism. (See "Overview" to this volume.) No sooner had Carter leaned in the trilateral direction than the

---

*In a 1976 article in *Fortune*, for instance, Schlesinger charged that the weight of responsibility unavoidably placed on the United States "to curb the growth of Soviet power will not disappear merely because the American public has become tired or has become *absorbed in its domestic concerns*...Our allies and dependents overseas recognize their reliance on the firmness of American policy—and the will of the American public to continue to fulfill our historic responsibilities." Schlesinger asserted that our allies have become apprehensive about American steadfastness because "*Our internal preoccupations* and our *political divisions* of recent years have at least suggested a *growing infirmity* of American policy." (Emphasis the author.)

Democrats' traditional cold warriors began a counteroffensive. Organizing around opposition to the SALT talks and other tension-reducing efforts, groups like the Committee on the Present Danger have successfully forced Carter to move towards the right. Though largely excluded from top decision making positions with the administration (James Schlesinger, the former Secretary of Energy, was an important exception), Cold War Democrats have seized upon Soviet maneuvers in Africa and elsewhere to push Carter's policies in the direction of confrontation. Although they lost on the B-1 bomber, they can take credit for such developments as: a stiffening of the U.S. position on SALT; the transformation of human rights language from a critique of Latin American dictators to an anti-Soviet crusade; the decision to accelerate development of the cruise missile, and, more importantly, the M-X; and Carter's decision to expand U.S. civil defense efforts.

There are other good reasons why the trilateralists have been unable to outflank the militarists. The military/space sector has become an important part of the U.S. economy, and many members of the Trilateral Commission have important ties to the armaments industries or to the communities in which they are located. Because of their emphasis on Europe and the Middle East the trilateralists are as hostile to the Soviets as traditional cold warriors—they just see the advantages of selective cooperation on peripheral issues. The trilateralists would like to cut defense spending, but they are no more prepared to surrender U.S. military supremacy than the Reaganites. Indeed, given their commitment to U.S. dominance *within* the trilateral framework, they really have no choice but to strengthen U.S. military capabilities—and especially its NATO-oriented forces. Thus Carter has advocated a substantial increase in defense spending even while affirming the need for budget cuts to control inflation. Without the flamboyant rhetoric and pugnacious style of Reagan, in other words, the Carter Administration is heading for a renewed Cold War, with U.S. defense intellectuals and policy makers solidly behind it. (For closer examination of the failure of trilateralists to bring about a cooling of the Cold War, but rather, oversee the reverse, see Alan Wolfe Part VIII.)

The Domestic Impact of Resurgent Militarism

We now turn to our final, and ultimately most important question: what effects, now and in the future, will resurgent militarism have on our day-to-day lives. For no matter how deeply concerned we may be by recent developments in foreign policy, we can hardly expect to arouse meaningful public opposition so long as these issues are seen as being disconnected from our daily lives. It is essential, therefore, that we examine the domestic economic and social consequences of the impending Cold War. The economic consequences of escalating military spending are dire, although the myopic eye sees only the benefits reaped by a few privileged corporations and communities. True, the infusion of Pentagon funds into a company may temporarily boost the sagging fortunes of a particular locale, but in the long run it will have recessionary effects on the economy as a whole. Military spending increases inflation because it generates goods which cannot be recycled into the economy. Military spending contributes to both inflation and stagnation by rewarding corporations for maximizing their costs of production through "cost-plus-fixed-fee" contracts (rather than, as in conventional capitalist enterprises, seeking to reduce costs through efficient use of technology and materials), thereby promoting waste and chronic cost overruns. Furthermore, by feeding industries that are so capital-intensive, military spending creates fewer jobs than an equivalent amount of civilian spending, and what jobs it does create are both unstable and disproportionately highly skilled.

Militarism's exacerbation of economic ills, coupled with the declining competitiveness of U.S. goods in the world market (caused in part, by the diversion of U.S. scientific and technical resources from the civilian to the military sector) and the increased prices of oil and other raw materials, means that stagnation and inflation are likely to remain with us indefinitely. And, to the degree that military expenditures consume public resources, needed social programs will be reduced commensurately—a process that has already begun with the new Carter budget plan. Needless to say, the biggest losers in this process are those who suffer the most already: poor people, people on fixed incomes, and those unable to find work.

There are secondary consequences as well. High unemployment rates divide worker from worker. Union members see affirmative action for women and racial minorities as intolerable competition for scarce jobs. The hard-won gains of the 1960s in the areas of civil rights and equal opportunity are jeopardized; advances are simply out of the question. Groups fighting for public funds are forced to compete with each other for the leftovers of an economic pie already carved up and consumed by militarism.

Militarism also leaves its stamp upon the cultural and social fabric of our nation. A garrison society turns irresistibly toward authoritarian methods; it promotes the centralization of society, the mystification of expertise, and repression of nonconformist styles and beliefs. Military preparations require unassailable secrecy, and thus, in the name of national secrecy, the power of the military and the presidency grows, with a commensurate loss in self-government.

The growing sophistication of military systems makes it easy for political decisions to be disguised as technical matters and thus further removed from public discussions and debate. By controlling the terms of discourse, the national security elite obscures the real choices open to us and thereby insures that the decision making process will become increasingly undemocratic.

Since, in an era of economic stagnation, rising military expenditures inevitably consume funds needed for social programs, large-scale repression may ultimately be needed to quell resistance to further cuts in already dwindling public services. Indeed, by ordering layoffs of municipal workers and encouraging the public to lower its expectations, the prevailing authorities have already instilled an atmosphere of insecurity and resignation in many communities. And when such self-induced repression fails, there is always the imperative of national security to legitimize the use of more forceful measures, such as those contained in proposed revisions of the Criminal Code.

There is also danger of more blatantly ideological repression. A new McCarthyism, predicated on inflated estimates of the Soviet threat, might provide a way to mobilize popular support military, or at least to neutralize the opposition. Such a campaign would surely appeal to those ideologues who feel a nostalgic attachment to the original Cold War epoch—when such disquieting issues as racism, sexism, and environmentalism posed little challenge to the prevailing social order. As economic conditions deteriorate, such a campaign might also appear attractive to those of the middle and lower-middle classes who fear the loss of their jobs and traditional styles of living. Such a campaign, by focusing attention on an external specter, would also provide a way of making domestic problems seen less important; it would provide a facile remedy to the "crisis of confidence" in prevailing institutions and would simultaneously provide an excuse for disciplining the media. But even without explicit orchestration from the top, the media recently have been enthusiastically publicizing the Right's distorted assessments of Soviet military power, thereby discouraging substantive public debate on such issues as SALT and the procurement of new strategic weapons.

All struggles for social progress, then, must confront the new militarism; anyone who fights for a change in national priorities must confront the argument that "national security" requires higher defense expenditures, even at the expense of long-overdue social reforms. Moreover, everyone working in this country for social and economic justice will have to join in the struggle against resurgent militarism and interventionism or risk the ruination of all their efforts in a new round of Cold War hysteria. Those who propose real changes in American society must therefore address the issues of militarism and foreign policy head on. We can no longer evade them; *foreign policy is inseparable from domestic policy*. And the fundamental issues of foreign policy will be placed on the agenda for public discussion *only* if we place them there.

We are all potential casualities in a new Cold War. We must bring these issues into every possible political arena: into electoral campaigns, political parties, unions, social movements, and churches. The entire structure of U.S. foreign and military policy must be understood and challenged if we are to achieve a livable future. We must recognize that there is no division between domestic and foreign policy, no way to separate ourselves from our nation's actions around the world. We cannot create a decent society at home so long as national priorities are distorted by militarism and its antecedents. If resurgent miltarism is *not* stopped, the likelihood of nuclear war will surely increase, while inflation and unemployment—with all their attendant social ills—will worsen.

It was only a long and concerted campaign of many different groups using a diversity of tactics that made possible the end of the Vietnam War.* Now that political triumph must be repeated—to put a halt to the devastating worldwide impact of U.S. foreign policy and to save our own society from the paralyzing exigencies of a Cold War and the catastrophic global consquences of a hot war.

---

*Some action is underway: The Coalition for a New Foreign and Military Policy (a national coalition of 41 religious, labor, public interest, and progressive organizations) and the Mobilization for Survival are two broad coalitions dedicated to ending the arms race and promoting social needs.

PART V
MAKING CAPITALIST DEMOCRACY MORE GOVERNABLE: TRILATERALISM AND THE "CRISIS OF DEMOCRACY"

Trilateralists have acknowledged what most Western economists and political scientists deny: "issues related to economics are at the heart of modern politics." What is the historic relationship between politics and economics, capitalism, and democracy? What is the trilateral view? This section examines the two-faced trilateral response to popular mobilization, class conflict, and the political/economic crisis of capitalist democracy. The first article focuses on the anti-democratic face and examines the trilateral report on the governability of democracy. The second focuses on the reformist face as it is turned toward labor-management relations. The last article argues that energy policy is central to the trilateral program for restructuring the economy and consolidating the role of the state in economic planning and examines opposition within the capitalist class.

Reduced to their simplest terms, Labor and Capital are men with muscle and men with money—human beings, imbued with the same weaknesses and virtues, the same cravings and aspirations...Capital cannot move a wheel without Labor nor Labor advance beyond a mere primitive existence without Capital. But with Labor and Capital as partners, wealth is created and ever greater productivity made possible.

—John D. Rockefeller, Jr.*

...Our enemies are the socialists among the labor people and the anarchists among the capitalists.

—Ralph Easley, founder of the
National Civic Federation, 1909**

*"Labor and Capital—Partners," *Atlantic Monthly,* January 1916, excerpted in *The Annals of America,* Vol. 14, "1916-1918: World War and Prosperity," pp. 23-24.
**Quoted in James Weinstein, *The Corporate Ideal in the Liberal State 1900-1918* (Boston: Beacon Press, 1968). Weinstein analyzes the role of the National Civic Federation (NCF), the leading organization of the new corporate liberalism of the Progressive Era, providing an excellent historical case study of the two faces of corporate capitalism: reformist and repressive. Corporate liberalism rejected the prevailing doctrine of laissez-faire (government nonintervention in the economy), favoring state intervention to promote economic stability. Rather than extend the late nineteenth century period of violent strike-breaking and ruthless repression of worker organizing, the NCF sought to accommodate rising trade unionism and populism by promoting "responsible," conservative unionism and promoting the notion of "social responsibility" as advocated by middle class reformers. Radical and socialist unions, and the Socialist Party (led by Eugene Debs), however, were repressed harshly by the state. Using the Espionage Act of World War I, thousands of members of the IWW (International Workers of the World), socialists, and other antiwar activists were imprisoned and socialist and pacifist publications were confiscated from the mails. NCF reformism was opposed by small and middle-range manufacturers led by the National Association of Manufacturers (NAM).

chapter one

CAPITALISM SHOWS ITS FACE: GIVING UP ON DEMOCRACY
*Alan Wolfe**

Save for some cataclysmic exceptions, capitalism and democracy have generally been linked, especially in the 20th century. To be sure, certain sectors of the business community have always retained a submerged fear that the masses would rise up and elect to office irresponsible demagogues who did not understand the necessity of industrial leadership, but that fear took second place to the perceived advantages of a democratically organized society. The major benefits were two. First, liberal democracy made a sharp separation between the economy and the political system, one in which the formal equality promised within the latter ("one man, one vote") actually sustained a rampant inequality within the former. Working classes, in short, accepted political rights in return for a general sacrifice of economic ones. Secondly, liberal democracy seemed to offer just enough hint of fairness to be seen as legitimate by the majority, yet also provided dominant groups with enough control to serve their needs as well. Other things permitting, democracy and capitalism could actually work to strengthen each other.

Other things, as the world should know by now, do not always permit. If democracy and capitalism had been strongly linked as ideas, so that one was literally inconceivable without the other, they would have both lived and perished together. But their connection

*Alan Wolfe is author of *The Rise and Fall of the 'Soviet Threat': Domestic Sources of the Cold War Consensus* (Washington D.C.: Institute for Policy Studies, 1979); *America's Impasse: The Rise and Decline of Cold War Liberalism* (forthcoming Pantheon Books); *The Limits of Legitimacy: Political Contradictions of Contemporary Capitalism,* (Free Press, 1977), and *The Seamy Side of Democracy: Repression in America,* (David McKay Co.). He teaches sociology at Queens College, New York. This article originally appeared in *The Nation,* 29 November 1975.

was far more practical than theoretical, raising the possibility that, when conditions changed, those who supported one ideal would come to be critical of the other. The Left first made this separation: to a significant part of the socialist movement, the dream of democracy, which it loved, had become perverted into the nightmare of bourgeois democracy, which it detested. Genuine democracy, it was argued, would be realized only when capitalism was abolished. Yet this separation of concepts, while tantalizing in theory, did not mean much in practice, since no socialist movement was strong enough or courageous enough to actually put this vision into practice, except in certain countries where a Western democratic tradition had never really taken root. Of far greater interest, then, is a second separation that occurs a bit later in Western history. For it is not difficult to turn the socialist argument on its head and suggest that the realization of genuine capitalism can be achieved only when democracy is abolished. The lack of a true fit between democracy and capitalism makes that a permanent possibility, though the argument will be advanced only under exceptional conditions.

Social and economic conditio· s in the United States since 1970 have led a number of beneficiaries of U.S. capitalism to question their allegiance to political democracy, and that raises the thought that we may be in the midst of precisely such "exceptional conditions." Two trends seem to have clashed to bring on the new war against democracy. *First, the economy itself is in trouble, unable to deliver the prosperity that has always been the main argument in favor of capitalism.* With private capital no longer able to generate enough investment to guarantee the accumulation necessary to keep the system afloat, the state became more and more involved in the economy on behalf of private capital. But, as James O'Connor points out, in *The Fiscal Crisis of the State*, that merely shifts the problem from one area to another since government assistance is, almost by definition, a confession of the failures of capitalism, and aid of this sort goes far to destroy the ideal that the government is a neutral, benevolent force concerned with the interests of all.

While this was taking place, a second trend made itself felt—*large numbers of people appeared to be taking democracy far more seriously than they ever had before.* The war in Indochina was stopped essentially by popular opposition. Two presidents were forced out of office because of their uncanny ability to violate popular conceptions of what is proper and what is improper. Politics as usual became the surest way to political defeat. In short, at the moment when capitalism no longer seemed to be working, democracy was just beginning to work. As one fails and the other succeeds, the inherent differences between them emerge, so that those whose main stake lies in preserving a capitalism that is no longer viable are forced to become critics of a democracy more alive than ever. This conjuncture of forces, which seemed headed toward a preliminary head as early as the election of 1976, has led a number of leading intellectuals to revise their once accepting attitude toward political democracy.

Perhaps the first, and certainly the most significant, shot in the new war against democracy is the Report of the Trilateral Task Force on Governability of Democracies, made public in May 1975. (Formal publication in a revised version appeared in late 1975; the analysis contained here is based on the original unpublished version obtained from the Trilateral Commission's headquarters in New York.)

Two features of this report are immediately striking. One is its pessimism, for the dominant tone of U.S. political sociology since the 1950s has been aggressively optimistic. Thus, S.M. Lipset, who could proclaim in *Political Man* (1960) that liberal democracies had attained the good life, now finds, in recent reflections in *Commentary*, that those very societies are in crisis, though characteristically he blames their problems more on those removed from power than on those who hold it. *The Crisis of Democracy* accepts this neo-pessimism completely, preferring the vision of Celine to that of Pangloss. While the old optimism and the new pessimism are in reality two variations on the same theme—both are equally ahistorical, unanalytic, apocalyptic and afraid of class conflict—the shift from one to the other does betoken an increasing conservatism among leading social thinkers. The other and quite related feature of the report is the unmediated authoritarianism of the new approach to liberal democracy. In *Political Man*, to use that marvelously suggestive book again as an example, it was the working class which was considered intolerant, disposed to be impatient with the indirectness of democratic procedures. *The Crisis of Democracy* fli-flops this proposition as well, for it ironically reveals a professoriat possessing all the impatience and intolerance once attributed to the people who cleaned their offices.

Pessimism and authoritarianism pervade the report of the Trilateral Commission from start to finish. It is divided into four sections: one on Europe, another on Japan, a third on the United States and some concluding remarks about structural changes. The European section, written by Michel Crozier, and the American, by Samuel P. Huntington, are the more interesting, though the concluding recommendations are the most controversial. In both Europe and the United States, all the traditional agencies of what political scientists call political socialization are seen as falling apart. People are no longer deferential, accepting as inviolate what established authorities tell them. The value structure of society has changed, and new expectations have revolutionized political life. Crozier, for example, paraphrases Jurgen Habermas's *Legitimation Problems of Late Capitalism* when he notes that traditional standards of rationality in the West, such as the distinction between ends and means, have begun to disintegrate. Cut loose from ties of obedience and traditional values, people begin to make political demands on the state. The result is an overload of inputs which cannot be met by government. Consequently, in Crozier's words, "the more decisions the modern state has to handle, the more helpless it becomes."

Huntington carries Crozier's pessimism yet further. What he calls the "democratic surge of the 1960s" was a challenge to all existing authority systems. As people became politicized, their disappointment was inevitable because democratic societies cannot work when the citizenry is not passive. The result is a substantial withering away of confidence in government. Huntington, like many other political analysts, makes great use of the University of Michigan's Survey Research Data, which shows both a dramatic decline of public trust in government between 1964 and 1970 and an equally sharp rise in the feeling that government is run only by and for the rich.[1] (See chart in appendix.) An accompanying decline of faith in the party system, combined with the inability of presidents to finish their terms, produces what Huntington suggestively calls a "democratic distemper" which hinders the political system from carrying out its traditional policies, both domestic and foreign. If the system is to correct itself, this "excess of democracy" must be reduced. There must be an emphasis on the fact that the "arenas where democratic procedures are appropriate are limited." Individuals and groups should be cooled out, since a functioning system requires "some measure of apathy and noninvolvement." In general, the demand is for "balance":

> A value system which is normally good in itself is not necessarily optimized when it is maximized. We have come to recognize that there are potentially desirable limits to economic growth. There are also potentially desirable limits to the extension of political democracy. Democracy will have a longer life if it has a more balanced existence.

In order to restore this balance, the authors make a number of controversial proposals. First, they strongly endorse mechanisms for economic planning. Noting that "the governability of democracy is dependent upon the sustained expansion of the economy," the report implicitly argues that the only way to make people recline in political apathy is to increase their income, and this task is too important to be left entirely to the operation of market mechanisms. The authors' hopes for planning are as much political as they are economic, for to them a workable capitalist economy and democratic acceptance are totally linked.

Second, the report calls for stronger political leadership. Sentiments which one would have thought dead after Vietnam and Watergate are dramatically reborn: "The trend of the last decade toward the steady diminution of the power of the president should be stopped and reversed. The president clearly has the responsibility for insuring national action on critical matters of economic and foreign policy. He cannot discharge that responsibility if he is fettered by a chain of picayune legislative restrictions and prohibitions." Some people never seem to learn; the seeds of a new Watergate have been planted, even before the old roots have been fully ripped out.

Third, the report calls for attempts to put some life back into dying political parties; it endorses governmental aid to parties, but calls for balance in the sources of campaign finance. The decisions of governments to finance elections to themselves—a recent feature of American, Italian, and German politics—is one more sign of the inability of traditional institutions like parties to win support.

Fourth, restrictions are proposed but never exactly specified on the freedom of the press. ("But there is also the need to assure to the government the right and the ability to withhold information at the source.") Fifth, education should be cut back because the democratization of education, minimal though it has been, has raised expectations too high. Assuming that education is related to "the constructive discharge of the responsibilities of citizenship," then "a program is necessary to lower the job expectations of those who receive a college education." On the other hand, if citizenship training is not the goal of education, then colleges should be turned into vast job-training centers. Sixth, the report calls for "a more active intervention in the area of work," since alienation must be attacked at its roots. German experiences with co-determination are rejected in favor of state aid for experimentation with new forms of work organization. Finally, supranational agencies of cooperation are encouraged among the major capitalist powers, including the mobilization of private groups (like the Trilateral Commission) to share "mutual learning experiences."

The unusual bluntness of *The Crisis of Democracy* violates a taboo of U.S. society, which is that no matter how much one may detest democracy, one should never violate its rhetoric in public. Consequently this report has generated a full-scale controversy within the Trilateral Commission itself. When it was formally presented, at a conference in Kyoto, Japan, on 30 and 31 May 1975, numerous Commission members from the United States and Europe denounced it as too pessimistic, and some even urged that the Trilateral Commission, like Nixon with his report on marijuana, repudiate its own study. In a major speech, Ralf Dahrendorf, now head of the London School of Economics, aligned himself with the critics, saying, "I am not, contrary to many others today, pessimistic about the future of democracy." One of the few members who did not take a position on the controversy was David Rockefeller, who put up the money for the Trilateral Commission. Although one can obtain a general feeling of Rockefeller's attitude toward democracy from the behavior of his Chase Manhattan Bank during New York City's fiscal crisis, it would have been interesting to have had his views officially on record—and that is undoubtedly why he declined to divulge them.

The bitterness of the Kyoto debates reveals that liberal democracy still has its partisans, that establishment intellectuals by no means unanimously share a developing disdain for it. Yet despite the evident sincerity of those within the Trilateral Commission who have objected to the Crozier-Huntington analysis, one cannot escape the feeling that their commitment to democracy is as much tactical as it is principled, that they are prepared to retain democratic structures only until their breakdown is further advanced. The seriousness with which *The Crisis of Democracy* has been discussed, even by those who object to it, confers upon its ideas a certain legitimacy, making reasonable what only ten years ago would have seemed an outrageously extremist position. Just as during the war in Indochina, the Defense Department continued to adopt options which it had only shortly before dismissed as extreme, so Western intellectuals are now calmly discussing hypotheses which they once associated with lunatic fringes. But for all their illiberalism, it is the authors of this report, and not their critics within the Trilateral Commission, who have made the richer analysis of the contradictions, limitations, and ambiguities of late capitalist societies. To understand why that is the case requires a short digression into recent neo-Marxist attempts to formulate some insights into the nature of the capitalist state.

In the writings of people like Jurgen Habermas and Claus Offe, critical theorists who have had a major influence on both German and North American social scientists, the state is called upon to perform simultaneously two functions that are quite contradictory. On the one hand, given the fact that any capitalistic society will have capitalists, the state will be expected to help them. What Habermas and Offe call the *accumulation* functions of the state encompass all the ways by which governments become involved in helping private industrialists to accumulate more capital and therefore presumably to make more money. Unlike the early period of capitalist development, which expressed a highly articulated, though rarely applied detestation of government, contemporary capitalists very willingly recognize their dependence on the state. Government aid to corporations, macroeconomic policy, banking, regulatory commissions which actually formulate corporate policy and government support for research and development—these are only a few of the ways by which the state involves itself in the accumulation process in a society dominated by firms which dwarf entire competitive industries of a century ago.

But in addition to all this, Habermas and Offe recognize another function. In order for a government to be a government, it must be supported by all the people, not by just one class. The state therefore has a *legitimation* function as well as an accumulation one; it is responsible for obtaining mass loyalty to the system. Just as accumulation has moved from the realm of the private corporation to that of public agencies, legitimation becomes centralized as well. Families, neighborhoods and private associations play a smaller role in structuring obedience; education propaganda agencies and the bureaucracy become much more active.

The theoretical notions associated with this version of critical theory were given precise empirical application by James O'Connor in his important book, *The Fiscal Crisis of the State*. O'Connor argues that the tendency to intensify both the accumulation and the legitimation function is at the root of the current U.S. budgetary crisis. Greater governmental involvement in accumulation costs money since it makes fiscal demands upon the state and, at the same time, intensifies the need for legitimation, since such giveaways must be explained one way or another. Legitimation, in turn, costs money, and that sets off something of a vicious circle. The state is placed in an impossible situation: if it tries to fulfill its accumulation function, it loses legitimacy, but if it aims for legitimacy, it may harm the process whereby capital is accumulated. The attempt to do both things at once, though expensive, becomes the least offensive option, not the best possible decision. Political struggles are turned into fiscal priorities, and social conflict tends to resemble a race to the last line of the balance sheet.

Positing a deep conflict between the legitimation and accumulation functions of the capitalist state is only a starting point for understanding the nature of government activity, but it is a more fruitful place to begin than any other that has been advanced. Testimony, of the most ironic sort, to its importance is the attempt by the authors of *The Crisis of Democracy* to adopt these essentially Marxist ideas for their own different purposes. Faced with a bankruptcy of their own ideas, conservative defenders of U.S.

society—especially those more interested in keeping that society together than they are in defending ideas which they know are no longer relevant—turn with increasing frequency to their ideological opponents for their basic concepts. A society which grew by appropriating physical labor can apparently try to preserve its growth by appropriating mental labor as well.

Of all the sections of *The Governability of Democracies*, the one showing most clearly the attempt to use neo-Marxist ideas for conservative purposes is the analysis of the United States, for Huntington accepts the basic premise of a contradiction between the accumulation and the legitimation function of the capitalist state. Like his Harvard colleague Daniel Bell, Huntington finds O'Connor's book important enough to merit some reflection.[2] There is no doubt, Huntington agrees, that demands on government, symbolized by both warfare and welfare, are responsible for the state's budgetary problems, and that consequently the fiscal dilemmas of the capitalist state have a social and political root. But then, almost as if he were afraid to find any more agreement than necessary with Marxist writers, Huntington differentiates himself from O'Connor, Habermas, and Offe in two ways. First, he spuriously assigns different relative weights to each of the functions and second he finds the cause of their current intractability in a different place.

In the approach to the state developed out of critical theory, accumulation and legitimation exist in a roughly balanced equilibrium. Any change in one is also associated with a change in the other, especially in late capitalist society when political and social crises tie the two functions ever closer. Huntington's first attempt to differentiate himself from O'Connor misses this essential point. "What the Marxists mistakenly attribute to capitalist economics, however, is in fact a product of democratic politics," Huntington notes. Such a conclusion must be based on a misreading of the Marxists, however, for the whole point of their enterprise is to suggest the very definite links between demands on the state which grow out of democratic politics and fiscal irresponsibilities caused by capitalist economics. O'Connor, for example, emphasizes time and again that only one of the ingredients of the fiscal crisis is a breakdown of the private accumulation system; the other includes such democratic matters as pressure from civil servants, demands for state services like welfare, and public expectations about equality and fairness.

Indeed, if anyone is guilty of assigning too much weight to one of these functions over the other, it is clearly Huntington, for in his perspective, accumulation becomes so important that it is not even mentioned. The expectation that the state will support capitalists in their drive for profits is so totally accepted by the authors of *The Crisis of Democracy* that the only question becomes one of how best to insure its success. Both macroeconomic and foreign policy, euphemisms for the accumulation function, are seen as being in danger because of new attitudes toward government. It was to preserve these essential parts of the accumulation process that the report was written in the first place. The point is neither to attribute problems of capitalism to democracy or problems of democracy to capitalism but to understand the interrelationship of both forces to each other under current conditions.

Huntington's failure to deal with the interrelationships between the functions of the state means that to the degree that he accepts accumulation, he must perforce denigrate democracy. His argument that only less democracy can save democracy is scholastic at best, since what he wants to save is only the shell, not the actual content, of democratic government. Like some mid-nineteenth century industrialists, the authors of this report equate genuine democracy with socialism, anarchism, and every other nightmare they can conjecture. While there is little evidence currently present in the United States to suggest that the working class is about to take up arms in the cause of socialist revolution, the passive developments that worry Huntington and his colleagues—the breakdown of conventional attitudes, public cynicism toward existing government, decreased party identification and increasing violence, to name a few—all could signify a crisis of legitimacy and therefore make their fears realistic. Those who benefit from an existing order have every right to worry when that order loses support and comes to be viewed with suspicion and cynicism.

By polarizing accumulation and legitimation as he does, Huntington severely restricts the options available to him. One easy way to remove some of the legitimacy problems of contemporary capitalistic societies, for example, would be to make them more legitimate—deceptively simple, of course, because then they probably would no longer be capitalist. The easiest way to make large numbers of people happy with their political system is to give them, or allow them to take for themselves, the power, participation and equality needed to make the notion of citizenship meaningful. Yet Huntington's fear of just this alternative is what prevents him from advocating anything of the sort. His failure to question the need for accumulation as it takes place at present locks him into defending an indefensible position. One could, in contrast to him, reverse the priorities by assigning legitimation greater importance than accumulation. But that alternative accepts Huntington's polarities, even while reversing them. An approach based on the interconnections between the two functions of the state would lead in a different direction, toward an understanding that democracy can be preserved, not by doing away with accumulation but by democratizing it. Industrial societies, for better or worse, accumulate in one way or another. But the way makes a substantial difference. Applying the logic of democracy, not only to the public world to which it has traditionally been consigned but to the private world as well, would resolve much of the tension between these two functions. Earlier in European history, the response to those who were deprived by industrialization was to urge them to enrich themselves; the notion, essentially, was that accumulation could serve as its own legitimizing mechanism. Now we have come full circle, for the inability of class-based capitalist societies to win acceptance suggests that legitimation must serve as its own accumulating mechanism. In other words, if the process of capital accumulation is not subject to popular control, we may wind up with a society that not only is illegitimate but also disaccumulative.

A second point where Huntington's approach to the state differs from those of the neo-Marxists is on the factors which are seen as causing an intensification of the contradiction between accumulation and legitimation. To Huntington, the cause of the "democratic distemper" lies not so much in anything that governments have been doing lately but more in changing patterns of political participation. Whereas Marxist writers are likely to emphasize contradictions within the ruling class, Huntington hardly ever considers those in power; it is citizens, not leaders, who are responsible for the current instability of what Maurice Duverger has recently called "pluto-democracy." For example, Huntington is particularly concerned about the increase in political participation among Black Americans. Attributing it, rightly, to their heightened group consciousness and generalizing from that, he concludes that greater education is not what makes for greater participation, but the degree to which an individual or group develops a preoccupation with political questions. The rhetoric of democratic values begins to be taken seriously. As Huntington notes, "For much of the time, the commitment to these values is neither passionate nor intense. During periods of rapid social change, however, these democratic and egalitarian values of the American creed are reaffirmed. The intensity of belief during such creedal passion periods leads to the challenging of established authority and to major efforts to change governmental structures to accord more fully with those values." Democracy, in short, begins to work.

Huntington recognizes that political consciousness is the crucial determinant of the current legitimacy crisis of the state. The conclusion that follows from this is that the root cause of the political instabilities of modern capitalism lies in the changing nature of popular conceptions about political life. If all workers were to go on strike, if they were to withhold their labor power, nothing could be produced. Similarly, if all citizens were, in a sense, to go on strike—to withhold their allegiance to the system—no politics as usual would be possible. While neither of these situations has come about, the Trilateral Commission's report emphasizes the possibility of the latter. In short, it is possible to argue that the declining ability of the state in advanced capitalist societies to meet both its accumulation and legitimation functions has been caused not only by the declining ability of private capital to reproduce itself but also by the increasing tendency of more and more people to condemn political behavior that violates their standards of decency and fairness. The state faces both a fiscal crisis and a legitimacy crisis, and the two eventually become so intertwined that they become one. Each component is essential, but it is a mistake to emphasize either at the expense of the other.

One way to interpret what has been taking place is to argue that, tired of politics as usual, citizens of countries like the United States are refusing to allow themselves to be a party to conduct which they consider outrageous. The fact that it is now possible to openly criticize the CIA and the FBI and not be run out of town is one example; indeed, it is commonly heard in Washington these days that people are so far ahead of Congress on such issues that the process has only begun. This change in popular attitude by no means signifies a total breakthrough to a new society. It is much clearer what people do not want than what they do, and despite widespread public disenchantment, no politician—except a few on the Right—has crystallized support into an alternative vision of how to organize the U.S. But it would also be a mistake to view this disenchantment as a passing phase. When most politicians are seen by the public as more unfavorable than favorable, when problems cry for solution but no solutions are offered, when the greater the crisis, the greater the assurance that nothing is wrong—when all this takes place, the question of legitimacy must be seriously raised.

The warning that comes across clearly from a reading of *The Crisis of Democracy* is that some people with access to the center of power now understand that the change in popular attitudes toward government will necessitate a rapid dismantling of the whole structure of liberal democracy. What should be the popular response to their authoritarian proposals for resolving the crisis of democracy? Is it counterproductive to come to the defense of an order which has its own severe limitations only because one's enemies want to replace it with something even worse? It would be more than ironic if civil liberties, which were won by the dispossessed in bitter struggles for their dignity, were to be left to the dispossessed to defend as ruling groups undermine them. Something more positive than a simple defense of the status quo must be advanced, for when the Right is moving as fast as it is now, to stay in the same place is to fall behind. The fact is that conditions have rarely been better for a decisive move in the direction of a more humane political system, and the reason has everything to do with the issues that worry the Trilateral Commission. The changing patterns of political perception and participation which Huntington views as causing an excess of democracy must be encouraged. The pessimism of the Trilateral Commission should be the optimism of everyone else. If ruling groups feel they are losing power, it is only because everyone else is gaining it. If their world is crumbling, ours should be being built. Their fears are in reality our opportunities.

Because public disenchantment runs deep, no way out of the political impasse can be discovered through cliches and slogans, either from the reform politicians or from sectarian groups on the Right and Left. This is not the time to debate whether plan X or plan Y does more for the American people, but it is the time to let the American people control the discussion. What we should be working toward is the creation of new structures, not new programs, for only structures which democratize the entire accumulation process will be able to generate the new political energy and imagination necessary to turn the negative disenchantment we see all around us into a positive and constructive political system. The Trilateral Commission has unwittingly given us an analysis that can help us in this task; if we don't take advantage of its unintended generosity, we may find ourselves the victims of its warped values and constricted imagination. Using its analysis for our own purposes seems the best way to avoid that fate.

FOOTNOTES

1. See Arthur H. Miller, "Political Issues and Trust in Government: 1964-1970," *American Political Science Review*, September 1974.
2. See Daniel Bell, "The Public Household—on 'Fiscal Sociology' and the Liberal Society," *The Public Interest,* Fall 1974.

Appendix
Government Run by Few Big Interests or for Benefit of All

	1958	1964	1966	1968	1970	1972-Pre	1972-Post
For benefit of all	76.3%	64.0%	53.2%	51.2%	50.1%	43.7%	37.7%
Few big interests	17.6	28.6	33.3	39.5	40.8	48.8	53.3
Other, depends	1.0	4.0	6.3	4.8	5.0	2.5	2.5
Don't know	5.1	3.5	7.2	4.5	4.1	5.1	6.5

Questions: (1) 1958: Do you think that the high-up people in government give everyone a fair break whether they are big shots or just ordinary people, or do you think that some of them pay more attention to what the big interests want?

(2) Other years: Would you say the government is pretty much run by a few big interests looking out for themselves or that it is run for the benefit of all the people?

Original Source: University of Michigan, Center for Political Studies, election surveys.
Found in *The Crisis of Democracy*

chapter two

SOCIAL DEMOCRACY AND AUTHORITARIANISM: TWO FACES OF TRILATERALISM TOWARD LABOR

William Tabb*

One of the key themes which runs through this book—indeed it is suggested in the very title, *Elite Planning for World Management*—is that the Trilateral Commission is an institution, some say *the* institution created by the most powerful of the world to shape our collective destiny. But today the economic movers and shakers appear to be the Howard Jarvises and Tom Kemps. Rather than the polity being seduced by a corporatist vision of social democracy— which promises a bountiful welfare state where government business and labor amiably cooperate—we are witnessing an assault on the interventionist state. Labor is not being bought off, but rather the victim of "one-sided class warfare."** Those on the Left who had predicted a rise of corporatist national economic planning would seem to have missed the boat.

I will argue that the Trilateral Commission and the forces it represents are alive and as well as can be expected. To coin a phrase, they are still making history but they are not free to do so exactly as they choose and it is important to see the ways in which their restructuring design for the world economy is being resisted on different fronts. First, and at present most dramatically, trilateralists face opposition by members of their own class. Second, by the working classes of the world, a resistance that takes different forms in

---

*William Tabb is Associate Professor of Economics at Queens College, City University of New York, and author of *The Long Default: New York and the Urban Fiscal Crisis*. He is co-editor, with Larry Sawers, of *Marx and the Megapolis* (NY: Oxford Press, 1978).
**United Auto Worker's president, Douglas Fraser, angrily accused the business community of waging a "one-sided class war" when he resigned from the Labor-Management Group, a presidential advisory body.

different national and sectoral contexts. Third, by laws of motion which do indeed constrain all actors in history; capitalists feel the brunt of the limits capitalism sets on its own development.

The theme of this article is that there are two faces to trilateralism. One is the social democratic face which calls for international accommodations to ease tensions which might interfere with the smooth flow of international trade and investment and which favors domestic reform, national planning, social control of investment, and accommodation to trade union participation. This first face confronts the new Right and old-style conservatism and seems to the latter to be an appeaser, soft on communism and unprincipled on domestic social issues. The other side of trilateralism is less benevolent. It is an elitist, authoritarian alliance of the most skillful exploiters of labor power on a world scale, playing one group of workers off against another to perpetuate the dominance of monopoly capital. Competitive national capital and labor are both quite right not to trust the Trilateral Commission's smiling face of progressive internationalism. On the other hand, I believe, radicals especially have tended to give almost exclusive attention to the Huntington "excess of democracy" theme in trilateral ideology (see Wolfe) and have remained largely unaware of the degree to which trilateral policy agendas resemble social democratic and even socialist transitional programs in many respects. The less well-known but equally dangerous social democratic face is the subject of this article.

The Roberts Report*

The tri-lats (I shall use this term for the Trilateral Commission ideologues) predict that the problem of unemployment may be much more intractable in the future since there is growing evidence that technological developments will be far from labor intensive. Since they believe it will be possible to secure large increases in manufac-

*I will draw extensively on the Draft report of the Trilateral Commission, Task Force on Industrial Relations, *Continuity and Change in Industrial Relations Systems in Western Europe, North America and Japan* since at the time of this writing the final report had not yet been published. The draft report was part of a joint study conducted by the Trilateral Commission and the Atlantic Institute for International Affairs (based in Paris). The principal author is Benjamin C. Roberts of the London School of Economics. The two other task force members, one from the United States and one from Japan (as is the Commission's mode of operation), are George C. Lodge, professor of business administraion at the Harvard Business School and Sueaki Okamoto, professor of industrial relations at Hosei University, Tokyo. The draft report, dated 14 March 1978, was completed after extensive consultation with experts from the three regions; it was first presented as the basic working document to a Toronto seminar of the Canadian members of the Commission which met from

turing output with a shrinking labor force, then, assuming it is not possible to create the appropriate number of new jobs in the tertiary or service sector—it is likely that all industrially advanced economies will face endemic unemployment in the period ahead.[1]

The fear is that workers will respond to the growing unemployment with demands for greater job security. Moreover, the tri-lats are afraid that not only leftists but non-Left unions as well, may strongly oppose the idea that they should accept a significant element of joint responsibility for the efficient management of the enterprise. By sticking to the traditional antagonistic relation—perceiving the union role as protecting workers interests and that of management as profitably running the organization—the unions will cause great difficulties for capitalism. Why is this? Because if unions attempt to secure the best possible settlement in working conditions, wages, and benefits they will impede the flexibility required for economic growth. Old-style unionism and old-style management both impede progress in the trilateral view. The tri-lats are thus critical of "strongly motivated entrepreneurial employers bent on making a success of their enterprise [who] hold firmly to the belief that they must be in sole command."[2] What is needed, they assert, is for conflict to give way to cooperation. If the dynamic readjustment of world production which they envision is to take place, the resistance to economic, technological, and organizational change must be undercut. The divide between workers and managers must be closed.

The tri-lats recognize that their view of the need for cooperation as the future orientation of society "is sharply contested by those who hold to the belief that class conflict is not only inevitable, but under private capital ownership the necessary stimulant in the process of dialectical change, that will ultimately lead to a socialist system of production and a classless society."[3]

Unlike most members of the business community, the tri-lats view is that *they can only wield power by sharing it.* Management by agreement rather than management by command is more effective. Tri-lats are pragmatic not fanatically ideological in the defense of their class interests. The tri-lats fear the power of rank and file workers who wish to mitigate the harsh effects of management's unilateral decision making with regard to the introduction of new machinery and broader investment policies. The advantage tri-lats

---

11-13 June 1978 in Washington, D.C. This allowed members the occasion to reflect on the report in the context of wider tri-lat discussions and only later was the report finalized and distributed by the Commission. The report is reviewed in *Trialogue #18,* Summer 1978 along with discussion on energy and wider economic matters.

see in talking through such proposals with union bureaucrats is that they can be persuaded that such developments are necessary. The unions in turn are in a better position to explain to their members why workers cannot prevent progress given the realities of international competition and so on —forestalling potential worker resistence. Thus the tri-lats see trade unions as an important tool of their own class rule.

The progressive wing of the capitalist class has long understood the limits of an authoritarian management style. Forcing workers to submit to the imperatives of the maximum output solution irregardless of circumstances can create a rebellious, uncooperative workforce and the ensuing costs of coercing acceptable labor behavior may be high. As the tri-lat report suggests, "A succession of studies showed convincingly that employees would respond to money, but only up to a certain point. To secure the full cooperation of employees, it was necessary to satisfy other needs that were related to their role and status, to the nature of this work process and its environment. From these studies developed the idea of enlarging and enriching the job and of developing autonomous workgroups." And the report significantly goes on to say "In the development of these programs, the initiative came almost entirely from management."[4] Efforts to involve workers have been important as a method of breaking down distrust and dissatisfaction. Workers, may however, view these reforms for what they are: efforts to increase productivity and increase the rate of exploitation—extracting more surplus value and increasing employee responsibility with little or no adjustment in corresponding pay levels.*

It is important to understand that the tri-lats are liberals in the tradition of the National Civic Federation (NCF) and the Progressives,** working for closer class collaboration, under the hegemony of their own enlightened leadership, in order to minimize the needless conflicts which might arise through the simple pursuit of self-interest in the face of dynamic change. Today, as always, the

---

*ed. note: The following case illustrates the insidious nature of management-style "job enrichment." In a California electronics firm women workers were given slightly more complex tasks which were now rotated frequently. The "enriched" jobs were no more skilled or fulfilling but they did require greater concentration and were less easily habituated. The women demanded the old jobs back, angrily asserting that "the old firm already had their hands" and now the bosses "wanted their minds as well"—and for what? They preferred the "mindless" jobs which at least allowed them to socialize amongst themselves and think about more important things as they worked.

**See note preceeding this section.

future requires creative adjustment. Those who dig in their heels and try to protect their present position are doomed to fail. However, their attempts can be costly to all. The tri-lats think dialectically and accept the inevitability of change. They too believe humankind need not be the victim of history but can seize the time and make history, not totally as they would like, but within the constraints of the historically possible. The tri-lats embrace much of the Marxist method but given their class interests they stand with Bernstein and later day social democrats in the belief that capitalists and workers can work together and that progress can be made through gradualism. Such a policy, by embracing some reforms *within the capitalist system,* can, in their view, prevent socialism.

One common social democratic measure, employee shareholding, has a history that goes back over a century. Its original aim was to give employees a direct interest in the firm and, as the tri-lat report notes, it was often linked to the condition that employees should not belong to a trade union. The contemporary variant is not explicitly anti-union but "most companies with these schemes hold the belief that if the employee is a shareholder his attitudes toward the company will be more cooperative and understanding of the realities of business finance and therefore less inclined to listen to those who advocate continuous conflict as the only route to the classless society." An interesting formulation! That is, token stock ownership and cooperation is suggested as an alternative root to the classless society. In 1968, for example, the French government introduced a law obliging all companies with more than a hundred employees to set aside into an employee fund a share of gross profits, calculated in relation to the value added by the firm's work force. The tri-lats applaud such reforms. They are also pleased to work with social democrats who encourage a gradual extension of workers' power through securing a redistribution of capital and who believe that giving the unions a greater degree of control over the economic environment is socialist. But, the *quid pro quo* is that workers must behave "responsibly."

The tri-lats appear to be sympathetic to union leaders who must convince their members that showing restraint on pay demands and accepting higher levels of productivity (which is likely to put them out of work) is somehow in their best interests. Moreover, the tri-lats seem sensitive to the need of allying with rank and file workers who are less committed to ideology and more concerned with the prospect of financial gain. The tri-lats would try to bypass shop stewards and union leaders with more radical political orientation by appealing to individual worker self-interest. The difficulty with this, of course, is that it is precisely because capital offers the workers so little and wants them to take still less that their ideological alternatives lack appeal. Workers do not become militant because of abstract arguments but because their exploitation under capitalism and, thus, class struggle is real and continuous for them. The tri-lats would work to ameliorate the worst employment abuses and offer cooperative, shared, negotiated settlements. The strategy has been most successful in West Germany, and in the stronger more prosperous Northern European economies generally, where workers could be conceded more. In the present period of general economic decline with deepening crisis for weaker capitalist nations the deal is harder to make (and even harder to keep). At the same time it is not exactly easy sledding for the Left, as we will see below.

The European Examples

In Europe the larger political context is social democracy which has given the unions a stake in the success of government. Not strong enough to govern in their own right, the communist parties of Italy and France must either overtly or tacitly allow the continuance of capitalist-dominated governments or face chaos. They are forced to cooperate one way or another in ways the U.S. radical Left criticizes easily, often without really grasping. The tri-lat Report recognizes the problem faced by the Eurocommunist unions.

> Having to take the national interest, as well as the interest of their members into account has posed serious problems for the unions. It has called into question their bargaining role, forcing them to refrain from using their bargaining power to the full. This has not always been achieved, and when it has, it has not been without bitter internal divisions of opinion, and it has often not been easy to convince rank and file members that it was necessary to exercise restraint.[5]

In the Scandinavian countries and Northern Europe generally (Germany, Holland, and Switzerland), a tri-lat favored policy of employer-employee accord has until very recently resulted in labor peace, efficient introduction of new technologies and amicable settlement of differences within a framework of cooperation and class conciliation. Britain, France, and Italy remain troublesome. The tri-lat strategy in these countries is clear enough: give the unions greater participation. Rather than something to be feared by employers such collaboration is to be welcomed. As the tri-lat report asserts: "There is a widespread belief among employers, governments and the general public that having achieved the right to participate in the making of national economic decisions, unions cannot continue to behave as if this development had not occurred."[6]

Sweden, the showcase of social democracy, has carried the

program furthest. While 90 percent of industry is privately owned, a significant 6 percent is the property of a strong cooperative movement (and 4 percent is state owned). Over half of the Gross National Product is redistributed through state expenditures. By indirect yet very tight steering of the private economy Swedish capitalism has been kept exceedingly competitive. Backward firms are not sheltered; they are forced to innovate or are driven out of business by intense competition. Investment and labor market policies are used to recycle capital and labor to more productive uses. There is no talk of the need to protect widow and orphan stockholders. They are already helped by the Swedish welfare state as are displaced workers who are retrained and relocated in new jobs at government expense. All of this worked remarkably well in a prosperous world economy. At the same time it is clearly not socialism. Capital is privately held and owned by a narrow strata. Work relations, while somewhat more humanized, fit the same hierarchical alienated patterns, and class lines are as tightly drawn as found elsewhere in the capitalist world.*

Various forms of worker participation in management—or co-determination—exist throughout Europe. The longest traditions of works councils are to be found in West Germany and Italy where corporatism emerged earliest. The German scheme has been most successful. Works councils were established in Germany in 1952 along with equal employee representation on supervisory boards in coal and steel enterprises. The effort was made to displace worker interest in trade unionism with a dependence on cooperative rather than conflictual agencies of representation. The works councils' influence is based on the acceptance of their *advisory* role by management and limited by the management view of "efficient" enterprise. If cooperation fails—workers cannot act independently to protect their interests. They cannot call strikes.

Similarly representation on the board of directors has helped management rather than created worker control. The German system of electing supervisory board representation is complicated. Like the framers of the U.S. Constitution (who wanted to protect against the direct popular vote) the drafters of the German system established an electoral college procedure for large enterprises. The electoral college elects the supervisory board members. At least one

---

*In the protracted period of structural crisis we are now witnessing, even Sweden is finding it must move forward to real socialism or slide backward. Swedish social democrats are splitting on this fundamental issue making that country's politics especially fascinating to follow.

representative of the salaried employees (as distinguished from hourly wage workers) and one from the senior executives must be elected on the worker half of the board. The chairman of the board is elected by a two-thirds vote of the board which of course requires labor-management agreement. If this is not forthcoming the shareholders' representatives are free to elect the chairman and deputy chairman by a simple majority. Since the chair breaks deadlocked votes by casting a second vote this in effect leaves power in contested issues on the side of capital. Moreover, German unions are far less disposed to fundamentally disagree with capital. Unions own one of the largest banks in the country, the largest construction company, and are large investors in other enterprises. They see their success tied to the future of a strong German capitalism. The supervisory board at Volkswagen, for example, has shown the importance of co-determination in enabling the company to make a large reduction in its German labor force—handling the situation "without degeneration into bitter social conflict."[7] Further, by negotiating with the works council rather than the union the company avoids the union having as much influence on basic wage and benefit issues despite their strong statutory role in co-determination. The German unions have declared that their aim is not to change the nature of the state. They fully accept the private ownership of capital. Under such conditions co-determination has a clear meaning. It is not a tool in the transition to socialism as some would argue. It is a tool of capitalist domination.

In Holland a works council structure has resulted in a growth of worker power. These councils came to be radicalized under labor pressure and consulting has given way to increasingly conflictual negotiation. This has been even more true in Italy with the reintroduction of works councils in 1953. While the idea was that these consultative committees would deal with minor welfare questions; act as vehicles to gain acceptance for productivity improvements (e.g. speedups and reorganizations, to which workers might otherwise object); and act as a safety valve and early warning system for management when troubles developed, in fact the militance of Italian workers and their ingrained Marxist sense of class struggle meant these co-optive organs were soon radicalized. Indeed, they offer a local arena in which Catholics, communists, and socialist workers have learned to work together, forcing greater cooperation at higher levels between their respective political parties.

The tri-lats conclude that in every other country capitalist managers are prepared to recognize that in the future workers will have greater rights—to elect members of the board of directors, to extend the powers of workers councils at the plant level, to bring more and more management prerogatives into the arena of collective bargaining. The European Economic Community (or Common Market) is busy trying to create a European company law so that the global corporations will be able to operate free of current national limitations. The EEC believes this would mandate that employees are seen to have interests in the functioning of enterprises "which can be as substantial as those of shareholders." Only the U.S. seems to lag behind; most unions aren't even asking for the rights the more enlightened European employers are clamoring to give their workers.

The shift from conflict to consensus which the tri-lats see as so crucial is resisted by neanderthal trade union leaders who prefer to see capitalists act like capitalists so they can do battle in traditional business union fashion. It is almost always the employer who wants to initiate greater employee participation. The U.S. situation can be contrasted to developments elsewhere in that the U.S. labor movement does not vie for political power directly but seeks to reward its politician friends who often turn out to be quite fickle in reciprocating such friendship. The writers of the tri-lat report seem quite perplexed. Both management and especially labor seem to resist rational extensions of class collaboration into the realms of co-determination. The individualistic ethic dies hard in the U.S. The corporate planners do not seem to understand why "everyone" doesn't see the advantages of "communitarian" relations.

In Western Europe, as the tri-lat report on industrial relations systems notes with approval, there is widespread belief that the role of management and the rights of workers should be established by law rather than through collective bargaining. The broad social contract should include public consensus and unity concerning acceptable labor-management relations. Much of the U.S. Left, especially that identified with the Democratic Socialist Organizing Committee (DSOC) and other social democratic tendencies within labor and the Democratic Party, look to just such a statist solution of legislated rights for workers within the context of basically unaltered social relations, class division and highly centralized negotiation between representatives of labor and management.

The report declares of the 1973 steel agreement (between the United Steel Workers Union and the 10 top steel companies) and particularly the 1977 contract: "This settlement failed to bring labor costs into line with productivity but had the companies insisted on doing so, the experimental agreement may well have collapsed. It is also probable that unemployment in the industry would have gone up more quickly had a strike occurred."[8] The Report argues that problems like falling productivity and employee alienation "could be tackled through the collective bargaining process, but it is unlikely that American management would be easily persuaded to give to unions the participative rights the unions in Sweden now enjoy under the co-determination of Work Act, nor is it likely that the American Congress would be prepared to pass such an Act."9

The Politics of Restructuring

The accommodationist social democracy of Cold War liberalism which had dominated the Democratic Party since the end of World War II seems on the defensive and appears to be rejected by much of the business community (see article by Wolfe in the final chapter). The Trilateral Commission's more up-to-date version, essentially a revitalized and updated Establishment liberal position, revises old-style liberalism most clearly in its international analysis and is most undeveloped in its domestic aspects. Politically, the trilateral position is having a more difficult time gaining acceptance than the earlier variant. Postwar liberalism, personified in Hubert Humphrey's simultaneous stance of anticommunism at home and cold war toughness abroad, combined with domestic subsidization of corporate accumulation and a modernizing liberalism, disarmed both the right wing racists and the radical Left. Trilateralism's vehicle, Jimmy Carter, has moved to a negotiated toughness with labor befitting a less secure U.S. ruling class-bargaining and accommodating in a less grand style. (See Tabb Part IV.) A no-growth world economy calls for restructuring and endless negotiations in which the system has far less to offer than before. Its dynamic is one of continued rapid growth for the global corporations—as they penetrate all industrial sectors and regional economies which can be integrated into an overall accumulationist design but which leaves in ruin formerly economically viable areas and firms whose markets and functions have been usurped by the multinationals. In an important sense right wing politics feeds on the discontent of the victims of this process—small business pushed to the wall; a shrinking middle strata which has come to include fairly large capitalists who are not large enough to survive; many white collar workers who identify the problem as the unions, and union workers who see their increasing taxes as going to social spending to help "them." That the emotional life-style issues—abortion, busing, pot, sexual preference, and gun control—have been the focal point of so much working class rage may be because these aspects of liberalism form the only face of the emerging social order that clearly violates cherished mores. The multinational corporations are too confusing a phenomena—they bring new products and a so-called higher standard of living (but also shoddy merchandise, planned obsolescence, pollution and other forms of ecological disaster). They are the dynamic sector of the economy creating jobs (but they are the owners of the runaway plants and the destroyers of worker skills and dignity). They pay the taxes because they are where the money is (but they avoid their fair share of taxes by blackmailing communities and nations on pain of leaving them without income if concessions are not granted).

The potential for change, however, clearly exists in the U.S. The movements of the 1960s can be seen as an omen of this potential to disrupt business as usual and raise demands which cannot easily be met within the system's limited confines. A decade later it even appears that organized labor is learning.

Labor is beginning to learn that electing Democrats is not really all there is to winning political objectives. With a Democratic president and a majority in both houses of Congress, labor has experienced one major setback after another in Washington. Perhaps most important was the defeat of the proposed Labor Law Reform Bill in June 1978. Following defeats on a badly wanted construction site picketing bill and lack of action on health and employment legislation, the chief lobbyist of one major union commented after the November 1978 election, "We have to devote most of our effort to keeping bad things from happening."

The number of National Labor Relations Board representation elections which unions have been winning has been going down. Indeed, in 1977 unions lost more certification contests than they won. The number of decertification elections they lose has also been increasing—they lost three out of four in 1977.

Labor has also become less able to deliver to its members even in their traditional area of strength—wages. In 1978 wage increases in the big negotiated settlements averaged only 6.5 percent over the life of the contract while prices rose by 8 percent. The unionized worker has not been doing very well in real purchasing power. Over the 1970-77 period the rise in real hourly compensation was lower than in any other industrialized capitalist nation. Adjusting for the slower rise in output per labor hour, the rise in unit labor costs in the U.S. was still below all other industrialized nations.

The tri-lats are aware that one reason for the lower rates of increase in real labor costs for the U.S. is that U.S. trade unions have been so strongly contained under the influence of capitalist ideology. They have been weakened by racial divisions, anticommunism has been a powerful internal deterrent to union militancy, and the lack of working class political formations viably contesting for state power in the electoral realm leaves capitalist ideology relatively intact. On the other hand, the fragmentation of U.S. labor into relatively autonomous national unions, and in some cases locally autonomous ones, makes centralized wage bargaining along the Swedish model, or even political bargaining as in Britain, for instance, impossible. As the global capitalist crisis worsens, however, these accommodations are more difficult, as Thatcher's election in Britain and Palme's defeat in Sweden during the late 1970s indicate.

Trilateral Social Democracy

The tri-lats are hopeful that as large U.S. based firms do business in Europe they increasingly learn "how to do it" and that Americans who initially express considerable scepticism concerning worker participation come to see that their fears are unwarranted. It really does work. The result of co-determination is successful co-option, not the chaos skeptics had predicted.

The tri-lats see the future as bringing all countries closer together as market forces compel the gradual eradication of national differences. They expect that while the social relations of production will retain some locally unique characteristics, there will be strong pressures for legislation of corporate-labor rights and responsibilities, and industrial relations generally, to grow more and more alike.

In Europe the trend toward industrial democracy as we have described it above has already resulted in works councils representing all employees, in employees being represented on the boards of directors of corporations, and for labor-management joint responsibility for job enlargement as well as corporate investment decisions. Terminological confusions, however, abound and the formal collaboration which appears structurally similar masks extreme differences between the countries of Western Europe.

U.S. corporations who have done business in Europe have been educated in the process. The typical European legislation which forces corporate disclosure of information on its future plans relating to the introduction of new methods of production, expansion and closing of plants, and other changes which affect workers, are first viewed as intolerable, but over time the firms come to live with (and profit by) this new form of industrial relations.

The differences between the liberal trilateral approach to industrial relations and the more confrontationalist class struggle approach of most U.S. employers has its counterpart in the discussion of national economic planning. Just as most employers see little to recommend itself in trilateral accommodation to unions and prefer to slug it out with labor from their position of class monopoly of the tools of production, so too they see little to be gained from larger versions of social contracts which call for public discussions of investment priorities and state intervention in capital allocation. From their individual perspectives they are probably correct in their opposition. Just as in industrial relations the trilateral perspective stresses the importance of rapid technological change and the importance of winning worker cooperation to its introduction; so in the national economic planning debate it is again the flexibility to structure far-reaching economic transformations to meet crises and turn adversity into opportunity which is at the heart of the trilateral approach. Most businesspeople see themselves as losers in these world-shaking structural transformation. It is the global corporation which will gain at the expense of firms oriented towards more freely competitive markets and those dependent upon national markets who look to the government to protect them from the very dislocations the tri-lats are trying to finesse.

Class Struggle as the Democratic Distemper

The integration of national capitals as well as the continuance of intercorporate rivalries requires new forms of coodination to prevent disruptions from the losers in the process. To the exent that the legislative branches of the different nation states are not securely under their dominance, multinationals show a preference for unofficial forms of cooperation and negotiation. The reason state planning of the kind many on the Left perceived as inevitable has not come about is because intra-capitalist rivalry between national and petty capital on the one side and multinational forces on the other is not going at all well for the tri-lats. The political process is too open. The forces which oppose them are too active in politics at the local and hence congressional level for the tri-lats to be at all sure that they could achieve some version of social democratic rhetoric and redistribution to please the Left (over the opposition of most of the rest of the business class) or the control over investment necessary for promoting technological innovation and "enhancing the U.S. competitive position in world markets" (that is, pursuing policies favorable to them).

In terms of labor, the tri-lats basically want a free hand in introducing new technologies and are willing to pay a price for it. What frightens them is old-style unionism which sees its role as negotiating hard to obtain for members as much of the gain from productivity increases as they can. The tri-lats want these profits for reinvesting—to keep growing to widen their technological leads and to reinvest in facilities elsewhere in the world. That is why the stress on productivity and competitiveness is such a mystification. The industrial relations policies they favor are tools in a more sophisticated ideological domination of labor.

That what the tri-lats are after is the acceptance of European-style cooperation rather than merely lower wages for U.S. workers is suggested by a comparison of wage costs, fringe benefits and productivity trends in the U.S. versus the other major capitalist countries. The lack of competitiveness of U.S. products does not seem to be captured in such crude indices of comparative performance. Wages are increasing faster everywhere else in the advanced capitalist world; so are unit labor costs (after accounting for fringe benefits). The problems perceived by the tri-lats are qualitative—the increasing failure of the system in the U.S. to properly socialize the working class, and the unruliness of minority communities, women, and youth.

Samuel P. Huntington's views on democracy (see Wolfe Part V and the Overview) did not take long to become the consensus view. John Herbers starts a three-part series on "Governing America" on the front page of the *New York Times* with what might be a quote right out of *The Crisis of Democracy*. He writes:

> The United States is becoming increasingly difficult to govern because of a fragmented, inefficient system of authority and procedures that has developed over the last decade and now appears to be gaining strength and impact, according to political leaders, scholars, and public interest groups across the country.[10]

Accommodation does not extend to militants and trouble-makers as *The Crisis of Democracy* makes clear.

Looking at the present political line up, we are faced with a deceptive portrayal of the major conflict. On the one hand, a far-sighted trilateralism, which sees the world economy in fragile condition and calls for accommodation, compromise, and mutual concern for the general welfare in getting through this difficult period; on the other side, all those who would pursue selfish interest at the general expense—labor unions asking for more when for them to get more would mean less for everyone else, government bureaucrats who don't want to cut their programs and exercise fiscal restraint in the face of rising and intolerable deficits, and profiteering firms which refuse to submit to a general contract view. People should refuse to accept this dichotomy. *The social contract orientation of the tri-lats is a maneuver to get what they want and call it a public interest solution.* The selfishness of unions is no more than an effort not to get screwed as they did in the last wage-price controls (which controlled wages far more than prices and profits). The public sector cuts are an effort to make the poor and the service recipient bear the brunt of the crisis.

While perhaps not a very novel note to end on, the purpose of this article is not to develop a comprehensive strategy for the Left but rather to point out what is often presented as the Left alternative—national economic planning, capital rationing through the political process, agreements on wage and price controls, greater worker participation in corporate management—are the policy phrases of the most powerful wing of the capitalist class. The Left must develop an alternative analysis and realistic *transitional* programs which cannot be confused with—or co-opted by—the monopoly capitalists. That is, we must not confuse a social democracy of a corporatist sort with a Left program of economic democracy and class struggle which may include tactical demands for necessary transitional reforms.

FOOTNOTES

1. Draft report of the Trilateral Commission, Task Force on Industrial Relations, "Continuity and Change in the Industrial Relations Systems in Western Europe, North America and Japan," 14 March 1978, p. 17.
2. *Ibid.,* p. 18.
3. *Ibid.,* pp. 17-18.
4. *Ibid.,* p. 46.
5. *Ibid.,* p. 21.
6. *Ibid.,* p. 22.
7. *Ibid.,* p. 27.
8. *Ibid.,* p. 55.
9. *Ibid.,* pp. 52-54.
10. John Herbers, "Deep Government Disunity Alarms Many U.S. Leaders," *New York Times,* 12 November 1978.

The Trilateral View on Energy and Social/Political
The Trilateral View on Energy
and Social/Political/Economic Change

"Indeed the debate over energy policy itself has become a forum for debating the shape of 'post-industrial' American society."
—*Energy: Managing the Transition*
(Trilateral Report, 1978)

There can be little doubt that more serious shortages of energy and more drastic adjustment of economic patterns and social lifestyles lie ahead.

Economic factors will by themselves induce certain changes. *But the situation will call for a considerable degree of voluntary cooperation and of acceptance, voluntary and involuntary, of governmental regulation of an increased sector of personal life...*

There will surely be a slower overall growth of the economy, a restructuring of production, a high rate of investment, and a retreat from some of the more extravagant features of our consumer society. The cult of the automobile and the current methods of constructing, heating and cooling buildings can hardly remain unaffected. *In essence, there will be a reallocation of capital, labor, technology, and available supplies of energy through the economics of scarcity.*

It is a real question, therefore, whether the necessary sacrifices will in fact be accepted by powerful elements in the body politic, be they politicians, civil servants, trade unions, businessmen, or an undefined mass of ordinary citizens. In such cases, there is instability and turmoil whether a government tries to face the crisis or to avoid it. *We foresee growing extremism, both of the right and of the left, which will feed on this instability.*

Each nation, of course, will have to make its own decisions on how the necessary elements of social discipline, governmental control, and changes in customary modes of living can be reconciled with the vital need to preserve civic freedoms and democratic institutions. [Italics ed.]

—Trilateral Commission, 1974

323

chapter three

"GUIDED MARKETS": CARTER'S ENERGY PLAN AND THE RESTRUCTURING OF U.S. CAPITAL

Allen Kaufman & Patrick Clawson*

In 1974, the Trilateral Commission issued two major papers on the energy crisis[1] which spell out the belief that the age of cheap hydrocarbon fuels is over and that a search for alternate sources of energy is necessary, even though the transition to a new age of energy will be difficult.[1] Prices of all forms of energy will continue to rise through the end of the century and beyond. In the reports' estimation, higher energy costs will further weaken the stagnating economies of the trilateral nations and increase competition among them. At the same time the rising energy prices will exacerbate the already serious financial indebtedness of the underdeveloped nations to the advanced industrial nations. The economic difficulties of the transition are portentially so great that the reports predict the increasing possibility of major political upheavals unless proper leadership is provided. An attempt to ensure such leadership is made by the reports, through a series of recommendations, one of which proposes greater state control over energy consumption in the trilateral nations.

The Trilateral Commission reports summarize their recommendations to the advanced nations as follows: "The consuming nations should intensify and coordinate their efforts for the more efficient use of energy, setting specific targets and working out plans for investment technology and public policy to achieve them."[2] In April 1977 President Carter announced his first energy program to Congress. Although it does not address the international issues raised by the Trilateral Commission reports, it reflects their major recommendation concerning the need for national energy management. The categories of energy efficiency and planning adequately describe the two major goals of Carter's energy program. (See Garitty.)

---

*Allen Kaufman has a Ph.D. in History from Rutgers University. Pat Clawson teaches in the Department of Economics, Seton Hall University and has a Ph.D. in Economics from the New School for Social Research.

The program delineates several means by which energy can be more efficiently consumed. The first is an energy conservation effort which is to be initiated through such diverse programs as establishing more rigorous federal standards for transportation vehicles and appliances and by creating federal grants for public facilities to make energy conserving rennovations. To prolong the supplies of oil and natural gas Carter's plan recommends that utilities and industrial facilities convert from gas and oil to coal and that the use of nuclear energy be expanded. He also proposes to explore alternate sources of energy (such as solar) in an effort to conserve supplies of fossil fuel.* Still under the rubric of efficiency the plan recommends that natural gas prices slowly be raised. It explains that the federal regulations of gas have kept prices at a low level and have encouraged wasteful consumption.

The Administration's intent to manage and project future energy usage is evident in the recommendations for designing an energy management system and the proposal for promoting research and development. These proposals are consistent with the regulatory functions of the federal government in other areas. However, the oil well head tax would extend the government's power beyond a regulatory one. Simply stated it would place a tax on new supplies of domestic oil and raise the price of U.S. oil to the world market level. This tax could be considered part of Carter's conservation strategy since it would foster more frugal consumption of oil. The major result of this tax, however, would be to transfer enormous revenues from the oil companies to the federal government. With those revenues the government could have an impact on the economy that would far exceed its present regulatory powers. It is no wonder that when Carter announced his energy plan he considered the oil well head tax the crux of his program.

Carter's energy plan will mean higher energy prices and, consequently, declining real wages for the working class. The Administration admits that, under the plan passed by Congress, natural gas prices will rise by over $25 billion from 1979 through 1985

---

*Environmentalists, most notably Barry Commoner, have correctly observed that Carter's conservation measures merely shift the economy from one source of energy to another. The plan itself does little to guarantee in general the efficient consumption of energy.

The main shift in energy sources will be from petroleum to nuclear fuels—not coal, propaganda from the Energy Department notwithstanding. Besides posing grave health risks, nuclear power plants require massive investments—investments for which consumers are being forced to pay through rate increases. The nuclear power industry is concentrated in the hands of old money firms such as GE (a manufacturer of power plants) and Gulf (a supplier of uranium).

when prices will rise further (other estimates of the cost range up to $50 billion).[3] Little of the opposition to the energy plan has come from workers, however. Workers' resistance cannot explain the plan's long delay in Congress. The principal opposition has come from sectors of the capitalist class who object to the minimal increase in the price of natural gas and the substantial oil well head tax. These forces killed the oil well head tax by freezing it in committee and forced a compromise on the deregulation of gas.

The delays in Congress and the death of the oil well head tax were lamented by Carter and his staff as well as by the Trilateral Commission. In the summer of 1978 the Trilateral Commission issued yet another report evaluating the trilateral countries' efforts to control their consumption of energy.[4] For the most part the report praised Carter's plan—which closely resembles the trilateral program—stating that it shows "the clear determination that the federal government should assume the leading role in planning and directing the nation's energy policy in a comprehensive manner."[5] The report, however, deplores the political machinations that have prevented the federal government from assuming this role of economic planner under the aegis of the energy program.

President Carter anticipated the opposition of some sectors and admonished all concerned Americans to make the necessary sacrifices to overcome the nation's current crisis. His startling rhetorical demand in his address before Congress that the American people wage a "moral equivalent of war" against the energy crisis echoes the Trilateral Commission's estimation that rising energy costs will create "a situation not unlike those of war."[6]

Below we shall explore Carter's energy plan in terms of the increasing state intervention that is required to resolve both the energy crisis and the economic crisis which has plagued the Western nations and Japan for nearly a decade. It is assumed that the energy crisis itself is not the simple result of a limited supply of fossil fuels but rather the outcome of capitalist economic relationships which periodically produce profound economic and social crises. Radical thinkers, thus, are not persuaded by President Carter's call for the moral equivalent of war against nature's meanness. They continue to insist that the only real solution to the energy crisis is class struggle— with the ultimate goal of establishing socialism, a system in which natural resources will be used to satisfy human needs in an ecologically sound manner; not the drive for profit.

The Disputes Over the Energy Plan

The disputes between President Carter and Congress on energy policy indicate a deepening political crisis in the U.S. ruling class. The major antagonism can be described as the conflict between that faction known as *new money* and that known as *old money*. The determinants of these factions include political, economic, and ideological factors as well as geographic considerations. Broadly speaking, we see that the Snowbelt (the industrial Northeast) interests oppose the Sunbelt interests (the Southwest). Economically, the more established and larger *Fortune* 500 corporations have quite different interests from more rapidly growing but smaller firms. Politically and intellectually, the liberal intellectual circles from which the Trilateral Commission were drawn are at odds with conservative groups. On international issues, those capitalists who are more involved in foreign investment have emphasized cooperation with the rising powers of Western Europe and Japan. Less internationally oriented capitalists see as realistic direct U.S. domination over the entire world; they favor, therefore, brinksmanship confrontation with the USSR. The distinction between the two sectors is not absolute; sometimes factions are pulled in one direction by one force and in the other direction by a different interest. Therefore, the camps of old and new money are not to be understood as simple static historical designations, but as complex dynamic terms which include multiple variables.

The principal division between these groups is economic. Old money is likely to be concentrated in the more established *Fortune* 500 corporations and to be rooted in the metal transforming industries of the Snowbelt, such as steel and auto, which are on the decline nationally. New money is generally associated with the rising industries of the Sunbelt, such as electronics and data processing. ("Silicon Valley," near San Francisco, where the microprocessing industry has a large base, is a prime example). This division, however, is not so simple that one can list industries belonging to mutually exclusive camps. New technologies continually blur old distinctions between industries, e.g., the current merging of computer and telephone industries. Firms in declining industries shift their focus into new fields, further obliterating a neat distinction between old and new money. The complexities are well illustrated by the petroleum industry. The major oil companies—the Seven Sisters— are generally tied to old established families such as the Rockefellers; these firms are heavily involved overseas and have supported business liberalism including cooperation with the rising powers of Western Europe and Japan. Yet these companies have been diversifying into new industries. The smaller companies—whose revenues may reach into the billions of dollars per year—have few ties to the old money families. Nevertheless, they are largely dependent on domestic production and consequently are less internationally oriented. They generally favor cold war brinksmanship politics.

New money has generally been associated with conservative and reactionary political tendencies, typified by Barry Goldwater in 1964 and Ronald Reagan's 1976 & 1980 presidential bids. Political and ideological factors, thus, must be included in a distinction between old money and new money.*

This paper argues that the conflicts of interest between old and new money not only helped formulate Carter's energy plan, but also forebode its demise. Carter's original proposal to limit the price increase of natural gas demonstrated his bias towards old money interests located in the Snowbelt. The oil well head tax proposed in Carter's original plan would have transferred billions of dollars from new money interests to the federal government and ultimately to firms favored by the state. In other words, old money wants to use its influence over the state both to protect its declining industries (such as steel) and to provide the profits with which to take over the rising new industries. New money was understandably opposed to this plan. Its proposal, following the tenets of laissez-faire doctrine, was to have its competitors bear the losses through deregulation of natural gas and oil prices so that new money could emerge as the dominant faction of U.S. capital. New money is therefore opposed to state planning, precisely because planning is being used by old money to shift the burden of the crisis.

*ed. note: There have been numerous attempts to distinguish between factions of the ruling class, the old money/new money or Yankee/Cowboy thesis, as Kirkpatrick Sale and Carl Ogelsby popularized it, being one. In "The Traders and the Prussians," (*Seven Days* 28 March 1977) Michael Klare proposes an alternative analytical framework. Although tentative, Klare's model is extremely useful in locating the Trilateral Commission within a brief but highly informative analysis of intercapitalist conflict. The Traders refer to the multinational corporations and banks behind the Trilateral Commission. The Prussians signify the "more domestically oriented" capitalists associated with the National Security Establishment: "an alliance of Pentagon leaders, arms producers, rightwing politicos, intelligence operatives, and some domestic capitalists."

Zbigniew Brzezinski pointed to divisions within the ruling class when he wrote in 1973 (when the shocks of Vietnam were still reverberating within the Eastern establishment) "Uncertainty about America's world role has been intensified by the almost simultaneous waning within American society of the relatively cohesive Eastern elite which hitherto has served as the source both of inspiration and leadership for America's more focused post-World War II engagement in world affairs. The disintegration of this group, its loss of self-confidence, its generational splits, go hand in hand with the appearance in American society of new groups aspiring to leadership. *These groups reflecting new economic interests and located in the Far West and Middle West*, have supplied some of the personnel for the new Nixon Team..." [Italics mine.] "U.S. Foreign Policy: The Search for Focus," *Foreign Affairs*, July 1973, pp. 713-714.

There is a battle in Congress over every minor appropriation, with each side demanding a funding formula that will benefit their respective interests. Carter's energy plan was heavily weighted toward the interests of the Northeast. As it emerged from Congress, the energy plan was much more oriented towards a free market solution to the energy crisis. Congress—especially the Senate, where the Southwest has disproportionately more representatives—systematically altered Carter's proposals to make them more beneficial to the Southwest.

There was considerable opposition to Carter's energy plan from within old money interests. Old money corporate opposition to the energy plan has reflected the different concerns of corporate managers and political leaders. Business executives are concerned with the profits of their individual firms; political leaders have to respond to diverse pressures and must view the interests of the capitalist system as a whole. The management of the major corporations do not want to cede power to government officials. The business world was upset over the energy plan's proposal to shift considerable control over investment and technological innovation to the government. Determined to maintain their economic control, many old money corporation officials led an ideological attack on the energy plan. The plan was said to interfere with the market system and consequently to endanger the American way of life. The ideological attack had the effect of supporting the position of new money in favor of free markets in energy. Interestingly, the most vociferous attack on Carter's energy bill came from Mobil Oil normally associated with old money.[7]

In addition to splits between old and new money, and within old money between corporate management and political figures, there have been various other forces at work shaping Carter's energy program. Government policies are not dictated by the capitalist class, nor are political disputes based purely on economic self-interest. The conflict over the energy plan has been influence by non-ruling-class groups, including some environmentalists and consumer advocates who have long opposed the big oil companies. These groups, to varying degrees, have favored greater state intervention. On the other hand, the antigovernment rhetoric of corporate opposition to the Carter plan is shared by right wing groups like the antibusing and anti-ERA/abortion organizations. This convergence creates the potential for a powerful right wing political force. Thus the Carter energy plan was entangled in political and ideological divisions going far beyond the conflict over energy management between old and new money.

Free Markets Vs. State Planning

Within the complexities of the political debates on energy policy, three general positions on the question of state intervention seem to have emerged. The first, a welfare state position, has yet to be presented here while the others have already been mentioned: the laissez-faire position associated in the energy debate with new money and the guided markets position offered by Carter in support of old money.

The principle organ for the welfare state position can be identified as the Committee for National Economic Planning. Its members include Wassily Leontief, Leonard Woodcock, John Kenneth Galbraith, and Robert Heilbroner. This grouping would like to see the formation of an Economic Planning Board which would coordinate long-range planning of federal departments and agencies, as well as prepare an economic growth plan for the U.S. as a whole. Its objectives would include, according to a 1977 *Fortune* article, "full employment, price stability, equitable distribution of income, efficient utilization of public and private resources, balanced regional and urban development,"—a number of well-meaning demands that are utopian under capitalism.[8] In order to accomplish these objectives, Leontief would use "selective control of capital and credit flows, tax exemption, or even direct public investment."

Needless to say, these social democrats are not the most influential in making government policy. For the most part they have been isolated from the mainstream thinking and decision making within the ruling class (even though this group is responsible for a number of important bills including the now mutilated Humphrey-Hawkins full employment bill).

In contrast, the laissez-faire position may have recently gained in popularity as a result of the alleged failures of the federal antipoverty programs in the 1960s and of the contention that the federal budget deficit contributes to inflation. The non interventionist position has a certain amount of ideological and political clout, as the middle class and small and medium-scale business have generally resisted government regulation of the economy. On the one hand, these groups associate state intervention with monopoly use of government agencies to protect markets from intruders; on the other hand, these groups associate state intervention with a welfare state which they perceive as providing special breaks to the working class and minorities. The major economic group vigorously opposing state intervention has been the oil interests associated with the Southwest. In the place of government regulation of the industry, the new money interests want to see domestic oil price controls eliminated. It is their contention that if prices would be set by the international market, then oil and gas companies would have sufficient incentive to find new domestic reserves of energy.

Since new money's oil investments are largely domestic, deregulation would favor it over old money. As we mentioned before, old money opposes deregulation. The political forces associated with old money agree that higher prices may open new domestic oil reserves, but in themselves, they argue, new reserves will not ensure that the U.S. will become less dependent on foreign sources and that the U.S. will be able to overcome future energy bottlenecks. Moreover, additional domestic oil wells, it is argued, do not guarantee the development of new sources of energy or energy efficient technology; nor do domestic oil sources generate the new investment patterns needed to accelerate the current slow growth economy in the Northeast. To fulfill these goals, state mangement is required, according to old money politicians.

Guided Markets

In addition to free markets and state planning, there is a third position on the question of state intervention in the economy. This is becoming the dominant position within old money. It was set forth by Charles Schultze, the chairman of Carter's Council of Economic Advisers, in the Godkin lectures at Harvard in December 1976. Schultze's talk was reprinted in the May 1977 *Harper's*, and the Brookings Institution, the main think tank of the liberal wing of the ruling class published it as *The Public Use of Private Interest*. Schultze accepts the notion that the market may, in certain cases, not perform optimally, so that state intervention is both necessary and positive. In fact, the historic trend, according to Schultze, seems to demand more state intervention.

Does this mean that Schultze agrees with Leontief or some other standard state planning position? No, it does not. Schultze makes crystal clear that he dissents from the traditional position on state intervention which he labels a command-and-control model that is grafted onto the "private enterprise incentive-oriented system, usually in the form of a regulatory apparatus." Schultze finds this type of intervention questionable for both economic and political reasons. First, this type of intervention undermines the consent arrangement of the marketplace which minimizes the need for coercion. To have regulatory agencies coerce people to act against their will is a position that Schultze finds contrary to good political and economic logic. Second, the command-and-control position is unable to function properly because it cannot obtain either accurate or sufficient data. Third, the command-and-control apparatus

creates too many political problems since the state becomes responsible for the dislocations and the suffering of the market place. When
the free market pushes people out of jobs, lowers living standards,
etc., there is no one to blame but nature. Finally, the system of
government that has developed in the U.S. is so restrictive in its
regulatory functions that it narrows the range of economic activity
and is unable to promote technological innovation.

Although the command-and-control form of intervention is not
right for U.S. capitalism, Schultze says that a second variety of
planning is. He describes this variety as the modification of the
"informational flow, institutional structure or incentive pattern of
the private system." Essentially, this modification is carried out
through various fiscal policies at the discretion of the state—such as
taxes, rebates, subsidies, etc. The intent of these policies is to make
actions desired by the state on the part of business or individuals
profitable and nondesired actions unprofitable. Schultze gives a
number of examples, one of which is the voucher system for funding
higher education (each student receives a voucher, which s/he can use
at any accredited university). According to Schultze, in approaching
planning from this angle, one essentially retains all the political and
economic advantages of the market (not to mention the ideological
obfuscation which the market affects on the real nature of class
relationships).

Schultze's essay does not have a program for the energy crisis.
The details of this position were perhaps first made known through
an article in *Fortune* magazine in February 1977—two months
before Carter's plan was finally drafted and presented before
Congress. The article, "My Case for National Planning," was written
by Thorton Bradshaw, president of Atlantic Richfield. Like
Schultze, Bradshaw disassociates himself from the Leontief-
Woodcock group. Bradshaw's call for national planning is based on
the nonexistence of a market mechanism in oil (OPEC controls the
market); the inability of the market to guarantee new sources of
energy; and the political/military necessity to be free of foreign oil
dependency. Following Schultze's notion of modification of the
private system. Bradshaw suggests incentives and disincentives
through taxes and subsidies that more or less resemble the Carter
plan released months later.

Thus, we see that Carter's energy plan is not a simple makeshift
response to the energy crisis. It has been evolving within the ruling
class as a potential program by which to resolve the political and
ideological difficulties in establishing national economic priorities.
Politically, the plan has aspects which seemingly cut through many of
the controversial consumer issues that are related to energy, such as

partial maintenance of price regulation on crude oil in order to prevent windfall profits. Moreover, Carter's strategy of market modification is designed to comfort small and medium-scale business, the middle class, and organized labor that the market is still functioning and that the state is above class interests. Most important from the perspective of the old money capitalists who support Carter's plan, the plan would put the state in control of restructuring industry—the state would decide which industries get subsidized and which get taxed.

Capitalist Crisis and State Intervention

The growing debate on state intervention has been spurred by more than the specific crisis in energy. For the past decade, the overall U.S. economy has experienced economic stagnation. While the effect of the economic slowdown has been experienced differentially in the Southwest and the Northeast, the fact remains that the U.S. economy is not as robust as it was in the 1960s. Economic theorists have acrimoniously debated the reasons for the crisis and the mechanisms for recovery. The contending positions around the energy proposal are based implicitly on differing solutions for capital's economic crisis.

The free markets approach (championed by Milton Freedman and others) assumes that the market system, left to itself, automatically produces full employment and optimal growth. Economic crisis is then said to be the temporary result of an outside shock to the market system, e.g., a war or an oil price rise. Given time, the markets will adjust back to full employment, say the free marketeers— although the adjustment may take years or decades, as in the Great Depression. This theory must account for the frequent economic crises under capitalism through ad hoc explanations for each individual crisis. However, the frequency and regularity of economic crisis is an indication that crisis is actually a product of capitalism, not of an external shock. Free markets produce a cycle of crisis giving way to full employment returning to crisis. Free market economists see the energy crisis as the product of government interference in the market; the crisis could be resolved if only the government left the market alone. The notion that there could be a free market in energy in the modern world is amusing. Each of the Seven Sisters (Exxon, BP, Shell, Texaco, Gulf, Mobil, and Socal) have sales larger than the GNP of nearly all countries. The oil companies determine the free market according to their interests, subject to increasing control by the governments of OPEC and of major Western powers. Deregulation means more power to gigantic firms, not a return to a freely competitive market. (See Table 1 in Overview.)

The most common explanation for economic crisis has been that crisis is caused by lack of demand or underconsumption. Keynesians argue that capitalism's underconsumption problem can be resolved by stimulating demand through increased investment and government spending. The implicit assumption behind the Keynesian solution to economic crisis is that there is a potentially infinite amount of credit, such that government and corporations can borrow at will. The only limit on demand then becomes the *will* of the ruling class, animal spirits, as Joan Robinson so colorfully and accurately puts it. If only capitalists *wanted* to get out of the crisis, if only they acted as if there were no crisis (by investing fully), then there would be no crisis.[9] Capitalists are hardly so all-powerful as to be able to determine the pace of accumulation and the level of state expenditures without worrying about any constraints.The attempt to borrow without limit causes monetary crisis, inflation, and currency fluctuations. By focusing on demand exclusively, underconsumption theories overlooked the problem of production. Keynesian economists have therefore been largely uninterested in the debate about energy shortage. The energy proposals, according to mainstream Keynesians, are basically irrelevant to resolving the U.S.'s economic difficulties. These economists have been upset that the dispute over energy policy have prevented action on other economic proposals.

The most basic laws of capitalism are those which pit workers and capitalists against each other in the struggle over the division of income. Economists who have mastered only these elementary laws ascribe crisis to a profit squeeze stemming from an increase in the workers' portion of national income. Capitalist crisis becomes, then, the time when growing unemployment (the reserve army of unemployed) is used as a club to beat wages back to a minimum, with the state intervening to speed the process. There is certainly some truth to this theory of crisis resolution via lower wages. The profit squeeze focus is inadequate, however, for this would argue that capitalism will generally seek to reduce wages; once wages have reached the physical subsistence level, capitalism would fall into permanent crisis. The profit squeeze theory is incompatible with capitalism's tendency to raise the standard of consumption of the working class.[10] Carter's energy policy proposals are understood by profit squeeze theorists as a means to reduce wages, e.g., by increasing prices consumers must pay. As we indicated above, reducing wages is only a small part of the plan. The conflicts over Carter's proposals can not be explained through the profit squeeze theory, since both the guided market and the deregulation plans would raise prices to consumers. More must be at work here than simply a struggle over the division of income between wages and profits.

For different reasons, economists of the free market, under-consumptionists, and profit squeeze schools would each attack Carter's energy plan. Is the plan then economically unsound? No—rather, each of these theories of crisis are inadequate for reasons sketched above. Marx demonstrated that the key to capitalism's health is the production of profits, and Carter's proposals are based on increasing production of profits. The fundamental mechanism for increasing profits under mature capitalism is through higher productivity.[11] By producing at higher productivity, the capitalists are able to reduce the value of each particular commodity (i.e.. the same amount of physical goods is cheaper to produce—it has a lower real price). The amount of time during the working day which is spent to produce enough commodities, the sale of which will cover the worker's wage bill, is reduced, with a corresponding rise in the time of production which goes toward the capitalists' profits. The higher productivity which allows for higher profits.is primarily derived from the application of new technologies. The general upward leaps in profits which resolve a crisis come from the development of new more productive industries which replace the older industries as the engines of economic growth. Rivalry among firms grows sharp in an economic crisis as each strives to outlast competitors. The largest corporations have the funds to develop new technologies and to run the risks of entry into new industries where technology is rapidly developing.

Capitalist economic crises are resolved through restructuring which eliminates the marginal producers (devaluing their capital) and raises productivity. The restructuring of capital must be planned according to the interests of capital as a whole, not left to the whim of chaotic and unpredictable market forces. The last decade has seen an enormous increase in state intervention in the accumulation and production process in the U.S. State intervention has gone far beyond traditional Keynesian monetary and fiscal policy. Environmental impact studies have involved the state in every major investment decision and also in decisions around production technologies. Loan guarantees, industrial safety regulations, energy useage directives—year by year, the state becomes more immediately involved in major corporate decisions. President Carter's energy plan is an extension of state guidance for the economy. The move to a state-guided economy comes not from any deep-rooted ideological commitment to planning, but from the harsh realities of capitalist economic crisis. Carter's rejection of open state planning in favor of indirect planning through guided markets reflects the strong opposition to increased direct state intervention.

Energy and the International Situation

The United States' declining international strength exacerbates domestic economic difficulties. OPEC's economic power illustrates this point. The oil price rises of the early 1970s were made possible by U.S. weakness. Faced with a growing threat from West European and Japanese competitors, U.S. capitalists supported the rise of OPEC oil prices in 1971. Western Europe and Japan, heavily dependent on imported oil, had to pay higher prices while U.S. industry was relatively insulated. Once the OPEC governments discovered how easily they could enforce a price rise, they kept on raising the price. The oil companies were willing partners since their profits rose along with the price (compounded with spectacular short-term profits due to inventory revaluation and artificial shortages). Realizing its increasing dependence on oil imports and its inefficient use of energy relative to other competitors, the U.S. strongly opposed the later price increases. Times had changed from the mid-1950s, when the U.S. government implemented its energy policy of high oil company profits by overthrowing the popularly elected Mossadegh government in Iran. In the 1970s, the U.S. was unable to bring sufficient force to bear to reverse the oil price increases. Efforts at a common front among the Western powers fell apart as each country pursued its own interest; no one country was strong enough to force all to follow a joint strategy. The OPEC cartel continues to fix prices and to divide markets with the aim of increasing income for each producer. (See Bird.)

Higher energy prices have revealed that U.S. capitalism has become technologically less advanced in key areas compared with German and Japanese capitalism. The inefficient use of energy in the U.S. is a symptom of the U.S. decline. The U.S. capital stock is old and unproductive. While West German and Japanese industrialists were investing in massive new factories, the U.S. ruling class was forced to pour billions into arms expenditures to defend the global empire (over $200 billion in the Indochina War alone). The U.S. ruling class is now demanding that the burdens of the crisis be shared; the West German and Japanese rulers resist strenuously. The pressure on U.S. capitalists is greatly increased by the threat from Soviet capitalism. The USSR is still more backward technologically than the U.S. in nearly every area, but it is rapidly catching up. The nature of the propaganda in the U.S. press has led many to overlook the tremendous gains of the Soviet economy in the last few decades.

Economic competition from other powers creates pressure to boost productivity quickly, which is possible only if more profit is readily available. In short, U.S. capitalists face a tremendous capital shortage if they are to maintain their hegemonic position in the world. The New York Stock Exchange estimate of one trillion dollars above what would normally be generated seems a reasonable figure for capital requirements to restore international competitiveness and a return to full employment. So far the funds have simply not been forthcoming. Investment in industrial capital has been weak since 1974. Corporations were over-indebted then; they had to use profits to reduce debt instead of funding new investment. Corporations have not been able to raise new equity capital because the stock market has been sickly. In any case, inflation and economic uncertainty have made corporations unwilling to invest. The U.S. economy is unlikely to return soon to the more rapid growth characteristic of the 1950s and 1960s. The energy situation contributes to the sustained economic stagnation, which in turn exacerbates efforts to resolve the energy shortage through the introduction of new technologies. U.S. capitalists have no easy path out of their present quandry. The attack on the working class' share of income is being carried out with vigor and it will escalate even further as capitalists attempt to save themselves and their system.

Postscript

Since this article was written in the summer of 1977, Carter's energy program has been altered and extended in ways that can be understood through the analysis presented here. The Windfall Profits Tax, Synfuel Corporation, and Energy Mobilization Board (see Garitty) may be seen as the newest arenas for the continuing struggle by old and new money for the power promised by energy profits. Carter's moral equivalent of war begins to look more like a specter of the real thing as conflicting interests prevent the political will needed to resolve the United States' deepening economic crisis.

FOOTNOTES

1. John C. Campbell, Guy de Carmoy and Shinchi Kondo, "Energy: The Imperative for a Trilateral Approach" and "Energy: A Strategy for International Action," in *Trilateral Commission Task Force Reports 1-7: The Triangle Papers, A Compilation of Reports from the First Two Years of the Trilateral Commission* (New York, 1977).

2. *Ibid.* p. 110.

3. The Department of Energy's Applied Analysis Natural Gas Pricing Proposal Team estimates that revenues of natural gas producers will rise by $29.5 billion through 1985, under a moderate geological assessment.

4. John C. Sawhill, Hanns W. Maull, and Keichi Oshima, *Energy: Managing the Transition*, The Trilateral Commission, June 1978.

5. *Ibid.* p. 50.

6. Campbell, *op.cit.*, p. 125.

7. For instance, the minors—petroleum firms besides the Seven Sisters—strenuously attacked the energy plan. These small oil and gas firms depend primarily on domestic petroleum production, so they had much at stake in the debate over the price for domestically-produced gas and oil. All sides agree that price of oil and gas sold to U.S. customers should be raised to the world market price. The debate was between the current regulated domestic price and the world market price, as opposed to the new money proposal that the producing companies should get the extra income. The major oil companies—the Seven Sisters—were not particularly involved in the debate, except for Mobil. The majors will not particularly benefit from the increase of U.S. prices. Their main source of profits is international operations. In so far as U.S. production expands, the Seven Sister's control over imports becomes less valuable. Furthermore, the majors have diversified into other energy fields (e.g., Exxon's move into the coal industry), so that they would benefit from a reduced reliance on U.S.-produced petroleum.

8. Tom Alexander, "The Deceptive Allure of National Planning," *Fortune,* March 1977, p. 150.

9. For the notion that certain "Crises are really investment strikes" see John Gurley, "Unemployment and Inflation," *Monthly Review,* December 1977.

10. The profit squeeze theory would imply that capitalism prospers the most where wages are the lowest. An obvious counter-example would be the post World War II U.S.

11. Marx showed that profits come from paying workers less than the value workers add to the product. The difference between the value of workers' wages (more exactly the value of labor power) and the value added to the product is the capitalist's surplus value. One way that capitalists raise surplus value is by lowering the *value* of the goods the workers recieve—which is not the same as lowering the *amount* of goods the workers receive. Marx called surplus value produced through lowering the value of the workers' labor power "relative surplus value."

PART VI
TRYING TO KEEP THE WORLD SAFE
FOR INTERNATIONAL BUSINESS

Trilateralism has not altered three central aims of Western policy toward the Third World: securing raw materials, markets, and stable friendly regimes. This section analyzes the trilateral response to changing Third World (and world) realities. As Philip Wheaton argues, "the West hopes to discard its colonial robes while maintaining its neocolonial throne." In the Middle East, trilateral strategy entails co-opting the oil rulers and defusing the Palestinian struggle. In Southern Africa—demilitarizing the liberation struggle and modernizing apartheid. In Latin America—democratization, economic aid, and counterinsurgency.

I was in the East End of London yesterday and attended a meeting of the unemployed. I listened to the wild speeches, which were just a cry for "bread, bread, bread," and on my way home I pondered over the scene and I became more than ever convinced of the importance of imperialism...My cherished idea is a solution of the social problem, i.e., in order to save the 40,000,000 inhabitants of the United Kingdom from a bloody civil war, we colonial statesmen must acquire new lands to settle the surplus population, to provide new markets for the goods produced by them in the factories and mines. The empire, as I have always said, is a bread and butter question. If you want to avoid civil war, you must become imperialists.

> —Cecil Rhodes, British financier, colonialist, and imperialist, 1895—Rhodesia and Rhodes scholar are two of his namesakes.*

I think that whenever we have the possibility of contributing toward development what we are doing, really, is creating stable conditions under which American goods and services will eventually be desired. My approach to Africa is in some ways like the Japanese approach to Asia, and my approach to foreign aid is not necessarily humanitarian. It is in the long-range interest of *access to resources and the creation of markets for American goods and services.* [Italics ed.]

> —Andrew Young, ambassador to the U.N., before the Senate Foreign Relations Africa Subcommittee, 6 June 1977.

*Related by William Stead, as cited in Lenin, *Imperialism: The Highest Stage of Capitalism.* International Publishers, 1939, p. 79.

chapter one

CO-OPTING THE THIRD WORLD ELITES:
TRILATERALISM AND SAUDI ARABIA
*Kai Bird**

It is no coincidence that in the decade of the energy crisis those intellectuals with an *internationalist* perspective on global trade issues have come to dominate the U.S. foreign policy community. Nothing underscores the trilateral interdependence of North America, Western Europe and Japan more than their competition for stable energy supplies. In a world of vastly constrained resources, it is argued, the three major industrial powers must not jeopardize their growth by cutthroat competition for oil. Rather, stable trading partners must be found in the Third World—where much of the world's excess oil reserves remain—who can be depended upon both to supply us with energy and buy from us enough manufactured goods and services to offset higher energy costs.

It is this willingness of the new U.S. leadership to cooperate with a number of developing regional powers—to strike a trading bargain with their ruling native elites—that is distinctive about U.S. diplomacy in the 1970s.[1] President Jimmy Carter's trilateral approach to foreign policy—an outgrowth of his participation on the Trilateral Commission—is actually a mandate to co-opt a few of those larger, resource-rich Third World nations into an expanded economic system.

This perception of the opportunities available to the trilateral powers in the Third World is brazenly articulated by Tom Farer in an

*Kai Bird is assistant editor of *The Nation*. He has spent ten years in the Middle East, both as a student and then a reporter writing for *The Far Eastern Economic Review, Foreign Policy, The Washington Post, The Los Angeles Times* and other publications. This article is adapted from "Co-opting the Third World Elites," *The Nation*, 9 April 1977.

October 1975 article of *Foreign Affairs* entitled, "The United States and the Third World."* He observes first:

> *There was a creaming off and co-optation of the natural elite of the working class* [in America]. Some members were drawn off early by opening the channels to higher education. Their followers were pacified in very small measure by vicarious participation in the structure of power and in very large measure by receipt of slightly increased shares of a very rapidly growing pie. *There is no evidence that any existing wealth was redistributed.* [Italics ed.]

Farer goes on to suggest, by analogy, that the managers of the three major capitalist societies—North America, Western Europe and Japan—can hope to co-opt and divide the Third World in the same way:

> For the most part, Third World elites are even less committed to human equality as a general condition of humanity than we. They are talking about greater equality between states. And in their largely authoritarian systems, the state is they...The central fact is that *the overall number of people who have to be given a stake in the essential structures of the existing international economic system is relatively small.* [Italics ed.]

Farer argues that a strategy of accommodation with a few Third World regional powers can effectively diffuse the strident demands of the current North-South negotiations. Saudi Arabia, Iran (sic), Brazil, Venezuela, Mexico, Nigeria, India and Indonesia are cited as the cream of the Third World—countries rich in natural resources and ruled by middle class native elites who have for the most part broken all ties to the impoverished masses in the countryside. Farer points out that, though many of these native elites have suffered personal humiliation at the hand of Western colonialism, their immediate economic aspirations are quite compatible with the existing international economic system. (See **Girvan**.)

Thus, to stabilize the international order, the United States must apply balm to the personal sores induced by past colonial humiliations and allow the native elites of these regional powers a very small measure of "vicarious participation in the structures of power," and "slightly" increased shares of the world's economic growth.

---

*ed. note: Tom Farer is a member of the Inter-American Commission of Human Rights of the Organization of American States and former special assistant to the assistant secretary of state for Inter-American Affairs. For futher discussion of Farer's views see the article by Philip Wheaton in this volume.

It does not matter that the vast majority of humanity will remain outside the economic system. Redistribution of present wealth and decentralized democracy have no place in such a system—and to the trilateralists both ideals are deemed disruptive.

The assumption behind such a conciliatory approach to Third World elites is that the leadership which might supplant them could be much more substantively detrimental to basic U.S. interests. Unlike the more conservative wing of the foreign policy establishment represented by Kissinger's crisis-management diplomacy, the liberals take a longer view. William Maynes expresses their concern in the July 1976 issue of *Foreign Affairs*. Maynes, a former secretary of the Carnegie Endowment for International Peace, has since become assistant secretary for international organizations at the State Department. In this position Maynes has played a leading role in U.S. relations with the United Nations and in the North-South dialogue. He writes:

> Like the moderate leadership in the American civil rights movement in the late 1960s, however, the moderate elements in the Third World have gone years without victories and urgently require some to prove that a moderate course can produce results. Otherwise, we can expect the extremists of international politics to take over.

It is in this context that our relationship to the Arab oil producers—and Saudi Arabia in particular—is considered of crucial importance by the trilateral policy makers. Of all the regional powers singled out by the trilateralists for special attention, none pose as many political ambiguities as does Saudi Arabia. Unlike any of the other major oil producers—Iran and Venezuela included—the Saudi rulers are not immediately confronted by internal demands in the form of millions of hungry and expectant citizens. In lieu of these internal political pressures, oil production decisions are simply a reflection of Saudi diplomacy. This is the heart of the much publicized U.S.-Saudi *special relationship*. Underlying Carter's entire energy program is the assumption that the Saudis can continue to be persuaded to produce oil at nearly three times the rate necessary to meet their external payments.

While the Saudi monarchy is by definition politically conservative, ardently anticommunist, and naturally aligned to the West, nonetheless the Saudis do bring with them to this special relationship a capacity for independent political action unlikely to be duplicated anywhere else in the Third World. The foremost Saudi concern, of course, is to see that a comprehensive settlement of the Arab-Israeli dispute be achieved in such a way as to diffuse the various radical tendencies at work in the Middle East—and without being perceived by the Arab masses as having abandoned the Palestinians or reneged on the basic ideals of Arab nationalism. These Saudi objectives no doubt in part explain why the Carter Administration has given a peace settlement in the Middle East such high priority.

It is not the price of oil as such but increased supply, that is linked by the Saudis to a Middle East peace settlement. The goal of U.S. diplomatic efforts in the Middle East is not to lower oil prices but to insure staple supplies. Christopher Makins, then deputy director of the Trilateral Commission, told the *New York Times* on 19 October 1976 that the price of oil will in the long-term depend on the cost of producing alternative fuels. By this measure, the world market price of standard crude set by OPEC (Organization for Petroleum Exporting Countries) is already underpriced. For this reason, one can assume that whatever happens in the political realm, oil prices will not decline. Rather, they will continue to climb throughout this century, placing serious constraints on industrialized economies in the capitalist world.

Given the dependence of the trilateral powers on oil and the concentration of world reserves in the Middle East, price is simply a function of the budget requirements of the oil producers. Saudi Arabia controls the entire system because it is the only OPEC country with a significant shut-in capacity. The Saudis may have a potential production capacity of around 18 million barrels per day, but are currently producing only 8.5 million barrels per day. (During the Iranian crisis of 1978-79 the Saudis responded to trilateral needs by temporarily increasing production to 10.5 million barrels per day.) Without Saudi Arabia's 108 billion barrels of proven reserves, the world would run out of oil well before the forecast year of 2017. All other OPEC nations are producing at maximum capacity; some, like Kuwait, will soon begin a steady decline in production. Even Mexico's announcement of greatly increased proven reserves is not expected to alter the picture much: it will take many years before sizable quantities of Mexican oil are available on the world market. And, in any case, Mexican export capacity will probably never match Saudi exports today. Only Saudi Arabia has the political option to cut supplies indefinitely without cutting its national budget.

The trilateral powers are more vulnerable currently than ever before to the oil weapon. United States oil imports have tripled since the 1973 oil embargo, while domestic crude production is down 12 percent. More than 40 percent of the oil consumed in the United States in 1978 was imported. Even more disturbing to the authors of Operation Independence is the shift toward greater reliance on Arab OPEC oil and away from non-Arab sources. Imports of Saudi oil increased 45 percent in 1975, while imports of Canadian oil actually declined 21 percent. By 1976 Saudi crude alone accounted for more than 23 percent of U.S. imports.

The Saudis are the only members of OPEC who can afford, or who want, to use their oil supplies as a political weapon. Such was the case at the December 1976 OPEC conference in Doha, when the Saudis decided to increase their production levels in the face of universal OPEC opposition. Most energy experts predict that Saudi Arabia alone must increase its production each year by at least a million barrels a day just to meet normal world demand. Trilateral reports on energy cite CIA estimates that Saudi production will have to rise to 17 to 24 million barrels per day if world energy demands are to be met in 1985. This would require at least a 50 percent increase in production and would push Saudi oil revenues to more than $100 billion annually.

The trilateral approach to international energy policy recognizes the intravulnerability of the three major industrial powers to a Saudi production cutback, and the United States' trilateral allies are uneasily aware that their supplies of Saudi crude oil are directly contingent upon President Carter's willingness to impose a comprehensive Middle East peace settlement. Dr. Mason Willrich, director of the International Division of the Rockefeller Foundation, told an audience of energy experts at Princeton University: "In discussions we have had with our European and Japanese allies, they have emphasized that they want the United States committed to stable Saudi imports—for their own protection."

The major strategy, according to the trilateralists, is to entangle the Saudis with the Americans and assure them a stake in the established economic order. Genuine co-optation of Saudi Arabia entails the creation of a credible regional power. No one in Washington's small foreign policy clique talks about it publicly, but Saudi energy resources, military muscle and investments in Western industry will give it considerable influence in whatever world order emerges from the trilateral vision. This influence already extends beyond the Arab world. All of Black Africa today receives more foreign aid from Saudi Arabia alone than from the United States. (The Saudis allocate more than 13 percent of their gross national product to foreign assistance, compared to only 29 percent by the United States.)

The traditional U.S.-Saudi special relationship and Carter's current policy of mutual entanglement with the oil regimes is thoroughly documented in a number of Trilateral Commission reports: *Energy: A Strategy for International Action; Energy: The Imperative for a Trilateral Approach; OPEC, the Trilateral World, and the Developing Countries: New Arrangements for Cooperation,*

1976-1980; and *Energy: Managing the Transition.*[2] These reports outline a policy of cooperation with the oil producers on questions of both energy and a Middle East peace settlement:

> The Trilateral countries have to recognize that the question of the supply of oil cannot be separated from the existence of political conflict in the Middle East. The prospect that a new crisis would bring a new reduction or cutoff of Arab oil and again drive the consuming nations apart highlights the need for an early settlement and for an agreed American-European-Japanese approach to it.[3]

One report specifically rules out the possibility of military action against the oil producers and says "attempts to deny food or other supplies will court political disaster."[4] The U.S. special relationship with the oil producers, says another of the trilateral reports on energy, "should accord to them a place in international economic councils commensurate with their increased economic status."[5] This is a clear reference to the "vicarious participation in the structure of power" spoken of by Tom Farer.

There are immediate and long-range costs to any policy that attempts to guarantee oil supplies from the Middle East, but the trilateral reports boldly state what no politician has been willing to tell the U.S. people:

> The building of petroleum-related industries such as refining and petrochemicals in the producing countries is natural and inevitable. The consuming countries should provide help, *even though the temporary effect will be to add to OPEC's bargaining power, create competition for their own industries, and aggravate their situation regarding the cost and supply of oil products.*[6] (Italics added.)

There are two sides to the Saudi-U.S. special relationship: assured stable supplies of oil for the trilateral industrial powers is only half of the relationship. A much more important factor in understanding the nature of this alliance is the recycling of Saudi revenues back to the U.S. market. The fact is that U.S. multinational corporations have benefitted disproportionately from Saudi oil revenue expenditures on U.S. goods and services.

A look at the larger picture illustrates that the special relationship has been anything but one sided. During the period from 1974-77 the U.S. purchased $106 billion worth of goods and services from OPEC countries. But during the same four year period, more than $108 billion of OPEC petrodollars were returned to the United States.[7] Seventy billion dollars of this total represented purchases of U.S. goods and services. The remainder was invested in the United States, largely in the form of bank deposits or purchases of U.S. Treasury bonds and corporate securities.

The primary goal of trilateral policy in the Middle East is to maintain this exchange of oil for goods and services. It is in this context that the Iranian revolution and the precedence it establishes for a slower pace of modernization, raises a serious challenge to the trilateral managers. The loss of Iran as a regional power willing to produce oil at full capacity and to reinvest its petrodollars in purchases of U.S. arms and industrial plants is a substantial setback to Washington. The possibility of a similar political upheaval in Saudi Arabia is more remote for the simple reason that the Saudis do not face these kinds of internal security problems. But the declines in Iranian oil exports can only compound the difficulties in persuading the Saudis that they should continue to export oil at nearly three times the rate necessary to meet their external payments.

The trilateralists are acutely aware of this problem. A July 1978 Trilateral Commission report, *Energy: Managing the Transition*, acknowledges, "Within the Saudi government there is opposition to raising production further because of the lack of domestic need for expanded current revenues. There is a feeling that domestic expenditures have increased too quickly, engendering waste and fueling strong inflationary pressures in that country."*

In response to these pressures the United States has made every effort to institutionalize the special relationship Two organizations exist through which American interests in Saudi Arabia are guarded. The U.S.-Saudi Joint Commission on Economic Cooperation, administered by the U.S. Treasury Department, has a mandate to insure the recycling of Saudi petrodollars through an ambitious $140 billion industrialization program. The other institutional pillar of the special relationship is, of course, the Arabian American Oil Company (Aramco), representing Mobil, Exxon, Texaco, and Standard Oil of California.

The U.S.-Saudi Joint Commission was founded in 1974 to provide the Kingdom technical and managerial assistance. Today, it directly administers nearly $800 million worth of development projects in the country. The Commission works in close tandem with the Saudi Planning Commission in the implementation of a $140 billion Five Year Plan.

A great deal of business is at stake. Bechtel Corporation, for instance, is supervising the construction of a $20 billion dollar

---

*ed. note: Oil Minister Yamani was blunt about the Saudi Program to expand production capacity: "it is not really in our interest. It is only in the interest of the West that we are carrying out this expansion." (*Time* 22 May 1978).

industrial park at Jubail on the Arabian Gulf. And in what is the largest industrial project ever undertaken by a single company, the Fluor Corporation will build the plants necessary to process enormous natural gas reserves into fuel for local industry. This particular project is an excellent example of how trilateralists so hope to entangle the Saudis that they could no longer conceive of cutting back on oil exports. Currently, the Saudis flare (burn-off) the large amounts of natural gas associated with oil production. But when the extensive petrochemical industries fueled by natural gas have been built, any decline in oil production with an accompanying decline in natural gas production would seriously cripple local industry. Each new industrial project in Saudi Arabia is thus a deterrent against any politically motivated oil embargos.

The process of entanglement proceeds on other fronts. The Saudis have been made to recognize that no currency other than the U.S. dollar can handle the large transactions involved in marketing their oil. By conducting their business in the American currency, the Saudis have become the primary backers of the U.S. dollar as *the* gobal trading currency. And finally, as a regional power of increasing importance in the Middle East—with a particularly urgent military role with the overthrow of the Shah of Iran—the Saudis will be supplied with ever more sophisticated armaments and assistance in training and expanding their small army. In 1978 alone, the Saudis contracted some $4.8 billion worth of U.S. weapons (and are scheduled to receive 60 F-15 advanced jet fighters valued at $2.5 billion). Even apart from their crucial role in the Arab-Israeli conflict, the Saudis will in the future play an interventionist role in places like Oman, North and South Yemen, Lebanon, Pakistan and Eritrea.*

Thus unknown to the American people—and without any real public debate—quiet alliances are being negotiated (supposedly on their behalf) to secure necessary natural resources, and oil in particular, that are controlled by the autocratic elites of a few regional Third World powers.

The other bridge between the trilateral powers and regional powers like Saudi Arabia is the multinational corporation. Aramco is still an appropriate conduit for trilateral diplomacy, though the oil fields themselves have long been nationalized. "In the energy field," says Dr. Mason Willrich, "we have to forge an alliance between the

*ed. note: Saudi Arabia has intervened in Africa on past occasions. In the Spring of 1977, for instance, Saudi-financed Moroccan troops helped crush a revolt against Zaire's strongman, Mobuto Sese Seko.

federal government and the oil companies. Our long-term energy shortage problems are so serious that we ignore oil only to our own peril. One of the major problems will be to persuade the American people that they are not being ripped off."

Aramco has created a company state in Saudi Arabia over the last forty years—much as Delaware is a preserve of the Du Pont Co. But Aramco has had the farsighted political good sense to forgo confrontation tactics in its dealings with the Saudi elite. The company has never humiliated the royal family and never blatantly usurped sovereignty, as did the French and British colonialists in the Middle East. The company has made itself indispensable to the production and marketing of oil, without openly transgressing the strict boundaries of Saudi culture and religion. Aramco long ago recognized the royal family's right to regulate the pace of modernization—a decision which allows the Saudi elite to manage gradually increasing demands for political participation.

In return, the Saudi monarchy has provided the company with long-term security in a country of unusual political stability. Even while the Saudis were negotiating 100 percent ownership of the oil fields, Aramco continued to express unshaken confidence that its special relationship with Riyadh will continue for many years.

James V. Knight, Aramco's vice president in Washington, D.C., told National Reports, 9 October 1976, a Washington magazine on government affairs and policy, "Rather than the so-called nationalization being a case of 'throw the rascals out,' you might say that Aramco is being strengthened all the time. They [the four oil company partners] are going to continue to market oil."

Aramco is a strong structural factor conducive to Saudi cooperation with the trilateral powers. But there is always the danger that the volatile nature of the Arab nationalist movement could radically alter this special relationship. Saudi relations with the United States are more fragile than they appear; for one thing, they are clouded by a U.S. de facto alliance with Israel. Whatever their affinity to U.S. economic interests, the Saudis are subject to the same political imperatives of any Arab state. The trilateral foreign policy strategist recognizes that regional powers often inherit compelling cultural or political ideals, which, if violated, would jeopardize their domestic political consensus. Such is the case with Saudi views over the status of Jerusalem or the demands by Palestinian Arabs for a national homeland. Thus the Palestinians represent an internal political threat to the Saudi monarchy—at least to the extent that the broad political consensus behind the throne would shatter if the royal family was perceived to have betrayed the Palestinian cause. On the other hand, the successful establishment of a leftist and secular state in Lebanon or Palestine-Jordan threatens the Saudi monarchy as well as trilateral interests.

It is out of this contradictory desire to protect their identity in the Arab community and simultaneously maintain the status quo that Saudi diplomacy can be understood.

In 1976 they forced an abrupt end to the Lebanese civil war—first intervening to prevent a complete victory over the Christians by a coalition of leftist Muslim Lebanese and Palestinians, and then intervening again to save the PLO from annihilation. And they forged a reconciliation among Egypt, Syria and Jordan for the sole purpose of bringing a united Arab front—including a beleagured PLO—to the brink of a comprehensive peace settlement with Israel. The Camp David accords negotiated by President Carter are part of this process, though the U.S. Administration was no doubt surprised by Saudi demands that the accords include a more explicit timetable on the withdrawal of Israeli troops and the holding of elections in the occupied territories. (The Camp David affair may well have been one of those issues where the trilateral managers in Washington misjudged the willingness of their Third World regional power to violate a domestic political imperative.)

The settlement the Saudis envision is probably very close to the kind of peace outlined in a 1975 Brookings Institution report ("Toward Peace in the Middle East"), signed by both Zbigniew Brzezinski and William Quandt, his former Middle East aide at the National Security Council. The Brookings report endorses a Palestinian state or entity in the West Bank and Gaza, with perhaps nominal Arab or international sovereignty over the Old City of Jerusalem. The Saudis probably are counting on the creation of a right wing autonomous Palestinian state in the West Bank and Gaza that excludes the Marxist elements in the PLO, and is perhaps loosely federated with the Hashemite Kingdom in Jordan.

A moderate, cooperative Saudi monarchy cannot indefinitely survive—much less continue to supply more than half of the United States' increased oil needs—without a comprehensive Middle East peace settlement. And because the Saudis could be maneuvered by events into politically motivated cutbacks in oil production, the trilateralists can be expected to work very hard to negotiate an Arab-Israeli settlement. Even so, more important to the special relationship than these political factors is the economic entanglement of the Saudi Kingdom into the trilateral system. If the trilateralists are successful—which is by no means a foregone conclusion given precedence set by the Iranian revolution—a new industrial power will be built in Saudi Arabia which, given a stake in the U.S. market, could become a major pillar of the Western economic system.

Editor's Postscript: Saudi Arabia's internal calm was shaken by the taking of the Grand Mosque in Mecca during November and December 1979 by several hundred armed followers of a movement challenging the legitimacy of the ruling family. After heavy fighting and casualties on both sides, the rebellion was squelched on December 3. The *New York Times* of 28 January 1980 reports that an elite French antiterrorist unit played a key role in advising and arming the Saudi assault forces.

FOOTNOTES

1. See Michael Klare, "The Traders and the Prussians," *Seven Days*, 28 March 1977.
2. See *Trilateral Commission: Task Force Reports: 1-7: A Compilation of Reports from the First Two Years of the Trilateral Commission* (New York: New York University Press, 1977) Task Force Reports 5, 6, and 7: "Energy: The Imperative for a Trilateral Approach" (1974); "Energy: Strategy for International Action" (1974); and "OPEC, The Trilateral World, and the Developing Countries: New Arrangements for Cooperation, 1976-1980" (1975). Also see *Energy: Managing the Transition*, The Trilateral Commission, 1978.
3. "Energy: A strategy for International Action," (1974) Task Force Report 6, contained in *Trilateral Commission Task Force Reports: 1-7*, p. 145.
4. *Ibid.*
5. "Energy: The Imperative for a Trilateral Approach," *op.cit.*, p. 117.
6. "Energy: A Strategy for International Action," *op. cit.*, p. 147.
7. Harry Magdoff, "The U.S. Dollar, Petrodollars, and U.S. Imperialism," *Monthly Review*, January 1979, p.9.

chapter two

APARTHEID AND TRILATERALISM: PARTNERS IN SOUTHERN AFRICA
Carolyn Brown*

Introduction

One of the greatest challenges to trilateralism and the U.S. government has come from Africa, a region of the world which only in 1958 came to warrant a "special desk" at the State Department. Throughout the 1960s Washington supported the white settler governments in Southern Africa. Heeding Option 2 of National Security Study Memorandum (NSSM) 39, the Nixon Administration misjudged the potential of Southern African liberation movements and reasserted its support of the minority regimes: "the whites are here to stay and the only way that constructive change can come about is through them."** Assuming that Africans would be unable to win social and political justice through armed struggle, the Memorandum outlined a two-pronged strategy for the U.S.: (1) remove certain sanctions against the minority governments and integrate them more closely with the Western economies, with the intent of influencing them to *gradually* incorporate Blacks within the governing process; and (2) strengthen linkages (such as increased aid) with Black-led

---

*This is an edited version of a longer paper on underdevelopment, trilateralism, and Southern Africa (written for this volume) which is available from the author. Carolyn Brown teaches African Politics at the State University of New York at Stony Brook. She is completing a doctoral thesis in African History on labor in the Nigerian Coal Mines, at Columbia University. The author wishes to thank Alem Habtu for helpful comments on the original draft of this article.
**ed. note: The classified 1969 Memorandum outlined five policy options for Southern Africa. Option 2 warns that political violence by Blacks will only lead to chaos and increased opportunities for the communists. NSSM 39 is reprinted and analyzed in Mohamed A. El-Khawas and Barry Cohen, eds., *The Kissinger Study of Southern Africa* (Westport, CT: Lawrence Hill, 1978).

regimes in the region in order to win them over to the U.S. position and have them assist in "convincing" the liberation movements of Angola, Mozambique, Guinea-Bissau (then three Portuguese colonies), Zimbabwe (Rhodesia, a British colony until minority leader Ian Smith declared unilateral independence in 1965); Namibia (South West Africa) and Azania (South Africa), that negotiated decolonization was the most "fruitful" path.

Events in Southern Africa quickly nullified Option 2. In 1974-75 the Portuguese people overthrew the fascist Caetano regime and the Portuguese territories—the "keepers of the gate" to Southern Africa's minority white regimes—swiftly achieved independence. The U.S. found itself exposed in Angola where it had been supplying covert assistance to those weaker factions of the Angolan "nationalist" movement backed by South Africa and Zaire: Holden Roberto's FNLA and Jonas Savimbi's UNITA.* In December 1975 and January 1976 the U.S. Congress terminated all aid to the FNLA and UNITA—then fighting the MPLA postindependence government in Angola—against the wishes of Ford and Kissinger.

Events in Angola thrust African liberation into the headlines. The problem for the trilateral states was no longer one of stopping this movement for change. Rather, the task became one of *redirecting change* to permit a neocolonialist solution.

This article will review the stakes of the trilateral countries in Africa generally and South Africa in particular; analyze the international and regional role of the South African economy; discuss apartheid; and explore the current process of "reform" in South Africa by which South Africa's "enlightened" business and political leaders, transnational corporations, and trilateral states hope to splinter and overcome rising Black resistance.

The Trilateral Mineral Stake

Africa's contribution to the past and present economic development of the trilateral regions is consistently underplayed. Just as most historians (with some notable exceptions, such as Eric Williams, author of *Capitalism and Slavery*) ignore the impact of the slave trade on the industrialization of Europe and North America,

---

*See Nathaniel Davis, "The Angola Decision of 1975: A Personal Memoir," *Foreign Affairs*, 57: 1 (Fall 1978) and John Stockwell, *In Search of Enemies: A C.I.A. Story*, (New York: W.W. Norton and Company, 1978). Davis was .assistant secretary of state for African Affairs in 1975, director general of the Foreign Service 1973-75 and ambassador to Chile 1971-73. Stockwell was head of the CIA's Angola operation.

most analysts claim that recent investments and trade with Africa are an insignificant contribution to the continued wealth and development of West European and North American capital. Africa illustrates the paradox of "underdevelopment" (see Girvan): the countries rich in sought-after mineral and agricultural resources are poor in national income; the per capita incomes of most African countries are among the lowest in the world.

The trilateral states have developed a major reliance on Africa's mineral resources which partially explains their concern with political developments on the continent, especially the mineral rich areas of Central and Southern Africa. Trilateralists fear liberation movements which might cut off their supplies of these crucial minerals or, more likely, change the terms of trade making them less favorable to international capital. While the colonial economy they inherited demands continued links with South Africa and the trilateral states, the long-term goal of governments in Mozambique and Angola is to end these ties of underdevelopment.

Many people, at least since the 1973-74 energy crisis, are aware of the significance of the oil rich nations of North Africa (which most Western scholars and policy makers amputate from Africa and graft on to the Middle East), and to a lesser extent, of the oil resources of Angola, Nigeria and Gabon. Less well known by the public is that a large number of critical minerals necessary for industrial production are concentrated in Zambia, Zaire, Zimbabwe, Namibia and South Africa—chromium, manganese, cobalt and platinum are key materials in producing metal alloys such as steel—along with strategic imports like uranium.

The degree of reliance on African mineral exports varies with the import needs of the particular trilateral state. Japan, a resource-deficient industrial state which lacks historical ties with Africa, is rapidly increasing its Africa trade. Japanese exports to Africa jumped from $207 million in 1955 to $5.9 billion in 1976. African exports to Japan, mostly oil and raw materials, rose from $63 million in 1955 to $2.1 billion in 1976.[1] France, which in 1977 relied on Africa for 8 percent of its total import needs, receives 42 percent of its strategic imports from the French-speaking countries of Africa including 100 percent of its uranium and 63 percent of its cobalt. French military bases are located near the sources of these strategic imports.[2] When trilateral interests in Zaire were threatened in the Shaba crises of 1977 and 1978 France (and Belgium) intervened militarily with U.S. and West German support.* France has also

---

*Zaire is a major producer of copper, cobalt, and industrial diamonds. The March 1977 and May 1978 assaults on mineral-rich Shaba province (formerly Katanga

been deeply involved in Chad, Mauritania and the Central African Republic.*

The U.S. relies on Africa for a major percentage of most critical mineral resources: manganese ore, 41 percent; ferromanganese, 32; cobalt, 77; platinum, 33; chromite, 30; ferrochromium, 58; vanadium, 56 percent.

South Africa supplies the trilateral states with many critical industrial minerals, giving Pretoria great strength in averting economic sanctions. It produces more than half of the world's gold and platinum; holds over half the world's known reserves of platinum, vanadium, chrome and manganese ore; and is one of the top three producers of uranium, diamonds, and asbestos. In 1979, South Africa supplied the U.S. with 27 percent of its imported gold.

Evaluating the degree of trilateral dependency on African and South African minerals is above all a geo-political question. In the cases of some strategic minerals, the Soviet Union is the only major

---

province) by Katangese exiles disrupted mineral production and threatened the Mobutu regime. Under Mobutu, Zaire's foreign debt has reached enormous proportions. In 1979, Zaire fell $1 billion in arrears in repayment of its *$3 billion in foreign loans.* Throughout the Summer and Fall of 1979 private and public lenders met together to reschedule Zaire's debt and set conditions for subsequent assistance. The International Monetary Fund (IMF—see article by Phillips) negotiated a harsh stabilization plan and the trilateral states and banks forced Mobutu to accept almost total administrative control over the economy by a group of IMF advisers from the trilateral states. (Such direct financial control is reminiscent of the role played by New York City's bankers through the Emergency Financial Control Board). Dr. Erwin Blumenthal, former director of the West German Bundesbank, became principal director of Zaire's central bank, La Banque de Zaire. Foreign officials oversaw the Finance Ministry and the Belgian government stepped in to reorganize the Customs Department. IMF-decreed wage freezes, currency devaluations and other measures have had a devastating impact upon Zaire's impoverished population. The trilateral goal is to buttress the Mobutu regime while restructuring the national economy. Recent strikes and mounting political instability threaten to bring down the repressive Mobutu regime and thwart trilateral designs.[3]

*ed. note: Shortly after France helped oust the Central African Republic's self-proclaimed Emperor Bokassa (and replaced him with David Dacko), *New York Times* correspondent Flora Lewis examined France's presence in Africa: "during an impromptu television session with young West Germans in Bonn last week, Valery Giscard d'Estaing was asked whether France maintained its presence in Africa to seek economic advantage. The French president was visibly irritated. The countries where France has intervened, [sic] he said, are 'among the 24 poorest in the world—they have no natural resources, no mineral resources [sic] and live on French aid."So, he concluded, the question was 'insulting and stupid.'" A chart appears in the article showing France's extensive military presence in Africa as reported by the Institute for Strategic Studies. (Flora Lewis, "Bokassa Affair Hits Nerve in the French African Policy," *New York Times,* 7 October 1979.)

producer outside of Africa. Thus it is essential, in the minds of U.S. planners, that major African producers remain within the West's sphere of influence. South Africa ranks fourth among the world's nations in known reserves and exports of minerals necessary for industrialization. If the Soviet Union is eliminated, South Africa becomes the third-ranked supplier in the capitalist world. South Africa's importance is underscored when one considers that the world's number one mineral-rich nation, the United States, is deficient in certain key minerals such as vanadium.* South Africa exports more strategic minerals to the U.S. than any other country except Canada. South Africa itself is second only to the USSR in mineral self-sufficiency excluding oil—which shall be discussed below—and a few minor minerals.[4]

Mineral Imports From South Africa
Percentage of Total Imports as of January 1979

Mineral	U.S.	U.K.	West Germany	France	Japan
Platinum group	25	37	—	22	38
Vanadium	57	60	50	31	62
Chrome (ore)	chromite 91	30	29	17	37
Ferrochrome	35-40	15	43	20	87
Manganese (ore)	9	43	52	40	43
Ferromanganese	35-40	27	14	—	—
Antimony (ore)	44[a]	95	50	14	15
Vermiculite	na	100	14	19	100
Copper	na	4	10	1	21
Nickel	na	—	11	14	21
Asbestos	3[a]	—	—	—	35
Fluorspar	na	—	—	—	23

[a] 1973-1976 figure

Chart compiled by Carolyn Brown and Holly Sklar

Sources: "South Africa: Does the West need the minerals?" Africa Confidential 20:2 (17 January 1979), p 6 and Sandy Feustel, "African Minerals and American Foreign Policy," Africa Report 23:5 (September-October 1978), p. 17.

*ed. note: Uranium is another mineral of which the U.S. has huge reserves—much of it on Indian lands as Michael Garitty points out in Part IV of this volume—but not enough to meet the needs of U.S. industry and the military. The largest uranium mine in the world is at Rossing, Namibia, now under South African control. The Rossing pits lie just outside of Walvis Bay, Namibia's only deep water port and a potential source of oil (from its continental ridge). South Africa does not want to give up formal control over Walvis Bay in the settlement for an independent Namibia. See "Twilight on the Namib Desert," Africa 85 (September 1978), p. 16.

South Africa: The Exceptional African State

Trilateral policy toward South Africa reflects the pivotal economic, strategic, and political role which South Africa enjoys in southern and east-central Africa; a role which multinational corporations continue to nurture with tacit approval by their home governments. Whereas most foreign investment on the continent is in mineral and resource extraction, first-stage manufacturing, or the import of semi-processed goods for last-stage assembly; in South Africa, massive infusions of foreign capital (begun in the late 19th century with the gold rush) have built a highly integrated economy composed of capital goods manufacture, and chemical, metal, and petroleum processing.

Long-time cooperation by multinational corporations in building a strong industrial base has helped cushion South Africa against potential international economic sanctions to condemn apartheid. Moreoever, diversified industry has enabled South Africa to expand its markets in African states whose economies have been tied to South Africa since colonial times. This dependent relationship is expressed in the uneven trade balance between South Africa and Black Africa which South African propaganda uses to discredit the political condemnation of South Africa by these same countries. Pretoria particularly emphasizes its linkages to (penetration of) the Mozambican economy, linkages rooted in Mozambique's colonial legacy of technological dependence on South Africa and participation in the migratory labor system supplying South African mines. In short, multinationals have assisted South Africa in producing its own center-periphery system in Southern Africa, a structure which the trilateral states hope will be decisive in moderating the region's continuing political struggles.

South Africa has the distinction of being Africa's only "developed industrial" state. Yet, unlike the "developed" trilateral states, the majority of its population is incapable of forming a strong internal market because their wages are held so miserably low. While the small internal market of highly paid white South Africans was sufficient to support the initial industrialization thrust in the post-World War II period, by the 1970s this market was saturated and South Africa had to look toward external markets in Africa, the West, and industrializing Third World countries like Taiwan, Mexico, and South Korea. The recession of 1973-75 hurt South Africa's external market in developed states, however, and Pretoria's economic planners focused their attention on Black Africa against which it has a great competitive advantage.

Black workers pay the price of white South Africa's economic development, as will be seen below. But apartheid has many contradictions. The South African economy began to feel the impact of the recession in late 1975. The decline in the economy's growth rate to under 2.5 percent threatened to pose serious political problems; a 5 percent rate of growth was seen as necessary to absorb Black youths entering the labor force and accommodate rising military expenditures.[5] Oil prices increased just as South Africa, in anticipation of an oil blockade, began to stockpile petroleum. In 1976 the price of gold fell 100 percent, from $200 per ounce in 1974 to $100; foreign exchange reserves plummeted. The collapse of the Portuguese empire in 1974-75 exposed South Africa's flanks to hostile liberation movements in Angola and Mozambique and guerilla war in Namibia and Zimbabwe escalated, prompting Pretoria to raise military expenditures. Mounting imports, needed to complete the industrialization drive, increased in cost while South Africa's markets in Western Europe, Japan, and the U.S. contracted because of the recession.[6] The economy, which in the 1960s and early 1970s had grown at a rate of 5.7 percent was stalled in 1977 (with a zero rate of growth in Gross Domestic Product).

Contradictions generated by the oppression of Black labor deepened. South Africa experienced shortages of skilled labor—a logical consequence of job reservation and the exclusion of Black workers from the skilled labor job categories.* This shortage was especially marked in the mining industry, which demands a core of highly skilled technicians to supervise a large semi-skilled and unskilled Black labor force. The shortage was heightened in 1975 when migrant labor was cut back from Angola and Mozambique, causing a shortage of unskilled labor as well. In 1977 South African recruitment efforts in Western Europe, the U.S. and Australia—historical sources of skilled labor—failed to attract sufficient miners to fill the skilled positions. Meanwhile 1977-78 immigration trends indicated that for the first time in 18 years *emigration* of skilled workers from South Africa exceeded immigration.**

Apartheid has been challenged politically as well as economically.The 1976 uprising in Soweto (a Black township of one million) spread to other townships and demonstrated the explosive anger of the Black community. Under severe repression the liberation struggle

---

*In 1924 white miners went on strike in the Rand protesting the substitution of more expensive white labor by cheaper Black labor. As a part of the settlement the South African government passed a law reserving many job categories for white workers only.

**More whites left South Africa in the first seven months of 1978 than in the entire year of 1977. (*Financial Mail,* 10 August 1979, pp. 538-539.)

has shifted from a non-violent movement toward expanding guerilla activity, in urban centers as well as rural areas. That foreign investors distrust Pretoria's capacity to contain the liberation struggle is evident in the sudden—albeit temporary—drop in investment and loans following the Soweto uprising. Trilateral business and political leaders increased pressure on Pretoria to modify the more glaring aspects of apartheid. Internationally, antiapartheid forces used official forums such as the U.N. and the International Labor Organization to voice their condemnation of the regime.

These economic and political strains provided the impetus to "modernize" the mechanisms of control over the Black population. The need for reform of apartheid was especially clear to the mining interests and the multinationals engaged in processing and manufacturing. The problem for the state is: how to achieve economic reforms without disrupting white minority rule through the full admission of Black political participation. The government's attempted balancing act has generated a political storm over the direction of the state and economy.

Before reviewing recent political developments in South Africa we must analyze further the South African economy and its role as an outpost of transnational capitalism in Africa. Six aspects of the political economy of South Africa will be explored: the critical role of the mining sector, especially gold; the role of the state in promoting the interest of South African based capital; the role of transnational capital in developing the diversified manufacturing sector; the military-industrial complex; the super-exploitation of Black labor; and the *Bantusans*, the officially designated "tribal homelands" of the Black majority.

Mining and Gold

Ever since the late-nineteenth century, when gold and diamonds were discovered on the Witswatersrand and in Kimberley, the mining sector has been key to the profits which have provided the financial base for economic diversification and industrialization. The mining companies encouraged legislation which robbed the African peasantry of its land, making it an impoverished working class.[7] Under the Native Land Act of 1913, 80 percent of the land was seized by the mining companies and white farmers. With the coming to power of the Afrikaner Nationalist party in 1948, racism became engrained in the South African political, social and economic fabric through the policy of apartheid.*

---

*Apartheid's ideological basis is the claim that South Africa's cultural and racial heterogeneity will never permit a truly *multiracial* state; but that each ethnic group, if

South Africa's gold is not conducive to mechanization, but depends upon super-exploited Black labor for its extraction (miners often have to scrape ore with their hands from veins with threads one inch thick.)[8] Uranium, 99 percent of which is found in the gold mines, is exploited mainly as a by-product; but is of major political-strategic importance to South Africa both as a source of nuclear power and as a critical export. Price hikes in 1978 and 1979 increased the export earnings of gold, platinum and iron. In 1978 gold contributed 56 percent of the country's total mineral export earnings.[9] Gold topped $500 per ounce in 1979 and shot up to over $800 per ounce in January 1980.

Gold is an invaluable asset to the economy. As the director of Consolidated Gold Fields explains:

> The possession of an export article..with the attributes of gold, which all the world wants, is a great advantage to a young country. Gold as a final means of settling international indebtedness can enter through doors which import controls close to other commodities. And hence, from the establishment of the Union, South Africa could pay, without undue difficulty, for the capital goods it urgently needed to expand its total productivity.[10]

Skyrocketing gold prices came at an opportune time. South Africa was again confronted with rising oil prices after the revolutionary government of Iran cut off trade; formerly Iran supplied 90 percent of the country's oil (the Shah had never participated in the Arab League boycott of South Africa called in retaliation for supplying arms to Israel during the 1973 Arab-Israeli war).

The mining sector is highly monopolized. Seven large interlocking mining/finance houses dominate the production of minerals in South Africa and dependent Namibia. An examination of one of the seven, Anglo-American Corporation—which mines gold, diamonds, coal, copper, platinum and other minerals and has substantial industrial investments—reveals the extent of their international linkages. Charter Consolidated, Anglo's main international arm, owns the Malaysia Tin Mining Corporation, tin and wolfram mines in Europe, and has diversified investments throughout Australia, North America, continental Europe, and Africa. Only 34.4 percent of its 1979 profits were earned in South Africa.*

Anglo-American is linked with United States capital through

given its own territory and "nation," can participate in a 'multinational' South African society.
*Charter has interest in several South African companies: Selection Trust (25.8 percent), Minoroco (20 percent), Anamint (20 percent) and Amcan (24.8 percent). See Financial Mail 27 July 1979, p. 37.

Englehard Minerals and Chemicals Corporation, the world's largest refiner and fabricator of precious metals. (Anglo-American owns 32 percent of Englehard's common stock and 20 percent of the preferred stock.) The late Charles Englehard, company founder, was instrumental in promoting U.S. investments and loans to South Africa before and after the Sharpeville massacre in 1961 through his new African-South African Investment Corporation. He had close ties with both the Kennedy and Johnson Administrations.[11]

Foreign investment in the mining sector has *not* slackened in response to events like Soweto. On the contrary, foreign investors remain attracted to mining because of a high rate of profit made possible by the low costs of a large nonunionized and mostly migrant labor force, a well developed transport system, and cheap electric power (generated by price-controlled coal and government incentives.)[12] A major portion of an anticipated 20 percent increase in U.S. capital expenditures in South Africa—$277 million in 1979, as compared to $230 million in 1978—was slated for the mining sector, much of it thought to be in uranium.[13]

Private South African capital, the South African state (through state corporations called parastatals) and the transnational corporation comprise the triumvirate which dominated the South African economy. In most cases, foreign-based multinationals participate in joint ownership of the mines with South African giants. But foreign firms are often responsible for providing *all* management services. For instance, 39 percent of Palabora Mining Company is owned by the British firm Rio Tinto Zinc Corporation. Rio Tinto Zinc manages Palabora and the Namibian Rossing mine.**[14]

Since the nineteenth century Britain has provided the vast majority of South Africa's foreign investment but U.S. and non-British European companies have been investing heavily. Since 1974 the Japanese have been restricted by Japanese law from any direct investment in South Africa. Nonetheless, they participate in the mining sector through long-term sales contracts and by arranging financing in international markets.* This link is crucial for mineral-deficient Japan, the trilateral state most dependent on South African mineral exports.

*The Japanese steel industry—led by Mitsubishi whose president is on the Trilateral Commission; Nippon Steel, the world's largest steel producer; and Kawasaki Heavy Industries—is heavily involved with the South African steel and iron parastatal ISCOR. Under an agreement with ISCOR, Japan is to receive two-thirds of South Africa's 15 million tons of iron ore. In return Japan has supplied financing, technicians, plant and equipment and agreed to participate in five major development projects designed by the South African government: Sishen-Saldanha Bay Development project (iron ore), St. Croiz Island Facility Expansion Plan (manganese
**ed. note: Rio Tinto is heavily represented on the Trilateral Commission.

Manufacturing

Foreign direct investment outside the mining sector has increased in response to government incentives and rising production costs in the foreign investors' home countries. In manufacturing, trilateral states concentrate their interests in different sectors. British investment is found in a broad spectrum of sectors ranging from motor vehicles to chemicals to metals to computers. However, its top share in direct investments has been declining relative to those of U.S. and West German transnationals.[15] British investments are generally interlocked with parastatals and private corporations such as Anglo-American and Lonrho, the London-Rhodesian company which is the largest industrial-financial holding company in South Africa. Imperial Chemicals, the giant chemical firm, has 42 percent equity in South Africa's African Explosives and Chemical Industry, AECI, the second largest commercial explosives company in the world. South Africa is Imperial's second largest market after the U.S.[16]

U.S. manufacturing investments are more often directly held with 100 percent equity: "Four out of five dollars (80 percent) invested in manufacturing and nine out of ten dollars (90 percent) invested in trade are directly held."[17] U.S. investment is expanding most rapidly in high technology industries such as uranium processing, computers, and chemicals. Almost 98 percent of the total U.S. investment in machinery manufacturing in Africa is in South Africa.[18] U.S. and British computer firms like IBM, ICI, Burroughs, Control Data, and Sperry-Rand hold much of the computer market in South Africa.[19]

Computers are essential for the modernization of South Africa's internal repressive apparatus and its military establishment. They are used in missile and weapons deployment, nuclear weapons production, control and tracking of satellites, aircraft navigation, communications, surveillance, and other forms of counterintelligence. Several computers are in use at the Departments of Justice, Prisons, Interior and Labor.[20] The business community uses computers in banking and finance, as well as in manufacturing and mining. Computers help compensate for the shortage of skilled labor and avoid upgrading Blacks.[21]

---

ore), Richards Bay Expansion including a new railway link from Witbank (coal), ISCOR's Expansion Plan Corange River Project (electricity). See Yoko Kitazawa, "From Tokyo to Johannesburg," Programme to Combat Racism of the World Council of Churches and Interfaith Center for Corporate Responsibility. (1 February 1975) p. 5. Also, U.N. Commission on Transnational Corporations Activities of Transnational Corporations in the Industrial Mining and Military Sectors of Southern Africa (22 March 1979).

Although Japanese government policy has prohibited direct investment in South Africa, since 1974 Japan has continued—and deepened—its trade and technical assistance with South Africa. South Africa today is Japan's number one African trading partner. Long-term purchasing agreements, Japanese assistance in arranging export and import credits, licensing and supply of technology for South African development projects—all permitted by Japanese law—characterize Japan's relationship with South Africa.[22] Japan's thirst for South African minerals is seen in the increase of South African exports to Japan from R181 million in 1970 to R762 million in 1978, a nearly 400 percent increase.* In the same period, Japanese exports to South Africa jumped from R221 million in 1970 to R824 million in 1978.[23] Moreover, Japanese businesses have increased their investments in South Africa's nominally independent "tribal homelands," a practice that has not attracted much attention from anti-apartheid forces in Africa and Western countries.[24] In short, Japanese law is characterized more by what it allows, than what it prohibits.

West German investors, ranked third after the United Kingdom and the U.S., are especially attracted to South Africa. West German labor and freight costs are among the highest in Europe, and West Germany sees its South African subsidiaries as a means for developing an export base throughout the southern hemisphere, including Latin America:

> The managing director of Deutz...explained that rising labour and freight costs in the Federal Republic of Germany had led the parent company to decide to concentrate manufacture of components at whichever of their several plants around the world had the lowest costs and export the parts to sister plants and assembly centres elsewhere. He made it clear that the relatively cheap labour and material costs in South Africa were "an advantage" in this new approach by his company.[25]

Today Volkswagen cars assembled in South Africa are reexported to other African nations. U.S. firms, like General Motors and Ford also envision South Africa as an important export base.

Multinational corporations assist South Africa by transferring technology. The importance of technology transfers is evident in the fact that over 40 percent of South Africa's Gross National Product expansion from 1957 to 1972 was related to "product innovation and introduction of technological knowhow."[26] Foreign investments in

*In 1978, for example, Japan bought 45 percent of South Africa's platinum output and 30 percent of South Africa's coal exports. (Nigel Bance, "Can South Africa Bring Back Foreign Capital?" *Euromoney Supplement* (June 1979), pp. 7, 11.

high technology industries help decrease the economy's dependence on Black labor and fit neatly into the government's "separate development" policy which advocates the relocation of excess laborers to the "homelands"—"removing the unemployment problem"—while retaining a higher skilled labor force in the "white" territories.

But before reviewing South Africa's "tribal homelands" or Bantustan policy we must first discuss the role of government intervention in the economy, especially the role of the parastatals.

Role of the South African State in the Economy

The South African government follows a policy of frequent and direct intervention in the economy, seeking to transform the mining and agriculturally-based economy into a diversified industrial economy that can resist international economic pressures. The establishment of state-owned corporations known as parastatals is a cornerstone of this policy. According to Jennifer Davis, an exiled South African economist, parastatals are designed to (1) establish large enterprises which, because of the amounts of capital required and the low yields generated, are unattractive to private investors; (2) give the government control over the exploitation of natural resources which, it is feared, private enterprise may deplete; and (3) meet the military or strategic requirements of the state.[27]

Parastatals are found in all areas of the economy: electrical and nuclear power generation, EXCOM; shipping, SAFMARINE; oil refineries, NATREF; uranium enrichment, UCOR; steel and iron production, ISCOR; oil, coal and gas production and distribution, SASOL; chemicals production, SENTRACHEM; armaments production, ARMSCOR.

During the recession the government used parastatals to borrow in international financial markets.[28] Parastatals provide energy (electricity), transport and vital military armaments at reduced prices and thus subsidize foreign-based and domestic capital.* Pretoria is encouraging foreign investment in certain parastatals. Many transnational corporations, for instance, are participating in the massive $7 billion dollar SASOL III (SASOL II extension) coal-to-oil conversion plant.**

---

*South Africa pays the price for subsidized industrialization and a "laagered" economy. The present financial problems of the steel parastatal, ISCOR, are illustrative. In June 1978 ISCOR showed an unprecedented loss of R73.3 million which it felt was caused by both "social-political manufacturing and the repayment of loans. The government has therefore begun to divest itself of certain subsidiaries and begun to sell them to private investors." *Financial Mail* (6 July 1979) p. 22.

**This plant provides South Africa with a means of alleviating its dependence on

A second means of government intervention in the South African economy is legislation which dictates stringent terms for foreign involvement compared with other non-trilateral countries, again demonstrating the exceptional nature of South Africa's economy. Profits made by foreign companies may be repatriated to the home country; capital may not. One-third of all insurance and pension funds must be invested in government bonds, bonds which are used to finance the huge defense expenditures. Banks are likewise obligated to purchase these bonds with a certain percentage of their profits. The law also requires South African participation in transnational subsidiaries.[29]

In strategic industries like munitions, motor vehicles, electronnics, oil and nuclear energy, government efforts to lessen dependence on foreign investment has met with varying degrees of success (e.g. the largest auto supplier, Sigma, is 75 percent owned by Anglo-American). The electronics industry, crucial for weapons production and modernization of technology throughout the economy, remains dependent on foreign inputs. This is one of the bottlenecks in the armament industry's drive to be self-reliant which the government is attempting to overcome. ARMSCOR, now the largest armament industry in the southern hemisphere, has gone heavily into debt to expand the domestic arms industry in the wake of the international arms embargo.* ARMSCOR has made progress in transplanting arms technology from the trilateral states but it is still criticized inside South Africa for being too reliant on foreign suppliers (in 1979, 62 percent of ARMSCOR's military hardware was purchased from South African suppliers[30]).

Oil, not armaments, may be the Achilles heel of the South African economy. Although petroleum represents only 20 to 25 percent of South Africa's overall energy needs, it is crucial to certain sectors of the economy such as transport. Agriculture, which is

---

imports of oil and the expensive spot market. The Fluor Corporation, a California-based engineering firm, is the major contractor. The U.S., is looking to South Africa for technical assistance in their own development of similar plants. The synfuel technology was originally developed in Hitler's Germany, an interesting coincidence given South Africa's pro-Nazi sympathies during the war. (See Fluor; Building Energy Self-Sufficiency in South Africa, Southern Africa Perpectives No. 5 (1979); John Burns, "S.A. Plunged Into Oil Crisis, Seeks Ways to Cope," New York Times (13 August 1979); "South Africa to 'Mine' More Oil," New York Times (8 March 1979).

* ed. note: On embargo violations see Western Massachusetts Association of Concerned African Scholars, ed., U.S. Military Involvement in Southern Africa (Boston: South End Press 1978), Part III. Also see "More Arms Smuggling to South Africa Exposed," Southern Africa, January 1979 and reports in the Vermont Rutland Herald on the U.S.-Canadian munitions company Space Research Corporation.

becoming more mechanized, will be increasingly dependent on oil. The oil industry is controlled by five transnational corporations: Royal/Dutch Shell, British Petroleum (part-owned by the British government), Caltex, Mobil and Total. They control 85 percent of the import, refining, marketing and distribution of petrol and petroleum products and 91 percent of the service stations. Four major refineries (three run by transnationals and one by NATREF) produce 95 percent of South Africa's oil and 100 percent of the oil of South African dependents Namibia, Lesotho, Botswana and Swazi.[31]

The government has adopted five major policies to reduce oil dependency:(1) promotion of SASOL II and III coal-to-oil conversion plants;(2) encouraging conservation and a shift to alternative energy sources, namely coal and nuclear energy;(3) stockpiling of oil reserves (much more difficult and costly with the cut off of Iranian oil);(4) acceleration of nuclear power development; and (5) legislation forcing oil companies to comply with government directives to supply oil in case of war or other national emergencies.

Nuclear energy is highly dependent on foreign technology. West German and U.S. firms have played a key role in transfering technology used in uranium enrichment. Early in the 1960s the first nuclear research reactor was built by a U.S. company and until 1976 the U.S. supplied South Africa with enriched uranium. Since 1978 an experimental plant at Valindaba has been in operation with the assistance of German firms.[32] The role of U.S.-based transnationals in the South African nuclear industry makes a mockery of Washington's public concern about South Africa's alleged explosion of a nuclear device in October 1979.*

Bantustan Policy

The foundation of South Africa's industrial miracle is the sophisticated process for controlling a super-exploited Black labor force, much of it migrant labor created by apartheid's policy of "separate development." The apartheid policies of the present Nationalist Party government are the culmination of centuries of disenfrancisement, repression, and exploitation of the indigenous African population. In South Africa, in contrast to other African

---

*The New York Times, (26 October 1979) reported that satellite sensors had detected a "low-yield nuclear explosion" on September 22 in the Indian and South Atlantic Ocean near South Africa. South Africa denied exploding a nuclear device and suggested that the explosion resulted from an accident on a Soviet nuclear submarine, an idea the White House quickly rejected, according to the New York Times 28 October 1979.

nations, there is virtually no subsistence agricultural sector. The Pass Laws and other so-called Influx Control Legislation, which carefully regulate the mobility and employment of all Blacks have given South African capitalists an unusual capacity to shift labor resources as needed.

But at the same time, large scale production is promoting the homogenization and unification of the work force. Recognizing this inherent political danger the state is promoting the retribalization of the African working class, in large part through the revival of archaic social divisions or the *invention* of artificial ones.* South Africa's "Grand Apartheid," the Bantustan system, is one means by which the white minority hopes to solidify and extend artificial cleavages and thus continue to "divide and rule" the Black majority.

Under the banner of "separate development" the government has appropriated 86.3 percent of the land, encompassing the richest agricultural and mineral areas, for the nearly million whites who constitute 18 percent of the population.**The fifteen million Blacks were left 13.7 percent of the land, recently divided into nine "homelands" made up of widely scattered parcels of land. KwaZulu, the Zulu "tribal homeland," is made up of some 188 parcels of land totalling just over 2.2 million hectares, (1 hectare equals 2.471 acres) separated by several miles of white territory. The Bantustan system is not even consistent with the government's own fabricated ethnic divisions: the Xhosa group has two homelands, Transkei and Ciskei, while the Pedi and Northern Ndebele share a single one. In short, the Bantustans reflect "the European" view of African traditional culture rather than the reality.***33 (Afrikaner scholars also argue that their ancestors settled South Africa before the Blacks got there!)

Over time each tribal homeland is to be granted "independence" by the South African state. At the time of "independence" all the "citizens" of a homeland then residing in white areas will get full civil rights in the homeland and become "aliens" in white South Africa. Since the 1970 Bantu Homelands Citizen Act (No. 26) Blacks have

---

*Prior to the colonization of "South Africa" the African peoples of the region had consolidated into multi-ethnic political units led by such leaders as Tshaka, and Mosheshe. See, for example, Walter Rodney, *How Europe Underdeveloped Africa* (London: Bogle-L'ouverture Publications, 1972).
**The Native land Act, No. 27 of 1913 and Native Trust and Land Act, No. 18 of 1936.
***Nearly all of the supposed "tribal groups" are related, with similar lifestyles and a common history, and many anthropologists divide them into two basic linguistic groups, the Nguni and Sotho speakers. Nguni and Sotho are two closely related Bantu languages.

had no political and civil rights; any such rights are available only in their "independent homelands." In 1976 the Transkei became the first homeland to be granted its pseudo-independence; no countries have recognized it.*

The Bantustans are located in splintered, resource-deficient areas, which are virtually incapable of being either agriculturally self-sufficient or otherwise viable economically. Bantustan residents must try to find employment in South Africa's urban centers, the border industries located in white areas adjacent to the Bantustans, or in so-called "growth points" for future industry within the Bantustans. The government's much-touted policy of decentralizing industry into the Bantustan areas is a fraud. The Bantustans lack sufficient infra-structure to support industrialization (water, energy, transport, and communications networks) and have inaccessible or unpredictable supplies of raw materials. The real aim of the decentralization policy is to speed the removal of Blacks from the urban industrial areas (Western Cape, Port Elizabeth-Uitenhage, Durban-Pinetown, and the Southern Transvaal).

Bantustan population statistics are divided officially into two major categories: *de facto* and *de jure*. *De facto* population is the number of inhabitants actually residing in the homeland. *De jure* includes the number of Africans living in designated white regions or other Bantustans. According to studies by the South African Institute of Race Relations, none of the Bantustans has more than 67 percent of its *de jure* population.[34] In six of the nine homelands less than half the "tribal" population lives in the Bantustan. The average annual income of the Bantustans is among the lowest in Africa: in 1974 on the four largest Bantustans it was $97 per year, in comparison with $180 in Nigeria, $510 in Zambia, and $120 in Tanzania.[35] The infant mortality rate is high, approaching 50 percent on many Bantustans. As more Blacks are relocated, conditions will deteriorate further.**

---

*South Africa is so intent on making this "independence" appear real that it launched a massive publicity campaign. A Madison Avenue advertising firm, Sydney S. Baron was contracted for the publicity which included a "Spirit of '76" ad in the *New York Times*. Andrew Hatcher, the Black former public relations expert of President Kennedy assisted with the account. Anthony Sampson, "Pretoria's Scandal," *Newsweek,* 2 April 1979.

**Let's look at this situation more closely. In 1954 the Tomlinson Commission produced the major Bantustan study and found that 30 percent of all Bantustan land was badly eroded and 44 percent moderately eroded. Population density was higher than most African countries, ranging from 61 per square mile in Bophuta Tswana to 173 in Kwazulu.[36] In the ten year period from 1960 to 1970 forced-removal policies and resettlement schemes increased the total population from 4 to 6.9 million,[37] making the food burden on the Bantustans even more unbearable

Africans have been brutally colonized and made foreigners in their own country. The Bantustans were never meant to have economic or political autonomy, but to operate as satellites of the pivotal South African economy. Their inhabitants are to form a migrant labor force—moving to the "foreign land" of South Africa to work in the mines and industries for a specified period, living in barracks without family members who must remain in the Bantustan, stripped of political and civil rights. South Africa is fond of comparing this arrangement with the condition of migratory workers (from Southern European countries like Italy, or from the Caribbean, Asia, and North Africa) in countries like West Germany, Britain and Switzerland, or with that of so-called "illegal aliens" or undocumented workers in the United States. But a more accurate comparison would be with Native Americans and the reservation system.

The South African Reform Process

Many critics of apartheid have been caught off balance by the South African government's recent reform program. I shall argue that these reforms primarily serve the expansion of transnational enterprise and South African capital. The reforms create a "new" image for South Africa while actually strengthening the system of political repression and economic exploitation.

In the struggle against Portuguese colonialism a new element emerged in Africa's anti-colonial tradition. Peasants, workers, and other progressive sectors of the society not only contested the repressive colonial structure but went beyond to express strongly antiimperialist and anticapitalist sentiments. Legislation (the 1924 Industrial Concilliation Act and the 1953 Bantu Labour Settlements Act No. 48) denying registration and bargaining rights to Black unions and prohibiting strikes by Blacks failed to stop a wave of strikes which culminated in 1973 with over 361 instances of strikes and work stoppages involving 90,000 workers.[38]

In June 1976 it took several days to suppress the Soweto uprising and over 600 people—many of them children who had demonstrated first against a government decree to enforce Afrikaans as the teaching language—were killed. Soweto threatened South Africa's image of stability and control over the oppressed Black masses and galvanized the Black liberation struggle.

More recently, despite the extensive use of the Internal Security Act provisions banning Black trade union organizing, Black and multiracial unions have experienced a resurgence. In the spring of 1979 a multiracial independent trade union federation, FORSATU (Federation of South African Trade Unions), representing an estimated

30,700 members,[39] began to draw membership from the fraudulent "parallel unions."* In October 1979 the Consultative Committee of Black Trade Unions (CCBTU), representing 10,000 members, announced it would form SABLATU, the Association of South African Black Trade Unions. Black workers asserted their freedom to affiliate with nonrecognized unions. FORSATU also asserted its right to affiliate with political parties despite a clear government policy forbidding such activity. Denial of the right to strike, refusal to recognize Black unions, and the use of repressive legislation to crush the Black trade union movement have been condemned by the progressive sectors of the international trade union movement through words and action.**

The futility of jeopardizing the whole future of South Africa's capitalist economy by staunchly defending what are seen as outmoded aspects of apartheid has long been recognized by certain sectors of the South African business community. This "enlightened" business position championed by Harry Oppenheimer, chairman of the Anglo-American company, has been strengthened by the specter of another massive uprising like Soweto, the collapse of the Portuguese empire, the international antiapartheid movement and the failure of the grand attempts to clandestinely influence international public opinion.

The "Muldergate" Information scandal revealed a secret government slush fund which, among other things was used to help defeat leading U.S. congressional critics like Senator Dick Clark (D-Iowa) in 1978; influence the ICFTU to call off a threatened shipping strike against unloading South African goods; play "dirty tricks" to harass the British antiapartheid movement; and back John McGoff, conservative U.S. businessman and long-time lobbyist for South Africa, in an unsuccessful attempt to buy several major U.S. and UK newspapers.[40] The totality of the scandal may never be known, but it revealed the importance South Africa places on an improved

---

*Parallel unions, sponsored by the white Trade Union Council of South Africa, were set up following the 1973 strikes by whites for coloreds in the same sector of industry. They are usually paper organizations, with no full time officers to handle complaints and are often staffed by white or colored unionists. See *Africa Confidential,* 20: 10, 9 May 1979.

**For example, in 1978 British Leyland's Rover Confederated Shop Stewards Committee called for an action against South African goods, citing the 1976 loss of some 50,000 jobs and the possible loss of an additional 30,000 while Leyland expanded its investments in South Africa. They demanded recognition of the Black union MAWU (Metal and Allied Workers Union), an end to British investment in South Africa and a halt to Leyland-South Africa's supplying of spare parts to the British parent company. *Africa Confidential* (17 February 1978).

international image. Long-time Prime Minister Vorster and Minister
of Information Connie Mulder were forced to resign in disgrace,
clearing the way for reform-minded Pieter Botha, now prime
minister, and Pieter G. Koornhof, minister of cooperation and
development (formerly called minister of Bantu affairs), to assume
leadership in the ruling Nationalist Party.

The pillars of Pretoria's reform program are two commission
studies, each initiated in June 1977. The two commissions—
Wiehahn, on industrial relations, and Riekert, on "petty" apartheid
and influx control—are attempts to adjust the mechanisms of white
domination over the Black population and to permit continued
super-exploitation of Black labor.

The prestigious Johannesburg *Financial Mail*—voice of the
"liberal" business community—commented on 18 May 1979:

> The government has thus finally acceded to demands from the
> business sector to build up and stabilize a labour aristocracy and a
> black middle-class in the major urban areas.

Since the process is unfolding at the time of this writing it is not clear
what the total legislative package implementing these proposals will
look like. But we can look more closely at the reports themselves.

The first of six sections of the *Wiehahn Commission Report* was
made public in early May 1979. Wiehahn recommended registration
of Black trade unions including migrant workers, but excluding
agricultural and domestic workers (sectors where 80 percent of the
work force is Black). The criteria for registration, and its revocation,
are left to the discretion of the Minister of Labour. Once registered,
Black unions would be subjected to the same restrictions placed on
"colored" and white unions: auditing of finances; scrutiny of membership lists; control over constitution and membership; no affiliation
with political parties.[41] The report calls for protection of the rights of
minority groups (white workers) through tough unfair dismissal
laws, training and re-training, relocation allowances for transferred
workers, development of "fair employment practices." White workers will have a veto over Black apprenticeship in skilled labor
positions and on industrial councils and plant floor workers-
employers advisory groups.

These provisions and others would have the effect of: splitting
the Black workers' movement into a group of workers who are
eligible for unionization rights and those who are not; arresting the
momentum of the multiracial independent trade union movement
and the Black trade union movement; isolating the unions from the
political influence of South African liberation movements; controlling the mobilization of the Black working class by making the

surveillance of all aspects of trade union activity a requirement for registration and legitimization; scoring a bargaining point with international critics campaigning for divestment and in support of trade union rights.

The second pillar of the reforms, the *Riekert Commission Report*, proposes revisions in the influx control laws which restrict the presence of Blacks in designated white urban areas and industrial centers, recommends wider opportunities for Black commercial groups, and advocates greater Black involvement in government administration boards.[42] Simultaneously, however, Riekert calls for an increase in removals of "unlawfully resident" urban Blacks and their relocation to the Bantustans.

Riekert recommends that no Black remain in urban areas without a job and approved housing* and advocates tougher penalties for employers hiring an illegal urban Black. This process has already been implemented. Pieter Koornhof increased the employer fine from R100 to R500 per illegal employee. Employers immediately laid off thousands of workers as increased police raids in search of illegals accelerated and "repatriation" of Blacks to the poverty-stricken Bantustans was speeded up.[43]

Individual farmers and employers would no longer conduct their own recruitment of Black labor but go through government labor bureaus, which would absorb the unemployed "legal" Black urban residents before seeking outside labor. Riekert wants Black businesses to be allowed in some areas for multi-racial entrepreneurs and raised the possibility of limited access to white areas. Black community councils would have the "right," prohibited by previous apartheid legislation, to admit white businesses in Black townships. Blacks would be permitted to participate in regional administrative boards which develop plans for township development and, with the Economic Development Corporation, encourage light service industries and trade in Black areas. But this new independence carries new responsibilities and added burdens. Employer contributions which subsidized the paltry services in Black areas will be phased out, with their costs to be born by Black township communities themselves.

Riekert and Wiehahn seem to advocate the creation of a so-called "middle-strata" in the Black community, the rationale being that given a stake in the apartheid system this Black elite would then defend the status quo against challenges from the larger Black

---

*"Approved housing" will be difficult to find, given a 141,000 unit Black shortage since December 1977 and an anticipated shortfall of 132,000 in 1981. (*Financial Mail* 11 May 1979.)

population. Another rationale for the reforms is that they will permit expansion of the internal market.* In reality, however, the number of Blacks who will benefit economically from the reforms is so small that the effect on the internal market would be negligible. Further, even those few Blacks who are the reforms' beneficiaries will not be permited *political* participation in the South African state.

It appears then that the primary purpose of the reforms is to create an illusion that apartheid is being dismantled while in actuality the system is being strengthened. An improved *international* image would smooth the way for expansion of South Africa's *export* market in Black Africa. At the same time it is hoped that a co-opted Black elite of professionals, managers, and skilled workers will serve as a safety valve for the pressure which has been building rapidly since the Soweto uprisings.**

Transnational corporations, aware that some trade union activity can assist capital, have promoted legitimation of Black trade unions. But this does not mean they will permit a meaningful trade union movement to develop. Transnationals and the South African state are attempting to co-opt trade union activity and divorce it from political struggle. Wiehahn- and Riekert-type reforms are weapons to split the Black community, but in so doing they intensify existing contradictions. South Africa is aware of the security consequences of the transference of large numbers of "illegal urbans" to the Bantustans. While mass removals will relocate the political problem posed by a mobilized Black working class to the tribal territories, it is precisely in the rural areas where the ANC (African National Congress) and PAC (Pan Africanist Congress), the banned liberation movements, are most active. The *Financial Mail* asks bluntly:

> Can the grand new strategy work? Perhaps in the short term, government will succeed in co-opting a significant number of

---

*To illustrate: some South African businessmen are supporting a scheme to electrify Soweto, a Black community of one million with no electricity and running water, with the hope of marketing electrical appliances there. (See *Financial Mail* 20 July 1979).

**Harry Oppenheimer, in his 1979 Chairman's Address, suggested a scheme to expand the Black middle class: "One of the programmes being undertaken is a scheme, ambitious in concept and likely to be difficult of execution, to recruit, educate, train and develop high-quality black matriculants who will form a pool of potential managers in the financial and engineering fields which are at the heart of our business. Known as the undergraduate cadet scheme, it has been made possible by the cooperation of the University of Witwatersrand...it will cost rather more than R3 million over the next five years. We look upon this as an investment in the widest sense, for once the scheme has proved itself it will be made available to other employers and educational institutions in the country."

> urban blacks—not to active support of apartheid, but at least in the sense of *neutralizing (with the aid of Jimmy Kruger's security police)* any futher trouble in the townships. [Italics ed.]

Seeming to predict the long-term consequences of the new policies, it continues:

> Huge pools of unemployed, resentful people in the Bantustans, *who are themselves now formally excluded from the new system, are likely to be fertile recruiting grounds for insurgents.* It is easy to skip across the borders into Mozambique, Swaziland, or Botswana, and thence into training camps elsewhere in Africa or in communist countries. Indeed, this has already been happening, as the spate of Terrorism Act trials over the past few years testifies. Perhaps insurgency will remain limited until the situations in Rhodesia and South-West Africa have been resolved. But gradual escalation of such activity (backed by the communist countries), rather than urban revolution, seems the most likely long-term scenario.[44] [Italics ed.]

Nonetheless, the reforms are a last opportunity for South Africa and its trilateral allies to preserve a system of labor exploitation that is extremely profitable to capital. Trilateral states are hoping that these modifications diffuse international criticism of transnational investors and permit a "moderate alternative" to the militancy of the South African liberation movement to develop. They are willing to go farther than the South African state, in winning over potential allies through even more far reaching reforms in apartheid. South Africa hopes that the reforms will stimulate further economic growth and help break down South Africa's political and ideological isolation from its Black African neighbors, permitting deepening penetration of their economies and the economies of Africa as a whole.

The success of the reforms in accomplishing these goals will depend less on the vision of their architects and more on the consciousness and mobilization on the part of the Black South African masses.

National Liberation and Anti-Imperialism in Africa: Challenge to Trilateralism

The political crisis in Southern Africa has generated a policy crisis in trilateralism. In the United States this policy crisis is most often portrayed as a struggle between the "Africanists" of the State Department and the United Nations Mission, and the "globalists" in the Department of Defense, the intelligence community and the National Security Council. Both sides see the rising power of the national liberation movement and the incorporation of anticapitalist and antiimperialist ideology as dangerous. Where they differ, is in how to handle this growing threat and insure the long-term ideological, political, and economic dominance of capitalism. Former UN Ambassador Young, who appeared to believe that communist ideology only takes root among Blacks when they are denied a share in the wealth, tended to minimize the influence of socialist states and ideology. Accordingly, if the trilateral states would embrace the poverty-striken African masses, sponsoring more "development" projects and forcing South Africa to eliminate the repressive apartheid system, the influence of anticapitalist ideologies could be minimized.

Young expressed these sentiments in testimony before the Senate Foreign Relations Committee in 1976:

> ...the best thing the Communists have going for them is the presence of racist minority regimes in Southern Africa. If those were no longer there, there would no longer be any need for the weaponry which the Soviet Union supplies and the issue would be one of development. When it comes to development, I would say that our track record is as good as anybody's.

It is the two-pronged character of the liberal Young approach which is often confusing. By championing development, Young is championing trilateral interests:

> I think that even among so-called radical countries, such as Mozambique and Angola, there is a realization that if they are going ever to be nonaligned countries, it is going to *require their opening a part of their economy to Western involvement and influence.*[45] [Italics ed.]

Young knows that Angola and Mozambique have inherited economies which are oriented toward South Africa and the West. The task for the U.S. and other trilateral states is to ensure that these linkages are maintained—albeit in modified form. Moreover, trilateralists understand that most African states, while far from being anti-capitalist, are critical of the U.S. for not exerting more pressure on minority regimes in Southern Africa and they stress their communality of interests with regional "new influentials" like Nigeria. But there are two sides to the coin: trilateral states must also be receptive to African concerns. Nigeria has both political and economic motivations: as long as South Africa dominates the regional economy it leaves little room for involvement by other major African states. Likewise, the Black African states in Southern Africa cannot expand their economies in the face of a dominant South African economy.

The so-called "globalists"—Kissinger is the outstanding mentor—see the socialist component of African liberation movements as an outcome of manipulation by foreign socialist states for their own geopolitical reasons. They therefore advocate a hardline against Cuban and Soviet activity in Africa, misrepresenting the fact that the Cubans and Soviets have been *asked* to assist legitimate governments and internationally recognized liberation movements. The common flaw of both the Africanist and globalist position is their inability to see the depth of antiracism and antiimperialism within the indigenous liberation movements.

Since the qualitative shift to armed struggle in the African nationalist movement, the trilateral states have attempted to demilitarize the African liberation struggle—not the minority regimes—and force a negotiated solution The most recent manifestation of this policy is the Zimbabwe Agreement. (See Nesbitt). Similarly, trilateral states are pressing a resolution to the Namibian crisis that would arrest the armed character of the struggle and bring SWAPO (South-West African People's Organization) and South Africa to the negotiating table. (South Africa has refused to make the necessary concessions even though SWAPO has assented to the Namibia Plan.)

As the new decade of the eighties progresses, developments in South Africa itself will intensify. It remains to be seen whether the trilateral-backed South African reform effort will revitalize the minority regime—or hasten its demise.

Editor's Postscript: On 1 June 1980, ANC guerillas conducted their most daring and successful operation ever, making simultaneous attacks on two heavily guarded SASOL oil-from-coal conversion plants and causing millions of dollars in damage. This year (1980) has seen massive popular protest, including a boycott by mixed-race and Indian students against the inferior education in the Black, "colored," and Indian school systems. And, as *Southern Africa* (June 1980) reports:

> The student rebellion wasn't the only new wave of resistance to apartheid. It coincided with the largest and most militant surge of strikes by black workers since 1973. And in both schools and factories, renewed resistance struck a damaging blow to Prime Minister P.W. Botha's claims that apartheid reformed can mean apartheid preserved. For the high school and college students and urban factory workers who were marching and picketing represented precisely those sectors of the black population [and mixed-race and Indian population] envisioned as a buffer against rebellion in Botha's "total strategy" [of militarization, economic expansion, and "reform"].

FOOTNOTES

1. "South Africa: Does the West Need the Minerals?" *Africa Confidential,* 17 January 1979, pp. 3-4.
2. "France: New Oil and Minerals Strategy," *Africa Confidential,* 28 March 1979.
3. Carey Winfrey, "The Coming Months are Key to Future of Bankrupt Zaire," *New York Times,* 13 November 1979; "Zaire: Can the IMF Succeed?" *Africa Confidential,* 3 January 1979; "Zaire: IMF Contradictions," *Africa Confidential,* 19 September 1979; "Zaire: IMF Loses Hope," *Africa Confidential,* 20 June 1979; *Africa Research Bulletin,* 20 September 1979.
4. Paul Cheeseright, "U.S. Fears Dependence on Africa for Minerals," *Financial Times,* 16 October 1979; "South Africa: Does the West Need Minerals," *Africa Confidential,* 17 January 1979, pp. 3-4.
5. "Who Cares About Foreign Investment?" 25 November 1977 cited in Jennifer Davis, "U.S. Dollars in South Africa: Context and Consequence," *Southern African Perspectives No. 3* (1978), p. 4.
6. Davis, *op. cit., p. 4.*
7. Colin Bundy, *The Rise and Fall of the South African Peasantry,* (London 1979).
8. Francis Wilson, *Labour and the South African Gold Mines,* (London, 1972), pp. 16-17.
9. *African Research Bulletin,* 15 April-14 May 1979, pp. 5105-5106.
10. As quoted in Ann and Neva Seidman, *U.S. Based Multinationals in South Africa,* (Westport, Ct.: Lawrence Hill, 1977), p. 50.
11. *Ibid.,* p. 89.
12. U.N. Commission on Transnational Corporations (UNCTC), *Activities of Transnational Corporations in the Industrial, Mining and Military Sectors of South Africa,* (22 March 1979), p. 40.
13. "South Africa: Multinationals Stand Firm," *Africa Confidential,* 15 December 1978.
14. UNCTC, *op. cit.,* p. 19.
15. *Ibid.*
16. Ann Seidman and Neva Makgetla, *Activities of Transnational Corporations in South Africa,* (New York: U.N. Centre Against Apartheid, May 1978), p. 27.
17. *Ibid.,* p. 7.
18. *Ibid.,* p. 17.
19. See Seidman and Makgetla, *op. cit.,* p. 47 and Richard Leonard, *Computers in South Africa: A Survey of U.S. Companies,* (New York: The Africa Fund, November 1978).
20. Leonard, *op. cit.,* pp. 7-8.
21. Seidman and Makgetla, *op. cit.,* p. 46.
22. Edward A. Olsen, "Japan Building Bridges to Africa," *Africa Report,* March-April 1980.
23. Nigel Bance, "Can South Africa Bring Back Foreign Capital?" *Euromoney* supplement, June 1979, p. 7.
24. Olsen, *op. cit.*
25. Seidman and Makgetla, *op. cit.,* p. 35.
26. Lindsey Phillips, "No Easy Walk to Freedom," *Working Papers,* March-April 1979.

27. Davis, *op. cit.*

28. Corporate Data Exchange, *U.S. Bank Loans to South Africa,* (New York, 1978).

29. UNCTC, *op. cit.;* Seidman and Makgetla, *op. cit.*

30. *Financial Mail,* 25 May 1979, p. 683.

31. Bernard Rivers and Martin Bailey, *Oil Sanctions Against South Africa,* (New York: U.N. Centre Against Apartheid, June 1978).

32. UNCTC, *op. cit.,* p. 31. For a brief history of the role of trilateral-based transnationals in the nuclear industry by a South African business publication see "Uranium: South Africa's Secret," *Financial Mail,* 13 July 1979, pp. 115-116.

33. Barbara Rodgers, *op. cit.,* pp. 18-19.

35. *Ibid.,* p. 29.

36. *Ibid.,* p. 20.

37. *Ibid.,* p. 31.

38. David Davis, *African Workers and Apartheid,* (London: International Defense and Aid Fund), p. 25.

39. *The Economist,* 6 October 1979.

40. See Anthony Samson, "Pretoria's Scandal," *Newsweek,* 2 April 1979 and Karen Rothmeyer, "The McGoff Grab," *Columbia Journalism Review,* November-December 1979.

41. See *Weihahn Commission Report* and National Union of South African Students, "Wiehahn: Exposing the Contradictions," Summer 1979.

42. This discussion is based on *Africa Research Bulletin,* 1-31 May 1979 and *Financial Mail,* (11 May and 18 May 1979)

43. *Financial Mail,* 13 July 1979.

44. *Financial Mail,* 18 May 1979.

45. Hearings before the sub-committee on African Affairs of the Committee on Foreign Relations, U.S Senate, (6 June 1977).

chapter three

TRILATERALISM AND THE RHODESIAN PROBLEM: AN EFFORT AT MANAGING THE ZIMBABWEAN LIBERATION STRUGGLE

*Prexy Nesbitt**

What we have achieved is a masterpiece as a politico-diplomatic exercise. No one ever believed that we could get the internal leaders to agree to so much...whereas we were alone, we now have the advantage of authentic black nationalists defending our political position.**

The 1978 "Zimbabwe Rhodesia"*** constitution and subsequent elections of April 1979 can be interpreted in light of trilateralist principles. The constitution and elections were not the creations of White Rhodesia alone. They also resulted from two historic initiatives by the West: first, joint efforts by Britain and the United

*A *postscript,* written in May 1980, extends this earlier analysis of trilateral strategy. Prexy Nesbitt and Holly Sklar want to thank Tamara Danish for copyediting their final draft of this article. Prexy Nesbitt is research secretary for the World Council of Churches Program to Combat Racism. He was previously Director of the Africa Project of the Washington D.C. Institute for Policy Studies. For two years he was associate director of the American Committee on Africa. He has lived, worked and studied in the Southern African region for over 4 1/2 years beginning in 1965. The views expressed in this article are the author's own.

**Co-Minister of Defense Picker K. Van de Byl speaking to an all white, closed door audience when Muzorewa first began to cooperate with Ian Smith's government. *The Times* (London) 8 May 1978 quoted in Nazir Ahmad, *Abel Muzorewa: An Autobiography*, an unpublished paper available from the IPS Africa Project.

***ed. note: *Zimbabwe Rhodesia* is the name given the country under the constitution approved by the white settlers. *Zimbabwe* is the African Name—the name for the independent nation under true majority rule. *Rhodesia* is the colonial name, after Cecil Rhodes, who led the first plundering expedition which claimed the area for the British Crown; he became the colony's first administrator. In this paper, *Rhodesia* is used in reference to the settler regime, especially the military apparatus. *Zimbabwe* signifies the African majority. *Zimbabwe Rhodesia* is used where appropriate in reference to the Muzorewa/Smith government.

States culminating in the 1977 Anglo-American plan for Zimbabwe and, second, collaboration on Namibia between the U.S., Britain, France, West Germany and Canada (the so-called Contact Group), also beginning in 1977. These initiatives are part of a larger set of events which includes: the August 1977 African journey of then British Foreign Minister David Owen and then U.S. Ambassador to the United Nations Andrew Young; the February 1978 trip of Patriotic Front leaders Joshua Nkomo and Robert Mugabe to Malta for talks with U.S. and British officials; and the 1978 meeting of trilateralists Carter, Vance, Mondale, and Brzezinski with South African Foreign Minister Botha. A host of politicians and private organizations in the U.S. and Britain—ranging from the British Anglo-Rhodesia Society to North Carolina Congressman Jesse Helm's tax-exempt foundation to the Institute of American Relations and the Center for a Free Society—have also had a hand in shaping the so-called Internal Settlement.

The constitution and elections are the basis for an illusory (i.e. having the appearance of majority rule) neocolonial structure which would serve as an alternative to a seizure of state power by a genuine national liberation movement: the Patriotic Front (PF), consisting of the Zimbabwe African National Union (ZANU) and the Zimbabwe African People's Union (ZAPU). Like the white settlers, trilateralists seek to avoid an "excess of democracy" in Zimbabwe. However, the newly elected prime minister, Bishop Abel Muzorewa, and his white settler-dominated Cabinet represent only a modified application of the trilateral method to the Southern African scene. The constitution and elections were too plainly cosmetic. They were broadly perceived as resulting in the same white structure with Black faces (Zimbabweans have called Muzorewa a "blacksmith"). Because the elections of April 17-21 were judged neither free nor fair and because the new constitution maintains the white settler community's economic and political hegemony, the hoped for lifting of sanctions by the international community did not follow.

Furthermore, the elections to bring peace to Zimbabwe have neither ended the war nor renewed the ragged economy. On the contrary, since the elections the *escalating* war has strained the economy even further. The *Washington Post* reported on 30 September 1979 that Zimbabwe Rhodesia's war effort was costing $1.6 million daily. And the Salisbury-based correspondent for *The Economist* reported shortly after the elections that it was the war-related problems—the transport bottleneck, balance-of-payments problem, shortage of skilled labor—that were creating a stagnant economy, not the application of sanctions by an equivocating international community. "So long as the war continues—and escalates," he wrote, "the capacity for increased production simply does not exist."[1]

There has been an accelerated call-up for military service to bring the number of Rhodesian soldiers to over 100,000, an increasing proportion of them being Blacks. On the other side, by September 1979 there were 30 percent more Patriotic Front guerillas operating inside the country than had been the case only six months earlier. The PF guerillas have succeeded in bringing large tracts of land under their administrative control—penetrated only intermittently by large Augusta-Bell helicopters—and have carried out successful operations in Salisbury, the Capital. Some 2,000 of Rhodesia's 6,100 white farms have been abandoned;[2] whole communities have disappeared. The period around the election itself witnessed high monthly death tolls of 800 to 900 people and by August 1979 that figure would climb to over 1,000. At the same time some 1,000 or so whites were emigrating monthly.*

There is an additional by-product from the war. The PF guerillas have succeeded in paralyzing the international business community. Foreign capital is watching as closely as the PF, the telling statistics of white emigration, gross domestic product, and foreign exchange. A recent report of the United Nations Economic and Social Council assessed the over-all situation in Rhodesia:

> Many foreign interests are reportedly prepared to expand their operations once the political situation stabilizes. For the moment, however, very little investment activity, foreign or local, is taking place. During the past year, almost no new foreign capital has been invested in the once dependable mining sector and the search for new minerals has practially stopped.[3]

The Muzorewa solution has failed to achieve a central objective of trilateralism in Africa: managing or at least stemming the advance of the radical liberation forces and, in Henry Kissinger's words, "preventing the radicalization" of the situation.**

---

*Official figures state that since January 1979 the country lost 9,973 whites for the 2,268 whites who immigrated. (*The Star*, Johannesburg, 6 October 1979.) The *immigration* figures are consistently exaggerated by the Rhodesian Government in an attempt to retain what foreign capital remains.
**In testimony before the House of Representatives, International Relations Committee Hearings, 17 June 1976, Kissinger argued:

> With the end of the Portuguese era in Africa, pressure was building on Rhodesia, regarded by the Africans as the last major vestige of colonialism. Events in Angola encouraged radicals to press for a military solution in Rhodesia.
>   With radical influence on the rise, and with immense outside military strength apparently behind the radicals, even moderate and

In the sections below we shall discuss the following: the political/military background to the April 1979 election; foreign capital interests in Rhodesia; the election and the Muzorewa government; the ramifications of the Carter/Young policy toward Rhodesia upon domestic politics, with a special focus on the growing role of Black Americans; and the general strategy of trilateralism toward Southern African liberation movements, as applied to the specific case of Zimbabwe.

Background to the April Elections

On 15 September 1978, in a speech delivered in Maputo, President Samora Machel of Mozambique lamented: the Front Line States* and Africa as a whole had allowed British and U.S. envoys to deceive the Front Line presidents; the latter had accepted the intentions of the West as being one with those of Black Africa in seeking to terminate the illegal Smith regime. (A white minority government led by Ian Smith defied calls for majority rule by unilaterally declaring independence from Britain in 1965.)

Even from the perspective of imperialism, Machel pointed out, apartheid in South Africa, colonialism in Namibia, and settler rule in Zimbabwe were all anachronisms. Continuing his analysis (perhaps addressing himself to certain of his Front Line colleagues), he observed:

> Our candor and the sincerity with which the Front Line states tried to advise the British and Americans, enabled imperialism to improve its strategy, enabled imperialism to maneuver so that, till now, it has managed to maintain the illegal Smith regime.
>
> *The main objective of the imperialist action is not to overthrow Smith. The main objective of imperialism is to destroy the liberation movement*, to destroy any form of organization which enables the people to liberate themselves.
>
> Imperialist strategy has been, after all, extremely coherent.

---

responsible African leaders—firm proponents of peaceful change—began to conclude there was no alternative but to embrace the cause of violence. By March of this year, guerrilla actions took on even larger dimensions. We saw ahead the prospect of war fed and perhaps conducted by outside forces; we were concerned about a continent politically and economically estranged from the West; and we saw ahead a process of radicalization which would place severe strains on our allies in Europe and Japan. (p. 8)

*The five Front Line States are: Tanzania, Botswana, Angola, Mozambique and Zambia. At the 1979 meeting of the Organization of African Unity (OAU), the Front Line States were once again endorsed to speak for and act on behalf of the entire OAU.

Imperialism has two operational detachments in Zimbabwe: Smith and his lackeys and Great Britain and its partners. *The operational strategy is always to have ready two solutions: an internal solution and an international solution.*

When one of the alternatives is about to reach a solution to the problem, imperialism sets in motion the other alternative.[4] [Italics ed.]

There is a long history of meetings, conferences, and agreements which substantiates President Machel's contention that imperialism always keeps these two solutions at the ready, with the main objective being to prevent the Zimbabwean liberation movement from gaining power. Beginning with the talks between Smith and Prime Minister Harold Wilson aboard the H.M.S. Tiger—held one year after Smith's unilateral declaration of independence in 1965—and extending to the Fall 1979 talks at Lancaster House in London (taking place as this article was written), there have been repeated Western efforts at negotiating a solution to the Rhodesian problem. At times talks have been bilateral, brief, informal, or secret, as when on 2 August 1977 Andrew Young had a chance meeting with Patriotic Front co-leader Joshua Nkomo in Guyana and followed it up with a trip by Nkomo to Washington and New York. At other times, such as in the October 1976 Geneva Conference, talks have been formal, extensive and involved all of the various parties, including the Front Line States, with the support of the United Nations.

For the Patriotic Front and its African supporters—especially the Front Line States and, increasingly, Nigeria*—the talks and conferences are largely tactical. That is, they are modalities which should assist in transforming the status quo. What President Samora Machel said in a 1978 speech to members of the United Nations in Maputo could just as well have been expressed by the leadership of ZANU or ZAPU. Speaking to the audience which included both a U.S. and a British delegation, Machel remarked:

We totally reject the idea that the path of armed struggle and the path of negotiations are either mutually-exclusive alternatives or contradictions in the process of national liberation. We do not love war but we believe that, when the contradiction is antagonistic and insoluble, only war makes peace.

Our people have a saying for this: "you can't make tea without boiling water."

*Nigeria, Tanzania, Zambia and Australia were the countries which pressured Britain into convening the Lancaster House Conference. Nigeria's takeover of British Petroleum just before the August 1979 Commonwealth Conference was one more instance of Nigeria exerting its muscle and showing its growing power as one of the Third World's "new influentials."

Talks are an important factor for victory but they are not the decisive factor.

For Smith (and more recently for his successor/collaborator Muzorewa) the talks and conferences, whether secret or open, are means to try and *preserve the status quo.* To date Smith and his colleagues have refused to consider the means of genuine transfer of power and the dismantling of the mechanisms by which some 250,000 whites exploit some 7,000,000 Blacks. Rather they have attempted to use the talks and (abortive) agreements as part of a strategy to split the PF and impede any growing momentum, diplomatic or military, which the PF might be enjoying at a particular time.

For the trilateralist West, particularly the U.S. (though by tacit agreement Britain, because of its responsibility as the colonial power, is usually the central actor*), the meetings and talks up to and including Lancaster House 1979 signify a process of management. Trilateral leaders would be the first to say that the status quo situation of white settler hegemony has to be altered. But other experiences in Southern Africa, especially in Angola, and throughout the Third World, have taught them that the key problem is one of shaping the nature of change, i.e., avoiding the "chaos" of revolutionary change. On 3 July 1979, when Henry Kissinger was asked about his plan for Rhodesia as secretary of state, he told the *Washington Post:* "My plan was to co-opt the program of moderate evolutionary reform, that is to say majority rule and minority rights." Speaking from the same posture of managing change, Andrew Young answered a question about U.S. involvement in Africa by saying:

I don't think you can blame us for that [the fact that the war was still going on in Zimbabwe]. See we were in a supportive role— supporting Africa and Britain, in trying to find a political answer to the problem, and I think we have remained true to that. But other changes have come about that we were not in control of.[5]

*This is true only as long as the British are adequate to the task. According to the *London Observer* of 21 October 1978, at the point at which the Lancaster House Conference almost collapsed over the issue of whether a new government should assume the costs of compensating departing white settlers for their land, it was a secret intervention—reportedly at the request of President Nyerere of Tanzania and Shridrath Ramphal, the Commonwealth Secretary—by Carter and Vance promising the funds that salvaged the Conference. I suspect the Carter Administration did not require much prodding to proffer the funds—part of a multi-donor program. In fact, such assistance was planned under the Zimbabwe Development Fund envisaged by Kissinger in 1976. To say that the funding was being done at the request of the African parties just provides better cover for the managerial initiatives.

It is important to note one fundamental difference between the Kissinger approach and the Carter/Young approach. The latter seems to be much more trilateralist. Whereas Kissinger maintains that the best thing to do with the radical nationalists (what he calls the "ideological radicals," a category into which he places Mugabe but not Nkomo) is to *isolate them,* Young and Carter feel that it is best to *maximize contact* in the belief that the radical nationalists ultimately "want to share in the productivity of the American way of life."*

But differences aside, there has been a consensus on one key point regarding Rhodesia: the need to maintain the interests of the multinational corporations operating there in the face of the growing military threat from the PF's fighting forces. How great is that threat? Is there any possibility that the Patriotic Front will take power through a military victory?

The thirteen years of war have been a bitter and cruel affair. The strategy used by the Rhodesian Forces—similar to that of the U.S. forces in Vietnam—has been to terrorize the civilian population away from the support they have consistently given the guerillas, whom they fondly call "the Boys."** Some indication of the extent to which this type of counterinsurgency has failed is provided by the fact that the Patriotic Front has today a pool of close to half a million refugees in the neighboring countries of Mozambique, Angola, Zambia and Botswana from which to draw political cadre and military recruits.

Likewise, the fact that South Africa assumed an increasingly overt role in the war is a direct indication of the Front's effectiveness. It has been known and reported for some time that South Africa is materially involved in the war in Zimbabwe, just as it has intervened in Angola and Mozambique. South Africa continues to wage a war

---

*The anecdotal pastor Young illustrated this point beautifully in a recent speech to the Houston, Texas Trade Associations:

> I remember when we sat down with the Patriotic Front when they agreed to elections run by the British and supervised by the United Nations—something which Ian Smith and Bishop Muzorewa never would agree to one of the things that happened was a big, burly guy comes over to me and put his hand on my shoulder and said, "I need to talk to you." I didn't know him. As big as he was I was kind of nervous. He pulled me off to the corner. He was in his battle fatigues, long bearded. He was supposedly one of their military commanders from out in the bush. He pulled me off on the side and said, "What really happened to the Oakland Raiders?" I said, "what do you mean?" He said, "they were supposed to be Super Bowl this year, what happened?" (Remarks by Andrew Young, Houston Trade Association, 18 May 1979; reprint available from United States Mission to the United Nations, New York, NY.)

**Please note when this term is affectionately used by Zimbabweans, they are making reference to both men and women in the Patriotic Front's fighting forces.

of aggression against Angola, both directly and through its extensive support of UNITA. South Africa has aided Rhodesia with equipment (in February 1979, for instance, South Africa supplied Rhodesia with Mirage jets for its attack upon ZAPU camps in Angola), $50 million in monthly bank loans[6] and with personnel. But the South African military is worried that Muzorewa's forces are outnumbered and out-experienced by the guerillas. A spokesman stated, "I don't see how they'll [Muzorewa forces] win unless they get more manpower." On 24 September 1979 Prime Minister Botha told a Capetown National Party meeting:

> We have an interest in the stability north of us. If confusion and chaos are created for Rhodesia by outside forces, I want to warn that the South African parliament will have to consider what steps we are going to take because we do not want and we cannot afford confusion on our borders.*

A month later, on October 22, Zambian President Kenneth Kaunda alluded to one of South Africa's steps to preserve stability when he told a visiting Iraqui delegation how Zambian forces were (thus far) "containing" some 1000 Rhodesian and South African troops operating in Zambian territory.[7]

South Africa is, indeed, very concerned about their "kith and kin" to the north; but their concern is not altruistic. Rhodesia is, as the International Defense and Aid Fund describes it, a "sixth province of South Africa." There would be more and more troop commitment and escalated intervention by South Africa in Rhodesia because:

> Political and business confidence in South Africa is intimately bound up with the survival of Bishop Abel Muzorewa. Whether South Africa sets itself on a path of even more moderate economic growth is now probably more dependent on what happens at Lancaster House in the next few months than on any other single factor.[8]

Foreign capital is also assuming a more active profile in Rhodesia. The present Rhodesian economy is the product of Western capital, South African capital, and, to a lesser extent, of white settler farmers. From the moment Cecil Rhodes first planted his feet on

---

*Cited in the *Washington Post*, 29 September 1979. Another aspect of the confusion Botha may have been alluding to is the growing morale problem with Rhodesian security forces. The London *Guardian* (29 August 1979) pointed to an increasingly bitter internecine quarrel when it headlined a story that the most effective Rhodesian counterinsurgency force, the Selous Scouts, were preparing "to resign and leave Rhodesia."

Zimbabwean soil in 1890, Rhodesia has been a "company" country. As the Southern African Bureau of the U.S. Agency for International Development acknowledged in its February 1977 report:

> The role of the multinational corporation in the Rhodesian economy is dynamic and pervasive...A concern of the new government will be its relationship to these corporations and the role it believes they should play in the future Zimbabwe...larger firms produce over 80% of Rhodesia's manufactures and most of these are probably multinationals, integral parts of the world economy (p. 273).

Observers report that many multinationals in Rhodesia have announced cutbacks in operations.[9] It is in the mining sector particularly where one finds striking cutbacks by British companies like Rio Tinto Zinc and Lonrho, and South African companies like Johannesburg Consolidated and Lomagurdi Smelting and Refining, a subsidiary of the Anglo American Corporation. Earlier, U.S. multinationals such as Union Carbide and Foote Mineral Company were forced to curtail their chromite production because of the 1977 repeal of the Byrd Amendment.* It has been argued that the pressure of international sanctions (passed by the United Nations Security Council on 16 December 1966 and extended in 1968 into a total economic boycott) and subsequent investigation into alleged violations by the U.S. Treasury Department have caused U.S. oil companies like Caltex and Mobil to curtail their activities in Rhodesia. But the real dynamic of the oil trade, i.e., *indirect* supply, was accurately portrayed in a 25 June 1978 London *Observer* feature: "Oil Chiefs Bust Sanctions."** The companies had been providing oil to Rhodesia via South Africa (through subsidiaries and cooperating South African firms) throughout the period of 1966 to 1978.***

Slowly but steadily, information is emerging about the economic and political activities of the multinationals Eschel Rhoodie, the former South African government official who initiated South

---

*The Byrd Amendment, passed on 10 November 1971, had lifted the ban on the import of so-called strategic and critical minerals from Rhodesia, including chrome. On 18 March 1977 Carter signed P.L. 95-12 amending the 1945 UN Participation Act and halting the importation of Rhodesian chrome.

**ed. note: Without these oil transfusions the Smith regime could never have survived; the economic and military machinery would have ground to a halt. Besides Mobil and Caltex, collaborating oil companies included Royal/Dutch Shell and British Petroleum, 51% owned by the British government.

***See Martin Baily and Bernard Rivers, *Oilgate: The Sanctions Scandal* (London: Hodder and Stoughton, 1979).

Africa's Watergate-type scandal, revealed that he worked with leading executives of the Alleghany Ludlum Industries (a large U.S. importer of chrome from South Africa and Rhodesia) to secretly contribute over 1½ million dollars to Bishop Muzorewa and his lieutenant, James Chikerema. In fact, Muzorewa has been the beneficiary of much company largess.* What the foreign investors want in Rhodesia is reflected in this statement from an article in the *London Observer* of 21 October 1979: "...to bring this nasty war to an end, and so save possibly hundreds of thousands of lives, give the white Rhodesians some chance of retaining a stake in the country and prevent the economy from being totally wrecked *as were those of Mozambique and Angola.*" [Italics mine.] For the moment, the corporations have lined up with the Muzorewa government. Much of their activity in Rhodesia is channeled through their South African subsidiaries or in tandem with the South African government. Thus multinational corporate interests often coincide with those of South Africa.

The corporate perspective is like that of Kenneth Adelman, a noted African affairs "expert," who recently argued for more U.S. military expenditure in Africa.**

> Given this background of instability [in the current African era], the economic development that both Africans and Americans yearn for can only grow from a foundation of security.[10]

The Election and Election Results

> He insists that it was the white farmers who made possible the election that put Prime Minister Muzorewa into power this year by organizing farm workers and local people in the countryside,

---

*Recently, it has been reported that Muzorewa received approximately $100,000 from the Lonrho Corporation.[9] During the summer of 1977 and shortly after his selection as Rhodesia's new prime minister, Muzorewa and his colleagues were contacted by a number of influential corporate executives. The Mobil Oil Corporation hosted a reception for the Bishop in New York and The Cummins Engine Company flew him to Indiana to discuss his plans for rebuilding the Rhodesian economy.

**I hasten to add, though, that the multinational corporations are not just one vast leviathan. There are clear differences between them, and some corporate chiefs like Tiny Rowland and Lonhro Company (the London Rhodesian Company) seem to take a more long-term—more trilateralist—view on the Zimbabwe Rhodesia problem than do some of the less sophisticated and worldly actors like E.F. Andrews and Alleghany Ludlam of Pittsburgh. The stakes are very high for Tiny Rowland (perhaps this accounts for a relatively more long-term perspective.) *The Guardian* (London) reported 11 November 1978, that Lonrho and another company, Liebigs, owned between them, over "two million acres of ranching land."

assuring them that there would be no repercussions if they voted and transporting them to voting places.*

Muzorewa's election as the first Black prime minister of white-ruled Rhodesia was the second stage of a process which began when the white settler community—representing 4 percent of the entire population—voted approval of a constitution which guarantees white privilege under a facade of "majority rule."** Muzorewa's election was an exercise carried out by the occupying colonial force in Rhodesia; much of the country was under martial law. David Cante described the election in his article in *The Nation*:

> the army and the armed police made it clear that they were in business to get people to vote...in Matibi the majority of the voters were herded in by patrols...in Joni village in Mangwerde, people were warned that if they did not vote their village would be bombed...[12]

While Ian Smith and the white settler leadership were still basking in the glow of their new-found prodigies, the arrangement began to unravel within the African community. The private armies of Reverend Sithole, Chief Chirau and Muzorewa—the parties to the internal settlement agreement signed with Smith on 3 March 1979—have been a source of terror and misery to the Zimbabwean peasantry since early 1978. The flames of alienation and anger toward the purported authentic Black nationalists felt by Zimbabweans (especially those in rural areas) have been fanned by actions taken by the new government: extending martial law provisions, detaining more people, practicing even more vicious torture than had occurred under the previous all-white government.

Under the emergency regulations of 1976, continued by the Muzorewa government, special court martials or military courts were created. By 1979 there were a minimum of 1,851 political prisoners, i.e., those convicted of supporting the liberation struggle (caught carrying food on the road, for example); thousands of others were imprisoned as criminal offenders. According to ZAPU sources, 200 of this number were awaiting execution by hanging at the end of 1978. In fact, under the State of Emergency regulations summary executions were often carried out in the field by the six different forces on the government side, including Auxiliary Forces like

---

*White Rhodesian farmer Colin Cook interviewed by Carey Winfrey, *New York Times*, Thursday 27 September 1979.
**As the American Committee on Africa recently commented: "There is not a single chapter in the entire constitution which demonstrates even the potential for the transition to majority rule in Zimbabwe."[11]

Muzorewa's private army.* With this record of atrocities in mind:

> More and more Zimbabweans call Muzorewa and other black beneficiaries of the internal settlement *Zvimbgawasungata*—the Shona term for "hunting dogs." As Zimbabweans explain the significance of the term: It is a stray dog with no owner. Anyone who cares can take it hunting for the pot. Once it catches an impala or a hare and kills it, the hunter takes the meat home and chases the dog away. It does not eat any of the meat it kills.[13]

The coalition government is coming apart. Starting with the resignation of Co-Minister Jusice Byron Howe, and continuing through some dozen separate cases, key members of both Muzorewa's UNAC party and of his government began to resign in protest. The Bishop's government is not adequate to the task of neutralizing the Patriotic Front and rebuilding the economy. A white farmer in the Rhodesian Highlands expressed his disappointment in Muzorewa's conciliatory approach at the Lancaster Conference: "I think he's made a great mistake. He put all his cards on the table."

The essence of the situation, however, is that the mistakes are less those of Muzorewa than of his backers. The Bishop's nominally independent government cannot address the hardships of war, white privilege, and rural exploitation which all Africans face daily. It cannot confront the reality of deeply institutionalized racism.** Hence, while it might have been an adequate "African" solution, the Muzorewa government as constructed by Smith, the National Front, and their Western allies fails as an enduring neo-colonial solution. Says Byron Howe:

> People in our country have been looking for evidence that the agreement is leading toward majority rule. Now they have

---

*Even Muzorewa's colleague was not immune. In August members of Reverend Sithole's private army charged that government troops and airplanes massacred over 300 people as they stood unarmed, waiting for government troops to pick up their discarded weapons.[14] New information about the character of Muzorewa's security forces is available in the detailed study by the British Anti-Apartheid Movement, *Fire Force Exposed: The Rhodesian Security Forces and their role in Defending White Supremacy* (London, October 1979). A significant conclusion of the study is that the "Rhodesian security forces, in short, are incapable of playing any positive role in a genuine transfer of power to the people of Zimbabwe as a whole, and must be disbanded."

**A good example: the Muzorewa government has explicitly said that it will leave the present economic infrastructure intact. The state-run Agricultural Finance Corporation in 1975 gave an average line of credit to Rhodesia's 6,000 white farmers of $18,000. It made available an average credit of $2.00 to the 600,000 African farmers. For more on this, see Michael Bratoon, "Settler State, Guerilla War and Rural Underdevelopment in Rhodesia," *Issue*, Spring/Summer 1978, pp. 56-7.

evidence to the contrary. Far from adjusting toward majority rule, Smith and his machinery are trying to cheat us, to take us for a ride, and to cheat the whole world. They believe in the substance of power remaining in white hands, with the shadow of authority passing to blacks.[15]

U.S. Policy Toward Zimbabwe and Domestic Politics

As Howe indicates, the world is watching events in Zimbabwe, the United States as closely as Britain. Within a nine month period, all of the major actors in the Smith/Muzorewa government visited and lobbied in the United States. The major media, especially television, began to give regular coverage to Zimbabwe; some, notably the *Washington Post* and the Columbia Broadcasting System augmented the number of its personnel stationed in Africa.

Shortly before resigning from his United Nations post, Andrew Young responded to the question posed by *Encore*, a Black American magazine, "How important do you think Rhodesia will be as a campaign issue?" He said:

> Very important. Because the Republicans have decided that Zimbabwe is the new racial code word for "Let's keep the niggers in their place." In 1968, you remember, it was crime in the streets," in 1972 it was "busing," in 1980 it is Rhodesia.[16]

The debate over whether to send an official election observer team from the U.S., the elections themselves, the visits of Smith and Muzorewa to the U.S., the illegal transfer of a number of U.S. made Huey helicopters and Cessna airplanes to Rhodesia via Israel*—all these events took place in rapid succession in 1979. Each of them presented the Carter Administration and its program for Africa with a new set of domestic challenges.

Beginning with the 1975-76 mobilization protesting U.S. intervention in Angola and continuing into the Carter Administration, prominent Black American individuals and organizations have been carving out a role in determining the shape and direction of U.S. policy and action in Africa. The publication of Kissinger's "whites are here to stay" policy memorandum (see introduction to Brown's article); revelations about the CIA's activities in Africa (extensively chronicled in books like John Stockwell's *In Search of Enemies: A CIA Story*, 1979); and the 1976 Soweto uprising in South Africa galvanized Black and mixed organizations toward renewed levels of

---

*Jim Hoagland, "11 Bell Copters Said Smuggled Into Rhodesia." *Washington Post*, December 15, 1978. also see, *Fire Force Exposed: The Rhodesian Security Forces and Their Role in Defending White Security, op.cit.*

activity. In 1977 the NAACP sponsored a major factfinding trip to Africa and issued a report calling for sanctions against South Africa as well as Rhodesia. Andrew Young's demonstrated concern with Africa in his highly visible position of UN Ambassador helped many Black institutions deepen their awareness and sharpen their position. But above all, it was the founding of *TransAfrica* which signalled the dawning of a new period of Black concern with Africa.* Founded in 1977, an outgrowth of the 1976 Black Congressional Caucus' *African American Manifesto on Southern Africa* (an official declaration endorsing the concept of armed struggle by the Southern African liberation movements), TransAfrica rapidly became a nationally-based membership organization functioning as a Black American lobby on international affairs.

Thus, the Carter Administration, while attempting to implement its trilateralist solutions to what it calls "the arc of crisis stretching across Southern Asia to Southern Africa," has to contend with the domestic ramifications of policy decisions. When the State Department permitted Smith, Sithole and Muzorewa to visit the U.S. in October 1978 and July 1979, mass counter demonstrations were held in every city in which they appeared. When President Carter considered lifting the sanctions against Rhodesia, in the spring of 1979, as directed by the 1978 Case-Javits Amendment, he was confronted with a maintain-sanctions campaign organized by TransAfrica, the Washington Office on Africa, and some thirty-odd other groups organized into a coalition called the Southern Africa Working Group. Black American publications like the *Amsterdam News* and the *Detroit Chronicle,* and media organizations such as the National Negro Publishers Association systematically pressured Carter to abide by the March 8 UN Security Council decision which declared the election fraudulent and urged member states to refrain from sending observers.

The potential significance of the Black American community in influencing Western policy toward Africa was underscored by a

*There is no intent on this author's part to assert this is a new development. On the contrary, the long history of Black American concern and involvement with Africa and the Caribbean   seen in the work of leaders like Marcus Garvey, W.E. Dubois, Paul Robeson, Malcolm X and Alphaeus Hinton   is a subject which is in need of more exhaustive attention. The difference is that with the Carter Administration the potential for influence is greater, largely because Carter owes an electoral debt to Blacks for having received over 85 percent of the Black vote in 1976. Not only is there a strengthened Black American constituency. It is a Vietnam-sensitive Black American constituency; people who, like most U.S. citizens, are disinclined to be involved in another Vietnam-like intervention. On this see a novel by Randall Robinson, director of TransAfrica, called *The Emancipation of Wakefield Clay* (Bogle l'Overture Press, London, 1978) and "Resurgent Militarism" by Klare et. al. in this volume.

November 9-11 Conference on Southern Africa sponsored by the British-American Ditchley Foundation. This quiet counterpart to the Lancaster Conference was convened for twenty-five to thirty individuals from Western Europe, Japan, and the U.S.* in order "to focus on the question of coordination of Western Democracies' policies, and ways in which they might help bring about effective long-term solutions to the serious problems of the area Southern Africa." Several Black Americans, among them TransAfrica Director Randall Robinson, were invited. When they declined the invitation because no Black South Africans had been asked to participate,** the Ditchley Foundation began frantically "combing the woods" (Ditchley's words) to locate Black Americans who might cooperate. This incident illustrates the critical importance Western policy makers and corporate strategists attach to winning Black American legitimization of their activities on the African continent. In addition, the attendance by leading corporate executives, diplomats, media chiefs, and academics signifies the urgency with which they are trying to develop new strategies toward Southern Africa hand in hand with a rationale for public consumption.

Lobbying by Black groups and traditional progressive allies like the American Committee on Africa (called "liberationists" by the CIA-linked Georgetown University Center for Strategic and International Studies, CSIS) is not easy. Besides the perennial problem of inadequate financing, TransAfrica and other groups have to compete against a sophisticated, interconnected, and well-financed lobbying effort being waged by various forces hoping to see the exisitng Muzorewa government recognized and sanctions lifted immediately. Among the U.S. forces actively promoting the Smith/Muzorewa

*Among the participants were: Keith Douglas Scott, Australian Ambassador to South Africa; Christopher Laidlaw, Chairman of British Petroleum; Anthony Tuke, Chairman of Barclays Bank, President of the British Bankers Association, and a Trilateral Commissioner; Neil Forster, Director of Bristow Helicopters; Anton Rupert, Chairman of the Rembrandt Group of Companies, South Africa, and Director of the South Africa Reserve Bank; Francis Vale, Public Affairs Director of Rio Tinto Zinc; and the Managing Director of Royal Dutch Shell. Attending also were Richard Moose, U.S. Assistant Secretary of State for African Affairs; Shiro Saito the Asia Area Chief of the *Japan Economic Journal*; Jerome Caminada Foreign News Editor of the *London Times*; David Harrison, Producer for BBC Television; Chester Crocker, Director of African Studies at the Georgetown University Center for Strategic and International Studies; and William Foltz, Director of the Council on Foreign Relations' Africa Project.

**Later one Black South African "industrialist," i.e. factory worker, and one "Cape Town Colored" were asked to come.

option are: from the corporate world, Union Carbide and Allegheny-Ludlum Industries; from the Congress, Senators Dole (Kansas), Helms (North Carolina), Hayakawa (California) and Representatives Ashbrook (Ohio), Schweiker (Pennsylvania) and De Concini (Arizona); from the church community, the Texas Methodists and the Christian League of Southern Africa; and from the political Right, many of which maintain full-time professional lobbyists,* the Liberty Lobby, the American Rhodesian Association, the Friends of Rhodesia and the Association of Americans to Save Africa. Many of these U.S.-based prointernal settlement forces have international links. For instance, as mentioned above, Allegheny Ludlum's president, E.F. Andrews, collaborated with the South African government in making secret payments to Muzorewa.** The Friends of Rhodesia, Inc., is closely linked to the official Rhodesian Information Office which maintains an office in Washington in spite of the sanctions. CSIS (mentioned above), a major promoter of Smith and a moderate Black solution, was found to be directly linked to Britain's Institute for the Study of Conflict, which in turn has direct links to British police and army training institutions.[17] (See note following Thompson's article for further discussion of these ties.)

It is within this matrix of domestic and international forces that the Carter Administration must try to apply its trilateralist principles to the Zimbabwean national liberation struggle. Zbigniew Brzezinski, told the 1979 annual convention of the American Society of American Society of Newspaper Editors:

> In the mushrooming cities of the Third World, congested and rootless populations are more susceptible than ever to political mobilization. Nationalism is increasingly imbued with ideologial content, intensifying the desire to assert both national and social goals.
> Cumulatively, traditional global relationships are undergoing profound changes in a context of extraordinary diversity.

---

*Some indication of the resources available to the professional lobbyists (Neville Romaine is the most famous Rhodesia lobbyist) is seen in a recent revelation about lobbying in Washington to get more U.S. arms for King Hassan and Morocco. *Africa News,* 19 October 1979, reports that chiefly through the Washington D.C. public relations firm, DGA International, Morocco spent a million dollars in the 1978-79 year attempting to buy the support of the U.S. government and the public.
**Andrews' perspective is quite clear. He said in 1976: "The question is what can the private sector do with an eye to keeping Rhodesia...in the Western sphere as opposed to the Soviet and Cuban sphere?" *Africa News,* 25 October 1976. For the full story see *The Christian Science Monitor,* 9 October 1979, and *Southern African Magazine,* July/August 1979, p. 21.

The role of the United States in that context *is paramount*, but *no longer predominant*.

It follows that our central goal must be to *import positive direction to change* by creating for it a stable and increasingly cooperative framework.[18] [Italics ed.]

How does the U.S. manage to cooperatively play a "paramount, but no longer predominant" role?* Several approaches are visible in the Carter response to congressional pressure to lift sanctions during the Spring of 1979 and in the U.S.—British relationship in organizing the Lancaster House Constitutional Conference. First, in exemplary trilateralist fashion, the Carter Administration permits Britain to play the Matt Dillon marshall role at Lancaster House, with the U.S. appearing as the faithful deputy Chester.** Second, Carter makes certain that to whatever extent possible the U.S. is given very low profile; role-playing the silent deputy as well as the faithful one. Third, the Carter and Thatcher Administrations pursue steps which assure them maximum flexibility, for in the post-Vietnam era it is flexibility and not raw muscle power which characterizes the winner. The appointment of Lord Carrington, the British foreign secretary as Lancaster House Conference chairman, insured that trilateralism and corporate interests would be well served.*** The Lord served as Britain's secretary of state for energy in 1974 and was the minister of aviation supply from 1971-74. He is now or has been a director of the following multinationals: *Rio Tinto Zinc Corporation,* Australia and New Zealand Bank, Hambros Bank, Barclay's Bank, Amalgamated Metal Company and the Cadbury Schweppes Company. And if this background is not enough to ensure that he is a good, skillful and neutral chairperson, he has the additional qualifications of being a past member of the Trilateral Commission (See "Who's Who on the Trilateral Commission") and the president of the British-Iran Society.[19]

---

*What did Brzezinski have in mind? *Webster's New World Dictionary* (College Edition) defines paramount as "ranking higher than any other, as in power or importance; chief, supreme." Predominant means having ascendancy, authority, or dominating influence over others. ed. note: It would seem Brzezinski had confused these terms until another nuance is considered this time in *The American Heritage Dictionary of the English Language.* The second definition of predominant is: "most common or *conspicuous;* prevalent." [Italics ed.]

**The reference is to the famed Western *Gunsmoke*. Dillon is a giant blockbuster. Chester is diminutive but faithful to his leader.

***Ed. note: Carrington is seen as the guiding light of reason in Thatcher's Conservative Government in so far as international politics are concerned. His appointment as foreign secretary was a sign there would be little, if any, break with the policies of David Owen, his predecessor in Callaghan's Labor Government with which the Carter Administration had had good rapport.

Charlie Cobb, a journalist covering the Lancaster House Conference, described the third approach—flexibility—quite aptly when he explained British moves at the conference:

> In deciding its next move meanwhile, the British government is wrestling with conflicting pressures from African states on the one hand and right wingers in the Conservative Party on the other. Last week's party conference showed there is still strong sentiment that the Muzorewa government should be recongized. Thatcher's government does not dissent from this goal but seeks maximum flexibility on timing and tactics.[20]

U.S. Secretary of State, Cyrus Vance, employed the same approach when he explained Carter's 7 June 1979 decision not to lift sanctions. Besides emphasizing cooperation with Britain, his remarks were filled with phrases like "not rushing forward," letting "the situation evolve," maintaining "the ability to communicate with all the parties to the conflict." He commented that whatever one's interest in ideology, all concerned shared one common positive feature: a desire for "peaceful change in Southern Africa." In short, the Carter/trilateral approach is to make the best of a tension-wrought high-stake situation, like Zimbabwe, through accommodation rather than confrontation.

Concluding Perspectives on Trilateralism, Zimbabwe, and African Liberation

Whatever the outcome of the Lancaster Conference*—which will see either new elections including the Patriotic Front or a deal struck between Britain and the Muzorewa government, however inadequate—there are certain conclusions we can reach about the West's strategy for Zimbabwe and about the broader question of trilateralism and African liberation movements.

Trilateralists attempt to defuse conflict. Their strategy is that of initiating dialogue with their enemy—certain that ultimately the sheer economic hegemony of the international capitalist system will neutralize, by coercion and co-optation, the ideological fervor of the nationalists. The U.S. and Britain are maintaining positions in the

---

*The Lancaster House Conference which began in London 8 September 1979 was a ninth attempt at a negotiated solution to the Rhodesian problem. Although officially hosted by the British government, the conference was the production of a compromise with African nations, especially the Front Line states, at the August Commonwealth Conference meeting in Lusaka. All parties were present at the Lancaster Conference including military representatives from both the Patriotic Front and the Rhodesian government. Besides the European members of the Commonwealth the Lancaster Conference also clearly had the full backing of the Carter Administration.

Zimbabwe-Rhodesia conflict which maximize their flexibility. They are distinguishing between short-term and long-term objectives. Neither wants to see a Zimbabwe run by the Patriotic Front. But both governments—unlike the right wing within the Tory Party (the Conservative Party headed by Margaret Thatcher), or that in the United States like the American Enterprise Institute for Public Policy Research (AEI)*—would at the present moment stop short of heavy and direct military intervention to prevent the Patriotic Front from coming to power. Unlike many in their own constituencies, the Carter and Thatcher administrations argue that in the long run the Patriotic Front, especially the Joshua Nkomo element of the Front, can be managed.

U.S.-British strategy *vis-a-vis* Zimbabwe pursues another approach which is reflective of the essence of trilateralism, i.e., the use of regionally influential countries like Tanzania and Nigeria as power brokers in managing change. That approach counts on manipulating the very real pressures felt by the Front Line states. *New African* (September 1979) quoted Julius Nyerere, the president of Tanzania, as having said that the reason he decided to back the British Lancaster House initiative was that it was the last chance for a peaceful settlement and that if it failed he could "foresee Rhodesia becoming another Mozambique." He went on to give his assurance that the Patriotic Front would not be an obstacle to the new initiative. Patriotic Front leaders want to make their own decisions independent of the West and even the Front Line States, or their socialist allies; but they are dependent on the latter for sanctuary and political and material suppport.

What is behind Nyerere's comment? On the one hand, Nyerere wants to see the war end.** Just as earnestly he is committed to seeing

---

*AEI, with a board of directors which includes people like Melvin Laird, William Colby, Barry Goldwater, Clark Clifford and John von Johnson of *Ebony* magazine, openly argues for a higher U.S. military profile in Southern Africa because of Africa's vital role in maintaining U.S. global interests. Although AEI stops short of advocating commitment of U.S. combat forces, it nonetheless urges increased planning preparation and expenditure so as to have such an option easily available at various locations in sub-Saharan Africa. See Palmer "U.S. Security Interests and Africa South of the Sahara," *AEI Defense Review* II: 6, 1978, pp. 2-43.

Also see the forthcoming report by Bob Lawrence and Holly Sklar, *U.S. Africa Policy for the 1980's: What the Think Tanks are Thinking*—covering AEI, Georgetown Center for Strategic and International Studies, as well as the more "liberal" Rockefeller Commission on Southern Africa and Council on Foreign Relations.

**The war has been long and costly to Tanzania which has provided the PF with support and training facilities. It has been even more costly to Tanzania's neighbor to the South, Mozambique. At the time of this writing for instance, Rhodesian

genuine majority rule in Zimbabwe. On the other hand, Nyerere is faced with a Tanzanian balance-of-payments deficit expected to reach $350 million by the end of the fiscal year 1979/80. Tanzania is awaiting a decision about needed supplementary financial assistance from both the International Monetary Fund (IMF) and from the World Bank, to which it is heavily indebted, giving the World Bank a larger and larger role in development planning and financing. Debt pressures increase the leverage which the trilateralist West currently holds over "new influentials" like Tanzania.

Zambia and Botswana face similar predicaments, only their situations are worsened by their historical economic dependence upon South Africa. So too is the case with Angola and Mozambique which inherited not just poverty, underdevelopment and war-time destruction, but also economies which were deliberately tilted so as to serve the Witwatersrand (South Africa) industrial mining complex. (See Carolyn Brown.) Add the costs of daily military aggression, vicious bombings and helicopter forays from South Africa and/or Rhodesia* which cost the lives of some four Mozambicans or Angolans and many Zimbabweans daily; the 150,000 Zimbabwean refugees which the Mozambican economy is sustaining; and the 500 million dollars in railroad and other revenues Mozambique has lost since it closed its border in compliance with the UN sanctions against Rhodesia in March 1976; and a stark picture emerges of the pressures upon the Front Line States.** The trilateralist states play upon these pressures in their quest to harness the radical nationalist fervor of the Patriotic Front's armed struggle.

Trilateralism in Africa today faces a grave dilemma. Domestic constituencies prohibit the use of traditional solutions, such as military interventions—which, as in the case of Vietnam, do not always prevail. At the same time the liberation movements of Zimbab-

---

mercenaries led Portuguese settlers, ex-Frelimo (the governing Party) supporters and South Africans, and captured the central town of Macossa. (*The Guardian*, London, 23 October 1979)..
*South Africa and Rhodesia both have raided refugee camps and PF quarters in Zambia and Botswana reaching even into the Zambian capital Lusaka, to attack, for example, Nkomo's residence. But consistently the brunt of the most viciious aggression has been reserved for sites in Angola and most especially, Mozambique. During the London Conference Salisbury cut off shipments of corn from South Africa via the Southern Rhodesia railway to Zambia, for added leverage over Zambian President Kaunda. See Michael Holman, "Why Salisbury is Squeezing Kaunda," *Financial Times*, October 24, 1979.
**ed. note: Zimbabwe Rhodesia carried out extensive military attacks against Mozambique and Zambia throughout the London Conference. See, for example, *New York Times*, 4 November 1979.

we, Namibia, and South Africa have developed a momentum which poses a radical threat to the world capitalist system. Thus, trilateralism turns to new partners and new solutions: new influentials like Tanzania are used as peace agents, the defenders of stability and world order. Colin Legum, a veteran participant/observer of events in Africa, recently summarized the trilateral approach in Africa:

> This new Western approach to the problems of the region contained five major elements. First, every stage of planning and implementing the two initiatives involved close consultation with the African states, most directly concerned—the five Front-line States (Tanzania, Zambia, Mozambique, Botswana and Angola), as well as Nigeria. Second, in the case of Rhodesia and Nambia, the leading liberation movements (the Patriotic Front and Swapo, respectively) were brought directly into the negotiating process. Third, the stated objective was to achieve majority rule. Fourth, the agreed aim was to defuse the violence; while not condemning the armed struggle, the premise of the diplomatic approach was that armed violence, was not necessarily the only road to majority rule. Fifth, explicit opposition to the introduction of big power politics into the region. (The justification for the Anglo-American role was that both counties were already involved in the area and could use their leverage positively. Meanwhile, no new foreign powers should be brought in as this would complicate the negotiating process and impede the achievement of majority rule.)[21]

Trilateralism will persist, devising other strategies, calling on other countries. As Samora Machel, quoted earlier in this paper, states: "when the internal solution doesn't work, they turn to the external one."

But the liberation movements also have their strategies and counterstrategies. By their very nature, the participants in liberation movements besides being excellent teachers are also excellent students. Recently Patriotic Front co-president, Robert Mugabe, answered a question about the common work of ZANU and ZAPU. As with the PF's consistent demonstration of flexibility at the Lancaster Conference, the response by Mugabe showed that the West's trilateralism is among the subjects he mastered. He said, showing patience and confidence:

> We try to work on a political level against the strategy worked out by Britain and the United States. Since the Kissinger Plan, Geneva Conference and the Anglo-American proposals, we resisted the bid to create a neo-colonial state in the country. We have also had the same diplomatic drive on the Zimbabwe question. That is at the political level. The joint [military] operations that we envisage are intended to balance the cooperation we have at the political level.[22]

Postscript (May 1980): The months between the start of the Lancaster House Conference on 8 September 1979 and Zimbabwean independence on 17 April 1980 witnessed a renewed effort on the part of the trilateral nations to manage Zimbabwean liberation. The Patriotic Front emerged from this contest with successes in two new arenas: the diplomatic arena and the electoral arena.

Throughout the constitutional discussions, cease-fire, elections, and transition period, the brazen manner in which the British, represented mainly by Lord Carrington and later by Lord Soames, the colonial governor, conducted themselves led many to suspect that the British strategy was to provoke the Patriotic Front into walking out of the negotiations so that a more "legitimized" solution could be conducted with Muzorewa. The Lancaster talks were formally ended on December 15, *without* the approval of the PF leaders. Muzorewa, however, was totally unacceptable to the Front Line States and the larger Organization for African Unity, which in July 1979 had formally reaffirmed its support for the PF as the sole legitimate representative of the people of Zimbabwe. Likewise, the role of the Commonwealth Secretariat was also crucial in seeing the negotiations initiated and followed through, intervening at critical junctures to gain concessions for the PF and facilitate the agreement, and later protest the British electoral bias.[23]

On 21 December 1979, the Lancaster House Agreement was signed by Robert Mugabe and Joshua Nkomo for the Patriotic Front, Bishop Muzorewa representing the Salisbury Administration, and Lord Carrington for the British Government. A cease-fire was set for December 28 and elections scheduled for late February. Even before the Agreement was signed the trilateral nations moved together to normalize relations with Rhodesia. On December 12 Lord Soames arrived in Salisbury to assume the post of colonial governor and Britain quickly dropped sanctions against Rhodesia to pressure the PF and bolster the Salisbury regime. On December 16 President Carter ended sanctions through executive action. France and Japan followed suit in the next few days. Britain and the U.S. were condemned by the United Nations Security Council for ending unilaterally UN-imposed sanctions before the UN did so.

On 22 December 1979 the London *Daily Telegraph* exulted that "Lord Carrington had pulled off Britain's greatest diplomatic coup of the decade."[24] But within two months the seedy side of diplomacy was revealed. Under direct orders from Prime Minister Thatcher and Lord Carrington, a massive surveillance operation was conducted. The British used Rhodesian security to interpret the African languages while also keeping the Rhodesians informed. Tapped telephones, bugged rooms, and monitored diplomatic communications were "why Lord Carrington could conduct the conference on the basis of brinksmanship. The intelligence services told him where the brinks were."[25]

In spite of British, Rhodesian, and South African maneuverings (often in violation of the Lancaster Agreement) before and during the election period—including detention of PF, especially ZANU candidates; secret funding by South African and multinational corporations; a strong South African military presence;[26] a pattern of dirty tricks by Rhodesian units; assassination attempts against Mugabe; a media campaign against ZANU and favoring Nkomo, and especially Muzorewa; intimidation and violence against the population by Muzorewa's expanded auxiliary force;[27] freedom of activity for Rhodesian security forces and their deployment by the British against PF guerillas (alleged at times by the very same Rhodesian security forces to have violated the cease-fire);[28] the delayed repatriation of 250,000 refugees from Mozambiques, many of them ZANU supporters—in spite of transparent attempts to subvert the electoral process, ZANU won a resounding victory. Led by Robert Mugabe, ZANU won nearly 63 percent of the popular vote and gained 57 seats in the 100 member House of Assembly (which reserved 20 seats for whites). ZAPU, led by Joshua Nkomo, won 24 percent of the vote and 20 seats. Muzorewa was finished.[29] The path ahead for Zimbabwe will be difficult; the battle against neo-colonialism is only beginning.[30] But the progress of the liberation movement thus far points to a strong future for Zimbabwean liberation.

A closing word about the Southern African regional situation is in order. On 18 December 1979, Prime Minister Thatcher affirmed the trilateral objective before the Foreign Policy Association in New York:

> The Lancaster House Agreement could prove a major step towards a peaceful evolution and away from violent revolution in Southern Africa. We are encouraged to persevere with the Five Power initiative to achieve an all-party settlement in Namibia.
>
> In this context I want to say a particular word about South Africa. There is now a real prospect that the conflicts on South Africa's borders, in Rhodesia and Namibia, will shortly be ended. This, combined with welcome initiatives on South African domestic policies, offer a chance to defuse a regional crisis which was potentially of the utmost gravity, and to make progress towards *an ending of the isolation of South Africa in world affairs."* [Italics mine][31]

In the Spring of 1980, Zimbabwe joined other African nations of Southern Africa in Lusaka to affirm their commitment to coalesce into a self-reliant regional entity, reducing the economic dominance of South Africa and countering Pretoria's strategy to form a constellation of dependent states around it.

FOOTNOTES

1. *Economist*, 26 May 1979.
2. *Times of Zambia*, 14 June 1979.
3. Report of the Secretariat: ECOSOC, UN, *The Activities of Transnational Corporations in the Industrial, Mining and Military Sectors of Southern Africa,* E/c.D/5l, (22 March 1979), p. 35.
4. President Samora Machel, "The Position of the People's Republic of Mozambique *vis-a-vis* the Evolution of the Situation in Southern Africa focusing on Zimbabwe," a speech delivered in Maputo, Mozambique on 15 September 1978.

Full text available from Mozambique Information Agency, P.O. Box 896, Maputo, Mozambique.

5. *West Africa*, No. 3244, 17 September 1979, p. 1683.

6. *Africa News*, 19 October 1979.

7. Reuters (Lusaka) 23 October 1979.

8. John Kore Berman "South Africans Miss Golden Opportunities" *The Guardian* (London), 21 October 1978.

9. *Zimbabwe News*, March-April, 1978.

10. Kenneth Adelman, "Africa's Security Needs," *Wall Street Journal*, 9 August 1979.

11. ACOA/Africa Fund, *The "New" Rhodesian Constitution: The Illusion of Majority Rule*, (New York, 1979), p. 4.

12. David Cante, "Black Votes, White Power: The Sham Election in Rhodesia," *The Nation*, July 14-21, 1979.

13. Quoted from "Puppet Show in Salisbury," *Zimbabwe News* (publication of Zimbabwe African National Union), 10:2, 1978.

14. "Sithole Forces Allege Rhodesian Massacre," *International Herald Tribune*, 19 August 1979.

15. Byron Howe quoted in the *Christian Science Monitor*, 8 May 1978.

16. *Encore*, 2 July 1979, p. 9.

17. Fred Landis, "Georgetown's Ivory Tower for Old Spooks," *Inquiry*, 30 September 1979, p. 9.

18. Speech at New York Hilton, 1 May 1979.

19. In addition to "Who's Who on the Trilateral Commission" also see Counter Information Services, *Sellout in Zimbabwe, Anti-Report No. 24*, (London) 1979.

20. *Africa News*, 19 October 1979, p. 10.

21. Colin Legum, *The Western Crisis Over Southern Africa*, (New York: Africana Publishing Company, 1979), p. 4.

22. Interview, *Southern Africa*, September 1979, p. 5.

23. See David Martin and Lawrence Marks, "Man Who Saved Rhodesian Deal," *The Observer* (London), 9 December 1979, and Colin Legum, "Report Rebukes Soames," *The Observer*, 6 April 1980.

24. David Adamsen, "Coup of the Decade by Carrington," *Daily Telegraph* (London), 22 December 1979.

25. Barrie Penrose, "Minister's Phone was Tapped by Secret Services," *The Sunday Times* (London), 3 February 1980. Also see Duncan Campbell, "Big Brother's Many Mansions," Part II, *New Statesman*, 8 February 1980.

26. See *Washington Post*, 1 December 1979, and the January 1980 Congressional Hearings "The President's Report on Rhodesia," especially the testimony of Richard Moose of the State Department Africa Desk.

27. See James MacManue, "A Nightmare Awaiting the British Governor," *The Guardian* (London), 28 November 1979.

28. "Governor Orders Rhodesians to Curb Rebel Infiltration," *New York Times*, 31 December 1979.

29. See David Caute, "The Battle for State Power," *New Statesman*, 7 March 1980.

30. See D.G. Clarke, *Foreign Companies and International Investment in Zimbabwe*, (London: Catholic Institute for International Relations, and Gwelo, Zimbabwe: Mambo Press, 1980) and United Nations Conference on Trade and Development (UNCTAD), *Zimbabwe: Towards a New Order: An Economic and Social Survey*, UNCTAD/MFD/1/UNDP PAF/78/010/1980.

31. Text of Prime Minister Margaret Thatcher's speech, "The West in the World Today," Foreign Policy Association, New York, 18 December 1980.

chapter four

TRILATERALISM AND THE CARIBBEAN: TYING UP "LOOSE STRINGS" IN THE WESTERN HEMISPHERE
*Philip Wheaton**

Introduction

Essential to any geopolitical definition of a region, such as the Caribbean,** is an understanding of the external forces which help shape it. The Caribbean has long been subject to exploitation and containment, first by European powers—England, Spain, and to a lesser extent, France and Holland—and later, by the United States. While there exist considerable cultural and linguistic differences between the Caribbean island nations, they all share a cruel heritage of slavery and colonialism. The United States has been the dominant imperial power in the region since ousting Spain in 1898. Economically, however, England remained paramount until World War II and played a large role in the Spanish-speaking colonies as well as the English-speaking colonies it controlled. As the British gradually conferred independence and dismantled their colonial administrations, the U.S. quickly moved in to fill the ensuing power vacuum (for example, a U.S.-Jamaica defense pact was signed in 1963, the year

*Philip Wheaton is co-director of EPICA, Ecumenical Program for Inter-American Communication and Action, Washington, D.C.
**The Caribbean includes the following: Antigua, Bahamas, Barbados, Belize, Bermuda, Cuba, Dominica, the Dominican Republic, Haiti, Grenada, Guadeloupe, Guyana, Jamaica, Panama, Puerto Rico, Santa Lucia, Trinidad and Tobago, and the Virgin Islands.

403

following Jamaican independence). Today the Caribbean is a region shaped politically, economically, and socially by its forced containment within the U.S. sphere of influence (Cuba alone has successfully revolted). England's formal departure, therefore, did not produce a post-colonial situation but a neocolonial situation which continues through the present.

In this article we will be analyzing the contemporary form of neocolonialism in the Caribbean and the impact of trilateral strategy as implemented by the Carter Administration. First we must look more closely at the interwoven history of British and U.S. imperialism.

Historical Linkages Between British and American Imperialism

A number of crucial reference points are helpful in understanding the relationship between British, American (and Spanish) imperialism in the Caribbean. First, during the eighteenth century, the British sugar industry in the West Indies—particularly in Barbados, Jamaica, and Grenada—was outproducing and outconsuming the combined industries of colonial U.S. and Canada. From England's perspective, sugar was king, and it was the accumulation of capital from this sugar industry that fueled the British Industrial Revolution.[1] Enormous profits were wrenched from the livelihoods of hundreds of thousands of African slaves, whose grandchildren and great-grandchildren today make up the majority of the Caribbean peoples; the native Indian peoples were largely exterminated by the colonialists. An antagonistic relationship has existed between Britain and the United States from as early as the Molasses Act in 1733 and it was the American Revolution which finally broke the monopoly of the British West Indies sugar trade.

Second, the United States moved into the Caribbean as an imperialist power much earlier than is generally realized. For example, in 1825 the U.S. effectively warned Simon Bolivar, the South America liberator, against sending an army to free Cuba and Puerto Rico from Spain. And between 1856 and 1865 the U.S. militarily invaded the Isthmus of Panama five times.[2] These interventions were executed in order to secure the Isthmus for the Panama Railroad Co., a private U.S. firm, and thus promote U.S. trans-oceanic travel from the East coast of the U.S. to the Oregon Territory and to the gold in California—as part of the empire-building underway on the continent, wreaking havoc on the native Indian and Mexican cultures. Tensions mounted between the U.S. and England (which enjoyed continued naval superiority) as a result of these interventions and earlier events. They were resolved through treaty negotiations which prescribed for the use and control of Panama and Central America. In many respects, the United States became an imperial power long before most of its citizens saw their country as an international actor.

Third, the United States went to war with Spain in 1898 in response to growing domestic economic problems which the government hoped to ease through the lucrative enterprise of foreign expansionism. The blowing up of the U.S. Maine in the Havana Harbor was in all probability an incident staged deliberately by the U.S. in order to justify the Spanish-American War. Cuban independence fighters were nearly victorious in liberating their country from Spain before the U.S. intervened with the alibi of anti-Spanish colonialism.

Then the United States arbitrarily annexed Puerto Rico as spoils of war in the Paris Peace Treaty although there had been no fighting there. In a similar fashion, the U.S. only aided the Panamanian independence fighters in August 1903, after the Colombian Congress (which administered Panama's territory) had refused to allow the United States to build a canal across the Isthmus. The new Panamanian leadership was forced to respect the U.S. interpretation of the Treaty of 1903 which Colombia had rejected. The interest of the U.S. in each of these cases was not to save the Caribbean peoples from Spanish colonialism—as so loudly exclaimed—but to establish Caribbean bases for its own imperialist expansion into the region.

Fourth, during World War II, the United States made it clear to the British (in conversations between Franklin D. Roosevelt and Winston Churchill) that colonialism was no longer appropriate in the Caribbean.[3] The accord they reached included the development of a West Indies Federation under Anglo-American auspices. This was a direct countermove to a similar initiative first advanced in 1935 by the indigenous Caribbean Labor Congress (CLC). These two groups, the CLC and an Anglo-American Commission met separately in Kingston, Jamaica in 1947 to determine whether such regional development would be Caribbean controlled, through worker pressure and participation, or imperially imposed by foreign governments. Although the West Indies Federation was never implemented, the CLC initiative was quickly suppressed through an anticommunist campaign undertaken by the American Institute for Free Labor Development (AIFLD). Their main foe at the time was the democratically elected, pro-labor, socialist leader Cheddi Jagan of Guyana.

Fifth, there was a climactic juxtaposition of events in the Caribbean during the late 1950s and 1960s. The English-speaking islands achieved independence during this period, inspiring two key struggles against colonialism and imperialism in the adjoining Spanish-speaking region. These were the Cuban Revolution in 1959 (which successfully defended itself against the U.S.-directed Bay of Pigs invasion in 1961) and the invasion of the Dominican Republic by over 20,000 U.S. troops in 1965 to counter forces attempting to reinstate the 1963 Constitution and restore Juan Bosch to the presidency. (See Lisa Wheaton.)

> President Johnson's initial justification of U.S. intervention was "to give protection to hundreds of Americans who are still in the Dominican Republic and escort them safely back to this country." However, four days later after thousands of men had come ashore, the president justified the intervention as a way to prevent "the establishment of another Communist government in the Western Hemisphere." In fact, the evidence seems conclusive that the prevention of another Cuba was the real explanation from the beginning of the intervention.[4]

These two events—the one progressive (liberating and socialist); the other regressive (repressive and dependent capitalist)—clearly illuminate the depth and nature of the conflict in the Caribbean. Progressive English-speaking Caribbeans reflecting on these events initially believed their countries would not fall under the same shadow of U.S. imperialism. But now, especially since the 1973-75 period, they clearly understand that they do.

Change from Colonial to Neocolonial Domination

The postcolonial history of the Caribbean[5] actually refers to the post-British colonial era. During this period the dependent national ruling classes (landowners, businessmen, and professionals) quickly assumed control, filling the power vacuum created internally by the British departure. In fact, such transitions of power were normally arranged before formal independence actually took place. The post-independence leadership experimented with new forms of government, economic planning, and social development—sometimes in progressive, sometimes in regressive ways. The populace pressed the new leadership for social reforms which would provide more jobs, a better standard of living and justice. The generally negative response to these initiatives destroyed the myth that somehow with the passing of colonialism traditional class relations and economic exploitation would be eliminated. Obviously this did not occur. The heightened level of popular expression and progressive experimentation on the part of some of the new leaders caused the national economic elite to attempt to exercise greater control over the situation along with multinational corporations and banks. Increasingly, the United

States intervened indirectly and directly to shape the direction of change.

The experience of having parameters imposed from above and outside has heightened the political consciousness of many Caribbeans about the nature of neocolonialism and imperialism. It was a process that moved progressive Caribbeans from a state of resignation before a fading colonialism, to hopes of self-determination and independent development, to a more sobered and more systematic understanding of the pervasive nature of imperialism. Just as it took the U.S. Marine invasion of Santo Domingo to make Dominicans antiimperialist; so, for example, the harsh conditions imposed on Jamaica by the International Monetary Fund have heightened antiimperialist sentiment there. In sum, Caribbean consciousness has developed from one of anticolonialism, especially antiracism and pro-Africanism, into an antiimperialist, and, in some nations, a prosocialist orientation, between the 1960s and the 1970s—as the primary focus switched from Britain to the United States. Furthermore, this growing awareness has corresponded with the creation of numerous Caribbean antiimperialist organizations in the United States and Canada, which have helped transform this local and regional movement into one of hemispheric solidarity.[6]

Trilateral Strategy as Implemented by the Carter Administration

No analysis of the Caribbean can ignore the fact that changes have taken place in the U.S. approach toward the region since Jimmy Carter assumed the presidency. These differences are exemplified by the more conservative and confrontational approach of Kissinger, Nixon, and Ford, on the one hand; and the more liberal, conciliatory approach of Brzezinski, Vance, and Carter. However, we must immediately correct any notion that this implies some substantive change in the direction of U.S. policy. Rather, it represents a change in tactics in response to altered historical conditions. The goal is the same: to maintain U.S. hegemony over the region and, indeed, to integrate the Caribbean region even more closely into the U.S. sphere of influence and into the control of the trilateral powers.

Trilateral strategy holds that the Western industrialized nations must back away from, or openly oppose, old-style colonialism. It is quite clear that this is a strategy of the Carter Administration. As is described elsewhere in this book, this is not a coincidence but a result of the interconnection between the Carter Administration and trilateral leadership. In applying this anticolonial policy to Southern Africa, the Carter Administration has been faced with the contradiction of opposing white minority rule there while maintaining U.S.

colonial outposts in the American Hemisphere. Thus, if President Carter could say, as he did in his Notre Dame speech, that colonialism is dead, it became encumbent upon Carter's Administration to begin to affect changes in these colonial outposts—or risk undermining the impact of the worldwide stance. Henry Kissinger was aware of these contradictions and their dangers as well (for example, it was precisely this awareness that led Kissinger to sign the unsuccessful, Eight-Point Agreement with Panama's Foreign Minister Tack in 1974, following the 1973 UN decision in favor of Panamanian control over the canal). However, now the situation is far more urgent and thus the *mode* and *speed* of confronting these problems has changed under Carter.

Below we will discuss the four major elements of trilateral strategy, as executed by the Carter Administration, toward the Caribbean: modification of colonialism; nonconfrontational politics multilateral developmentalism; and human rights promotion based on so-called political neutrality.

Modification of Colonialism

The United States has two obvious colonial enclaves in the Western Hemisphere, both in the Caribbean: Panama and Puerto Rico. U.S. imperialism thus faces this dilemma—how to modify these colonial contradictions without jeopardizing hegemonic control over the region? In the case of Panama, it is now clear—with the dust of the treaty debates behind us—that the actual result of those treaties is a minimal modification of colonialism, not its uprooting. We note that the treaties stipulate that the U.S. is to maintain its existing military bases *indefinitely*; that the U.S. will be directly involved in the defense of the Canal until the year 2000; that the U.S. and its "zonian" citizens have been granted extraordinary rights over the use and disposition of certain lands in the Canal Zone; that the U.S. will dominate the Panama Canal Commission which will operate the Canal until the year 2000. Moreover, the terms of the neutrality treaty are purposely ambiguous; the U.S. claims the right to intervene militarily *after the year 2000* to guarantee canal security. Moreover the U.S. reserves the right to build a sea-level canal in Panama as a substitute for the present canal (this is linked to the energy policy of the Carter Administration and the need to transport petroleum from Alaska to the East coast of the U.S.).[7] Even this rather paltry modification of colonialism is more a future projection than a present reality.

What is of prime importance is that the debate over the new treaties has masked the central concern of the United States regarding the Isthmus; this refers to what a leading Panamanian economist has called the "Platform of Transnational Services."[8] One component of the platform is the Colon Free Port, the second largest free port in the world—where 600 multinational corporations enjoy special conditions such as tax-free benefits and where over 50,000 paper or brass-plate offices are set up to carry out paper transactions (e.g. altering the destination, ownership, and prices of products moving through the canal) resulting in millions of dollars in added profits for multinational corporations, insurance agencies, etc. Another component is the enormous hemispheric banking center at Panama City—consisting of more than eighty foreign banks well representative of the trilateral nations and their operations through-out Latin America. The goal of the treaties is to stabilize Panama—politically, economically, and militarily—so that the functioning of the Platform of Transnational Services will be guaranteed. It is this neocolonial system that the U.S. Treaty negotiators were concerned with defending, not the Canal Zone, which has become a glaring symbol of U.S. imperialism, nor the antiquated canal itself. Terence Todman, assistant secretary of state for Inter-American Affairs, expressed these intentions clearly in 1977:

> ...*Panama is a hemispheric bastion of free enterprise*, hosting a large number of international businesses and seventy major U.S. banks...
>
> ...In terms of U.S. defense interests, perhaps the most important aspect of these Treaties is what they don't do—they don't limit in any way our freedom to draw upon our whole range of military options to act in defense of the Canal in any way we find necessary.
>
> ...Instead of wondering whether next year will bring a new outbreak of civil disturbances, or mounting U.S.-Panamanian tensions, or unforeseen Panamanian demands, or the stopping or starting of negotiations with uncertain outcome, *we will be able to look forward to 22 years of stability and cooperation under our own control, and every reason to expect a continuation of the same stability and cooperation thereafter.*[9] [Italics ed.]

A modification of Puerto Rico's colonial status is another item high on Carter's Latin American agenda. A crisis has been building there ever since 1965-67 when the Free Associated State or Common-wealth of Puerto Rico became highly unstable. The development model upon which the Commonwealth was based—called Operation Bootstrap, but totally dependent on U.S. inputs—was a failure. It disintegrated precisely 15 to 17 years after its initiation; that represents the time period of tax-free status which had been granted to U.S. companies moving to Puerto Rico in the late 1940s and early

1950s. Largely because of the cessation of that special privilege many of these companies left the island to seek higher profits in the Dominican Republic, Haiti, and elsewhere. With that exodus, the Commonwealth model fell into disarray as capital-intensive industries replaced the older labor-intensive industries. Since 1968, no political party has been able to survive more than one term in office. The much heralded Compact of Permanent Union, an attempt to bolster the Free Associated State, was never enacted; it failed to move out of the House Subcommittee in 1976 and its proponent, Governor Hernandez Colon of the Popular Democrats (PPD), lost that year's election. In addition, there is constant pressure from the Puerto Rican *Independistas* and other forces opposing affiliation with the U.S.[10] These forces were successful in persuading the United Nations Decolonization Committee to bring the question of Puerto Rico's status (whether it should be officially regarded as a colony of the United States and treated as such) to the floor of the General Assembly in 1978.

Obviously, some modification of Puerto Rico's status is in order. The question for the U.S. government is in which direction to move and how best to progress: towards greater autonomy for Puerto Rico (few observers believe that the U.S. would willingly allow Puerto Rico to achieve full independence) or towards statehood—the integration of Puerto Rico into the Union as the 51st state. Proof that this latter option is being seriously considered is readily available. Just before Carter took office, President Ford issued a surprising announcement in favor of statehood from Vail, Colorado. Within six months after Carter's inauguration two studies emerged from the Library of Congress which analyzed the transition from Commonwealth Status.[11] In addition, and more significantly, HEW has prepared a 10,000 page report on Puerto Rico, anticipating its proximate incorporation into the United States. These steps are part of an orchestrated plan to win public acceptance of Puerto Rico as a state; a move tentatively scheduled for 1981 or shortly thereafter.

There is no easy neocolonial solution for Puerto Rico. The United States continues to treat it as a colony. For example, the U.S. Navy continues to bomb the inhabited island of Vieques and surrounding fishing waters as part of military training operations,[12] the FBI continually harrasses progressive Puerto Ricans in the U.S., and police repression in Puerto Rico continues. "In 1975, the *New York Times* reported that 'ninety-eight percent of all the food, raw materials and manufactured goods consumed here are imported from the mainland and 85 percent of the island's exports go to the mainland.' "[13] The mainland, of course, is the United States. The cost Puerto Ricans bear for generating more profits for U.S. business is extremely high; low wages, severe unemployment, and poor living standards are the norm. The environment suffers as well; worsening industrial pollution is another of the many corporate gifts to the island. While statehood is purported to eliminate colonialism, in actuality it would represent the ultimate colonization of the Borinqueno people.[14]

Non-Confrontational Politics

Another basic trilateral strategy is that of non-confrontational politics, coupled with aggressive economics. Three themes are illustrated in Brzezinski's well-known book, *Between Two Ages*, which bear upon this policy. First, that a confrontational approach as advocated by Kissinger is unworkable and, thus, taboo; that the U.S. must take the Third World seriously; and, that the U.S. can only resume its role as world leader on the basis of Western unity and cooperation with the multinational corporate elite. It is only when we understand the differences as well as the similarities between the Kissinger and Brzezinski approaches that we can appreciate the change in U.S. policy toward the Caribbean. A key example, the case of Jamaica between 1976 and 1977, is analyzed below.

Two major policy changes were adopted by Jamaican Prime Minister Michael Manley mid-way through his first term in office. First, in the Spring of 1974, he began a program to gradually nationalize bauxite (of which Jamaica is one of the world's leading producers). Second, that fall, he instituted his political program known as "Democratic Socialism." The combined actions generated a vicious U.S. response comparable to the campaign launched against Salvador Allende in Chile. That is, a strategy of economic destabilization was implemented which involved the shutting off of multilateral loans and private bank loans, a decline in U.S. aid, and other measures in the context of a growing economic boycott led by the U.S. against Jamaica. A campaign of political destabilization was begun before the 1976 elections. This series of political actions was triggered by a Christmas visit by Kissinger to Jamaica in 1975 during which he asked Manley to stop backing the Angolan MPLA (which the U.S. was covertly opposing) and to accept the harsh conditions of the International Monetary Fund in return for an end to the economic boycott. Manley rejected both demands. Within a few months, Operation Werewolf, directed by the CIA with the help of the JLP, the oppostion party, was begun.[15] The results were catastrophic for Jamaica: so many people were killed, wounded or driven from their burned-out homes during the ensuing disorders that Manley was forced to invoke a state of emergency in June 1976. Fortunately, however, the CIA strategy backfired—partly due to an expose by Philip Agee on CIA activities in Jamaica which appeared at the time. Manley went on to win a popular mandate for Democratic Socialism with an overwhelming victory in the popular elections of December 1976 for his second term in office.

Carter rejected such brazen tactics and stopped all forms of political harassment of the Manley government. Nevertheless, when Rosalynn Carter visited Jamaica in the summer of 1977 she urged Manley to accept the conditions of the IMF. By April of that year, Jamaica's economy was in such a state of crisis as a result of continuing economic destabilization that Manley accepted certain IMF conditions in return for aid. A year later, in May 1978, he was forced to capitulate to full IMF demands; such harsh price, wage, and budget controls were imposed upon the Jamaicans that Manley's democratic socialism program is in jeopardy.[16] (See Phillips.) This illustration shows how the Carter Administration practices nonconfrontational politics while successfully employing the economic pressures used by previous administrations in order to maintain neocolonial control.

Multilateral Developmentalism

The unstable social conditions in many Caribbean countries today are the direct result of serious economic problems such as poverty, unemployment, seasonal underemployment, etc. What are obviously needed are appropriate internal development programs— encompassing heightened agricultural production and nationally directed industrial growth. Long recognizing this need and desirous of creating a stimulus for such development, without outside influence, various regional strategies have been attempted by the Caribbean peoples. Two of these are the Caribbean Free Trade Association (CARIFTA), created in 1968, and the Caribbean Community and Common Market (CARICOM), which evolved out of CARIFTA in 1973. CARIFTA and CARICOM have been constantly frustrated by disagreements over goals and by the reluctance of the larger countries to share advantages with their smaller neighbors. Fomenting this national and class competition is pressure from U.S. imperialism and the Western economic community in the context of the world economic crisis.[17]

When Carter took office a decision was made by the Department of State to promote a regional economic program led by the trilateral nations—thus circumventing Caribbean proposals. By mid-1977 a Caribbean Task Force had been established by the State Department "precisely to focus on economic development problems of the Caribbean...through aid flows both bilateral and multilateral in nature."[18] What is noteworthy about this strategy is that both Jamaica and Guyana were singled out as problem areas, representing examples "of this Administration's willingness to *tolerate* economic models which are not necessarily our own and which we would not advocate but with which we are prepared to live."[19] [Italics added.] The responsibility for implementing this development strategy was turned over to the World Bank; a preliminary planning meeting took place in December 1977, followed by the first formal meeting of the "Caribbean Group for Cooperation in Economic Development" on 25 June 1978. Both of these conferences were held in Washington, D.C., not in the Caribbean! According to the World Bank, the Caribbean Group for Cooperation in Economic Development was established:

> ...to serve as a mechanism for the coordination and strengthening of external assistance to the Caribbean and for the continuing review of national and regional activities related to economic development in the area.[20]

The donor nations to provide such external assistance are the U.S., Canada, France, the Federal Republic of Germany, Israel, Japan, the Netherlands, Norway, Spain, and the United Kingdom.

The crucial point about this Western-dominated multilateral strategy is that it supplants, and in many respects, co-opts, indigenous regional development plans envisaged by an independent CARICOM. Furthermore, the agency will restrict relations between the Caribbean region and Cuba. Africa and the Socialist bloc by tying loan eligibility to trade restrictions with countries outside the Caribbean Group for Cooperation.

Human Rights Campaign and Political Neutrality

A fourth element in the Carter Administration's new approach to the Caribbean is a strategy of deploring human rights abuses while maintaining a posture of supposed political neutrality. Although the U.S. government may loudly protest abuses, such protestations are hollow without a strong stance with respect to full democratic rights. In fact, the issue of democratic rights is the key indication as to whether Carter is serious about human rights or whether it is merely a ploy to bolster Carter's standing and improve the tainted image of the U.S. It is here where the capitalist system and moral concerns come to an impasse since, today, dictators and military regimes have become the principal guarantors of capitalism and anticommunism in the Caribbean.

The failure of the Carter Administration to take a forthright stand wherever democracy is being threatened or in crisis is not, of course, limited to the Caribbean. Early in his administration, for example, Carter supported Anastasio Somoza in Nicaragua as well as Balaguer in the Dominican Republic. He praised each of these repressive rulers for their "progress" in the area of human rights. Because events in the Caribbean are less publicized and, thus, less well-known than events in South and Central America—like the Nicaraguan Revolution—the connection is not always drawn with the Caribbean. Events in Grenada and Guyana are two glaring examples of this media and public oversight.

In 1977, the fascist government of Eric Guery in Grenada invited Chilean military advisers to the country in a move which appeared to represent efforts by the Chilean Junta to establish an anticommunist base in the Caribbean. Grenadian troops were trained in Santiago and sophisticated weaponry was imported from Chile. In the case of Guyana, strongman Forbes Burnham—originally placed in power through the help of the CIA in overthrowing democratically-elected Cheddi Jagan—staged a dubious 1978 referendum by which the Burnham-dominated Congress was converted into a constituent assembly. The assembly has power to draft a new constitution which will not have to be approved by any future plebiscite. It is, in effect, a referendum to end all referendums and it was vigorously opposed and denounced by all liberal and progressive sectors in the society, including the church. There was no comment from the White House in either of these cases.

While the State Department may argue that such a hands-off approach is in keeping with its policy of political neutrality and nonintervention, the fact is that such a policy is selectively applied. The United States intervened in the Dominican Republic in 1965, in Jamaica in 1976, and it will continue to do so under Carter wherever there is a threat to capitalism and a possible opening to communism. As we have argued above, brazen intervention tactics are normally rejected by the Carter/trilateral approach in favor of diplomatic pressures or, if necessary, economic destabilization programs. Generally, the U.S. attempts to do this indirectly through multilateral agencies such as the IMF or the World Bank. The Caribbean is highly instructive in this regard because it is an area of particular concern for the present administration and a good arena for evaluating these tactical changes. More importantly, through this new strategy the Caribbean is being just as effectively integrated into the U.S. sphere of influence as it was under the more crude oppression of earlier imperialism.

Accommodation: The Ideology of Neocolonialism

The preceding examples clearly illustrate a U.S. neocolonial strategy that is being actively pursued and applied in the Caribbean region. It is equally important, however, to assess the ideology that accompanies this strategy. The positive side of Carter's rejection of confrontational tactics entails some adjustment on the part of the West to the unified anticolonial stance of Third World countries and the development of a policy of accommodation by the United States. One of the chief spokespersons for this neocolonial ideology is Tom Farer—a member of the Inter-American Commission of Human Rights of the O.A.S. (Organization of American States) and former special assistant to the assistant secretary of state for Inter-American affairs.

Farer orginally outlined his thesis in a paper entitled: "The United States and the Third World: A Basis for Accomodation." In this paper he frankly admits that any policy modification is a tactical adjustment, the goal of which is to preserve the capitalist system:

> What must be defended in the large is an economic system which rewards the capitalist virtues of investment, innovation, hard work, and sensitivity to the shifting needs and preferences of consumers. As Lincoln Gordon [former U.S. ambassador to Brazil] recently noted, this is one of the reasons why a comprehensive system of "price indexing" should be unacceptable: "If world demand is shifting away from a given commodity,...what is needed is a structural shift in...production and exports to items in stronger demand." Preservation of the incentives to practice those virtues is essential because without them the world's product will shrink. That is bad for the North, worse for the South, and absolutely destructive of any possibility of accommodation.[21]

The anathema shown here to price indexing is interesting given the fact that Farer's article was published in October 1975, one year after the bauxite price-indexing arrangement initiated by the Manley government. Farer's statement that without these pro-capitalist virtues the world's product will shrink is, of course, false. What would shrink under price indexing is the capitalist share of wealth as the balance of profits and resources was redistributed. To date this has not occurred in real terms to any notable extent, but a symbolic victory was achieved. Manley's action, for instance, was a sign to the Caribbean of what a Third World rebellion might look like and capitalism was not pleased.

The goal of accommodation to the Third World, argues Farer, is to co-opt the spirit of solidarity which anticolonialism has generated. This accommodation implies an anticolonial posture on the part of the

U.S. which would help lessen the distrust rightly held by Third World countries against the West and would provide a basis for cooperation:

> If anticolonialism as defined above, is in fact, the paramount source of cohesion in the Third World, one necessary consequence is the intense links it forges among all the issues which it touches. Hence, the successful accommodation of U.S.-Third World differences in some issues would necessarily enhance the prospects of accommodation all along the line.[22]

The goal of such anticolonialism is to pave the way for a smoother pattern of neocolonialism. According to Farer, Western nations, and particularly the United States should no longer *speak* and *look* like colonial powers by *appearing to change* they will have greater flexibility to act in their own interest:

> A second corollary of the main proposition[accommodation]is the importance of gestures. It is not only what the United States does that matters; what it says also counts. After all, some of the most damaging humiliations of the colonial relationship were a function of Western rhetoric and the patronizing and contemptuous attitudes which it embodies and to a considerable extent continues to embody.[23]

Conclusion

The changes taking place in the Caribbean are not changes which benefit the mass of the population. They are not changes in the direction of growing self-determination by individual nations nor toward the strengthening of regional ties. Where relations are developed with progressive countries, such as Cuba, or liberated nations in Africa, the U.S. is cool or hostile to them. In this transition from British colonialism to U.S. neocolonialism, we have observed a strengthening of U.S. hegemony under the trilateral strategy which prefers economic aggressiveness to militarism and direct political threats. This neocolonial approach is even more insidious than its parent because it pretends inter-American partnership and good will but only under conditions that are acceptable to the United States.

If we look at the Caribbean in relation to the rest of the hemisphere, we are witnessing a move on the part of U.S. imperialism to tie up some loose strings in an area heretofore somewhat disregarded. Here, as elsewhere in the Third World, the West hopes to discard its colonial robes while maintaining its neocolonial throne.[24]

Editor's Postscript: On 13 March 1979, the government of Eric Gairy was overthrown. Maurice Bishop became prime minister of the People's Revolutionary Government of Grenada. In October 1979 Carter announced a new program of U.S. intervention in the Caribbean, as described in the conclusion to this volume. So far, 1980 has witnessed the bombing of the stadium in Grenada, which Prime Minister Bishop survived unhurt but many others were killed or injured; a violent destabilization campaign in Jamaica, including attempts on the life of Prime Minister Manley and a coup attempt against the PNP government; the assassination of Walter Rodney, internationally-respected scholar and a leader of the Working People's Alliance of Guyana, followed shortly by a new IMF loan arrangement for the Burnham government although it had failed in meeting previous IMF criteria.

FOOTNOTES

1. Eric Williams, *Capitalism and Slavery,* (London: Andre Deutsch, 1964), pp. 114-116.
2. EPICA, *Panama: Sovereignty for a Land Divided,* (Washington D.C., 1976), p. 11.
3. Trevor Munroe, *The Politics of Constitutional Decolonization* (Kingston: University of the West Indies, 1974), p. 27.
4. Inserted by the editor from Cole Blaiser, *The Hovering Giant: U.S. Response to Revolutionary Change in Latin America,* (University of Pittsburgh Press, 1976, p. 246. Internal quotations are from U.S. Department of State Bulletin, 17 May 1965, p. 738 and pp. 744-48 respectively.
5. See Michael Manley, *Politics of Change* (Washington, D.C.: Howard University Press, 1975).
6. For example, the Guyanese Defense Committee, the North American Federation of Grenadian Organizations, the U.S. Committee for Human and Democratic Rights in the Caribbean, etc.
7. For an analysis of the treaties see *Treaty for Us, Treaty for Them* (Washington, D.C.: EPICA, 1977), pp. 5-6 and p. 14.
8. Mario R. Villalobos, "Un Tratado Para Ellos," *Dialogo Social* (Panama City, October 1977), p. 33 ff.
9. From remarks by Todman to the Conference of UPI editors and publishers Puerto Rico, 13 October 1977, cited in *Treaty for Us, Treaty for Them*, p. 21.
10. See *Puerto Rico: A People Challenging Colonialism* (Washington, D.C.: EPICA, 1976).
11. See Peter B. Sheridan, "Puerto Rico: Commonwealth, Statehood or Independence?" and William A. Lansill, "Puerto Rico: Independence or Statehood?" (Washington, D.C.: Library of Congress, 1977).
12. The people of Vieques have long struggled to get the U.S. Navy, which occupies four-fifths of the island off their land. The Vieques Fisherman's Association has been protesting the bombing of the island and their fishing waters. Many *Viequenses* have been killed or maimed as a result of the bombings and "practice" assaults, and many *Viequenses* and their supporters have been arrested for protesting the naval actions. For information contact the Center for Constitutional Rights in New York, and EPICA in Washington, D.C.
13. Cited in *Puerto Rico: A People Challenging Colonialism*, p. 30.·
14. See Manuel Moldonado-Denis, *Puerto Rico: A Socio-Historic Interpretation,* (New York: Vintage, 1972) and Louise Cripps, *Puerto Rico: The Case for Independence* (Cambridge: Schenkman Publishing Co., 1974).

15. "CIA and Local Gunmen Plan Jamaica Coup," *Counterspy* 3:2, (December 1976), p. 36.

16. See *Jamaica: Caribbean Challenge* (Washington D.C.: EPICA, 1979).

17. William G. Demas, "Essays on Caribbean Integration and Development," ISER (University of the West Indies, 1976).

18. From Remarks made by Sally Shelton, assistant undersecretary of state for Latin American affairs, in "U.S. Policy Towards the Caribbean," a speech published by the Institute for Policy Studies, Washington, D.C. February, 1979, p. 1.

19. *Ibid.,* p. 7.

20. World Bank News Release, 26 June 1978, Washington, D.C., p. 1.

21. *Foreign Affairs*, October 1975, p. 93.

22. *Ibid.,* p. 85.

23. *Ibid.*

24. For a more extended analysis of trilateralism and especially Carter/Trilateral strategy toward the Third World see Shank, Wheaton, and Lockwood, "Jimmy Carter's Foreign Policy, Human Rights and the Trilateral Commission," (ACTS Washington DC, September 1977).

chapter five

"DEMOCRATIZATION" IN
THE DOMINICAN REPUBLIC
*Lisa Wheaton**

Introduction

Since mid-1978, a decided shift in U.S. government policy has occurred toward the Dominican Republic, until recently under military dictatorship. It can be defined as a process of democratization, in which the Carter Administration's human rights campaign is a highly visible element of this democratization strategy.[1]

The recent Dominican national elections of May 1978, wherein the Dominican Revolutionary Party (PRD) achieved an electoral victory over Joaquin Balaguer, reveal this U.S. policy shift in support of democratization. When Dominican military forces intervened in the vote count, the U.S. stood by and called for "free, honest, and open" elections, and opposed military intervention. This is a startling action for anyone having monitored U.S. military and economic support of the Balaguer regime over the last twelve years. The last time the "constitutionalists" had a chance at a popular victory, the United States responded with 20,000 marines to restore the military regime, as we shall see below.

Democratization is a political face-lift for the undemocratic economic and political practices found in a country whose economy and politics are determined by foreign interests, just as the Human

*Lisa Wheaton works with the EPICA Task Force, a program of the Council on the Caribbean and Latin America of the National Council of Churches.

Rights campaign is a face-lift for the U.S. government's sagging moral image. The strategy is rooted in the trilateral solution to problems between the industrialized West and Third World countries such as the Dominican Republic. The Trilateral Commission calls for:

—The end to "old-fashioned colonialism...neo-colonialism, paternalism, and tutelage;"

—The need to promote "cooperation" between all nations in order to avoid "disassociation," particularly by the developing countries;

—The need to promote and manage the interdependence of the world, to more successfully integrate nations into an interdependent system.[2]

Speaking of the role of the trilateral nations in international politics, Commissioners argue that "their aspirations should go beyond merely *coping* with future events to *shaping* these events."[3] [Italics mine.] Democratization is an attempt to shape the political and economic system of the Dominican Republic and other countries. To fully comprehend these recent events some historical background is necessary.

U.S. Economic and Military Presence: 1844-1930

U.S. intervention in the Dominican Republic began in the late 1880s when individual commercial interests acquired land to participate in the sugar industry, the mainstay of the economy.* There was a constant struggle for national power from the 1844 independence until 1900 when foreign interests, particularly the U.S., moved in to singularly control the Dominican economy. As a stabilizing measure the U.S. dollar was imposed as the national currency in 1905. By 1912, the U.S. National Bank was established, and in 1917, the International Banking Company of New York arrived.

By 1916, claiming civil war had broken out and insisting that the U.S. was responsible for stabilizing the situation, the United States Marines intervened in Dominican politics establishing martial law and a U.S. military government. Despite opposition from Dominican President Jimenez, the United States remained in the country, continuing its military rule for the next eight years. Within weeks of the Marine invasion, the Central Romana Sugar Refinery (under the

---

*During the last half of the 19th century, foreign interests—Cuban, Italian, Puerto Rican, and North American—came to dominate the agricultural base of the country's economy. Power in Dominican society was then held by the large landed aristocracy (or *latifundistas*) who were closely linked to, or part of, the commercial exporting sector.

Puerto Rico Sugar·Company) and the Grenada Fruit Company, both U.S. business interests, were established. There was an immediate effort to disarm the Dominican Armed Forces as well as the civilian population, and to re-establish a U.S. trained National Guard.

The National Guard, created and controlled by the U.S. military and representing the strongest organized military force in the country, remained to safeguard U.S. interests after formal military withdrawal in 1924. In 1930 President Horacio Vasquez (in office from 1924) was ousted by National Guard Chief Trujillo, because of his "excessive democratic tendencies." Trujillo held the presidency for the next thirty-one years.

Trujillo and the Consolidation of Capital: 1930-1961

Trujillo came to power with the support of U.S. corporate interests. One-third of the country's sugar was produced by the U.S.-owned Central Romana refinery, while another 20 per cent was controlled by La Casa Vicini, wealthy national land owners. Sugar made up 54.8 percent of all exports.. Trujillo's own assets in 1930 were relatively small, amounting to no more than two middle-sized *fincas* (or farms).[4]

Trujillo's long-run goal was to reduce, if not altogether end, the role of foreign economic interests in the Dominican economy and consolidate national wealth under his personal rule.*

But economic control alone would not guarantee Trujillo's power. When he came into the presidency he began to carry out a major campaign of torture and death against his opponents. Most people—wealthy and poor—feared for their safety if they did not concur with the "Benefactor's" plans. Under such harsh repression, little serious political opposition grew between 1930 and 1961. Formal opposition parties were outlawed. In the 1930s, Trujillo formed the Dominican Party (PD) to which every government employee was obligated to belong in order to continue working. Local power aspirers had to go through the Trujillo-controlled

---

*To do so he carried out two basic economic policies which were not initially threatening to U.S. investors whose wealth was heavily concentrated in the sugar and banking industries. First, he focused on building up the internal market for local and foreign goods. Second, he passed laws and entered into business agreements allowing him to monopolize certain industries. Trujillo gained control of those industries providing basic necessities to the Dominican people such as clothing, shoes, cement, some foodstuffs and certain exporting industries like tobacco and coffee. Industrialization of the economy was stimulated.

economic and political structure to establish themselves.* Early in his rule, Trujillo welcomed foreign investment in the country; so as far as the U.S. was concerned he did not represent a threat and the U.S remained only marginally involved in domestic politics. It would not be until after 1950 when Trujillo's mounting economic wealth began to infringe on U.S investments that the Benefactor's days were numbered.

Between 1940 and 1950, Trujillo began to seriously expand his economic control to the foreign-dominated banking sector for the first time.** By 1950, Trujillo controlled almost all of the economy—estimates range from 65-85 percent—except for the important sugar industry. With sugar untouched, U.S. investment more than doubled between 1946 and 1955, rising from $84,170,440 to $201,491,411.[8] But in other industries, e.g., tobacco, U.S. investments were restricted.

In 1950, Trujillo established a competing sugar refinery in Rio Haina.***By 1961, when Trujillo was assassinated by members of his own army, he controlled 51 percent of the total investments in industry.[7] With sugar untouched, U.S. investment more than doubled assassination, controlled less than 42 percent of the investment.[9] Clearly for the United States, Trujillo no longer served the expansion of U.S. capital in the Dominican Republic.

U.S. Economic Investment and Political Control: 1961-1978

Trujillo's death brought about a temporary power vacuum. Vice-President Joaquin Balaguer, took over until the Trujillo family and associates were forced to leave the country. National elections held in late 1962 brought formerly-exiled Juan Bosch to power. Bosch, leader of the Dominican Revolutionary Party (PRD), received his support from the middle and lower classes. The U.S. government supported Bosch as a candidate, seeing him as a new democratic leader that could help carry out the Alliance for Progress and other democratic programs in Latin America designed to stabilize political

*When the first phase of concentration of political and economic power was over—about 1938—Trujillo departed for Europe. It is a real reflection of the power structure he had created that during his one year abroad, no attempt was made to bring down his regime. The National Guard, by then his "personal army," took care of any individual group who chose to oppose his policies.[5]
**He not only acquired the National City Bank and all of its branches—a bank traditionally tied to the sugar interests[6]—but established the Reserve Bank of the Dominican Republic in 1941 along with the Central Bank of the D.R. which distributed and regulated Dominican currency.
***The Cuban Revolution of 1959 put further pressure on the United States to secure its sugar markets.

unrest and expand U.S. economic interests. With Trujillo out of the way, the U.S. was ready to move in unchallenged.

But Bosch had his own plans. In 1963, he moved to reform the Constitution, increasing the rights of peasants and limiting the power of foreign interests and national landowners. This caused a major national crisis and Bosch was toppled at the hands of a military coup. U.S. President Kennedy, who conditionally supported the military triumvirate which took over following the coup, ordered all economic and military aid to the Dominican Republic suspended when his terms were not accepted.[10] Nonetheless, the Pentagon, the CIA, and the sugar interests continued to back the new Trium-virate.[11] Donald Reid Cabral, known as a CIA agent and nicknamed "el americanito," was appointed to head the government.

Kennedy was assassinated in November 1963. Johnson's in-auguration brought the official reinstatement of U.S. military and economic aid to the Dominican government and the encouragement of private investment, with the intention of stabilizing the situation.[12] Little by little Trujillo's wealth was transferred to the private sector. U.S. Agency for International Development (AID) projects sprung up and new loans were approved. These actions were predecessors to the major U.S. corporate and banking investments that had not yet entered the phase of massive foreign participation in the economy that would characterize the policy of the future Balaguer regime.

In the meantime, Juan Bosch, then living in exile in Rio Piedras, Puerto Rico, initiated the signing of the Rio Piedras Pact which affirmed the decision to bring down Reid Cabral and to return to the 1963 Constitution. Anti-Trujillo officers of the Dominican military supported the Pact and prepared for an armed take-over of the Dominican capital, Santo Domingo. Representatives of the U.S. government visited Bosch in Puerto Rico to notify him of their intention to support neither Reid Cabral nor Bosch's "Constitu-tionalists," but rather to back the conservative military following of Army General Elias Wessin y Wessin.[13]

The Constitutionalists took power on April 25, 1965; the PRD Secretary-General, Francisco Pena Gomez, announced the victory over the National Radio Station.* The military lost no time in sending in tanks to stop the takeover. Their communique to the Johnson Adminstration (through U.S. Ambassador Tapley Bennett)

---

*At this time the Constitutionalists controlled the National Palace, the Ozama Bridge (principal entrance to the city from the east), the National Radio Station, and major neighborhoods. With their power centered at the San Isidro Air Force Base, just outside the city, the conservative generals maintained constant communications with their U.S. colleagues.

was that the choice was between "castroism and democracy"[14] President Johnson immediately sent in 400 marines from bases around the Caribbean; within five days, some 20,000 additional marines were called in.* After heavy fighting and bombing by the U.S. and Dominican conservative forces, 2,500 civilians lay dead.[15]

In July 1965, a truce was signed by the Constitutionalist government and the conservative military leaders under the auspices of the Organization of American States (OAS). Many Dominicans were opposed to such an agreement which they saw as a farce, given U.S. domination of the OAS.[16] A provisional government was set up following U.S. specifications headed by Trujillo's exambassador to the U.S., Hector Garcia Godoy.**The provisional government, totally dominated by U.S.-backed conservative *militares*, held elections in 1966. Former vice-president to Trujillo, Joaquin Balaguer, won over PRD leader Juan Bosch under circumstances of massive election fraud.[17] Balaguer, who had formed the Partido Reformista (PR), immediately changed the Constitution to eliminate the clause that prohibited presidential reelection.

During the twelve years that Joaquin Balaguer held the presidency, the U.S. government sought to create their kind of stability in the Dominican Republic: through massive development programs; land seizures; control of the sugar production, mining, tourism; military aid; and repressive and disruptive labor practices.[18] Most revealing about the death of Trujillo and Balaguer's rise to power is the monumental increase in U.S. investments in the Dominican Republic. In 1961 when Trujillo was assassinated, foreign investment, primarily from the U.S., had reached US$150 million in the Dominican Republic.[19] This represented a little less than one-half of the total capital invested in industrial businesses in the D.R. By 1975, the investment figures had risen to $411 million in direct investment. If we add the estimated AID funds—approximately $500 million from 1962-1967—the figure of U.S. investment rises to somewhat under $800 million. This does not include the fact that the Dominican Republic received from the U.S. the highest amount of aid per capita in Latin America for police training in 1966. The total military assistance for 1963 to 1968 came to $10.3 million. Total funding from the United States during the Balaguer regime must have surpassed the $1 billion mark.

---

*The marines landed to the west of the capital while the Dominican military were on the east side at San Isidro Base. The Constitutionalists were caught in between.
**General Wessin y Wessin was given a diplomatic post in the United States while Constitutionalist leader, Colonel Caamano Deno received a similar post in London.

Foreign investment and foreign aid are seen as two principal solutions to the instability of Third World nations. In reality, they are moneymaking ventures as well as tools of control. For example, between 1965 and 1974 the Overseas Private Investment Corporation (OPIC) guaranteed investments for forty-seven different U.S. companies ranging from $40,000 to $185,000 each.[20] Three major industries were developed, expanded, and controlled by North American companies:

Company	Industry	Country of Origin	Total Capital Investment
Gulf and Western Corporation	sugar/tourism/cattle	U.S.	$200 million (by October 1974)
Rosario Resources	mining (gold)	U.S.	$41 million (1962-1970)
Falconbridge Nickel	mining (nickel)	Canada	$190 million (1962-1970)

These investments developed out of deepening ties with the Balaguer government. From 1966 (the year Balaguer became president of the Republic) to 1971, the following measures were established to encourage foreign investments: Investment Bank Law (1966); Industrial Incentive Law (1968); Farming Policy Law (1970); Free Zones Law (1970); Mining Law (1971); Tourist Incentive Law (1971); Mortgage Banks Law (1971).[21] Of all of these, the greatest incentive was (and is) the creation of the tax-free zones, or *Zonas Francas*. Just as the island of Puerto Rico serves the United States corporate sector with its fifteen to twenty year tax-free status, these free zones—largely projects of the Gulf and Western Corporation and the Dominican government—eliminate U.S. corporate tax requirements, national tax commitments, minimum-wage standards, environmental guidelines, and fair labor practices. While workers are paid 40¢ an hour, the Gulf & Western Corporation recently listed annual assets for 1978 at over $4.2 billion.[22] The tax free zone is a veritable slave labor camp.

Along with U.S. investments in 1966 came massive Agency for International Development (AID) funding. According to David Fairchild, assistant program officer for AID in the Dominican Republic from 1966 to 1967:

...of all the AID money given to the Dominican governments since 1962, $100 million to $180 million were grants and will never be repaid. Since 1962, betwen $500 million and $600 million have been involved in the total aid program. Per capita, that was the heaviest AID program in Latin America.[23]

Fairchild points out that USAID funded every last penny of the public projects for roads, lights, streets, water and housing for two years (1966-1967)—all part of the infrastructure for business expansion. Not only that, but, according to a leading Dominican economist, AID played a key role in developing formerly state-controlled industries into agencies autonomous from the government's State Council.[24]

National Bank for Housing, and the Dominican Agrarian Institute. This process accentuated the growing imbalance of political power bases in the country and provided the U.S. with further control.

But U.S. intervention on the economic level apparently was not enough security for the U.S. CIA and AFL-CIO penetration of the labor movement became one of the most active areas of U.S. intervention in the Dominican Republic. This active period began as Trujillo's power came to an end. Because of Trujillo's lack of cooperation with the AFL-CIO,[25] the U.S. was even more anxious to help the AFL-CIO move in under new Dominican leadership.[26] One of the most dramatic examples of the U.S. antidemocratic labor campaign was its destruction of the independent sugar cane worker's union, the Sindicato Unido (SU), a coaliton of 33 agricultural and industrial unions.*

By 1978, the situation in the Dominican Republic was economically and socially tense. Balaguer's personal terrorist youth gang, La Banda, slaughtered over 2,000 people in the early 1970s. Freedom of the press, freedom to organize, freedom to take opposing political views were not part of the Dominican reality under Joaquin Balaguer. Against the massive influx of U.S. investment and aid programs, a stark picture is painted in looking at the reality of Dominican society: by May 1978 (election month) officially counted unemployment stood at 30 percent; minimum wages were 30¢ an

---

*While buying up the Central Romana refinery in 1966, the Gulf and Western Corporation sought to destroy the SU. The company had the union's lawyer arrested and soon after he "disappeared." Eighty-three labor leaders were arrested. The company threatened workers by cutting back on the harvest time from seven to five months. To complete the process, the person asked to replace the SU at Central Romana with a company-controlled union was Damilo Brito Baez, once a high official of the CIA-funded Dominican union known as CONATRAL; Brito Baez was also known as a "strong-arm man of the AFL—CIO."[27]

hour in urban areas and 20¢ an hour in the countryside. Inflation stood at 14 percent. Dominican external debt amounted to almost $800 million and the U.S. bought up 66.6 percent of all exports.[28] According to eyewitness accounts, children commonly found their meals in garbage cans.

It is amidst this misery that Balaguer launched the fourth and heaviest political campaign of his 12-year period as president. Prior to the elections, he visited President Carter in Washington and promised to hold free elections. In May 1978, over 2 million Dominicans registered to vote in what turned out to be one of the biggest surprises for U.S. foreign policy in a long time.

New U.S. Policy of "Democratization": 1978 to the Present

Presidential elections were held in the Dominican Republic on 16 May 1978. For the first time in over a decade, it looked like an opposition party might have a chance at national power in the Dominican Republic. The PRD forces, with the majority of the middle and working classes behind it and with the U.S.-Balaguer promise to carry out "free and honest" elections, were more than hopeful of a PRD victory. They were determined to avoid any incident that would give Balaguer and the conservative military forces an excuse to subvert the election procedures.

Vote counting began at 6:00 p.m. By late evening, the PRD was clearly the leader in the Santo Domingo area. Reports not yet received would eventually reveal that even the more conservative areas in the north supported the PRD. Suddenly, at 4 a.m. the next morning—with the vote count still going on—all national radio and broadcasting stations were turned off. The voting process had been blocked! Voting tabulation was halted by the military, led by Army General Neit Nivar Seijas who opposed a PRD victory. Hundreds of fraudulent practices had already taken place the day before as the *Partido Reformista* (PR) unsuccessfully tried to assure themselves a victory. Direct military intervention was a last-minute attempt to keep Balaguer in power by essentially carrying out a coup against the incoming winner, the Dominican Revolutionary Party.

During the following week, calls and letters from national as well as international political leaders called for an immediate resumption of the vote counting. On 19 May 1978, Secretary of State Vance notified Balaguer that attempts to subvert the elections would seriously impair relations between the two countries.[29] Neither Balaguer nor the U.S. had expected a PRD victory. The military's attempt at a coup and the stalling of the resumption of vote counting meant that both the U.S. and Dominican power structure needed time to plan their strategy. Needless to say, the final vote count which was finally resumed on 27 May 1978 came out in favor of the PRD. As a last attempt to save the old regime, Balaguer carried out a final antidemocratic measure against the incoming party: an impromptu announcement on July 8th by the Central Elections Board (JCE) claimed that an error had been made in the counting of winners of Senate seats; the JCE immediately transferred four PRD seats in the Senate, where it had a majority, and give them to the PR, making it the majority party. The PRD called for a general national strike to protest the blatant acts of fraud, but it could not undo them. With PRD President Antonio Guzman ready to come to office in August 1978, Balaguer continued his last minute ploys to maintain a *balaguerismo* without Balaguer. The now PR-controlled Senate passed laws giving the military unilateral power to investigate subversive activities. Also passed was permission for the president to choose military officers for government posts for only a two year period, as opposed to the indefinite periods assigned in the past.

Why did the U.S. government stand quietly by and watch their candidate lose? Why did the U.S. support a party that is a member of the social democratic Second International—a party it twice removed, once through the 1963 coup and once through a 1965 military invasion?

Part of the explanation is that the United States has a new human rights policy which it did not have in 1965. What the Alliance for Progress did for John F. Kennedy's popularity in Latin America,[30] the Human Rights Campaign is supposed to do for Carter. The U.S. government avoided direct intervention in the 1978 elections because it wanted to promote the Carter human rights policy of nonintervention and nonconfrontation, the course earlier recommended by trilateralist planners. (See Philip Wheaton).

The second reason for U.S. actions is that the PRD is not the party it used to be. The U.S. can live with the PRD; it no longer needs a dictator like Balaguer to promote its interests. In 1965 the PRD called for a return to the constitutionalist government of 1963, the enemies of the constitution being the large landowners and foreign control of national industries. Interestingly enough, in the recent election the presidential and vice-presidential candidates, Antonio Guzman and Jacobo Majluta, represent the large landowners and foreign business interests, respectively. They replaced two more progressive party leaders, Jorge Blanco and Francisco Pena Gomez, who had both been considered for these posts. The PRD also recently eliminated its previous resolve to nationalize foreign companies, and instead took the stand:

That the PRD develop a strong Dominican bourgeoisie, that

would be the base that would allow the PRD to govern for many years.[31]

This is not the same PRD that carried out an armed constitutionalist revolt against the military and U.S. marines in 1965, and whose leaders were harassed, imprisoned, and killed during the Balaguer regime.

That is not to say that the PRD's arrival to power has not brought about important changes. The century-long environment of military repression has been ended. Freedom of the press has been extended and most political parties are allowed to operate freely. Likewise, trade unions have seen a lifting of repressive antilabor tactics. In short, politically the PRD has brought about a degree of liberation called for by the Dominican people.

One of the most positive changes in the Dominican Republic at the political level is the dismissal of over 200 prominent military leaders and some 250 less well known military officials, all former collaborators of the Balaguer regime. This signaled Guzman's most clear-cut break with the past regimes since it had been the corrupt Dominican military leaders who had maintained the regimes in power. Another important change is the legalization of trade union organization. Such was the repression in the past that it has been estimated that between August and December of 1978, ten to fifteen new trade unions a month have been formed. On 8 September 1978, a major amnesty law was passed, effecting some 500 political prisoners, many of them progressive labor leaders.

But this freedom has gone only so far. When PRD Secretary-General Pena Gomez called on workers "to tighten their belts" in 1978,[32] at a time when wages still remained very low while the unemployment level was over 30 percent, he was playing into the hands of the domestic and foreign business leaders who hoped to keep the pace of social reform at a level which served, rather than threatened, their interests. The openness of the new regime brought many workers out on strike in hopes that things would be different. From September to December 1978, many strikes were carried out in the sugar cane fields and the government responded forcefully. When a major demonstration was planned by the General Confederation of Workers (CGT) at Gulf & Western's Romana refinery, the CGT secretary-general, Francisco Antonio Santos, was jailed and the workers were prohibited from holding the event. At the beginning of October 1978, 509 workers went out on strike at the Sabaneta Dam construction site; they were demanding company payment of a special allowance projected by the Labour Code at the end of the project. Eighty-nine of the protestors were immediately arrested.

Very soon after, fifteen women were detained who had demonstrated in protest of the arrests. Despite appearances and promises, political freedoms have not been fully restored to the Dominican people.

Contrary to the political situation, the economic situation has hardly been altered. Most reforms have served to *increase* the economic privilege, power, and income of the Dominican upper classes and enhance the foreign business interests in the Dominican Republic. Not once since his inauguration in August 1978 has Antonio Guzman even discussed the possibility of eliminating the tax free industrial havens in the Republic. What is more, Guzman's Administration includes high-ranking officials of two of the largest foreign corporations in the Dominican Republic: Eduardo Fernandez, a Gulf & Western Corporation vice-president, is now president of the Central Bank of the Dominican Republic; and Gaetan Boucher, president of the Falconbridge "Dominicana" Company, directs the State Sugar board which controls approximately 60 percent of all sugar production and exports.[33] In a March 1979 meeting of London bankers, the Dominican government presented its economic strategy. It plans to focus attention in the following areas: improvement of living conditions; priority to agricultural production; development of infrastructural projects; development of the tourism industry; balance-of-payments deficit; better use of national economic agencies.[34]

All of these measures are aimed at resolving some of the immediate difficulties faced by the national government. The first item has not been dealt with except for salary increases for public employees. Numerous loans have been solicited or granted for both national crop-diversification efforts and infrastructural projects. In the last five months, the Dominican Republic has received $210 million in U.S. loans and $7 million from the Federal Republic of Germany. Total loans outstanding equal $350 million.[35] In 1979 tourism was up 24 percent from 1978 according to National Director of Tourism and Information Victor Cabral; the Board of Tourism just received $2 million to carry out a heavy publicity campaign to further promote the industry.[36]

As to the last two measures, they have been dealt with indirectly through attempts to increase government revenues from and participation in foreign-run industries.* Another PRD campaign promise

*For example, in the case of Rosario Resources Company, a gold-mining operation, a bill was recently submitted to the Dominican Congress calling for a progressive tax on Rosario in order to reduce profits for the company and increase revenues for the Dominican government. Due to increases in the price of gold, Rosario Resources

pointing toward increased national control over resources is the transfer of lands held by the Gulf & Western Corporation to the Dominican government. Within a month after the national elections, Guzman (by that time clearly the winner of the presidency) pointed out that although he would never go so far as to nationalize the Gulf & Western Corporation's holdings, the Dominican government would try to obtain part of the Central Romana lands for small fruit production.[38] Gulf & Western would seem to be open to such a move given their previous interest in establishing a company-controlled, but supposedly worker-owned Agricultural Company of Central Romana for which a significant land "transfer" would be carried out.[39] Both the Gulf & Western plan and the Guzman proposal raised hopes of further measures to realize Guzman's campaign call for an end to the large landownership system and movement towards bringing more Dominicans relatively more economic power, thus strengthening the national economy.

Though in the immediate sense, these moves to strengthen the national economy appear as an advance forward for the general population, in actuality they also reflect a new corporate strategy which eyes greater consumer purchasing power as one of its most coveted goals. This entails, as one journalist referred to it, "developing a stabilizing middle class"[40] that opens up the national market and allows more people a stake in the economy.

Conclusion

As the PRD and Guzman moved into power, the Dominican Republic took on a new significance for U.S. leaders. They found that, though the PRD was (and is) officially a social democratic party it was not going to make any radical changes such as nationalizing industries and carrying out a truly progressive land reform. Although the PRD called for an end to all political repression and has extended freedom of the press and the legal right of most political parties to organize, it has not gone so far as to let labor unions and other political organizations carry out their full range of democratic functions. The Guzman/trilateral hope is that, on the one hand, the traditional reasons that cause people to protest, will be eliminated; while on the other, that labor unions and other democratic political organizations will be kept in line with a combination of concessions and more subtle repression. As far as the U.S. is concerned, the PRD has the potential to defuse the potentially explosive masses.

---

received an additional income this year (1978-1979) of $24 million, compared to $18 million last year.[37]

What is called a non-confrontationist policy by the Carter Administration is being carried out in the Dominican Republic. This policy aims to nurture a seeming respect for human rights and foster cooperation and participation in more *predictable* negotiations—i.e. "conflict avoidance"[41]—*before* becoming militarily over compromised as was the case in the Dominican Republic in 1965.

According to many observers, the Dominican Republic, insofar is as evident, represents a successful model of government: renewed democratic politics, growing economic autonomy, regional economic cooperation in the Caribbean, and a favorable policy *vis-a-vis* the United States in particular. Compared to the varying attempts of non-confrontation in Jamaica (where the International Monetary Fund was used to moderate the development of a progressive government; see Phillips) and in Nicaragua (where the U.S. unsuccessfully attempted to intervene under cover of the Organization of American States), the Dominican transition has gone smoothly. It seems that with the victory of the conservatized PRD, stability and democratization could not have been easier and more favorable to the United States government and Western corporate interests. Nonetheless, the corporate strategy to enlarge the middle class, create new needs and sell more products, and pacify labor must ultimately fail. The political consciousness of the Dominican people—which led to Balaguer's defeat—will not be suffocated under an illusion of political and economic democracy.

It is important to remember that the Dominican people, the government, and the PRD are not totally unified in support of Guzman's present policies. Recent clear splits between the Guzman Administration and the more progressive PRD leadership (led by Jorge Blanco) is evidence of the former. According to reports from the D.R., a heated debate has erupted around the failure of the Guzman government to follow the PRD economic program as a result of pressure on Guzman "from several sectors to do nothing of the sort."[42] Moreover, great numbers of mass protests by organized and unorganized workers, political organizations, and even certain PRD leaders protesting Guzman's policies reveal mounting dissatisfaction with the new government, no matter how welcome initially by many sectors of Dominican society.

The Dominican people officially elected the PRD; the Dominican upper classes, the Armed Forces, the U.S. Government and Western business were forced to accept that reality. As the 1982 elections approach it is likely the Dominican people will again force a change—at the Senate level, where the conservatives maintained control through fraudulent means, and perhaps, at the presidential level as well—more firmly moving the country toward political and economic democracy.

FOOTNOTES

1. See for example, Sally Shelton, "U.S. Policy Towards the Caribbean," transcript of a speech given at the Institute for Policy Studies, Washington, D.C., 22 February 1978, and Kai Bird's article in this volume.

2. *Towards a Renovated International System*, The Trilateral Commission, 1977.

3. *Ibid.*, p. 18.

4. Juan Bosch, *Composicion Social Dominicano* (Santo Domingo: Impresor Arte y Cine, 1970).

5. Richard Barnet, "Dictatorship, Democracy, and the U.S. Intervention," *Intervention and Revolution* (New York: New American Library, 1972), p. 8.

6. Jose des Castillo, Miguel Cocco, Walter Cordero, Max Puig, Otto Fernandez, and Wilfredo Lozano (Estudios y Documentacion del Caribe, EDOC); "Corporaciones Multinacionales; La Gulf & Western en la Republica Dominicana; (Santo Domingo: Taller, 1974), p. 8.

7. North American Congress on Latin America (NACLA); "Smoldering Conflict: Dominican Republic: 1965-1975," *Latin American Political Report*, 9: 3 (New York: NACLA, April 1975).

8. Franklin J. Franco: *Republica Dominicana: Clases, Crisis, Comandos* (Cuba: Casa de las Americas, 1966) p. 80.

9. Carlos Maria Gutierrez, *El Experimento Dominicano* (Mexico: Editorial Diogenes, S.A., 1974).

10. *Ibid.*, p. 142.

11. Franco, *op.cit.*, pp. 162-165.

12. See Gutierrez, p. 144 and Barnet, p. 5.

13. Piero Gleijeses, *The Dominican Crisis* (Baltimore: Johns Hopkins University Press, 1978) pp. 179-184.

14. Gutierrez, p. 147.

15. *Ibid.*, p. 148.

16. *Ibid.*, p.148.

17. Gleijeses, pp. 261-265.

18. NACLA, pp. 4-5, pp. 13-28. See also, NACLA, "Dominican Republic: 'Military Democracy,' " *NACLA Report*, 8:4 (New York: NACLA, April 1974).

19. NACLA (April 1975), p. 4 (footnote).

20. *Ibid.*, p. 6.

21. Dominican Center of Information Exchange (CDII), *Breves Dominicanos*, 1:1 (Santo Domingo, May 1978) p.6.

22. Patrick Hughes, "Guess Who's Coming to Breakfast?" Slide Show/Tape Presentation (Packard Manse Media Project, Stoughton, Massachusetts, 1978).

23. NACLA, "U.S. A.I.D. in the Dominican Republic—An Inside View," *NACLA Newsletter*, 4:7 (New York: NACLA, November, 1970), p. 9.

24. del Castillo, et. al, p. 15.

25. NACLA (April 1975), pp. 14-15.

26. *Ibid.*,

27. *Ibid.*, p. 24.

28. CDII, pp. 13-14.

29. United Press International, "Balaguer Victory Claimed; General Strike Threatened," *San Juan Star*, 19 May 1978.

30. Barnet, p. 2.

31. "Discusion: Como debe de enfrentarse el conflicto obrero-patronal?" *Ahora*, No. 776 (Santo Domingo, 25 September 1978).

32. *Ibid.*

33. CDII, *Breves*, Vol. 5 (September 1978), p. 60.

34. Latin American Newsletters Ltd., "New Dominican Team Aims for Cautious Growth," *Latin American Economic Report*, 7:13 (London, 30 March 1979), p. 98.

35. "DR Sings $185 million," *Listin Diario*, Santo Domingo, 21 May 1979.

36. "Tourism," *Listin Diario* (Santo Domingo) 17 May 1979, p. 4.

37. CDII, *Breves*, 1:6 (February 1979) p. 68.

38. "El Presidente Electo:Sus Ideas, Sus Planes," *Ahora*, (Santo Domingo) 5 June 1978.

39. "Gulf and Western Dominican Unit Begins Program to Become Worker Owned Firm," *Wall Street Journal*, 8 February 1977, p. 11.

40. *New York Times* News Service, "DR fans anti-American fervor but this time it comes from the right,"*San Juan Star*, 30 May 1978.

41. *Towards a Renovated International System*, p. 19.

PART VII
MANAGING THE INTERNATIONAL
CAPITALIST ECONOMY

The world political economy has been transformed by the global corporation. This section begins with a vivid description of the global corporation and the international economy, including an examination of relations between the capitalist and socialist worlds, and an analysis of the meaning and consequences of Third World economic nationalism in general and OPEC in particular. Then the strengthened management role of the International Monetary Fund is examined with a case study of Jamaican debt dependency. Trilateral agricultural plans for Asia are analyzed followed by a comment on the food system in the United States by a family farmer. The goal of trilateral food policy, writes Dahlia Rudavsky, is to transform "the basic human need for food into a source of economic gain and social control." Indeed, economic gain and social control are inseparable goals of trilateralism.

American capitalism has brought more benefits to more people than any other system in any part of the world at any time in history.

—David Rockefeller*

Following World War II, the U.S. followed a very enlightened policy of free trade and free investment,...a very open world, and a very stable world. So this was one of the periods of freedom: freedom to invest, freedom to trade, freedom to have economic intercourse. Stability and freedom.

—Orville Freeman, president of Business International**

It is now apparent that the old order is indeed crumbling— but amid such disorientation that the world is confronted not with a new order but *a new global disorder...*

Whatever shape the upcoming system eventually takes, it is clear that the major decisions affecting the international economy of the 1980s will be made in Tokyo, Bonn and Riyadh [Saudi Arabia] *as well as in Washington...*

Looking back, the pivotal year in the American decline was perhaps 1973, a year that began with the United States military withdrawal from Vietnam and the final collapse of the American-dominated monetary system of fixed exchange rates. It closed with the quadrupling of oil prices by the Middle East-led oil cartel. *American political and economic hegemony had been successfully challenged.* [Italics mine.]

—Ann Crittenden, *New York Times International Economic Survey,* 4 February 1979.

*Quoted in Jack Egan, "Money Talks: An Interview with David Rockefeller," *New York,* 3 March 1980, p, 14.
**From an interview in the film *Controlling Interest* cited in Jack A. Nelson, *Hunger for Justice: The Politics of Food and Faith,* (Maryknoll, N.Y.: Orbis Books, 1980), p. 40.

chapter one

ECONOMIC NATIONALISTS VS. MULTINATIONAL CORPORATIONS: REVOLUTIONARY OR EVOLUTIONARY CHANGE?

Norman Girvan*

Towards a New International Order?

Suddenly, it seemed the multinational corporations were on the defensive. In the space of a few short months during 1973 the Organization for Petroleum Exporting Countries (OPEC) turned the tables on the giant oil companies and the Western nations and began calling the shots on the price of the most important commodity entering into world trade. For once, countries in the Third World were actively controlling the terms of their trade with the industrialized world and their powerful multinational corporations, instead of the other way around. What is more, the OPEC action inspired similar attempts from dozens of other Third World exporters of primary commodities. C. Fred Bergsten, an influential U.S. economist (assistant secretary of the treasury for International Affairs under Carter) spoke ominously of "the threat from the Third World," warning that in addition to the OPEC action:

> the seven leading *bauxite* exporters have formed the International Bauxite Association (IBA). Immediately thereafter, Jamaica forced a six-fold increase in its earnings. Other members are now beginning to follow suit...
>
> Six leading *phosphate* producers have tripled their prices, with further increases likely...

*This article originally appeared in *Multinationals in Africa*, (published for the Scandanavian Institute of African Studies, Upsala, Sweden, by Almqvist and Wiskell International, Stockholm, 1975). Norman Girvan is head of the Jamaican National Planning Agency. He has served as director of the Caribbean Center for Corporate Research in Kingston, Jamaica, and as adviser to several governments. His most recent book is *Corporate Imperialism: Conflict and Expropriation*, (New York: Monthly Review Press, 1976).

Four leading *copper* producers, through the Intergovernmental Council of Copper Exporting Countries (CIPEC)...have
announced that they will seize a greater share of the marketing of
copper; expand the membership of CIPEC to increase their
market power; and work directly with the producers of potentially substitutable metals to reduce the risks of cartelization to each...

The *tin* producers, through the International Tin Agreement, are seeking a 42 percent increase in the guaranteed floor
price maintained by its buffer stock. These countries maintained
an effective producer cartel before World War II.

The leading *coffee* producers, through a series of interlocking marketing companies and stockpile marketing arrangements, have seized control of world coffee prices. They were
confident enough of their success to let expire the International
Coffee Agreement, through which they had previously sought the
help of consuming countries to block price reductions.

Five of the leading *banana* producers, through the Organization of Banana Producing Countries, have levied sizeable taxes
on banana exports to boost their returns.

In addition, exporters of *iron ore* and *mercury* have been
meeting regularly. The four major *tea* producers have sought to
coordinate marketing and establish a floor price, and at least once
reached agreement on production quota. There are numerous
other primary products—including tropical *timber,* natural *rubber, nickel, tungsten, cobalt, tantalum, pepper,* and *quinine*
where effective collusion among producing countries is distinctly
possible...[1]

Nor does the new economic nationalism stop at attempts to
control the prices upon which depend the export incomes and,
through them, the economic livelihood of Third World nations.
Action on prices is seen as only one component of a general strategy
of securing control over marketing and ultimately production in the
resource industries which sustain Third World economies. State participation in ownership—whether the equity percentage is 20, 51, 60,
or 100—has in the space of the last few years become the order of the
day for these industries in the Third World. National economic
sovereignty, in short, is seen as inseparable from the objective of
greater equality in international economic power-relations. An outgrowth of this is the development of direct government-to-govern-
ment resource combination projects within the Third World which
seem to bypass the multinational corporations. In the Caribbean
three governments have agreed to develop aluminum production in
which Trinidad will supply natural gas for power, Jamaica will
furnish alumina and Guyana will provide both alumina and hydro-
electric power. Similar projects are announced by the OPEC states
almost daily.

Apart from the OPEC action on oil prices, two events perhaps more than any other dramatize the seemingly profound shifts which have taken place in international economic relations. One was the United Nations special session on raw materials, distinguished by the historic analysis of Algeria's President Boumedienne and marked by the passage—against the wishes of the West—of a resolution calling for a New International Economic Order.* The other was the huge loans by Iran—allegedly an underdeveloped country—to Britain and France, two of the leading industrial nations. The loans were to help these countries finance their balance-of-payments deficits, a problem normally regarded as a distinguishing feature of underdevelopment.

So is dependency dead, or dying? Is economic imperialism being decisively confronted? Is economic power slipping irretrievably from the grasp of the giant multinational corporations who will in the future have to share it on equal terms with national states in the Third World? Are we in fact witnessing revolutionary changes in the international economic system?

This article offers some interpretive observations in answer to these questions. Definitive conclusions are out of the question, if only because of our proximity in time to these events, at this writing but we can advance certain views and show the factors which have led us to the interpretation they present.

It is self-evident that we are witnessing important substantive changes in the structure and power relationships of the international economic order which prevailed up until the end of the 1960s. I

---

*ed. note: The NIEO is documented in the *Declaration and Programme of Action for a New International Economic Order* and the 1977 *Charter of Economic Rights and Duties of States,* passed by the United Nations General Assembly. The Group of 77, the bloc of Third World nations in the UN (originally numbering 77 and now over 115), sponsored the "Joint Declaration of the Developing Countries" before the 1963 UN General Assembly. The United Nations Conference on Trade and Development (UNCTAD) has been an important forum for the NIEO. The first meeting of UNCTAD was held in Geneva in 1964. UNCTAD V, the most recent, met in the Philippines in May 1979. Third World unity around reforming the international economic order was first formally expressed at the Asian-African Conference of Non-Aligned Nations (i.e., not tied to either the Western or Socialist bloc) held in Bandung, Indonesia in April 1955, where major principles of "Economic Cooperation" were established.

For a review of events leading up to and following the call for the NIEO see, for example, Orlando Letelier and Michael Moffit, *The International Economic Order* Part 1, (Washington, D.C.: Transnational Institute of the Institute for Policy Studies, 1977) and Geoffrey Barraclough, "The Haves and the Have Nots," (13 May 1977); "Waiting for the New Order," (26 October 1978); "The Struggle for the Third World," (9 November 1978) all in *The New York Review of Books.* On the Nonaligned Movement see A.W. Singham, ed., *The Nonaligned Movement in World Politics,* (Westport, CT: Lawrence Hill & Co., 1977).

believe that the most important aspect of these changes is the rise in the international economic power of certain Third World states relative to that of Western industrialized states. But I shall also argue that it is important to distinguish Western industrialized *states* from the multinational companies which are based in those states and with whom they have traditionally been assumed to share a common, if not identical, interest. It will be suggested that the assumption of an identity of interest between Western states and Western multinational corporations should no longer be made. Indeed, a working hypothesis of this article is that the rise in the relative economic power of some Third World states has been brought about—or, at least, permitted—by factors engineered by the multinational firms (MNCs).

I will argue that the solid achievements of the new economic nationalism do not in any way constitute a disengagement by these states from the system of internationalized capitalism. As a result the characteristic patterns of development and of income distribution implied by participation in that system are not being fundamentally altered. Furthermore, when one evaluates the process of strategy and counterstrategy being pursued by countries and companies, one finds no significant erosion in the power of internationalized capital as represented by multinational corporations. On the contrary, not only has the rise in the economic power of certain Third World states *vis-a-vis* Western states been permitted—if not actually planned—by the policies of the MNCs, but the new economic nationalism is also being turned by them to their advantage in the form of higher profits, reduced instability and more efficient long-term corporate planning. In the new international economic order now unfolding, certain Third World states can be accommodated as more equal children in a family where unmistakable and overall control is in the hands of a small elite corps of powerful multinational corporations. The quantitative and qualitative size, the resources and the power of these corporations, are growing with extraordinary intensity and at a rate faster than any other component of the international economy.

Finally, I believe that these developments are having a perverse effect: that side-by-side with a tendency for greater equality among states—a limited diffusion of international economic state power, as it were—is a tendency for growing *in*equalities between groups of people. This development, which really represents an acceleration of trends already existing, takes place both among Third World countries and within them. It makes even more anomalous than before the practice of lumping all Third World countries together, and of lumping together all the people of any one Third World country. Third World states and financially poor states are no longer interchangeable or identical; the distinction between affluent people and poor people within Third World countries has become more relevant than ever before. In short, we are in need of redefinitions, both analytical and terminological.

The Transnationalized Economy

When we speak of the multinational corporations we mean far more than that category of business organizations whose main distinguishing feature is that they all happen to operate in more than one country. We mean a large and rapidly expanding sector of the world economy characterized by a revolutionary new system of production and accumulation. The main features of this new system are diversified internationalized production under centralized control; massive size and huge financial resources of the basic institutional unit; technological dynamism and leadership; and high and continuously growing concentration of economic power. In a very real sense this new system now dominates the world economy, whether developed, underdeveloped, or socialist. Both quantitatively and qualitatively the MNC is continually enlarging and intensifying its sphere of operation and control; attempting to absorb, subordinate, or liquidate all other systems of production and accumulation. As a result, the expansion of this system is generating powerful tensions and contradictions— some of a traditional and familiar type, and others which appear to be altogether new. We will refer to this system as *transnationalized capitalism,* the specific contemporary phase of international capitalism which has emerged since World War II.

Quantitative indexes are not necessarily adequate measures of true economic significance or influence. But even the raw quantitative data speak loudly on the importance of the new transnationalized economy. The United Nations estimates value added in this new sector of the world economy at $500 billion in 1971, amounting to one-fifth of total GNP of the nonsocialist world[2] and exceeding the GNP of any one other country except the United States. Furthermore, all observers agree that the share of this sector in the world economy is growing rapidly. At least since 1950 its annual rate of growth has been high and remarkably steady at 10 percent, compared to 4 percent for noninternationalized output in the Western developed countries.[3] One apologist for the new system frankly envisages that within a generation some 400 to 500 MNCs will own something like two-thirds of the world's fixed assets.[4]

The emergence and expansion of this new transnationalized economy is rapidly making a mockery of such traditional concepts as national economy and the associated one of international trade and finance. Even by conservative estimates, the value of internationalized production[5] now exceeds the value of international trade and the former has therefore displaced the latter as "the main vehicle of international economic exchange."[6] But so-called international trade itself consists, to a growing extent, merely of shipments among branches and affiliates of MNCs rather than arms-length transactions on the world market. Such intrafirm transfers* already account for about one-quarter of all British exports and imports.[7] The intrafirm shipments of U.S. MNCs alone represented about 11 percent of total world exports in 1970,[8] and an estimated 33 percent of U.S. manufactured exports consist of parent-to-affiliate shipments.[9] As one observer put it "...the direct activity of international companies (has) become the single most important link between industrial countries, even though the notion that this (is) still trade continues to be the basis for national economic policy and thinking."[10] Overall, U.S. multinationals are responsible for 62 percent of the exports and 35 percent of the imports of manufactured goods of that country;[11] domestically, they account for at least one-third of U.S. economic activity.[12] It is also now accepted that U.S. MNCs are by far the principal influence on the U.S. balance-of-payments.[13] Furthermore MNCs generally have become the major actors on the international monetary scene to a degree that is frightening to many: at the end of 1971 they controlled no less than $268 billion in short-term liquid assets, "movement of only a small proportion of which could produce," and has produced, "massive monetary crises."[14]

What is important about the new transnationalized economy is not only its size and growing share in the global economy, but also the fact that it is charaterized by a high and unprecedented concentration of raw economic power. Power in the transnationalized economy derives first of all from a number of characteristics of its basic institutional unit: the multinational corporation. The first of these is the MNC's large size. The $36 billion-per-year turnover of the largest MNC, General Motors, is larger by far than the GNPs of the majority of member states of the United Nations, including such developed countries as Switzerland and Denmark. Of the ninety-nine largest economies in the world in 1970, forty of them were multinationals.[15] Given the rate of growth of MNCs, their size relative to that of national economics can only be expected to increase. (See Overview to this volume for tables comparing countries and corporations in 1970 and 1976.) The second characteristic giving rise to power is the wide spread of their activities, both over product lines and over

---

*ed. note: Intrafirm transactions are carried out at artificially manipulated transfer prices, resulting in lower taxes and higher profits for the firm, lower revenues for host governments and higher prices for consumers.

countries. Among the 187 U.S. MNCs selected for the famous Harvard Multinational Enterprise Study, for example, the median enterprise produced twenty-two products, and the average firm operated in over eleven foreign countries.[16] Diversified production and global operation mean tremendous flexibility for management and free the fortunes of the company from dependence on any one product or country. Third, these corporations operate on the very frontiers of technology. Compared to other companies they spend more on research and development, receive the bulk of government subsidies for technological development, and utilize more skilled and more specialist manpower;[17] and it is they who introduce the bulk of new products and new processes into the mainstream of economic life. The fact that consumers and governments want—or have been conditioned to want—what these firms can deliver implies that tremendous leverage flows from their technological prowess.

A fourth characteristic of the MNCs that is crucial to the understanding of the power dimension is the centralization of authority in the global corporate headquarters. Recently two celebrated empirical studies of management practices in MNCs have appeared, one on either side of the North Atlantic.[18] Whatever their differences, both studies are agreed on one finding: in all such corporations, power in relation to overall strategic decision making is concentrated in a small group of senior executives at the corporate head office. The key instrument in the service of this power is financial control. One consequence of this power is that large areas of global economic life—such as the distribution of production and employment among countries, the volume, value and direction of exports and imports, and the value and stability of national currencies—are falling increasingly under the control of a small number of committees of corporate managers. Another consequence is an increasingly uneven distribution of power and authority spatially across the globe. The late economist Stephen Hymer left us a vivid picture of where this development is leading us, a kind of corporate 1984. We can do no better than to quote him extensively:

> The modern multinational corporation has an elaborate vertical structure with many levels of intellectual work. The higher up the ladder, the higher the wages and status, the more abstract the level of planning, the longer the time horizons, the greater the scope for discretion and judgement. At bottom one supervises a few people, remains rooted in one spot, and deals with narrow specialties... operating activities (level III) spread themselves widely over the globe in response to the pull of men, markets and materials. Coordinating activities (level II), because of the need for white-collar workers, communications systems, and information tend to concentrate in large cities...Level I activities, the general

offices, tend to be even more concentrated than level II activities, for they must be located close to the capital market, the media, and the government...On the international level, the centralizing tendencies of multinational capital implies a world hierarchy of cities. High level decision-making will be centralized in a number of capitals—New York, Tokyo, London, Frankfurt, Paris, forming an inner ring between roughly the 40th and 50th parallel. These, along with Moscow and Peking, will be the major centers or radial points of strategic planning. Lesser cities throughout the world will deal with the day-to-day operations of specific local problems. These in turn will be arranged in a hierarchical fashion; the larger and more important ones will contain regional corporate headquarters, while smaller ones will be confined [to] lower level manufacturing activities.

The new international economy will be characterized by a division of labor based on nationality...Day-to-day management in each country is left to the nationals of that country, who, being intimately familiar with local conditions and practices, are able to deal with local problems and local government. These nationals remain rooted in one spot, while above them is a layer of people who move around from country to country, as bees among flowers, transmitting information from one subsidiary to another and from the lower levels to the general office at the apex of the corporate structure. In the nature of things, these people for the most part will be citizens of North Atlantic countries (and will be drawn from a small culturally homogeneous group within the advanced world), since they will need to have the confidence of their superiors and be able to move easily in the higher management circles. Latin Americans, Asians and Africans will at best be able to aspire to a management position in the intermediate coordinating centers at the continental level. Very few will be able to get much higher than this, for the closer one gets to the top, the more important is "a common cultural heritage." *The majority will be little more than middlemen helping to organize their countries' labor for sale abroad.*[19] [Italics ed.]

Finally, power in the transnationalized economy also derives from the collective characteristics of the community of MNCS taken as a whole. In any one industry, for instance, production is dominated by a small number of giant corporations operating across the entire spatial spectrum of the world economy. The consequence is an enormous oligopolistic market power on a world scale; but since the corporations in any industry almost always fix their prices in sympathy with one another, what is oligopoly in form becomes monopoly in fact. There is the distinct tendency for growing concentration in industries which are technologically dynamic and/or capital-hungry, such as computers, transport equipment and oil. All this must be seen in conjunction with the speed and frequency of mergers which produce giant world conglomerates, and of the formation of consortia for specific projects which blur the distinctions between allegedly competitive firms. Such developments take place not only among firms from the same home country but also and increasingly among firms of different nationalities. It is when we take the huge size, diversified production, technological dynamism and centralized global control of the individual corporation together with the collective market power of MNCs as a whole, that we begin to appreciate the growing sector of the world economy.

The Multinational Corporation and the Nation-State

At the same time, this power generates reactions from, and conflicts with, other capitalist groups and other classes which are increasingly threatened or subordinated by it. To some extent, these conflicts are manifested in the theme of "the multinational corporation vs. the nation-state." In the underdeveloped world this issue has long been an important one; it is put principally in terms of the subversion of national economic sovereignty which foreign ownership represents, and the set of reactions expressed broadly by the term *economic nationalism,* to be discussed below.[20] A relatively new phenomenon, however, is the emergence of this issue among countries such as Canada and Australia, which have most of the structural characteristics of economically developed countries, but have predominantly foreign ownership in their manufacturing and natural resource industries. Here the issue is posed in terms of the limited effectiveness of the traditional techniques of economic control and regulation in the context of what has been called a "branch-plant economy."[21] Labor is generally suspicious of the power and intentions of foreign corporations but conditioned to believe that they are an indispensable means of securing higher living standards, while different segments of national capital make tactical alliances with or against different segments of foreign capital depending on where they perceive their interests to lie. The nation-state is in a real sense buffeted between the powerful pull from the MNCs to adapt to the requirements of transnationalized capital by accepting a reduction in its sovereignty on the one hand; and on the other, pressures from opposing national groups and classes who see the nation-state as the principal remaining means of defending their interests. (See Block.)

What is striking is the even more recent emergence of issues of this kind among the developed metropolitan countries such as Britain, France, and the United States. These are the home countries of many (in the case of the United States, most) of the MNCs and are traditionally considered to share common interests with corporations based within them. The fact is that the growth of the power exercised by MNC executives over the international distribution of jobs and income growth, over the direction and value of trade and monetary flows, and over advanced technology, have considerably strengthened their bargaining power and their leverage over even the most powerful of nation-states. Governments, which are subject to pressures from small and medium-sized national capital and from labor, are uneasy at the shifting balance of power. Can the traditional loyalty of multinationals to their home country and its government still be counted on? Even this is by no means clear. The Royal/Dutch Shell Oil Company has its commercial headquarters in London, but "...the British authorities know fully well that substantial interference [in Shell's foreign exchange transactions in order to protect Britain's exchange reserves] would result in the group moving its commerical centre of gravity to the Netherlands."[22] The British/Dutch firm, Unilever, is reported to assure itself of cooperation from the British government in a similar way.[23] In the United States, the labor movement has for years adopted the view that U.S.-based multi-nationals acknowledge no national interest where the distribution of jobs is concerned: they are held responsible for the export of perhaps as many as 1.3 million U.S. jobs to areas of cheap labor abroad.[24] And this development is in turn said to be at least partly responsible for the structural deterioration in the U.S. trading position towards the end of the 1960s, which undermined the value of the dollar. To cap it all, the resulting speculation against the dollar which precipitated the devaluation of the early 1970s is ascribed in large part to the activities of U.S.-based multinationals, who were seeking to protect the real value of their billions of dollars worth of liquid assets.[25]

In that sense we seem to be witnessing a process of *de*national-ization of capital, a corollary of *trans*nationalization as corporations adopt a truly global view, wherever they may be, and favoring those governments which "offer them the biggest bribes."[26] The change since the time when Lenin wrote his *Imperialism, the Highest Stage of Capitalism* in 1916 has been a profound one, and should by no means be underestimated. Up to the time of World War I capital was international but corporations were (by and large) national. Capital exports took place mainly in the form of portfolio investments, financing more often than not locally-organized enterprises abroad in the production of primary products needed by the imperialist centers. In the imperialist centers, national, monopolistic, vertically-integrated corporations, closely allied with their governments, fought each other for access to the raw materials and the markets of the world. The important development since that time is the direct organization of production abroad by monopoly capital, providing itself directly with primary products and penetrating foreign markets more and more through foreign production rather than exports of finished goods. In the process, direct investment has displaced portfolio flows as the main form of capital export, and national companies have become world corporations.

Destructive rivalries between national capitals, which twice in the first half of the twentieth century generated world wars, are being replaced in large part by collusion, mutual market interpenetration and interlocking production and financial ties at the world level among MNCs of different nationalities. Political imperialism has been replaced by neocolonialism, the colony by the client-state. But even the client-state as such is becoming less necessary to transnationalized capital, as additional sources of leverage other than physical coercion or threat of it are available to be deployed against governments, national capital, and labor (i.e., the huge financial resources, international flexibility, and monopoly over advanced technology controlled by the multinational corporations). *The power of transnational capital today is the power to withhold or relocate investments from a country, thereby threatening it with the specter of economic stagnation and technological retrogression.* West Germany has no imperialist presence abroad of the traditional kind, but the head of that country's largest commercial bank surveys the future with confidence:

> A prime necessity...is the improvement of the investment climate in the developing countries themselves, as well as an improvement in the whole attitude towards private property and in particular towards business activity...In the longer term the necessary investment climate will be created by sheer force of circumstance, because automatically investment capital will flow to those countries providing the necessary conditions—and there are already a number of them. The others will undoubtedly learn the lesson and follow suit in their own interest.[27]

Exponents of the corporate ethic leave no doubt in the mind that the rise of the multinational corporation has, in their view, rendered the nation-state a technologically obsolete institution as a unit of economic decision making or a reference point for economic welfare. According to one, the nation-state should be considered as archaic, just as medieval institutions were at the time of the Renaissance.[28] The managing director of Shell insists that the MNC can contribute "...much both to the immediate national interest and to the *more sovereign interest* of world economic development."[29] Professor Raymond Vernon, director of Harvard's Multinational Enterprise Project, uses more academic and philosophical language, but the meaning is the same:

> It may be that, in the end, sovereign states will learn to live with a decline in their perceived economic power. But one marvels at the

tenacity with which man seeks to maintain a sense of differentia-
tion and identity, a feeling of control, even when the apparent cost
of the identity and the control seems out of proportion to its
value.[30]

In this view of the world, the concern for national economic sovereignty is regarded as some kind of traditional custom surviving from
a previous historical age, one which is quaint but fundamentally
inimical to progress; in much the same way as the colonialists in
Africa regarded the "natives'" attachment to village life as an anthro-
pological curiosity which was inimical to their own welfare because it
inhibited the spread of the money economy—i.e. colonial exploitation. Now it seems that governments in the developed countries,
like colonized Africans, will have to be reeducated as to what is good
for them.

MNCs and the Socialist World

Were Lenin alive today he would in all likelihood be less
surprised at the transnationalization of capital since 1916 than at its
success in incorporating the socialist world into its sphere of
operations. Perhaps with some understatement, the United Nations
report on MNCs noted that "the centrally planned economies...are
more involved in the activities of [multinational] corporations than a
cursory examination of the standard data might indicate."[31] Equity
participation by MNCs in these economies is obviously limited; even
so, it does exist on a small scale in Romania and Hungary and on a
growing scale in Yugoslavia, where up to 49 percent is allowed and
where the constitution protects such equity against expropriation.
But the principal form of MNC involvement in the socialist world in
through the sale of technology and co-production agreements.
Anaconda, expropriated by Chile in 1971, signed in 1972, a $1,000
million agreement with the Soviet Union for the development of the
latter's copper deposits, at the same time as the USSR proposed to
help Chile develop its nationalized copper industry. By 1975 about
one-half of Russia's passenger-car production would come from Fiat,
under a co-production agreement; [32] and Soviet citizens are now
drinking homemade Pepsi Cola faster than it can be produced by the
factory operating under license from the U.S. company. As of
January 1973 about *600* such co-production agreements were in force
between multinationals and socialist countries;[33] every day, the list
grows longer. Of former President Nixon it was often said that,
whatever his domestic crimes, his foreign policy achievements in
securing detente with the Soviet Union and China were substantial
and indeed revolutionary. It seems, however, that the major beneficiaries of this co-called revolution are likely to be U.S. MNCs.

According to *Time:*

> Sino-American trade has already taken a great leap forward. (In 1973) it will probably exceed $800 million, up from $92 million in 1972. In only three years, the U.S. has become China's second most important international trading partner, after Japan.
>
> *So far, the new link is proving to be a bonanza for U.S. firms;* the Chinese import nearly 15 times as much from the U.S. as they export. Among the biggest ticket items to date are some 4,000,000 tons of grain, ten Boeing 707 jetliners valued at $150 million, and eight ammonia plants to be built by M.W. Kellogg Co. for $200 million. The Chinese are also anxious to do business with giant American oil companies such as Exxon, Mobil and Caltex, and makers of petroleum and drilling equipment, including U.S. Steel International, Phillips Petroleum and Baker Oil tools...
>
> ...In January (1973) the government disclosed that the Chinese were willing to seek "deferred payment arrangements"— a euphemism for foreign credits—to pay for still more technology. This (indicated a) departure from China's previous policy (of) buying only what it could pay for in cash...[34] [Italics added.]

Evidently the celebrated Nixonian detente is nothing more than a means of facilitating the access of transnationalized capital to those areas of the world which had hitherto been closed to it.*

I do not thereby mean to imply that the role and effects of MNCs in the socialist world are the same as they are in the capitalist bloc. A convincing case can certainly be made that, at least for the present, the socialist countries are adapting technological inputs from MNCs to their own internally determined development process, rather than the other way around, as it is in the capitalist world. It is nevertheless the case that until recently the Soviet Union and China appeared to represent models of autonomous and self-reliant accumulation based entirely on technology which was either (1) internally generated or (2) universally known and freely available. The rapid growth of business between these countries and the largest and most technologically-advanced corporations has put an end to this model—whatever we might think of the merits or demerits of the socialist pattern of absorbing technology from the multinationals. One important question relates to how far such relationships can develop before the socialist countries themselves become subject to an international division of labor programmed for the world by transnationalized capital. It is certainly the case that some observers are frankly stating

---

*ed. note: The United States normalized relations with China on 1 January 1979. Since then the economic bonanza for U.S. firms has grown enormously. Trilateralist Leonard Woodcock is the new U.S. ambassador to China.

that many MNCs may well prefer to deal with socialist countries than with many of those in the capitalist world—particularly the under-developed part of it.[35] Socialist countries are seen to be safer and more stable: there is virtually no risk of expropriation, practically no strikes or labor unrest, little exchange risk since payment is made in cash or in kind, and they offer greater political stability than either the developed capitalist countries or the Third World. In short, the investment climate in socialist countries is superior.

The Meaning and Consequences of Third World Economic Nationalism

The advance of capital has, historically, always been marked by tensions and conflict, by new contradictions generated just as old ones are transcended. In short, it is a process which is dialectical rather than linear; and the contemporary period is no exception. One of the principal contradictions has been that between international capital (i.e., imperialism) and various social classes in the Third World. The phenomenon of Third World economic nationalism, which has burst with such vigor upon the international scene, has brought this contradiction again to the fore.

It needs to be emphasized that the contradiction is not new, only the apparent success of the Third World offensive. From the outset, the securing of the noncapitalist areas of the world into the orbit of the international capitalist system was only accomplished through the violent subjugation of their peoples with the political imperialism and gunboat diplomacy of the nineteenth century. Conflicts between Third World states and MNCs involved in their natural resource industries were evident as long ago as 1937-38 when expropriations of foreign oil companies took place in Bolivia and Mexico. Then, as now, country-company conflict tended to crystallize around a number of fairly well-defined issues. These included: (1) the issue of economic sovereignty posed by foreign ownership and decision making in a major sector of the domestic economy, (2) the state's share of the industry's surpluses, (3) the extent of local processing of the raw material and production of by-products and inputs, and (4) the existence of a foreign enclave physically, economically, and socially isolated from the national society and engaging in discriminatory or alien practices in relation to nationals.[36]

Behind these issues lie a variety of class interests and attitudes.[37] Imperialism is interested in the periphery (the Third World) principally as a source of primary products (food and industrial raw materials) which can yield substantial profits and help sustain the process of accumulation in the industrial-center countries. Accordingly, imperialism could not lead to any substantial economic development in the periphery of the type enjoyed by the center (the colonial and neocolonial powers). One consequence of this is the continuous impoverishment of the mass of the population in the periphery: peasants, workers, underemployed and unemployed. This lays the basis for a potential alliance (not always realized) among these impoverished classes, directed against imperialism for the purpose of disengaging from the international division of labor it imposes and toward the initiation of an autonomous development strategy geared to satisfying popular needs.

Another consequence of imperialism is the exclusion of the possibility of the emergence of a powerful, independent national capitalist class with a well-developed internal material base. Instead, a dependent comprador bourgeoisie emerges, structurally attached to international capital and confined to activities like local commerce, real estate, and light manufacturing industry. Usually it is assumed that this bourgeoisie is an internal ally of international capital, and defends the latter; but in fact its objective position is rather one of ambivalence. Normally it is true that this class allies itself with foreign capital in order to protect its privileged position relative to the rest of the national population. But there is no reason to suppose that it is objectively satisfied with the *weak, dependent,* and *junior* position it occupies in relation to international capital. On the contrary, where it perceives a configuration of international and domestic circumstances which provides the conditions for it to assert greater independence and to develop its material base internally there is every reason for it to take advantage of such opportunities. These conditions are provided when (1) the nation-state possesses sources of leverage over international capital and the center countries, such as the supply of vital products; and (2) a viable set of domestic class alliances can be constructed which range the nation as a whole against international capital. It need hardly be added that for such a project, the state machinery is an absolutely indispensable instrument used by such a class alliance in the struggle to secure greater surpluses from, and to *redefine*—if not necessarily revolutionize—the relationships with, international capital and the nation-states in the center. *The result is the phenomenon of economic nationalism expressed in the form of conlict between MNCs in natural resource industries and Third World governments.*

It is precisely because such conditions were lacking in the past that company-country conflicts have long been muted, and because they are now being provided in a significant number of Third World countries, that such conflicts are so widespread today. Let us remember that until the 1960s a large part of the Third World was under colonial rule, and the colonial state was of course in the direct service of imperialist capital. But even amongst the formally independent states, such as those in Latin America, the balance of power was tilted heavily in favor of the MNCs. A state which expropriated an imperialist firm could expect at the very least an economic blockade, such as took place after the Mexican and Iranian oil nationalizations in 1938 and 1952; and worse, a military intervention as happened in Guatemala in 1954, Suez (Egypt) in 1956, and Cuba in 1961. In addition, production technology and marketing outlets in these industries were so tightly controlled by the MNCs as to make it difficult and costly for a state to attempt to defy them and operate a resource-based export industry successfully. Finally, the development of a sizeable and sophisticated bureaucratic class in these countries was not as advanced as it is today.

Developments since the early 1960s have changed the picture. First of all, Third World states now have at their disposal new and powerful sources of leverage in international economic relations. To begin with the international political climate has changed with the rise of the non-aligned movement, the growth of the socialist bloc, and growing Third World participation in the United Nations. One need not exaggerate the significance of this, however, as the case of Chile (see Overview) demonstrates the lengths to which an imperialist government will go to preserve the policital conditions necessary for the free operations of its corporations. The concrete sources of additional leverage arise out of two factors. One is the rise within the capitalist bloc of Western Europe and Japan, and the emergence of the Soviet Union and China, as well, as major economic powers. This has meant an increased competition among the major industrial nations for the natural resources of the Third World and loosened the tight monopolistic control over production technology and markets exercised by the MNCs—especially those based in the United States. The other factor is the shortages of many primary commodities, especially those of strategic importance in high-growth industries, such as petroleum, bauxite, and phosphates in 1972-74.

At the same time, in most Third World countries there has been the rapid development and maturation of a technobureaucratic class based on the state apparatus. Where this occurs together with the additional leverage represented by the possession of strategic export commodities, it creates possibilities which allow the technobureaucratic class—in alliance with the traditional comprador bourgeoisie—to attempt to transform itself into a class of state capitalists in a project for national industrialization and development, using the additional surpluses from the export industry, with the mass of the population more or less coerced or mobilized into the so-called struggle against imperialism. Such countries as Saudi Arabia, Nigeria, Zaire, Zambia, Venezuela, and Trinidad-Tobago may fit this model to a greater or lesser degree.

But how far is this really a struggle against imperialism? I will argue that these developments imply *modifications* in the international capitalist order, as regards the role, the relative power and the relative degree of development of different groups of nation-states; but *without any fundamental change in the power of trans-nationalized captital and the pattern of unequal development* characteristic of the international capitalist system.

We must first of all reconcile the recent successes of Third World economic nationalism with the picture drawn earlier of the rapidly growing power of transnationalized capitalism in general. The apparent paradox can be easily resolved if we adopt a view which is (1) historical, (2) sectoral, and (3) dialectical.

At the same time as the balance of bargaining power in Third World natural resource industries has been shifting from the MNCs to host governments, the bases of dynamic capital accumulation in international capitalism has been shifting to entirely new activities and geopolitical areas. When World War I brought an end to the great nineteenth century boom in capital exports, the bulk of international investment was deployed in primary production in the periphery, and in the infrastructure (e.g. transport) needed to bring such products onto the world market.[38] Foreign investment in manufacturing was insignificant. Indeed it was the growth of *national* manufacturing industries in Western Europe and subsequently the United States which made necessary (and profitable) international investment in food, raw materials, and transport infrastructure. International investment in the periphery was not only necessary to support capital accumulation based on national manufacturing in the center countries, it was also an important basis of capital accumulation in its own right.

But since 1945 the pattern has changed rapidly. The bulk of new international investment since then has been in manufacturing and among the industrial center countries themselves.[39] This reflects the emergence of technology-intensive consumers' and producers' goods industries as the main bases of incremental capital accumulation in the contemporary period, and the growth of direct foreign investment by the large manufacturing corporations in the center countries (for the purpose of mutual interpenetration of each other's markets) as the principal form of international capital flow. This, of course, is not to suggest that primary production and the periphery are in any way expendable to contemporary international capitalism; far from it. Raw materials from the Third World are just as essential as before, perhaps more so, in order to permit the process of accumulation in the industrial center countries to continue. Nevertheless, the point is that the principal loci of capital accumulation is technology-intensive manufacturing and service activities (such as information processing and transmission) in the industrial center countries; and it is upon these activities that the rapidly growing power of transnationalized capitalism chiefly rests.

The implications of this point should be carefully considered: international capitalism is increasingly interested in a *reliable* and *adequate* supply of Third World raw materials for use in other industries and is relatively less concerned with the raw materials industries as sources of *direct* profit. This creates possibilities for a new alliance with national state capitalism in the periphery: Third World elites will provide raw materials in return for a much increased share of the surplus and a role in national industrialization (using technology from transnationalized capital). In other words, it creates possibilities for co-opting economic nationalism into the system of international capitalism, whose structure will in turn have to be modified to permit the accommodation.

To be sure, this process will not be a smooth one, free from all kinds of tensions and contradictions. The MNCs directly involved in the natural resource industries are unlikely to take a broad view of the interests of international capital as a whole, and may, at least initially, resist the demands of economic nationalism. Nonetheless, a distinct pattern has already emerged in which these corporations can and do accommodate such demands without incurring significant short or long-term losses—and indeed, in some cases, turn them to their advantage. One common strategy is to use the actions of producers as a justification for raising downstream or finished products' prices, scooping up even greater profits at the refining end. There is considerable evidence that this has taken place in the case of petroleum, as the hugely increased revenues secured by the OPEC countries have been accompanied by astronomical profits for the multinational oil companies.[40] Indeed, in this case there is a widespread conviction that the oil shortages of 1971-74 which permitted OPEC to exert so much leverage were in fact engineered by the oil companies themselves in order to secure higher prices and generate the enormous profits they claim are necessary to fund expansion in the industry. [41] A similar process has taken place in the aluminium industry.[42]

In another case—that of bananas—the corporations seem to have succeeded in getting the best of both worlds; that is, defeating the producer cartel's attempt to secure higher returns while at the same time raising downstream prices. In early 1974 seven Central and South American states formed a Union of Banana Exporting

Countries (UBEC) and proceeded to raise export taxes against the opposition of the major U.S. fruit companies. The companies retaliated by raising banana prices to the consumer by more than enough to pay the higher taxes, and by cutting back production and purchases from the countries concerned, eventually forcing the UBEC states to reduce or drop the new taxes. The result:

> ...in the end the big winner of the banana war may not be the seven members of the cartel but the two US fruit corporations. *Only a year ago (1973) the two companies' profit per box of bananas was only 20 cents.* But since the cartel boosted prices—and the companies retaliated by cutting back their purchases, the world price of bananas has increased by 40 percent. *And as a result of the shortage they helped create, the two companies are now making a profit of nearly 70 cents a box.* All of which goes to prove that sometimes organizing a cartel is just plain bananas![43] [Italics added.]

A second strategy is to secure the maximum benefits from equity participation by the Third World states.[44] This is done by negotiating favorable valuation and payment terms for the equity acquired by the state, expansion of the now "mixed enterprise" using outside financing, and reducing taxation and foreign exchange burdens. Through such devices an MNC can end up with a greater cashflow as a 49 percent shareholder (with the state owning 51 percent) than it did as a full owner; this was the case with the Chileanization of Kennecot Copper in 1967 and the Zambianization of the copper mines in 1969. Closely associated with this is a third strategy: that of specialization in the supply of support services to state enterprises, such as management, purchasing, and marketing. These can yield highly remunerative returns, since the fees are usually based on a percentage-of-sales basis. They also permit the MNC to retain a high degree of control over the state enterprise and indeed to regard it virtually as a member affiliate of the multinational corporate family. As a vice-president of Chase Manhattan Bank told a Conference of Industrialists and Financiers, sponsored by the UN's Economic Commission for Africa:

> Most successful (joint ventures) have been achieved without hard and fast requirements for certain rigid percentages of stock ownership. The important element is there be a meeting of minds at the beginning as to who does what—who manages and controls. Under these circumstances, a minority shareholder can in fact functionally not only manage but control the enterprise.[45]

A fourth strategy is for the MNCs concerned to diversify not only into the provision of support services but also into related industries. It is said that U.S. oil companies should more properly be called Energy Corporations: besides their oil interests they control vast coal reserves, more than half the U.S. uranium reserves and most of its natural-gas production.[46] Similarly, by the time Kennecot and Anaconda were expropriated in Chile, the former had acquired a substantial coal-mining interest and the latter was already a major aluminium producer. None of these strategies mean that country-company conflicts no longer exist. But they do mean that the MNCs involved in these industries have developed a fairly coherent and consistent formula for accommodating to economic nationalism and securing new alliances with the aspirant national capitalists in certain peripheral countries.

From the point of view of the wider interests in transnationalized capitalism, there are certain positive advantages to be gained if the Third World states progressively assume the functions of formal ownership and administration of the natural resource industries. At first, stability of primary product supplies was secured by direct ownership of these industries in the periphery by MNCs. But the rise of economic nationalism has made foreign ownership and control an explosive issue: what was at first an asset has now become a liability. *By ceding ownership to the Third World states, supplies may actually be made more reliable,* since the ownership issue will have been defused. The point was made in the following way by U.S. Senator Frank Church, in hearings before the U.S. Senate Subcommittee of Multinational Corporations, when he put the following question to the president of Reynolds Metals about the company's bauxite mines in the Caribbean:

> Would it have been possible for you to have contracted to secure that bauxite *on a different basis than equity ownership because it is that that is creating the highly intense nationalistic feeling?* Is there a way for your industry and other industries that are involved in the extractive field to do business in foreign countries without securing the form of ownership of the minerals or the metals or the oil or whatever that arouses these highly nationalistic feelings? If there is, I would think it would be both in the interest of your company and in the interest of our Government...We want to contrast our own pattern with the Japanese and Western Europeans to see what we can learn because we have to live with the political consequences of our acts and *I would hate to see all of Latin America go the route chosen by Chile and by Cuba.*[47] [Italics added.]

Typical of the model Senator Church probably had in mind is the project for the construction of one of the world's largest gas lique-facation plants by the Algerian state company SONATRACH, in which the bulk of the production was to be purchased by France, Belgium, and West Germany upon completion in 1977.[48]

Third World state ownership, moreover, makes the problem of

dealing with the labor force a government responsibility, and removes the MNCs from the politically vulnerable position of being a "foreign imperialist exploiter" of indigenous labor. With ownership, the national government directly assumes the risks of fluctuations in the international markets for the commodities concerned, a situation which could easily have adverse repercussions on them while benefitting the consumers and the MNCs.[49] Such factors indicate that transnationalized capitalism is capable not only of accommodating to Third World economic nationalism but also of turning it to its advantage by assigning it a specific role in the overall international system. From the point of view of Third World peoples, this shows the importance of analyzing imperialism not only in terms of *formal* ownership forms; but in terms of all forms of control and of the effects and consequences of the system as a totality.

Accommodating Economic Nationalism: the OPEC Example

In spite of the strategies referred to above, important problems and contradictions generated by the new economic nationalism remain to be resolved. These can be analyzed with reference to the OPEC experience. OPEC is the most important cartel, controlling massive financial flows, and represents a model upon which other Third World country-cartels have attempted to base their own behavior.

The most important problems relate to the financial power of the oil producing states, occasioned by massive transfers of monetary assets to their account at the expense of the major consuming nations, particularly Western Europe and Japan. These states are expected to accumulate the astronomical sum of $1,200 billion in monetary reserves by 1985.[50] At one level the problem appears to be technical: how to recycle petrodollars received by OPEC into the accounts of deficit countries and the international economy generally so as to prevent economic collapse and worldwide depression.

From this strictly technical point of view a reasonably coherent pattern of dealing with the recycling problem has emerged. To begin with, the so-called conventional market mechanisms are handling a large part of the petrodollars, i.e., the OPEC countries are placing much of the funds with the largest multinational banks, mainly U.S. and West European, who are in turn lending them back to deficit countries. (One of the results of this is to strengthen the hold of U.S. banks over Western European countries thus reinforcing the reassertion of U.S economic dominance over Europe brought about by the rise in oil prices.) To this must be added OPEC holdings of government securities in the Western countries. Another form of recycling is the large contributions by various OPEC states to the

International Monetary Fund and the World Bank. (See Phillips.) This relates to the use of the market mechanisms in that they involve chanelling funds to deficit countries through the intermediation of international financial institutions not under the direct control of OPEC states.

These forms can be distinguished from another category, which bypasses international intermediation entirely: direct loans by OPEC states to institutions and governments in deficit countries, both developed and underdeveloped. Iran leads the way in this regard pledging some $10 billion in over 12 countries,[51] followed by Saudi Arabia, which lent Japan some $1 billion in late 1974 on commercial terms. Such bilateral transactions include not only commercial lending and general aid but also massive deals for the purchase of capital goods, technology, and military equipment. The purchase of technology with petrodollars is also being carried out through direct transactions between OPEC states and the large MNCs. Gulf Oil, for example, is reported to be investing over $1 billion in natural gas liquefacation in a joint venture with the Nigerian government, which will itself contribute an even larger sum.[52] In the longer term such projects based on OPEC-MNC partnerships may well become one of the principal forms of petrodollar recycling. The director general of the Kuwait Fund for Arab Economic Development is reported to have told a conference sponsored by the Banker's Trust Company that:

> The Arab oil countries want to use their surplus revenues to set up joint ventures with multinational firms to industrialize their own countries and are not interested in projects aimed at simply lending their funds to oil-consuming countries...Kuwait and other Arab countries are particularly anxious to encourage direct investment in their own countries and...multinational firms offering such projects could be the main recipient of oil-producer investments.[53]

Associated with such partnerships is the emergence of another new phenomenon: that of direct equity investment by OPEC states in MNCs and Western enterprises generally. Iran's $100 million investment in Germany's Krupp Steel is only the initial trickle of what could become a flood, for the U.S. stock market is expected to absorb billions of petrodollars.[54]

It is evident that the process of recycling involves far more important changes than those connoted by such an innocuous term. A whole new network of linkages—financial, commodity, technological, and institutional—is being constructed between the OPEC states on the one hand, and the developed countries and the multinational corporations on the other. We can assume that this pattern will serve as the model for other Third World countries which succeed in generating large surpluses through their primary-product exports. These new linkages are designed precisely to ensure that the international economic order can continue to function without any catastrophic dislocation. Predictions that the international monetary system is capable of handling the petrodollar problem, although with some strain, bear ample testimony to this.[55] In effect, success in recycling petrodollars implies that the money eventually finds its way back into the international capitalist order and, in particular, into the cash flow accounts of the major MNCs. In that sense, the substance of the system will remain intact. What is changing, however, is the nature of economic relationships and power-relations among governments, and between governments and MNCs.

The rapid emergence of a new network of ties between the OPEC states and the major industrial consuming countries signals a new set of relationships which are not only qualitatively greater, but also qualitatively different from those that ruled in the past. They are based on far greater equality in power-relations than before: on a partnership between equals rather than that of a horse and its rider. Some might suggest that the huge reserves being accumulated by OPEC, which exceed those of Western European nations, will give the former an absolute superiority in economic power. Such a crude measure of economic power is nevertheless misleading, precisely because it is quantitative rather than qualitative. The industrial consumer countries possess the technology and the armaments that the OPEC states want to acquire, and to the extent that the former succeed in tying up the latter's reserves in their own monetary and real assets, then they will have as much leverage over OPEC, as OPEC has over them. Indeed, one implication of the new linkages is that there is emerging a growing reciprocity and mutuality of interest between the OPEC countries and the West. (See Bird.)

Accompanying the diffusion of financial power to the OPEC countries is a longer-term process involving the diffusion of physical productive capacity not only in light, but also in heavy manufacturing industry. The growing list of projects in these countries for the establishment of petrochemicals and other chemical industries, steel, nuclear power, military equipment and other basic or heavy industry indicates that their industrialization will be allowed to go beyond the limits of light manufacturing to which the majority of Third World countries have been limited. But this development should not be confused with an autonomous or indigenous industrialization strategy, for it is based on advanced technology from the advanced industrial countries themselves, who will also purchase much of the output of the new industries. It therefore constitutes a new form of integration with traditional center countries; one that complements on the level of production the integration being established on the level of finance. Such integration also allows the state capitalists in the OPEC countries a much more developed and meaningful material base than before, and will permit the emergence of an economic structure bearing at least a superficial resemblance to that of the industrial center countries. But the economic system will still be a dependent one, a vital component of the wider international capitalist system.

This new form of integration is associated with a new structure of relationships between OPEC states and the MNCs. Increasingly, these countries will purchase technology and goods from the largest and most technologically advanced MNCs, paying for them with surpluses generated either directly or indirectly by the activities of the oil MNCs which transport, refine, and market the oil produced by OPEC state enterprise or by joint ventures.

All this is of course to a certain extent an ideal scenario. The actual course of events has not been as smooth as that implied by the apparent neatness of the new structure of relationships which seems to be evolving. Nor will the future process necessarily be much smoother. For one thing, the evolving equilibrium between OPEC states and the MNCs is not necessarily a stable one: the Organization of Arab Petroleum Exporting Contries (OAPEC) has signalled its intention to move into the downstream end of the oil business,[56] thereby threatening the established position of the oil companies in areas such as oil well drilling and refining. Indeed, in the long run there is no necessary reason why the new class of petroleum state capitalists should limit their international ambitions to the oil business alone. It is not inconceivable that with their huge financial resources they would make a bid for their own place of near equality in the overall system of international capitalism as the Western Europeans and Japanese did in the 1960s, with all the accompanying tensions and strains which that provoked. President Ford and Secretary of State Kissinger led the saber-rattling against OPEC in September 1974, when such anxieties were high.[57]

Looking to the longer run, analysts from the U.S. note that country's growing dependence on raw materials and refer to "The Threat from the Third World."[58] While the rhetoric of these groups tends to be couched in terms of universalistic or technocratic concerns, such as the need to "curb inflation," to "restore the operation of the laws [sic] of supply and demand," and to "prevent a collapse of the world monetary system," it is the issue of power that really preoccupies them. As Vaughan Lewis puts it, "the parameters of power relations and of behavior patterns have been rudely disrupted, without their replacement by a new set which is clearly understood and respected by all."[59]

Contradictions among the different capitalists and power groups provide only one reason why the new evolving system is not necessarily a stable one. Another and more potent reason is that the new order shows every sign of accentuating, rather than reducing, the contradiction of increasing wealth accompanied by growing poverty on a world scale.

Equity and Polarization: A Global View

We have seen that Third World economic nationalism is succeeding in bringing about a diffusion of international economic power from the central developed countries to some raw material producing Third World states. But this diffusion is accompanied by a contradictory, reverse movement—one of growing concentration of incomes and economic power on the world level. The apparent paradox is easily reconciled if we adopt a global view, and one that is based on an analysis of classes rather than countries.

In 1974 *Newsweek* carried a cover story titled "Iran's Push for Power." The Shah used his country's $20 billion-per-year oil revenues in some very interesting ways. In 1973 alone he spent $4 billion on arms purchases from the United States; in the first nine months of 1974 he ordered some 289 jet fighters, 500 attack helicopters, 700 tanks, and six destroyers. He had also committed some $10 billion in aid, loans, and investments to governments and institutions in twelve countries, in order to "seek to expand his sphere of influence." In addition, the revenues financed the "opulent life-styles" of the royal family, the super-rich and the "flourishing business class," all of whom "frolic in striking splendour." Of course, large sums were also being plowed into Iran's "development"; but agriculture and industry were lagging and inefficient, the literacy rate was only 30 percent, and "most of the populace still survives on a diet of bread and vegetable oil." Not surprisingly the Shah found it necessary to maintain a secret police force (SAVAK) which was one of the largest in the world. Its full-time personnel was estimated to number between 30,000 and 60,000, but perhaps as many as 3 million Iranians—some 12 percent of the adult population—were occasional informers. SAVAK was credited with holding as many as 50,000 political prisoners and with carrying out hundreds of executions.[60] What did these Iranians think of their country's success in redistributing the world's wealth from the rich countries to the poor?*

*ed. note: The answer, of course, came loud and clear when the Shah, and then his hand-picked successor, were overthrown in the massive popular uprisings of 1978 and early 1979.

The Shah's extremely centralized and autocratic rule may not be a characteristic shared by most of the other mineral-rich countries, but the picture of state affluence based on mineral revenues, accompanied by continuing economic underdevelopment and class inequalities, is by no means atypical. As *Newsweek* puts it:

> For every sheik who spent last summer in the cool mountain air and tolerant moral climate of nearby Beirut, thousands of uneducated and ill-cared for Saudis sweltered in slums of Jidda and Riyadh. And the gap between rich and poor is as great in such oil-producing non-Arab nations as Nigeria, Malaysia and Indonesia.[61]

Even before the recent successes of OPEC, it had become clear that for the countries of the periphery, the mere receipt of huge amounts of financial flows by the state did not necessarily lead to a process of self-sustaining development, structural transformation and general improvement in living standards for the mass of population.[62] On the contrary, under certain conditions, it can serve as an obstacle to the achievement of these objectives. On the purely economic level, an abundant and reliable flow of mineral revenues provides foreign exchange which props up an economic system which is structurally dependent on imports, and removes the pressure and incentives for changes which would orient the system along more self-centered lines. Food can be imported, so that agriculture can remain backward and inefficient without generating a foreign exchange crisis; the same applies to manufactured goods. There is therefore no pressure to develop and apply an indigenous technology for the utilization of indigenous materials in a productive system geared to satisfying the needs of the broad mass of the population. Thus the divergence analyzed by Clive Thomas—that between the structure of resource use and the structure of demand—is unlikely to be narrowed in such a system.[63] We have seen that the considerable rise in revenues secured by raw material producing states has increased their capacity to undertake large projects in basic or heavy industry. These are partly based on domestic resources and partly on imported raw materials; but in all cases they are based on imported technology, are geared to exporting to the markets of the central industrial countries, and usually involve some form of partnership with the large multinational corporations. Thus they intensify integration with the center rather than reduce it; the divergence between resource use and demand widens as the system expands. And the system is capable of expansion so long as production and/or prices of the mineral-exports grow, or accumulated foreign exchange reserves hold out. Furthermore, this pattern of development is highly capital-intensive, and does not normally involve a real reorganization of the agricultural social economy. There is no evidence that it can solve the problems of un and under-employment and of rural poverty—*the* fundamental condition for an improvement in living standards for the mass of the population in these countries.

What is more, mineral revenues serve to strengthen immensely the power of antipopular political structures in these countries, which is the socio-political correlate of an economic system which excludes the mass of the population from effective participation. It is true that the nature of the political and social regimes in mineral-producing states appears to vary widely: from right reactionary (Iran under the Shah, Saudi Arabia, Indonesia) to left-progressive (Algeria, Iraq), to parliamentary democratic (Venezuela, Jamaica) and so on. These differences correspond to the exact nature of the class alliance and the dominant political ideology in different countries. But they hide a reality which is much less heterogeneous. In most cases the state plays an important and growing role in the economy, precisely because it is through state intermediation that mineral revenues are disposed of. The result is a powerful state or bureaucratic capitalist class. The variety springs from the fact that in some countries this class shares power with a dominant (or subordinate) royal or landed group, the military, or a middle class; in some cases it is the dominant economic class, while in others it remains junior to, and an adjunct of, the private capitalist class.

Mineral revenues provide the state bourgeoisie with the material resources to undertake a project of national capitalist development which will strengthen its own material base and at the same time reproduce the structure of dependence and social inequality; they also provide this class with the resources to coerce or bribe the rest of the population into accepting the pattern. In that context, the objective role of economic nationalism is to serve as an alternative to socialism and a socialist pattern of development, rather than as a complement to the latter. Nevertheless, both the precise nature of the process of socio-political development in these countries and the resulting contradictions deserve more comprehensive and subtle analysis than we are able to undertake in this article.

In the underdeveloped oil *consuming* countries, the rise in oil prices is manifested as a foreign exchange crisis which really represents an intensification of the balance-of-payments problem which is one of the most characteristic features of peripheral underdeveloped capitalism. The reflex reaction of the groups which control the state is to seek ways and means of mounting a salvage operation by cutting imports and raising additional foreign exchange receipts. In countries which produce strategic commodities currently experiencing shortages—such as bauxite and phosphates—there are evident opportunities to turn what might have started as a defensive action into one which follows the OPEC example, not only in terms of raising taxes and prices through cartel-like actions but also in terms of undertaking development of new types of industries under the initiative of a state bourgeoisie, with all the economic and social consequences that that implies.

In a large number of underdeveloped countries, however—countries having a large proportion of the world's population—such possibilities of raising fresh export receipts do not exist. Here the prospect must be for increasing foreign indebtedness and a reduced level of real imports, bringing about a contraction in the rate of economic growth. Who will bear the costs of adjustment in these countries? In a capitalist system those who are strongest will pay the least, passing on the costs in the form of higher prices and taxes, to others who are weaker and less capable of defending themselves: labor, especially unorganized labor, the underemployed and un-employed, and the peasants. Economic crisis and political contra-dictions in such countries, therefore, can only be heightened; the demise of the Selassie regime in Ethiopia is only the earliest manifes-tation of this.

Again, we cannot pretend that this one article begins to adequately analyze developments and possible resolutions in this group of countries. What we can say with some confidence is that those who wish to see, and struggle for, a more socially rational and just economic order should be careful not to mistake the achieve-ments of Third World economic nationalism for revolutionary change. The structure of the international capitalist order is being rapidly modified to permit the incorporation of a greater number of national capitalists. In the process, some capitalists in the central industrial countries have had to suffer a relative decline in their power and status. But at the same time the power of transnational-ized capitalism has not been significantly affected; indeed, new op-portunities have been created for MNC investment and market outlets. The tendency for greater equality in power relations between the center and OPEC-type states is accompanied by one of growing polarization: between OPEC-type states and other Third World states; between the ruling class and the greater population within OPEC-type states; and between the marginalized masses of the Third World, on the one hand, and the ruling classes of the whole world, on the other. Evolutionary changes must be compared continually with genuine revolutionary alternatives, alternatives which begin with the social, political, and economic needs of the marginalized people of the world as the *objective* of economic development and social change.

FOOTNOTES

1. C. Fred Bergsten, "The New Era in World Commodity Markets," *Challenge,* September/October 1974, pp. 34-35.

2. United Nations, *Multinational Corporations in World Development,* New York, 1973, p. 13. This refers to value-added of MNCs both in home and host countries.

3. Orville Freeman, president of Business International and former U.S. secretary of agriculture, quoted by U.S. Senate Committee on Finance, *The Multinational Corporation and the World Economy,* Washington, 1973, p. 3. The 10 percent figure refers to the rate of growth of production by MNCs.

4. Osvaldo Sunkel, "Transnational Capitalism and National Disintegration in Latin America," in *Dependence and Underdevelopment in the New World and the Old,* Norman Girvan, ed., Special Issue, *Social and Economic Studies,*, 22:1 (March 1973),p. 163,quoting A. Barber, "Emerging New Power: The World Corporation," *War/Peace Report,* October 1968, p. 7.

5. i.e., "production subject to foreign control or decision and measured by the sales of *foreign* affiliates of multinational corporations," United Nations, 1973, p. 13. [Italics added.]

6. *Ibid.*

7. Hugh Stephenson, *The Coming Clash: The Impact of the International Corporation on the Nation State,* (London: Weidenfeld and Nicholson, 1972), p. 4.

8. $35.6 billion out of a total of $309 billion. See U.S. Senate Committee on Finance, *Implications of Multinational Firms for World Trade and Investment and for U.S. Trade and Labor,* Washington, 1973, pp. 275, 279.

9. *Ibid.,* p. 275.

10. Stephensen, *op.cit.,* p. 4.

11. U.S. Senate Committee on Finance, *The Multinational Corporation,* p. 21.

12. Raymond Vernon, *Sovereignty at Bay: The Multinational Spread of U.S. Enterprises,* (New York, 1971), p. 13.

13. *Ibid.,* pp. 13-18.

14. U.S. Senate Committee on Finance, *The Multinational Corporation,* p. 6.

15. *Ibid.,* p. 8.

16. Vernon, *op.cit.,* pp.11, 285. The author also notes that the 187 firms concerned are "an extraordinary group, quite distinct in many respects from the rest of the U.S. corporate economy." (p. 11).

17. *Ibid.,* p. 12.

18. Michael Z. Brooke and H. Lee Remmers, *The Strategy of Multinational Enterprise,* (New York, 1970); John M. Stopford and Louis T. Wells, Jr., *Managing The Multinational Enterprise,* (New York, 1972).

19. Stephen Hymer, *Notes on the United Nations Report on Multinational Corporations in World Development,* United Nations, Geneva, 6 November 1973, (mimeo); see also Hymer, "Multinational Corporations and the Law of Uneven Development," in J. Bhagwati, ed., *Economics and World Order,* (New York, 1972).

20. See Hymer, "Multinational Corporations and the Law of Uneven Development," p. 37 ff.

21. See, for example, K. Levitt, *Silent Surrender: The Multinational Corporation in Canada,* (Canada, Macmillan Co., 1970).

22. Stephenson, *op.cit.,* p. 128.

23. *Ibid.,* p. 51.

24. On the most "pessimistic" assumption that in the absence of production abroad by U.S. MNCs, the market would have been supplied by U.S. exports. See U.S. Senate Committee on Finance, *Implications of Multinational Firms* (1973), p. 5.

25. See, for example, comment in *The Wall Street Journal,* 20 August 1971, cited in Stephensen, *op.cit.,* p. 123.

26. A Conservative Party spokesman is reported to have said, during the 1970 British General Election, that "some types of international industry go to those countries which offer them the biggest bribes and it will be necessary for the next Conservative Government to match these inducements." Cited by Stephenson *op.cit.,* p. 49.

27. Cited by Stephensen, *op.cit.,* p.12..

28. A. Barber, "Emerging New Power: The World Corporation," *War/Peace Report,* October 1968, p. 7, cited by Sunkel, *op.cit.,* p. 163.

29. Cited by Stephenson *op.cit.,* p. 58.

30. Raymond Vernon, *The Economic and Poltical Consequences of Multinational Enterprise: An Anthology*, (Boston, 1972), p. 19.

31. United Nations (1973), p. 21.

32. *Ibid.,* p. 22.

33. *Ibid.*

34. *Time,* 30 December 1973, p. 51. [Emphasis added.]

35. See, for example, "New Era for Multinationals," *Business Week,* 6 July 1974, pp. 73-74. The magazine quotes C. Fred Bergsten as remarking that "ironically, the multinationals probably will find that it's safer to operate in Communist countries than in some others."

36. See, for example, Norman Girvan, "Multinational Corporations and Dependent Underdevelopment in Mineral-Export Economies," *Social and Economic Studies,* December 1970, and Raymond Midesell, ed. and contributor, *Foreign Investment in the Petroleum and Mineral Industries,* (Baltimore, 1971).

37. For a useful discussion of class categories and class structure in the social formations of peripheral capitalism, see Samir Amin, *Contemporary Peripheral Social Formations, Unequal Development and the Problems of Transition,* (IDEP Reproduction, 1972).

38. See, for example, W. W. Ashworth, *A Short History of the International Economy* (London, 1952). Admittedly, this generalization holds most strongly where the United States, Canada, and Australia are regarded as part of the nineteenth century "periphery," which in a very important sense they were.

39. See, for example, United Nations (1973) p. 8-12. Some two-thirds of international direct investment were located in the developing market economies and manufacturing was the largest single sector, constituting 40 percent of the total.

40. See, for example, "Putting Heat on Big Oil," *Newsweek,* 4 February 1974, pp. 36-38.

41. *Ibid.*: Also Leonard Silk, "Multinational Morals," *International Herald Tribune,* 8 March 1974. It is also felt that the oil companies' allies in engineering the energy crisis were the U.S. Government which, following the dollar crises of 1971-73, wished to reassert U.S. economic dominance over oil-dependent Western Europe and Japan and the giant U.S. automobile companies (who wished to gain political leverage over the environmental lobby). For the first, see Samir Amin, "Towards a New Structural Crisis in the World Capitalist System?" *Multinationals in Africa,* Chapter 1. The point about the automobile companies was suggested in conversation by Ms. Kari Levitt.

42. In 1970-71 the international aluminum industry suffered from excess capacity due to overexpansion in the late 1960s. In early 1972 the leading aluminum multinationals took the lead in establishing the International Primary Aluminum Institute, which monitors production, inventories, and expansion plans throughout the capitalist world. Since that time the excess capacity has gradually been replaced by excess demand, and the companies are reporting high profits by 1974.

43. From "Carter Is Just Bananas," *Newsweek,* 26 August 1974, p. 38. See also "Multinationals: A banana brouhaha over higher prices," *Business Week,* 6 July 1974, p. 42.

44. See, for example, Paul Semonin, *Nationalization and Management in Zambia,* (DEP Reproduction, 1971), and Girvan "Multinational Corporations and Dependent Underdevelopment," *op.cit.*

45. Semonin, *op.cit.,* p. 14.

46. *Newsweek,* 4 February 1974, p. 36.

47. United States Senate Committee on Foreign Relations, Subcommittee on Multinational Corporations, *Hearings: 93rd Congress, 1st Session. On Overseas Private Investment Corporations (OPIC):* July-August 1973, Washington, 1973.

48. "Algeria to Build World's Largest Gas Plant," *Newsweek,* 16 September 1974.

51. In this connection see also William B. Quandt, "Can We Do Business With Radical Nationalists? (1) Algeria: Yes." *Foreign Policy* 7, (Summer 1972); and "Shortages: Risky Race for Minerals," *Time,* 28 January 1974, pp. 48-49.

49. See, for example, Theodore Moran, "New Deal or Raw Deal in Raw Materials," *Foreign Policy,* 5 (Winter 1971-1972). In this connection it should be noted that by October 1974 sources in the United States were predicting a fall in oil prices within two years, though not to the 1973 levels.

50. "Recycling the Petrodollars," *Newsweek,* 14 October 1974, p. 41; "Oil: The U.S. Talks Tough," *Newsweek,* 7 October 1974, p. 16.

51. "The Master Builder of Iran," *Newsweek,* 14 October 1974, p. 27.

52. "Gulf Oil to Tap Nigeria's Natural-Gas Resources," *Newsweek,* 27 May 1974, p. 36; "Saudi Arabia to Make Cheap Steel," *Newsweek,* 15 April 1974, p. 36; "Dow Chemical To Take Part in $500 Million Joint Venture in Iran," *The Financial Times,* 9 August 1974, p. 18.

53. "Priority Use of Oil Money in Development, Arab Says," *International Herald Tribune,* 18 September 1974, p. 9.

54. *Newsweek,* 14 October 1974, p. 43.

55. "Recycling the Petrodollars," *Newsweek,* 14 October 1974, pp. 41-43.

56. "Arab Drive For Bigger Oil Profits Continues," *Newsweek,* 27 May 1974, p. 36.

57. "Oil: The U.S. Talks Tough," *Newsweek,* 7 October 1974, pp. 15-18; "Coping with the Oil Cartel," *Newsweek,* 14 October 1974, pp. 25-26.

58. C. Fred Bergsten, "The Threat from the Third World," *Foreign Policy,* 11, (Summer 1972). See also "Shortages: Risky Race for Minerals," *Time,* 28 January 1974, pp. 48-49.

59. Comment at Society for International Development, Round Table on the Energy Crisis, Abidjan, 11 August 1974.

60. "The Master Builder of Iran," *Newsweek,* 14 October 1974, pp. 27-33.

61. From "Winners and Losers," *Newsweek,* 30 September 1974, p. 41.

62. For an analysis of this see Girvan, "Multinational Corporations and Dependent Underdevelopment," *op.cit.*

63. See Clive Y. Thomas, *Dependence and Transformation: The Economics of the Transition to Socialism,* (New York, 1974), especially chapter 2.

chapter two

RENOVATION OF THE INTERNATIONAL ECONOMIC ORDER: TRILATERALISM, THE IMF, AND JAMAICA

James Phillips*

In recent years, the International Monetary Fund (IMF) has become an important vehicle for the implementation of trilateralist economic and political policies in Third World countries. The fundamental work of the highly powerful U.S.-dominated IMF in supporting and strengthening policies of economic expansionism and so-called free trade for the industrialized West has fitted well with the basic policies of world economic management promoted by the trilateralists. Recent events in Jamaica will serve as a case study. But first we must review the IMF's origin, purposes, and policies.

IMF Origins

The Bretton Woods Agreement of 1944 accomplished an overhaul of the older international monetary system. The existing gold standard was not totally abolished but each of the major industrial nations agreed to defend the value of its currency by various domestic economic and monetary measures. National currency values were no longer allowed to adjust themselves automatically in relation to world trade. The U.S. dollar was clearly the strongest and most stable currency, and it quickly became the practical, day-to-day surrogate for gold as the standard for international currency exchange. Other currencies were readily convertible into dollars, and vice versa. This situation of convertibility continued until the early 1970s.

*James Phillips holds a Ph.D in Economic Anthropology and has lived and worked in the Caribbean for several years. He writes frequently on issues of Third World development.

The International Monetary Fund was founded as the institution responsible for implementing the terms of the Bretton Woods Agreement. In particular, the Fund was established to ensure currency exchange rate stabilization and to support and protect free trade and investment against tendencies toward protectionism. Each member nation of the IMF made contributions and could apply for assistance from the Fund in trying to achieve stabilization of their own currency. The lending policies of the Fund were determined by a board of directors representing the member nations, heavily weighted toward the major contributors. This large contribution/large vote arrangement ensured that the United States would be the dominant voice in policy operations.

A limited set of options were open to countries seeking to achieve currency stabilization. Five of the most important options include: use of national reserves; protectionist measures; revaluation of the national currency; anti-inflation measures; and longer-term development of the economic base (that is, of the productive level) of the nation. The IMF program, as it evolved during the 1950s, addressed each of these options as reviewed below.

One option open to a government trying to defend the exchange rate of its currency is to use some of its national reserves to "pay" the deficit in the short run. If the balance-of-payments deficit is chronic or long-term, however, continued use of reserves may quickly deplete the national treasury and make any realistic economic development program difficult or impossible. The IMF has supplied loans to nations to assist them in paying their balance-of-payments deficits so as to avoid extensive borrowing from national reserves. As long as most of the nations involved were industrial nations with a basis for reconstruction or rapid development—without a chronic balance-of-payments deficit—this IMF policy worked reasonably well. It was designed as a temporary measure for a temporary situation, such as that existing in Western Europe at the end of World War II. As time went on, the deepening problem of chronic undevelopment of the raw materials-producing Third World nations challenged this particular operation of the Fund and helped bring about changes in the style of operation and policies of the IMF during the 1960s. But even during the Eisenhower years (1952-60) there was a gradually increasing awareness among the political and financial elites of the industrial nations that the economic underdevelopment of much of the postcolonial world would bring strains in the future operation of the IMF. This realization reflected an inner contradiction inasmuch as the whole colonial system from which Western industrial nations drew much of their wealth was largely responsible for the underdeveloped state of much of the emerging postcolonial world. (See Girvan.)

A second option open to countries trying to manage the value of their national currency is to institute some forms of protection for domestic industries and export goods together with measures designed to discourage and reduce the importation of foreign goods and services. Tariffs and taxes on imports are the usual form of such protection. Several variations of this theme are possible, including a selective tariff schedule which taxes luxury imports but not imports of basic necessities (or vice versa), or which raises tariffs on all imported goods but grants a subsidy in the case of certain basic necessities. Decisions as to what measures to employ are normally highly political in character and reflect the demands—and power to impose those demands—of different sectors of the population at a particular time in relation to the national government. For example, a government may institute tariffs on luxury goods and subsidies on basic necessities if it wants to safeguard the interests of the poorer sectors of its population, even at the risk of alienating some of its wealthier citizens.

Programs of economic development are a third way of dealing with the problems of currency stabilization. Development addresses the underlying long-term economic problems which foster a chronic balance-of-payments deficit in a particular country. But while the IMF was not conceived as a major source for development funds, it could not continue indefinitely to loan to nations experiencing chronic payments problems, especially if those problems were rooted in the nation's economic structure. Thus, a regular institutionalized form of development assistance was established: the International Bank for Reconstruction and Development—commonly known as the *World Bank*—IMF's partner institution. During the 1950s, the focus of development aid turned from a revived Western Europe toward the emerging postcolonial nations of the Third World.

Control of inflation is yet another means of dealing with curency exchange rate problems. The IMF has consistently held to the view that inflation is a major threat to stable currency exchange since it erodes the value of a particular currency in relation to other currencies and especially in relation to goods and services on the world market. The IMF views inflation as an imbalance between the domestic supply of goods (productivity) and the supply of money, with too much money available for the goods produced. This situation can occur if a government expands the money supply, relying on deficit spending to cover expenses. The Fund's policy has been to try to return money to the government and to the more productive (i.e. profitable) private enterprise sectors at the expense of other sectors of the population, following a policy of tight money. In order to take money out of citizens' hands and return it to government and profitable business sectors a variety of measures are advocated, including tax and price increases and wage controls. The measures which the Fund has advocated over the years to deal with inflation are rationalized within the logic of traditional, orthodox capitalist theory; but tend to have immediately adverse effects upon the living standards of major sectors of the national populations, most notably poor and middle class people whose income is squeezed between wage controls and rising prices.

As the Fund lent increasingly to poorer, Third World nations, the question of the effects of anti-inflationary monetary policies on the poor became a more critical social and political question since the highly exploited non-industrial bases of former colonies within the Western trade system made rapid increases in productivity—and drops in inflation—more difficult to achieve. This situation also contributed to an increasing reliance upon force and repression by governments trying to impose IMF policies on sectors of its population already in desperate economic straits. Curtailment of popular protest against wage freezes, tax and price hikes, and the suppression of worker organizing and strikes in an effort to maintain or increase productivity provided a context of repression and continued violation of human rights. In recent years, these trends have continued at even higher levels.

A fifth option for a nation dealing with the problem of currency stabilization involves revaluation of its currency. This option brings us back to the two fundamental purposes for which the IMF was established: promotion of free and unrestricted world trade and stabilization of world currencies. It also brings us forward to a consideration of changes which took place in the world economic situation and in the policies of the Fund during the 1960s.

The promotion of free and unrestricted world trade had remained the primary purpose of the Fund; stabilization of national currencies is seen as a fundamental condition of free trade. The Fund has advised devaluation of a national currency in place of protective trade measures as a remedy for a chronic balance-of-payments deficit. After devaluation, it costs more, in terms of the national currency, to purchase foreign goods and capital. This increased cost is supposed to operate as a brake on foreign imports into the country.

In its early years of involvement with the reconstruction of the industrially-based economies of Western Europe, the Fund allowed a degree of protectionism against U.S. goods but not against U.S. capital investment in Europe. Later, as the Fund shifted its involvement more toward the Third World, the removal of protective barriers to trade assumed greater critical importance for the U.S. and Western European interests within the IMF directorate, inasmuch as these nations were major raw materials suppliers and potentially important markets. Maintaining the steady and cheap flow of essential raw materials reasserted itself as a primary focus of Fund policies.

Adjustment to Changing Conditions During the 1960s

The economic resurgence of Western Europe and Japan and the political emergence of the postcolonial Third World posed problems and tensions in the international order. The Western industrial powers, and the United States in particular, dealt with those changes in part through adjustments in the policy and operation of the IMF.

West European and Japanese firms invaded the U.S. market and competed for the growing Third World market. Moreover, European nations began to give aid and loans to Third World nations, becoming an alternative source of aid and strengthening economic ties to their former colonies. Third World nations began to use U.S. aid to repay debts to Western Europe or relied on U.S. aid to offset chronic balance-of-payments shortages incurred, in part, through buying European products. In effect, the U.S. saw itself as paying for Third World importation of European and Japanese goods. Additional tensions arose over the priority of debt repayments by those Third World nations which had incurred debts to West European nations or Japan as well as the U.S. Which nation should be repaid first? In short, the problem from the perspective of the U.S. was that the situation then unfolding gave Third World borrowing nations too much freedom to manipulate the system, to the partial advantage of Western Europe and the Third World and to the definite disadvantage of the U.S.

The political emergence of the postcolonial Third World created an additional problem, albeit of a different order: how to integrate these newly independent nations, most of which were "underdeveloped," into the monetary/financial system based on the Bretton Woods Agreement. In particular, the U.S. was concerned with extending its economic (and political) hegemony over the emerging Third World politically-independent nations without creating undue tensions with Western Europe and Japan.

The nature of these problems made it clear that an important part of the solution resided in streamlining and reforming the policy and operation of the IMF. The trend which emerged during the middle and late 1960s was reflected, above all, in the proposals vigorously supported by then Deputy Secretary of State for Economic Affairs, Douglas Dillon. One proposal was to increase the practice of "tied" aid: aid to a country under the condition that it be used by the country to buy U.S. goods and services. This proposal addressed directly the growing practice of using U.S. aid to pay for European goods. A second proposal advocated a consortium approach to aid, which involved increased coordination among donor nations about scheduling payments due them by recipient nations. Each donor nation would refuse to grant aid except on terms identical to those of other donor nations in the consortium. This proposal was aimed at reducing the degree to which recipient nations could play off donor nations against each other in an attempt to get better terms of aid.

Another trend was toward more program aid; that is, aid given with definite stipulations, often within the context of an overall program of economic planning, to which a recipient nation had to agree in order to obtain the aid or loans. Essentially, this practice of program aid, aimed at reducing the maneuverability and increasing the accountability of Third World recipient nations, was similar to IMF standby arrangements for meeting balance-of-payments deficits. We have already discussed some of the aspects of IMF policy which form the basis for standby arrangement accountability. Stated more explicitly, the program of accountability or "conditionality" generally includes IMF demands for:

(1) abolition or liberalization of controls on foreign exchange and imports by the recipient nation; that is, the reduction of any form of "protectionism" against U.S. or European goods, investment and free trade;
(2) devaluation of the exchange rate (currency devaluation);
(3) domestic anti-inflationary practices such as:
—control of bank credits, higher interest rates, and higher central reserve requirements;
—control of government spending; reduction of so-called "extravagant" social services and programs; increases in taxes prices; abolition of subsidies on consumer items;
—wage controls
(4) encouragement of foreign investment*

*ed. note: In *The Debt Trap: The International Monetary Fund and the Third World,* Cheryl Payer explains that import and foreign exchange controls are dismantled— even though they are meant to preserve precious foreign exchange—because they discourage foreign investors. In this manner, liberalization "is a measure which benefits the country's trading partners rather than itself." Other measures seem to fit this pattern. For example, "devaluation is intended to restrict imports by raising the price in domestic currency of ALL imports, and will (in theory) give imports a boost by permitting export producers to lower their selling price in foreign exchange without losing income in domestic prices." The country may be hurt for instance, when it is forced to pay for imported necessities for which there is no ready substitute

The IMF, in its standby arrangements with Third World nations, began to develop and pursue these demands as part of an overall program within which aid would be granted; without which aid would be denied. Aid could then be held up or cut off if a recipient nation failed to comply with or achieve one or more of these conditions or goals. Later we shall illustrate the devastating impact of such terms of conditionality by way of the Jamaican example.

A fourth and highly critical proposal for streamlining international finance during the 1960s was the use of IMF standby arrangements as "pilots" for further public and private lending to a recipient nation. The IMF standby arrangement became a test for the international financial lending institutions and private banks about the financial credibility of a particular recipient nation. Successful compliance with the standby stipulations and overall program earned the recipient country the IMF "seal of approval" necessary for further assistance. This is a critical point since the aid given by these other sources often proved to be far greater than that given by the IMF itself. Essentially, this meant that the IMF standby arrangement became a tight form of foreign control over the economic and financial policies of needy recipient nations.

Two other proposals for reforming the IMF had the effect of increasing the power, range, and flexibility of the Fund in dealing with the Third World. These included a 50 percent increase in the amount which the IMF could loan to borrowing nations and the formation of the International Development Association (IDA) to grant loans for development projects at easier terms than the regular multilateral and private bank sources. The IMF itself confined most of its loans to the elimination of balance-of-payments debts and to improving a nation's currency exchange position.

These proposals for streamlining the IMF were an attempt to resolve increasing tensions and problems within the Western world's political economy. The IMF was recognized to be a critical component of that political economy. The overriding goal of reform was to reaffirm and strengthen the fundamental purpose of the IMF itself and thereby strengthen the overall system. In 1967, George Ball, undersecretary of state for economic affairs under President Kennedy and now a member of the Trilateral Commission, clearly

---

at the higher prices while international buyers purchase the *same amount* of the country's primary product at the lower prices. All in all the measures bear most heavily on the poorer sectors of the population as prices rise, consumer subsidies are abolished, wages are kept down, social services are cut, and taxes increased. (New York: Monthly Review Press, 1974), pp. 33-34 and 17-18.

summarized the basic outlook from which this reform of the IMF proceeded:

> In these twenty postwar years, we have come to recognize in action, though not always in words, that the political boundaries of nation-states are too narrow and constricted to define the scope and activities of modern business.[1]

The Emergence of Trilateralism in the Early 1970s

The reform of the IMF during the 1960s did not resolve the problems arising from the economic resurgence of Europe and Japan and the political emergence of the Third World. By the early 1970s, the continued expansion of European (EEC) and Japanese industry began to have serious consequences upon both the U.S. trade balance and the position of the U.S. dollar itself.

In August 1971 Nixon promulgated his New Economic Policy, suspending the convertability of the dollar into gold and other reserve assets. This led to a devaluation of the dollar which was allowed to "float" in relation to other national currencies instead of remaining the fixed standard for other currencies. (See Frieden for an analysis of the so-called "Nixon shocks.")

What is important for the present discussion is that the New Economic Policy represented a direct attack upon the basic tenets of the Bretton Woods Agreement and, in particular, upon the fundamental purposes of the IMF. In attempting a nationalistic solution to the tensions and problems of the 1960s, Nixon's plan was the catalyst for more inclusive attempts —under the direction of trilateralists—to deal with the developing crisis of Western capitalism.

The IMF remained at the center of the international economic system. It is no coincidence that the trilateralists saw the Fund, and its further reform, as a powerful and necessary vehicle for the development of other trilateralist plans and proposals for international economic/financial management. It is critically important to remember that the power and impact of the IMF is not confined to corporate board rooms or private banking circles. The policies and operation of the Fund, and changes and reforms in those policies, affect the daily lives of millions of people in the Third World and in the trilateral world itself. The example below of Jamaica during the period of 1972-79 clearly reflects the impact of the IMF in human terms, and also points out the way in which the trilateralists have utilized the Fund as a potent vehicle of U.S. foreign policy and corporate interest in the Third World.

Jamaica, Trilateralism, and the IMF: 1972-1979

In March 1972, ten years after gaining formal independence, the

Caribbean nation of Jamaica democratically elected a new government to rule the island of two million people. The People's National Party (PNP), under the leadership of Prime Minister Michael Manley embarked on a program of mixed economic development, with increased government control over certain key sectors of the national economy (public transportation, utilities, etc.) alongside continued private enterprise. During his first two years in office, Manley instituted a program of economic development which had two basic goals. One involved gaining greater national control over Jamaica's natural resources and wealth, especially bauxite. The other involved using some of the wealth generated by these industries to finance social programs aimed at improving the lot of workers, the poor and unemployed. By October 1974, this program had evolved a coherent political philosophy which Manley and the PNP called democratic socialism.

Toward the first end—that of gaining greater control over its natural resources and wealth—Jamaica became a leading nation in the negotiations for a New International Economic Order at the United Nations, Conferences of Non-Aligned Nations and other international forums. In Jamaica Manley began to implement some of the basic provisions of the NIEO, moving toward more self-reliant development.*

Legislation was passed in June 1974 which altered the basis on which government revenue from bauxite mining—the nation's largest source of income—would be computed, implementing a

---

*ed. note: When the PNP was voted into power in 1972 the country's economic situation was bleak. An "industrialization by invitation" program begun in the 1950s (designed much like Puerto Rico's "Operation Bootstrap") in an attempt to solve national economic problems through massive foreign investment, attracted tourist, manufacturing, finance, textiles, food processing and other industries along with mining. The end result, however, was rising imports, higher foreign debt, severe unemployment (consistently over 20 percent), declining agricultural production, and foreign control over the economy. See Epica Task Force, *Jamaica: Caribbean Challenge,* (Washington, D.C., 1979), p. 34.

Economist Norman Girvan (a contributor to this volume) observes that the Jamaican bauxite industry expanded rapidly between 1950 and 1970 but resulting there and throughout the Caribbean were "mineral-export enclaves almost completely isolated from the host economies" which were wholly owned and operated by a small number of vertically-integrated transnational aluminum companies (production technology is capital-intensive) employing less than 2 percent of the total labor force. Very little taxes are paid on raw products and the companies import virtually all capital goods, equipment, and required materials. Jamaica's economic lot under the bauxite industry "was growth without economic development." See Girvan, *Corporate Imperialism: Conflict and Expropriation,* (New York: Monthly Review Press, 1976), pp. 117-121.

production levy (based on the selling price of aluminum ingot) in place of traditional taxation schemes based on the artificially low profits registered by the companies. (The companies did not take a profit loss: a tight aluminum market meant the companies could easily pass along the higher taxes to consumers in the form of higher prices.) This was a major event in the economic history of the island. Within two years, the income to Jamaica from bauxite increased more than fivefold and much of the new revenue was plowed into social programs and land reform efforts. At the same time, the government began negotiating with the major aluminum companies for the purchase of all their lands and 51 percent of their mining operations on the island. The U.S. aluminum companies together owned or controlled as much as one-third of the entire land mass of the island until the government began to buy back some of the land and negotiate for the rest.

During the rest of 1974 and the first half of 1975, Jamaica entered into negotiations with other major bauxite producing nations, and in July 1975 they formed the International Bauxite Association (IBA) with the aim of coordinating the production and maketing/sale of their bauxite. The IBA was conceived along the lines of OPEC and the producers' associations proposed in the NIEO Declaration—although the tone and content of member demands were much more moderate than OPEC. Its purpose was to give the bauxite producers better leverage in negotiating with the transnational aluminum companies and the consuming nations (largely the trilateral world).

Several facts about the bauxite industry in Jamaica made these moves of Manley's government particularly significant. Jamaica has consistently remained the world's largest or second largest exporter of bauxite, the mineral which is processed into aluminum. Aluminum is one of the thirteen critical strategic materials in the U.S. defense industry and one of the most common elements in the production of consumer and industrial goods. Jamaica supplies as much as 50 to 60 percent of all bauxite ore used by the U.S. aluminum industry. Jamaica remains the largest single supplier for the U.S aluminum companies—Kaiser, Reynolds, Alcoa, Revere—which, together with Alcan of Canada, controlled *all* of the bauxite industry in Jamaica until the government began to negotiate for 51 percent controlling interest. These facts show why Jamaica was in a fairly strong position to negotiate for more profits and increased control over the industry. They also reflect the power of the U.S. aluminum companies, and show why the companies and the U.S. government reacted as aggressively as they did against the moves by Manley's government.

Immediately after the bauxite levy was announced, Kaiser, Alcoa, and Reynolds filed (an unsuccessful) suit against Jamaica, charging breach of con'ract. The companies began to stockpile aluminum in the U.S. and to promote the recycling of aluminum products. But in November 1974, Kaiser agreed to sell 51 percent of its mining operations to Jamaica, and the following April, Reynolds did likewise. As was the case throughout the Third World with trans- actions of this sort, the companies maintained *managerial* control while the government assumed more of the operating risks. During 1975 and the first half of 1976, the companies turned increasingly from legal or indirect responses to direct economic actions against the Jamaican government and economy in order to subvert Jamaica's program of economic nationalism and democratic socialism. Shut- downs and slowdowns in production were ordered in several mining and plant operations on the island as the companies tried to wait out the Jamaican government by reducing the production level, and thereby reducing the size of revenues going to the government from the levy, while doubling their imports from Africa.

In 1975, a destabilization campaign—reminiscent of the one aimed at Allende's Chile—was launched against Jamaica. Jamaica was closed out of the international public and private lending market. Total U.S. assistance dropped from $13.2 million in 1974 to $2.2 million in 1976, and further AID assistance was embargoed. "Even though many in the State Department objected to what one mid-level official called an 'effort to cut Jamaica off at the knees,' observes one writer, the embargo on new lending remained in effect until the Carter Administration revoked it in early 1977."[2] Jamaica's credit rating with the U.S. Export Import bank dropped from a top to a bottom category. During 1976 the Jamaican Government was unable to secure a single private bank loan. Jamaican capitalists went "on strike" along with foreign capital, closing down the factories, cutting back production, and laying off workers. Emigrating wealthy Jamaicans smuggled an estimated $200 million from the island.

Meanwhile, toward the end of 1975 and during the first half of 1976, a concerted plan (later exposed as "Operation Werewolf") was put into effect by agencies within the U.S.—apparently including the CIA—acting in concert with forces within the JLP, the major opposition party (misappropriately called the Jamaican Labour Party). In January 1976, a series of increasingly violent events began. People by the dozens were burned out of their homes (whole areas were torched) while paid gunmen shot or threatened those trying to escape. Most of the victims were PNP supporters. Food supplies were poisoned, and rumors of poisoning of water supplies were rife. The police and Defense Force uncovered guns, explosives, and hundreds of rounds of ammunition of a kind never seen before in Jamaica. The violence escalated until Manley, exercising his constitutional powers, declared a state of national emergency in June, hinting strongly that outside forces were at work.[3] The foreign Western press, especially in the U.S., picked up on the theme of violence in Jamaica, often misrepresenting or distorting the actual facts of events. Later, Manley, his ministers, and the leaders of several other Caribbean nations (including Guyana and Barbados) charged that a plot to "destabilize" the Jamaican government was under way.

The campaign of fear and violence during the first half of 1976 had several important consequences for the Jamaican economy. It slowed production as fear and disturbance spread among the working population. It frightened any remaining potential foreign investors and financial leaders. It had a devastating effect upon the tourist industry, Jamaica's third most important source of revenue. In effect, the campaign of violence greatly aggravated the problems of the Jamaican economy, already in trouble because of the increase in oil prices (Jamaica imports all of its oil), the activities of the bauxite companies, and U.S. controlled or dominated public and private lending agencies.

It is clear that the purpose of these moves was either to frighten the Manley government into retrenchment from its more progressive and assertive policies of national resource sovereignty; or to topple the government entirely, replacing it with the conservative JLP. Kissinger's actions support this. In December 1975 Henry Kissinger (and many advisers) had arrived in Jamaica for a vacation. In off-the-record talks Kissinger reportedly told Manley that he could expect U.S. aid *if* Jamaica broke off relations with Cuba, withdrew support from the Angolan MPLA—which the U.S. was then covertly fighting—and moderated the domestic program of democratic socialism.[4]

But this strategy of political destabilization did not work in quite the way it was planned. After June the operation of the state of emergency did succeed in reducing significantly the level of violence, at least for a time. In December of 1976, the PNP and Manley were returned to power in a landslide victory, effectively ending, for the time being, hopes of an electoral elimination of Manley's government. The election, together with the PNP victories in the local elections the following April, clearly reflected strong and growing support for the PNP and Manley among the Jamaican people.

With the election of Jimmy Carter in the U.S. in November 1976, a definite change took place in U.S. policy toward Jamaica. The change reflects the differences between the protectionist, hardline policies, represented by Nixon, and the "free trade," soft-line policies of trilateralism, personified in Carter and his Cabinet. Under Carter the IMF became the vehicle for implementing trilateral policy toward Jamaica rather than the CIA. The IMF set out to complete the job which the destabilization campaign had begun.

What specific considerations led to this change in U.S. policy toward Jamaica beginning in early 1977? Some are apparent. First, the elections of 1976-77 showed clearly that, politically speaking, Manley and his government were still strongly entrenched in political power and popularity, and that, if anything, the previous efforts to destabilize the government had only strengthened Manley's mass-based political support. Second, Operation Werewolf had been exposed so that the Jamaican government and people became more sensitive to destabilization efforts of the kind seen in early 1976.* Third, Manley himself, faced with continuing economic and political pressures from within and without his party, made a series of political moves during 1977, which seemed to be a partial accommodation to the more conservative, foreign-capital-oriented interests in and out of Jamaica. (For example, Manley agreed to the resignation of several of his more radical ministers and close advisers.) Fourth, and perhaps more crucial, the economic condition of Jamaica had become serious enough to force Manley to make some immediate political decisions about the future orientation of the Jamaican political economy.[6] In other words, the economic effects of the many-sided destabilization campaign were such that, while it did not achieve the elimination of Manley's government, they did place the government in a weak economic position in relation to IMF and international financial and monetary community. To add to the economic toll of destabilization, the bottom fell out of the sugar market in 1976; sugar is Jamaica's prime agricultural export. Jamaica's foreign exchange reserves dwindled quickly, and the nation found itself saddled with a huge balance-of-payments deficit. This kind of economic weakness seemed to be the Achilles heel of Manley's government, and the place where the next U.S. efforts to deal with Jamaica would logically be taken. While the trilateralists may not have formulated the policies which precipitated the crisis in the Jamaican economy, they were quick to utilize the crisis as a context for reclaiming U.S. economic hegemony over Jamaica, via the IMF. How did this happen?

---

*In September, Philip Agee, a former CIA agent, came to Jamaica and warned of definite CIA involvement in destabilizing Manley's government. Agee listed names of members of the U.S. embassy and AID staffs which he said were known CIA operatives.[5] In addition, investigation of events in Jamaica was proceeding among circles—including congressional groups—in the U.S.

In mid-1977, after much debate and uncertainty—seemingly without an adequate alternative—Manley reopened negotiations with the IMF for assistance in addressing the developing balance-of-payments deficit, and salvaging the country's dwindling reserves. The government announced its own austerity program and emergency production plan, looking to these negotiations. In July, the Fund granted (U.S.) a $74 million standby loan, to be paid in four installments, and the U.S. government resumed aid to Jamaica which had been suspended under Nixon in 1975. As conditions for the standby arrangement, the IMF demanded 40 percent devaluation of the Jamaican dollar, a wage freeze, cutbacks of subsidies on basic commodities, and cutbacks in government spending on social programs. The devaluation would have meant additional profits for the aluminum companies, since they bought bauxite from their Jamaican subsidiaries in U.S. dollars. But the Jamaican government negotiated a two-tiered devaluation, managing to keep some foreign exchange-earning products, such as bauxite, at nearly the old exchange rate. Under pressure, the gap between this and the new rate was gradually eroded by further devaluations in October 1977 and in January 1978.

These IMF measures resulted in increased hardships for Jamaica's poor, who saw their living standard erode as prices jumped and wages remained frozen. They also resulted in political problems for Manley and his government, in at least two ways. It reduced his ability to fund social programs which were a basis of his support among the poor. It also aggravated ideological splits within the PNP—splits which deepened as the public debate over the IMF measures, and the government's acceptance of them, continued throughout 1977 and 1978.* In the face of IMF demands, Manley tried—and succeeded to some extent—to negotiate the easiest terms possible for the poor and working class. The government also moved to gain greater control over parts of the tourist industry by becoming the largest hotel owner on the island.

The worst was yet to come. In December 1977, the Fund cancelled the standby arrangement, claiming that Jamaica had failed to meet one of the technical stipulations: the amount of money in circulation in the national economy was several million dollars higher than the stipulated limit of $355 million. In other countries involved in similar standby arrangements the IMF had overlooked

---

*When it came to foreign policy, the Jamaican government remained staunchly progressive. Manley remained a vigorous spokesperson for the NIEO in international forums. In October 1977 Cuban President Fidel Castro visited Jamaica.

such a failure. Jamaica had met all other IMF targets but the IMF demanded that the loan be renegotiated. The Jamaican *Daily News*, in a two-inch, front page headline, called the decision "IMF SHOCKER." The economic effect was devastating, especially since the IMF withdrawal effectively held up further aid from other governmental and private sources. The IMF "seal of approval" had been revoked.

This maneuver of the IMF succeeded in weakening Manley's bargaining position. Several Cabinet ministers resigned over the next few months to be replaced by more conservative ministers, including a new finance minister who was better trusted by the representatives of international capital. Manley opened fresh negotiations with the Fund, and during 1978 a new $240 million loan was negotiated under far more stringent conditions than the old loan.[7] The new arrangement called for a further 30 percent devaluation of the Jamaican dollar and dropped the two-tier exchange rate. Price controls were lifted (allowing the price of basic food staples to rise dramatically); from May 1978 to June 1978 the overall cost of living leaped 13 percent. The IMF demanded a balanced budget, translating into further cuts in social programs, and even cuts in essential services. Most government ministries had to reduce their operating budgets, and there was talk of eliminating entire government departments during early 1979. The advances of the PNP in health care, nutrition education and other areas of social welfare are being undone. The IMF also demanded that the Jamaican government resort to added taxation measures to generate additional revenue. The government tried to place these taxes where they could be borne easiest: on larger businesses. But the IMF was also quick to demand that the government not frighten business expansion and development with heavy taxes on business enterprise. New taxes were placed on consumer items, including basic necessities. Wage restraints demanded by the IMF created a context of industrial tension, as workers struggling to maintain a standard of living against rising prices were forced to strike or engage in other militant actions. This, in turn, affected production levels and caused additional political problems for the government. The State Trading Corporation, which Manley instituted as a government agency to oversee and regulate importation of basic goods and necessities into the country and to try to provide basic items at reasonable prices, was attacked by the IMF with the support of Jamaican business and the JLP, which was concerned that it would unduly interfere with the flow of imports into the island.

Throughout 1978 and into the first half of 1979, the ongoing debate within Jamaica over the IMF has caused deeper rifts within the Jamaican political Left and the PNP itself. The overall political climate was embittered as the government and Manley himself were generally determined to make the IMF arrangement succeed, seeing it as a needed relief from the relentless deterioration of the Jamaican foreign exchange position and the runaway balance-of-payments deficit. In general, the right wing and center of the PNP support this determination. Opposition to further attempts to make the IMF arrangement work came from an unlikely combination of Right and Left groups, each with very different reasons for their opposition. The Right, represented by the JLP leadership in particular, has attempted to exploit the government's predicament to their own political advantage by blaming Manley for the economy's ruination and portraying Manley's acceptance of the IMF demands as a sellout of the interests of the poor by the PNP. For the most part, however, this hypocrisy of the JLP position is clear to the majority of poor and working class Jamaicans.

In general, the Left does not support further involvement with the IMF, pointing out that such involvement has already resulted in decreasing economic autonomy and increasing dependency on foreign countries—the U.S. in particular—as well as greater hardship for the Jamaican people. The economists of the Left also point out that while the IMF demands have resulted in a cost of living increase of 40-50 percent in 1978 and a 100 percent increase in the price of the most basic items on the island in the past three years, the overall economic postion of the nation is actually worse now than before the IMF intervened. This can be seen in terms of the economic goals basic to the IMF purpose in Jamaica: the foreign exchange position has not improved and the balance-of-payments crisis is worse than before.

Jamaica is deeper in debt than ever. IMF loans and subsequent loans from other funding sources do not lessen the country's debt burden but compound it. Between the end of 1976—before IMF negotiations—and 1978, Jamaica's foreign debt more than doubled. Jamaica must continue borrowing in order to service (pay interest and amortize) mounting debts. This is the meaning of the "debt trap" which progressive Jamaicans warned against.

All of this has led to an increasing sense that the IMF's standby arrangment, with its drastic demands, is an economic disaster for Jamaica, *a disaster which has political as well as economic purposes* for the Fund and for those who control it. What are these larger political purposes? They have to do with the trilateralist policy/strategy for dealing with nations such as Jamaica, by moving away from the confrontational, violent, destabilization program of Nixon and Kissinger, and toward a non-confrontational form of politics. The trilateralist strategy utilizes multilateral developmentalism and economic insitutions in an attempt to co-opt and integrate the economies of nations such as Jamaica into the larger Western-dominated system for which the IMF is a key regulator. (See Wheaton.)

What is in store for Jamaica as it struggles with IMF demands? At this writing the most common forecast, especially among the political economists and observers of the Left, is that Manley (or someone who takes his place) will be forced into ever sterner security measures in trying to enforce the IMF demands on an already long-suffering and increasingly frustrated and desperate population in the face of worker strikes and demonstrations. Already there are signs that the U.S. has reclaimed the economic and political hegemony which was challenged earlier by Manley's government. A new and larger U.S. consulate has recently been completed in Kingston. The USAID mission in Jamaica is now one of the largest in Latin America. Meanwhile, U.S. agencies have resumed aid to Jamaican development projects, and U.S. officials visit the island with cordial smiles and words of friendship and mutual cooperation.

The example of Jamaica clearly shows what the utilization of the IMF as a vehicle of trilateralist policy can mean. The people suffer most. At worst they starve, struggle, and die while the IMF systematically undermines their efforts for self-determination, and reinstates U.S. economic control over their lives and that of their nation. The tale would be bad enough if that were its conclusion. But the trilateralists have, during the past few years, initiated yet more reforms of the IMF, reforms designed to make the Fund an even more efficient instrument of U.S. and trilateral hegemony over the Third World. It is to these reforms we now turn.

Trilateralist Proposals for Further Reform of the IMF

Shortly after its establishment, the Trilateral Commission published its first full report; a program for reforming the international monetary system inherited from Bretton Woods. *Toward a Renovated World Monetary System*, co-authored by Richard Cooper, now undersecretary of state for economic affairs, states:

> The task before us is to renovate the monetary system so that it can do as well in the next two decades as it did in the two decades following the Second World War, recognizing that the underlying conditions at present are very different from what they were in the 1940s.[8]

It was no mere coincidence that the Commission was first and foremost concerned with the international monetary system. The formation of the Commission was a direct response to the threat which the trilateralists saw in Nixon's approach to the monetary crisis of the early 1970s. And the trilateralists immediately utilized the IMF, the center of the monetary system's operation, as a vehicle for implementing trilateralist policy toward Third World nations such as Jamaica. The Commission makes it quite clear that they are talking about reform and change within the IMF itself:

> ...we believe a serious attempt should be made to lodge respon-
> sibility for overseeing and in some cases managing the improve-
> ments sketched [in this report] in an international insitution,
> most logically a revamped International Monetary Fund.[9]

The Commission goes on to suggest that:

> ...the Fund must be given more authority than it now has in
> guiding balance of payments adjustments, it must be capable of
> responding to financial need more quickly, and in much larger
> magnitude than it is now able to do, and it must involve more
> actively the top policymakers of the leading countries.[10]

Three interrelated themes emerge from this trilateral report. One emphasizes the need for a more powerful and more flexible IMF to carry out a larger management role. A second theme emphasizes the need for cooperation and greater coordination of monetary and economic affairs among the "leading countries," predominantly the trilateral nations. A third emphasizes the desirability of a truly international monetary system—one without protective barriers to investment and trade—wherein the national economies of nations, especially Third World nations, would be more efficiently and totally integrated with the economies of the trilateral nations within a single monetary system. The system would be managed by the U.S. through the IMF with the assistance of a somewhat enlarged group of leading countries, including token participation by selected Third World powers. In short, the renovations depicted in this first report would accomplish more smoothly and subtly what reliance on the as-yet-unrenovated IMF has been slowly accomplishing in nations such as Jamaica: the reassertion and strengthening of Western capitalist control.

One specific proposal of the Commission in 1973 was to phase out the use of the dollar and other national currencies and reserves as means of redressing balance-of-payments deficits in the short run. As we have seen, within the older IMF/Bretton Woods scheme, one of the options open to a nation faced with short-term balance-of-payments deficit was to cover that deficit by paying the debt out of the nation's foreign reserves, in its own or some other currency. The Commission proposed that this practice be reduced and eventually eliminated. Instead of national currencies another form of reserve, called Special Drawing Rights (from the older IMF arrangement) or *bancor* (a term used by Keynes and adopted by the trilateralists) would become the basis for balance-of-payments redress. By creating such an international reserve which would be used specifically for addressing balance-of-payment problems among nations, a world monetary situation would be created which would reduce the current dependent interrelationship between flows of capital and investment on the one hand, and balance-of-payments problems on the other hand. That is, the elimination of national currencies, such as the dollar, from use as a reserve in dealing with payments balances allows the transfer and movement of large sums of capital (in national currencies) with far less disruption of the international monetary position of a particular nation. This is the near ideal climate for the kind of world economic order implied by George Ball in his 1967 description of the flow of international capital and his assertion that political boundaries of nation-states are "too narrow and constricted to define the scope and activities of modern business." Bancor would provide the economic/monetary basis for a world without political-national boundaries to business investment and expansion. This proposal for the use of bancor as a reserve for balance-of-payments deficits is itself a transitional measure, as the Commission implies:

> Eventually, bancor might circulate as a genuine international currency and be used as a medium for an intervention in international exchange markets...It would require widening the eligibility for holding SDRs, from central banks alone, to include other financial institutions and even individuals.[11]

An international currency would be inherently favorable to the already developed, industrialized nations, especially to the U.S., which holds tremendous political and economic power (despite balance-of-payments and currency problems). Poorer Third World nations would find themselves less able to gain, even in the short-run, from revaluations of their currencies or from playing off and trading in various national currencies. Their economies would be more easily and tightly integrated with those of the trilateral nations which would dominate the distribution of bancor/SDRs.

The other proposals for monetary reform set out by the Trilateral Commission in its first report are largely adjuncts to the proposal for the establishment of bancor/SDRs. One such proposal is for establishment of a "substitution account" within the IMF, wherein nations which hold large reserves of U.S. dollars (as a result of U.S. trade imbalances) could convert these dollars into bancor. This proposal has the double effect of furthering the establishment of bancor as an international reserve and of stopping the further deterioration of the position of the dollar. In essence, it would slow or eliminate the accumulation of very large sums of dollar capital (by governments, individuals, corporations, and banks) outside the U.S. itself.

The Commission also proposes additional specific measures to facilitate the acceptance of and conversion to bancor as a reserve for balance-of-payments adjustments. It advocates the establishment of a facility in the IMF for rapid short-term lending to countries confronted with the need to convert. The facility "would lend quickly and on short term any amount that a country seemed to require to defend an exchange rate that was threatened by a massive movement of funds."[12] This measure would further help to stabilize the world monetary situation while allowing transfers of large capital and reserve funds across national boundaries. The effect on poorer nations of such huge transfers would be minimized only at the expense of their incurring further indebtedness. This proposal supports and extends the proposal for establishment of bancor, and to the same end: it creates the monetary mechanisms for large-scale free flows of investment capital across national borders without disruption or collapse of national (especially Third World) economies. Such national economies would continue to function, albeit with increasing indebtedness, as investment and market outlets.

Further proposals along similar lines were made by the Trilateral Commission and associated individuals and agencies (e.g. the World Bank) during the period from 1973-1978. One of these appears in the 1975 Trilateral Commission report, *OPEC, the Trilateral World, and the Developing Countries: New Arrangements for Cooperation, 1976-1980.*[13] In this report, the Commission advocates the establishment of a "Third Window," which would lend to poor nations at concessional terms. This proposal within the World Bank was prompted by the increasing economic crisis which had been forming in 1974-76, and which threatened to severely disrupt the ability of some nations to meet their debt payments or to absorb further capital and market expansion by the trilateral world. The regular lending facility of the World Bank was not flexible enough to meet the immediate crisis of 1974-76. The "Second Window" of the Bank, the International Development Association, was financed through periodic replenishments from donor nations every few years. It could not meet the immediate crisis because its Fifth Replenishment was already committed and its Sixth would not occur for several years. Thus the Trilateral Commission advocated a new and temporary lending facility, a Third Window, which would "be an interim measure providing emergency financing over the next year while a larger Fifth Replenishment was being negotiated."[14]

This proposal, which was subsequently accepted by the World Bank, illuminates another aspect of trilateral renovation of the international monetary system; in particular it shows how the Trilateral Commission utilizes development assistance via the World Bank in conjunction with regulation of the monetary system by the IMF. (See Frieden.) The Third Window was meant to avert the economic disruption or collapse and default of various Third World nations in a time of severe economic crisis. While trilateralism seeks to endure greater integration of Third World national economies into a monetary system free for the flow of transnational (trilateral) capital and investment, the Commission also seeks to ensure that the economies of Third World nations remain sufficiently viable to absorb investment and to continue to provide a potential market for trilateral business. It is not in the interest of transnational business and capital to allow total economic collapse by Third World nations.

A 1976 trilateral report, *The Reform of International Institutions,* reiterates the need for a "substitution account" within the IMF for nations to gain rapid assistance in defending their currency exchange rate in the face of massive transfers of funds (capital or reserves). This proposal emphasizes the gradual development of a complex situation during the period 1976-79, one characterized by a continued trilateral push to restructure the world monetary order along lines ideal for transnational capital in the midst of a deepening world monetary and economic crisis which has seemed intransigent and nearly insoluble by traditional capitalist economic wisdom. Two further sets of proposals address this situation.

One set was advanced in 1976-77 by then U.S. Secretary of the Treasury Blumenthal, an early proponent of trilateralism. Blumenthal proposed that

> —IMF lending facilities be increased so as to provide a real supplement to private lending;
> —IMF lending be more closely coordinated with that of private banks, resulting in the merger of IMF and private bank lending in a single program;
> —lending programs, such as the IMF standby arrangement be subject to even tighter measures of accountability and control by the IMF over the monetary and economic policies of the recipient nation.

Blumenthal's first proposal was partially realized by the establishment of the so-called Witteveen Facility, named for the former managing director of the IMF. The Facility provides for a fund of $10 billion provided by fourteen of the wealthier nations in order to assist the poorer nations to repay their debts on loans from private banks. Essentially, Blumenthal's proposals are an attempt to use the IMF to support the private banks in lending to poor nations, while tightening the accountability and control of the IMF and the banks over the economic policies of their recipient nations.

Together, the Blumenthal proposals and the Witteveen Facility reflect the complex nature of the current situation, a situation which had changed since the original proposals for renovating the IMF were published in 1973. Formerly, the primary concern was for a more integrated and closely functioning system so as to provide the ideal climate for business expansion. Now, it is clear that the monetary and economic crisis of the Third World during the period 1974-76 was not temporary but permanent and growing, and that private banks and other financial sources would not be able to keep supplying loans and credits to Third World nations whose positions continued to deteriorate. A U.S. Senate report of August 1977 quotes the vice-president of Morgan Guaranty Trust Company warning that:

> ...the international commercial banking system cannot be counted on to continue to increase its international intermediary role at the pace experienced so far this year...limits to the ability of existing mechanisms to cope with this problem are being approached.[15]

In characteristic fashion, the trilateralists have been advancing proposals which would exploit the situation created by the current economic crisis—especially the need to support the private banks—in such a way as to further extend and strengthen the control, integration, and management of the international monetary and economic systems of the Western world. The Senate report mentioned above points out that:

> ...limited IMF resources and the willingness of the private banks to provide credit without strings have in the past undermined the IMF's ability to impose adjustment policies on its members. But now the private banks seem willing to stand behind the IMF in imposing tough conditions on future deficit financing. With their backing and the additional lending resources of the Witteveem Facility, the IMF would have much greater leverage.[16]

The report goes on to suggest what this will mean for recipient Third World nations:

> Once the public and private lenders join forces, deficit countries will be left with no alternative sources of financial assistance; there will be no escaping IMF conditionality, little choice but to accept whatever terms the IMF and private banks choose to lay down.[17]

As for the people in these countries the Senate report indicates lower living standards under IMF austerity measures imposed with repression:

IMF "adjustment" policies may also bring about a low standard of living, higher unemployment, a cutback in social welfare programs, and greater emphasis in filling the demands of the export market than on producing to meet the needs of the domestic consumer...while Fund recommendations may lead to the stated goal of reducing a country's payment deficit, and make it more creditworthy in the eyes of the banks, the steps a government has to take to carry out those recommendations can in many instances lead to heightened political tension and greater social unrest. In some countries, *governments may have to resort to political repression in order to carry out such policies.*[18] [Italics added.]*

In conclusion, it is clear that the IMF has consistently functioned over the years as a vehicle for increasing control over national economies, especially over emerging Third World economies by the United States, From the example of nations such as Jamaica and from the nature of the recent trilateralist proposals of Blumenthal and others, it is also clear that the deepening world economic crisis is being used as the condition for ever greater integration of national economies into a larger system, which through reformed IMF operation would provide the desired climate for transnational business. Such a "renovated" economic order can only lead to continued Third World dependency and relentless exploitation of people throughout the world.

---

*ed. note: The report discusses the harsh impact of IMF policies on people in Western industrialized countries as well as the Third World: "In the recent IMF negotiations with Britain over a $3.9 billion loan, the Fund demanded that the Labour Government make large cuts in public expenditures to reduce the budget deficit, cut taxes, hold down the money supply, and improve conditions for private investment. These demands led to a cabinet crisis, as the Left wing of the Labour Party threatened to walk out if the IMF's conditions were accepted. It appears that only the direct intervention of the U.S. Government convinced the IMF to modify its position, thereby averting a cabinet crisis and possibly the fall of the Callaghan Government. In Egypt, widespread rioting took place when the government announced, in accordance with IMF recommendations, large cuts in food subsidies. Although the troops Sadat sent into the streets quelled the riots, the Egyptian President also felt compelled to restore the subsidies. More recently, in Peru, the IMF's stiff demands for economic austerity measures, coming on top of earlier conditions pressed by the private banks, have created a deep split within the government, caused two finance ministers to fall, and led to widespread public demonstrations and strikes." (pp. 66-67.)

Editor's Postscript: Since this article was written, the political situation in Jamaica has become critical. In March 1980 the Manley government broke off negotiations with the IMF, rejecting the harsh new terms for further credit. January 1980 had found Jamaica in a poorer foreign exchange position than it was in 1977 before the IMF stabilization program! Political violence has flared since elections were announced for September 1980. A new destabilization campaign was launched to bring down the PNP government and put JLP leader Edward Seaga in power. In June the head of the right wing United Front Party was arrested with military collaborators for plotting a coup. The explosive events in Jamaica fit into a growing pattern of U.S.-backed destabilization, political repression and economic manipulation in the Caribbean and Central America, discussed in the postscript to Philip Wheaton's article and in the conclusion to this volume.

FOOTNOTES

1. George Ball, "Cosmocorp: The Importance of Being Stateless," *Columbia Journal of World Business,* II: 6 (November-December 1967).
2. J, Daniel O'Flaherty, "Finding Jamaica's Way," *Foreign Policy,* (Summer 1978), p. 154, cited in Holly Sklar, "Jamaica, Democratic Socialism and the IMF," an unpublished paper of 29 April 1979.
3. James Phillips, "Jamaica: A Repeat of the Chile Pattern?" *Christian Century,* 29 September 1976. Also see Ellen Ray, "CIA and Local Gunmen Plan Jamaican Coup," *Counter Spy,* December 1976.
4. Sherry Keith and Robert Girling, "Caribbean Conflict: Jamaica and the U.S.," *NACLA Report on the Americas,* XII (3), May-June 1978, p. 31.
5. *Ibid.* Also several newspaper articles.
6. EPICA Task Force, *Jamaica: Caribbean Challenge,* Washington, D.C., 1979.
7. "Caribbean Conflict: Jamaica and the U.S.," *op.cit.*
8. "Towards a Renovated World Monetary System," *Trilateral Commission Task Force Reports,* 1-7, Rapporteurs: Richard Cooper, Motoo Kaji, Claudio Segre, (New York: New York University Press, 1977), p. 4.
9. *Ibid.,* p. 21.
10. *Ibid.,*
11. *Ibid.,* p. 15.
12. *Ibid.,* p. 18.
13. Trilateral Commission Task Force Report No. 7, Rapporteurs: Richard N. Gardner, Saburo Okita, B. J. Udink (1975).
14. Charles B. Heck, "World Bank Establishes Third Window, Trilateral Commission Proposal Realized," *Trialogue,* No. 8, 1975, p. 7.
15. "International Debt, the Banks and U.S. Foreign Policy," Staff Report of the Subcommittee on Foreign Economic Policy of the Senate Committee on Foreign Relations, Washington, D.C., August 1977, p. 59.
16. *Ibid.,* p. 63.
17. *Ibid.,* p. 66.
18. *Ibid.,* pp. 66-67.

chapter three

THE GRIM REAPERS: THE TRILATERAL COMMISSION TAKES ON WORLD HUNGER

Dahlia Rudavsky*

The Trilateral Commission has developed a program for addressing the problems of "malnutrition and hunger," as described in their Food Task Force Report, *Reducing Malnutrition in Developing Countries: Increasing Rice Production in South and Southeast Asia.* A careful analysis of this report reveals the political interests of the Trilateral Commission as well as its perspective on the world hunger crisis.

In this article we will summarize trilateral thinking, examine its internal logic in view of trilateral interests, and criticize it in view of historical experience.

Trilateral interest in world hunger comes from a desire to maximize profits in the long run. Profit maximization is only possible in the context of social and political stability; thus, Commission members wish to diffuse the continual upsurge of social unrest and revolutionary activity that results from widespread hunger and malnutrition. Within a stable social climate, corporations can mold local economies to serve their interests, transforming the basic human need for food into a source of economic gain and social control.

The concern with unrest is summarized by former Trilateral Commission member Andrew Young:

> It is in the conditions of chaos, underdevelopment and poverty, and a wide gap between the "haves" and the "have-nots," that revolutionary and political tensions emerge, which in our time, inevitably will spill over to developed nations."[1]

*Dahlia Rudavsky is a lawyer and former director of Earthwork/Center for Rural Studies, a resource center on food and land in San Francisco, California.

The aspirations and initiatives of people Young calls the have-nots threaten Trilateral Commission members' interests. Protests, riots, and revolution in countries such as India, Bangladesh, Guatemala, and Nicaragua have become almost daily reminders that people will not stand for unceasing exploitation. Addressing the issue of hunger is one way to defuse these actions.

This perspective was clearly summarized by the president of the World Bank, Robert McNamara, speaking before the World Bank's Board of Governors in 1973:

> When the highly privileged are few and the desperately poor are many—and when the gap between them is worsening rather than improving—it is only a matter of time before a decisive choice must be made between the political costs of reform and the political risks of rebellion...Social justice is not merely a moral imperative. It is a political imperative as well.[2]

The underlying interest of Commission members is the increase of corporate economic gain and social control. From the report we read: "Increases in food production in Asia will contribute to the broadening of markets for industrial products in Asia."[3] Technological developments in Asia will "stimulate the economies of developed countries which export these goods and services." "Agricultural machinery modified for Asian agriculture (such as small tractors, power tillers, rice planters) will be necessary."[4] The newly created markets will absorb not only agricultural inputs, but also consumer goods. Of course, this sort of economic development is only possible in a climate of political stability.

The Commission's membership includes top executives from the world's largest farm machinery and grain trading companies.* These

---

*Agribusiness is well represented on the Commission. The agribusiness interests that are represented are among the largest firms, with extensive global reach and impressive control in their areas. Members include J. Paul Austin, chairman of Coca-Cola Company, William Hewitt, chairman of Deere and Company, Kenneth D. Naden, president of the National Council of Farmer Cooperatives, William R. Pearce, vice president of Cargill, Inc., and Lee Morgan, president of Caterpillar Tractor Company. (One Commission member involved in agriculture who is not from the U.S. is Michel Debatisse, chairman of the French National Farmers Union).

Coca-Cola is the world's largest soft drink beverage company, with 1976 sales of $3,032 million, 47 percent of the world soft drink market.[5]

Deere is the world's largest manufacturer of farm machinery, with 1974 sales of $2.5 billion, 33 percent of all farm machinery sold.[6]

The National Council of Farmer Cooperatives is a lobbying organization representing farmer-owned marketing and purchasing cooperatives, such as Sunkist Growers, California Canners and Growers, Land O'Lakes, Sun-Maid Raisins, and Dairylea.

members are interested in approaches to the problem of hunger which stave off revolution and make money. Concern with the reduction of hunger is not therefore motivated primarily by humanitarianism. Though these feelings may be present, they are often subordinated to corporate strategies for maintaining and increasing control over the world's resources and its people.

This overall goal is the background against which we must examine trilateral concern with hunger. Thus, whether the issue is food, or health care, or the rate of industrialization, we must examine how developing each of these areas serves to augment the concentration of control. As one agricultural economist has stated, making food available can be

> grasped as a part of a particular kind of strategy for dealing with the problem of the availability of labor. This strategy, in which income is improved in exchange for more work, we may call a strategy of "development." The alternative strategy, in which income is reduced in order to impose the availability of work through deprivation and poverty, we may call a strategy of "underdevelopment."[9]

In the strategy proposed by the Commission in its report, parts of the countryside are developed, but many people are driven deeper into poverty. The report's plan only makes sense if we understand that the Commission is not really trying to end hunger per se, but rather to neutralize the effect of hunger on its economic and political interests.

Thus, the major task of the Food Task Force Report is to devise a method of simultaneously defusing social unrest which challenges trilateral power and interests, while designing profitable solutions to current demands for food. In this respect the report does a thorough job.

The report lays out four ways to solve the problem of world hunger:

> Among the measures that developing countries can pursue to contribute to a reduction of their food deficits, the following should be considered:

Cargill is the world's largest grain trader and the twelfth largest U.S. corporation, with net worth of about $9 billion.[7]

Caterpillar, which has 1977 sales of almost $6 billion and profits of $445.1 million,[8] manufactures large earthmoving equipment. While its products are used primarily in construction, farmers in the western U.S. use some of these machines in farming. Caterpillar is a major contractor of the World Bank and other multilateral lending agencies which fund development projects involving road and dam construction.

a) Slow the growth of food demand by encouraging and supporting programs to reduce the rate of population growth.

b) *Improve income distribution and food distribution* both among income groups and among different regions within a given nation, so that the malnourished may have more food. *Substantial changes in income distribution may require sweeping political and economic reforms, which may not be imminent in many areas.* Since many of the poorest people live in farm areas, increasing farm productivity could have favorable effects upon the income of many who are malnourished.

c) *Increase food production.* This is a very complex process, involving both *more extensive and intensive use of land and water, increasing the availability of basic agricultural inputs (such as fertilizers and pesticides),* appropriate agricultural policies and institutions, and agricultural research. It should be firmly kept in mind that the yields of cereals and other crops throughout the world are far from being uniform, reflecting the uneven distribution of agricultural inputs and skills.

d) Reduce the present waste in the entire food system, from production to final consumption, Decreasing these losses requires substantial improvement of the post-harvest processing, transportation and storage system, and better control of pests.[10] [Italics added.]

Let's look at these specific proposals first in terms of their potential impact and secondly in terms of the trilateral choice to emphasize some and reject others.

First, the Commission considers the reduction of population growth rates. Population control problems have often failed in countries where they have been attempted without accompanying changes in social and economic structures. The Task Force realized this, and sets aside, at least for the time being, the notion that the "population explosion" is at the heart of the world food crisis.*

The food problem is closely linked with that of rapid population growth in the developing world, although population growth actually multiplies existing problems concerning food and other fundamental human needs *rather than* being their basic cause.[11]

---

*There is much debate about the alleged "world food shortage." In the past it was assumed that hunger was the result of too many people, and that the solution to hunger was limiting the number of people. Several recent studies refute this assumption. They persuasively argue that the world's absolute food supply is completely adequate to feed the world's population, and that the problem is not absolute supply, but inequitable *distribution* of food. Distribution is only a problem for poor people; with enough cash, consumers can order exotic foods from halfway around the world.

One might add that slowing population growth does nothing to improve the condition of people now alive who already cannot afford food.

The Task Force stops far short of calling for an end to, or even a reevaluation of current population control programs. In fact, it points out that "adequate medical facilities should be provided so that programs to reduce population growth rates may be adequately and rapidly pursued."[12] It does note, however, that these programs are not working well, and must be integrated into overall social and economic development if they are to succeed. The report focuses not on population control, but on overall ideas for economic development which are the context for population control programs.

The second option, "improving income distribution and food distribution both among income groups and among different regions," is the only option which treats world hunger as a problem of food distribution rather than absolute food supply. This view acknowledges that the problem is not a shortage of food per se, but a shortage of cash in the hands of poor people who most need it to buy food. The Commission is aware that cash is the critical element in ending world hunger:

> A basic distinction must be made between commercial food demand and nutritional requirements. For the very poorest of the world's population, increased food production and lower food prices alone will not be sufficient to eliminate malnutrition. Unless their incomes are increased, the very poor will continue to receive less than adequate nutrition, even if commercial demand is being satisfied at reasonable prices.[13]

The income level of the poor can be raised by fundamental economic change. However, "sweeping political and economic reform," as the Commission calls the necessary changes, have in the past not been in the long-term economic interest of Commission members. On the contrary, their goal is to increase their ownership and control of the world's productive resources, and to maximize their profits from these resources. Certainly changes which would return these resources to the masses of the world's people are not an acceptable option. This viewpoint is especially ironic since many Third World nations which now are net food importers were self-sufficient in food before colonialist forays by the developed world distorted their economies. In these incursions, land used to grow crops for local consumption was taken over and planted with crops for export to the colonizing country. By stating that "sweeping economic and political changes" are not "imminent," (or so they hope) the Commission cuts off discussion of economic change, except for a short qualifier tacked on: "Since many of the poorest people live in farm areas, increasing farm productivity could have favorable effects upon the income [thus the ability to buy food] of many who are malnourished."

This is a very important aspect of the report. It provides the first indication that although the Commission recognizes the need for higher incomes to attack hunger, only the option of increased productivity (which could improve income), and not income redistribution, is an acceptable solution. Again, keep in mind the Commission's concern with diffusing social unrest caused by hunger, in order to serve its constituency's direct economic interests. The Task Force is here developing a program which it feels meets both aspects of this concern, based on increased farm productivity.

The next option, (c), provides some clues to the details of this program. "Increase Food Production," through a more intensive use of land and water, including "increasing the availability of basic agricultural inputs (such as fertilizers and pesticides)." The report reminds us that "the yields of cereals and other crops throughout the world are far from uniform, reflecting the uneven distribution of agricultural inputs and skills."

Thus a translation of the need for more even income distribution to more even distribution of agricultural inputs and skills is neatly accomplished, through the notion that since "many of the poorest people live in farm areas, increasing productivity could have favorable effects." This solves the contradiction between the need to meet the demands of people to end hunger (which requires higher incomes) and the desire to avoid "sweeping social and political reforms." The solution outlined will ultimately benefit trilateral interests through the sale of Western technology for increasing food production.

The last option is another suggestion to increase use of Western technology, this time for storage and transport. Once again, increasing absolute food supply, not raising the income level of the poorest people, is seen as the solution.

The Task Force recommends going ahead with the last two options. "Of the four areas mentioned above, increasing food production and reducing crop and food wastes are those areas where strategies can be most readily implemented and can have the most immediate impact on nutrition."[14] The Commission has developed its overall strategy—to attack hunger by increasing incomes of the rural population by increasing rice production in Asia. It sets the goal of doubling Asian rice production by 1993. The balance of the report focuses on this goal.

The Commission chooses to focus on Asia for several reasons— it feels that "insufficiency of food supply will continue to be a chronic problem there."[15] The Commission feels that Asia is a natural, since many of the world's hungry people live there, and there is a large gap between current food production and potential output from the same land. Since Asia has little new land to bring into production, increased yields must be brought about by more intensive cultivation methods on land already in agricultural use. Thus, Asia is a fertile potential market for agricultural supplies from trilateral countries: "The income-creating effects that increase in food production will have on the peasants of Asia...should, in turn, contribute to the broadening of markets for industrial products in Asia."[16]

The report candidly mentions that many Asian governments believe that an increase in regional food self-sufficiency is a necessity. Through its plan, the Commission attempts to transform these aspirations for self-sufficiency into a new form of dependency—the adoption of agricultural technology requiring extensive use of industrial inputs.*

If we step back for a moment from the Commission's stated reasons for the food report, we can surmise other motivations beyond those stated outwardly.

It is curious that though hunger and malnutrition are problems plaguing most of the underdeveloped world, the food report targets one region. This is especially striking since Commission reports are generally characterized by broad policy statements rather than specific concrete plans for a particular area. It seems quite possible that Japanese Commissioners largely determined the content of the Food Task Force Report. Strong Japanese influence is apparent in the fact that while the report is attributed to one author from each of the trilateral regions, it credits three Japanese as consultants. These observations are clues to explaining why the report focuses on Asia.

The report can be seen as an attempt to encourage Japanese business and government to invest more of its capital elsewhere in Asia, instead of reinvesting it in the Japanese economy. The highly productive Japanese economy enjoys a phenomenally high rate of

---

*Third World officials often play into the Commission's scheme. In many cases, they, too, want to increase food production as a source of additional income for themselves and their associates, and as a means of controlling their people. Demands of these officials for higher prices and more advantageous trade terms for their products do not necessarily benefit poor people who need to raise their incomes to buy food. In other cases those in power may not act to accrue personal gain, but to pursue policies they consider best for their countries. For example, they may choose to appropriate the excess produced by agriculture to further industrialization rather than improve the lives of the peasants whose labor produced the excess. In both types of cases, rural people bear the brunt of undemocratic control, and often take action to change this state of affairs.

reinvestment, due in part to relatively small military and foreign aid expenditures. The high rate of reinvestment only exacerbates the degree to which the Japanese economy outstrips European and North American productivity. Trilateral thinkers wish to slow down the Japanese economy to bring greater parity among trilateral nations. Such parity would help insure the future of stable markets for products from all three regions. One way to help bring about the desired slowdown would be to expand Japanese foreign aid and private investment abroad.

Asia is Japan's realm of influence, and a likely candidate for aid. While the report doesn't explicitly state that a large portion of investment in Asia should come from Japan, it doesn't need to. Once the idea of massive capital investment in Asia is planted in the minds of major policy makers, it is likely that appropriate projects will be set up, and investment will follow.

A side benefit of massive Japanese investment coupled with humanitarian-looking aid projects might be an improvement in Japan's reputation with its neighbors. Asia is an important source of raw materials for Japan; giving aid ostensibly to "end hunger" might help mute the anti-Japanese feeling that now results from the obvious exploitation by Japanese business of other Asian peoples' land, resources, and labor.

Since rice is the main Asian foodgrain, and since, according to the report, it offers the highest yield among foodgrains under Asian climatic conditions, the Commission chooses to focus on rice production. The emphasis of the trilateral program is widespread irrigation development for land that is currently "inadequately irrigated" or "rainfed."

Irrigation development fits into a four-stage process of rural development, according to the Commission.

> *The first and the longest stage is that of primitive farming,* with reliance on traditional implements and practices and on rainfall for water. *In the second stage, the productivity of the land is improved* by irrigation, by the enhancement of soil nutrients through systematic incorporation of organic materials, by the more accurate timing of crop production, and by improved implements for cultivation. *The third stage is marked by the introduction of scientifically developed techniques.* Cultivation of dwarf varieties on irrigated land with chemical fertilizer and pesticides is a typical development of this stage. Another is the introduction of vaccines and dips to control livestock disease. *The fourth stage is the structural transformation of the rural economy,* which involves establishing the full range of institutions needed to support a high-productivity agriculture.[17] [Italics added.]

The irrigation development of stage two prepares the rural areas for stage three: effective use of "scientifically developed techniques," such as the products Commission members offer for sale. Thus, a major aspect of the rural development scheme involves bringing traditional farmers into the modern market economy to serve trilateral interests.

Nonetheless, it might appear that irrigation is a good idea, that it will improve the economic situation of all farmers involved, and that it can be separated from the rest of the plan if desirable. Who is to force the farmers with irrigated fields to change their methods of cultivation and to use more purchased inputs, or to defer structural change to the fourth stage? Perhaps irrigation, taken alone, will raise productivity and therefore the incomes of some of the world's poorest farmers.

If we examine the question closely, we will find that this isn't so. Irrigation, like any other technical innovation, cannot be evaluated apart from its social context. At best it will reflect existing problems and disparities; at worst it will exacerbate these.

This pattern was documented by Betsy Hartmann and Jim Boyce in the course of their research on food aid in Bangladesh. The World Bank had built 3,000 tubewells in Bangladesh, each designed to serve 25 to 50 farm families. In the village that Hartmann and Boyce studied, the one World Bank-funded tubewell was located on the land of the wealthiest landowner, who rented the use of this well to neighbors at an exhorbitant hourly rate. Hartmann and Boyce comment:

> At first we were surprised that the beneficiary of the World Bank's aid should be the richest man in our village, but on closer investigation we learned that this was not so strange. A foreign expert working on the project told us, "I no longer ask who is getting the well. I know what the answer will be, and I don't want to hear it. One hundred percent of these wells are going to the big boys. Each *thana* [administrative unit] is allotted a certain number of tubewells. First priority goes to those with political clout: the judges, the magistrates, the Members of Parliament, the union chairman. If any are left over, the local authorities auction them off. The rich landlords compete, and whoever offers the biggest bribe gets the tubewell. Around here the going price is 3,000 *taka* (less than $200)."

> An evaluation sponsored by the Swedish International Development Authority (SIDA), which helped to finance the tubewell project, confirms that the experience of our village was typical. The evaluator concluded after examining 270 tubewells: "It is not surprising that the tubewells have been situated on the land of the well-to-do farmers, or that it is the same well-to-do farmers who are the chairmen and managers of the irrigation

groups. It [would have] been more surprising if the tubewells had not been located on their land, with the existing rural power structure, maintained largely because of the unequal distribution of the land."

Given the social realities of rural Bangladesh, the outcome of the World Bank's tubewell project was entirely predictable.[18]

In nonsocialist Asia, 60 percent of the arable land is controlled by 20 percent of the landowners. Given this social reality, the outcome of the trilateral irrigation project is also entirely predictable.

The Commission's answer to this problem is that: "such inefficiencies cannot be removed unless leadership and discipline are developed in the rural community to organize its members for the protection of their common good and reconciliation of conflicting interests."[19]

This comment is rather cryptic; there is no reason that richer and more powerful farmers will share available water any more than they will share available land. The Commission is aware that equal use of irrigation water ultimately rests on a more equal landholding pattern:

> More basic is the problem of agrarian structure and land tenure. It has often been reported that community work programs are difficult to organize for irrigation projects that primarily benefit larger farmers and landlords. A recent study at the International Rice Research Institute suggests that the participation of community members in communal irrigation projects is greater and more uniform in a village where villagers are more homogenous in terms of tenure and farm size. If this is the case, redistributive land reform is critical not only for equity considerations, but also for the mobilization of local resources for sustained increase in food output under severe constraint of limited land resources.[20]

The Commission's Task Force is acknowledging that there may need to be a limited amount of land reform to insure that farmers will cooperate with the overall plans and schemes laid out by the Commission. But what will this land reform look like? The report does not explain this, nor how the needed land reform will be carried out. We know that "sweeping economic and political changes" are out of the question. Clearly eliminating the large landowner, restricting transnational corporations, and giving the peasants freedom to determine their own economic destinies is not what the Commission has in mind.* One gets the feeling that the Commission

---

*Like irrigation development, land reform can be organized to serve Trilateral interests.

A scenario for land reform that would follow the same sort of thinking that runs

would be quite willing to go ahead with the irrigation plan without ironing out these sticky details.

Athough the Commission raises all the problems inherent in its irrigation program, it attempts to rationalize them away, and then to point out further benefits of irrigation, like creating jobs for local unemployed workers: "Abundant manual labor has to be mobilized and effectively utilized with reasonable wages, which would greatly contribute to the solution of serious unemployment in rural Asia."[21] The notion of "reasonable wages" in areas of massive unemployment is not persuasive, since most experiences have shown that what actually occurs in such situations is starvation wages for back-breaking work which is primarily for the benefit of the already well-off. Workers are often given the choice of these low-paid jobs or starvation. While the Commission may see ditch-digging as a social benefit, those doing the work often see themselves cut off again from the fruits of their labor and from development planning that will benefit them in the long run. Once the irrigation works are completed, these landless workers are thrown back into unemployment.

A vast influx of capital into a society stratified into classes, without political change, (such as the $52 billion of this irrigation scheme), will produce the familiar pattern: the rich get rich and the poor get poorer.* If we examine the Commission's strategy of how to

---

through the irrigation scheme would involve distributing enough land to silence demands for justice without challenging farmers' dependency on the marketplace. For example, large feudal estates might be divided up and given to the more prosperous tenants. These small farmers would be released thereby from rent obligations, but would become beholden to new masters, (or old masters in new roles) to secure credit, inputs and a market for their products. These middle sector merchants and moneylenders are often tied into the international marketplace dominated by trilateral country corporations.

Such land reform would serve to divide the beneficiaries of the reform from subsistence farmers and the landless not reached by it. The gesture of dividing up some estates would dissipate demands for land, cause a realignment of allegiances in rural areas, and strengthen overall corporate control.

*This capital is given with strings attached. Most of the $52 billion investment in the Commission plan is to be given as *loans,* not grants.

> "We recommend that aid, in the form of grants, be provided for the training of additional personnel required for the development of irrigation projects and that part of the costs of surveys, feasibility studies and detailed designs be covered by grants and the *remainder financed on a liberal basis.*" [22]

Third World countries may have received about all the loan aid that they can stand:

> "By 1972, the underdeveloped countries owed over $150 billion to banks, governments, and lending agencies in the industrial countries. Each year a greater and greater portion of aid coming in must go out again just to repay loans received in previous years. By 1973, almost 40 percent of all

irrigate, we get a better insight into how this works.

Capital tends to go where it is most productive, where the return is greatest. The Commission's strategy for irrigation follows this pattern. It distinguishes between land that is inadequately irrigated, and can be improved at a cost of $400/hectare, and land which is totally without irrigation, and would cost $1,500/hectare to improve. Twenty-nine percent of the agricultural land in Asia falls in the first category, seventy percent falls in the latter, and one percent is adequately irrigated. This leads the Commission to prioritize as follows:[26]

> (1) *Top priority should be given to projects for which effects can be achieved quickly and cheaply,* including improvement of existing irrigation projects and pump irrigation, on a small or medium scale. Most of these projects fall in Alternative (C) on Chart 4 (page 38), converting inadequately-irrigated land. Full participation of local farmers is considered a great advantage in view of employment effects and other positive results of their involvement.
>
> (2) Medium-scale multi-purpose dams with provision for irrigation, hydropower, and flood control may require a consider-

---

> the official development assistance received by underdeveloped countries was spent on debt service payments on past 'aid.' "[23]

Political economist Cheryl Payer compares this system to peonage:

> The system can be compared point by point with peonage on an individual scale. In the peonage, or debt slavery system, the worker is unable to use his nominal freedom to leave the service of his employer, because the latter supplies him with credit (for over priced goods in the company store) necessary to supplement his meager wages. The aim of the employer-creditor-merchant is neither to collect the debt once and for all, nor to starve the employee to death, but rather to keep the laborer permanently indentured through his debt to the employer. The worker cannot run away, for other employers and the state recognize the legality of his debt; nor has he any hope of earning his freedom with his low wages.
>
> Precisely the same system operates on the international level. Nominally independent countries find that their debts, and their continued inability to finance current needs out of exports keep them tied by a tight leash to their creditors.[24]

This leash takes the form of creditors dictating terms of trade, monetary policies, even agricultural technologies. (See Phillips.)

One further point: the report proposes that the money necessary for its program be raised from a joint effort of the "developed" countries, OPEC countries, and multilateral lending agencies. ("You all put up the money and we'll figure out how to spend it.") OPEC's participation in decision making would be virtually nill.

The report fails to mention than OPEC countries contribute 3 percent of their total GNP to development aid, 8 times more than the developed countries of Europe and North America are now giving.[25]

able amount of construction machinery, cement, iron and steel, contractors' work and consultants' services, which in turn would stimulate the economies of developed countries which export these goods and services. These projects would normally belong to Alternative (B) on Chart 4, converting rainfed cultivated land to adequately irrigated land.

(3) Large-scale projects under consideration would be difficult to complete by 1993 as they require at least five years for surveying and designing plus another ten to twenty years for construction.[27] [Italics added.]

The land that is most productive now will get first attention. At the end of the Trilateral Commission project, 21 percent of the land remains totally unirrigated and 5 percent remains inadequately irrigated.[28]

The technical estimates and projections of the Task Force have been questioned even by colleagues who share its basic goals. Dr Montagne Yudelman, director of Agriculture and Rural Development at the World Bank, points out that "the estimate of costs seems to be too modest, the time horizon too short."[29] Instead of capital investment, he suggests better management of existing facilities. Assuming that he is even partially correct, and that the costs of the necessary inputs (concrete, steel, etc.) will indeed rise, then an even smaller portion of the targeted acreage will be reached by improved irrigation. The first target will be the 29 percent of the land that is currently "inadequately irrigated." This 29 percent may be the only land to be reached by irrigation.

Even the trilateral plan, in its most optimistic estimates, leaves 21 percent of the land untouched. The Commission predicts that this land will produce yields less than one-third as large as the irrigated land.[30] Among farmers with land, those benefited by the project will realize both an increase in the value of their now-improved land, and increased income through greater crop yields. Those whose land is not improved (the vast majority)* will become relatively poorer, both in the value of their land and in the value of their crops. Crop value

---

*Since land ownership in nonsocialist Asia is highly concentrated, this 21 percent of the land is occupied by more than a like proportion of landowning farmers. Sixty percent of the land is owned by the wealthiest 20 percent of the people, so four-fifths of landowners are crowded onto 40 percent of the land. These poorer landowners are less likely to have made technical improvements on their land, making it fall outside of the Commission's top priority for development. It is possible that up to *half* of the *landowning* population will be excluded from the trilateral plan. These relatively poorer landowners, together with the landless, make up a majority of the population of the countries targeted.

may be depressed by higher yields from the irrigated lands. Thus, the poorest group of farmers becomes even poorer. The landless must content themselves with the mythical benefits that supposedly will trickle down as the rich get richer.

Although irrigation is the primary program put forward in the report, there is another agenda operating at the same time. The first sentence of the report's discussion of irrigation give us a clue: "The new high yield varieties of crops are very responsive to irrigation."[31] This presumption of the use of high yielding "Green Revolution" seeds is apparent throughout the report. It is mentioned so often that it is clear that the irrigation project is merely a means of building the infrastructure needed to spread the Green Revolution further. Up until now, the Green Revolution has been adopted to only a limited extent, since a consistent, plentiful water supply must be available for higher yields. The report states openly that, in reviewing technical innovation in Asia, "irrigation conditions...defined the upper limit of use of MVs (modern, high yielding varieties of seeds) and fertilizer."[32] New irrigation works would potentially open up enormous new markets for these high yielding seeds, for fertilizers and pesticides and for thousands of other products mentioned by the Commission and controlled by a handful of transnational corporations.*

Since members of the Trilateral Commission represent sectors of the economy which have virtual monopoly control over the production and distribution of many of these basic inputs, they will be the long-term beneficiaries of these projects through increased future social control.

The adoption of Green Revolution technologies is plagued by the same pitfalls of increasing income disparities as the highlighted irrigation scheme. More affluent farmers who are able to make use of expensive imputs (paid out-of-pocket) will often have dramatically increased yields, leaving their poorer neighbors behind. A scholar of the Green Revolution, Keith Griffin, has found that

> those farmers who depend on rainfed agriculture are at a considerable disadvantage, particularly compared to those who are able to double-crop their land using irrigation. Farmers in rainfed regions use high yielding varieties on a minority of their land and obtain yields only two-thirds as high as those in the most

---

*The report foresees that expenses of Green Revolution inputs would be paid out of farmers' own pockets, since these inputs represent "current expenses to be paid out of current income."[33] All aid (grants and loans) given would go to irrigation projects. Therefore, only relatively affluent farmers could even consider using "modern" inputs, resulting in greater disparities in yields, and therefore, in income, between farmers.

favoured situation. Since the irrigated farms were more prosperous than the rainfed farms even prior to the introduction of the improved seeds, the new technology has led to an increase in inequality.[34]

This process leads to marginal farmers and tenants being driven off the land, greater concentration of landownership, and higher unemployment. As the numbers of landless swell, and competition for jobs increases, migration increases to already overcrowded cities. After documenting these consequences of the Green Revolution, Griffin summarizes its social impact: "The most significant consequences of technical change may have been to alter the distribution of income and class structure in rural areas rather than to eliminate malnutrition and agricultural shortages in urban areas."[35] Other studies of the Green Revolution reiterate this point.

A major problem with the Commission plan is the likelihood that more grain will be grown than people can buy. There's a solution, however. Excess grain can be fed to livestock that will be slaughtered for meat for the more well-to-do. There is one hitch, though, and that's the fact that rice is not the best grain for fattening livestock. This was anticipated by the Commission, and addressed in the Spring 1978 issue of *Trialogue,* the Commission newsletter. Kenzo Henmi, Dean of the faculty of agriculture at the University of Tokyo and a consultant to the Commission's Task Force, stated

> The importance of non-rice foods in South and Southeast Asia, and the fact that tens of millions of the poorest people there are not rice eaters, should not be forgotten when trying to assess the potential results of a program such as this. As the authors themselves point out, in a longer-term perspective, the importance of non-rice grains in total grain consumption will increase with the increasing consumption of livestock products among the Asian population.[36]

Historically, a pattern of grain surplus in the United States has led to an increased level of meat consumption. Only recently has this pattern spread around the world, a sign of the growing affluence of portions of the Third World population. This affluence can have a negative effect on the nutritional well-being of other portions of the population. In countries where poor people can't even afford to eat grain, if the affluent adopt a diet that will reduce the amount of grain available for human consumption, grain prices will be forced up beyond the reach of the poor. It is interesting that Henmi mentions together poor Asians whose diet is based on non-rice grains, and rich Asians turning to a meat-centered diet. He is using the existence of the non-rice-eating poor to justify cultivation of other types of grain, even though much of the grain grown would most likely be fed to livestock.

Another possible way to dispose of any grain that can't be marketed at "commercial rates" is outlined in the report:

> The developing countries must have a reasonable expectation that *export outlets* will be available on favorable terms for any exportable surplus of agricultural products that may be created and for processed and manufactured products to provide the foreign exchange required for the flow of imports of modern farm inputs, energy, and capital goods required for the expansion of agricultural output.[37]

In the trilateral plan, food is treated like any other commodity: those who can't pay won't eat. A surplus does not mean more food is produced than people can eat; rather, more food is produced than people can buy at the market price. Such food can be exported if international market prices are high enough. And if the world grain market is glutted, land planted to rice can be converted to more profitable crops.

Thus the Commission scenario is laid out: a model of agricultural self-sufficiency gives way to interdependence trilateral-style: Third World farmers and working people produce inexpensive raw and semiprocessed materials, including food, for trilateral corporations that provide finished expensive industrial products to the Third World. This scheme keeps Third World economies dependent, in debt, and unable to bargain as equals in the international marketplace. Within such a climate of scarcity and dependency, the conditions faced by poor and working people are likely to deteriorate.

In summary, the Trilateral Commission has developed a well-thought out analysis that realistically assesses the causes of hunger and analyzes how hunger helps and hurts trilateral interests. It has then developed a plan that can maximize the benefits and minimize the liabilities to these interests. On the one hand, by linking a decrease in hunger to increased income for some farmers, and by proposing a capital investment that contributes to a more technically advanced agriculture, the Commission has put forward a program that appears to address a serious world problem. On the other hand, it is clear that the increased production is based on inputs controlled by trilateral interests, well within the economic status quo. Thus the Commission manages to serve both short and long-term trilateral interests rather than the hungry people in question.

Although this program makes a tremendous amount of sense given the Trilateral Commission's analysis of the problem and the interests which it wants to serve, its solution is clearly not designed for, nor will it be in the interests of the people who are hardest hit by malnutrition. The poorest farmers and the landless—those people least likely to have enough money to buy food—are not helped. Nothing in the plan will raise their incomes.

But, as we have pointed out, the predominant goal of the trilateral plan is not to end hunger, so much as to maintain and increase corporate control. Thus, even if people remain hungry, so long as revolution has been dampened and corporate control has grown, the strategy will have succeeded.

Nonetheless, many people will take the trilateralists at their word, and criticize the Commission for not really dealing with the inequities that cause hunger.

The Commission anticipates this criticism:

> ...in view of *present power structures,* it is unrealistic to expect that (redistributive) land reform will be implemented effectively within the time horizon of this rice-production doubling program...
>
> In any case we should base our decisions on hard reality: what is desirable and what is feasible. Strengthening the organizational capacity of rural people and reforming agrarian society into more egalitarian forms are much to be desired. But it is not certain that these goals will be achieved in the short or medium run.
>
> *The difficulty in achieving social change, however, should not lead to defeatism about the prospects for the rice-production doubling program proposed here,* based primarily on irrigation facilities and modern inputs. We should not conclude that the program should not be implemented until we know how to reform rural society...Our plan will have the effect of injecting a momentum into rural society for inducing institutional innovation. *Of course, there is a danger that the momentum will result in some undesirable social consequences, such as unequal income distribution or polarization of the rural community.*
>
> Today, unless a major effort is made to increase food production in the form of a feasible program, *we are bound to lose what is now a dead heat between population and food supply: this will result in greater misery of poor people and greater social injustice.* In such a situation, *it is criminal not to undertake feasible programs, even though the social consequences are somewhat unpredictable.*[38] [Italics added.]

A revealing dialogue occurred at a Paris meeting at which the report was discussed. One participant stated that "special attention should be given to the potential impact of regional water supply differences on already existing regional disparities." A defender of the report responded, "This dilemma is ultimately a choice which has to be made by the Asian countries themselves: whether they want more rice at the cost of regional disparities, or shared misery."[39]

When pushed to admit that their plan may lead to greater economic injustice, the Commission conjures up the persuasive image of teeming masses of hungry people, even harkening back to images of the "population problem." This effective use of the "threat of hunger" is merely another trilateral tactic.

The Commission does not claim that its program is neutral. At the same time, its answers do not satisfy critics who claim its avoidance of fundamental change will doom its program to being a redistributive land reform favoring the rich. To silence critics, the Commission falls back on the popular misconception that the hunger problem is so immense that any contribution is progressive. It tells its critics that even clear inequities are acceptable given the alternative of mass starvation. These critics may not be aware that mass starvation may be even more likely if the trilateral plan is implemented.

In a sense, the Task Force is nothing new; like the Commission itself, the report is just the latest formulation of elite planning.* But somehow the repackaging seems to give impetus to new activity. The Asian Development Bank and the World Bank, among others, have thrown their verbal support behind the proposal (though with some proposed revisions).[40]** After all, the proposal fits right into their current strategies. These institutions wield enormous influence and capital. The report may be just the catalyst they need to implement the current phase of elite planning more widely.***

---

*Earlier elite planning developed the Green Revolution as a strategy for dealing with hunger through increased production. This work began at the Rockefeller-funded CIMMYT Institute, founded in Mexico in 1943.

The Green Revolution appeared to avoid the problems associated with trickle-down development, because it could be implemented on any size farm, at least theoretically. But in reality, the Green Revolution rarely benefited the poorest people any more than the trickle-down projects like huge industrial complexes. The poorest people still had no jobs, no land, or if they had any land, no money to purchase Green Revolution inputs. Nonetheless, the Green Revolution approach was extended to rice through research at the International Rice Research Institute, founded in 1962 as a joint effort of the Rockefeller and Ford Foundations.

**Others have followed suit. For example, the lead article of the 12 March 1979 issue of the U.S. Agency for International Development's *World Development Letter* begins:

"Irrigation may be the key to stepping up Third World food production. Some experts maintain that if India, Indonesia and Bangladesh, the big potential food importers, can irrigate their land efficiently, future food shortages can be cut drastically..." The "experts" are not named.

***A quick review of current publications of the World Bank and other international and governmental agencies reveals that they have taken up a new strategy, the "basic needs" approach to development. This approach, which has replaced the trickle-down theory of development, tries to raise the income levels of poor people directly, through employment, limited land reform, and so on. (Not by income redis-

A parallel process has occurred within the U.S. government. In June of 1978, President Carter announced plans to establish a Commission on World Hunger. He chose to make the first announcement of his plans (which were leaked to the press) at a private White House meeting with members of the Trilateral Commission. The official public announcement was not made until September, right around the time the Trilateral Commission report was scheduled to come out. The President's Hunger Commission will "coordinate the efforts of United Nations agencies with international organizations to combat starvation."[41] President Carter named Sol Linowitz, a Trilateral Commission member, to head his Hunger Commission. Among the appointees was Norman Borlaug, the agricultural scientist who won the 1970 Nobel Peace Prize for his pioneering work on the Green Revolution at the Rockefeller-funded CIMMYT Institute in Mexico. Another Carter nominee was Clifton Wharton, Jr., an agricultural economist and president of the State University of New York. Wharton has been described as "an old Rockefeller associate who has taken to evoking the spector of Lin Piao's rural guerilla strategy when calling for more [U.S. government funded] work in the countryside."[42] Other nominees included members of Congress and other public figures. The appointees with trilateral connections probably did their best to get Carter's Commission to follow the recommendations and analysis of the Trilateral Commission Food Task Force, but more progressive Hunger Commission members insisted on a different analysis. The resulting draft report lacked concrete proposals, indicating the dissension among members.[43]

Will the trilateral plan fulfill its primary goal of diffusing social unrest and revolutionary activity? The underlying source of the unrest, food priced beyond the means of poor people, has not been effectively dealt with. The identities of the poor people have changed, but the group itself has not been eliminated. It may even be enlarged by the plan.

In an exhaustively researched book about the Green Revolution in India,[44] Professor Francine R. Frankel documents how time and again, agricultural innovations without accompanying land reform have led many people to support political parties advocating basic economic and political change. The most significant result of the

---

tribution, however.) The trilateral plan fits squarely into the "basic needs" approach, as it appears to help raise income levels of poor people by helping them help themselves. As we have seen, the plan avoids the basic changes which would bring an end to hunger and poverty. The trilateral plan, like most "basic needs" schemes, offers some people the chance to participate in the world market instead of promoting self-sufficiency, economic independence, and political self-determination. "Basic needs" is a catchword for reformist plans which attempt to sidestep fundamental change.

Trilateral Commission food strategy might well be an acceleration of conflict between the beneficiaries of the new abundance and those left behind.

In such a case, the trilateralists (or their successors) will once again be faced with the threat of revolutionary activity. The next time, they may adopt a strategy which feeds more people* while maintaining their control over the world's productive capacity: the land, natural resources, and people's lives and labor. At that point, raising the standard of living of greater numbers of people will have become a necessary concession in the attempt to maintain the system of corporate domination. It will also be evidence of the growing strength of working people demanding more than a spare existence in a world in which they have created great wealth. People's realization of their growing strength will lead to demands for greater and more basic changes in the future.

What is the alternative to the trilateral plan? The whole problem with the Trilateral Commission is that it is a small, powerful, self-appointed group making plans for the rest of the world. Its plans for development or underdevelopment are intended to further its own ends. A development process controlled by the world's people would look very different.

When people around the world have taken control out of the hands of transnational corporations,** they have tended to focus attention on the areas of greatest hardship first. They have dramatically reduced malnutrition and infant mortality and increased food consumption within their societies. The price paid to control development has been years of war and hardship, since transnationals do not give up their power willingly.

Our role in this process can be active—not in designing development strategies for people who are much better equipped to do so themselves—but in supporting the efforts of Third World countries to seize control of their economies, and in educating ourselves and our friends to counteract the media distortions and falsehoods that surround the issue of hunger.

*This is what has occurred in the United States as a result of working people's demands for a decent standard of living. But since profit remains the main goal of the elites controlling the U.S. economy, these demands have not been fully met. In 1975 an estimated 20 million people suffered from poverty-related malnutrition in the United States, the richest country in the world.[45]

**Recent decades have seen socialist revolutions in North Korea, China, Cuba, Angola, Vietnam, Mozambique, and Guinea-Bissau. These countries contain 40 percent of the underdeveloped world's population. Their people have managed to distribute available food in such a way that no one goes hungry.

Even more important, we must do what we can to bring an end to large corporations' exclusive control over the wealth produced in this society. The power of corporate leaders in the U.S. is based on the wealth produced through the efforts of U.S. working people during the period of industrialization, and the continuing accumulation of wealth by the corporations depends on the continuing efforts of U.S. working people. Today, this continuing accumulation is being questioned. Farmers demanding a fair return for their production from food monopolies, and farmworkers and industrial workers demanding decent wages and working conditions, are challenging the perogative of large corporations to dominate economic development in the U.S. These initiatives deserve our active support, based on an understanding that in our "interdependent" world, an increase of popular control anywhere has a positive effect on democratic control everywhere.

If we are truly interested in ending world hunger, we will take concrete steps to attack its roots in our own society. We must understand continuing world hunger in the midst of abundance for what it really is: not a moral issue, certainly not an inevitable tragedy, but a measure of how far we have yet to go in creating an international society founded on democratic control, and committed to spreading prosperity and opportunity among the greatest possible number of people.

AFTERWORD: THE U.S. CONNECTION: CONVERSATION WITH A CALIFORNIA FARMER

The trilateral plan is premised on the notion that prosperity in the rural areas of Asia can be promoted through increased production As we have seen, the plan makes widespread use of products controlled primarily by U.S.-based multinationals, corporations that base their strength in the international arena on domination of the U.S. agricultural economy.

In order to better understand how Asian rural society might be shaped by the trilateral plan, we thought it might be useful to examine the lot of the farmers and farmworkers who make U.S. agriculture the most productive in the world. We asked a farmer from Colusa County, California, one of the most prosperous agricultural counties in the United States, to comment on how corporate domination affects him and his neighbors. Tom Stevenson is in his fifties and has farmed for twenty-five years. His family grows grain and sugar-beets on 800 acres. This is some of what he had to say:

"The farmer is getting the squeeze. Costs of the farmer are going up much faster than food prices for the consumer. As a result, he barely breaks even. You wouldn't put your money in a savings account for 4 percent interest, would you? Well, that's what the farmer returns on his investment when he farms, and that doesn't include any return for his labor in his costs.

"Some of our better farmers that didn't think they could ever be hurt are now in jeopardy. We're going to lose those farmers, and when they're gone, there won't be the productivity. You won't get the productivity out of corporate farming. Then you'll really see food prices go up. These farmers are having problems because their input costs have tripled in recent years—equipment, chemicals, fuel...and repairs, if you can even get the parts at all. Sure, labor costs are going up too, but people who work have got to make a living. Labor costs aren't nearly as big a factor as the inputs. These are the direct reasons these guys are in a bind.

"Of course, increased input costs wouldn't make any difference if you had the ability to pass them on, but we don't. The corporations set the price they will pay. So there the farmer is, caught in the middle.

"It has nothing to do with productivity...You produce more at a greater cost and still get less money than it cost you. Zero times ten is still zero, at least where I went to school...you've got to have a price, and that price has to reflect your cost plus a profit...

"If you have an operating debt this year, and you can't pay it back, then you capitalize it, borrow against your land. Then, the next year, you have a capital debt—in a sense, you're starting off the year brand new, but you're really not. You capitalized the debt—it's hidden, but it's there all the same. On the balance sheet it looks like you bought a ranch, or a new tractor, but you've got no new assets, you just owe more to the bank.

"If you're talking about farm problems, or labor problems, poor consumer problems, you have to go back to the root cause...agriculture in the United States is shaped by the multinational corporations and their particular needs, anything they can do to keep their costs down and profits up. They all want to get economic control for their own best interest—not your interest or mine.

"Trilateral is part of a worldwide plan. Their goals are to seek out anywhere in the world where they can produce their products the cheapest, and sell them into the highest market. The essence is to make a lot of money. They will do the same thing that a businessman in the United States will do. You'll shop for the cheapest tractor; they'll shop for the cheapest country, where they can get the most profit, exploit the people, exploit the raw materials—and any

industrial nation can't do without raw materials—so they naturally
want them cheap so they can make a profit at the other end.

"With labor it's the same way. They go into these countries and
they want nickel-an-hour labor. The only reason, I'm convinced, that
there's still agriculture in the U.S. today, is that they can't find it
cheaper anywhere else. And we're helping those guys—we're giving
them nickel-an-hour labor, our labor...

"They'll go into an area and give the people a nickel an hour—it
may be better than they got before, because before maybe they got
four cents and now they get a penny more—and they produce the crop
cheaper than they can buy it here. Then they come to us and say 'Well,
American farmer, you've got to produce as cheap as we can get
elsewhere; otherwise you've got to go out of business.' The end result
is that there will be no farmers left here.

"I heard a man from Castle and Cooke telling us what a great
job they're doing. He said they would be producing tomatoes in
Haiti, Nigeria, and Jamaica, of equal quality to our tomatoes, and
delivering them to New York. They try to tell us that they're helping
people by growing food and creating jobs, but when you get down to
what they're paying those people and the disruption of their
economy, they were really robbing them, plain and simple. The
Castle and Cooke man told us they were doing everything they could
within the administration to get rid of tariffs on imported tomatoes
and they did. Those tomatoes are coming in now...

"We used to condemn the slave ships when they brought over the
slaves from Africa. We haven't changed much, except now we're
bringing the goods instead of the slaves. It's the same type of labor.
So they tell farmers and farmworkers, 'You'd better straighten out or
we'll go to South Africa or somewhere...' As long as there's some new
area to exploit, they're going to do it.

"You have problems when there are very few at the top, and a
very large lower class. A wise man summed it up some years ago. He
said,

> I feel more anxiety today than even in the midst of war. As a
> result of the war, the corporations have now been enthroned, and
> an era of corruption will follow in the high places. The moneyed
> powers will endeavor to prolong their reign on the prejudice of
> man, until all wealth is aggregated in the hands of a few, and the
> Republic is destroyed...

That was Abraham Lincoln.

"And sure enough, they've got everybody fighting everybody,
the Black fighting the white. This has to change. The farmers and
ranchers and labor unions should be together going after the guy at
the top. That's the problem—nobody's focused on who's really

controlling the national economy. Everyone's focused on this little group, or that little group, or even that big group. But we all have basically the same problem. Who's doing this to us?

"Your government owes you something—our government does. It owes you a chance—the pursuit of happiness—it owes you the Preamble, an opportunity, and a fair price for whatever you do produce. Every worker is worth his hire...

"We're all in the same boat. It's just hard to tell people that and make them believe it. When are people going to say 'we've had it?' It's always happened that there comes a point where the people either give in and adapt, or they won't adapt, and they find their own form of adaptation... history has shown there's no other way. This is what Americans are looking at right now. Are we as farmers going to be extinct, are we as a country going to be like Spain in the eighteenth century, a country of consumers, unproductive, or are we going to hear a different story a hundred years from now from our graves? Maybe we'll hear, 'Oh, Americans...they had enough and decided to change history, so they revolted and got rid of all those people who were trying to control them...' And the same question that's facing us is facing all the other people around the world."

FOOTNOTES

1. Andrew Young, interviewed in the film *I Want to Live,* produced by the Windstar Foundation.
2. Robert McNamara, speech before the World Bank's Board of Governors in 1973, quoted in Betsy Hartmann and Jim Boyce, "Bangladesh: Aid to the Needy?" *International Policy Report,* IV: 1, May 1978, (Washington, D.C.: Center for International Policy, 1978), p. 14.
3. U. Columbo, D.G. Johnson, T. Shishido, *Expanding Food Production in Developing Countries: Rice Production in South and Southeast Asia, Report of the Trilateral Food Task Force* (New York City: The Trilateral Commission, 1978), p. 16. Page numbers refer to Discussion Draft prepared for the Trilateral Commission meeting in Bonn, Federal Republic of Germany, on 22-25 October 1977, entitled "Reducing Malnutrition in Developing Countries: Increasing Rice Production in South and Southeast Asia."
4. *Ibid.,* p. 48.
5. *The AgBiz Tiller,* No. 7, November 1977, p. 3.
6. Deere and Co. Annual Report, 1975.
7. Susan George, *How the Other Half Dies,* (Montclair, N.J.: Allenheld, Osmun & Co., 1977), p. 18.

8. Caterpillar Tractor Company Annual Report, 1978.

9. Harry Cleaver, "The Politics of Public Health and the International Crisis," *Review of Radical Political Economics,* Spring 1977, appendix.

10. Report of the Trilateral Food Task Force Report, pp. 4-5. Here and in later quotations, italics added for emphasis by the author of this article.

11. *Ibid.,* p. 3.

12. *Ibid.,* p. 6.

13. *Ibid.,* pp. 2-3.

14. *Ibid.,* p. 6.

15. *Ibid.,* p. 17.

16. *Ibid.*

17. *Ibid.,* p. 22.

18. Hartmann and Boyce, op. cit., p. 7. The Swedish source they quote is Per-Arne Stroberg, "Water and Development: Organizational Aspects on a Tubewell Irrigation Project in Bangladesh," Dacca, March 1977.

19. Report of the Trilateral Commission Food Task Force, p. 41.

20. *Ibid.,* pp. 42-43.

21. *Ibid.,* pp. 40-41.

22. *Ibid.,* p. 36.

23. UNCTAD, "Debt Problems in the Context of Development," 1974, p. 1216, quoted in Lappe & Collins, *Food First,* (Boston: Houghton Mifflin, 1977), p. 325.

24. Cheryl Payer, *The Debt Trap,* (New York: Monthly Review Press, 1974), pp. 48-49.

25. George, p. 217.

26. Report of the Trilateral Food Task Force, pp. 45 and 46.

27. *Ibid.,* p. 47.

28. *Ibid.,* p. 46.

29. "Agriculture at the World Bank: Interview with M. Yudelman," *Trialogue,* No. 17, (Spring 1978), (New York: The Trilateral Commission, 1978), p. 9.

30. Report of the Trilateral Food Task Force, p. 46.

31. *Ibid.,* p. 9.

32. *Ibid.,* p. 29.

33. *Ibid.,* p. 49.

34. Keith Griffin, *The Political Economy of Agrarian Change: An Essay on the Green Revolution,* (Cambridge, Mass.: Harvard University Press, 1974), p. 57.

35. *Ibid.,* p. 62.

36. *Trialogue,* No. 17, p. 15.

37. Report of the Trilateral Food Task Force, p. 69.

38. *Ibid.,*pp. 56-57.

39. "Comments on the Trilateral Food Task Forces Report," December 1977 May 1978, unpublished document, Trilateral Commission, p. 11.

40. *Ibid.,* pp. 1-2 and 3-5.

41. *The New York Times,* 18 June 1978, p. 13.

42. Harry Cleaver, "Will the Green Revolution Turn Red?" in Steve Weissman, *et al., The Trojan Horse: A Radical Look at Foreign Aid,* (Palo Alto: Ramparts Press, 1975), p. 196.

43. *Preliminary Report of the Presidential Commission on World Hunger,* (Washington, D.C., 1979).

44. Francine R. Frankel, *India's Green Revolution: Economic Gains and Political Costs* (Princeton, N.J.: Princeton University Press, 1971).

45. Select Committee on Nutrition and Human Needs, United States Senate, *Report on Nutrition and Special Groups, Part I* (Washington, D.C.: U.S. Government Printing Office, 1975), p. 3.

PART VIII
CHALLENGES TO TRILATERALISM
INSIDE THE TRIANGLE

The Trilateral Commission has called for cooperation between North America, Western Europe, and Japan, and is attempting to fashion appropriate policies for changing world realities. But as Fred Block shows in the article below a contradictory process of cooperation and rivalry marks the relations among capitalists and between trilateral states. Vested political and economic interests (within the capitalist class) oppose the trilateral approach to domestic and foreign policy. In a second article, Alan Wolfe focuses on the political problems faced by U.S. trilateral planners in their attempt to put trilateral plans into effect.

In the simplest of terms, the Trilateral Commission is an establishment booster club, a floating seminar for business and academic leaders...on a deeper level, the Trilateral Commission is an effort to reestablish consensus in the American foreign policy community where even the harmony of that small club was shattered by Vietnam.

—William Greider,
Washington Post, 16 January 1977

These words written for a project of the Council on Foreign Relations apply equally to the Trilateral Commission:

[It must] come to grips with strategies for modifying *the behavior of the relevant actors in the international community*— individuals, governments, agencies within governments, elite groups, industrial firms, interest groups, mass societies, and other groups and organizations at the subnational and transnational level. [Italics the authors]

—"The 1980s Project,"
7 March 1975*

---

*Draft Memorandum, cited in Shoup and Minter, *Imperial Brain Trust,* p. 256.

chapter one

TRILATERALISM AND INTER-CAPITALIST CONFLICT

Fred Block*

The emergence of the Trilateral Commission amid international capitalism's growing economic difficulties has rekindled an old debate. The debate centers on the capacity of the most powerful capitalist states to negotiate their differences in order to create a stable international economic order. On the one side are those who stress that the growing international integration of capitalist firms creates a common transnational interest among dominant capitalists and that this common interest can be the basis for negotiating a stable order. On the other side are those who insist that the crisis tendencies within capitalism will continually create circumstances in which capitalists in one nation will attempt to solve their problems through state actions, at the expense of capitalists in other nations. The argument is that policies designed to create national economic advantage (for example, protectionism, exchange rate manipulations, export subsidies) increase the likelihood of intercapitalist conflict as each nation attempts to improve its position to the detriment of the others.

*An earlier version of this paper appeared in *Marxist Perspectives*, Spring 1979. Fred Block teaches in the Sociology Department, University of Pennsylvania and is the author of *The Origins of International Economic Disorder*, (Berkeley: University of California Press, 1977).

While there have been many formulations of these opposing positions, the debate to this day still revolves around the rival formulations developed by Lenin and Kautsky in the period before World War I.[1] Kautsky, the leading theoretician of the German Social Democratic Party, argued for the possibility of ultraimperialism—a stable and cooperative organization of relations among the dominant capitalists. Against Kautsky, Lenin insisted that any period of cooperation simply indicates a truce in a perpetual war since, sooner or later, capitalists in one or more countries would grow dissatisfied with their share of the world markets, investment opportunities, and access to raw materials. These dissatisfied capitalists would pressure their government to push for a revision of the system of international cooperation. Demands for revision would most likely meet resistance, and the dissatisfied powers would use more and more aggressive tactics leading to sharpened economic conflict and heightening the possibility of interimperialist war.

That the debate has continued for so long is not surprising since the two positions talk past each other. The Kautskian interpretation could always treat a period of international capitalist cooperation as evidence of permanent stability, whereas the Leninist interpretation could always treat a cooperative period as a prelude to new hostilities. When the hostilities came, the former could always treat them as a moment of bloody aberration, the latter as proof of imperialism's fundamental instability. The argument continues apace for no objective methodological criterion satisfies adherents of both sides.

But there is growing evidence that neither of the polar positions is adequate. Efforts to interpret contemporary developments within either the Kautskian or Leninist framework have led to serious errors. On the one hand, those closer to the Kautskian position have exaggerated the impact of trilateralism on the Carter Administraton and on intercapitalist relations more generally. On the other, analysts close to the Leninist position have predicted escalating trade wars among the dominant capitalist powers without considering the factors that militate against increasing interimperialist conflict. In this article, I will try to demonstrate the inadequacies of these polar positions and argue for an alternative perspective recognizing a contradictory process of cooperation and rivalry.

Trilateral Mystique and the Decline of the Dollar

In recent years some observers have described the emergence of an international ruling class based in the 300 to 500 leading multinational corporations and banks.[2] (See Girvan.) Their common desire for a stable world economy far outweighs their competing interests. Hence, the small groups of people who own and manage these firms constitute an increasingly cohesive class. Initially brought into contact with each other through their business dealings, the people who own and manage these firms increasingly develop social and political ties—especially through organizations like the Trilateral Commission.

Consistently defending liberal economic principles (that trade and capital should be allowed to flow freely across national boundaries in response to market forces), the Commission opposes any drift towards neo-mercantilism—the deliberate use of governmental intervention to shape those flows in the interests of a particular nation.[3] The Commission's notorious study, *The Crisis of Democracy*, grew in part out of a concern that democratic institutions were making it difficult for political leaders to adhere to liberal economic principles in domestic and international economic policy[4] (See Wolfe Part V.)

The appearance of so many trilateralists in the Carter Administration seemed to provide powerful evidence of the validity of the international ruling class hypothesis. (See "Who's Who" for complete list.) But despite the strength of the trilateral connection, actual policies of the Carter Administration have strayed far from the principles of trilateralism. In fact, the Carter Administration has seen the prolonging of the most sustained deterioration of U.S.-Japanese and U.S.-Western Europe relations of the post-World War II period. On a series of interrelated issues—foreign steel imports, the Japanese trade surplus with the United States, the rate of economic expansion in Germany and Japan, and the declining value of the dollar—Carter Administration policies have exacerbated the level of tension with the other trilateral powers. In some cases, the violation of trilateralist policies has been blatant, such as with the reference pricing system for steel imports. In other cases, the U.S. has violated the spirit of trilateralism by attempting to exercise its power unilaterally, rather than engaging in the desired process of trilateral consultation and compromise.

The gap between the Carter Adminstration's trilateral origins and its actual policies has led one observer of the Washington scene to write, "The Trilateral idea...appears to have hit the floor soon after the Administration took office." This reporter goes on to quote a foreign policy official as saying, "The Trilateral idea is dead. It was just rhetoric."[5] By analyzing concrete policies we can better grasp the forces which shape rhetoric and reality.

Analysts in the neo-Leninist tradition were not taken in by the trilateral mystique; instead, they tend to minimize the importance of trilateralism except as a device to coordinate imperialist policies toward the Third World. Neo-Leninists tend to assume that corporate trilateralists are *insincere* in their expressed support for higher levels of international cooperation and argue that, in actuality, U.S. capitalists favor more aggressive governmental policies designed to improve their position at the expense of their trilateral competitors. Paul Sweezy and Harry Magdoff, for example, contend that the decline of the dollar in the period from July 1977 to the beginning of 1978 was part of a deliberate policy designed to gain a competitive edge for U.S. capitalists in international trade.[6] They imply that the policy reflected the interests of the most powerful U.S. capitalists.

If this were indeed the case, their anticipation of an intensifying trade war between the U.S. and other trilateral powers would be persuasive, since Japanese and Western European capitalists would be almost certain to demand compensatory actions by their own governments. Such compensatory actions would necessarily lead to further escalation by the U.S., and a full scale trade war would ensue. However, Sweezy and Magdoff's implication that big capital in the U.S. favored a competitive depreciation of the dollar is unproven and dubious. There is no evidence in the business press during 1977-78 of any significant business support for a reduction in the value of the dollar. On the contrary, the business press expressed continuing anxiety over the dollar's fall. At least a part of this anxiety can be traced to the interests of many U.S.-based multinationals that stand to lose from a declining dollar. Since these firms tend to service foreign markets through foreign-based production, rather than through exports, their actual sales would be only marginally influenced by a cheaper dollar. More importantly, they stand to lose significant sums of money in currency transactions when the foreign exchange markets are thrown into turmoil by a declining dollar. Furthermore, the large U.S. banks also risk considerable losses as declining international confidence in the dollar leads investors to shift their assets to banks in countries with stronger currencies.

A more plausible explanation of the dollar decline during 1977-78 centers on the domestic motivations of the Carter Administration. The Administration had been determined to sustain an economic expansion that would bring unemployment rates down from the potentially explosive levels reached during the Ford Administration. But pursuit of expansionary economic policies in 1977-78, with the rest of the world economy stagnant, created a substantial trade deficit. Throughout 1977, the Carter Administration sought to reduce the size of the deficit by convincing West Germany and Japan to expand their own economies more rapidly. The Administration argued that with all three locomotive economies—the U.S., Japan, and West Germany—expanding rapidly, business activity would pick up in the rest of the world economy. A global economic revival would mean the U.S. could expand without a devastating trade deficit because heightened foreign demand would boost U.S exports.

Acting in their own immediate national interests, the West Germans and Japanese refused to cooperate and allowed their economies to grow only slowly through 1977 and most of 1978.* With West German and Japanese demand for imported goods remaining depressed, the rest of the world economy stagnated, and the U.S. trade deficit reached record levels. The Carter Administration, however, continued its expansionary policies on the theory that any decline in the value of the dollar resulting from the growing trade deficits would act as an additional pressure on West Germany and Japan to step up their economic growth. The threat that West German and Japanese goods might be priced out of certain markets by a declining dollar was designed to convince the other trilateral powers that faster economic expansion would be the lesser of two evils. All pressures pointed in the same direction, since if West Germany and Japan sought to forestall the dollar's decline through massive interventions in the foreign exchange markets, they would risk inflationary growth in their domestic money supplies as the central banks accumulated huge quantities of unwanted dollars.[8]

In Sweezy and Magdoff's view, the depreciation of the dollar was designed to give U.S. firms a competitive advantage in a stagnant world economy. I am suggesting, instead, that the dollar's decline was an undesired consequence of the Administration's pursuit of domestic economic objectives. However, a secondary gain from the dollar's decline was increased pressure on West Germany and Japan. U.S. policy makers believed that if these two nations had succumbed to the pressure then the U.S. deficit would have been sharply reduced and the dollar's decline reversed.

In this context, it is possible to see why West Germany and Japan have not taken strong retaliatory actions. Despite their dissatisfaction with a declining dollar, they could hardly be enthusiastic about most of the remedies available to reduce the size of the U.S. deficit. In particular, if the U.S. attempted to reduce the deficit by pushing its economy back into recession, this would have closed off any prospects for a worldwide economic recovery that would revive the West German and Japanese economies. In short, the most

*West Germany and Japan refused to stimulate their economies for fear that such Keynesian expansionary measures would generate more inflation than real growth. Both countries preferred to wait for export demand to pull their economies toward a faster rate of growth. Their suspicion of Keynesian fiscal measures seems well grounded since it is likely that both economies require deeper structural changes to pave the way for resumption of rapid growth. For a discussion of the German case, see Fred Block, "The Stalemate of European Capitalism: Eurocommunism and No Postwar Order," *Socialist Review* 43, January-February 1979.

the Germans and Japanese could do was resist U.S. pressures to reflate their own economies and hope that the U.S. would moderate the speed of its expansion, enact measures to reduce its oil imports, and increase interventions on the foreign exchange markets to slow the dollar's decline. In light of these goals, sharp retaliatory actions hardly seemed to make sense.*

The State and Imperialist Relations

Underlying the explanation I have proposed above is the notion of divergence between the interests of powerful government officials or state managers and the interests of dominant capitalists or accumulators, which will be examined below. The Carter Administration pursued expansionary policies despite the fact that the resulting dollar decline and international currency instability had negative consequences for U.S.-based multinationals. The critical point is that neither the Kautskian nor the neo-Leninist lines of analysis allows the possibility for such a divergence. Both theories err by relying on an instrumentalist view of the state (i.e. the state is seen wholly as an instrument of the dominant class).[9] In the neo-Kautskian analysis, the dominant capitalists prevail directly on the state to pursue policies designed to increase interimperialist cooperation. The contrasting neo-Leninist view holds that the dominant capitalists direct the state to follow policies that serve their interests and create conflict with other powers. In neither analysis do state managers or other social classes play a significant independent role in determining policy outcomes. Both result in either/or positions: either there will be international economic cooperation or there will be international economic conflict. In reality, however, pressures for conflict and cooperation coexist with sufficient force to generate an indefininite stalemate.

The key factor in this stalemate is the divison of labor in contemporary capitalist societies between accumulators and state managers; this division gives rise to differences in interests and perceptions.**However, this division of labor occurs within a

---

*West Germany has found another way to respond to the dilemmas created by a declining dollar. With France it has revived the project of monetary unification within the European Economic Community. Their current plan, the European Monetary System, envisions greater stability among European currencies supported by a $20 billion fund. The immediate goal is to keep West German goods from being priced out of European markets as a result of the mark's rise against the dollar. Still, this cannot be understood simply as a realiatory action since it is linked to the historical project of European economic integration, and U.S. policy makers are divided in their assessment of whether the Franco-German plan opposes U.S. interests.

**By state managers, I am referring to the more powerful figures at the top of the state apparatus, whether they be in the legislative, executive or judicial branches. To be

structural framework that operates such that pursuit of self-interest by state managers tends to serve the long-term interests of capital. The self-interest of state mangers—their capacity to continue their own rule—depends on the maintenance of reasonable levels of economic activity because economic downturns make likely a change in administration and increasingly severe economic conditions undermine popular support for the reigning economic/political system. Hence, to serve their own interests, state managers have to act to assure reasonable levels of investment. This concern with the investment level provides a powerful disincentive against taking anticapitalist actions and provides a strong incentive for measures to improve the investment climate—measures usually in the long-term interests of capital.

If we recognize that state managers are concerned with preserving and expanding their own power, then it follows that they will be preoccupied with three interrelated goals: (1) to protect their nation's position within the international state system since those who preside over a decline in their nation's political, economic, or military strength are likely to find their own power diminished as their nation's freedom to maneuver internationally declines; (2) to maintain or restore reasonable levels of economic activity; (3) to build or preserve a political base of support that extends into the subordinate classes.*

---

sure, this is a heterogenous group whose interests are by no means uniform, but they share enough in common so that it is reasonable to speak of the interests of state managers. The interests of state managers involve a complex combination of personal interests (as with politicans who want to remain in office) and institutional interests (defense of the state apparatus or of particular bureaucratic entities within it). Although conflicts do emerge, two types of interests are generally mutually reinforcing.

Accumulators refer to the more powerful capitalists—whether owners or managers or both. While there is obviously a high degree of movement back and forth between corporate and government employment, my assumption is that one's current position largely shapes one's consciousness. Secretary of the Treasury Blumenthal, for example, thinks about economic policy differently than he did when he was president of a multinational corporation, and his orientation is likely to shift again when he moves back to the private sector. While there are clearly limits to how much views are likely to change, the demands of a particular position will have a powerful effect on one's approach to specific policy issues, such as the relative mix between internationalism and neomercantilism.

I have developed my ideas on the state in "The Ruling Class Does Not Rule," *Socialist Revolution*, No. 33 (May-June 1977), pp. 6-28.

*I do not mean to suggest a simple relationship between unemployment and political crisis, but it does seem true, particularly in conditions of advanced capitalism, that rising and continuing unemployment undermines the legitimacy of government.

Frequently, these goals are mutually exclusive. The defense of a nation's position in the competitive state system might require substantial diversion of resources toward military spending that could undermine domestic prosperity and weaken the administration's support base. The incompatibility of the second and third goals has been analyzed at length as a conflict between accumulation and legitimation.[9] (See Wolfe, Part V.) State managers have to juggle these often contradictory goals, and the struggle for priority takes the form of interagency conflicts over policy directions. Those at the top of the state apparatus will attempt to mediate these conflicts, but their final decisions will be strongly influenced by the particular balance of bureaucratic forces.

The decision in favor of reference pricing of steel illustrates this process. Reference pricing means that all imports of steel have to be priced above a certain minimal level. This blatant form of protectionism restricts the possible price competitiveness of imports. The Carter Administration was subject to a number of pressures before it responded with this policy initiative. The major steel firms, agitating for some kind of protection against Japanese imports, used various tactics—intensified lobbying, legal procedures against alleged Japanese dumping (selling steel abroad at a price lower than the cost of production in order to undercut the domestic producers in a given country) and the closing of older, less efficient steel works. Union pressure for protection also intensified as large numbers of workers were being thrown out of work by present and expected plant closings.

Despite the intensity of these immediate pressures, the Carter Administration apparently made its concessions to protectionism on the basis of two related long-run considerations. Firstly, it feared that the plant closings in Youngstown, Ohio and Lackawanna, Pennsylvania would be followed by others if the steel industry did not receive protection. Both industry and Administration knew that the next five to ten years would bring substantial increases in steel production in various low wage parts of the underdeveloped world. If free trade prevailed these *potential* imports, as much as current Japanese and European imports, threatened a major decline in domestic steel production. Obviously, the closing of additional steel plants would have worsened the already serious problems of unemployment in the Northeast and Midwest. But national security considerations were at least as important, for the prospects of substantial dependence on imported steel would leave the United States without assured access to an essential component in the production of armaments for conventional warfare.[10] The combination of an explosive situation, rising unemployment, and the national security effects of such a dramatic decline in the domestic steel industry forced the Administration's hand. In this case, the first and third goals—protecting the nation's international position and maintaining a domestic political base—required another lapse from liberal economic principles.

Yet, the state clearly confronts limits on its capacity to pursue neomercantilist economic solutions. If it did not, the fabric of international economic relations would long since have broken down into trade wars and worse. No one country, not even a superpower like the United States, can consistently dictate to all others. Neomercantilist policies provoke countermeasures, which can raise the stakes of intercapitalist competition dramatically. Thus, a government must calculate the effect of its policies on both the nation's international standing and domestic prosperity. The state's capacity to execute effective countermeasures in response to another nation's policies largely depends on its standing within the competitive state system. Japan, for example, could not afford—politically or economically—to take strong measures against the U.S. reference pricing actions on steel. It had to be content with lower level response: for example, retaining certain regulations on U.S. investment in the Japanese economy in the face of U.S. pressure for liberalization. Yet, in other instances even weak powers can exert effective pressure to force a strong power to abandon or modify its neomercantilist initiative.

The possibility of countervailing actions of other states imposes only a partial restraint on state managers, for a combination of differential state power and imperfect information can drive neomercantilist initiatives to the point where significant escalation of economic conflict could result. Here, the perceptions of the internationally oriented segments of the domestic business community come into play. These segments, while not unified, generally maintain some variant of a trilateralist ideology since their interests depend on the smooth working of the international economic system which they tend to regard as highly fragile. When their own particularistic interests are at stake, members of these segments rarely hesitate to pressure the state to violate liberal economic principles.*

*This point—the difference between particular interests and general interests—is essential. Another way of stating it is that these multinational firms depend upon the power of their home state to support them in their international activities. At the same time, they also wish to maximize their own freedom from interference by their home state and by other states. In this sense, their advocacy of internationalism is not abstractly ideological but rooted in practical considerations. This tension is captured well by Richard Barnet and Ronald Muller, *Global Reach* (New York: Simon and

But when they act as a group, their general interest in preserving the fabric of international economic cooperation exerts itself in the form of continuing support for liberal economic principles.

The shared perceptions of these internationally oriented segments tend to become a significant factor whenever an Administration moves in a strongly neomercantilist direction in an effort to resolve domestic contradictions at the expense of foreigners. Even when other nations cannot adopt effective countermeasures, the internationally oriented business community is likely to act as a "peace interest" and agitate for a reduction in tension.[11] It will use various types of influence, including the threat of a "decline in business confidence," which often translates as a drop in stock market prices and a slowing of new domestic investment. In short, these segments can fulfill their own prophecy by precipitating a domestic recession if the Administration refuses to reverse its policies.

A version of this scenario, entailing more subtle forms of business pressure, seems to have occurred in 1971 when Nixon's secretary of the treasury, John Connally, was acting aggressively to force Japan and West Germany to undertake substantial revaluations of their currencies. Even though West Germany and Japan had few effective countertactics to employ, U.S. internationally oriented business began exerting pressure for a modification of the Administration's policies.[12] The Nixon Administration made a significant retreat and was able to reach a settlement with West Germany and Japan. John Connally's tenure as secretary of the treasury did not last much longer; he was replaced by George Schultz in May of 1972.

Similarly, the Carter Administration's no-action dollar policy of 1977 and early 1978 led to increasing dissatisfaction in the internationally oriented business community. Editorials in the U.S. business press insisted that West Germans and Japanese were probably right to resist pressures for faster economic growth.[13] They also argued, with the Germans and Japanese, that the trade deficit problem arose from the Carter Administration's attempt to sustain too strong an economic expansion. This pressure from business circles did not force an immediate change in Administration policy, but it did weaken the government's bargaining position with West Germany and Japan. By late 1978, continuing business pressure—

Schuster, 1974), especially ch. 4. But it is precisely the dependence of firms on their home states that the neo-Kautskians fail to take into account. For a discussion of this weakness of neo-Kautskian scenarios, see *The Origins of International Economic Disorder* pp. 212-215.

most dramatically revealed by intensifying speculation against the dollar—forces the Carter Administration into a major policy shift. On 1 November 1978, the Administration announced a rescue package to save the dollar that included a commitment to massive intervention in the foreign exchange markets and a dramatic increase in domestic interest rates.[14] This upward shift in interest rates was widely seen as increasing the chances of recession, and thus jeopardizing the Administration's ongoing efforts to lower the rate of unemployment.

In situations such as this one, where state managers are pursuing neomercantilist policies and the internationally oriented business community is exerting itself as a "peace interest" urging greater international cooperation, it often remains unclear which group's policies are the more enlightened—that is, which are more sensitive to the long-term interests of capitalism. Neither group is responding to the needs of capitalism as a system; each is acting on its own short-term and long-term interests. The state managers are pursuing policies they regard as necessary for their continued exercise of political power, while the internationally oriented business interests are acting to insure their direct stake in an international economic climate in which they make money.

Often, faulty business perceptions of the fragility of the inter-national economy lead to overreactions against neomercantilist policy initiatives. More important, in opposing neomercantilist intitiatives, internationally oriented business opts for costly domestic policies—slowing down the domestic economy, cutting government spending, and allowing more workers to be displaced by imports. The pursuit of such policies endangers social peace and undermines the legitimacy of the capitalist system. But, even though state managers might be more rational in avoiding such costly domestic policies, the costs of intensified international conflicts are also potentially enormous. The ever-present danger is that neomercantilist policies will provoke an escalating conflict which would seriously damage the international trading and financial system and lead to a global depression—hardly an attractive alternative to a temporary slow-down of the domestic economy. In sum, it is not as though one side or the other has a monopoly on rationality; rather both state managers and business are caught in a continuing contradiction between the needs of the national political economy and the needs of capitalism as a world system.

Conclusion

In context of the preceeding analysis it should now be possible to unravel the complex relationship between Jimmy Carter and trilateralism, and formulate a perspective on future trends. It must be understood that from the start, the trilateral vision had a utopian dimension. There was never a realistic possibility of achieving the kind of economic coordination and cooperation that the trilateralists wanted, since the domestic costs of such coordination were so high for the nations involved—particularly the United States. This utopianism gave rise to a strange reversal: instead of the internationally oriented capitalists using an idealistic politician for their own ends, Carter used the idealistic trilateralists. Carter made maximal use of the Commission both before and after his election. (See Shoup.) Most importantly, the contacts that Carter had made within the business community helped reassure the business community that he could be trusted. The fact that Carter continued to face enormous distrust from the business community only goes to show how desperately he needed the kind of legitimation that the Trilateral connection provided.

But once his Administration was under way, Carter could then proceed to abandon trilateralism. To be sure, he still had to pursue policies to gain the confidence of the business community, but this he did by turning to more conservative domestic economic policies, without pursuing the other aspects of the trilateral platform.

But the corporate trilateralists will almost certainly have the last laugh on Jimmy Carter. Carter's efforts to move in a direction opposing trilateralism have already been frustrated. Rather than continuing his attempt to lower domestic unemployment by exporting it to West Germany and Japan, Carter is presiding over an austerity regime—including both budget cuts and rising unemployment. (See Tabb Part IV.) At this writing, it seems entirely plausible that his forced shift towards conservative economic policies will cost him a second term in the White House.

Yet this outcome is not completely satisfying to the corporate trilateralists either. To be sure, they favor domestic austerity over a turn towards neomercantilism, and they must be reassured that indirect economic pressure can force a president to make that choice. But the initial motivation for launching the Trilateral Commission was a recognition that reliance on such informal pressure and ad hoc measures was no longer adequate for the successful management of the world economy. The trilateral vision—the desire to create a stable structure of international economic cooperation—is rooted in an awareness that capitalism's economic difficulties can erode safeguards on free trade and foster a turn towards neomercantilism and escalating intercapitalist conflict.

The trilateralists can easily imagine circumstances in which state managers decide that the costs of defying the internationally oriented business community are less great than the costs of pursuing liberal economic policies that have a corrosive effect on the domestic social fabric.

This fear is rooted in the historical evidence of the 1930s, when state managers did opt for exchange controls, protectionism, and neomercantilism rather than liberal economic policies. They know it could happen again if continuing economic problems and radical political mobilization of either the Right or the Left dramatically increase the political and social costs to state managers of adherence to the existing international rules of the game.

It was to avert such an outcome that the trilateralists launched their ambitious project. But if the world economy remains mired in stagflation during the next five to ten years, the chances are high that the most sophisticated trilateralist interventions will not suffice to discourage state managers from pursuing increasingly aggressive foreign economic policies, making unbridled interimperialist conflict once more an historical reality.

FOOTNOTES

1. Karl Kautsky, "Ultra-Imperialism," *New Left Review*, No. 59. (1970, originally published 1914), pp. 41-46; V. I. Lenin, *Imperialism* (New York, 1939, originally published 1917). The issue was joined most directly in a debate between Martin Nicolaus and Ernest Mandel in *New Left Review* at the end of the 1960s. See Ernest Mandel, "Where is America Going", *New Left Review*, No. 54 (1969), pp. 3-15; Martin Nicolaus "The Universal Contradiction," *New Left Review*, No. 59, (1970), pp. 3-18; Ernest Mandel, "The Laws of Unequal Development," *New Left Review*, No. 59 (1970), pp. 19-40. Mandel's views are also developed in *Europe vs. America?* (London, 1970), and *Late Capitalism* (London: NLB, 1975), ch. 10. For other contributions to the debate, see Bob Rowthorn, "Imperialism in the Seventies— Unity or Rivalry," *New Left Review*, No. 69 (1971), pp. 31-54; Marty Landsberg, "Multinational Corporations and the Crisis of Capitalism," *Insurgent Sociologist*, VII (1976), pp. 19-33; Nicos Poulantzas, "Internationalization of Capitalist Relations and the Nation-States," *Economy and Society*, III (1974), pp. 145-179.
2. This argument is suggested by Landsberg, *Insurgent Sociologist* VII (1976), pp. 19-33; and by Stephen Hymer, "The Internationalization of Capital," *Journal of Economic Issues*, VI:1 (1972), pp. 91-112. It is developed explicitly in Jeff Frieden, "The Trilateral Commission: Economics and Politics in the 1970s," *Monthly Review* December 1977, pp. 1-18 which appears in updated form in this volume.
3. For expression of the Trilateral Commission's commitment to international cooperation and its opposition to neomercantilism, see the Task Force Reports.
4. Also see Alan Wolfe, *The Limits of Legitimacy* (New York: Free Press, 1977), for a discussion of this aspect of trilateralism.
5. Elizabeth Drew, "Brzezinski," *New Yorker*, 1 May 1978, p. 109.
6. See The Editors, "Comment on Frieden," *Monthly Review*, December 1977, pp. 19-22.
7. The Editors, "Emerging Currency and Trade Wars," *Monthly Review*, February (1978), pp. 1-7. Note that Sweezy and Magdoff do not explicitly address the relationship between capital and the state in the development of this policy, but a corporate interest in a depreciating dollar is implied.

8. See James O'Connor, *The Fiscal Crisis of the State* (New York, 1973), and Wolfe, *Limits of Legitimacy.*

9. The principle source for the critiques of instrumental views of the state is David Gold, Clarence Leo, and Eric Wright, "Recent Developments in the Marxist Theory of the State," *Monthly Review*, October 1975, pp. 29-43, and November 1975, pp. 36-51.

10. Emphasis on the national security component of the Administration's choice of reference pricing builds on an argument of Robert Keohane, "United States Foreign Economic Policy Toward Other Advanced Capitalist States: The Struggle to Make Others Adjust," to appear in Kenneth Oye, et. al., *Contemporary Issues in American Foreign Policy.*

11. The term "peace interest" is Karl Polanyi's, drawn from his discussion of the role of international banks in maintaining peace in Europe in the second half of the 19th century. See Karl Polanyi, *The Great Transformation* (Boston, 1975), pp. 9-14. Bruce M. Russett and Elizabeth C. Hanson, *Interest and Ideology* (San Francisco, 1975) provide some limited but suggestive evidence, based on surveys of internationally oriented businessmen, that supports this argument.

12. An editorial in *Business Week* argued for a moderation in the Administration's policies in the issues of 11 September and 25 September 1971. Hints of domestic business opposition to Connally's policies are provided in Robert Solomon, *The International Monetary System, 1945-1976,* (New York, 1977), pp. 200-201.

13. See, for example, *The Wall Street Journal*, 8 March and 30 March 1978, and *Business Week,* 6 March 1978.

14. *Wall Street Journal* 2 November 1978.

chapter two

REFLECTIONS ON TRILATERALISM AND THE CARTER ADMINISTRATION: CHANGED WORLD REALITIES VS. VESTED INTERESTS

Alan Wolfe

Two years into its first term the Carter Administration developed a foreign policy that seems in perfect continuity with its six predecessors. Hostility toward the Soviet Union has dominated public debate, interventions into Third World countries have been threatened, no fundamental effort has been made to bring the arms race under control, and covert agencies like the CIA remain ubiquitous. Little change has taken place during what has been called "the amateur hour" except for a slight quickening of the Cold War pulse.[1]

Such continuity confirms the suspicions of those who believe that the makers of U.S. foreign policy are all basically cut from the same cloth. Earl Ravenal, for example, a perceptive and articulate critic of U.S. foreign policy, has suggested that the Carter continuity should come as no surprise because the men who make his policies, even though sometimes viewed as dissenters from the Cold War consensus, yet adhere to the contours of the consensus in all basic respects.[2] Richard Barnet and Richard Falk, in a similar vein, have argued that if the postwar consensus on U.S. foreign policy did crack, which to them is dubious, it has rapidly been reestablished, so that little different can be expected from Carter compared to what came before. The U.S. will continue to export the Cold War until a fundamental restructuring of its entire society has been effectuated.[3]

I cannot disagree with the facts as these commentators see them. The persistence of Cold War attitudes and behavior patterns into the Carter Administration is self-evident; one has only to watch Harold Brown testify before Congress or listen to the latest inside information about Zbigniew Brzezinski's moves to know that the Cold War is alive and well in the Pentagon and National Security Council. But I can and will disagree with these observers over what the persistence of Cold War attitudes means. To me it represents not so much the success of U.S. policy makers in overcoming their differences to reestablish a consensus as a failure of the foreign policy establishment to come to grips with a changing world political economy. What I plan to argue in this essay is that the persistence of Cold War thinking itself is an indication of the degree to which the U.S. ruling class has lost control over its foreign policy making process.

At the nub of the issue is the interpretation that one gives to trilateralism. The writing and activities of the Trilateral Commission could be interpreted as window dressing, an attempt by a temporarily displaced elite to develop a reasonable coherence for its ideas so that it could come to power, at which point the fluff would be dropped because it would no longer be needed. Trilateralism, from this point of view, served its purpose once state power had been recaptured by the Democratic Party in 1976.

However, another view of the significance of the Trilateral Commission makes more sense to me. Recognizing that conditions in the world economy and domestic capitalism had altered during the 1960s, a group of elite policy planners met to hammer out a new series of foreign policy guidelines for a set of altered material constraints. Not blinded by an inappropriate chauvanism, they realized that foreign policy as usual—i.e., the Cold War—had become somewhat obsolete. At least nine major economic and political transformations—addressed throughout this volume—had established a new material context. To summarize: *First*, the U.S. had lost in Vietnam, thereby establishing military limits to a Cold War strategy of unreflective intervention. *Second*, U.S. control over the world monetary system was collapsing, and with it the ability of the U.S. to finance its overseas ventures at the expense of the Europeans and Japanese. *Third*, raw material producers were asking for higher prices for basic commodities, thereby transforming, in some degree, relationships between North and South. *Fourth*, facing stagnation, numerous economies were flirting with protectionism, thereby threatening free trade arrangements that had been of substantial benefit to U.S. manufacturers. *Fifth*, within the United States rising unemployment and persistent inflation had produced an economic situation that was pleasing very few and was undermining domestic harmony. *Sixth*, the economies of certain U.S. allies, especially West Germany and Japan, were moving into the vacuum created by the U.S. failure. *Seventh*, economic links between the United States and the Soviet Union were growing, as the latter became more dependent on U.S. wheat and transistors while the West had its eye on Soviet natural gas. *Eighth*, China was rapidly achieving major power status as its hostility toward the Soviet Union increased. *Ninth*, U.S.-based multinationals were establishing international economic links that, like the Rothschild banking empire of the nineteenth century, looked askance at political and military hostilities.

Each of these transformations had an effect on the Cold War posture of the United States. Military defeat in Vietnam meant that intervention would have to be more selective. A lack of control over the world monetary system made it difficult for the United States to spend unlimited amounts on arms for overseas use. Higher raw material prices contributed to inflation, and high defense budgets would intensify that aspect of the economy even further. Protectionist sentiment struck at the core of the liberal ideology that the U.S. was supposed to be defending in its foreign adventures. Rising unemployment and domestic disharmony contributed to a distrust of government that undermined the ability of governments to fight wars. The rise of West Germany and Japan meant that more attention had to be paid to economic conflicts, often at the expense of geopolitical ones. Economic ties between the United States and the Soviet Union contradicted the anti-Soviet hostility necessary to flame the Cold War. The entry of China into the picture destroyed the myth of monolithic communism so essential to earlier Cold War ventures like Korea. And finally, U.S.-based multinationals preferred to bring about their own conception of world order through trade and finance rather than relying on state-based methods like military intervention. The total effect of all these changes was to raise the issue of whether the Cold War as usual was the appropriate foreign policy stance of a revised U.S. capitalism.

The problem facing the U.S. foreign policy making establishment in the late 1960s and the 1970s was how to bring about a new approach to the world appropriate for changing material realities without at the same time alientating itself from the vested interests that prefer the status quo. While it is true that the economic realities within which U.S. foreign policy making was embedded had changed, it is also true that certain vested interests will resist change as much as they can. In postwar United States, conservative vested interests had entrenched themselves in two basic places. Within the government, a group of policy planners devoted to preserving the Cold War mood had solidified themselves in the

Pentagon, the armed services, the intelligence agencies, and other important bureaus. They had a self-interest in keeping the Cold War alive, to be sure, but they were also ideologues who genuinely believed in their anticommunism and were willing to pursue their passion whatever the economic consequences. And in the private sector, defense contractors and other major manufacturing industries connected to them (rubber, steel, etc.) could be counted on to support high defense budgets and Cold War assumptions. The problem for policy makers became one of revising the defense posture of the United States in such a way as to take account of changing material realities while at the same time making such changes palatable to these vested interests.

The Trilateral Commission became one of the elite agencies that sought to walk the narrow line between economic necessity and vested political power. From the start, its difficulties were enormous. If it moved too far toward change, attempting to bring the defense posture of the United States in line with changing world economic realities, it risked losing power and opening itself up to attack from the bureaucracy and the military-industrial complex. On the other hand, if it sought to solidify its position by making alliances with the vested interests, it would lose the ability to develop ideas or plans that could accommodate to the new realities. Elite planning under these circumstances requires a heroic combination of economic analysis and political cunning.

While the Trilateral Commission had numerous resources to bring about its goals, especially including Rockefeller money and access to state power in the Carter Administration, it has not succeeded. Little talk is heard of new policies and plans for a revised global order and instead the Cold War has been resumed. Why, with all its power and prestige has the Trilateral Commission been unable to bring about a transformation in U.S. foreign policy? Among the answers to this question, three factors would seem to be of special significance: the disjuncture between a rapidly changing economic universe and a conservative political one; the tendency of vested interests to prefer the *status quo* even to the point of their own suicide; and the inability of a fraction of the ruling class to pursue partial reforms under conditions when more wholesale alternations are necessary.

Economic Circumstances Change Far More Rapidly Than Political Structures

Although the economies of capitalist societies go through periodic convulsions—ranging from business cycles to long waves to structural transformations—political systems are expected to remain constant. It is a source of pride to Americans that their Constitution has been so little altered, yet if a businessman were to brag about a corporation that had operated according to the same procedural rules for two hundred years, he would be viewed as somewhat loony by his competitors. There will always be, in other words, a disjuncture between the rapid economic transformations that develop out of capitalist productive relationships (particularly on a world scale where planning is much more difficult) and a bureaucratic state apparatus at home that does not want even to acknowledge change, let along adjust to it.

What is true of political institutions is also true of polical attitudes. Citizens form their expectations about political society during periods when the economy is performing one way; when the economy reverses itself those deeply ingrained views often do not change. An entire generation that was brought up during the depression never quite adjusted to postwar prosperity, and a generation that has known postwar prosperity cannot bring itself to accept recent stagflation. Capitalist economies often perform like automobiles that are still moving backwards even though forward gears have been engaged.

These somewhat general thoughts must be of acute concern to elite managers during periods of rapid economic change. In the 1945-1948 period, for example, when a new world order under U.S. hegemony came into being, it was a major preoccupation of State Department policy makers to transform U.S. opinion. "The greatest danger to the whole postwar planning, second only to winning the war...", Secretary of State Cordell Hull had written, "is the question of securing the support of the electorate for our postwar course."[4] In this task policy makers of that generation had a major advantage. They could make a reasonable case that if Americans overcame their isolationist prejudices against imperialism, material benefits and the avoidance of depression would be their reward. Nonetheless, the architects of the postwar economic order devoted a tremendous amount of time to ensuring that political attitudes would keep pace with material transformations. In essence, they were forced to flame the Cold War in order to bring about the required transformations in both the structure of the U.S. state and popular attitudes compatible with U.S. domination over the world economy.

Compared to their predecessors, the planners of the Trilateral Commission had a much more difficult task. First of all, one scare campaign had already been used, making a second that much more difficult. (No matter how hard he tried, Carter could not convince the American public that the energy crisis was the moral equivalent of war; perhaps the Cold War was one war too many.) Secondly, the contraction of the world economy meant that the new message must emphasize restraint, and it is much harder to convince people to accept less than to force more down their throats. And third, the generation of the 1940s had a fairly clear political field, since the Right had been discredited by its profascist sympathies and the Left was being repressed through a concerted campaign. In contrast, the trilateralists faced a situation in which the Left did mobilize a popular campaign against the Vietnam War and in which the Right is stonger than ever. Under these conditions, the Trilateral Commission was never able to engage, let alone win, the battle for public opinion that its vision of a world order required.

Evidence for the inability of the trilateralists to transform democratic opinion and the structure of the state in order to put their plans into practice is pervasive, but the clearest example is the fate of Carter's energy legislation. West Germany has proven that it is possible to absorb higher energy costs without generating large-scale price increases if state direction of the economy permits a continuation of export-led growth. The West German experience frustrates U.S. global policy makers. Without a state-directed program for managing energy resources, the U.S. cannot even hope to recapture a competitive edge for its exports. Yet while export-led growth would be, as it was in the late 1940s, a boon to the economy as a whole, oil producers and their allies in the U.S. Congress, never known for their far-sighted vision, will block any program that does not include for them substantial *immediate* profits. Carter's only workable strategy in this context would have been to go over the heads of local elites to rally support for a trilateral energy policy, but this would have meant an attack on corporate privilege. Carter could not exercise that option, and he was forced to sit back helplessly as his best laid plans for a long-term energy policy were devastated by Congress.*

*ed. note: After 1978, Carter's energy program made rapid progress. In June 1980, however, Congress soundly defeated his proposed oil-import fee which would have been passed on to consumers as a 10-cent surcharge on a gallon of gas at the pump. The Energy Mobilization Board has been stalled by opponents whose power lies at the state and local level and who fear federal direction. (For more on Carter's (trilateral) energy program see Garitty, and Kaufman and Clawson.)

Two lessons were reenforced by the experience of the energy program in the eyes of global policy makers: Congress cannot be trusted to make policy and people cannot be trusted to know what is in their long-term interest. In other words, the energy experience reveals the degree to which trilateralism is in opposition to both the structure of the state and to democratic opinion. There is nothing surprising about this. Trilateral theorist Samuel Huntington mused on both these problems in *The Crisis of Democracy.*[5] The structure of the state has concerned Huntington for some time. Long before the Trilateral Commission was even an idea, he wrote an essay arguing that Congress was "local" and the executive "cosmopolitan" so that only the latter could be trusted with the national interest.[6] This is fully in accord with the Hamiltonian view of a strong president, directing economic growth for the benefit, even if against the desires, of a national capitalist elite.[7] The new ingredient for Huntington in his trilateral report was the explicitly antidemocratic sentiment that called for curbs on popular government in order to make capitalism function more efficiently. (See Wolfe Part V.) As he watched the popular preference for cheap gasoline interfere with both strategic interests in the Middle East and trade problems with Europe, Huntington, from his vantage point on the Naitonal Security Council, surely must have felt confirmed in his diagnosis.

The obvious solution to these problems for policy planners would be to concentrate power in the executive and to find ways of curtailing public opinion. This is a solution, however, that is not very feasible. For one thing, Nixon tried both strategies and was brought down, making it far more difficult for a candidate who ran aginst Nixonianism to do either. But there is another more important reason, for if Carter were inclined to perform a mini-coup from above, he would not allow mere political hyprocricy to stand in the way. The crucial reason why an antidemocratic attack is not in the offing has to do with a fundamental characteristic of U.S. politics, one that Huntington surprisingly misses. This is that in the United States democratic pressure often comes more strongly from the Right than it does from the Left, making it impossible for conservative elites, whether Republicans or Democrats, to control it.

In most countries throughout the world, large majorities are to be found in favor of the welfare state and governmental programs designed to redistribute income and curb private accumulation. To some extent this is true of the United States as well, where, despite strong sentiment for tax relief, majorities regularly favor a national health insurance system and other aspects of the welfare state. Yet in the United States, as I have argued at length elsewhere, social democratic tendencies have taken the form of military Keynesianism.[8] The politically acceptable method of providing a governmental stimulus to the economy and allowing some degree of social planning (from highways to education) was to do so under the rubric of national defense. A coalition was formed led by the Democratic Party and by progressives for warfare as well as welfare, so that in the United States both *national* security and *social* security are inextricably combined; the Rebublican Right, for example, has opposed both. From its inception circa 1946, the Cold War governmental machinery has been the creation of liberal and centrist Democrats and their allies in the unions and the university-military-industrial complex.[9]

The peculiar social democratic cast to Cold War liberalism has colored the nature of political discourse in the United States. Insofar as popular majorities can be mobilized for anything, they tend to be strongly supportive of one aspect or another of Cold War liberalism: hostility toward communism, support for the defense budget, and the promotion of U.S. chauvanism. This coloration confuses the nature of democratic opinion, since it results in popular pressure for a continuation of the status quo, not, as in Western Europe, demands in favor of extending social reforms. But just as Cold War liberalism confuses democratic pressure, it also is upsetting to anti-democratic sentiment. Conservative elites in Europe have an unambiguous program: they are opposed to the welfare state and, like the antitax politician Mogens Glistrup of Denmark, they are opposed to a defense establishment as well. In the United States, however, to oppose warfare is politically suicidal. Conservative demagogues, no matter how virulent their antistate rhetoric, must support the Cold War apparatus or find themselves cut off from the right wing businessmen that finance and legitimate conservative demagogues. In this highly unusual situation, one must attack the state but exempt one of the largest bureaucracies; rail against inflation but never mention the greatest cause; call for tax cuts yet demand an increase in defense costs; and denounce governmental inefficiency while ignoring cost overruns and guaranteed profits. It is difficult terrain in which to build a conservative reaction against the state.

Cold War liberalism is in many ways the major obstacle to an implementation of Huntington's cure for the "democratic distemper." Any attempt by this administration or any other to curtail democracy would, in the peculiar atmosphere of U.S. politics, entail the opposition of the huge complex that has organized around military Keynesianism. As Carter is finding out, a broad-based coalition involving labor, defense contractors, conservative intellectuals, former Cold War policy makers, intelligence operatives, and wealthy contributors to the Democratic Party has the power to block any initiatives in the direction of a new global stance for the United States. Moreover, these groups can do so by claiming the mantle of social democracy; it is they who favor jobs and Carter who opposes them; they who speak for the masses while the Administration is elitist; they who have the unions and the workers on their side while the trilateralists have the multinationals. The tremendous support that Cold War liberalism has in the Congress, in the bureaucracy, and in the public mind means that any attempt to centralize power will arouse the fury of those who first created and then kept alive through most difficult times the Cold War consensus. In the face of that, the antidemocrats on the Trilateral Commission have very little leverage to put into practice an executive-oriented, top-down administrative machinery. The reality of U.S. politics is that Cold War vested interests have co-opted democratic rhetoric more effectively than executive branch policy planners.

Unable to implement the recommendations of *The Governability of Democracies,* the Carter Administration finds itself at the mercy of a political system and a set of attitudes that refuse to adopt to new economic realities no matter how pressing. There is every reason to believe, as trilateralists like Cyrus Vance and Paul Warnke argued in 1976, that the persistence of Cold War patterns does irreparable damage to the U.S. economy in the form of inflation, negative trade balances, and support for unproductive investment.[10] Yet a sophisticated understanding of the sources of capitalist stagnation means little if a ruling class is unable to win political support for the programs necessary to rejuvenate accumulation. Carter, and the trailteralists who advise him, find themselves in the awkward position of having better theory than practice; understanding capitalism better than democracy, they know what they need to do but cannot figure out a way to do it.

Vested Interests Will Protect Themselves to the Point of Suicide

The tenacious hold that the doctrines of Cold War liberalism have on popular consciousness is reinforced by a propaganda campaign waged by vested interests that have benefitted from military Keynesianism. Government reorganization is such a compelling theme to executive-oriented elites because any plan for shifting power away from Congress or bureaucratic departments automatically involves breaking the power of obstructionist interests that have entrenched themselves in such comfortable resting places. This is why very class conscious administrations in twentieth century United States—Theodore Roosevelt, Wilson, F.D.R., Truman, and Kennedy—all have made a stab at attacking vested interests through the reorganization of the state. Truman, for example, after at first not realizing their significance, took an active part in the debates that unified the Armed Services, created the CIA, and gave the president overall supervision of U.S. imperial apparatus. The fight was a bitter one, but it was essential to wage it if a new administration was to create a state responsible for the worldwide exercise of U.S. power.

The very structure brought into being during the Truman Administration had become a problem by the time the Trilateral Commission was formed. Intelligence agencies had grown too unwieldy, disrupting the business of diplomacy and bringing about public disenchantment with imperial policies. Privileges reserved for the service branches in order to win their support for unification had gotten out of hand, as each one, lobbying for its own expensive toys, drove defense costs higher. The State Department, first rendered conservative during the McCarthy period, had become incapable of providing new ideas and needed a shaking up. In the bureaucratic swamp that dominated the making of national security policy, no overarching agency had merged to enforce discipline. Consequently, bureaucratically powerful cold warriors were operating unchecked, leading not only to duplication but to contradictory policies all over the globe. One of the main concerns of the Trilateral Commission was to reorganize the making of foreign policy so that some sense of order and consistency could be brought to the U.S. global stance.

Compared to the changes instituted by Roosevelt, Truman, and even Kennedy, Carter's attempts to control vested interests in Congress and the bureaucracy seem to have failed. Congress is unwilling to listen to him and has to be pushed beyond rationality to support even moderate changes in U.S. global posture (e.g. Panama). The intelligence agencies defeated Carter's first choice to revamp the CIA (Theodore Sorenson) and have proven themselves able to control the second. Defense Secretary Brown, with the exception of the B-1 bomber, has opted not to try and control wasteful weapons proliferation but is asking for ever growing defense budgets. An attempt by Carter people in the National Security Council to write an overall assessment of the U.S. global posture, which finally emerged as a document known as PRM-10, was torn apart by dissenting cold warriors. Rather than centralized, foreign policy under Carter has been so contradictory and directionless that the Administration seems more adept at fighting with itself than it does with the rest of the world.

In searching for answers to the failure of the trilateralists to bring about a centralized state apparatus that would be able to control and contain vested interests, one first looks to Carter's flaws as a leader, for the man's incompetence must lead sophisticated elite managers to gnash their teeth in frustrated silence. Yet the reasons are as much structural as they are idiosyncratic. Unlike the 1945-48 period, severe obstacles to a transformation of the state apparatus exist, particularly: the ratchet effect of state expansion and the necessity for choice imposed by declining economic conditions.

Economists use the term ratchet effect to describe a process whereby things do not return to normal at the same rate at which they become abnormal. For example, if a sudden burst of inflation hits an economy, when it settles down it will do so at an uneven rate, distributing itself in a herky-jerky fashion the way a ratchet controls a gear wheel. The metaphor describes political changes as well as economic ones. When the state goes through a sudden expansion, with new agencies and bureaus created, it establishes a bulwark that resists contraction when conditions change. In the immediate postwar period, elite planners discovered that they could centralize power away from specific interests by allowing the state apparatus to grow. The result was a dramatic increase in the size and density of the federal bureaucracy, particularly that part of it devoted to national security affairs. But when it becomes necessary to control that growth itself, which is the current problem, it is as difficult to bring down the size of government as it is to reduce prices. The state simply does not contract at the same rate at which it expands.

The consequences of the ratchet effect of government growth will be intensified when an expanding economy does not allow for an expanding state. Government spending, in a capitalist economy, is not always a panacea for economic stagnation. If conditions in the world economy are favorable, then it is possible for an increase in state spending to pump enough money into the economy to stimulate the private sector to invest. In 1945, conditions were perfect for military Keynesianism to work, and radical economists who explained why it was important to have a military budget in order to absorb an economic surplus were correct.[11] Moreover, military spending had a dual effect favorable to expansion, for not only did state spending fuel the economy, it also fueled the state. That is to say, the increased level of government spending drove the economy forward, and a driving economy allowed an expansion of the amount of government spending. Under these kinds of conditions, intense political conflicts could be bought off by allowing government to grow. When Truman or Kennedy wished to provide overall direction to the national security apparatus, they could do so without cutting back on the prerogatives of specific interests. Indeed, because of expanding economic conditions, they could hold out the "sweetener" of an increase in prerogatives in order to win support for centralizing mechanisms.

No such luxurious economic circumstances benefit the trilateralists. Unless there are frequent control mechanisms, which are politically difficult to impose on powerful institutions like defense contractors that have a lock on both the private sector and the public, government spending will at some point begin to tip toward unproductive expenditure and wasteful depletion, as other radical economists have argued.[12] When these tendencies are reenforced by a downturn in the world economy, as took place in the late 1960s, then the same military Keynesianism that once stimulated economic growth becomes an obstacle to its continuation.[13] At the same time, economic conditions that were favorable to the expansion of government turn in on themselves. A contracting economy no longer permits an administration to buy off conflicts between vested interests. Choices must be made, and as they are, preferences for one entrenched interest over another are made—such as the Army over the air force and navy in the defense budget for Fiscal Year (FY) 1979. When this occurs, all hell breaks loose. No vested interest is likely to accept without a struggle a diminution of its privileges.

What trilateralists are discovering as they set about trying to control the uncontrollable is a basic lesson about the difficulties of planning in a capitalist society. It has long been argued, both by Marxist and conservative economists, that an economic system based upon private investment decisions will resist planning. The nub of the argument is that any proposals that are strong enough to plan will be opposed by capitalists and any notions that are acceptable to capitalists will by their very nature not be capable of altering the economy. In a recent restatement of this position, Charles Lindblom described market economies as having all fingers and no thumbs (compared to socialist planning mechanisms that are characterized by him as having all thumbs and no fingers).[14] There is no reason to expect that answers have been found to this central contradiction of advanced capitalism. In many ways the contradiction has in fact intensified, for now, it can be argued, the same struggle has been extended to the state itself. Within bureaucratic apparatuses, tremendous conflicts between what is in the interest of the state as a whole and what is beneficial to specific sectors within the state are being fought out.

Under these kinds of conditions, those vested interests that have sawed off and claimed as their own a piece of public authority face a choice as an administration seeks to achieve centralization. They could decide, at least in theory, that what is in the long term interests of the state as a whole will ultimately benefit them and try to accept reform as necessary. If they try this tactic, however, they will discover what investors in the market know, that someone will take advantage of their generosity and undermine their position. Having an exclusive piece of the state is a most valuable form of property. As political scientists like Grant McConnell and Theodore Lowi have argued, public authority in the United States is clothed with private power; state actions are intimately connected with the privileges of all kinds of private constituents that exist solely off the benefits they receive from government.[15] Under these conditions, the option of accepting a long-term reform of the state apparatus is effectively closed in practice. Any bureau that tried to accept a change in the state as a whole would be outflanked and undermined by constituents demanding profit and privilege as usual. In short, the reason why vested interests will oppose centralizing reforms that would in the long-run benefit them is not because they are shortsighted and conservative but because the structural incorporation of the market into the state allows them no choice but to exercise a preference for their narrow privilege over rhetoric stressing their ultimate interest in reform. Advanced capitalism has not so much tempered the effects of the market by using the state as it has transformed the state according to the logic of the market. This is one of the reasons why planning, even at the elite level, is so often frustrated.

The contradiction between specific sectors of the state and the state as a whole has become so intense that any program of elite management will have to go through Herculean attempts to overcome it. The Trilateral Commission is not Herculean. As a planning body associated with a capitalist class, it can only go so far in trying to bring about long-term change. Neither in the economy nor the state is there an incentive structure that allows for long-term needs to be fulfilled. (See Block.) At some point the political costs of trying to force vested interests to change become so enormous that retreat becomes the only possible option short of an all out civil war within the state that would benefit all the enemies of the imperial order. The trilateralists found out how quickly that point can be reached. Their reforms were not especially far reaching. They wanted more free trade to stimulate the world economy; greater international cooperation on monetary matters; and changes within the structure of the U.S. state apparatus that would facilitate reaccumulation, for example. Yet the first means fewer short-term profits for U.S. manufacturers (at the expense of more efficient overseas industry); the second, less profit from currency speculation (in which quite a number of respectable banks are most likely engaged); and the last, a circumvention of the enormously profitable links between public agencies and private corporations. No substantial progress could be made toward any of these goals without curtailing privileges, which raises the question of what leverage the

Trilateral Commission had to wage a war on vested interests.

At this point a surprising irony enters the picture. It is possible to imagine one set of circumstances in which an elite planning body could undermine entrenched power in the state. If there were a strong working class, one highly organized into unions and willing to support a reorganization of capital, then an elite planning body might consider the use of its power in the electoral arena to force changes in the bureaucracy. Such a situation exists in Italy, and it helps explain why the leading Italian trilateralist, Giovanni Agnelli, has called for the incorporation of the Italian Communist Party (PCI) into the state, Trilateralism, an antidemocratic, procapitalist, heavily elitist movement, is in the awkward position of being dependent upon strong Left parties for its success. Without a strong Left, in other words, trilateralism has neither the will nor the political support to wage a war on vested interests. The very elitism and anti-working class nature of the U.S. branch of trilateralism is the most important reason for its impotence. (The U.S. ambassador to Rome, trilateralist Richard Gardner, for example, opposes the entry of the P.C.I. into government). Trilateralism could work only if it were willing to help organize and sustain the U.S. working class. No wonder that early in 1978 one high Carter official told the *New Yorker*'s Elizabeth Drew that trilateralism was already dead.[16] And many of its adherents would prefer it dead than accept a rejuvenated working class as the price of keeping it alive.

There is No Such Thing as a Partial Cold War (Just as There Can Be No Such Thing as a Partial Welfare State

From its beginnings, trilateralism adopted a time-honored approach to its basic dilemma. Caught between its need to adopt a vision and a fear that any change would threaten interests tied to the status quo, it chose to try and find a middle way. If the Cold War was causing economic problems, but there was going to be tremendous resistance to a relaxation of Cold War tensions, then the obvious solution was to go halfway, to try and create a partial Cold War. Similarly, if domestic demands on the state for power by ordinary people were too high, but if it were politically impossible to abolish either democracy or the welfare state, then what one needed was a partial approach. In its plans for both domestic political life and foreign policy, a distinguishing feature of most of the trilateral plans was their attempt to find a middle ground between unpalatable alternatives. As one trilateral report noted:

> ...an effective strategy must avoid either of two mistakes: (1) the excessive pragmatism of seeking to solve problems solely on a day-to-day basis; or (2) the visionary longterm approach that

does not concern itself sufficiently with the practical steps for achieving the ultimate goal. Both approaches to politics have much the same consequence: Both tend to support the *status quo*, the short-term approach by merely tinkering with the symptoms of the problem, the utopian by fleeing from the realm of the feasible. In the last analysis, both leave the real problems unsolved until breakdowns or explosive changes occur.[17]

The Commission's words are fully in accord with the general strategy of most ruling elites: in most places at most times, the pursuit of the middle road is the surest method of holding onto power for any fraction of an elite. But neither is this an iron law. From the Russian Mensheveks to the German Weimar Republic, there are numerous examples where the zealous pursuit of moderation failed to achieve political unity. And even in the United States, episodes like the McCarthy period stand out as instances where the middle ground collapsed. Under such circumstances, the middle path may well be the trilateralist's utopian option. Trying to find a balance where no balance can exist is hardly practical and realistic. Such, I will argue, is the situation at the present time, for it is inherent in the nature of both the Cold War and the welfare state that one must have them reasonably fully or not at all. Each establishes a logic that must be completed. Neither can exist halfway. The attempt to create a partial Cold War and a partial welfare state is bound to fail.

The Cold War itself is a halfway house between peace and an all out war. Yet its very ambiguity is what makes it integral. For a successful Cold War to exist, domestic populations must on the one hand be assured that, barring the most unusual circumstances, their way of life will not be threatened, yet at the same time be convinced that an international emergency requires their perpetual vigilance. In a peculiar sense an all-out war, if seen by the population as legitimate, requires a lower-level of ideological tension than a Cold War, for the existence of fighting and deprivation themselves constitute enough of an incentive to rally the people. But in a cold war situation, without death and disruption, ideological hostility must be intense or else passion will drain away and peace sentiments prevail. At the onset of the Cold War, Senator Vandenberg delivered his famous advice to Truman to "scare the hell out of the American people." The interesting point is that Roosevelt never had to scare people to fight against Hitler; a hot war and a genuine threat were all the scares that anyone needed.

It is naive to believe that one can relax tensions with the Soviet Union and at the same time keep alive a substantial part of the Cold War apparatus built up to sustain that tension. The failure of the trilateralists to learn this lesson can be seen in the astounding success of a cold war organization called the Committee on the Present Danger. After Carter took office, he appointed so many trilateralists to important policy making positions that he bypassed—some say snubbed—that aggressive group of Cold War fanatics that had worked for every Democratic president since Truman. Apparently frozen out of state power, the cold warriors counterattacked. Basing themselves on the unproved assertion that the Soviet Union was a clear and present danger to the United States—a notion that has more credence in the fantasy world of Washington politics than it does in the world as a whole—the Committee has forced Carter to kow-tow to its demands in one area after another.[18] Trilateral policy makers are in power, but the policies they are making belong to someone else. They have not found a middle road. Instead, trying to appease the cold warriors, they are bending over backwards to acknowledge that they too understand the dangers of the Soviet military build-up. Yet strange as it may seem, rather than co-opting the Right (as any such move would under normal circumstances), the *Right becomes stronger the more the center tries to woo it.* The price the trilateralists are being forced to pay in order to hold power is the public repudiation of their own ideas.

Even within the Trilateral commission itself, a backhand acknowledgement of the impossibility of a partial Cold War has been given. Although the Commission sought mightily to find a middle ground in East-West relations—publishing for example a report that sought to create the basis for U.S.-Soviet cooperation in a number of areas.[19]—it retreated in its comprehensive overview of the East-West situation. Commissioning such old-fashioned hardliners as Jeremy Azreal of the University of Chicago and Berlin's Richard Lowenthal to write its report, the Trilateral Commission fashioned a document that conceded little if anything to the cold warriors of the Committee on the Present Danger. The report indicates that a return to ideological hostility still remains the preferred method of dealing with the Russians.[20]

Azreal and Lowenthal (and the third author, Tohru Nakagawa of Japan) concede that the Soviet Union has sought at times to cooperate with the United States, acknowledge that there is an economic crisis in Russia, and even admit that Soviet military technology is behind that of the United States in a number of key areas. Nonetheless, the East-West crisis is for them the focal point of world power, and the United States must orient its strategic apparatus toward the Soviet Union. But the rationale for an anti-Soviet foreign policy can no longer by the irrelevant notion of Soviet expansion. Instead the authors seek a new set of arguments for the continuation of the old ideology.

The key issue is whether a stable world order has been created. Henry Kissinger made stability the hallmark of his policy, but these particular trilateralists take pains to remind us that stability is an illusion. If we accept stability, they argue, then we "confine the West to defensive goals and to a reactive political attitude." What we need is old-fashioned meddling, but in new-fangled garb: "the West should not be content to defend its fundamental values and seek to implement them on its own territory: it should set itself the objective to influence the natural processes of change that occur in the Third World and even in the Communist world in a direction that is favorable rather than unfavorable to those values."

Some idea of what this return to Wilsonian morality would mean can be seen in the example of Western Europe. Should the United States be concerned about Communist participation in Italian or French governments? Yes, this report argues, but not for the obvious reasons. The problem is not strategic but political. Communist participation would undermine attempts toward European integration and allow the Soviet Union to take advantage of rivalries among major capitalist powers. If this were to happen, the capacity of the West to present a united front to the rest of the world would be undermined, and therefore the West could less effectively meddle in order to promote its values. Eurocommunism is therefore seen not as a threat to the West's military power but to its political cohesiveness.

From this, it is a short step to the argument that the United States must build more weapons than the Soviet Union, not in order to defend itself but to preserve its political options. This is exactly what the report concludes, that the West should seek a nuclear strategic superiority that would be politically meaningful. This means that we should support arms control only if it is backed by military force, a position quite at odds with other trilateralists like Paul Warnke. This is the arms race with a vengeance.

Why does it seem impossible to escape the Cold War, even when economic conditions in the advanced capitalist world demand a relaxation of tensions? The answer lies in domestic politics, particularly in the power of the vested interests that reap short-term benefits from military spending. The web of half-truths and misperceptions that have sustained those interests since 1945 has grown to the point where it entangles almost every aspect of political life in the United States. A web of that encompassing a nature cannot be slowly unravelled by starting at its most completed end but must be brushed away with a decisive sweep of the hand. Short of that step, the web will entangle anyone that tries to limit it. Carter's only option in bringing about a new direction for U.S. foreign policy would have been to declare himself a peace president *a la* Sadat and simply refuse to play the anti-Soviet game. There is enough peaceful sentiment in the minds of ordinary people that such a gamble might prove successful. But a layer of intervening elites closely tied to Cold War methods of doing business stands in the way. Carter is not the man, and the Democrats not the party, to try it. Understanding that a limited approach to the relaxation of Cold War tensions failed before it even began, Carter moved more toward normality and became a Cold War president like the rest. He now understands what the Trilateral Commission at first did not, that a middle of the road position on the Cold War does not exist.

Much the same can be said for the welfare state. When *The Crisis of Democracy* was published it had a certain logical elegance that pleased academics but it contained political implications that frightened the politicians on the Trilateral Commission. Whatever secret fantasies one harbors about an anti-democratic coup, one never puts these notions into books and articles if one is considering public office. The immediate response on the part of the "realists" within the Commission was that even if Huntington's analysis were correct, governments would have to approach restrictions on democracy gingerly if at all. As was the case with the Cold War, a halfway approach seemed best: one that called for a halt to the expansion of the welfare state, sought fiscal integrity, called forth symbolic gestures to win public support, and spoke of an era of limited expectations and governmental incompetence. The welfare state would not so much be abolished as halted in its tracks while new solutions to social problems emphasizing markets would be developed.[21] (See Tabb Part IV.)

But, as it turns out, a partial welfare state is as difficult to realize as a partial Cold War. At stake in the debate over the responsibility of government, as Huntington pointed out, was not the economic issue of the fiscal crisis but the political one of the rights of ordinary people.[22] If the matter were simply one of trying to bring budgets under control, a middle of the road position might make sense, gradually curtailing expenditures and raising taxes. But if the issue is political, then the middle ground dissolves. On the one hand, social services establish certain expectations which, as Daniel Bell has noted, tend to rise.[23] Once they have been given social security, it is difficult to keep people from wanting health insurance. Even in the United States, the welfare state has never lost its popularity. On the other hand, any attempts by centrist factions to speak the language of fiscal responsiblity and restraint fuels a right wing reaction against the welfare state *in toto*. Reactionaries are simply better at tax-cutting rhetoric than centrist Democrats. If the public mood becomes one of seeking large-scale tax reductions, then political discourse will be led by the extreme Right, as already appears to be the case. Both Carter and California Governor Jerry Brown have learned that when they try to appear as conservatives, they undermine their own base in the middle and find themselves running after the Right, always trying to keep up with a mood that outstrips them.

For the moment the public mood seems to be one of mouthing the Right's rhetoric of tax cuts and limitations on government while electing Democrats to preside over the resulting mess. There is an apparent stand-off. The Right is frustrated because its ideas are being adopted as it is being excluded from power and the Democrats are frustrated because they are in power but unable to develop any ideas. This is not the kind of atmosphere in which ready solutions to contradictions are possible. It is one that allows Carter to fudge his position with somewhat more leeway than he can over the Cold War, but the underlying problem remains the same. If middle of the road forces push for a restriction on the welfare state, they will find themselves outflanked by the Right. But if they press for its continuation, they will have to extend the welfare state to more and more areas, especially including health care. Partial solutions and expediencies may result in some buying of time, but they are severely inappropriate for ending the stand-off.

In conclusion, the United States is faced with a situation in which the general policy positions adopted since World War II no longer seem to work. A ruling class strategy demands bold action. Yet any bold action will arouse intense political opposition. Caught in an impossible bind, U.S. trilateralists have resigned themselves to the inevitable and has dropped any pretense of bringing about a new world order, a revised global posture for the United States, or a restructuring of the state. Instead they have chosen to pursue politics as usual, including a rekindling of the Cold War and futile attempts to proves their fiscal responsibility. The status quo is preserved. The only trouble is that the present historical moment is one in which the most class-conscious planners know that the preservation of the status quo could lead to disaster. To the extent that nothing changes, including the Cold War, to that extent things will have to change. Elites can plan, but putting their plans into effect is far more problematic.

FOOTNOTES

1. Thomas L. Hughes, "Carter and the Management of Contradictions," *Foreign Policy*, 31 (Summer 1978), pp. 34-55.

2. Earl C. Ravenal, "Foreign Policy Made Difficult," in Richard Fagen (ed.), *Capital and the State in U.S.-Latin American Relations* / 1979, (Stanford: Stanford University Press, 1979).

3. Richard J. Barnet and Richard A. Falk, "Cracking the Consensus: America's New Role in the World," *Working Papers for a New Society* (March-April 1978), 41-48.

4. Cited in Alfred E. Eckes, Jr., *A Search for Solvency* (Austin: University of Texas Press, 1975), p. 63.

5. Samuel P. Huntington et al., *The Crisis of Democracy* (New York: New York University Press, 1975).

6. Samuel P. Huntington, "Congressional Responses to the Twentieth Century," In David B. Truman (ed.), *The Congress and America's Future*, (Englewood Cliffs: Prentis Hall, 1973), pp. 6-38.

7. For the importance of Hamiltonianism to Huntington see his book *The Soldier and the State* (New York: Vintage, 1964), pp. 270-71.

8. Alan Wolfe and Jerry Sanders, "Resurgent Cold War Ideology: The Case of the Committee on the Present Danger," in Fagen, *op. cit.*

9. The best account of the politics of Cold War liberalism is Franz Schurman, *The Logic of World Power* (New York: Pantheon, 1975).

10. United Nations Association of the United States, *Controlling the Conventional Arms Race* (New York: UNA-USA, 1976).

11. Paul Baran and Paul Sweezy, *Monopoly Capital* (New York: Monthly Review Press, 1967).

12. Seymour Melman, *The Permanent War Economy* (New York: Simon and Schuster, 1974).

13. An interesting variation of this argument is presented in James M. Cypher, "The Transnational Challenge to the Corporate State," *Journal of Economic Issues,* June 1979.

14. Charles Lindblom, *Politics and Markets* (New York: Basic Books, 1977).

15. Theodore Lowi, *The End of Liberalism* (New York: Norton, 1969); Grant McConnell, *Private Power and American Democracy* (New York: Vintage, 1970).

16. Elizabeth Drew, "Washington Journal," *New Yorker*, 31 March 1978.

17. Richard N. Cooper, Karl Kaiser, and Masataka Kosaka, *Towards A Renovated International System* (New York: Trilateral Commission, 1977).

18. For specifics, see Wolfe and Sanders, *op. cit.*

19. Chihiro Hosoya, Henry Owen, and Andrew Shonfield, *Collaborating With Communist Countries in Managing Global Problems* (New York: Trilateral Commission, 1977).

20. My quotations are from a draft report of the Trilateral Commission dealing with an overview of East-West relations.

21. For a presentation of these ideas see Charles L. Schultze, *The Public Use of Private Interest* (Washington, D.C.: Brookings, 1977).

22. Huntington et al., *op. cit.*

23. Daniel Bell, *The Cultural Contradictions of Capitalism* (New York: Basic Books, 1976).

PART IX
CONCLUDING PERSPECTIVES

Today the occasional touch of nostalgia for the past is simply a reaction to the great complexities that we confront.

—Zbigniew Brzezinski
Washington Post, 30 March 1980

Dealing with contradictions and conflicts is a tricky business, and if foreign policy objectives are to succeed, there has to be a global view of the world and an underlying steadiness and coherence to foreign policy. Consistency in every aspect may be impossible, but a pattern of fundamental logic is not.

—David Rockefeller
Wall Street Journal, 30 April 1980

By contrast with the relatively "simple" international system built under the aegis of the *Pax Americana* in the early post-war era, we now live in an infinitely more complex and diversified world, where the balance of power is no longer what some described as the clear zero-sum game of old between two super-powers, and where the United States is no longer such a dominant economic power. "Yet," in the words of an American speaker, "we still seem to be acting as if the prevailing power relations were the same as in the 1950s." This...endangers the very fabric of the trilateral relationship.

—The Trilateral Commission
*Trialogue,*Spring 1980

TRILATERALISM AND THE MANAGEMENT OF CONTRADICTIONS: CONCLUDING PERSPECTIVES

Holly Sklar

That trilateralism is weaker in some areas and stronger in others can be seen from the preceding articles. But those observers who believe that trilateralism is "dead" are either mistakenly defining trilateralism as a *static* set of tactics and strategies which have been overcome by world events, or are engaging in wishful thinking.[1] As *New York Times* economic columnist Leonard Silk puts it:

> Trilateralism survives, based on the need for a concentration of thought and power among those whose interests closely cohere in a disorderly world.[2]

In 1980, all three of the leading slates for president and vice-president of the United States include trilateralists: Jimmy Carter and Walter Mondale, George Bush, and John Anderson. The 1980 elections will be discussed in greater detail later in this article, but two things are clear: First, trilateralists have shaped private ruling consensus, government policy, and public opinion in the past, and they will continue to do so in the future. Second, the *parameters* of "responsible" political discourse and policy have been tightened even as the field of contending establishment candidates has grown. Noam Chomsky helps illustrate this point with his remarks on the nature of thought—and policy—control in a capitalist democracy:

> ...the propaganda apparatus does not merely stake out a position to which all must conform—or which they privately oppose. Rather, it seeks to determine and limit the entire spectrum of

*I wish to thank Karen Anderson, Ros Everdell, Jeff Frieden, Nancy Goulder, Leah Margulies, Carol Schneider, Keith Sklar, and Bill Tabb for their comments and criticism on earlier drafts of this article, and Lydia Sargent and Michael Albert for editorial assistance on the final draft.

thought; the official doctrine at one extreme, and the position of its most vocal adversaries at the other...The democratic system of thought control is seductive and compelling. The more vigorous the debate, the better the system of propaganda is served. Since the tacit unspoken assumptions are more forcefully implanted, an independent mind must seek to separate itself from official doctrine and from the criticism advanced by its alleged opponents—not just from the assertions of the propaganda system, but from its tacit presuppositions as well, as expressed by critic and defender.[3]

In some respects, the general position of the ruling class in the United States has been strengthened, even as the fault lines of power struggle within the ruling class have widened.

How can we integrate the multi-faceted discussion of the Trilateral Commission and trilateral strategy presented in this volume with an understanding of fast-paced world events and come away with a viable evaluation of trilateralism and a meaningful outlook on the future?

I believe that the key to examining trilateralism is the notion of contradiction: contradictions within the ruling class, contradictions internal to the capitalist system, and, most importantly, contradictions between trilateral goals and peoples' needs and aspirations.

In their grandiose attempt to manage world events and preserve transnational corporate power and property, trilateralists are opposed by capitalists with different material interests, the rival Soviet superpower, and the growing forces of national and popular liberation. And they are stymied by a capitalist economic system which is mired in stagflation. Moreover, trilateralists themselves often disagree on the best tactics with which to pursue agreed upon goals and strategies. These conflicts are based on different perceptions of the same events reflecting their different experiences and *particular* interests and concerns.

Trilateralists serving in government are subject to the norms of the bureaucracies of which they are a part. Elected politicians are buffeted between the demands of their constituencies and their allegiance to trilateral principles. Sometimes they change constituencies when the balance becomes impossible; more often they bend trilateral principles. As far as government policy is concerned it is also important to be aware that trilateral success in one area may mean failure in another. There are several examples of this: successful measures to redistribute more wealth from the working and middle classes of the U.S. to Corporate America and thus foster capital accumulation will undermine the legitimacy of the current administration and erode the legitimacy of the overall political/economic system; the successful co-optation of Arab OPEC nations and the assurance of long-term stability in the Middle East entails recognition of the right of the Palestinians to self-determination and this recognition would undercut the West's staunchly anticommunist allies in Israel's ruling party. The Cold War posturing used to press the implementation of the Rapid Deployment Force and draft registration and hike military spending has derailed Salt II.

In sum, trilateralism is not a computerized dictatorship, but a dynamic alliance among powerful individuals and power blocs. And, as David Rockefeller admits, "dealing with contradictions and conflicts is a tricky business." Below I will examine trilateral strategies, and U.S. policy in particular, in light of central conflicts and contradictions in the economic, political, and social realms. I argue that at the level of international economics, trilateralists are trying to manage a shift in the division of labor between trilateral and Third World nations and to overcome the crisis of stagflation. Their perscription for reconstructing the U.S. economy exacerbates the contradictions between economic accumulation and political legitimation. In the Third World trilateral planners are trying both to accommodate the momentum for national liberation *and* preserve pro-West, anti-Soviet regimes. Meanwhile, trilateral nations are partners and rivals at the same time, and the U.S. swings between accepting the trilateral need for collective management and reasserting U.S. supremacy. Our discussion of these and other contradictions will set the stage for a closer look at the 1980 U.S. presidential elections and the outlook for trilateralism and social change in the 1980s.

Monopoly Capitalism, the International Division of Labor, and Stagflation

We have seen that the name of the major league capitalist game is to monopolize resources, productive facilities, technology, and markets on a worldwide scale—to accumulate capital. But the accumulation process is anarchic, irrational, and crisis prone. Corporate managers think first of their firms and second of the larger capitalist system. Their cumulative profit-centered actions—like swiftly transferring assets from a weakening dollar to stronger currencies—may have a harmful effect on the larger capitalist system.* In short, there is weakness as well as strength in the monopolization and interdependence of capital. Political economist Joyce Kolko writes:

---

*Some one *trillion* dollars is circulating in the fast-paced, unregulated Eurocurrency market.

...the consequences of this concentration of capital, the centralization of decision-making, and the further *de facto* integration of
the world economy leaves the national economies yet more
swiftly vulnerable to a crisis that might begin in another part of
the world. Hence it contributes to the destabilization of the
capitalist economy on a world scale.[4]

One of the potential crises given much attention in recent years is
the possibility of a wave of defaults by Third World governments on
their massive debt. More than half the debt—estimated at between
$400 and $450 billion— is owed to private banks. A few borrowers
owe the bulk of the total sum; Brazil alone has a foreign debt of over
$50 billion.[5] Heavily indebted, industrializing countries like Brazil
depend increasingly on their ability to export manufactured goods.

Since the 1960s, with the proliferation of runaway shops,
environmental regulations in the trilateral regions (with especially
heavy pollution in Japan), and the rise of Third World economic
nationalism, there has been a shift in the international division of
labor such that more industrial activity is being undertaken in the
Third World.* A handful of the "newly industrializing countries" like
Brazil, Mexico, Saudi Arabia, and the "New Japans," South Korea,
Taiwan, and Singapore, have won promotions to higher slots in the
international division of labor. They have become what trilateralists
call "international middle class countries."

Trilateralists reflect on the implications of industrial growth in
the Third World in the task force report, *Industrial Policy and the
International Economy*.[7] The report observes that an expansion of
Third World production of capital-intensive goods (like steel, autos,
and shipbuilding) will aggravate the problems of counterpart
industries in the West which are already suffering from overcapacity,
i.e., the ability to produce more than the world market demands. The
situation of overcapacity itself reflects a structural contradiction of
capitalism between unlimited production and restricted consumption[8] (low wages and automation-induced unemployment, for example, lower the costs of production but depress demand for consumer
goods).

Any strains in adjusting to Third World industrialization, says
the report, must be seen in terms of the overall benefits of world

---

*For example, Third World crude steel output increased from 2 percent of world
production in 1950 to approximately 11 percent in 1977. The share of the Third
World in global industrial production rose from 9 percent in 1955 to 12 percent in
1977. From 1950 to 1977 the Third World's share of manufactured goods imported
by the most advanced capitalist countries increased from 4.9 percent to 7.3 percent.[6]

industrialization. Certain adjustment strains are highlighted:

> ...While such a process [of industrialization] would take many decades and perhaps even some centuries to spread through the world as a whole, some countries, including such major economies as Brazil and Mexico, could relatively soon reach the ranks of the industrialized. It is not too early, therefore, for thought to be given to the implications of this for international institutions, including in particular the OECD, and for the world balance of industrial and political power; and to consider what strain may be placed on the world's resources as the number of industrialized countries increases until they contain, perhaps, one half or three quarters of the population of the world, and even eventually the whole of it, instead of between a sixth and a quarter of it at present...

"The areas of future growth for the more advanced" countries are not the "mature technologies" (such as steel) but the high-profit, skill-intensive, science or information-based industries (known as "software" or tertiary sector). Economic restructuring of the industrialized capitalist nations is necessary if Third World industrialization is to be accommodated. Basic industries must be *deindustrialized* while the future-growth areas are promoted: finance, management (e.g. management contracts with, and control over, Third World state-owned enterprises and joint ventures), data-processing, computers, aerospace, microelectronics, petrochemicals, energy, and biological engineering.

The strains of accommodating Third World industrialization are magnified in the current situation of general economic crisis. Capitalism has historically followed a cycle of boom and bust, expansion and stagnation: industrial prosperity from the late 1840s through the early 1870s; the Great Depression of the period between the mid-1870s and the mid-1890s; shaky expansion through World War I and the 1920s; the Great Depression of the 1930s; rapid growth from World War II through the mid-1960s; stagnation since the 1970s, with the worst recession since the 1930s occurring in 1974-75.[9]

Stagflation is the most significant feature of the current phase of capitalist crisis. Historically, inflation has risen along with the expansion of production and employment, but fallen off during periods of idle productive capacity and unemployment. The growth of monopoly capitalism is an important factor in the co-existence between prolonged persistent stagnation and rampant inflation. There is an upward pressure, rather than a downward pressure, on prices under monopoly capitalism. In the absence of competitive market forces, giant firms are free to *administer* prices.[10] They are also able to buy labor peace with relatively high wages which are passed along to consumers in the form of higher prices.

Inflation has increased with spiraling military spending; the rise in business and consumer debt; government deficit-spending to keep pace with the escalating demands of the welfare/warfare state; the shift from a dollar-based system of fixed exchange rates to a floating currency exchange system; and the rise in oil prices, estimated to "have multiplied fourteen or fifteen-fold, by conservative estimates."[11] The high cost of energy is good for oil-producers, oil companies, international banks, multinational companies doing business in the Middle East, and armament dealers; but adds to the debt of non-oil producing nations and deepens the slowdown of economic growth in the West.

The corporate prescription for curing inflation has been recession, unemployment, and austerity imposed through cutbacks in social spending and restrictive monetary policy, a prescription which in reality rewards the chief inflation makers: monopoly firms, the military-industrial complex, international banks. More recently, there has been a rising chorus for what is called *reindustrialization,* which extends the "anti-inflation" prescription into a broader offensive to revitalize the ability of U.S.-based multinationals to compete in the shifting international division of labor.

A "New Social Contract" for Economic Reconstruction: Accumulation vs Legitimation

In keeping with the trilateral policy of bringing "responsible" labor leaders on board to execute antiworker/anticonsumer policies, the Carter Administration signed a National Accord with Big Labor in 1979 which was "personally drafted," *Business Week* tells us, by Treasury Secretary G. William Miller and trilateralist Lane Kirkland, then secretary-treasurer of the AFL-CIO and now its president.[12] *Business Week* says this about "Carter's Bid to Buy Labor:"

> labor has become a full participant in the anti-inflation program it has shunned for the past year. Top union leaders agreed to serve on a 15-member tripartite board that will set voluntary second-year wage standards. The AFL-CIO executive council also, for the first time, endorsed tough anti-inflationary rhetoric including a call for "a period of austerity for Americans" during which "continued constraint is required on the overall levels of price and compensation increases."[13]

Paul Volcker, the Trilateral Commissioner appointed by Carter to head the Federal Reserve System, is quite clear about the corporate accumulation prescription: "The standard of the average [sic] American has to decline."[14] This is quite a turnabout from the postwar promise of continual economic prosperity.

At the June 1980 Venice summit meeting, the big seven trilateral leaders affirmed that "the reduction of inflation [and not unemployment] is our immediate top priority" and that "Determined fiscal and monetary restraint is required to break inflationary expectations."

> This will require shifting resources from government spending to the private sector and from consumption to investment and avoiding or carefully limiting actions that shelter particular industries or sectors from the rigors of adjustment.[15]

The trilateral approach to economic restructuring under centralized planning has received a strong boost from corporate leaders. In a special June 1980 issue *Business Week* proposed a program for "The Reindustrialization of America" which contains key elements of the trilateralist strategy. The term "reindustrialization" is misleading in that *Business Week* is "reaching conclusions about which industries can flourish and which must be allowed to vanish."[16] "If necessary," says *Business Week,* "an institution comparable to the Reconstruction Finance Corporation of the 1930s should be set up to channel credit into reindustrialization." It calls on "business, labor, and academic leaders" to "establish a forum to hammer out a new social contract for the U.S." Special efforts, say *Business Week,* should be made to bring minority groups on board. But revitalizing the U.S. economy will take decades and so:

> The drawing of a social contract must take precedence over the aspirations of the poor, the minorities, and the environmentalists. Without such a consensus, all are doomed to lower levels of living, fewer rights, and increasingly dirty air and water."[17]

Business Week follows the trilateralists in calling for a new "partnership" between labor and management "to build the new workplace" and increase productivity, especially of export industries.

> At the center of the new consensus must stand the recognition that each social group will be measured by how it contributes to economic revitalization. Each group's income must be related firmly to its economic achievement.[18]

Unions representing highly organized monopoly sectors like auto and steel formed the backbone of the postwar welfare/warfare state consensus. The former head of the United Auto Workers, Leonard Woodcock, for example, is a member of the Trilateral Commission and Carter's ambassador to Peking. But with basic industries in a depression the conflict between workers—employed and unemployed—and the owners of the means of "economic achievement" is intensifying. In 1980 more than one-third of all auto workers were unemployed. (During the Great Depression of the 1930s, one out of every four workers was unemployed.) Historically the auto industry has employed directly or indirectly one out of every six workers in the U.S.

Many laid-off workers will not be rehired. They are not being retrained for the modern information-based high-technology economy, but are being shunted from the assembly line to the unemployment line. After all, this is a throwaway society. Like our nonrenewable natural resources, human beings are not being recycled.

In *The Crisis of Democracy* trilateralists argued that democratic aspirations must be limited.[19] Now trilateralists and their partners in the business world are insisting publicly that economic aspirations must be limited. Rather than competing over how to distribute an expanding output of goods and services, says *Business Week,* "all social groups in the U.S. today must come to understand that their common interest in returning the country to a path of strong economic growth overrides other conflicting interests" (such as full employment, occupational health and safety, social welfare, consumer and environmental protection, and the survival of local and nationally-based smaller businesses).

Corporate America demands public sacrifice for private profit in the name of the national interest. Recession is the opening wedge for a fundamental restructuring of the economy in the 1980s. To the extent that the U.S.—and international—capitalist system is reconstructed under the banners of fiscal conservatism and reindustrialization, capitalism may be propped up for another period of accumulation. But conditions have changed since the rapid growth of postwar *Pax American* which mitigate against a repeat performance. And underlying structural contradictions, such as the contradiction between unlimited production and restricted consumption, would reassert themselves more vigorously.

The overall capitalist system is much like the agricultural system within it. Agribusiness keeps inventing more "productive" varieties of crops, but they are based on capital-intensive inputs like fertilizer, irrigation, and insecticide, and are increasingly vulnerable to disease, generations of stronger insects and human-made disasters like depletion and pollution of ground water and erosion of the top soil. So too, with the international capitalist system as each crisis brings forth planned and unplanned mutations in the system and a new growth spurt, but leaves the system more and more vulnerable to internal and external challenges.

Conditions are ripe for intensification of the contradiction between capital accumulation and political legitimation and a resurgence of the conflict between labor and capital.

Anti-Communism and Accommodation:
A Conflict of Priorities for Policy Toward the Third World

By the end of Carter's first term it had become commonplace to criticize U.S. foreign policy for being in "deep disarray." National Security Adviser Zbigniew Brzezinski has protested this characterization vigorously, arguing that U.S. policies "have been both coherent and consistent." The problem, says Brzezinski, is that the U.S. is trying "to do two things:"

One: to make the United States historically more relevant to a world of genuinely profound change; and secondly, to improve the United States' position in the geo-strategic balance with the Soviet Union.[20]

But there is a contradiction which arises between the goals of making the U.S. more "relevant," by accommodating change in the Third World, and maintaining or improving the geo-strategic balance with the Soviet Union, which entails supporting pro-West, anticommunist regimes however unpopular and unstable they may be. This contradiction is illustrated by Brzezinski's remarks in Algeria in the Fall of 1978 at the celebration of the anniversary of the Algerian Revolution. (Two weeks earlier the White House had reversed prior policy and approved arms sales to Morroco which is engaged in a conflict with Algeria over the Western Sahara; Algeria is backing the national liberation force, Polisario, in its struggle to liberate the Western Sahara, a former Spanish colony which Morocco annexed illegally.)

Brzezinski, reports the *New York Times,* had a dual mission: "first, to assure Algiers that the United States is eager to improve political and economic relations and regards as constructive Algeria's role in the movement of nations professing nonalignment." Second, to make it clear that, while the U.S. favors a political solution to the struggle for the Western Sahara, "the United States will not let its friends [like Morocco's King Hassan*] be overrun." Brzezinski "named Israel, Thailand, and South Korea as [other] examples of this determination" and said "that the policy had world significance and was not limited to northwest Africa." Brzezinski explained:

the United States now accepts that what he called the 'Euro-centric' era of the world had ended. By the end of the century, 85 percent of the world's people will be in Asia, Africa and Latin America, and they will be politically organized...The United

---

* How has Hassan been a friend? In 1978, for example, the U.S. flew 1,500 Moroccan troops into Zaire (along with 1,000 French and Belgian paratroopers) to keep Mobutu's regime in power.

States, Mr. Brzezinski added, is not trying to build dams against the forces of history but rather to channel these forces in a positive direction.[21]

When it comes to a "positive" shaping of the "forces of history" in the Third World, there are tactical differences among trilateralists which relate to the two sides of the contradiction sketched above. Carter policy is commonly portrayed as a tug-of-war between the "globalists" led by Brzezinski and the National Security Council, who view all world events through the lenses of the U.S.-Soviet rivalry, and the "regionalists" based in the State Department and United Nations, who emphasize legitimate national/regional concerns. Before being forced to resign their posts, Cyrus Vance and Andrew Young championed the regionalist/accommodationist approach.

The *common* goal of trilateral policies toward the Third World is to promote neocolonialism. Says Young:

> ...I don't think the U.S. has but one option [in Southern Africa] and that's neocolonialism. As bad as that has been made to sound, neocolonialism means that MNCs will continue to have a major influence in the development and productive capacities of the Third World...I just think capital and technology happens to be in the hands of the people who are called neocolonialists...[22]

Since resigning his UN post, Young has been practicing what he preached. His new corporation, Young Ideas Inc., promotes increased trade with Third World nations.

> "Basically what we're doing," Mr. Young said, "is getting to know government leaders, finding out what their development plans are and helping them find the American corporations that can help them." The goal is a stable international economy with America in "its rightful role as the senior partner in a worldwide corporation."[23]

In the face of socialist liberation forces, the trilateral accommodationist strategy is to shore up shaky regimes while seeking to install as conservative an alternative as possible. If the worker/ peasant-based popular struggle has advanced such that antiimperialist socialist forces are victorious in the face of trilateral measures of counterinsurgency, reform, and co-optation, then trilateral nations will move to the next line of defense: attempt to arrest the transition to socialism by promoting a neocolonial "mixed economy" or state capitalism. At this writing, the clearest illustrations of this trilateral policy are found in Zimbabwe and Nicaragua.

The pre-election *Manifesto* of ZANU, the governing party of independent Zimbabwe, states:

> In working towards the socialist transformation of Zimbabwean society, a ZANU (PF) Government will, nevertheless recognize historical, social and other existing practical realities of Zimbabwe. One of these existing practical realities is the capitalist system which cannot be transformed overnight.[24]

Among the weighty practical concerns facing the new government is the repatriation of some one million wartime refugees, the reconstruction and construction of schools, hospitals, and other services, land distribution, and wage increases for Blacks. By pulling the strings of aid and corporate investment, London, Washington, and other trilateral states will attempt to ensure that whatever transformation of the status quo does occur, it remains within the bounds of neocolonialism.

The Carter Administration fought strong right wing opposition to win congressional approval for aid to Nicaragua in an effort to keep the Sandinista government from becoming dependent on the socialist bloc for desperately needed reconstruction assistance. But the bulk of the aid is not going directly to government agencies for use in reconstructing the war-devastated/Somoza-pillaged nation; it is being channeled to the private business sector.

From Human Rights to Rapid Intervention

It seemed at the start of Carter's first term that the United States would attempt to compensate for its loss in police power with a heavy dose of preacher power or "human righteousness."[25] However, by 1979 Carter seemed eager to lead the West on a new military crusade. The Caribbean is a case in point.

In October 1979, Carter used the issue of Soviet troops in Cuba, "discovered" after being there with U.S. knowledge for seventeen years) to announce the establishment of a permanent Caribbean military task force based in Key West, Florida, and increased military maneuvers in the Caribbean. U.S.-Cuba relations would not advance toward normalization. Rather, the U.S. would increase surveillance, maintain the economic embargo, and flaunt stepped-up activity at Guantanamo where a U.S. naval base occupies 45-square miles of Cuban territory.*

When Carter announced the new military steps for the Caribbean, he also pledged to increase economic assistance "to insure the ability of troubled peoples to resist social turmoil and possible Communist domination." The domino theory has been resurrected in

---

*See editor's postscripts to Philip Wheaton's article in Part VI and James Phillips' article in Part VII for an update on other dangerous events in the Caribbean.

Central America with the "fall" of Nicaragua, mounting instability in El Salvador, Honduras, and Guatemala, and concern for the long-term stability of Costa Rica, Panama, and Mexico. It may not be long before the economic and military assistance, and the counter-insurgency teams now in El Salvador, give way to direct military intervention in the Caribbean and Central America with the same rationale of helping people "resist social turmoil and possible Communist domination."[26]

It is important to understand that the accommodationist approach remained dominant in the first half of the Carter Administration not just because it was accepted as the best approach, but because in the post-Vietnam era it was in many respects the only viable alternative. The *Wall Street Journal* makes this point in an article on U.S. efforts to "influence Central American Unrest" which was bluntly subtitled "Policy Is an Anti-Left Blend of Cash, Human Rights, Help for a Bloody Junta:"

> Unable to rely on moderate regimes in the region and unwilling to intervene militarily as it did in the Dominican Republic in 1965, Washington is increasingly relying on American aid for leverage. "Our use of aid is pure behavior modification," says one U.S. career diplomat in Central America. "U.S. dollars are rewarded like lumps of sugar to good little countries and withheld for shock value from stubborn, naughty countries."[27]

The brakes on U.S. interventionism in the post-Vietnam period have become known as the "Vietnam Syndrome." Treatment to cure the Vietnam Syndrome has been initiated on all fronts: rehabilitation therapy for the CIA; draft registration; refurbishing regional gendarmes like Egypt and Morocco; a rerun of "the President Knows Best;" self-censorship by press and politicians who don't want to be branded unpatriotic and irresponsible; guns-over-butter budgets; scapegoating Iran and OPEC as the cause of oil and gasoline woes; calling the Middle East a region of "vital interest" to be defended by military force; Cold War II.

Establishment policy makers have learned some lessons from Vietnam, but they want the public to unlearn them. That is, policy makers will attempt to avoid direct military intervention in the Third World but want the public to be ready to applaud increased military spending and a revitalized CIA "just in case" foreign intervention becomes necessary. In short, a "crisis of democracy" in the form of popular opposition to presidential (imperial) prerogative should not be one of the "unknown variables" in contingency planning.

The Soviet intervention in Afghanistan gave Carter, Brzezinski, Brown, and company the opportunity to extend the public reach of U.S. interventionism from the U.S. backyard to the oil fields of the

Middle East. And, as Michael Klare warns, "future intervention will have to be fought with much more precision, speed and ferocity than anything we have ever seen."[28] Hence, the push for the Rapid Deployment Force. Afghanistan provided the rationale for the draft, the real aim of which is to provide war pawns for protecting the vital interests of global corporations.[29]

The Rapid Deployment Force maintains the dangerous illusion that wars to preserve the "national interest" will be quick and relatively painless for the larger public: the "brave warriors"—as Carter called the troops of the "humanitarian intervention" in Iran—would march off, the public would watch these modern crusades on T.V., and the dead warriors would return for burial in manicured cemeteries. But the civilians shot in the crossfire and decimated in the bombing runs, the children napalmed, the land devastated would belong to the "foreign enemies."

Unfortunately. technocratic delusions are the rule, not the exception. Trilateral leaders and their advisers pride themselves on managing *complex* problems. The rapid, surgical strike force goes hand in hand with "winnable" nuclear war and the "peaceful atom" of nuclear power. Zbigniew Brzezinski and George Bush[30] are two trilateralist advocates of the limited nuclear war option (to be fought, of course, in the Third World or Europe). In a 1977 *Washington Post* interview Brzezinski defended the "political" deterrent value of nuclear superiority and refuted the interviewer's suggestion that a two-sided U.S.-Soviet nuclear exchange might make the "regeneration of human society" difficult if not impossible:

Well, first of all, that really is baloney. And I do emphasize the importance of the deterrent effect, namely, that no one should ever calculate that they can launch a nuclear attack on someone without suffering the consequences. As far as human society and all that is concerned, it sounds great in a rally. The fact of the matter is—and I don't want this to be understood as justifying the use of nuclear weapons, because we don't want to use them and we're not going to use them first in an attack—the fact of the matter is that if we used all our nuclear weapons and the Russians used all of their nuclear weapons, about 10 percent of humanity would be killed. Now this is a disaster beyond the range of human comprehension. It's a disaster which is not morally justifiable in whatever fashion. But descriptively and analytically, it's not the end of humanity.[31]

The Physicians of Social Responsibility have painstakingly refuted "the facts of the matter" assumed by Brzezinski, Bush, and other limited-nuclear war advocates. Their studies show that "medical 'disaster planning' for nuclear war is meaningless" and that "there is no effective civil defense." "Most 'survivors' would die" and

"Recovery from nuclear war would be impossible."[32]

In August 1980 the press reported on the Carter Administration's revised nuclear (and re-election) strategy promoting U.S. ability to fight a "prolonged but limited" nuclear war with the Soviet Union. It embodies the "counterforce" doctrine described earlier in this volume. Secretary of Defense Brown told Walter Cronkite in an interview at the Democratic Convention that anyone familiar with "the facts" would support the "evolutionary" policy directive. The strategy (elaborated in Presidential Directives 59 and 53) calls for more costly and sophisticated war technology such as the MX missile system and for "more effective procedures" for protecting civilian and military leaders. Neither the State Department nor the Arms Control and Disarmament Agency were involved in formulating the new policy. The strategy is based on the double delusion that nuclear war can be limited to "precise nuclear strikes" against "military targets" and that there can be adequate protection for the survival (and procreation?) of those people and things which count most, namely government, military, business leaders, and necessary civilian technicians, along with industrial and communications capacity. The stronger the illusion of technological control and self-security felt by the war planners and corporate leaders, the more thinkable and likely nuclear war becomes.

Policy makers like Brzezinski and the military-industrial complex in general are wholly irresponsible "as far as human society and all that is concerned." They will go on playing their MAD games of Russian roulette and nuclear hide-and-seek until stopped—or until we all lose. The resurgent U.S. antidraft/antiwar movement is linked with the antinuclear movement and has a growing antiimperialist content ("hell no, we won't die for Texaco"); it is an important sign of popular dissent from the warfare state ideology.

Trilateral Relations: Partnership and Rivalry

Trilateral leaders are both doctor and patient. The more trilateralists take their own medicine of mutual consultation and coordinated policy, the more effective will be their broad trilateralist prescription for world management. But (as Block argues), a contradictory process of cooperation and rivalry lies at the heart of relations among trilateral nations. The enduring economic stagnation of the trilateral world is kindling a resurgence of protectionism. *Business Week* warns of "Neo-Mercantilism" in the eighties:

> Three decades of open, free trade that permitted the multinationals to blossom are giving way to a period of neo-mercantilism...the cooperative effort to create an interdependent world economy—a hallmark of the postwar period—is being replaced

by what appears to be a free-for-all among industrial nations trying to grab or preserve as much as possible for themselves of the shrinking pie.[33]

Not even a rosy economic outlook would suffice to sustain a cozy trilateral partnership, however. There is stress built into the very structure of the triangle. It is not equilateral: the "third leg," the Japanese-West European relationship, is weak. "Where commonality of purpose has been evidenced between Japan and Western Europe," says Richard Ullman of the CFR, "it has often been catalyzed by common opposition to actions and policies of the United States."[34]

Most important the U.S. still seems to want to have its cake and eat it too by defining trilateralism as a process of West European-Japanese consensus around U.S. initiatives. Some "collective" managers are more equal than others.

Nothing illustrates the U.S. tendency to demand cooperation without exercising consultation better than U.S. policy throughout the U.S.-Iran crisis of 1979-1980 (continuing at this writing) and Carter's rush into Cold War II. Carter's reckless use of the hostage issue and the Soviet intervention in Afghanistan to grease his domestic electoral tracks has shaken the trilateral allies. Nixon's reelection hysteria culminated in Watergate. Carter's last stand might be World War III.* But Carter's electoral preoccupation is not the only explanation for shifts in U.S. policy.

Behind the U.S.-Iran crisis are conflicting state, corporate, and private interests. The late Shah had friends at Chase Manhattan Bank and in the highest echelons of trilateral power. David Rockefeller and Henry Kissinger played instrumental roles in arranging the Shah's exile and shaping U.S. policy toward Iran. The massive Pahlevi family fortune is stored in Chase accounts, in U.S. government securities, and elsewhere in the international banking system.[36] The Iranian government had filed suit in New York against the deposed Shah, alleging that an estimated $56.5 billion was stolen from the Iranian Treasury. A financial/political scandal of vast proportions is brewing over the late Shah's billions.

The Carter Administration froze Iranian assets under U.S. jurisdiction in large part to appease Iran's creditors (Chase etc.). The

---

*Ironically, when Jimmy Carter met with Commissioners at the time of the June 1978 plenary gathering in Washington, D.C. he reportedly told them: "if the Trilateral Commission had been in business after World War I, the world might have cancelled World War II."[35]

freeze upset non-U.S. trilateral banking interests, and established a dangerous precedent for international monetary relations. It heightened OPEC insecurity about the safety of their already inflation-eaten petrodollars in Western accounts, prompting conversion of some dollar assets into gold and other currencies, and further undermining the dollar's strength as an international currency.

Trilateral relations were further shaken by the abortive U.S. raid on the embassy in Teheran—and whatever else the secret plans called for—in the name of the U.S. hostages. However, the goal of the so-called "humanitarian" intervention was not to save the hostages. Rather, the action put the hostages in grave danger. The aim was to vindicate "U.S. honor," preserve the prerogative of intervention, rescue Carter's presidency, and, most likely, support a counter-revolution and cover up Western collaboration in the pillage of Iran's resources and oppression of the Iranian people under the Shah.

The intervention came just as trilateral allies had reluctantly backed more stringent and comprehensive economic and diplomatic sanctions against Iran, precisely to forestall U.S. military action. The resignation of Secretary of State Vance, in dispute over the use of military intervention in Iran and the increasingly confrontationist approach of U.S. foreign policy, intensified West European and Japanese fears of reckless unilateral intervention on the part of the U.S. Vance preached little, but practiced trilateralism (in relation to the trilateral allies, the Third World, and the Soviet Union) with far more consistency than Carter and Brzezinski, both of whom have fallen lower in trilateral esteem, as we discuss later.

When he did preach, at Harvard University 5 June 1980, Vance railed against the "dangerous new nostalgia" for the bygone *Pax Americana*. "It is far too easy, in an election year, to let what may seem smart politics produce bad policies." Vance restated the basic trilateral foreign policy position: preserve military balance with the Soviet Union, ratify SALT II, and forge a "common law of competition" based on both deterrence and cooperation; support peaceful change and peaceful resolution of conflict in the Third World, the likely "cockpit of crises" in the coming decade, through negotiations such as those leading to settlement in Zimbabwe, increasing security and development assistance and participating constructively in North-South negotiations; strengthen the Western alliance and encourage the U.S. to consult and adjust course "for the sake of a common purpose."[37]

The Carter Administration has attempted to use the crisis atmosphere surrounding Iran and Afghanistan as an opportunity not only to reassert U.S. power *vis-a-vis* the Third World and Soviet Union, but also to reassert U.S. dominance over its trilateral allies.

West Germany values highly its expanding trade with the Soviet Union and friendly relations with East Germany. Western Europe and Japan are more dependent on Persian Gulf oil than is the U.S.

U.S. propaganda notwithstanding, the real threat to the oil flow and Middle East stability is not Soviet "expansionism/aggression." Rather it is U.S. brinkmanship in the area and the failure of U.S. policy makers (especially in an election year) to press Israel to come to terms with the Palestinian right to self-determination.

West European leaders are vigorously promoting their own framework for peace, calling for PLO "association" with negotiations and recognition of the Palestinian right to self-determination. Before the West European initiative was announced, the Trilateral Commission met in London in March 1980. *Trialogue* Spring 1980 reports that the "theme which clearly dominated" the discussion on the Middle East

> was the *central nature of the Palestinian issue* in our efforts to move, beyond the Camp David agreements, closer to a true settlement in the Middle East. [Italics theirs.][38]*

A "Former British Diplomat" expressed trilateral aspirations with this observation:

> I think it would be foolish of the Israelis to assume that the Palestinians can never be brought to become neighbors. Our own experience of decolonization has often been that those who were our greatest enemies can turn out in time quite differently: Kenyatta [Jomo Kenyatta, first president of Kenya], for example, once seen as the most terrible of the terrorists we ever had to deal with, became the archetype of a moderate Commonwealth statesman; we cannot guarantee that this will also happen in the case of Mugabe, but there are promising signs. One ardently wishes the Israelis could be brought at least to *consider* the same possibility. [Italics theirs.][39]

In 1972 Brzezinski had criticized Nixon-Kissinger foreign policy for "taking by surprise both friends and enemies alike."[40] Ironically, Brzezinski turned out to be far more adventurist than Kissinger. At the Commission's 1980 London Plenary, the Carter Administration's tendency to "act now, consult later" came "under particular scrutiny"[41]

Trilateral business and political leaders are reminding the Carter Administration—and the next administration—that the United

---

* *Trialogue* Summer 1980 has been devoted entirely to the Middle East and a special trilateral task force on the Middle East has been established which is due to report to the Commission's next plenary conference on 29-31 March 1981.

States cannot expect loyal cooperation from the allies without mutual respect and consultation. In the Summer 1980 issue of *Foreign Affairs,* Giovanni Agnelli, a founding member of the Trilateral Commission's executive committee and chairman of FIAT, comments on the state of the trilateral alliance before presenting "A European View" of East-West trade:

> The United States and the whole West are facing particularly hard times. Detente between the superpowers has come to a standstill; world peace is in jeopardy, and mistakes now can be more hazardous than ever before. The time has come to speak as candidly as possible, to avoid dangerous misunderstandings among Western partners and allies...as a former Japanese Foreign Minister [and fellow member of the Trilateral Commission's executive committee], Kiichi Miyazawa, recently put it, there is today a special "need for America to acknowledge the plurality of interests of the allies and accept its consequences... The definition of the interests of the alliance on any issue has to become a collective exercise."[42]

Detente (and Salt II and accommodation with the Third World are cornerstones of trilateralism. Jimmy Carter is a political engineer who has bungled the job for which he was recruited.

The 1980 U.S. Presidential Elections

> The life of every human being on earth can depend on experience, judgement, and vigilance of the person in the Oval Office. The President's power for building and his power for destruction are awesome. And that power is greatest exactly where the stakes are highest—in matters of war and peace...the President of the United States is the steward of the nation's destiny.
> —Jimmy Carter's acceptance speech, 1980

As this book is going to press it is clear that Jimmy Carter is again the Democratic nominee for president. "Billygate"—the scandal involving Billy Carter's oil dealings with Libya and White House use of Billy as a liaison with the Libyan government over the issue of the hostages in Iran—provided only a brief preconvention drama. The Carter Administration has a good record of keeping its super-clean anti-Watergate image as it keeps potentially volcanic scandals from erupting as more than passing tremors: the indictment of Budget Director Bert Lance for banking fraud and his quick resignation; the implication of Treasury Secretary G. William Miller in the bribery activities of Textron, his former company; the "Peanutgate" involving Carter warehouse and campaign finances.

Carter has increasingly lost trilateral support with his mismanagement of the U.S.—Iran hostage crisis and his inept handling of relations with Congress. He is held in low esteem by important trilateral leaders like Helmut Schmidt. Trilateralists with a stake in a second term for the Carter Administration remained, unsurprisingly loyal to Carter's reelection campaign. Zbigniew Brzezinski appears to have slipped in his competition with Henry Kissinger for chief trilateral national security manager, with his irresponsible foreign policy antics (like being photographed looking through gun sites at Soviet positions in Afghanistan), his overdone Cold Warrior posturing, and his role in Billy Carter's dealings with Libya over the hostages in Iran. The broadest corporate support and trilateral momentum is not behind Carter. It is behind the Bush/Reagan ticket.

George Bush

In *The Carter Presidency and Beyond,* Laurence Shoup captioned a section on George Bush "The Jimmy Carter of the 1980 Election?" Bush tried to repeat Carter's successful strategy of starting early and campaigning as an "outsider."[43] As the primary season began it looked like he might capture the Republican nomination. David Rockefeller gave him his support.[44] The media celebrated his early Iowa "momentum." But George Bush dropped out of the primary competition before the final "super Tuesday." The reason has more to do with right wing opposition to his membership on the Trilateral Commission and association with the Eastern Establishment, than liberal opposition to his stands on "winnable" nuclear war and other aspects of domestic and foreign policy.

Bush was pegged by his conservative critics as an "Eastern liberal Rockefeller Republican," in the tradition of the late Nelson Rockefeller who lost his quest for the Republican presidential nomination in 1964 to the conservative standard-bearer from Arizona, Senator Barry Goldwater. Right wing groups like the Florida Conservative Union mounted a massive ad campaign to make sure voters knew that "the same people who gave you Jimmy Carter want now to give you George Bush." The aim of Rockefeller and company "is to win the presidential game 'whether the coin comes up heads or tails.' "[45] The ad campaign was effective in New Hampshire, Alabama, Florida, and Illinois. According to veteran political correspondent Martin Schramm, two of the pivotal issues in the New Hampshire primary were "gun control and Bush's former membership in the Trilateral Commission."[46] To the Trilateral Commission's right wing critics, the Rockefellers and the Eastern Establishment stand for appeasement of the Soviet Union. "Interdependence" is seen as a euphemism for a totalitarian "one-world government" serving the multinational corporations.

Trilateralists couldn't capture the Republican nomination in 1980 so they put plan B into effect: if you can't beat 'em, co-opt 'em. George Bush's selection as Reagan's running mate was a victory for the Eastern Establishment/trilateral forces over Reagan's more conservative advisers and constituency. *Time* magazine sighed with relief that "Reagan settled for the logical choice, George Bush."[47] The choice of Bush came after an intensive round of Kissinger shuttle diplomacy to get former President Ford to join the "dream ticket." The Ford/Kissinger conditions were too high, however: the appointment of Kissinger as secretary of state and reorganization of the executive branch giving Ford a major share in presidential authority and decision making.[48]

There were earlier signs that Reagan was responding to the appeals of the Republican "moderates." Before the convention, he had vetoed the advice of his Right/new Right aides and retained Bill Brock, a member of the Trilateral Commission, as chairman of the Republican National Committee in the interest of party unity. A closer look at Reagan's top supporters/advisers reveals that most are "moderate" Republicans and a significant number are members of the Trilateral Commission. Reagan's campaign director, William J. Casey, is a New York lawyer who was head of the Securities and Exchange Commission under Ford. "Though he hates the label," writes *Fortune,* "Casey is a bona fide member of that ephemeral conservative bogeyman, the Eastern Establishment."[49] Longtime Reagan promoter Justin Dart, of Dart Industries, is a member of the Business Roundtable's policy committee.[50] (The Roundtable is a lobbying/policy arm of the United States' largest corporations.)

Casper Weinberger, a Trilateral Commissioner and vice-president of Bechtel Corporation, is a top Reagan economic adviser. Other trilateralists include: Anne Armstrong, co-chairwoman of the Reagan campaign and (long-shot) possibility for the vice-presidential slot; Carla Hills, co-chairwoman of the task force to develop a program to help the housing industry; and Senator William V. Roth Jr., who chaired the Republican platform panel on economic policy. Three other top economic advisers on the Commission are Arthur Burns, former head of the Federal Reserve; Paul McCracken, chairman of the Council of Economic Advisers under Richard Nixon; and David Packard, chairman of Hewlett-Packard. Packard gave $88,438 to help launch the Trilateral Commission; Bechtel Corporation donated money to the Commission between 1976 and 1979. (See Part II section on funding.) McCracken serves on the Committee to Fight Inflation which was formed in June 1980, and is headed by Arthur Burns and supported by the American

Enterprise Institute. Other Committee members include: Reagan advisers George Schultz, president of Bechtel and John Connally's replacement as Nixon's secretary of the treasury, and William Simon, former secretary of the treasury, and Carter's former secretary of the treasury, W. Michael Blumenthal. The Committee to Fight Inflation supports Reagan's view that "inflation is largely a consequence of government actions" in response to "excessive public demands for the good things in life" like higher living standards, welfare, and environmental and health and safety protection. The Committee does not support the across-the-board tax-cutting policies of Representative Jack Kemp and Senator Roth embodied in the Kemp-Roth plan which Reagan endorses.[51] The Committee would prefer to reduce business taxes, as Kemp-Roth do, but without the general reduction of personal income taxes by 30 percent over three years.

Jack Kemp is said to be the only bona fide member of the New Right among Reagan's top advisers and right-wingers promoted him for vice-president. But even Kemp says, "I believe in the global economy, there is one economy," and sees protectionist measures like tariffs as understandable from an emotional point of view, but wrong economically. "It's raising taxes on international transactions to put barriers between Mitsubushi and you." About the Republican Party's international economic stance, Kemp says:

> It is heterodox. We were the party of protection and nationalism, and now there are some places in the platform where it actually talks about internationalism...Not in Trilateral sense, which really offends all sorts of people, but in the sense that we recognize that somebody who buys a Coca-Cola in New Dehli—part of the dime goes to the shopkeeper in New Dehli, part of the dime goes to Atlanta, Georgia, and part of the dime goes to a sugar plantation in Jamaica. Capital and ideas and trade and credit are fungible, and we need fewer barriers, not more.[52]

Think tanks which are more conservative than the Trilateral Commission, Council on Foreign Relations, and the Brookings Institution are prime recruiting grounds for a Reagan Administration: the American Enterprise Institute (AEI), Georgetown University Center for Strategic and International Studies (CSIS), and the Hoover Institute. But again the trilateralists will be exercising influence. CSIS chairman David Abshire has been on the Trilateral Commission since 1973 and is also a director of AEI. Anne Armstrong is vice-chairwoman of the CSIS Advisory Board and a member of the executive committee. Other trilateral CSIS associates are Henry Kissinger and William Roth Jr. (who is more trilateralist on some policies than others.[53]) Arthur Burns is AEI distinguished scholar in residence. Other trilateralists affiliated with AEI are D.

Gale Johnson, Paul McCracken, David Packard, Mark Shepard Jr., and Marina v.N. Whitman.

Reagan's top foreign policy adviser and possible successor to Brzezinski as National Security adviser is Richard Allen of the CSIS. Allen makes clear in an interview with the *New York Times* that Reagan's foreign policy will be more conservative than the Carter Administration's but not the "shoot from the hip" militarism that Reagan is accused of.[54] Reagan foreign policy will take a less accommodationist, more anticommunist approach to change in the Third World; the Republican Platform (which is in many respects more conservative than Reagan due to the control exercised by right wing delegates over its composition) criticizes the Carter Administration for aid to Nicaragua, for example. While economically, the trialteralists and Reagan's top policy advisers may have less differences than meets the press, they are further apart when it comes to relations with the Soviet Union and the arms race. Reagan is opposed to SALT II. The forces behind Reagan based in the Sunbelt defense industries will promote a spiraling arms race far beyond the level seen as reasonable by most trilateralists.

Reagan's economic advisers represent *Fortune* 500 companies like Bechtel, and not the National Association of Manufacturers. But Reagan's strength among small businesmen and nationally-based industrialists, and his increasing success among blue collar workers lends itself to a "new social contract" for protectionism, not corporate free trade. At the same time, his growing blue collar base conflicts with the traditional Republican antipathy toward organized labor. Like the Democrats, the Republicans would have an Administration which is visibly divorced from the needs and demands of its constituency.

John Anderson

The trilateralists had two men running for the Republican ticket. John Anderson, a member of the Commission since 1973, remained in the presidential race as an "Independent." Political commentators are stumbling over themselves to ring out the era of political parties and ring in the age of television democracy. Anderson, perhaps, is the test product: a "demopublican" packaged in an "Independent" wrapper and promoted with Carter's old slogan "Why Not the Best?" Anderson is more articulate than the other candidates but he speaks the same language: corporate capitalism.

Anderson has the support of prominent trilateralists like George Ball. Few people outside the Carter camp are calling him a spoiler, leaving him plenty of space to become a "viable" and "serious" contender. The *New York Times* captioned its 13 January 1980

editorial on Anderson "Why Not the Best?" and encouraged voters to
give him a chance in the primaries to show his worth. The *Times* gave
him the highest marks on energy, their "most important policy test"
for 1980 candidates.

Anderson, like Carter circa 1976, is being packaged as a fiscal
conservative and a social and foreign-policy liberal. He has been
called a "born-again progressive" and this year's "Mr. Conscience."
The last election's born-again Mr. Honesty told poor women denied
medicaid funds for abortion that "life is unfair." Carter's new slogans
are "I've had four years to learn," "I'm doing the best I can..." "Trust
me," and "I do not intend to lose."

Anderson has argued that while he is a strong advocate of
reduced federal spending—he sees government as the main inflation
culprit—he insists he "would never try to reduce the budget on the
backs of the poor." He likes to say he "wears his heart on the left and
his pocketbook on the right." Debating his Republican rivals in Iowa
Anderson said the only way they could simultaneously balance the
federal budget, cut taxes, and increase defense spending was "with
mirrors." Perhaps Anderson would use mirrors to keep heart and
pocketbook together.

His record leans heavily on the side of the pocketbook when it
comes to matters of concern to workers, women, minorities, cities,
the poor, elderly, and handicapped. Two journalists who have
scrutinized Anderson's record spanning two decades in Congress
have argued that his "understanding of the problems of the poor,
minorities, and women is confined to 'due process' (ERA, Civil
Rights)...He want Blacks to be able to sit at lunch counters anytime
and any place, but their ability to actually buy food isn't his
problem."[55] When it comes to energy, he has been a strong advocate
of nuclear power projects and of conservation through higher prices.
Anderson's "National Unity Campaign" fundraising letter contains
no reference to labor in the summary of his national program. No
wonder, Anderson has consistently voted antilabor. For economic
advisers, Anderson has turned increasingly to Felix Rohatyn, the
investment banker who has overseen New York City's IMF-style
financial "reconstruction" through austerity and corporate incentives as chairman of the Municipal Assistance Corporation.[56]

Edward Kennedy

Ted Kennedy, the other leading Democratic candidate would
have seemed the perfect trilateral candidate: national security
embodied in his S1 Criminal Code Revision and internationalist
outlook plus social security evident in his National Health Plan and
strong liberal/labor constituency. But what was good for the sixties
and possible in the seventies is anathema in the eighties.

Like the trilateralists, Kennedy has called for "a new economic partnership" between government, business, labor, and academia to "reindustrialize" the U.S. He was supported by trilateralist Robert Roosa and Walter Heller, a University of Minnesota economics professor. Kennedy proposed an "American reindustrialization corporation," taking its cues from the New Deal, and a massive public and private "Marshall Plan." But Kennedy's plan calls for a higher dose of government spending, a lesser dose of austerity, and a stronger role for labor than the trilateral bankers are prescribing. As he put it at the Democratic Convention:

> "If we could rebuild Germany and Japan after World War II, then surely we can reindustrialize our own nation and revive our inner cities in the 1980s."

The witch hunt the media led against Kennedy in the primaries was a symbolic attack on sixties-style liberalism—and perhaps an attack on *noblesse oblige*. But at the Democratic Convention Kennedy gave what Walter Cronkite called a "redeclaration of liberal Democratic principles," calling for "economic justice" and full—and safe—employment and implicitly rejecting the austerity program of the Carter Administration. Carter won the nomination by running against the Ayatollah and the Kremlin, but Kennedy won the Convention over to a reaffirmation of liberalism as the soul of the Democratic Party.

The parameters of "responsible" political discussion have been narrowed on the Left and extended on the Right. While the Reagan/Bush ticket is to the left of the far Right Republican Platform, Carter is to the right of the progressive liberal Democratic Platform. Kennedy's strong and steadfast support from labor, Blacks, and women forced Carter to fill his speech with references to jobs, social welfare, and FDR's New Deal, but they were offset by his emphasis on the military and on the *complex* nature of today's problems and tasks (Carter's self-defense). The stark Carter nominating speech given by Florida's Governor Graham painted a truer picture of Carter than Walter Mondale's rendition of Kennedy's speech. During Graham's speech Amnesty International led a demonstration against his advocacy and enforcement of the death penalty. Carter was booed loudly when he pointed with pride to draft registration.

Carter claimed to have put eight million people to work in the last four years. But he neglected to say that some ten million people are out of work. And youth unemployment (sixteen to twenty-one years) is 16 percent, or 3 million people, the heavily disproportionate share of whom are inner city people of color. Employing Andy Youngs and Donald MacHenry's will not erase that fact.

There was talk of walk-outs throughout the convention, parti-

cularly from Black, women, and labor delegates. William Winpi-
singer, president of the International Association of Machinists and
the most radical head of an AFL-CIO union, did lead a number of
Kennedy delegates out of the convention hall. How many Kennedy
delegates will go over to John Anderson and how many to Barry
Commoner of the Citizen's Party remains to be seen. But one thing is
clear: if progressives outside the triparty system don't forge challenging economic, political, and ideological alternatives in the next
few years, the 1984 election the Kennedy delegates are longing for will
bring the corporate authoritarianism depicted in Orwell's *1984*.

Toward the Future

In the United States and throughout the trilateral world,
trilateral planners have had to bend more to the Right than to the
Left. The Right has significant political clout particularly at the local,
state, and congressional levels and within the military-industrial
complex. Trilateralists were able to overcome heavy right wing
opposition and win congressional approval of the Panama Canal
Treaties, the Zimbabwe settlement, and aid to Nicaragua. But in
general, events in 1980 have added weight to Alan Wolfe's law of
political motion for the seventies: "the more the center tries to woo
it," the stronger the Right becomes, and the further to the Right the
center must shift.

A struggle is being waged between the factions of the capitalist
class whose vested interests are served by protectionism and super-
militarism and the global banks and corporations whose profits and
power depend upon international free trade, detente, and accommodation with Third World economic nationalism. What is occurring is not just a battle over short-run profits and power alignments—
taking place within, between, and outside the Democratic and
Republican Parties. We are seeing a struggle over the shape of the
national division of power, the international division of labor, and
the nature of the role of the state in the process of capital acumulation
for the coming decades.

Trilateralists are maneuvering to strengthen the forces of
internationalism within the governing arm of the Republican Party
but they still face a deep problem. They cannot launch an ideological
attack on backward capitalists, lest they look too much like socialists
with their calls for centralized economic planning and enthusiasm for
worker participation schemes. The parameters of responsible politics
in the United States are so narrow that even the 1972 McGovern presidential candidacy made people see Red. A true trilateralist offensive
would undermine the ideological domination of capitalism which has
helped close out a Left alternative. For a centrally planned corporate

capitalism is a far cry from the glorified free enterprise system. While the Right would scream about the impending "one world government," others may ask: if there's to be centralized planning why should it be in the hands of the corporate elite and not democratically controlled? If the pie is no longer expanding, why should more be distributed to Exxon and less to the "average American" and the poor.

The worldwide power of trilaterlism rests upon the domestic power of the ruling classes of the trilateral countries, particularly the U.S. That power has been made all the more secure because of the intricate way in which ruling class power is exercised in capitalist democracies: from subtle ideological manipulation, to co-optation through symbolic reform, to selective systematic repression, to periods of wholesale political repression. The fact that a white male high school dropout has a better chance of finding a job than a Black male or female high school graduate, while "Blacks, Puerto Ricans, Chicano/as, and American Indians are thrown in prison at over twice their proportion in the general population" are two sides to the same coin of economic and political repression.[57]

The "Red scare" of the McCarthy period, and the Cold War generally, greatly narrowed the parameters of "responsible" political discussion and action. We must not allow this to happen with Cold War II.

Reeducation is crucial to challenging the ideological domination of corporate capitalism and along with it political and economic domination. Progressive people cannot forget that most people in the United States and other countries do not have knowledge of, or access to, newsmedia, films, documentaries, and so forth outside the mainstream media, or exposure to speakers and educational events outside of television and mainstream church and school activities. The spread of alternative views (alternative to the allowable pro's and con's of mainstream debate) and alternative programs which can reach those who want changes, but see no realistic alternatives or fear those they do see, cannot be taken for granted but must be worked at.

Take the media packaging of the decades of the sixties and seventies for public consumption, as an example. The decade of the seventies has been dubbed the "me decade" and portrayed in the media as a decade of apathy—in contrast to the "protest sixties." It is in the ruling class interest to promote the myth of apathy and exalt "me" consciousness over social/political consciousness. Who can the "me generation" refer to? Those relatively affluent children of the sixties and seventies with *options,* who leapt from hippy or student radical into the "hippoisie." For them the feminist idea of "the personal is political" became a convenient excuse for careerism and hedonism.

The "me decade" symbolizes the value-consuming democracy of consumption described in the overview to this volume. Them that pays...gets it packaged (like year-round organic vegetables). Them that can't pay...don't get. Social change serves corporate capitalism if it is managed and packaged properly. Today business is eagerly cultivating the two-income "urban homesteaders" of the eighties who are pushing out the city poor and working class (consciously and unconsciously) to make way for themselves and the luxury shops which service them.

We must supplant corporate his/story with our/story. The decade of the seventies can be described by other names besides the "me decade": the grassroots decade, the decade of women's liberation and gay liberation. On the campuses the antinuclear and "divest now from South Africa" movements put the lie to the myth of student apathy. The seventies also saw a resurgence of rank and file labor militancy; rural protest by family farmers and farm workers; urban housing coalitions fighting gentrification and urban removal; struggles against sterilization abuse and violence against women. Internationally, national liberation swept aside the "me" nationalism of orchestrated decolonization.

Trilateralism has no passionate ideology to offer in place of the expanding consumption community. Its elitism is transparent. The more capitalism becomes bankrupt materially, the more it appears bankrupt ideologically. The capitalist promise of individual freedom goes hand in hand with the promise of individual prosperity; not the reality of declining living standards, rising crime, deteriorating health care, and polluted environment suffered by more and more people. The question is whether people will be mobilized to improve their condition under the umbrella of the Right or the Left, toward fascism or towards true democracy and socialism.

The ruling class hopes to channel frustration and anger in the United States over declining living standards and hurt national pride into a license for authoritarianism at home, and interventionism abroad. Provisions in the Federal Criminal Code Revision (grandson of S1) and the Energy Mobilization Board are designed to derail popular dissent and give a "fast track" to state repression and corporate profiteering. Domestic paramilitary and political shock troops—the Klan, Nazis, Right-to-Life forces—are striking out more viciously. The CIA and Rapid Development Force have been given the congressional seal of approval.

The eighties have opened with the urgency of the antidraft movement and race rebellion in Miami. We will have to fight hard to protect and extend democratic rights and civil liberties and oppose state repression at home and abroad. In 1981 the U.S. will likely try to impose statehood—an internal settlement—on Puerto Rico (the

Republican platform takes an explicitly pro-statehood position). But from Puerto Rico to the Philippines, from El Salvador to South Korea to South Africa, the struggle for liberation is intensifying.

Trilateralism will not roll over and play dead—or drop dead from a case of acute contradictions. We need a viable counter-strategy and a forceful alternative program. This book is not a guide for action but a tool for action. We have decoded establishment press, business magazines, and trilateral reports and commentary to demystify ruling class alignments, power, policies, and propaganda. These are tools we hope people can share with others. We have tried to build a foundation for seeing how local issues link up with national and international issues and for seeing particular struggles in terms of the larger power structure.

In July 1980 I participated in the International Survival Gathering sponsored by the Black Hills Alliance, a coalition of traditional Indians and activists, white ranchers and farmers, and antinuclear activists. The strength of this broad coalition and the diversity of the many thousands who attended the Gathering in South Dakota reflect the urgency of our task: to ensure the very *survival* of Indian peoples and the entire human race and to protect the earth for the generations to come. Farmers and ranchers tell us that the family farm is on the verge of extinction and that the water necessary for drinking and raising crops and cattle is being rapidly polluted and depleted by corporate misuse. Urban communities are wards of the corporate system of distributing water, housing, heat, food, and jobs, and are being uprooted at the whim of corporate redevelopers. All of us live under the threat of nuclear annihilation. To bring this point home—adjacent to the ranch site of the survival gathering was a Strategic Air Command Base and B52s and F15s made repeated runs over the ranch. But the gathering reaffirmed a sense of peoples' power not our helplessness; and it gave us a strong sense of the interlocking nature of our struggles.

We cannot enter the eighties competing over reformist programs, constituencies, and scarce funds. We need to build a unifying pro-gressive movement which is rooted in the daily struggles of our workplaces and communities, but which evolves a broad long-range resistance. If we are divided from each other and afraid and unable to challenge the power of corporate capitalism, our collective destiny of destruction will be determined for us by trilateral managers and right wing forces. Can we forge an effective strategy of popular resistance and a dynamic vision of social change? I believe we can—and we must.

FOOTNOTES

1. See the references to reporter Elizabeth Drew's remarks in the articles by Fred Block and Alan Wolfe in Part VIII.
2. Leonard Silk, "New U.S. View of the World," *New York Times* Economic Scene, 4 May 1979.
3. Noam Chomsky, "The Secular Priesthood: Intellectuals and American Power," *Working Papers* (May-June 1978), p. 31.
4. Joyce Kolko, *America and the Crisis of World Capitalism* (Boston: Beacon Press, 1974), p. 36.
5. Michael Moffitt, "The Third World: Deeper in Debt," *The Nation*, 5 July 1980.
6. See Raul Fernandez, "Third World Industrialization: A New Panacea?" *Monthly Review*, May 1980, p. 14.
7. John Pinder, Takashi Hosomi, William Diebold, *Industrial Policy and the International Economy* (New York: The Trilateral Commission, 1979).
8. Paul Sweezy, "The Present Global Crisis of Capitalism," *Monthly Review*, April 1978, p. 10.
9. For a highly readable historical analysis of this process see David M. Gordon, "Up and Down the Long Roller Coaster," *U.S. Capitalism in Crisis* (New York: Union for Radical Political Economics, 1978).
10. See Paul Sweezy, "Whither U.S. Capitalism?" *Monthly Review*, December 1979, pp. 4-5.
11. Robert LeKachman, "The Crash of 1980," *The Nation*, 5 July 1980, p. 15.
12. On Kirkland's corporate connections, see "Lane's Friends," *The Nation*, 19 January 1980.
13. *Business Week*, "Carter's Bid to Buy Labor," 1-5 October 1979, pp. 32, 34.
14. Steven Rattner, "Volcker Asserts U.S. Must Trim Living Standards," *New York Times*, 18 October 1979.
15. Text of the Declaration of the Venice Economic Summit Meeting," *New York Times*, 24 June 1980.
16. "The Reindustrialization of America," *Business Week*, 30 June 1980, p. 56.
17. *Ibid.*, p. 146.
18. *Ibid.*, p. 86.
19. See Samuel Huntington, "The Governability of Democracy One Year Later," *Trialogue* No. 10 (Spring 1976), pp. 10-11.
20. Richard Burt, "Brzezinski on Agression and How to Cope With it," *New York Times*, 40 March 1980. The themes of managing contradictions, coherence, and incoherence are also developed in Hedley Bull, "A View from Abroad: Consistency Under Pressure," and Stanley Hoffman, "A View from at Home: The Perils of Incoherence," *Foreign Affairs*, 57: 3 (1979), pp. 441-491.
   For useful analysis of the differences between Brzezinski, Kissinger, Vance, and Young, and of the divergences between Brzezinski's theory and practice, see Elizabeth Drew, "A Reporter at Large: Brzezinski," *New Yorker*, 1 May 1978 and Herman Nickel, "Why 'Zbig' Is not Quite on Top of the World," *Fortune*, 23 April 1979, pp. 71-75.
21. "Brzezinski in Algiers for Anniversary, Plans Assurance on Sahara War," *New York Times*, 1 November 1979.
22. Chicago Press Conference, 17 November 1976, Clergy and Laity Concerned.

Also see Jonathan Power, interview, "The Thoughts of Andy Young," *The Observer* (London), 9 September 1979.

23. Howell Raines, "Politics, Lectures and the Third World Competing for Andrew Young's Time," *New York Times,* 4 April 1980.

24. *ZANU (PF) Manifesto,* ZANU Mission, (211 East 43rd Street: N.Y.). On the evolution of national liberation struggles, see Nzongola-Ntalaja, "Internal Settlement, Neo-colonialism and the liberation of South Africa," *Journal of Southern African Affairs IV:2* (April 1979).

25. This expression is used by Andrew Kopkind in "None Dare Call It History," *Working Papers,* May-June 1980, p. 12.

26. See Robert Armstrong, "El Salvador—Why Revolution," *NACLA: report on the americas,* XIV: 2, March-April 1980 and "El Salvador" Part II, *op.cit.,* July-August 1980.

27. Karen Elliott House and Beth Nissen, "Southern Strategy: U.S. Tries to Influence Central American Unrest But Finds Task Tricky," *Wall Street Journal,* 1980. Also see Elizabeth Farnsworth, "Keeping the Caribbean Safe from Castro," *The Nation,* 15 December 1979, pp. 616-618.

28. See Michael Klare," Curing the Vietnam Syndrome," *The Nation,* 13 October 1979, p. 340. Also see, Klare, "The Brown Doctrine: Have R.D.F., Will Travel," *The Nation,* 8 March 1980, pp. 257, 263-266.

29. For good analyses of the drive for the draft and draft resistance, see Bertram Gross, "The Citizen's Guide to Draft Deterrence," *The Nation,* 29 March 1980, pp; 359-362.

30. Anthony Lewis, "Thinking About the Unthinkable," *New York Times,* Op-Ed, 13 February 1980; citing Robert Scheer, "Interview with George Bush," *Los Angeles Times,* January 1980.

31. Jonathan Power, interview, "A Conversation with Brzezinski," *Washington Post,* October 1977.

32. Physicians for Social Responsibility, (P.O. Box 295, Cambridge, Mass. 02238); Advertisement in *New York Times,* 2 March 1980, p. 22E.

33. "Neo-Mercantilism in the 80s," *Business Week,* 9 July 1979.

34. Richard Ullman, "Trilateralism: 'Partnership' For What?" *Foreign Affairs,* October 1976, p. 3.

35. William Greider, "Trilateralists: Big Tycoons on Defensive," *Washington Post,* 19 June 1978.

36. See Bill Paul, "Chase Bank and Others Face Court Challenges on Huge Loans to Iran," *Wall Street Journal,* 28 March 1980; Claudia Wright, "Buried Treasure at Chase Manhattan?" *Inquiry,* 7 April 1980, pp. 12-15.

37. "Text of Vance Speech at Harvard on Foreign Policy," *New York Times,* 6 June 1980.

38. *Trialogue,* Spring 1980, p. 16.

39. *Ibid.,* p. 17.

40. Zbigniew Brzezinski, "U.S. Foreign Policy: The Search for Focus," *Foreign Affairs,* July 1973, p. 715.

41. John B. Oakes, "The Trilateral Way," *New York Times,* op.ed., 10 April 1980.

42. Giovanni Agnelli, "East-West Trade: A European View," *Foreign Affairs,* Summer 1980, pp. 1016-1017.

43. Laurence H. Shoup, *The Carter Presidency and Beyond,* (Palo Alto, Ca: Ramparts Press, 1979), p. 233.

44. Jack Egan, "Money Talks: An Interview with David Rockefeller," New York, 3 March 1980, p. 14.

45. Florida Conservative Union quoted in Francis X. Clines, "Ads Turn Foreign

Affairs Group," *New York Times*, 10 March 1980.

46. *Washington Post*, 20 February 1980.

47. "The G.O.P. Gets Its Act Together," *Time*, 28 July 1980, p. 10.

48. Ed Manguson, "Inside the Jerry Ford Drama," *Time*, 28 July 1980, pp. 16-19.

49. *Fortune*, 19 May 1980, p. 82.

50. Shoup, *op.cit.*, p. 222.

51. Steven Rattner, "13 Former U.S. Economic Officials Join to Combat Chronic Inflation," *New York Times*, 22 June 1980.

52. Alexander Cockburn and James Ridgeway, "Reagan's Gamble: Can Calvin Coolidge Make Peace with FDR?" *Village Voice*, p. 13.

53. See "Statement of William V. Roth Jr. Before Wilmington Rotary Club," *Congressional Record*, 93rd Congress—1st Session, 10 December 1973, pp. 42839-40.

54. Richard Burt, interview with Richard Allen, "Reagan's Foreign Policy—From Someone Who Knows," *New York Times*, 29 June 1980.

55. Joe Conason and Jack Newfield, "The Great Anderson Hype," *The Village Voice*, 19 May 1980, p. 20.

56. See Steven Rattner, "Anderson's Economics," *New York Times*, 11 May 1980.

57. See Lennox Hinds, "Political Prisoners in the United States," *Africa*, September 1978. Also see Peter Biskind, "Political Prisoners U.S.A.," *Seven Days*, 8 September 1978.

BIBLIOGRAPHY

Trilateral Commission Task Force Reports: The Triangle Papers

The first seven reports are available in a single combined volume, *Trilateral Commission Task Force Reports: 1-7* (NY: New York University Press, 1977)

1. *Towards a Renovated World Monetary System* (1973)
   Trilateral Monetary Task Force
   Authors: Richard N. Cooper, Motoo Kaji, Claudio Segre
2. *The Crisis of International Cooperation* (1974)
   Trilateral Political Task Force
   Authors: Francois Duchene, Kinhide Mushakoji, Henry D. Owen
3. A Turning Point in North-South Economic Relations (1974)
   Trilateral Task Force on Relations with Developing Countries
   Authors: Richard N. Gardner, Saburo Okita, B. J. Udink
4. Directions for World Trade in the Nineteen-Seventies (1974)
   Trilateral Task Force on Trade
   Authors: Guido Colonna de Paliano, Philip H. Trezise, Nobuhiko Ushiba
5. *Energy: The Imperative for a Trilateral Approach* (1974)
   Trilateral Task Force on the Political and International Implications of the
   Energy Crisis   Authors: John C. Campbell, Guy de Carmoy, Shinichi Kondo
6. *Energy: A Strategy for International Action* (1975)
   Trilateral Task Force on the Political and International Implications of the
   Energy Crisis   Authors: John C. Campbell, Guy de Carmoy, Shinichi Kondo
7. *OPEC, The Trilateral World, and the Developing Countries: New Arrangements
   for Cooperation, 1976-1980* (1975)
   Trilateral Task Force on Relations with Developing Countries
   Authors: Richard N. Gardner, Saburo Okita, B. J. Udink
8. *The Crisis of Democracy* (1975)
   Trilateral Task Force on the Governability of Democracies
   Authors: Michel Crozier, Samuel P Huntington, Joji Watanuki
   (NY: New York University Press, 1975)

The next six reports are available in a single combined volume, *Trilateral Commission Task Force Reports: 9-14* (NY: New York University Press, 1978)

9. *A New Regime for the Oceans* (1976); Trilateral Task Force on the Oceans
   Authors: Michel Hardy, Ann L. Hollick, Johan Jorgen Holst, Douglas M.
   Johnson, Shigeru Oda
10. *Seeking a New Accommodation in World Commodity Markets* (1976)
    Trilateral Task Force on Commodities Issues
    Authors: Carl E. Beigie, Wolfgang Hager, Sueo Sekiguchi
11. *The Reform of International Institutions* (1976)
    Trilateral Task Force on International Institutions
    Authors: C. Fred Bergsten, Georges Berthoin, Kinhide Mushakoji
12. *The Problem of International Consultations* (1976)
    Trilateral Task Force on Consultative Procedures
    Authors: Egidio Ortona, J. Robert Schaetzel, Nobuhiko Ushiba
13. *Collaboration with Communist Countries in Managing Global Problems:
    An Examination of the Options* (1977); Trilateral Task Force on Constructive
    Trilateral-Communist Cooperation on Global Problems
    Authors: Chihiro Hosoya, Henry D. Owen, Andrew Shonfield

14. *Towards a Renovated International System* (1977)
   Trilateral Task Force on a Renovated International System
   Authors: Richard N. Cooper, Karl Kaiser, Masataka Kosaka

The following reports are available from the Trilateral Commission

15. *An Overview of East-West Relations* (1978)
   Trilateral Task Force on East-West Relations
   Authors: Jeremy R. Azrael, Richard Lowenthal, Tohru Nakagawa

16. *Reducing Malnutrition in Developing Countries: Increasing Rice Production in South and Southeast Asia* (1978)
   Report of the Trilateral North-South Food Task Force
   Authors: Toshio Shishido, D. Gale Johnson, Umberto Colombo

17. *Energy: Managing the Transition* (1978); Trilateral Energy Task Force
   Authors: John Sawhill, Keichi Oshima, Hanns W. Maull

18. *Collective Bargaining and Employee Participation in Western Europe, North America and Japan* (1979); Trilateral Task Force on Industrial Relations
   Authors: Benjamin C. Roberts, George C. Lodge, Hideaki Okamoto

19. *Industrial Policy and the International Economy* (1979)
   Trilateral Task Force on Industrial Policy
   Authors: William Diebold, Takashi Hosomi, John Pinder

20. *Major Payments Imbalances and International Financial Stability* (1979 draft)
   Trilateral Task Force on Payments Imbalances
   Authors: Masao Fujioka, Bruce MacLaury, Alexandre Lamfalussy

21. *Trade in Manufactures with Developing Countries: Reinforcing North-South Partnership* (due Fall 1980); Trilateral Task Force on North-South Trade
   Authors: Albert Fishlow, Sueo Sekiguchi, Jean Carriere

22. *Employment, Technological Progress and Industrial Change* (due Fall 1980)
   Trilateral Task Force on Labor Market Policies
   Authors: Heinz Markmann, Tadashi Hanami, Richard Nelson

23. *The Trilateral Countries and the Middle East* (due Spring 1981)
   Trilateral Task Force on the Middle East
   Authors: Garret Fitzgerald, Arrigo Levi, Joseph J. Sisco

Trilateral Commission Publications, Documents, and Memoranda

Trialogue, The Trilateral Commission's Quarterly of North American-European-Japanese Affairs

Trilateral Commission *Annual Reports*

Constitution of the Trilateral Commission, April 1973

The Trilateral Commission (prospectus), 15 March 1973

"The Trilateral Policy Program: A Report on Present and Prospective Trilateral Task Force Work." Memorandum from Zbigniew Brzezinski, 18 September 1973

Financial Statements: The Trilateral Commission (North America): "Schedule of Cash Receipts for the Three Years Ended 30 June 1976"; "Support, Year Ended 30 June 1978"; "Estimated Receipts and Expenditures for Second Triennium, 1 July 1976-30 June 1979"

The Trilateral Commission: A Private North American-European-Japanese Initiative on Matters of Common Concern. General Brochures.

Trilateral Commission Lists of Members

Selected Readings on Trilateralism and Related Topics
Books

Assman, Hugo, ed. *Carter y La Logica del Imperialismo*. 2 vols. San Jose, Costa Rica: EDUCA, 1978

Baran, Paul and Paul Sweezy. *Monopoly Capital*. New York: Monthly Review Press, 1966

Ball, George W., ed. *Global Companies: The Political Economy of World Business*. Englewood Cliffs, NJ: Prentice-Hall, 1975

Block, Fred. *The Origins of International Economic Disorder*. Berkeley: University of California, 1977

Brzezinski, Zbigniew. *Between Two Ages: America's Role in the Technetronic Era*. New York: The Viking Press, 1970

Camps, Miriam. *The Management of Interdependence: A Preliminary View*. New York: Council on Foreign Relations, 1974

Chomsky, Noam and Herman, Edward S. *The Political Economy of Human Rights*. 2 vols. Boston: South End Press, 1979

Centro de Investigacion y Docencia Economicas (CIDE). *La Comision Trilateral y la Coordinacion de Politicas del Mundo Capitalista*. (Special edition of *Cuadernos Semestrales: Estados Unidos: Perspectiva Latinoamericana*). Mexico City: CIDE, 1977-8

Collier, Peter and David Horowitz. *The Rockefellers: An American Dynasty*. New York: New American Library, 1976

Crozier, Michael; Samuel P. Huntington; Joji Watanuki. *The Crisis of Democracy: Report on the Governability of Democracies to the Trilateral Commission*. New York: New York University Press, 1975

Domhoff, G. William. *The Powers That Be: Process of Ruling Class Domination in America*. New York: Vintage Books, 1978

——— *The Higher Circles: The Governing Class in America*. New York: Vintage Books, 1970

Dowd, Douglas F. *The Twisted Dream: Capitalist Development in the United States Since 1776*. 2nd ed. Cambridge, Mass.: Winthrop, 1977

Edwards, Richard C., Michael Reich and Thomas E. Weisskopf, eds. *The Capitalist System: Radical Analysis of American Society*. 2nd ed. Englewood Cliffs, New Jersey: Prentice-Hall, 1978

Habermas, Jurgen. *Legitimation Crisis*. Boston: Beacon Press, 1973

Hayter, Teresa. *Aid as Imperialism*. Baltimore, Maryland: Penguin Books, Inc., 1971

Katznelson, Ira and Mark Kesselman. *The Politics of Power: A Critical Introduction to American Government*. 2nd ed., New York: Harcourt Brace Jovanovich, 1979

Klare, Michael. *Beyond the 'Vietnam Syndrome': U.S. Interventionism in the 1980s*. Washington D.C.: Institute for Policy Studies, 1980

Kolko, Joyce. *America and the Crisis of World Capitalism*. Boston: Beacon Press, 1974

Lawrence, Robert and Holly Sklar. *U.S. Africa Policy for the 1980s: What the Think Tanks are Thinking*. Washington D.C.: Institute for Policy Studies. Forthcoming.

Letelier, Orlando and Michael Moffitt. *The International Economic Order*. Part I. Transnational Institute/Institute for Policy Studies, Washington D.C., 1977

Linoberg, Leon, et. al. *Stress and Contradiction in Modern Capitalism*. Lexington, Mass., 1975

Magdoff, Harry. *The Age of Imperialism: The Economics of U.S. Foreign Policy.* New York: Monthly Review Press, 1966

———*Imperialism: From the Colonial Age to the Present.* New York: Monthly Review Press, 1978

———and Paul M. Sweezy. *The End of Prosperity: The American Economy in the 1970s.* New York: Monthly Review Press, 1973

Melman, Seymour. *The Permanent War Economy: American Capitalism in Decline.* New York: Simon and Schuster, 1974

Mermelstein, David, ed. *The Economic Crisis Reader.* New York: Vintage Books, 1975

Miliband, Ralph. *Marxism and Politics.* New York: Oxford University Press, 1977

——— *The State in Capitalist Society.* New York: Basic Books, 1969

O'Connor, James. *The Fiscal Crisis of the State.* New York: St. Martin's Press, 1973

Owen, Roger and Bob Sutcliffe, eds. *Studies in the Theory of Imperialism.* London: Longmans, 1972

Payer, Cheryl. *The Debt Trap: The International Monetary Fund and the Third World.* New York: Monthly Review Press, 1974

Piven, Frances F. and Richard A. Cloward. *Regulating the Poor.* New York: Vintage, 1971

Poulantzas, Nicos. *Political Power and Social Classes.* London: New Left Books, 1973

Radice, Hugo, ed. *International Firms and Modern Imperialism* (Selected Readings) Baltimore, Maryland: Penguin, 1975

Schiller, Herbert I. *Mass Communications and American Empire.* Boston: Beacon Press, 1969

——— *Communication and Cultural Domination.* New York: International Arts and Sciences Press, 1976

Shoup, Laurence H., and Minter, William. *Imperial Brain Trust: The Council on Foreign Relations and United States Foreign Policy.* New York: Monthly Review Press, 1977

Shoup, Laurence. *The Carter Presidency and Beyond: Power and Politics in the 1980s.* Palo Alto, California: Ramparts Press, 1979

Singham, A.W., ed. *The Nonaligned Movement in World Politics.* Westport, Conn.: Lawrence Hill, 1977

Sweezy, Paul M. *The Theory of Capitalist Development.* New York: Monthly Review Press, (1942 1st ed.), 1970

Union for Radical Political Economics. *U.S. Capitalism in Crisis.* New York: URPE, 1978

Weinstein, James. *The Corporate Ideal in the Liberal State: 1900-1918.* Boston: Beacon Press, 1968

Williams, William Appelman. *The Contours of American History.* Chicago: Quadrangle, 1966

Wolfe, Alan. *The Limits of Legitimacy: Political Contradictions of Contemporary Capitalism.* New York: Free Press, 1977

——— *The Rise and Fall of the 'Soviet Threat': Domestic Sources of the Cold War Consensus.* Washington D.C.: Institute for Policy Studies, 1980

——— *The Seamy Side of Democracy: Repression in America.* New York: McKay, 1973

Special Publications, Transcripts, Bibliographies, and Unpublished Papers

American Friends Service Committee. Transcript of a Consultation on Trilateralism and its Implications for New England, *The Trilateral Commission: Presentations by James Phillips, Holly Sklar, Howard Wachtel*. Cambridge, Mass.: AFSC, March 1979

"Analysis of Trilateral Commission Study on Industrial Relations." Washington, D.C.: International Association of Machinists, 1978

Becker, Steven M. "Making the Energy Transition: Notes on the Trilateral Approach and the Carter Energy Plan." Unpublished paper, Columbia University, 12 December 1978

Carter, Jimmy. "Campaign Speech to Chicago Council on Foreign Relations." 15 March 1976

Cist, Arturo and Gregario Iriarte. "From National Security to Trilateralism: Reasons for the Carter Administration's Stance on Human Rights in Latin America." La Paz: Bolivian Permanent Assembly for Human Rights, 1977

Cohen, Barry. "The Black and White Minstrel Show: Carter, Young and Africa." *Spokesman Pamphlet* No. 58. Nottingham, England: Bertrand Russell Press, 1977

Dolbeare, Kenneth M. "Alternatives to the New Fascism." Amherst: University of Massachusetts, 1976

Donkersloot, Hans. *Bibliography of Trilateralism in International Politics*. Amsterdam: Political Institute, University of Amsterdam, 14 August 1979

Freitag, Ruth S. *Selected List of References: The Trilateral Commission*. Washington, D.C.: Library of Congress

IDOC Bulletin No. 11-12. "The Trilateral Commission." Rome, Italy: International Documentation and Communication Centre, November-December, 1977

Kesselman, Mark. "The Crisis of American Political Science: From Apologetic Pluralism to Trilateralism and Marxism." Unpublished paper, Columbia University, August 1979

Laidlaw, Ken and Roy Laishley, eds. *The Global Theatre: Presenting the New Manipulators: The Trilateral Commission*. London: International Coalition for Development Action, 1977

Lockwood, Ted, Duane Shank, and Philip Wheaton, "Jimmy Carter's Foreign Policy: Human Rights and the Trilateral Commission." Unpublished paper, Washington, D.C., July 1977

Bill Moyers Journal. Transcript of "The World of David Rockefeller." WNET/Thirteen, New York, 7 February 1980

New York CIRCUS. *Trilateralism* (four articles). New York: New York CIRCUS, 1980

Rudavsky, Dahlia, ed. *Planning for International Agriculture: The Trilateral Commission Takes on World Hunger*. San Francisco, CA: Earthwork/Center for Rural Studies, May 1979

Periodicals (excluding articles appearing in this volume)

Allen, Mark. "James E. Carter and the Trilateral Commission: A Southern Strategy." *The Black Scholar* 8 (May 1977), pp. 2-7

"America and the World." *Foreign Affairs*. 1978 and 1979 (Special year-end volumes)

Ball, George. "Cosmocorp: The Importance of Being Stateless." *Columbia Journal of World Business* 2:6 November-December 1967

——— "Trilateralism and the Oil Crisis." *Pacific Community* 5:3, pp. 335-347

Barnet, Richard J. "Carter's Patchwork Doctrine." *Harper's.* August 1977, pp. 27-33

——— and Falk, Richard A. "Cracking the Consensus: America's New Role in the World." *Working Papers.* March-April 1978, pp. 41-48

Barraclough, Geoffrey. "The Great World Crisis I." *New York Review of Books* (NYRB). 23 January 1975

——— "The Haves and the Have Nots." NYRB. 13 May 1976

——— "Wealth and Power: The Politics of Food and Oil." NYRB. 7 August 1975

——— "Waiting for the New Order." NYRB. 26 October 1978

——— "The Struggle for the Third World." NYRB. 9 November 1978

Bergsten, C. Fred. "The Threat From the Third World." *Foreign Policy.* No. 11, Summer 1973

Bliss, Shepard. "Jimmy Carter: Trilateralism in Action." *WIN.* 30 June 1977

Blum, Bill. "Trilateral Mind Games: The Commission in Action." *WIN.* 30 June 1977

Bowles, Samuel. "Have Capitalism and Democracy Come to a Parting of the Ways?" *The Progressive.* June 1977.

——— and Herbert Gintis. "The Invisible Fist: Have Capitalism and Democracy Reached a Parting of the Ways?" *American Economic Association* 68:2 (May 1978)

Brzezinski, Zbigniew. "America in a Hostile World." *Foreign Policy* No. 23 (Summer 1976)

——— "Half Past Nixon." *Foreign Policy* No. 3 (Summer 1971), pp. 3-21

——— "The Trilateral Relationship." *SAIS Review* 18:4 (1974), pp. 4-12

——— "U.S. Foreign Policy: The Search for Focus." *Foreign Affairs* 51:4 (July 1973), pp. 708-727

Bull, Hedley. "A View From Abroad: Consistency Under Pressure." *Foreign Affairs* 57:3 (1979), pp. 441-462

Burnham, Walter Dean. "Reflections on the Crisis of Democracy in the United States." *Trialogue* No. 12 (Fall 1976)

Business Week. Feature Articles: "Neo-Mercantilism in the 80's: The Worldwide Scramble to Shift Capital." 9 July 1978; "New World Economic Order." 24 July 1978; "The Decline of U.S. Power." 12 March 1979; "The Past, the Present, the Future." 3 September 1979; "The Reindustrialization of America." 30 June 1980

Chomsky, Noam. "The Secular Priesthood: Intellectuals and American Power." *Working Papers.* May-June 1978, pp. 30-31

——— and Herman, Edward S. "The United States Versus Human Rights in the Third World." *Monthly Review.* July-August 1977

——— "Trilateral's Rx for Crisis: Governability, Yes; Democracy, No." *Seven Days.* 14 February 1977

Cooper, Richard N. "A New International Economic Order for Mutual Gain." *Foreign Policy* No. 26 (Spring 1977)

Cox, Robert W. "Ideologies and the New International Economic Order: Reflections on Some Recent Literature." *International Organization* 33:2 (1979)

Drew, Elizabeth. "A Reporter at Large: Brzezinski." *New Yorker,* 1 May 1978

Egan, Jack. "Money Talks: An Interview with David Rockefeller." *New York,* 3 March 1980

Falk, Richard. "A New Paradigm for International Legal Studies: Prospects and Proposals." *Yale Law Journal* 84:5 (April 1975), pp. 969-1021

Farer, Tom. "The United States and the Third World: A Basis for Accommodation." *Foreign Affairs.* October 1975

Ferguson, Thomas and Rogers, Joel. "Another Trilateral Election?" *The Nation* 28 June 1980

Gwin, Catherine B. "The Seventh Special Session: Toward a New Phase of Relations Between the Developed and the Developing States?" in *New International Economic Order: Confrontation or Cooperation Between North and South*, Sauvent, Karl P. and Hajo Hasperflug, eds., Boulder, Colorado: Westview Press, 1977

Hajime, Takano. "Rockefeller's Men in Tokyo: A Guide to the Japanese Membership of the Trilateral Commission." *AMPO*. 10:1-2, pp. 40-41, 61

Hoffman, Stanley. "A View From at Home: The Perils of Incoherence." *Foreign Affairs* 57:3 (1979), pp. 463-491

"How the Trilateral Commission Got Started." *The Electronics Journal* 4:3 (April 1979)

Hughes, Thomas L. "Carter and the Management of Contradictions." *Foreign Policy* No. 31 (Summer 1978), pp. 34-55

Hymer, Stephen. "The Internationalization of Capital." *Journal of Economic Issues* VI:1 (1972), pp. 91-112

"Imperialism and the State." Special issue of *Insurgent Sociologist*, 7:2 (Spring 1977)

"International Economic Survey." *New York Times*, 4 February 1979

"Intervention." *The Nation*. A Special Issue. 9 June 1979

"Interview with David Rockefeller, Takeshi Watanabe, and Georges Berthoin." *Freeman Digest*, February-March 1979

"Interview with George Franklin, Parts 1 and 2." *Freeman Digest*, February-March 1979

Judis, John and Wolfe, Alan. "American Politics at the Crossroads." *Socialist Revolution* 7:32, pp. 9-39

Karpel, Craig S. "Cartergate: The Death of Democracy." *Penthouse*, November 1977

——— "Who Runs Jimmy Carter?" *Oui*, September 1977

——— "Cartergate II: The Real President." *Penthouse*, December 1977

——— "Cartergate III: The Thoughts of Chairman Brzezinski." *Penthouse*, January 1978

——— and James Davidson. "Cartergate IV: The Inflationists." *Penthouse*, February 1978

——— "Cartergate V: The First Hundred Lies of Jimmy Carter." *Penthouse*, April 1978

Klare, Michael. "The Traders and the Prussians." *Seven Days*, 28 March 1977, pp. 28-29

——— "U.S. Military Strategy After Vietnam." *Monthly Review*, March 1974

——— "Curing the Vietnam Syndrome." *The Nation*, 13 October 1979

Latham, Aaron. "Carter's Little Kissingers." *New York*, 13 December 1976

Linowitz, Sol M. "Estados Unidos y America Latina: Proximos Pasos." *Center for Inter-American Relations* No. 20 (December 1976)

Lydon, Christopher. "Jimmy Carter Revealed: He's a Rockefeller Republican." *Atlantic Monthly* 240:1 (July 1977), pp. 50-57

Manning, Robert. "A World Safe for Business." *Far Eastern Economic Review*, 25 March 1977

——— "The Making of a President: How David Rockefeller Created Jimmy Carter." *Penthouse*, September 1977

Martin, Patrick. "Rocky's U.N.—Is Politics Too Important to Be Left to Politicians?" *Macleans*, Canada, 17 October 1977

McCue, Marian. "A Well-Connected Peanut Farmer." *Seven Days*, 26 July 1977

Minter, William. "From the Folks Who Brought Us Light at the End of the Tunnel." *Seven Days*, 14 February 1977

Moorehead, Caroline. "An Exclusive Club, Perhaps Without Power, But Certainly With Influence: The Bilderberg Group." *The Times*, London, 18 April 1977

Morris, Roger. "Jimmy Carter's Ruling Class." *Harpers*, October 1977

Novak, Jeremiah. "The Trilateral Connection." *Atlantic Monthly*, 15 July 1977

Peterzell, Jay. "The Trilateral Commission and the Carter Administration." *Economic and Political Weekly*, 17 December 1977

Petras, James and Rhodes, Robert. "Reply to Critics." *New Left Review* No. 101-2 (February-April 1977), p. 153

——— "The Reconsolidation of U.S. Hegemony." *New Left Review* No. 97 (May-June 1976)

——— "President Carter and the 'New Morality'." *Monthly Review*, June 1977

Roth, William V. "Statement of Senator Roth Before Wilmington Rotary Club." *Congressional Record*. 93rd Congress, 1st Session, 10 December 1973, pp. 42839-40

Scheer, Robert. "Jimmy, We Hardly Know Y'All." *Playboy*, November 1976

Serfaty, Simon. "Brzezinski: Play It Again Zbig." *Foreign Policy* No. 32 (1978), pp. 3-21

Sewell, James P. "Trade-Offs of Trilateralism." *International Perspectives* No. 61, (May/June 1977), pp. 30-34

Shearer, Derek. "The Carter Administration: The Best and Brightest Recycled Economics: Boardrooms and Backrooms Provide Us the Usual Suspects." *Seven Days*, 14 February 1977, pp. 4-5

"The Trilateral Commission." *Congressional Record*. 95th Congress, 1st Session. 19 January 1977, S1104-1109

"The Trilateral Elite." *Newsweek*, 24 March 1980

"The Trilateral Energy Study: A Discussion with Frank Tugwell." *World Issues* 6:1 (February-March 1979)

Thompson, Carol B. "The Trilateral Commission: An Attempt to Regenerate Imperialism." *Maji Maji*. University of Dar Es Salaam, Tanzania. No. 33 (March 1978)

"Trilateralists at Top—New Foreign-Policy Elite." *U.S. News and World Report*, 21 February 1977

Ullman, Richard H. "Trilateralism: 'Partnership' for What?" *Foreign Affairs*, October 1976

Urencio, Claudio C. "La Estrategia Trilateral y los Paises en Desarrollo." *Comercio Exterio*. Mexico. 29:11 (November 1979)

Vorontsov, Bennady. "Trilateralism—New Imperialist Strategy." *New Times* No. 43. Soviet Union (October 1978)

Watson, Russell, Bruno Hall and Scott Sullivan, "Life at Brzezinski University." *Newsweek*, 9 May 1977

Weissman, Steve and Robert Eringer. "The World's Most Exclusive Club [Bilderberg] Gets Down to Business." *Seven Days*, 6 June 1977

"We've Been Asked, Trilateral Commission: How Influential?" *U.S. News and World Report*, 22 May 1978

Wolfe, Alan. "The Two Faces of Carter." *The Nation*, 18 December 1976, pp. 648-652

——— "Carter Plays at Hawks and Doves." *The Nation*, 24 June 1978

——— "The Trilateralist Straddle." *The Nation*, 31 December 1977, pp. 712-715

Wright, Erik Olin. "Alternative Perspectives in Marxist Theory of Accumulation and Crisis." *The Insurgent Sociologist* No. 6 (Fall 1975), pp. 5-39

Newspapers

Alponte, Juan Maria. "Mexico y la Trilateral." *Uno mas Uno*. Mexico. 25 April 1979

———— "La Casa Blanca y la Comision Trilateral." *Uno mas Uno*. Mexico. 12 February 1979

Bowie, Robert R. "Trilateral Cooperation." *Christian Science Monitor*, 31 October 1973

Buckley, William F. Jr. "George Bush's 'Secret' Past." *Washington Star*, 8 March 1980

Calleo, David P. "What Has Gone Wrong?" *New York Times*, 21 May 1978

Clark, Tim. "Trilateralists Pose No Threats, Says Abel." *News-Sun*, 12 January 1979

Clines, Francis X. "Ads Turn Foreign Affairs Group Into Florida _____." *New York Times*, 9 March 1980

Duffy, Gloria. "Shaping Carter's World View." *Washington Post*, 15 August 1975

Goshko, John M. "Trilateral Group Studies Merger." *Washington Post*, 18 January 1978

Greider, William. "Trilateralists to Abound in Carter's White House." *Washington Post*, 16 January 1977

———— "Trilateralists: Big Tycoons on Defensive." *Washington Post*, 19 June 1978

Gwertzman, Bernard. "Vance Bids the U.S. Adjust to New Era." *New York Times*, 1 May 1979

Halloran, Richard. "Trilateral Unit Criticizes Official Plans on Energy." *New York Times*, 15 June 1978

Johnstone, Diana. "Une Strategie Trilaterale." *Le Monde Diplomatique*, 23 November 1976

Kristol, Irving. "The Trilateral Commission Factor." *Wall Street Journal*, 16 April 1980

Lagos, Gustavo. "De La Politica Del Poder de Kissinger al Humanitarismo Planetario de Carter." *Mensaje* 260 (July 1977)

———— "El Impacto Mundial de La Ofensiva Ideologica de Carter." *Mensaje* (September 1977)

Lewis, Anthony. "Through a Glass Darkly." Op./Ed. *New York Times*, 28 February 1980

Lewis, Paul. "A White House Supply Depot: The Trilateral Commission." *New York Times*, 13 February 1977

Novak, Jeremiah. "New World Economic System Dawns." *Christian Science Monitor*, 14 February 1977

Oakes, John B. "The Trilateral Way." Op./Ed. *New York Times*, 10 April 1980

Power, Jonathan. "The Thoughts of Andy Young." *The Observer*, London, 9 September 1979

———— "A Conversation With Brzezinski." *Washington Post*, October 1977

Reston, James. "Japan Demands Equality." *New York Times*, 2 March 1973

———— "The New Leaders." Op./Ed. *New York Times*, 9 May 1979

Rockefeller, David. "Foolish Attacks on False Issues." Excerpts from Remarks to the Los Angeles World Affairs Council. *Wall Street Journal*, 30 April 1980

Rosenfeld, Stephen S. "The New Multinational Establishment." *Washington Post*, 6 June 1975

Schram, Martin. "The Guns of the N.H. Skirmishing." *Washington Post*, 20 February 1980

Scheer, Robert. "Brzezinski: Profound or Banal?" *Los Angeles Times*, 23 January 1977

Silk, Leonard. "Carter and Key Advisors Among the Trilateralists." *New York Times*, 6 January 1977

——— "Multinationals Versus the State." *New York Times*, 22 June 1978

——— "New U.S. View of the World." *New York Times*, 4 May 1979

"The New Atlantis." *The Economist*, 5 May 1973

"Transcript of President's Address to Country on Energy Problems." *New York Times*, 16 July 1979

Whitman, Marina V. N. "Carter's Trilateral Conspiracy." *Christian Science Monitor*, 7 February 1977

INDEX

This index covers names, places, and selected terms. Because U.S. foreign policy and the Carter Administration are discussed repeatedly throughout this book, readers are advised to check under particular subject headings and consult the table of contents. Also see listings under Nixon, Ford, Kennedy, Johnson, Roosevelt, and Eisenhower. All text and notes are indexed except the "Who's Who on the Trilateral Commission" which contains a separate table of contents.